Adulthood and Aging

Adulthood and Aging

an interdisciplinary, developmental view

Douglas C. Kimmel

The City College
City University of New York

WILEY

JOHN WILEY & SONS

New York · Chichester · Brisbane · Toronto · Singapore

Acquisition Editor	Deborah L. Moore
Managing Editor	Joan Kalkut
Production Manager	Joe Ford
Production Supervisors	Marcia Samuels, Nancy Prinz
Copyediting Supervisor	Deborah Herbert
Photo Researchers	Elaine Bernstein, Joelle Burrows
Photo Research Manager	Stella Kupferberg
Designer	Sheila Granda
Manufacturing Manager	Jane Bennett

Cover Paul Jenkins, *Phenomena Veil of Vespers*, 1970. Sotheby's, Inc., New York. Courtesy Collection Edward Totah Gallery, London.

Library of Congress Cataloging in Publication Data:

Kimmel, Douglas C.
    Adulthood and aging : an interdisciplinary, developmental view /
Douglas C. Kimmel. — 3rd ed.
        p.   cm.
    Includes bibliographical references.
    ISBN 0-471-63580-4
    1. Adulthood — Psychological aspects. 2. Aging — Psychological
aspects. 3. Adulthood. 4. Aging.   I. Title.
BF724.5.K55   1990
155.6 — dc20   89-38339

Printed in the United States of America

10 9 8 7

Printed and bound by R.R. Donnelley & Sons, Inc.

To my parents, Mary and Rudy Kimmel
My partner, Ron Schwizer
And all who grow older

Preface

There is a demographic revolution underway in the world as older age groups increase much more rapidly than in past decades. Meanwhile, young adults produce, reproduce, and strive to reach the apex of their abilities. Middle-aged adults continue to control the political and economic power in society. Surprisingly, these important years of the life span have only recently begun to receive the detailed attention they deserve.

In writing this book, my goal has been to create a text that will serve as a useful introduction to this field and will also be personally relevant to many readers. In addition, I hope it will raise the level of awareness about this period of life and about the issues involved in growing older in a changing society. I have attempted to contribute some new ideas, to encourage thinking, and to raise important questions. Since most readers of this book will be using it in college courses, it includes chapter outlines, key words, chapter summaries, and a glossary. Review questions, which may help organize students' study for exams, have been included at the end of each chapter. An instructor's manual is also available.

It may be noted that the order of chapters follows a general chronological progression, although each chapter focuses on a specific aspect of adult development. Thus the earlier chapters (3 to 6) are somewhat more relevant to young and middle adulthood, and the later chapters (7 to 9) emphasize issues of older adulthood and aging. Of course, the subsections of the chapters may be reorganized to follow a strict chronological framework. Likewise, the chapters can be assigned in any order since each chapter is essentially independent.

This third edition, similar to grandchildren in the human life cycle, represents considerable change, but also resembles the first two editions in significant ways. Every chapter has been revised to be relevant, current, and responsive to the recent changes in our society and to the new developments in the field of adulthood and aging. Among the major changes in content are the following:

There is an entirely new chapter devoted to cognition, intelligence, memory, and wisdom in adulthood.

A new section on psychology and health has been added in the chapter on biological aspects of aging.

Recent studies on women's midlife development have been integrated with the discussion of Levinson, Gould, and Vaillant in Chapter 3.

Menopause and the sexual response cycle are now integrated into the chapter on families and single adults; other material from the previous chapter on sex differences in the life cycle has been integrated into discussions of gender differences throughout the book, including a discussion of androgyny in the chapter on personality.

Alzheimer's disease, Medicare Catastrophic Health Care Coverage, AIDS, and other emerging issues are discussed.

Sensitivity to ethnic differences, sexual orientation, and ageism has been strengthened.

I have revised all of the chapters to ensure that this edition is new and fresh, and to include current references.

Language has also been updated. For example, African American is used when discussing ethnic differences as a parallel with other groups such as Mexican American, Irish American, or Japanese American. When census data are described, or comparisons are made with Whites or Hispanics, however, the more general term Black is used. A similar change is the use of *gender* instead of sex; the term *sex* is restricted to discussions of sexual activity or clear biological differences between males and females.

As in the first edition, the book remains unique in the field of adulthood and aging in at least three ways.

First, it applies the *developmental* approach as a systematic framework for viewing these adult years; thus, it focuses on issues of change and continuity throughout the years of the adult life cycle.

Second, it approaches the study of adulthood from an *interdisciplinary perspective*, by emphasizing the interaction of psychological, sociocultural, and biological aspects of human development. The central theoretical framework is the interactionist perspective; this includes the interaction of these interdisciplinary aspects of development as well as the interaction between individuals and their environmental niche.

Third, the Interludes provide a challenging opportunity to bridge the gap between theoretical concepts and the real world, by focusing on actual adults who are living rich and varied lives. The longitudinal Interludes also call attention to the developmental processes of change and continuity over time.

The Interludes also have been updated. George was reinterviewed at age 43; Murray was interviewed again at age 64 — thus, these longitudinal cases now span 15 years. There is a new interview with David, a 65-year-old man whose wife developed Alzheimer's disease 10 years ago. All of the original interviews have been retained, although the second interview with Murray has been shortened and appears in the same Interlude as the third interview.

The approach and much of the information I present reflect my study at the University of Chicago, my teaching at a multicultural urban college, and my work with various committees at the American Psychological Association. I am deeply indebted to Bernice L. Neugarten, whose course in adult development provided the initial outline for my conceptualization of the study of adulthood, and to the other faculty members of the Committee on Human Development. I am also indebted to the other pioneers in the field, whose research and teaching created the study of adult development and aging, and to the more recent cohorts of researchers in the field, whose data and ideas are reflected in countless studies cited in this book. And I am grateful to my students and colleagues at City College and the Graduate Center of City University who have read, criticized, discussed, challenged, and encouraged my ideas. I am especially grateful to the seven persons who were so open to my questions in the interviews and shared part of their lives with us. Harry Charner asked to be mentioned by name.

The following reviewers were especially helpful in the preparation of this third edition:

Cameron Camp III
University of New Orleans

John Cavanagh
Georgia Technical University

Amye Warren-Leubecker
University of Tennessee — Chattanooga

Sarah O'Dowd
Community College of Rhode Island

George Rebock
Johns Hopkins University

Seth Kalichman
University of South Carolina — Columbia

George Hampton
University of Houston — Downtown

Janet Matthews
Loyola University

Cynthia Berg
University of Utah

John Neulinger
City College of New York

The editors and staff of John Wiley were an excellent team to work with. Ronald W. Schwizer provided invaluable assistance with a variety of tasks involved in preparing this book.

I feel that adulthood and aging will continue to emerge as a significant field of study, and I hope that this book will be useful in a variety of contexts. For example, I use it as a basic source book in my undergraduate and graduate courses in psychology. It would also be appropriate in interdisciplinary programs in human development or in lifespan development. Graduate programs in geriatric social work, nursing, and social gerontology may also find the book a useful text or resource. I encourage my undergraduate students to connect the text with individual people by discussing the Interludes in class and by working as volunteers in senior citizen centers, nursing homes, friendly visiting services, other programs with adults, or by interviewing persons of varying ages.

Most of all, I hope that this book is good reading, and that it encourages continued growth of the knowledge about adulthood and aging.

Douglas Kimmel
New York

Contents

Adulthood and Aging

CHAPTER 1

Pablo Picasso, *La Vie*, 1903. © 1989 ARS N.Y./SPADEM.

Adulthood: Developmental Theory and Research

hy study adulthood and aging? The first reason is to understand the nature of life span human development in our complex society, which, we should note, has several negative ideas about this later period of development. Some people may feel that it is a dull and unexciting time of life, compared with childhood or adolescence. Many may think it is depressing because it involves aging and our society often teaches us that aging is not as positive as youthfulness. Others may feel that infancy and early childhood are more important than adulthood because after a certain age people are not susceptible to various influences that can affect the rest of their lives. And finally, sometimes people think aging, senility, and death are all mixed up together so that if you get one, you get all three. As we will see, each of these ideas is untrue and should be challenged. They represent a false myth or inaccurate stereotype about adulthood and aging that we describe as *ageism*.

Second, more people are living much longer than ever before. This is creating a variety of new opportunities and challenges within our society. For example, politicians are seeking new ways to fund the programs that have been established to ensure financial security and medical care for our elders. Working people worry that they will have to pay too much to support the elderly and won't have the same benefits when they become old. Part-time job opportunities that used to attract young people now attract retired people. And who will care for the growing number of very old people? Thus, as citizens and as family members, we need to understand the variety of effects this worldwide aging revolution may have during our lifetime.

A third reason to study this topic is a very practical one. The growing number of people who are living to old age are creating a variety of employment opportunities for younger people. These include the range of human service fields (medicine, nursing, psychology, physical therapy, and social work) as well as occupations that are related to retirement (advertising, market research, recreation, travel, and leisure). Knowledge about adulthood and aging will be relevant to each of these careers, and mandatory for those in the human service field.

Fourth, most people plan to become older themselves. They also have older friends and family members. Studying this topic can help one understand and plan for one's own development and the aging of others. In particular, there are a number of personally relevant and practical topics about the adult and aging years included in this book. These include: choosing a career, the midlife transition, birth of the first child, sexual behavior, Alzheimer's disease, retirement, grandparenthood, widowhood, nursing homes, and bereavement.

Finally, it is interesting and useful to understand more about adults because they control the political and economic power in society. They achieve success, they experience frustration, and they grow older. On one hand, some may wish to be in such a position of power one day themselves; on the other hand, some may wish to understand those who are in such positions today. This book cannot provide a "how to do it" guide, but it can provide a perspective for those who want to understand adults and adulthood.

Throughout this book we use an **interdisciplinary perspective** to understand adult development. This perspective involves the ability to change "lenses" to get different views. Sometimes we use the lenses of a psychologist, sociologist, anthropologist, or biologist. Each of these fields, or disciplines, has important information

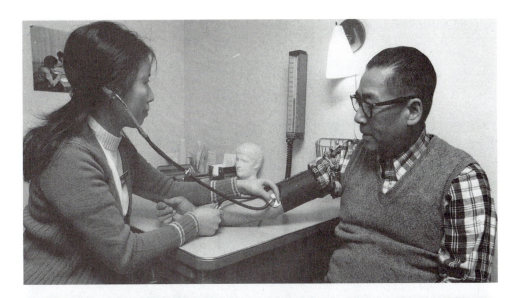

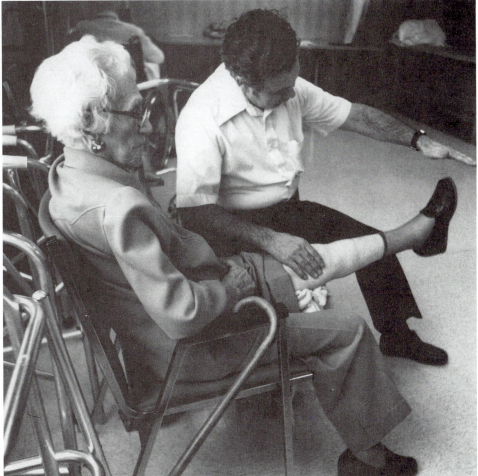

Careers in gerontology include positions in medicine, nursing, psychology, physical therapy and social work.

Adults hold most positions of power in society; studying adult development can help one understand adults and their various social roles.

and a unique viewpoint on adulthood and aging. Frequently we note that psychological, social, cultural, and biological processes *interact* to produce the phenomenon we are investigating. This becomes especially clear in the "interludes," where individuals talk about their lives; their individuality, social network, cultural background, and physical health interact to produce the unique person we encounter there.

The **developmental perspective** focuses on all the factors that interact to cause growth and change throughout the life span. For example, if we seek to describe the differences between young adults and middle-aged persons, we need to consider the psychological, social, cultural, and biological forces that influence these groups of individuals in different ways. Thus, the developmental perspective integrates the interdisciplinary viewpoint as it focuses on individuals growing and changing as they become older. The developmental perspective also stresses the *patterns of stability and change* that describe characteristics of individuals in general at particular points in their life cycle. The concepts of adolescence, midlife transition, or postretirement suggest that there are general developmental themes for individuals during these phases of life. Thus, this perspective tends to stress general developmental trends that apply to many people, but perhaps do not apply equally to everyone. Once these developmental themes are recognized, however,

individual variation may be examined to understand a particular person in a specific sociocultural network at a specific time in life.

Life Span Human Development

Philosophers, writers, and social scientists have suggested a variety of views on the nature of the human life cycle. One of the most common views is the analogy between the seasons of the year and the stages of life: spring is the time of growth and coming into bloom; summer is the time of maturity and greatest productivity; autumn is the time of harvest and culmination; and winter is the time of decline and death. Each season is beautiful in its own right; each is unique; there is a definite progression from one season to the next; and one complete cycle prepares the way for the next. Of course, this analogy is too simple to describe human development, but in a poetic way it captures much of the essence of various developmental theories: **development** is progressive, sequential, and follows the same pattern generation after generation; it is also circular in the sense that as each generation matures, it sows the seeds for the next generation.

There have been a variety of different concepts of development throughout history. Artists in ancient Egypt, for example, portrayed children as wearing a sidelock of hair that is known as the "sidelock of youth"; in contrast, old people were portrayed with groups of three wrinkles at the corner of each eye. Shakespeare offered a poetic, but satirical, view of human development as a series of seven stages.

> All the world's a stage,
> And all the men and women merely players.
> They have their exits and their entrances,
> And one man in his time plays many parts,
> His acts being seven ages. At first the infant,
> Mewling and puking in the nurse's arms.
> And then the whining schoolboy, with his satchel
> And shining morning face, creeping like snail
> Unwillingly to school. And then the lover,
> Sighing like furnace, with a woful ballad
> Made to his mistress' eyebrow. Then a soldier,
> Full of strange oaths, and bearded like the pard,
> Jealous in honor, sudden and quick in quarrel,
> Seeking the bubble reputation
> Even in the cannon's mouth. And then the justice,
> In fair round belly with good capon lin'd,
> With eyes severe, and beard of formal cut,
> Full of wise saws and modern instances;
> And so he plays his part. The sixth age shifts
> Into the lean and slipper'd pantaloon,
> With spectacles on nose and pouch on side,
> His youthful hose, well sav'd, a world too wide
> For his shrunk shank; and his big manly voice,

Turning again toward childish treble, pipes
And whistles in his sound. Last scene of all,
That ends this strange eventful history,
Is second childishness and mere oblivion,
Sans teeth, sans eyes, sans taste, sans everything.

As You Like It, Act II, scene vii

Certainly Shakespeare painted a cynical and stereotyped view of human development (and spoke only of men, not women), but the seven stages are quite similar to the ones currently used: infancy, childhood, adolescence, young adulthood, middle age, old age, and senescence. Shneidman (1989) noted that other historical descriptions have included between 3 and 12 stages; some have been linear, others have been cyclical. More modern versions have adopted twentieth-century analogies, including the spiral such as the famous gallery of the Guggenheim Museum of Art in New York City: one follows a path that circles repeatedly through various themes of development throughout life, each time at a different level.

Let us take a closer look at the life cycle in today's society. Consider the line in Figure 1.1 as a schematic representation of the human life span. It emphasizes the *progressive* and *sequential* nature of human development. That is, development progresses in only one direction (from birth to death) and it generally follows a sequence of predictable events for most people. Certain events are age-related because they reflect biological development — such as puberty or menopause. Other events are clearly linked to age in our society such as beginning school, being able to vote, drive a car, or drink alcohol, becoming a grandmother, and receiving Medicare. In general, biological development plays a more important role in age-related events during infancy and childhood than during adulthood; and social influences play a more important role in determining age-related events in adulthood. Some personally important events may not result directly from either social or biological sources, however. Consider, for example, falling in love for the first time, being born again as a Christian, or learning of a classmate's death.

One useful analogy is to think of the lifeline as a representation of a journey with a number of interesting places and crucial junctions along the way. Some years ago when travel was slower, roads were commonly marked with *milestones* or mileposts to mark off each mile traveled. Many people tend to mark off their progress through the life cycle in a similar way. We are consciously aware of our

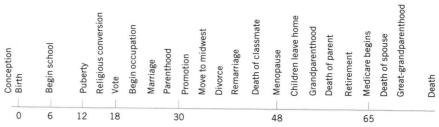

FIGURE 1.1 A human lifeline.

progress during the past year, and celebrate birthdays or New Year's Day to mark off another year. So the notion of milestones in human development is appropriate. When we think of the life cycle we often mark it off with developmental milestones and, in fact, often celebrate these milestones — such as graduation, marriage, or retirement. Let us define a **milestone** as an *event* (not a general goal) that stands out in one's memory, or in one's future plans, as a significant turning point, marker, or personal reference point.

The *lifespan perspective of development* is useful for studying adulthood and aging. It points out the fact that individual adults have a personal history and pattern of milestones that is unique. It emphasizes the dual processes of change and continuity that describe development throughout life. It calls attention to the interaction of "internal" (biological or psychological) forces and "external" (social or cultural) influences. Moreover, it alerts us to seek general patterns of development that may apply to specific groups of individuals, or perhaps even to most people in a particular culture. Finally, it asks whether there are universal patterns of development in all cultures; and if so, what produces them.

Developmental Theories of the Life Cycle

Theories of the human life cycle seek to explain the nature of growth and the patterns of change in individuals from birth to death. They clearly assume that adults continue to develop and change after adolescence. Since development is assumed to occur in a sequential progression, the goal of developmental theories is to understand the nature of that sequence and to explain why it progresses in the manner it does. Often, developmental theories take the form of a series of stages that follow each other in sequence.

In this chapter we discuss different theoretical models of life span human development. Although we cannot discuss every theory that has been proposed, we have selected seven that reflect important themes in our Western view of human development. (Different cultures view human development in different ways; see examples in Chapter 9.) The theories of Bühler, Jung, Erikson, and Levinson involve a sequence of *stages*. The dialectical approach described by Riegel focuses on the process of *change* throughout life. In contrast, Costa and McCrae emphasize the *stability and continuity* of lives over time. The pluralistic perspective suggested by Baltes and his colleagues integrates several elements of the views of development that do not involve a sequence of stages. The first three models (Bühler, Jung, and Erikson) are classic theories that have had wide influence; the last four are receiving greater attention among researchers today.

Bühler's Theory of the Course of Human Life

Charlotte Bühler and her students studied the course of human life from biographies and autobiographies collected in the 1930s in Vienna. They developed a methodology for analyzing these biographies to reveal an orderly progression of phases on the basis of changes in events, attitudes, and accomplishments during the life cycle.

They were also interested in examining the parallel between the course of life revealed in the biographies and the biological course of life.

They noted five biological phases: (1) progressive growth—up to age 15; (2) continued growth combined with the ability to reproduce sexually—age 15–25; (3) stability of growth—age 25–45; (4) loss of sexual reproductive ability—age 45–65; and (5) regressive growth and biological decline—age 65 on (Bühler, 1968). Based on their studies of 400 biographies, they proposed five phases of life that correspond to these five biological phases (Box 1.1). We assume that the ages are only approximations and that they reflect socially defined events such as retirement and biologically defined changes such as menopause.

Frenkel, one of Bühler's students, described the developmental progression in these words:

> The young person just passed through childhood—the first phase of life—makes the first plans about his life and his first decisions in adolescence or shortly afterwards. Here begins the second phase of experience. It is characterized first through the fact that the young person wishes to acquire contact with reality. He experiments with people and professions. An "expansion" of his person takes place. Also characteristic for him is the temporary nature of his attitudes as to what his life calling will be. . . .
>
> At the end of the second phase . . . the individuals have become clear as to their definite attitude toward life. . . . During the third phase, vitality is still at its high point, while direction and specification are now also present, so that very often this time is found to be the culmination period for subjective experiences.
>
> The transition to the fourth phase very often is introduced by a crisis, since at this point the unfolding of the individual powers has come to a standstill, and much has to be given up which depended upon physical aptitude or was connected with the biological needs. Contrary to the descent of the biological curve and the experiences which are connected with that, we find here an ascending scale by virtue of new interest in the results and productivity of life. . . .
>
> Finally, in the fifth phase we find more strongly mentioned age, premonitions of death, complaints of lonesomeness, and often those in this phase are occupied with religious questions. This last period contains experiences of a retrospective nature and

---

BOX 1.1   Bühler's Five Phases of Life

Age	Phase
0–15	Child at home; prior to self-determination of goals.
15–25	Preparatory expansion and experimental self-determination of goals.
25–45	Culmination: definitie and specific self-determination of goals.
45–65	Self-assessment of the results of striving for these goals.
65 up	Fulfillment of goals or experience of failure; previous activities continue, but in late life there may be a reemergence of short-term goals focusing on satisfying immediate needs.

Source: Based on Horner, Althea J. The evolution of goals in the life of Clarence Darrow. In C. Bühler & F. Massarik (Eds.), *The course of human life*, p. 65. New York: Springer, 1968.

considerations about the future, that is, about oncoming death and one's past life. The balance-sheet of life is drawn up, so to speak. (Frenkel, 1936)[1]

In general, this view emphasizes the parallel between the biological process of growth, stability, and decline and the psychosocial process of expansion, culmination, and contraction in activities and accomplishments. Often the biological curve is ahead of the individual's psychosocial curve; for example, a reliance on mental abilities allows a person to continue a high degree of productivity for several years after physical strength has begun to decline. Also there is considerable individual variation, since one person may become highly productive later in life and reach the psychosocial culmination phase several years after reaching the biological culmination period.

More recent formulations of this theory emphasize changes in motives or goals during the adult years. Raymond Kuhlen (1964) proposed that the growth-expansion motives (such as achievement, power, creativity, and self-actualization) dominate an individual's behavior during the first half of life. These motives may change during a person's life, however, if they have been relatively satisfied (e.g., the need for success or for sex), or because the person moves into new social positions (such as becoming a mother or the president of a company). In addition, with advancing age there may be "a shift from active direct gratifications of needs to gratifications obtained in more indirect and vicarious fashion" (Kuhlen, 1964). Bühler (1968) focused on the process of setting goals for one's life. For example, goals become gradually established during the first two decades of life that ideally lead to self-fulfillment during the culmination period. Some zestful individuals may reexamine these goals and strive for new goals during the fourth phase but, for most individuals, the goals probably shift to stability and retirement in the second half of life. She concluded from her studies that a sense of not having fulfilled one's goals was more important than biological decline in triggering maladjustment in old age.

This view of adult development suggests that the life cycle may be seen in terms of two general tendencies — growth-expansion and contraction — with a major turning point somewhere during the middle years. Bühler placed the turning point during the period of self-assessment following the culmination phase of midlife (about age 40 – 45). Kuhlen considered the turning point to be less clearly defined. It may result from satisfaction of the earlier growth-expansion motive that allows the emergence of other motives, or it may result from physical or social losses, from the sense of being "locked into" a situation, or even from the changing time perspective that results from having lived over half of one's life. We find a similar idea in the theories proposed by Jung and by Levinson.

Jung's Concept of the Stages of Life

Whereas Bühler's view of the life span grew out of a systematic study of biographies, and Kuhlen's concepts were based on considerable empirical research, Jung's view

---

[1]Reprinted with permission from *Character and Personality* (now *Journal of Personality*. Copyright © 1936 by Duke University Press.

of the stages of life was based primarily on his clinical work and his theory of psychology.

Carl G. Jung, one of the pioneers in the development of psychotherapy, worked for many years with Sigmund Freud. He developed a theory of psychology that, unlike Freud's theory, included a life span view. He began his discussion of the stages of life with *youth*, the period extending from after puberty to the middle years (age 35 - 40). Jung was interested in problems of the psyche, and although it may seem strange that he does not include childhood, he argued that while the child may *be* a problem to parents, educators, and doctors, normal children do not *have* problems of their own — only the adult "can have doubts about himself" (Jung, 1933).

In his view, the period of youth involves giving up the dreams of childhood, dealing with the sexual instinct and feelings of inferiority, and, in general, widening the horizon of life. The next important change begins between the ages of 35 and 40:

> At first it is not a conscious and striking change; it is rather a matter of indirect signs of a change which seems to take its rise in the unconscious. Often it is something like a slow change in a person's character; in another case certain traits may come to light which had disappeared since childhood; or again, one's previous inclinations and interests begin to weaken and others take their place. Conversely — and this happens very frequently — one's cherished convictions and principles, especially the moral ones, begin to harden and to grow increasingly rigid until, somewhere around age 50, a period of intolerance and fanaticism is reached. It is as if the existence of these principles were endangered and it were therefore necessary to emphasize them all the more. (Jung, 1933, pp. 12–13)

He saw neurotic disturbances during the adult years as an indication that the person was attempting to carry the "psychology of the youthful phase" into these middle years — just as neurotic disturbances in youth reflect an inability to leave childhood behind.

In old age Jung saw some "deep-seated and peculiar changes within the psyche" (p. 14). He noted a tendency for persons to change into their opposites, especially in the psychic realm. For example, he suggested that older men become more "feminine" and older women become more "masculine"; and he pointed out "an inexorable inner process" that "enforces the contraction of life" (we discuss these points in detail in Chapter 8). In general, he argued that "we cannot live the afternoon of life according to the programme of life's morning; for what was great in the morning will be little at evening, and what in the morning was true will at evening have become a lie" (p. 17).

Jung felt there must be some purpose in human life continuing into the late years, such as the caring for children. But what is the purpose of life after this has been accomplished? Is the purpose to compete with the young, as so often happens in our society? Jung pointed out that in most primitive societies the old people are the sources of wisdom, the "guardians of the mysteries and the laws . . . [in which] the cultural heritage of the tribe is expressed" (p. 18). In contrast, he felt we no longer have any clear sense of meaning or purpose in old age. Thus we try to hang on to the first half of life, clinging to youth instead of looking forward. Jung argued that many people reach old age with unsatisfied demands, but it is "fatal" for such persons to look back. It is essential for them to have a goal in the future. This suggests that the reason that all the great religions hold out the hope of an afterlife is to make it possible for one to live the second half of life with as much purpose as the first half. Jung recognized that modern men and women have become accustomed to disbelieve in life after death, or at least to question it, and that we cannot know whether there is an afterlife. But he argued that "an old man who cannot bid farewell to life appears as feeble and sickly as a young man who is unable to embrace it" (p. 20). He felt it is psychologically positive "to discover in death a goal towards which one can strive, and that shrinking away from it is something unhealthy and abnormal which robs the second half of life of its purpose" (p. 20). He suggested that in the second half of life the individual's attention turns inward, and that this inner exploration may help individuals find a meaning and wholeness in life that makes it possible for them to accept death.

Erikson's Ages of Life in Adulthood

Like Jung, Erik Erikson studied with Sigmund Freud and based his theory of human development primarily on clinical experience. However, his **eight ages of life** (Erikson, 1950, 1968, 1976) represent a series of crucial turning points stretching

Erik Erikson (1902–   ).

from birth to death; thus it is more comprehensive than any of the views presented so far. Unlike Jung, Erikson's stages emphasize childhood development; and the first five stages are largely expansions of Freud's stages of psychosexual development to include social influences.

Although we focus only on the later stages of his theory that deal with youth and adulthood, the earlier stages, in his view, are like building blocks upon which the later stages depend. Each stage presents a new challenge—we might say a new point of "turbulence" in the "stream of life" that must be negotiated successfully. Following our metaphor, if one's "raft" is severely damaged during one of the early turning points, the later turbulent points will be more difficult to negotiate. In this sense, Erikson's framework provides one view of the "river of life" and its major turning points and forks, so that we have a sense of the crucial challenges for individuals at various points through their lives.

We use this river metaphor because it seems appropriate on two levels: first, it expresses the sequential, progressive course of an individual through the eight turning points; and second, it suggests that this framework may be a simplified overview, from a great height as it were, of the general course of the life cycle. The theory is very difficult to test empirically, yet it provides a useful descriptive framework for understanding some general issues and changes during the adult years.

Each stage in Erikson's conception of the life cycle represents a struggle between two conflicting tendencies, each of which is experienced by the individual (Box 1.2). Thus, each stage is expressed by two opposite qualities, linked by the word *versus*:

> Versus is an interesting little word. . . . Developmentally, it suggests a dialectic dynamics, in that the final strength postulated could not emerge without either of the contending qualities; yet, to assure growth, the syntonic, the one more intent on adaptation, must absorb the dystonic. (Erikson, 1976, p. 23)

A **dialectical interaction** is one in which there is a tension between two or

---

BOX 1.2 *Erikson's Eight Ages of Human Life*

	Opposing Issues of Each Stage	Emerging Value	Period of Life
1	Basic Trust versus Mistrust	Hope	Infancy
2	Autonomy versus Shame and Doubt	Will	Early childhood
3	Initiative versus Guilt	Purpose	Play age
4	Industry versus Inferiority	Competence	School age
5	Indentity versus Identity (Role) Confusion	Fidelity	Adolescence
6	Intimacy versus Isolation	Love	Young adulthood
7	Generativity versus Stagnation (Self-Absorption)	Care	Maturity
8	Integrity versus Despair (and Disgust)	Wisdom	Old age

Source: Based on Erikson (1976).

more opposing forces; the result of that interaction is a new *synthesis* that reflects, not the sum of the forces, but a resolution of them in a way that is different from the original separate forces. In Erikson's theory, each dialectical conflict between the two opposite qualities is eventually resolved by a synthesis that represents one of the basic human strengths: *hope, will, purpose, competence, fidelity, love, care, wisdom.* The dialectical struggle is both conscious and unconscious within the individual. It involves both inner (psychological) and outer (social) processes. The psychosocial strengths that result are "an active adaptation rather than a passive adjustment" of the individual in a social environment, so that "they change the environment even as they make selective use of its opportunities" (Erikson, 1976, p. 25).

Each of the eight periods of the life cycle "has its stage of ascendence when physical, cognitive, emotional, and social developments permit its coming to a crisis" (Erikson, 1976, p. 24). The term "crisis" does not mean emotional distress, but instead a crucial issue that comes to fruition during a particular period of development. This sequential progression through the stages involves considerable overlap between them, however.

> Nobody . . . in life is neatly "located" in one stage; rather, all persons can be seen to oscillate between at least two stages and move more definitely into a higher one only when an even higher one begins to determine the interplay. (Erikson, 1976, pp. 24–25)

For the final stage, death itself functions as a kind of higher stage.

Since our concern is with adulthood, we discuss only the later stages in Erikson's scheme, although each builds on the strengths of the earlier stages.

Identity versus Identity (Role) Confusion

Erikson's fifth stage arises with the beginning of puberty and the increasing social demand to find one's role in life as a sexual, productive, responsible adult with a reasonably consistent set of attitudes and values about oneself. It may also reflect the adolescent's increasing ability to think abstractly, cultural values about individuality, and social definitions of gender roles.

The positive (or syntonic) side of the struggle is a sense of **identity**: a sense of continuity and consistency of oneself over time. The negative (or dystonic) side is a sense of confusion about one's identity or role — a lack of certainty about who one is, or about the part one is playing in the scheme of life.

The resolution of this stage involves experiencing both of these opposing tendencies within oneself and in relation to one's social environment. From that dialectical struggle emerges the psychosocial strength of *fidelity:* "the ability to sustain loyalties freely pledged in spite of the inevitable contradictions and confusions of value systems" (Erikson, 1976, p. 25).

An early period of this stage involves the overlap between Industry versus Inferiority (stage 4), when children are engaged in learning many of the skills they will need as adolescents and adults. The later aspect of this stage, when a sense of one's identity begins to emerge, overlaps with the next stage, Intimacy versus Isolation.

Intimacy versus Isolation

According to Erikson, the individual does not become capable of a fully intimate relationship until the identity crisis is fairly well resolved. **Intimacy** is a mutual relationship of affection and trust that involves full appreciation of each other's uniqueness and separateness. Thus, one needs to have a reasonably clear sense of who one is and the part one is playing in life — developed through the dialectical struggle described earlier — before one can fuse one's identity with another person successfully. Attempts to achieve intimacy earlier are frequently mixed up with identity issues and involve seeking to define oneself through a relationship with another person.

> Sexual intimacy is only part of what I have in mind, for it is obvious that sexual intimacies often precede the capacity to develop a true and mutual psychosocial intimacy with another person, be it in friendship, in erotic encounters, or in joint inspiration. The youth who is not sure of his identity shies away from interpersonal intimacy or throws himself into acts of intimacy which are "promiscuous" without true fusion or real self-abandon.
>
> Where a youth does not accomplish such intimate relationships with others — and, I would add, with his own inner resources — in late adolescence or early adulthood, he may settle for highly stereotyped interpersonal relations and come to retain a deep *sense of isolation*. (Erikson, 1968, pp. 135–136)

Resolution of this stage involves the dialectical struggle between the opposing tendencies of intimacy and isolation. The psychosocial strength that emerges from this struggle is *love*. The early period of this stage involves an overlap of Identity versus Identity Confusion with Intimacy versus Isolation. The latter period involves an overlap with Generativity versus Stagnation.

Generativity versus Stagnation (Self-Absorption)

This seventh stage of life may be the longest, because it refers to **generativity**, which may be defined as having left one's mark by producing something that will outlive oneself in some way, usually through parenthood or in occupational achievements. The struggle is between a sense of generativity and the sense of stagnation or self-absorption. As in all the stages, an individual may be involved in these issues as well as those of the previous stage, or in addition to those of the next stage. The outcome of this stage is *care* — "the widening concern for what has been generated by love, necessity, or accident" (Erikson, 1976, p. 24).

Integrity versus Despair (and Disgust)

The final stage is brought on by a growing awareness of the finitude of life and of one's closeness to death. The crucial task during this stage is to evaluate one's life and accomplishments. The sense of **integrity** reflects an affirmation that one's life has been a meaningful adventure in history. The opposite is the sense of *despair* or disgust: an existential sense of meaninglessness and a feeling that one's life was wasted or should have been different than it was. The dialectical struggle between these two opposing themes is the essence of this period and produces *wisdom:* "the detached and yet active concern with life itself in the face of death itself, . . . it maintains and conveys the integrity of experience, in spite of the decline of bodily and mental functions" (Erikson, 1976, p. 23).

Limitations: *Women and Non-Western Men*

Carol Gilligan (1982) pointed out that Erikson's model of development focuses exclusively on male patterns. Although he notes sex differences, his conception of the life cycle is defined by male experience.

> The problem that female adolescence presents for theorists of human development is apparent in Erikson's scheme. . . . The preparation for the successful resolution of the adolescent identity crisis is delineated in Erikson's description of the crises that charac terize the preceding four stages. Although the initial crisis in infancy of "trust versus mistrust" anchors development in the experience of relationship, the task then clearly becomes one of individuation . . . separateness . . . autonomy . . . [and in] adolescence, the celebration of the autonomous, initiating, industrious self through the forging of an identity based on an ideology that can support and justify adult commitments. But about whom is Erikson talking?
>
> Once again it turns out to be the male child. For the female, Erikson (1968) says, the sequence is a bit different. . . . While for men, identity precedes intimacy and generativity in the optimal cycle of human separation and attachment, for women these tasks seem instead to be fused. Intimacy goes along with identity, as the female comes to know herself as she is known, through her relationships with others.
>
> Yet despite Erikson's observation of sex differences, his chart of life-cycle stages remains unchanged: identity continues to precede intimacy as male experience continues to define his life-cycle conception. (Gilligan, 1982, pp. 11–12)

Certainly his conception does not describe the life cycle issues in all cultures, either. In Japan, for example, the traditional emphasis has been on interdependence, collectivism, empathy, and introspection instead of autonomy, equality, individuality, and aggression for both women and men (Lebra, 1976).

The later stages of generativity and integrity seem to encompass both typical female and male patterns. However, it is likely that they also are more fused with intimacy than Erikson's model suggests for women and for both men and women in some cultures.

Thus it may be wise to use Erikson's theory with a narrow instead of a broad brush. That is, it is a circumscribed, not universal, model of human development. It has been supported, however, by a major study of middle-class men from age 20 to 47 in the United States (Vaillant, 1977).

Levinson's Analysis of Developmental Periods

Daniel Levinson and his colleagues (1976, 1978) developed a model of adult development that, like Bühler's, was based on biographical interviews. Although his data analysis revealed a series of stages, or developmental periods, they differed from those described by Bühler and by Erikson. On one hand, although Levinson's model shares a midlife turning point with Bühler's theory, it reflects social development more than biological change as her theory did. On the other hand, Levinson's stages consist of periods of transition *alternating* with periods of calm, unlike Erikson's model. Also similar to Bühler and different from Erikson, this model ties the developmental periods to specific chronological age. We discuss these data in detail in Chapter 3. His stages are:

Early Adult Transition — age 17–22

Entering the Adult World — age 22–28

Age 30 Transition — age 28–33

Settling Down — age 33–40

The Midlife Transition — age 40–45

Entering Middle Adulthood — age 45–50

Age 50 Transition — age 50–55

Culmination of Middle Adulthood — age 55–60

Late Adult Transition — age 60–65

Late Adulthood — age 65

Riegel's Dialectical Analysis of Development

A different perspective on the nature of human development is presented in the dialectical approach proposed by Klaus Riegel (1976). Whereas the other theories we have discussed view development as a series of stages through which individuals progress, Riegel focused on the developmental processes of *change.*

He proposed that there are four major dimensions of development: inner-biological, individual-psychological, cultural-sociological, and outer-physical (Box 1.3). Each of these dimensions is constantly interacting with the others and with other elements within the same dimension. For example, psychological *maturation* reflects biological development, social expectations and attitudes, and economic conditions of life; if any of these change, the entire system is affected. Likewise,

---

BOX 1.3 *Examples of the Four Major Dimensions of Development That Produce Transitions through the Process of Dialectical Interaction*

Individual-Psychological	Individual-Biological	Cultural-Sociological	Outer-Physical
Maturity	Puberty	Social attitudes	Economic conditions
Emotional feelings	Health	Social expectations	War
Independence	Height	Opportunities	Urban/rural living

Source: Kimmel & Weiner (1985), Box 1.1, p. 16. Reprinted with permission.

psychological maturation affects other psychological characteristics. Therefore, each dimension may bring change, create problems, raise questions, or bring transitions in the life cycle.

This fourfold progression is obviously complex. Changes in one dimension are not always synchronized with changes in other dimensions. There is usually some degree of conflict between the dimensions. In addition, major changes in any of the dimensions will bring a confrontation between that dimension and the other dimensions. If this confrontation brings a major reorganization of the other dimensions, this may be seen as a period of *developmental transition* for the individual. The *dialectical interaction* among these dimensions is the essence of development as the individual grows older.

> Inner-biological progressions lead the individual away from home, to work, marriage, and parenthood. . . . Most of these events will be well synchronized with progressions along other dimensions. For example, many individuals marry when they are mature enough, when they have the appropriate psychological stature and intention, and when the social conditions are conducive and appropriate. In other instances such a synchronization is not achieved. Individuals marry without having reached a sufficient level of maturity; others may have attained the proper level but fail to find the right partner. Thus, the inner-biological and individual-psychological progressions are not always synchronized with the cultural-sociological or outer-physical conditions, for example, with the traditions and laws about marriage or the reduced availability of marriage partners after wars. (Riegel, 1976, pp. 693–694)

The synchronization of these four dimensions may be studied in the interaction of two or more persons, such as in families, or in relations between individuals and social groups. Even natural catastrophies (outer-physical dimension) may produce disruption to the synchronization of these dimensions for individuals, groups, and societies. All of this occurs over time.

Thus, this approach involves dialectical interaction of major dimensions of human life through time. It provides a perspective for the study of life span human development and calls attention to the complex nature of adulthood and aging. However, this view of development as a process of ceaseless change is very abstract, so it may be helpful to think of it as the process underlying specific developmental stages.

Stability of Development

In contrast to the emphasis on stages, change, and transitions in development, several studies have suggested that the basic structure of an individual's personality remains fairly stable over long periods of time; we discuss this in detail in Chapter 8. In particular, Costa and McCrae (1980b) reported that when personality traits are measured, there was little evidence of developmental change for most people. For example, their research found no evidence for a midlife crisis in a study of men, in contrast to Levinson's model (we discuss this in Chapter 3). Other studies likewise have found no compelling evidence to support a series of developmental stages during adulthood (Haan, 1981; Vaillant, 1977). Thus, Costa and McCrae (1980b)

Four interacting dimensions in Riegel's dialectical perspective are not always in synchrony. For example, lesbian co-mothers show that individual-psychological and inner-biological progressions are not always synchronized with cultural-sociological progressions such as the traditions and laws about marriage.

concluded that developmental theory should focus less on change and more on traits that remain stable during adulthood.

> Instead of looking for the mechanisms by which personality changes with age, we should look for the means by which stability is maintained. Are traits genetically determined, and therefore as stable as genetic influences? Do individuals choose or create environments that sustain the behavior that characterizes them? Are we locked into our nature by the network of social expectations around us? Do early childhood influences continue to operate beyond the reach of corrective experiences? (Costa & McCrae, 1980b, p. 81)

The contradiction between this stability model of adult development and the stage models discussed earlier may be less significant than it appears, however. We all recognize that important characteristics of individuals remain relatively stable over the lifetime. Our parents, friends, and co-workers may go through some important changes, but they usually do not change into different people than they were before; we discuss the simultaneous processes of stability and change in Chapter 2. Costa and McCrae (1980b) measured personality traits (including neuroticism, extraversion, and openness) that might be expected to persist over time, even in the face of developmental transitions, milestones, or crises (such as marriage, divorce, parenthood, changing jobs, becoming middle-aged, or retirement). In fact, in one study with 233 men between the ages of 35 and 79 they found that those who experienced more symptoms of a midlife crisis were not more likely to be middle-aged, but they were higher on the measure of *neuroticism*—both at the time of the study and also in a previous study 10 years earlier. Thus, some persons may be more likely to experience considerable crisis in their lives than other people with different personality patterns; in either case the personality patterns remain stable.

Pluralistic Approach to Development

An integrative model of life span development was proposed by Baltes and several of his colleagues (Baltes, Cornelius & Nesselroade, 1980; Baltes, Reese & Lipsitt, 1980; Baltes & Willis, 1979). There are several important themes in this model. First, developmental processes may begin at any point in life; likewise, they may differ in their duration, impact, and termination (Figure 1.2). Therefore, not all developmental processes begin at birth, during childhood, or early adulthood; some begin in old age. Second, not all developmental processes follow a straight line as has been implied by the stage theories described earlier. In fact, some developmental processes may be *curvilinear*—that is, important both early and very late in life, but not in between; for example, one generally has more potential leisure time without work and child-care responsibility in childhood and old age, compared with middle adulthood. Vice versa, some processes are less important in childhood or old age than in early and middle adulthood; for example, one usually has greater athletic ability during early adulthood than during either childhood or old age. Third, many developmental processes begin at various ages, increase to a maximum level, and decline only slowly if at all, as long as the individual is healthy. Fourth, there is considerable variation between individuals in development and this variation *increases* with age, particularly in adulthood and old age.

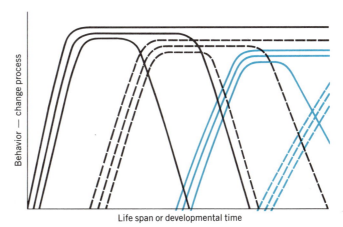

FIGURE 1.2 Hypothetical examples of life span developmental processes. Developmental functions (behavior-change processes) differ in terms of onset, duration, termination, and directionality when charted in the framework of the life course. Moreover, developmental change is both quantitative and qualitative, not all developmental change is related to chronological age, and the initial direction is not always incremental (see also Baltes, Cornelius & Nesselroade, 1980). (*Source*: Baltes, Reese & Lipsitt (1980), Figure 1, p. 73. Reprinted with permission from the *Annual Review of Psychology*, Volume 31, © 1980 by Annual Reviews Inc.)

Thus, development is **pluralistic** in that it begins at different points, and follows different courses depending on the aspect of development in question. Moreover, it is pluralistic in that the influences on development take different forms. According to the integrative model proposed by Baltes, Reese, and Lipsitt (1980), three general types of influences can be identified:

1. *Normative Age-Graded:* Biological and sociocultural influences that are linked fairly clearly with age, such as physical maturation during childhood or typical events during adulthood involving the family, education, and occupation.

2. *Normative History-Graded:* Environmental, cataclysmic, and social change influences that affect most members of a culture; their effects may differ for persons who are younger or older at the time of the event; examples include war, economic depression, major epidemics, or modernization of the society.

3. *Nonnormative:* Significant events that affect a particular individual, but do not occur for most people; examples include accidents, atypical career changes, temporary unemployment, winning a lottery, religious conversion, and divorce.

The impacts of these three general types of influences interact over time, differ among individuals, and vary for different behaviors, according to this model. Baltes, Reese, and Lipsitt (1980) speculated that the age-graded influences have greater impact early and late in life; the history-graded influences have their peak impact during adolescence; and the impact of nonnormative influences increases steadily from childhood to old age. We discuss normative age-graded influences in Chapter 2 and nonnormative influences in Chapter 3.

Conclusion

These theories of development during adulthood provide some useful outlines for understanding human development from a life span perspective. They indicate some of the ways in which persons in the second half of life might differ from persons in the early years of adulthood. They also sensitize us to some of the typical influences on development during the adult years. Some of these theories also suggest a possible midlife crisis when the growth and expansion trends of the earlier years are replaced by consolidation and, eventually, contraction of social participation in the later years. Other models, however, suggest no particular link between any specific age and developmental change.

The first three perspectives (Bühler, Jung, and Erikson) tend to be very general and also idealized. That is, they do not give much indication of the ways in which cultural differences, gender differences, social-economic status, or individual uniqueness interact with this general developmental progression. In a sense, they describe a process of development that leads toward the ideal of "human fulfillment" or "successful aging" as it is defined in the middle class in our society. For other persons, fulfillment or successful aging may mean physical survival and providing one's children with at least a reasonable chance for survival. For some, aging means illness, poverty, and isolation with little opportunity for fulfillment or success. It should be stressed that there is more *individual variation* among adults and older age groups than among younger age groups; thus, there is no single path to successful aging.

Riegel's dialectical model, although potentially providing a framework to analyze the effects of unique biological, sociocultural, psychological, and environmental influences of development, is not well enough defined to do more than suggest the directions future research should take. The pluralistic model proposed by Baltes and his colleagues incorporated several of these influences. Yet, it also provides a perspective rather than a specific model for future research.

The focus on stability of personality traits by Costa and McCrae is clearly a model for future research. The developmental processes suggested by Baltes are probably responsible for much of the stability, as well as the change, in individual lives over time.

In addition to the question of change versus stability in adult development, Levinson's research and theory calls attention to a very interesting issue. The men in his study were all born at about the same time (roughly 1925–1935) in the United States. This raises two important questions that we discuss in the remainder of this chapter.

First, if these developmental theories are useful guidelines for understanding the human life cycle, does it make an important difference whether that life cycle began in 1900, 1930, or 1960? That is, what is the effect of the interaction of an individual's life cycle with historical time, which reflects social and environmental influences that may affect these patterns of development?

Second, since empirical research can help us better understand the patterns of adult development, how does a life span developmental researcher study the course of human development? For example, would we learn the same things about adult development if we were to study young people and people their parents' age as we would if we were to study the same group of people when they were 20 and again when they were 45? Probably not — unless children grow up in ways that are very much like their parents. Either way, however, historical influences can affect these developmental processes, so we begin with that discussion.

Individual Life Cycles and Historical Time

An individual's developmental progression through the life cycle is only one source of age-related change. We have outlined some of the central biological and social age-related events that influence and serve to "time" the individual's progression through the life span. We have also discussed the changes that various theorists believe occur with age. But the historical time line that intersects with a person's lifeline is another age-related dimension that affects the individual's progression through the life cycle.

Recalling the lifeline described in Figure 1.1, we will now intersect it with the historical time line (Figure 1.3). Persons age 80 in 1990 were born in 1910 during a period in the United States of peace and isolation from world conflicts. They were at the forefront of the industrial expansion after the First World War and have lived to see horses and steam power replaced by space shuttles and computers. Obviously

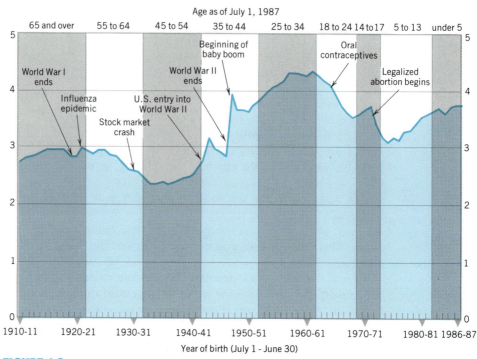

FIGURE 1.3 Number of births, by year, 1910 to 1987, and relationship to 1987 age groups. Shows effects of historical events on birthrate. (*Source*: U.S. Bureau of the Census, 1988, Figure 2, p. 2.)

a great deal has changed that has affected their patterns of development. Life expectancy has increased dramatically. Average length of education has increased by several years. Also, our complex technological society has made life for the elderly both easier and more difficult at the same time: the telephone, medical advances, and labor-saving appliances have helped many elderly to lead rich lives; but the fear of crime in cities, complicated Medicare forms, and rising costs have been troublesome for many also.

If you are a college-age student today, your grandparents were probably born between World War I and the Great Depression. They learned the interdependence of the nations of the world, but, most of all, they learned that economic security and material possessions may evaporate for reasons beyond their control. They may have gone to school during the depression and their early socialization experiences that influence later attitudes and values took place during this period of inadequate material resources. They lived through World War II, perhaps fought in it, when the security of the United States was felt to be directly threatened, and the material products of the expanding economy continued to be in short supply. It is interesting to talk with people who grew to adulthood during this historical period, for life was very different then (Elder, 1974). One study that followed men and women who were born in 1900 found that middle-class women appeared to benefit from the hardship of the depression, as measured by life satisfaction in their seventies, perhaps because they learned self-reliance skills that assisted them into old age.

"Hooverville" in New York City during the Great Depression of the 1930s.

Working-class women, and men did not show any such benefit, however (Caspi & Elder, 1986). This was also the period that gave rise to several of the theories of adult development and is the period to which the subjects in Levinson's study grew up.

With the atomic bomb came the end of the World War II and the beginning of the "nuclear age." Everyone born after the mid-1940s in the United States has experienced not only the economic growth of the country and the increased abundance of the middle class but also the omnipresent threat of nuclear war. Your parents were probably born after the World War II. They have lived through historical experiences unprecedented in their immediacy as a result of television and news coverage via satellite. Their world has not only experienced an amazing technological revolution and shrinkage in the effective size of the earth, but also has begun exploring far beyond our own planet.

There can be no doubt that great historical changes have occurred during the lives of individuals currently living, and that the pace of these changes is rapid and escalating. We can predict confidently that one important aspect of growing older in our society will continue to be an increasing complexity in the tasks and skills required of adults. Speculate for a moment about a retirement community on the moon that is especially attractive because of its low gravity, or visiting your grandchildren's computerized library of school books in electronic files.

Cohort Effects

A **cohort** is a group of people born at about the same time—for instance, in 1920, or between 1920 and 1929. Obviously, this group of people grows older together so that the cohort moves through the life span together. Each cohort experiences somewhat similar historical influences. These shared experiences can have an effect on the attitudes, values, and worldview of those individuals living through them. For example, individuals born after World War II could not have been influenced by the Great Depression of the 1930s in the same way their parents were. Many observers have noted differences in the value of money, feelings about the security of savings, and the importance of self-reliance between persons who were born before the depression and those born after World War II. The impact of this historical event is found only for those persons whose family experienced marked economic deprivation, however; predepression socioeconomic status and family interaction patterns also influenced the long-term effect of the 1930s depression on individuals (Elder, 1974).

In addition, different cohorts of individuals are affected by historical experiences in different ways because each cohort of persons is a different age when the experience occurs (cf. Stewart & Healy, 1989). For example, the Vietnam War had a very different effect on young people than it did on children or older adults because it was the cohort of Americans between 18 and 25 during the 1960s and early 1970s whose lives were most directly affected by that war. Although the Vietnam War affected all young people to some extent, it clearly affected those who actually fought in the war to a much greater extent. Recently, attention has been directed to the special problems and issues faced by Vietnam veterans that are different from those faced by earlier cohorts of veterans. In general, such historical events help to

The war in Vietnam affected those young people of draft age more than other age groups.

form individuals and each cohort of individuals carries its own experience of history through the life span. In that sense, these effects are more enduring than the historical conditions that brought them about.

Development, then, may be seen as a series of cohorts moving through the life span. As members of the cohort die, the group shrinks in size until only a few survivors are left. Therefore, studies of any age group involve studying the survivors of their particular cohort.

A visual example of these cohorts moving through the life cycle is shown in the population profile of the United States (Figure 1.4). This profile represents a "snapshot" of 18 different cohorts of men and women in 1986. If this "snapshot" were taken again in 1991, each cohort would have moved to the next higher age group (except for the 85+ group), and each group would be somewhat smaller (especially the older cohorts) because some would have died.

Note the "bulge" in the groups between age 25 and 39 (those born between 1947 and 1961). This is the so-called *baby boom* that followed the end of World War II. As men came home from the war and women left the factories where they had worked, they began having children. Since the economy was expanding and the country was optimistic, having several children was popular and the mother did not work for pay unless she had to. Fewer infants died than previously because of medical advances such as sulfa and penicillin. The postwar population bulge will continue to move through the lifeline; the leading edge of this bulge is age 45 in 1992. The baby boom has generated a wide range of pressures for this cohort that

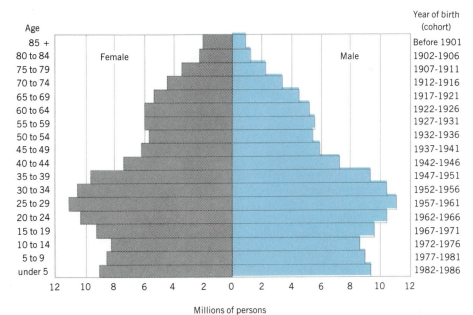

FIGURE 1.4 U.S. population by age, sex, and year of birth: 1986 (*Source*: U.S. Bureau of the Census. Estimates of the population of the United States by age, sex, and race: 1980 to 1986. *Current Population Reports* Series P-25, No. 1000 (February 1987).)

has had to compete with a large number of age-mates at each step, in overcrowded schools, college scholarships, getting a job, and buying a home. Some demographers see this cohort as under unusual stress because of this competition and link this to the high rates of divorce, suicide, and drug abuse among this generation (Easterlin, 1980). In addition, since they are expected to live longer than past generations, this cohort will eventually swell the ranks of the aged, placing great strain on Social Security, Medicare, and retirement housing.

Beginning around 1960, however, the birth rate began to decline and college-age students today were born into a cohort characterized by a low birth rate. In contrast to the baby boom cohort, today's generation of students would be expected to have relatively less competition for employment, education, and promotion. Because of their low birth rate cohort, they will live in a different demographic world than their high birth rate parents. We can predict that their lives will be affected by this particular *cohort effect*.

Historical Period (Time) Effects

Whereas many historical events affect one generation, or one age group (cohort), more than others, some historical events affect the entire society in relatively equal ways. For example, the invention of the automobile, electric light, transistors, and jet airplanes has affected the entire population. Similarly, improvements in medical care, nutrition, and sanitation have affected all people regardless of their age or cohort. To be sure, cohort differences still exist even within these large-scale changes, but we must consider these historical changes in understanding adult development.

A dramatic example of this kind of historical effect is the increase in *life expectancy* (Figure 1.5). In 1900 the average baby would have been expected to live 32½ years if he was a Black male; a Black male born in 1985 would be expected to live an average of 65 years — twice as long! The increase in the number of years the typical Black female baby is expected to live has been even greater — from 34 to 74 years! Similar increases in life expectancy have occurred for White babies. This extraordinary increase in life expectancy has resulted primarily from medical advances that have eliminated the major diseases that caused death in children. At one time, children were not given a name until they had survived smallpox because so many died as a result of it; today smallpox has been eliminated throughout the world. Other diseases require inoculations to prevent them, but children can now be readily protected. Similar medical advances have markedly reduced the effects of diseases that once killed young and middle-aged adults, such as pneumonia, tuberculosis, and influenza. Most of these changes have occurred since World War II. As a result, whereas only 19 Black and other nonwhite male babies out of every 100 born in 1900–1902 survived to age 65, 62 Black and other nonwhite male babies out of every 100 born in 1984 are expected to survive to age 65; the change is even more dramatic for Black and other nonwhite females and also quite significant for White males and females (Figure 1.6). In fact, almost as many men and women are likely to live to age 85 in 1984 than they were to reach age 65 in 1900.

Until recently the picture has been different for those people who do survive to

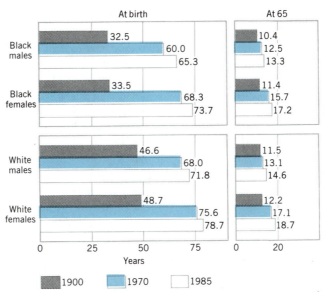

FIGURE 1.5 Life expectancy at birth and at age 65 by race and sex, in 1900, 1976, and 1985 in the United States. Most of the increase is the result of reduced childhood mortality; the increase for older persons is much less dramatic, but there has been a significant increase since 1970. (*Source*: National Center for Health Statistics. *Health, United States, 1986*. DHHS Pub. No. (PHS) 87-1232. Washington, DC: Department of Health and Human Services (December, 1986).)

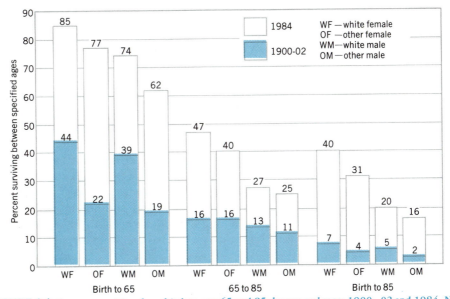

FIGURE 1.6 Percent surviving from birth to age 65 and 85, by sex and race: 1900–02 and 1984. Note that the proportion of women and nonwhite men surviving to age 85 today is comparable to the proportion surviving to age 65 in 1900. (*Source*: National Center for Health Statistics. Vital Statistics of the United States, 1984, Vol. II, Section 6 (Lifetables), March 1987. Reprinted from U.S. Senate, 1987–1988, Chart 1–12.)

age 65. Clearly, they have always been the healthiest, strongest, and luckiest members of their cohort—otherwise, they would not have outlived so many of their contemporaries. Also, until recently, medical science had made little progress in preventing and curing the diseases of old age, especially as compared with the success against many diseases of childhood. As a result, life expectancy did not increase as dramatically for persons at age 65 as it did for persons at birth earlier in this century (Figure 1.5). However, by 1980 life expectancy at age 65 had begun to increase significantly for this age group also. This change reflects a dramatic reduction in deaths from heart and artery disease that has resulted from greater awareness of healthful behaviors such as better diet, more exercise, and less cigarette smoking, as well as improved medical treatment.

Women clearly live longer than men, in general. They have also benefited more from the general improvement in health, nutrition and living conditions than men have. The reasons for this are not clear, but we discuss some of them in Chapter 7. The result is that women, compared with men, are more likely to be widowed, less likely to remarry late in life, and more likely to live alone in old age.

These general historical changes make the experience of adulthood and aging different today than it was in the past; and they will make the experience of aging different in the future than it is today. They reflect changes that affect all people living during a particular historical period. However, these changes in health, nutrition, technology, or level of education can affect some cohorts more dramatically than others although they generally affect all persons. That is, *development* (age) interacts with *cohort* (year of birth), and both interact with the effects of *historical period* (time).

To take a simple example, young adults are taller than children and are also taller, on the average, than old people today. The difference between the height of children is obviously the result of development—young children are not fully grown. However, nutrition affects growth so that young people today often grow to be taller than their parents. Similarly, adults today are taller than adults in earlier historical periods. Thus, differences in physical stature are *cohort effects*. Young adults are taller than older people today since older people did not grow as tall when they were growing up because of less adequate nutrition earlier in this century. In addition, older persons may lose some height in the later years as a result of muscular weakness and loss of connective tissue or changes in the bone (see Chapter 7); therefore, age differences in stature reflect both cohort and developmental effects. Individual genetic influences are also important, of course.

As this example illustrates, historical and cohort effects make the analysis of developmental change among individuals who are living in a changing world very complex. In the next section we discuss the ways developmental research deals with this issue.

Developmental Research Methodology

To understand adult development and aging, social scientists conduct **empirical research:** observation, inquiry about individual's experience, and carefully designed experiments. Empirical methods test ideas and speculations about adulthood with data from direct observation or experience. Examples of empirical methods that are often used are interviews, questionnaires, tests of particular skills, and experiments under controlled conditions. An adequate number of participants must take part in the study so that the results are unlikely to occur by coincidence. *Nonempirical* research, in contrast, might include speculations or impressions based on casual conversations, patients seen in a practice, or reports from informants. Nonempirical research may be useful, but it is not possible to judge its validity objectively. The type of research and the manner in which it is carried out are prescribed by the scientist's professional and ethical standards (e.g. *Ethical Principles in the Conduct of Research with Human Participants,* American Psychological Association, 1982). Research on aging can raise several important ethical and pragmatic considerations that deserve particular attention (Kimmel & Moody, in press; Schaie, 1988).

The central focus in **developmental research** is a systematic emphasis on change over time. For example, one might hypothesize that individuals in one period of life differ from individuals in another period, or that individuals change from one stage of life to another. This developmental hypothesis may reflect the interdisciplinary framework described earlier. This approach would lead one to study the interaction of biological, cultural, psychological, and sociological processes on an individual during a particular developmental phase. An example of a fully interdisciplinary study might include the effects of health, social participation, personality, and cultural attitudes about aging on the level of satisfaction older people experience in different countries of the world. Most developmental research does not involve all these different perspectives, however.

Much of the information in this book is based on empirical research, often from a developmental perspective. Likewise, information about adulthood and aging on television and in newspapers or magazines frequently is based on this type of research. Thus, it is useful for us to take a close look at this type of research, and at the meaning of age in psychological research.

The Meaning of Age in Developmental Research

Chronological age provides a convenient index of the passage of *time*. It may not be a very meaningful indicator of development, however. At best, it measures the number of revolutions that the sun has made around the earth since a person was born. At worst, it can be exaggerated or reduced by the individual if there are no accurate birth records available. For example, some studies of supposedly very aged persons turned out to have participants who were not as old as had been thought (Palmore, 1984).

Moreover, age provides a sensible measure of development only when the process being studied is *time-dependent* and begins at a particular chronological age. For example, biological growth can be measured fairly well by chronological age. In contrast, advancement in a career may also be time-dependent, but is not necessarily related to chronological age, as "child proteges" or "late bloomers" illustrate. In addition, some developmental events may be *time-independent* since they can begin at any point in time. Such events might include a serious physical illness, accident, or stroke of good fortune. Although these may be milestones, as discussed earlier, and influence the person's development, they are not related to chronological age. An illustration of these differing patterns was shown earlier in Figure 1.2.

Chronological age is most clearly seen as an *index* of a large number of factors that interact to produce development. It is an index of biological, psychological, social, and self-perceived changes that take place over time. Age alone does not cause these changes; it is an index of the speed with which the changes take place. Thus, the goal of developmental research is to replace *age* with an understanding of the time-dependent and time-independent processes that bring about the changes that take place through the course of the human life cycle (Birren & Renner, 1977).

This does not mean we should discard age as a variable — it may be the only one we have available for describing changes that occur over time. It does mean that we should look behind "age" to see the time-dependent and time-independent processes that cause development. For example, there are apparent age differences between 20-year-olds and 40-year-olds, including greater occupational achievement, family responsibilities, and experience. These differences are not *caused* by age; instead they are the result of social, biological, and psychological changes in addition to having lived longer and accumulated more experience.

Alternate Measures of Age

We might illustrate this idea by considering the different kinds of "age" that are relevant to human development. **Biological age** could indicate the person's level of biological development and physical health. It might be measured by a "treadmill" test that measures a person's maximum heart rate during exercise, perhaps in combination with other physiological tests. **Psychological age** reflects the person's level of psychological functioning, perhaps measured by psychological tests or by the progression through a series of developmental stages such as the ones proposed by Erikson. **Perceived age** would indicate how "old" the person feels ("young," "middle-aged," or "old"). **Social age** indicates the person's passage through the socially defined milestones of development (working full-time, marriage, parenthood, grandparenthood).

It is easy to imagine that one person who is *chronologically* 35 years old may be *biologically* 65 (overweight, high blood pressure), *psychologically* 45 (intellectually mature, has set goals to achieve before retirement, has a sense of intimacy and generativity), and is *socially* 21 (still training for a profession, unmarried, no children). This person's *perceived age* may be "young adult." Thus, chronological age alone may not provide very much information about the particular individual.

In many ways *perceived age* may be more useful than chronological age and of particular interest to the psychologist because typically it reflects the person's perception of the combination of social, psychological, biological, and chronological age. One person may feel, act, and look like an adult (and others would respond to that person as an adult) at age 16; another person might not feel like a full adult until he or she finishes graduate school at age 30. Similarly, one person of 70 may feel "old" and be in poor health, unable to get around very much, and another

One individual may be chronologically old, but act and feel much younger.

70-year-old may feel ''middle-aged'' and be as active and vigorous as a typical 45-year-old. This measure of age may be the most relevant one for the individual and also especially important for understanding the unique person in his or her psychosocial environment.

Age Simulation Exercises

One method to discover the time-independent and time-dependent processes behind the index of age was suggested by Baltes and Goulet (1971). They proposed that **age simulation** may be used to manipulate systematically the conditions under which age differences are found.

For example, if we find that 75-year-old men perform less well in a dart-throwing experiment than 25-year-old men, we do not know what may have caused this age difference. But we could manipulate some relevant conditions such as the amount of light. Let us assume that the 25-year-old men perform as poorly when the light is dim as the 75-year-old men under normal lighting conditions; and that the 75-year-olds perform as well as the 25-year-olds when the lighting is increased. We could then suspect that this age difference reflects differences in perceptual ability and indicates that older men require brighter light to perform this task than younger men require. Alternatively, it might be that lighting makes no difference, but when the older men are asked to stand closer to the board they score as well as the younger men, suggesting that physical strength is an important difference. Again, it might be that if older men are allowed to practice for an hour they do as well as the young men, suggesting that the age difference reflects practice effects.

We might then *simulate* these age differences (experimentally cause the young men to perform like the old men and vice versa) by varying the lighting level, the distance the dart must be thrown, and the amount of practice to discover the relative contribution of each variable.

This age simulation methodology thus allows an investigator to experimentally manipulate the factors that might reasonably be thought to affect the performance and to identify the factors that may be responsible for the age differences that are found. However, Birren and Renner (1977) pointed out that this procedure does not necessarily reveal the cause of the difference, since the variables that are manipulated may only simulate, but not reproduce, the actual age changes.

Cross-Sectional and Longitudinal Research Strategies

To investigate the processes that cause change to occur with age, it is obviously important to identify the changes that occur with age. The most apparent — and the easiest — way to find age differences is to gather a sample of persons of differing ages, give them questionnaires, tests, or interviews that are appropriate for the question, and compare the results. This research design is called a **cross-sectional study**, since it is based on a cross section of ages at one point in time. The differences found in this way are called *age differences*.

A second approach to studying the index of age is a **longitudinal study.** In this research strategy, a group of subjects is selected, appropriate for the question being studied, and is given a series of questionnaires, tests, or interviews *periodically over several years*. (An easy way to remember this is that *long*itudinal studies take a *long* time.) Differences found between individuals at different ages are called *age changes*. For example, the Grant Study (discussed in Chapter 3) began in 1938 with 268 selected male college students; extensive physical, physiological, and psychological examinations were conducted during the college years. After graduation, each respondent was sent a questionnaire every year until 1955, and every two years after that. All were interviewed during 1950–1952 and the sub-sample of 1942–1944 graduates was interviewed again in 1969 when their average age was 47 (Vaillant, 1977). The report of this study demonstrates that this technique allows the examination of individual differences and the ways in which different individuals change as they grow older.

A **sequential study** involves a combination of cross-sectional and longitudinal strategies and requires a sophisticated statistical procedure to analyze those factors that change with age, those that reflect the year the study was conducted, and those that reflect the year the person was born (Schaie, 1977). This is important because we would expect that younger adults are different from older adults (age), older people are different today from those a decade ago (time of the study), and adults born in the 1940s are different from those born in the 1930s (year of birth).

Longitudinal sequence is a technique that follows a group of subjects for a few years, possibly over a period of time that might represent a developmental turning point such as marriage, parenthood, menopause, or retirement (Baltes, 1968). This allows the investigator to assess some change with age and individual differences without committing the subjects and the investigator to a full longitudinal study.

There are disadvantages to each type of study. Among the problems in *longitudinal* studies are: (1) Participants may drop out during the course of the study and possibly distort the representativeness of the sample. Moreover, these dropout rates may be relevant to the variables being investigated. For example, subjects with lower intelligence or poorer health may be more likely to drop out of the study; this type of *selective dropout* can distort the results. (2) These studies take a long time and it is very expensive to contact and study the participants over a number of years. (3) The measures the researcher used at one age (in childhood or adolescence) may not be relevant at older ages since the important issues for individuals' lives vary as they progress through their lifeline. Also, as science progresses, new techniques become available to measure the variables of interest.

Sequential and *longitudinal sequence* techniques have many of these same problems, although they do not necessarily require as long a period of study as longitudinal studies, which may last decades.

Cross-sectional studies do not measure age-related changes in the same individuals; they only measure age differences between groups of people. Thus, they cannot separate the effects of age differences from changes caused by social and historical changes during the individuals' lives. These *cohort effects*, described earlier, are especially important to examine in developmental research. We discuss their effect in the next section.

Age, Time of Study, and Year of Birth (Cohort)

Since the bulk of data about adulthood and old age is based on cross-sectional studies, it is important to take a closer look at the implications of the differences between cross-sectional and longitudinal studies and to examine the difficulties implicit in cross-sectional studies.

A cross-sectional study by age is illustrated by any of the vertical columns in Figure 1.7; for example, C, G, K, N, P. It is apparent that a study based on such age groups will provide information on age differences (from 30 to 70) in 1990. Many of the problems encountered in longitudinal studies will be eliminated by collecting all the data for the study at one time. However, it is important to note that the difference between the groups of respondents is not only age but is also their *year of birth* or cohort. That is, a 70-year-old in 1990 was born in 1920, but a 40-year-old was born in 1950.

Previously, we discussed the importance of social, historical, and cultural changes for the individual's development through the lifeline. Now it may be seen that a cross-sectional study does not separate the cultural-historical influences from the age differences. That is, *age* and *year of birth* are confounded in a cross-sectional study: the effects of one cannot be separated from the effects of the other.

	Year Measured			
Year Born	1970	1980	1990	2000
1920	(A) 50	(B) 60	(C) 70	(D) 80
1930	(E) 40	(F) 50	(G) 60	(H) 70
1940	(I) 30	(J) 40	(K) 50	(L) 60
1950		(M) 30	(N) 40	(O) 50
1960			(P) 30	(Q) 40
1970				(R) 30

Figure 1.7 Illustration of hypothetical cross-sectional and longitudinal studies, showing that chronological age reflects the interaction of year of birth and year of measurement.

Thus, any age differences may be partly or entirely caused by cultural or historical differences. For example, the combined effect of improved medical care and nutrition, increased education, the depression of the 1930s, and World War II may explain many differences found among the five samples in the 1990 cross-sectional study (C, G, K, N, P). That is, the age difference may be associated primarily with the year of the individual's birth rather than with actual age-related factors. Recall that the effects of "year of birth" are called *cohort effects,* since a cohort is a group of individuals born at about the same time.

In contrast, longitudinal studies (such as A, B, C, D in Figure 1.7) hold the year of birth constant so that whatever effects might be caused by cultural-historical changes are not a factor confounding the age changes in the study. However, these longitudinal studies also confound two variables: *age* and *year of measurement* (time). For example, a change such as decrease in cigarette smoking or an increase in exercise in the population between 1970 and 1990 may counteract an age-related increase in heart disease and a variety of related physiological measures.

One way to assess the influence of these interrelated variables of year of birth and year of measurement is to compare persons of the same age (e.g., A, F, K, O in Figure 1.7). Although this does not provide any information on age, it does provide data on the combined influence of social-historical (time) factors and cohort effects. If all three types of data are obtained, Schaie (1977) has developed a statistical procedure for separating the effects of time, cohort, and age.

A variety of problems may limit the usefulness of these complex techniques, however (Kimmel & Moody, in press; Nesselroade & Labouvie, 1985; Schaie & Hertzog, 1985). The wise reader will want to consider issues such as the following:

1. Are the samples similar in important ways? College students, retired executives, and nursing home residents differ in many ways in addition to age.

2. Do the variables measure the same concept at different ages? For example, a study that requires participants to repeat a list of words or numbers may be a test of attention span at one age and be a test of memory at another age.

3. Were the samples recruited in ways that might affect the study? A "volunteer" sample may differ from one that is paid for participation and this may differ by age. Samples matched for education, health, or marital status may reflect different proportions of the population at varying ages.

4. Social-historical change and cultural background may affect the willingness of respondents to report sensitive information such as sexual behavior or physical abuse by a spouse or family member.

5. Changes in personnel, slight alterations in the experimental procedures, and different experience or motivation of the research staff may affect longitudinal measurements of the same variables.

In general, ideal research methodology carefully considers the appropriateness of the sample for the study, selects a suitable set of measures that are both *reliable* and *valid* in the sample, and discusses the conclusions in terms of the limits of the methodology (Schaie, 1988). No single approach is necessarily better in all circumstances and we must examine each study carefully to describe its implications and limitations.

Example: Change in Intelligence with Age

An important illustration of the differences between longitudinal and cross-sectional studies, and of the influence of cultural-historical factors in cross-sectional findings, is the change in performance on intelligence tests with age. The Wechsler Adult Intelligence Scale (WAIS) was given to a nationwide cross-sectional sample to "standardize" the scores for age differences (Wechsler, 1955). It was found that people in their twenties made the highest scores and that each age group after age 30 scored lower. However, when we consider the average number of years of education for each cohort in the study, we see that the score on the intelligence test corresponds closely with the amount of education (Figure 1.8). This suggests that the cohort factor of educational achievement explains much of the difference between the age groups in test performance. It is therefore sensible to assume not

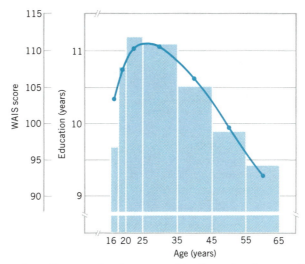

FIGURE 1.8 Comparison of cross-sectional measure of intellectual performance by age with the average education of the subjects. Vertical bar represents years of education for each panel of subjects; dot represents average WAIS total score for that same panel. (*Source*: Based on Wechsler (1955), Tables 5 and 10. Copyright © 1955 by the Psychological Corporation. Adapted and reproduced with permission.)

that people become less intelligent as they grow older but that this cross-sectional study confused age differences with cohort differences. Thus, cross-sectional studies *underestimate* the level of intelligence in the later years under the present social conditions of greater educational attainment for young people compared to older people.

In contrast, longitudinal studies find that performance in IQ tests increases at least to age 50 or 60; it declines moderately during the seventies and eighties (Botwinick, 1977). However, several factors need to be considered that suggest that these results *overestimate* the level of intelligence in later years. Selective dropout rates probably raise the average score, since the more highly intelligent are less likely to drop out. The longitudinal studies had higher average scores at younger ages than the cross-sectional studies, indicating that more able respondents were included and they may retain their IQ level longer than less able respondents. Also there is evidence of a general increase in IQ test performance between the 1930s and 1960s for people of the same age, using a test called the "Army Alpha" designed during World War I (Owens, 1966). In addition, the amount of time between the end of school and the test point (the longer the time, the lower the score), and the decreasing relevance of the type of questions asked on IQ tests, may also lower the scores of older respondents.

It seems reasonable to conclude that the change in intelligence with age is neither the decline indicated in cross-sectional data nor the increase shown for the highly intelligent subjects in longitudinal studies. Instead, it is bounded by the cross-sectional findings at the bottom and by the longitudinal data on the top and probably lies between these two extremes (Figure 1.9).

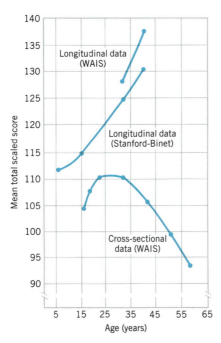

FIGURE 1.9 Comparison of longitudinal and cross-sectional data on changes in intelligence performance with age. Longitudinal data were based on the same sample from age 4 to age 42; two different intelligence tests were used in the last two testings. (*Source*: Longitudinal data from Kangas & Bradway (1971), Table 3. Copyright © 1971 by the American Psychological Association. Cross-sectional data from Wechsler (1955), Table 10. Copyright © 1955 by the Psychological Corporation. Adapted and reproduced with permission.)

We discuss aging and intelligence in more detail in Chapter 4; the point here is that cross-sectional and longitudinal studies may find very different results on the same variables. This example is only one of many that can illustrate the complex interaction of social-historical change and age-related studies of adult development. Other examples include research on sexual behavior, political attitudes, and gender roles.

Since our task is to understand adulthood in a changing society, the following chapters examine the interacting effects of social, historical, psychological, biological, and individual change as they affect adult development. Because the effect of social factors is so thoroughly intertwined with developmental change, we begin with a discussion of the psychosocial processes of development in the next chapter. But first we pause for an "interlude" — a sequential interview with a man who was age 27 in 1973 when he was first interviewed; he was 43 at the time of the latest interview in 1988.

Chapter Summary

1. Many of the events that mark the individual's progression through the sequence of adult development are socially defined as being related to age — such as permission to vote, the "best age" to marry or have children or to retire.

2. As people look back over their lives, or as they plan for the future, they see some events that stand out as especially important markers or turning points in their life cycle; we call these *milestones*.

3. The life span perspective of development emphasizes the dual processes of change and continuity that describe development throughout life. It calls attention to the interaction of "internal" (biological or psychological) forces and "external" (social or cultural) influences. It alerts us to seek general patterns of development that may apply to specific groups of individuals and it asks whether there are universal patterns of development in all cultures.

4. Several theories of life span human development have included a focus on adulthood; however, it is important to consider the effects of socioeconomic status, historical conditions, ethnic variation, and gender differences before accepting any as applying to *all* people.

5. Bühler's theory emphasized goal-related psychosocial expansion, culmination, and decline paralleling biological growth, stability, and decline.

6. Jung described a major change in life around the ages of 35 to 40; he suggested that an individual's attention turns inward, life tends to contract, and men become more "feminine" whereas women become more "masculine" during the second half of life.

7. Erikson viewed human development as a series of eight stages, each involving a dialectical struggle between two opposing tendencies; the synthesis that results produces one of the eight enduring characteristics of human life.

8. Levinson described four phases of development during early adulthood,

alternating between relatively stressful periods of transition and relatively stable periods; similar phases are thought to occur in middle and late adulthood.

9. Riegel's perspective focused on the process of change instead of stages of equilibrium; in his view, development results from the dialectical interaction of four major dimensions of human life.

10. Costa and McCrae suggested that the basic structure of an individual's personality remains fairly stable over long periods of time. However, some persons may be more likely to experience considerable change in their lives than other people with different personality patterns.

11. The pluralistic perspective noted that development begins at different points and follows different courses depending on the aspect of development in question; also the influences on development take different forms. There is considerable variation between individuals in development and this variation *increases* with age.

12. Since chronological age reflects when individuals were born and the historical period through which they have lived, differences between people of different ages do not necessarily indicate developmental change; they could reflect historical effects.

13. A *cohort* is a group of people born at about the same time in history. Cohort effects interact with time-dependent developmental processes and with historical changes to produce differences between young, middle-aged, and older people.

14. Historical change may also produce effects that influence all persons living through a particular historical period. These effects include improved nutrition, greater awareness of healthful behavior, and better medical care that have increased life expectancy today.

15. Chronological age is a convenient index of an individual's development. Age itself does not produce changes, however; biological, psychological, social, and other influences produce these changes.

16. Developmental research is often cross-sectional (by age), using groups of persons of various ages at one point in time; these studies need to be examined carefully for possible cohort effects.

17. In a longitudinal study a group of subjects participates periodically over several years; often only one cohort is studied so they may not be representative of persons born at other times. A sequential study involves a combination of cross-sectional and longitudinal strategies. The longitudinal sequence technique follows a group of subjects for a few years.

18. The comparison of cross-sectional and longitudinal studies of changes in intelligence test performance during adulthood clearly shows the importance of considering the potential significance of cohort effects in all studies of adult development.

Key Words

age simulation
biological age
chronological age
cohort
cross-sectional study
development
developmental perspective
developmental research
dialectical interaction
eight ages of life
empirical research
generativity
identity

individual variation
integrity
interdisciplinary perspective
intimacy
longitudinal sequence
longitudinal study
milestone
perceived age
pluralistic model
psychological age
sequential study
social age

Review Questions

1. List several reasons for studying adulthood and aging.

Concept of the Life Cycle

2. What is a milestone?

3. Draw a lifeline for your own life up to the present, marking the milestones you have passed (refer to Figure 1.1). Then extend that lifeline into the future, imagining the future events that would be milestones in your life.

Theories of the Life Cycle

4. What characteristics do the theories developed by Bühler, Jung, and Erikson have in common?

5. What are the major themes of the Bühler and Kuhlen models?

6. What is the essence of Jung's view of adult development?

7. Define the four crucial turning points (or stages) during adulthood in Erikson's theory.

8. Name the four dimensions of development proposed by Riegel and describe his system of dialectical analysis.

9. How can people remain stable in their personality pattern and also change in some ways?

10. What are the major ways in which development is pluralistic, according to Baltes?

11. Cite some criticisms of the general developmental theories of adulthood.

Individual Life Cycles and Historical Time

12. Place yourself, your parents, and your grandparents on separate individual

lifelines (similar to Figure 1.3) and compare the historical events that each generation directly experienced.

13. How does living during these different historical periods affect your grandparents, your parents, and you?

14. What is a cohort? What are cohort effects in developmental research?

15. Why has life expectancy at birth increased more than life expectancy at age 65 since 1900 (refer to Figure 1.5)?

Developmental Research Methodology

16. What is the meaning of age in developmental research?

17. Give an example of each of the following: biological, psychological, social, and perceived age.

18. Define cross-sectional and longitudinal research. What are two advantages and two disadvantages of each method?

19. What does the example of change in intelligence with age demonstrate about the importance of cohort effects? What other examples can you think of that also demonstrate this point?

George, AGE 27

George is the first of six case examples to be presented in this book; taken together, these examples represent a series of views of the life span from early adulthood to old age. Each is an edited transcript of an interview that lasted one to two hours. Six interviews were conducted by the author during the spring of 1973: George, age 27; Theresa, age 34; Murray, age 48; Joan, age 67; Henry, age 75; and Mrs. K., age 89; George was interviewed again in 1988 at the age of 43; Murray was reinterviewed in 1979 at age 54 and in 1989 at age 64. Follow-up information is available for all except one of the other respondents. These individuals do not represent "typical" adults—whatever that might mean; instead, they were selected to represent a range of adults—in age, social class, and life-style. One respondent lives in a nursing home; another lives in Harlem and has five grandchildren; one man is a successful modern dancer; another is a successful executive; and another is a waiter looking forward to retirement; the sixth respondent is a young working mother.

The interview was designed to explore the major milestones and crisis points during the respondent's adult life. Questions about the family, the occupation, thoughts about the future, and reflections about the past were central issues that were explored. The questions are indicated by italics in the text; the respondent's own words are used throughout with a minimum of editing or grammatical correction. All of the names have been changed, and basic identifying names and places have been changed to ensure anonymity.

One important characteristic of these interviews is that the respondents knew how they were to be used. Thus, the information is censored by the respondent to the extent that each tended to present his or her life in a relatively positive light under these conditions. To be sure, negative aspects and crises are discussed also but, in general, these interviews are revealing the more integrated, better understood, and socially acceptable aspects of their lives. Of course, this is a characteristic of well-functioning persons who have a reasonably good understanding of their strengths and shortcomings and who do not dwell on their failures or weaknesses. However, one should read these cases with a healthy mixture of skepticism and openness. Although there is probably much under the surface that is less positive, the strengths and ability to cope with mistakes, conflicts, and flaws are as important for understanding human functioning as any "deeper" conflicts and frustrations may be. In short, these are *developmental* interviews that are exploring the contours and milestones of human life; they are not clinical interviews attempting to uncover neurotic or unconscious psychodynamic conflicts.

At the time of this interview, George was a 27-year-old man who had moved to New York to join a dance company after graduating from college. He makes no secret of his gay life-style and has been living with his lover (Rick) for several years. By almost any standards he is successful and has a promising career ahead; he is comfortable with his life-style and, as he puts it, they live very well. His parents have accepted his homosexuality and his lover and take considerable pride in his accomplishments. Yet he feels unfulfilled in an important way that seems to be puzzling and disturbing to him.

This case raises a number of questions. What does it mean to be a "normal" adult? Why did the milestones and crisis points he selected to discuss stand out in his memory? In what ways has his gay life-style affected the developmental milestones of young adulthood? Was his decision to become a dancer a usual example of vocational choice? How did the interviewer's focus on *milestones* lead him to react? Did this developmental focus conflict with his perspective? What effect did historical changes in attitudes about homosexuality have on his life? How well do Erikson's theory about the ages of life and Riegel's dialectical perspective fit George's life?

As you look back over your life, what are some of the milestones that stand out? In terms of just profession, in terms of personal life? Do you want specifics? *Yes.* What made me choose my profession? *Was that a milestone?* It certainly was, I became a dancer out of the blue, literally—overnight. It wasn't my first dance class as such that made me become a dancer, because, although I enjoyed it very much, I knew I loved to dance. I've known that all my life. I had never seen dancers performing to even know there was such a thing as dance, other than ballet. I remember seeing [a famous dancer] on stage, watching him perform. I can even picture one thing that he did that just so struck me, absolutely hit me, and was such a fabulous thing to be able to do. I said "I want to do that." *Do you remember the time that you saw him do that?* I remember the exact moment. I can see it right now, I can picture it happening again—the exact moment in a particular dance—it was one particular solo that I remember as breathtaking. *And that was the turning point for you?* I look back and that's

what I remember, so that's a milestone for me, what one would have to call a milestone. . . .

Other milestones. I don't know, they just flow in. . . . Probably teachers I consider milestones in shaping my personality. My speech teacher in high school was very elemental in how I think today. He was a superb teacher, ultra-conservative. His political views just turn my stomach, but he was such a fabulous teacher that as a teacher he could overcome some of these . . . well, almost fascistic views. He was just a great teacher. He developed many things that I didn't know existed as such. The drama department was nothing in high school. He was a vital force, a vital person. And an English teacher . . . as I struggled to find my own identity as a homosexual, besides my identity as a person, as George. Just this little thing she did that made me realize that homosexuals as a class can be accepted by respected people. She called me in quite late in the semester just for a little talk. She was having some terrible times of her own, in terms of her lover of some 40 years, who I assume was her lover, a woman who lived with her for 40 years, who was dying of cancer. This was a very traumatic period for her. And she called me in and she said, "George, I just want you to know that I understand." She didn't say understand what. "And as far as your English grade, don't worry about it. I understand you're having problems and you'll have many more. This is some way I can help you. But you don't have to worry about your English grade." And that was it. She never said what or anything else, but of course I understood and she understood. I'm a sentimental slob and, of course, tears and all of that, but it was just a beautiful moment to know that there was. . . . It was the first time I was confronted, outside of a doctor situation. I did have psychiatric care in school. Here was someone who was not . . . I was not talking to in a medical way which is ugh, dry . . . even when you're probing inner problems, and because, I guess the way I think—I become so clinical as a person probing these problems and so far outside of them that I never feel a sense of satisfaction or of real searching, as I did with this teacher.

Anyway, other milestones. Oh, I'm sure I have some. Oh! Telling my folks I was gay was a milestone. Partly because of the way they responded (laughs). *When did that happen?* I was a junior in college. It was at the breakfast table, where in our family "great events" occur. 'Cause that's where most of the talking happens. And I finally just said, "Mom, Dad, I have something I just have to say, have to tell you." I told them I was gay. They both sighed, the two biggest sighs of relief you ever heard. And I was perplexed until they explained that they'd known for years. They never said how they'd known, I've never asked. And they just knew some day that I would tell them, and they just hoped that I would express my trust that they felt I had in them—which I do—could express it enough to say, "Folks, I am different than what we consider a norm," and that was about the way I said it. What could they say besides "Whew! Golly, you finally trusted us enough to tell us," and they were so pleased. That began a great chapter in our parent–child relationship. I still am their child. I love being their son, not a child, well yes, child, meaning offspring, not meaning adolescent.

Okay. More milestones. Can you think of some other areas maybe that would interest you? Or that would be relevant? Or that would help me remember? *What about more recent milestones? Like coming to New York?* Well, coming to New York wasn't really a milestone for me because that was so planned, so matter-of-fact that I was going to do it, that it wasn't really a milestone. Let me see. My life has been going so according to schedule lately, and so very planned. My working life I mean. *You planned everything out at some point back?* It seems to have evolved that way, you know.

Because I'm going in the direction with goals, specific goals in mind and I'm going that way and nothing has really detoured me off. My traveling has been very exciting. I wouldn't call any of it a milestone because I think of a milestone as changing, as a point where I can say from here on there is a real change. Richard, in a way maybe, I could call a milestone, meeting him and settling down with him; that's something I always wanted; even though maybe other people wouldn't interpret it that way, I've always been a very settled down kind of person. And we've just integrated our lives together, so it didn't really change my life or his, I don't believe. Other than it fulfilled for each of us something we needed and wanted. But again not a milestone. *It sounds like in a very real sense, once you made the decision to become a dancer, then somehow the rest of it is kind of an unfolding and fairly continuous.* Oh, yes; very much, very much a kind of an unfolding kind of thing. I went ahead and graduated from college, came to New York, studied, moved into the dance company, and have been working ever since as a dancer. Now I have started for the past year and a half getting jobs of my own, teaching dance last summer; and I have two offers to do teaching this coming summer, both for one-month periods. That would be two months of very well-paid teaching I might add, and do very well for myself in terms of building my own career. It's still all part of an unfolding. I live well now, very well.

As you look back over your life, have you changed much do you think, or has it been pretty similar all the way through? I was going to say I haven't changed. That's silly, of course I've changed. I've changed a lot. But to me, I'm still just me. And that me has always been here and present. Just different facets of it are more evident now as opposed to other facets which were more evident then, which I'm sure are still part of me, and could in the future be shown again. I have not changed as a person. Because people are such complex beings, like great crystal, the different sides are shown at different times, and at different angles, and because of different presences and outside influences, different things are seen. If nothing but green lights are shining on something, it's going to appear green, no matter what color it is. It's going to be changed. And yet it itself is not changed. It is still whatever it is. Take away the green lights and it's still there. So, I have not changed. I may appear different and seem to show different things.

We've been talking about milestones. What about crisis points? Have there been any crisis points that stand out? Yes, I've had a lot of crises. Do you want some of them? *Yes.* Well, younger crises, the natural crises of growing up, going through puberty, adolescence. I was a very nervous child. I'm still highly strung, but I just express it in very different ways. *Adolescence was a difficult time for you?* Oh, terrible. But, it is for everyone. I just probably expressed it more obviously than most children do. Through eighth, ninth, tenth, eleventh, twelfth [grades] and the first year of college I had my annual spring nervous breakdown, for which I had to be shuttled off for a time. Because it might have built to the point where I couldn't, in the course of my everyday things, I could not handle myself. *What do you mean by "shuttled off"?* Well, sometimes it just meant going home for a few days, staying away from everyone. The last couple of years of high school and the first year of college it meant running off to the hospital. I just became that bad. So, just getting out of my mainstream, away from my peer group, which is for me where the real pressures are. The people I work with now is where the real pressures are. *Was that partly because of your homosexuality?* I thought so at the time. I look back now and I say maybe it is, or was; maybe it was because I was gay; but it was because I felt so extraordinarily different, and was treated as someone very very different, and because I had some

very sick high school and junior high counselors. I know now; then I didn't know. I trusted them and they simply could not cope with it. I'm an open person. I tell people how I feel. In eighth grade I said, "I'm in love with that boy" and my counselor simply could not cope with it. He didn't know what to do, so it turned out he did all the wrong things. He said, "No, you're not," and such other stupid things, or "That's wrong." So my feelings of being different were constantly being reinforced by the very people who should have been helping me. *You say "different." What do you mean "different"?* How was I different? How do I consider myself different? *I gather that was more than just being gay.* Well, we don't know what being gay means as an adolescent, I don't think. We're all growing up and we're all changing. I didn't seem to be changing the way I saw the people around me changing. I always felt, especially from my male peers, that I was not like them. I didn't know why. And I was angry because I wasn't like them. Sometimes this anger was in terms of fighting and I would fight. Sometimes it was in terms of crying. I was extremely high strung, emotional; I'm still emotional. I'll cry. I did just Monday night, after talking to Mom. Just knowing what pain she was in talking to her on the phone [in the hospital]—she could hardly communicate—it just killed me. Tears just streamed down my face. I couldn't control it. Other boys were not so emotional. And so, I was ridiculed. And ridicule at 15 is tough, very tough.

Any other crises? Any other crises. Ah, I should go back to my building of my personality, because of my strong Christian background, I think I have a double set of morals inside of me that is constantly having trouble. I do not even understand them both. One comes from life and I lived it so far, and one comes from the morals that I've been taught. Maybe we all have these, probably. *Somehow these Christian values are in conflict with the values that you live with day by day?* Right. And to add on to that, the ideas and values that I live with day by day I consider correct. How can they both be correct? I don't know. This is my problem. And I admit this, because I have said to myself many times, if I did not truly believe what I was doing was correct, I wouldn't be doing it. And yet, at the same time, I will acknowledge to myself that I believe this, whatever it is, is wrong or not right, and yet I'm doing it. I don't know how to justify that and I don't know if I can. These are the kinds of philosophical questions one justifies, maybe never. *Is a lot of the content of this conflict sexual?* Part of it is. Like, just today I read something in the [New York] *Post* that deeply disturbed me — a Catholic priest saying that one cannot be a Christian and be a homosexual. That's intellectually sick, but inside me, I say maybe he's right. Yet, I know he's not right, and yet I can still believe he could be right. You know, there's an example of what I mean. *Can you think of another kind of example that is not sexual?* Yeah . . . abortion. I do not believe in abortion, and yet there are arguments that I have to agree with *for* abortion. How can this be resolved, because I can argue both sides and believe both sides? Absolutely believe them. And that is not compartmental thinking. *You really believe both and are caught in between.* Right, I truly believe both sides are correct.

Have there been any crisis points in your relationship with your family?   Not really. Some childish things. Nothing really recently. I've never run away from my family or anything like that as a child. *You said at one point when we didn't have the recorder on that your mother was in the hospital.* Yeah, she is. *Is this a serious matter?* It's not, now, as it's turned out, thank goodness. Oh, I see what you mean, a crisis in those terms. No, there's not even been any in those terms, no. Were my Mom and Dad, and they're not young, to die, that could be critical to me, I believe. Not permanently hurt, or upset by it, but I would be truly hurt because I love them as human beings,

I want them to be around, to enjoy them. It's such a very selfish thing to be saying, but it would be such a personal loss; the reason I can say that is because I know how fully they've both lived, and that in terms of them, there's no loss. They could both have died tomorrow, and they have lived very full lives. I think their lives may have been fulfilled a long time ago, and this is just all the frosting on the cake. I know a few young people who are such good people that their lives are fulfilled and that everything they do, the goals they reach, their quests and so forth are just growing beyond them. A tree can be a tree at two foot high, and can be a whole tree, and there it is — but if it grows to be 50 feet high it's just all grand and fabulous. *Is that somehow the way it is for you? Do you feel that way about yourself?* I'd like to think it were true, but it's not, no I'm not.

Before you changed [the topic] I was going to say that I have a romantic ideal in my psychic sexual fulfillment that I do not have. And I have had about three maybe four boys, and I knew that they were my desired sexual outlet, who, in my eyes could have been the fulfillment of that psychic sexual need. And, as yet, it still goes unfulfilled. And whether it even can be fulfilled, I don't know. And whether any of these boys could have fulfilled it I've no way of knowing. I just know that there are people who I have said to myself or even to them, "I love you," and it has not gone beyond. It has not been a fulfillment of that "I love you." *It never turned into a relationship?* Right. *So then your relationship with Rick is not one of these?* No, it's not, because my relationship with Rick is very fulfilled. I wouldn't give it up for anything. I have questioned it before. But I've only questioned it because I think it's healthy to question. I would not give it up for any of these ["ideal" boys] because this is something I truly need, want, have found, and am not going to let go of. So, I truly love Rick. But this thing, whatever it is in my head that I call a need; right now I call it a need for Bill or before him it was another Bill. Whatever that is in me, I don't know. I guess I'll have to find out, if I ever do. Don't people as they all grow older have unanswered questions, about themselves, about their living? It is almost accepted there will be unanswered questions in my life. I won't know everything. I'll see through the glass darkly and it get clearer, but will never be gone.

How long have you and Rick been to-gether? Five years last November, and this is February . . . a long time. *Have there been any crisis points in that relationship?* Oh, yes, several (laughter). *Do you regard it as a marriage?* I suppose so. I look on it as very similar to the relationship that my parents have. Because we're two people who want to live together and are greater because we're together; and that's perhaps, what a marriage is. *Have there been some crisis points?* Yes, there have been crises. For example, when we first got together we were still discovering each other, and I'm sure you know that one doesn't understand someone else immediately. We must all make concessions. That's a good word, it doesn't have to be a bad word. All have to make concessions if we are going to live with someone else. None of us can perfectly fit into someone else's life; such a thing doesn't exist. It takes you a while to find out how you must act or react to someone else before you can be together. Now, considering this I was talking about earlier — I don't know if I'll ever find [that "need"] fulfilled, like for example [with] Bill. Richard has had some real troubles because he feels that maybe somehow he's to blame for not "fulfilling" me. I, of course, say that's silly, because I don't even know if I can be fulfilled; how could you blame yourself for not fulfilling me? Then maybe I am fulfilled, and this other is a manifestation of some other problem. It has nothing to do with *fulfillment* as such. These are all possibilities that a person must face in their own lives. So, this has been a crisis a couple times — where he has

felt outrageous jealousy, what I consider outrageous jealousy, and then self-pity after thinking about it because he felt that he was inadequate. So, this has been a crisis. But, there have been no others as such. We hardly even argue anymore. We do get mad at one another and it's usually silly; but we forgive so quickly anymore, so easily. I'm glad, and I think he's glad that we both know that we can get mad at one another and just get outraged and throw things, and be furious, and even shout and it doesn't matter. That's very important to both of us because we're both volatile people; and to know that we don't have to be anything else or anybody else when we come into this house. When we come home we can be ourselves; we can be angry, we can literally take out our day's frustrations on each other, which we do do, both of us. The night before last, both of us had horrible, frustrating, interminably long days. And we both came home at different times, outraged, and we both took it out on the other one (laughter). But that really didn't matter, you know; we were cuddling and having a good time.

How long did you know him before you decided to move in with him? The whole thing was so gradual that it's really hard to tell. There's no date I can list of having moved in because I had two apartments; I lived here sort of and still had my other apartment. Some nights I slept there; eventually I slept here more than there, and then eventually I sublet that one out and eventually got rid of that one completely and then only lived here; but this was all so gradual that there's no way to say. I knew when I met him that I was interested. Here's a point that I think is very interesting. He is more like my best friends that I went to college with than any of my previous lovers ever were. He is more like the people I wanted to spend time with than the people I spent [time] in bed with, which is an interesting point. I knew he was bright and that probably attracted me to him more than anything else, because he's just so exceptionally bright. That's very important to me.

I gather that neither of you have any children. No. *Do you resent that?* No, I don't. That's interesting timing on that question, because just a couple days ago I was reading about adoption. And also, someone else had been talking about a way man is immortal is by having children. And I tried to think about that; what that meant to me. I said maybe I should worry about that. I'm a good worrier. Maybe I should think about that too. Would I some day worry about my own immortality and would not having a son make that hard for me. Well, I thought and I said, "What about the people who do not have children and who adopt?" I know from experience that they consider them their children every bit as much. And yet, if they were to think about it intellectually, I'm sure they would have to say, "No, I'm not passing myself on." And so I say this doesn't really interest me — having children — I don't particularly want children. I know that I will probably do a great deal of teaching in my life and I can be a grander father to more people that way. Already, the list of people, young men in general, even young ladies who have written to me after I've been somewhere teaching and said, "You have changed my life." And that, you know . . . how much greater father can I ever be than to have people tell you that you've changed their lives. Just a couple days ago I got a letter from a boy in Iowa who, after seeing me and talking with me in class — this was his first dance class ever — he's changed his whole life. He's come out, told his family. I was the first homosexual he met who was proud; not proud to be gay, that's so dumb — who was *proud* and who was a homosexual. Because I must make a distinction between saying I am not ashamed of being gay, and I am proud of being gay. I'm not proud of being gay any more than a heterosexual is proud of being heterosexual. But I am not ashamed of being gay any more than a heterosexual is ashamed of being heterosexual. There

is a big, big difference there that I think is very important, [in contrast] to the idea currently in vogue that I'm gay and I'm proud that I'm gay. I think that's silly. They're making the wrong thing important in their lives. So, this young man has dropped out of school, applied to another school which has a big dance department; it's in the West; he'll be going to study dance. He's been accepted there already. It really changed his life. [I've received] several page letters. This has happened to me several times. And I couldn't feel more of a father than that. I wouldn't want to be. I'm not interested in bringing more children into the world; we've got enough and therefore I can, as a father, in terms of a father, in the old Biblical sense of a father, I can father people. I'll be doing more than most people do.

In terms of your occupation as a dancer, have there been any milestones or crisis points? Oh, I've almost quit several times, if that's what you mean. I almost quit the company I'm currently in. But that's, that's still in grappling with knowing the situation I am in is not perfect, and I must be continually aware that I have to be there — this may sound crass and I don't mean it to sound crass — to get out of it what I can get out of it. Now I'm *giving* a hell of a lot too. So, that's why it's not crass to be getting out of it what I can get out of it, because I'm also giving every bit as much as I'm getting out of it. But I am there to get out of it what I can. And so, sometimes a really bad situation will arise; some personal thing with the director, some impossible tour situation — because touring can be impossible. And I'll say, "What am I doing? Why am I doing this? I'm not enjoying this. I've got to get out," and then I say, "No; my greater goals are more important and are satisfied better and can be reached better by staying." So I stay, although that's how I get over these kinds of crises. One of the most exciting personal things that happened to me arose out of my being a dancer besides the applause — which is the greatest thing in the world for me — was meeting Mr. and Mrs. Shah, the Shah of Iran, which was so exciting. I am excited by great people and I really felt I was in the presence of two great people when I met them. I am middle class, bourgeois, mid-America . . . I shouldn't . . . forget that. That is my background. I think it's important I remember that this is from where I came. I've been lucky. I just this morning made a list of countries I've been to — twenty-five of them. That's pretty impressive. And, it's unusual for someone from my circumstances and background. And in that way I can appreciate it even more because I can say, ''This is unusual. I have gone beyond myself in some way.'' In some ways I am a better person for it. How could a son of a multimillionaire be proud at my age of having traveled all over the world when he can do it at will?

Thinking back to when you first came to New York and started dancing with the company, how was that? Was that a crisis point in some way? Well, it was planned. It was all planned. I just did it. It was exciting. I loved it all. I was thrilled by everything. Golly, eager? Was I eager!

How did you come to the point of deciding that you were going to come to New York and be a dancer? I was always going to come to New York as long as I can remember. Someday I was going to go to New York. For many years I said that I was going to come to New York and be an actor. Practically, I never said that. I said things like, in ninth grade, you know, it's time to make a report on what you're going to be when you grow up, and I said I was going to be an accountant; and another time I was going to be something else, because I always thought of myself as a very practical person. But I always said to myself, ''Someday I'm going to go to New York and be an actor.'' So that's how I got to college, thinking in those terms. Then I discovered dance. For me this somehow seemed even better, and even greater; I could see more fulfillment, and as it

turned out that's where it looks like I belonged. And so I did come to New York, not as an actor; I came as a dancer.

How does your future look in terms of your career as a dancer? How do you see it developing? Well, if we only knew what lies ahead. I know what I want, I know what my goals are, and I know that's what I'm striving for. I value myself as an artist and a dancer, they are two very different things, which gets back to some basic philosophy of what a performer is. Is the performer an artist or is the performer a craftsman? Just to make things simple, I'll say the performer is a craftsman for me and I value myself as an artist. And therefore, I have to do my art; my art is theater. And so I'm working toward that goal. I'm a dancer; I work all the time to get better, to become continually a better technician and a better performer or craftsman, and I'm also learning the art of dance. I practice it as a craftsman with increasing craft ability, knowing that I also have artistic abilities. How good they are? All I can say is that what I have done so far artistically has been successful. I just hope that by continuing that I'll be more successful. That's what I'm working toward — which may mean my own company or maybe being part of another company. Maybe it will eventually lead its way from dance as such. *What are your career goals?* I don't know what it is specifically. I know that it will be in the theater. It may not even be as a performer. I don't know. I'll find out what peaks I can reach as a performer. And there's the age variable. One gets better as they get older. It's through sheer doing that one gets better. So, for my age I will be able to judge my peak as an artist. But, I don't know if it will even be in dance; it might be in some other form of theater. I don't know.

Has the way people reacted to you changed over the years? I'm still different. I still feel very different, and think I am treated as such. People are not ready for candid observation and conversation. People are not ready to be touched. If I want to touch someone I do; I get in trouble with it sometimes—male or female. Or, to say, "I love you" or to say, "I want to go to bed with you," or to say any everyday little thing, they're not ready for that kind of candidness, and I am. I am that way and I don't think it's wrong. If I thought it was wrong, I would have stopped it. So I will continue doing it, even though it offends people. I will say, "Okay, I'll watch myself under certain circumstances." If I think there will be long-range problems by my being candid or being open, or being too emotional, then I say, "Okay, George, don't. This is the time to say no. . . ." I am still different, and I'm treated differently; but now I kind of like being different because I have met enough people to whom that differentness was not bad, it was exciting, and I found out that the people to whom it seemed exciting were more the people I liked, were more the kind of people I was interested in. And the people who found it offensive were the people I didn't care about anyway. *So it's not so much that the people respond to you differently in general, but that you've found more people who respond to you the way you want them to respond.* Yeah, it's one of the reasons I probably love New York City. It's a huge city and I love big cities. I'm excited by them. I'm excited by many people. For me maybe it takes many people to find the few I want to call my peers, that I want to be my associates.

Would you say that you've got a pretty firm sense of who you are right now? Do you know who you are? Oh, that's a hard one. Let me think. . . . I know *exactly* who I am. *Who are you?* I'm George and my friends all know. That's all I can say. I am complex. I am simple. I'm emotional. I'm volatile. Creative. I'm an S.O.B. I have a nasty temper at times. I love sex. I love giving; I love receiving. I love beautiful things, and I even like some ugly things. I think I'm open. I don't have a closed mind, and yet I know that at times I will absolutely shut everyone and everything off because I think they're wrong, which is a closed mind, as closed as you can be. So I know that's part of me too. I'm opinionated. I'm educated. All those opinions mean things to me. Do I think I'm right? Darn right I think I'm right! If I didn't think I was right I would do different things and say different things. Am I always right? Oh, no! I'm not always right. That's been obvious through my life. But when I did it I thought I was right, or I wouldn't have done it, whatever it is at the time. *Have you always felt that way about yourself, that you really knew who you were? Or was there some time when you began to get more of a sense of really knowing who you were?* Probably always thought I knew who I was, but I can look back and say I hadn't the foggiest idea who I was when I was 15, 16, 17, 18, . . . 19, . . . 20, . . . 21. And I'm sure at 35 I'll say, "George you had no idea really what you were at 27." Now I think I do. That's what I hope maturing is; that's what I hope wisdom is—all of which I want. I'm not mature. God knows I'm not mature (laughter), but it's not bad to be immature because when I'm mature I'll probably be dead (laughter). Because maturing means "full," "the end," maturing is the top, and I hope I don't reach the peak until I'm gone. I want to reach the peak on my death bed.

Do you sometimes think about death? I guess. Death's death. Someday, maybe soon, maybe not. It doesn't matter. It really doesn't. I have wanted to die, so I guess then it mattered. I have enjoyed myself so much that I don't think I want to die right now, because it's so fabulous; but, at the same time I've said, "Maybe this would be a good time." But, I'm going to die; I hope it's not painful for someone else. Or I hope it's as painless as it can be. Death always seems to cause pain to the living. I assume mine will, because I know there are people who care. I know Rick cares. If I were to die tomorrow he would be very very hurt.

My family would be very hurt. But, this is why, even though I thought about suicide because I was suffering a pain which I don't understand, I said, ''Well, when I die I want to hurt as few people as possible. And if I die now by killing myself it would probably hurt as many people as possible, so I don't want to die.'' But . . . I'm not dead yet. So, that's about it. *Do you sometimes look over your life and review where you've been, what you've done?* I love memories, if that's what you mean? I value memories greatly. I have such fabulous memories! They are very important to me. . . . I love to go over them, I love to reexperience. My life has been exciting! And sometimes exciting-bad. And even then it was exciting. I wouldn't trade it. That doesn't mean it couldn't have been different or couldn't have been better, and even maybe wished it had been better, but the whole thing I wouldn't trade. I value my past.

Is sex as important to you now as it used to be? Yes. *More, about the same?* About the same. I don't have as much, yet it's still very, very important. Seriously important, not frivolously. I love sex. I love to talk about it. I love to do it, even though I don't do it much, because it is so much a part of every person. It is a great expression of giving and taking between two or more people. And sometimes, just one — giving yourself — because I enjoy masturbation, too. . . . I enjoy fantasizing. Oh, my fantasies when I masturbate are extraordinary, they're beautiful. If you wanted to find a fault you could probably say I fantasize too much in my life. That's probably my greatest fault, as I see it. One of the things I would change is, perhaps, I would be more real — fantasize less. Although I enjoy my fantasies, so I doubt that I will. *Why are you having sex less now than you used to?* Partly because I know I can get it when I want it. So, the urge to be constantly in there fighting for it — it's hard work — sex can be hard work too. You go in there and prove

yourself, which all of us, I think, tend to do, especially in more frivolous circumstances. I know that if I see a boy I want sexually, I can probably have him 99 times out of 100, straight or gay. I don't have to prove that anymore. So, I'll see a pretty boy and say, ''Oooh, I'll have to go to bed with him,'' and I just don't put out the effort that it might take, because I have lots of things to do, and the rewards of just having conquered someone are not always equal to the effort involved. I know I could probably do it, and I have lots of other things to do, and I do the other things. *How about your relationship with Rick in terms of sex; are you having less sex now than you once did?* Oh, yes. We don't have sex very often. *Why is that?* Well, I'm not really sure. I know it's probably a good thing, but once again, we don't have to perform for one another. We both work extraordinary hours, we're tired, so when we have it it's because we want it, and for no other reason. Oh, there are some times when one of us wants it and I know we just do it for the other one, just to please the other one. I've been too tired and Rick has really wanted sex, and I say, ''Oh, okay.'' I hope he doesn't . . . well, intellectually we both know we do that, but I hope he doesn't know when it has happened, because I want to please him and I know it wouldn't please him if he thought I were doing it out of obligation. And, the same for him. I know he's done it for me. I don't know when . . . I have no particular times in mind. I have sometimes known afterwards when he's told me, like the next day . . . ''Oh, I really didn't want to . . . I was so tired last night. I hope it wasn't too bad.''

In general, in your life, do you have a sense of being particularly productive, of leaving or having left your mark? Yes, I think it's obvious by the things I've said. *I guess you've also said this before, but has life been a meaningful adventure for you?* Very. Yes, I've also said that, yeah. *You are pleased with how its been?* Pleased, not satisfied, pleased. *What are some of the things you'd like to change?* About my life? I would like to understand why I think I love Bill. I'd like to understand that . . . or why I think I need him, and need him to love me, because I don't understand that. I would like to learn a better way of being candid without insulting and hurting, which sometimes I do. But it is usually of more value for me to be honest than not to hurt. So sometimes I'll say things and other people will say, "You shouldn't have said that," and I'll say, "It needed to be done. Somebody had to say it." *Finally would you say that your life is different now than it was a year or two ago? Have you changed? Are you different now than you were a year or two ago?* No, I'm not different at all. I know more. I have a greater understanding of some things; not as great as it will be next year. I hope it's better next year. I hope I understand more. I have to grow in wisdom. I want to be wise, truly wise; what I consider wise. I want to be generous. I can be more generous. *What would you like to be doing in five years?* Exactly what I'm doing right now . . . getting ready for another New York season . . . whatever that may mean. That could mean a hundred things.

It was not possible to interview George again in 1979 because of his busy schedule; however, I did talk with him long-distance by telephone for a few minutes. At the age of 33, he had been in the dance company for 10 years and had just returned from one of his many extended foreign tours with the company. He and Rick have now been together for 12 years. He finds that the long periods of separation while he is away on tour are more difficult now than they used to be, since the relationship seems to be even more important in his life than it was 6 years ago; he recently traveled several thousand miles to be at home when Rick had an operation, but then had to return to the company. When asked about milestones and crisis points,

he reported that they had bought a house 5½ years ago; this brought a period of strain in their relationship because of the financial difficulties that were involved. Another difficult period was when they no longer had sex, partly because Rick was drinking alcohol while using prescribed tranquilizers. Rick eventually stopped drinking, no longer takes the tranquilizers, and has lost 40 pounds; their sex life has also been reestablished.

I asked George about his feeling of being unfulfilled and his fantasy about Bill that he discussed in the interview 6 years earlier. He responded that Bill is still important in his fantasy life, but he now understands its significance better than he did earlier, at least at an intellectual level. Part of this feeling involves the "romantic fantasy" that he feels occurs in heterosexual relationships as well as in homosexual relationships. Another part of it is a kind of identification with someone who is not gay; Bill is predominantly heterosexual. At least intellectually, he now understands that the values and attitudes of his upbringing made him feel that being gay was wrong, or unfulfilling. Thus, Bill represents being liked and accepted by a heterosexual man; and the feeling of being unfulfilled has something to do with the stigma of being homosexual. Although he understands these feelings, he still recognizes that they are not fully resolved emotionally.

He reported no particular change or transition when he turned 30, but does feel a great deal of relief at having "grown up" and being further away from the many problems he had when he was younger. The problems he felt even 10 years ago took a great deal of his energy, but now he feels that he is able to use that energy for work and living, since it is being drained less by emotional problems. He has just completed choreographing a new work that was performed by a group of dancers and is looking forward to his eleventh season with the company.

CHAPTER 2

Psychosocial Processes of Development

*I*t is a common observation that individuals change in important ways during the adult years. Yet, even as they pass through the milestones of adult development, most people also remain unchanged in many ways. If we were to attend our high school reunion several years after graduation, we would certainly notice this. One old friend might have become a successful businessman and gained a sense of competence and power that contrasts with his happy-go-lucky attitude in high school; yet he would also be recognizably similar to the boy we knew years ago. Another old friend may have changed from the prom queen we remember to a brilliant research chemist; but she is still the outgoing, popular, and engaging person we remember. How does this happen? It is such a common phenomenon that we seldom examine it closely. However, it is puzzling. How do persons change while they also remain fairly similar to the person they were earlier in life? We refer to this as a process of *simultaneous change and stability* in adult development.

This chapter focuses on these processes of change and stability from a **psychosocial perspective.** That is, we examine the interaction of individual development and social influences. We see the adult as an individual in interaction with others in society and we believe this interaction process is central to an understanding of the age-related changes that occur in adulthood.

Of course, biological, economic, environmental, and political factors also may influence adult development; these are discussed in later chapters. These factors *interact* with the psychosocial processes we discuss in this chapter. It is important to note that an **interaction** of changes is not necessarily the simple addition of one change to another; instead the result is likely to be different from the sum of the parts. For example, menopause (a biological process) or winning a lottery (an economic event) or experiencing ageism (a political reality) *interact* with the psychosocial process of adult development. The meaning of this type of interaction is best defined by the outcome, not by the collection of factors that produce it.

We begin this chapter with a summary of important ideas developed by George Herbert Mead about the psychosocial interaction of individuals with others. He viewed the human individual as a social being with a mind and an individualized self that are created by the active interaction between the individual and society. We select this perspective because it emphasizes that the individual is *active* in the complex pattern of interactions instead of a passive respondent to social, cultural, or biological change. It is also consistent with our view that adults actively select many aspects of their physical and social environment and are affected by their assimilation of that environmental experience. We also see adults as actively affecting their social and physical environment and being changed in that experience.

The next two sections focus on additional social-psychological concepts that are vital for understanding the process of adult development. These include social roles, norms, and the process of socialization during the adult years.

The final section of the chapter discusses three questions that are central to the study of adulthood and aging. (1) Is there any age-related sequence to the changes during the adult years; if so, what factors serve to regulate this sequence? (2) What is the effect of *experience* on the individual—for it is this accumulation of "experience" that is the most obvious result of living a long time; and how does it affect the person? (3) What are the processes by which individuals change; and what processes are involved in the stability of individuals over long periods of time? Our approach to these questions and to the processes of development in adulthood is a psychosocial one. Thus, the processes of change, stability, timing or regulation of development, and the accumulation of experience seem best understood in terms of the individual interacting with others in social interaction.

Symbolic Interaction Approach to Adulthood

George Herbert Mead was a philosopher at the University of Chicago from 1894 until his death in 1931. He was especially interested in describing the process of social interaction, the nature of the self, and the relationship between mind, self, and society. He argued that humans evolved as social beings and that their ability to interact with one another through symbols (such as language or gestures) was particularly important for understanding the nature of the human self—thus, his approach became known as **symbolic interaction.**

One of Mead's teachers was William James, the influential early American psychologist. Mead was a colleague of John Dewey, a major leader in education, and of W.I. Thomas, a sociologist, during the time that the "Chicago School of Sociology" was evolving among a star-studded faculty at the University of Chicago.

Mead's scholarly writing was devoted primarily to philosophical and psychological issues. He was 40 years old before his first major paper appeared and he had not published a single book when he died at the age of 68. However, graduate students in sociology at the University discovered his unique ideas a decade before his death and "flocked to his classes" (Strauss, 1964). After his death, these students published their collected notes as well as his own notes and unpublished writings in his posthumous book, *Mind, Self, and Society,* in 1934. These Chicago sociologists succeeded in carrying his ideas into the mainstream of sociology by 1939. Many of his concepts influenced modern sociology and his ideas may also be found in the writing of psychologists (such as Carl Rogers) and psychiatrists (such as Harry Stack Sullivan).

Symbolic interaction theory remains a current sociological framework, but its influence has not been a dominant one for many years. However, his approach is especially useful in describing the complex interpersonal and intrapersonal processes that characterize adulthood. We use his ideas frequently throughout this book.

Perhaps his approach may best be seen as a framework or perspective for understanding human interaction. It is not the kind of theory that allows us to predict behavior, but it helps us to understand it better. It is an approach that describes human functioning in society and provides useful concepts for conceptualizing the process of social interaction. Its main advantages for the study of adulthood are: (1) the focus on the individual's inner experience; (2) the emphasis on the continual capacity for change; and (3) the significance given to social processes for the understanding of human functioning.

We discuss several of Mead's central concepts, emphasizing the importance of the self and self-consciousness for understanding adulthood.

The Self

The **self** is probably a uniquely human characteristic that requires the capacity to interact with other persons in social settings through the use of communication and language, according to Mead. The self is different from the physical organism. It is not present at birth. It develops through the process of social experience and social communication, and it continues developing and changing throughout one's life. Thus, the self is not a "thing" a person has, but it is a *process* that requires human interaction to come into existence and is continually developing and changing.

The self consists of two interacting aspects, in Mead's view. One aspect is called **I**; it involves *experiencing, awareness,* and *consciousness of oneself. I* is "that-which-experiences" (James, 1892). Thus, thinking and feeling are *I* processes: thinking is the *experience* of a thought; feeling is the *experience* of an emotion. The major characteristic of *I* is that experiencing occurs only in the present moment, in a moment-by-moment "stream of consciousness" (James, 1892). Once the experience or awareness can be put into words, or thought about, or told to another, it is no longer *I.* This is because *I* would then—at that moment—be experiencing and reacting to words or thinking about the previous experience. Thus, this aspect of the self is pure *process:* it is always changing, fleeting, existing only in the present moment. This provides a continuing source of creativity, surprise, and novelty to the self.

Although the term *"I"* is awkward and easily confused with other more common uses of "I" (perhaps it should be called "E" for experiencing), Mead probably chose *I* because it is the subjective term for the self, and *I* is purely subjective. *I* is private and cannot be examined because it is always changing as moment-to-moment experience occurs. This component of the self has often been ignored by other writers who consider only those aspects of the self that can be measured or counted or examined. *I* is not like an observable phenomenon; it it our experiencing of those "things" that others are counting, categorizing, and studying.

The other component of the self in Mead's view is the *me* (the objective word for the self). The **me** consists of all the characteristics of the person that can be seen, examined, touched, measured, or listened to: it is the body, the behavior, the gestures, clothing, words, personality characteristics, hair color—everything that can be seen.

In summary, the self consists of two components that are in continual interaction with each other. The *me* consists of all the objective characteristics of the self (Jewish, tall, woman, mother, lawyer, etc.). *I* consists of the person's experience *at that moment. I* experiences the *me* and is conscious of other people's reactions to the *me;* the *me* often shows the experiences of *I* through words, facial gestures, and so on. The self is *I,* the *me,* and the continual interaction between these two aspects (Figure 2.1).

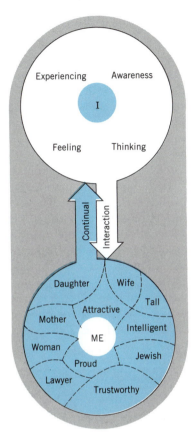

FIGURE 2.1 The self consists of *I* and *me* in continual interaction. *I* is entirely private or subjective; the many characteristics of *me* are seen by oneself or by others in social interaction.

Development of the Self

At birth, the infant cannot be said to possess a self, according to Mead. However, the origins of the experiencing, or *I*, aspect of the self would seem to be present: the infant experiences hunger, wetness, thirst, and pain as fleeting moment-by-moment experiences. Infants cannot conceptualize these experiences into thoughts, cannot express them in gestures or words, and cannot comprehend their own objective existence, so there is no *me* component of the self for the first few days or weeks of life. But soon the origins of the objective, of *me,* aspect of the self begin to appear. For example, infants begin to understand that the thumb is part of themselves, whereas the pacifier or blanket is not, by sucking the thumb and experiencing both the mouth sucking on an object and the thumb being sucked. Gradually, the objective aspect of the self begins to develop as children develop the ability to perceive that they are an object distinct from other objects.

The development of language greatly advances the development of the self because it provides the ability to communicate through the use of what Mead called **significant symbols.** These are words or gestures that have essentially the same meaning to everyone involved in the social interaction. Of course, some of the infant's cries and gestures may serve as significant symbols to those people who are caring for the infant—the "I'm hungry" cry, or the "I'm wet" cry—but the development of language brings a major advance in the development of the self. Children are able to talk to themselves, talk about themselves, and understand others when they talk about them. Thus, children become able to think about the objective (*me*) part of themselves and also become able to express their inner experiences (*I*) to others through the use of language.

During childhood, the self develops through social interaction with others and grows in complexity as the child's cognitive development allows greater understanding of the subjective (*I*) and objective (*me*) aspects of the self. Mead noted that some of the people with whom the child interacts are *significant others* in the sense that they are particularly important for the child's developing sense of self. For children, significant others usually include parents and other important models. Adults also have significant others who are particularly influential in the continuing evolution of the self during adulthood.

By adolescence, the person has learned to respond to several others at the same time—as in the game of baseball where one's behavior must be affected by the other players on the field—and has developed the ability to think in terms of

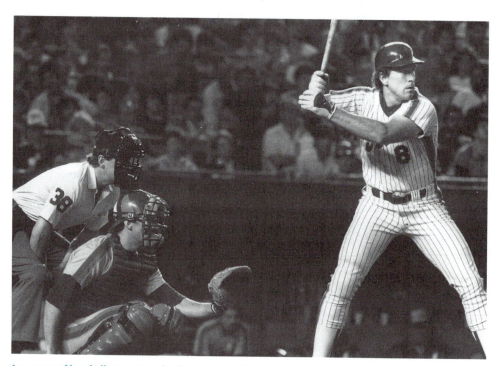

In a game of baseball one must take the attitude of the other players in order to anticipate the strategy of the opponents and the way one's teammates will react.

abstractions. This allows adolescents to consider the *generalized other*—that is, "others in general," or "society"—as one additional influence on their sense of self (Kimmel & Weiner, 1985, chap. 3).

Adults may also be very much aware of society's attitudes, so that the generalized other remains an important influence on the evolution of the self throughout the adult years. The process by which the attitudes of others affect the self is called "taking the attitude of the other."

Taking the Attitude of the Other

A central characteristic in the development of the self involves the skill that Mead called **taking the attitude of the other.** This means understanding as fully as possible the other person's experiencing. In simple terms, it is what we mean when we imagine ourselves in another person's shoes.

In social interactions one or more individuals are communicating with each other through significant symbols (language, gestures, etc.). One person's self—*I* and *me* in interaction—is communicating with the other person's self (Figure 2.2). Frank's *I* is experiencing his own *me* and Sally's *me;* and Sally's *I* is experiencing her own *me* and Frank's *me.* If Frank takes the attitude of Sally, Frank watches, listens, and senses Sally's *me* as a reflection of Sally's experiencing. Frank cannot see Sally's *I,* but Frank can see Sally's *me* and can guess what Sally is experiencing or feeling or thinking about Frank if Sally gives enough clues. Frank can then compare Sally's perception of Frank's self with Frank's own perception of himself. We describe this process in detail in the next section by its technical term, *self-consciousness.*

Mead argued that the self develops through this process. As in a sensitivity or consciousness-raising group where one provides feedback to another on how each sees the other, so also one's self develops through the process of receiving information from others about oneself. This involves *taking the attitude of others toward oneself,* or imagining how one looks through the eyes of another. Sometimes an-

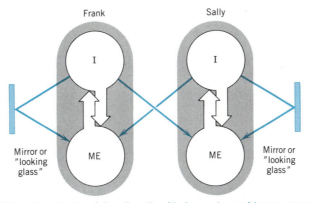

FIGURE 2.2 Taking the attitude of the other. Frank's *I* experiences his own *me* and Sally's *me;* Sally's *I* experiences her own *me* and Frank's *me.* If Frank takes the attitude of Sally toward himself, Frank tries to guess how Sally's *I* is experiencing Frank's *me* and compares this with the way his *me* appears to himself. Both see their own *me* as if they were looking at themselves in a mirror.

other person is actively involved in this process, as in feedback in a group. Or sometimes one simply looks in the mirror (in reality or imagination) and reacts to oneself as if one were another person (the concept of the "looking glass self"; Cooley, 1911). Sometimes one might take the attitude of the *generalized other* toward oneself in the sense of imagining how "society" would react to oneself.

One example of a man who suddenly realized he was middle-aged illustrates the way in which taking the attitude of the other toward oneself may bring about a change in the way one sees oneself.

> The realization suddenly struck me that I had become, perhaps not an old fogy but surely a middle-aged fogy. . . . For the train was filled with college boys returning from vacation. . . . They cruised up and down the aisles, pretending to be tipsy . . . boisterous, but not obnoxious; looking for fun, but not for trouble. . . . Yet most of the adult passengers were annoyed with them, including myself. I sat there, feeling a little like Eliot's Prufrock, "so meticulously composed, buttoned-up, bespectacled, mouth thinly set" . . . Squaresville. (Harris, 1965)

This middle-aged man is looking at himself from the point of view of another — perhaps a college student, perhaps an adult passenger, or possibly as if he were watching himself from across the aisle. From that perspective he realized that his *self* looked like a "middle-aged fogy."

Although taking the attitude of other is crucial for the development and change

The majority of social interactions are routine.

of the self, we probably do not use this process very often in ordinary social interaction. It is most useful when an individual is trying to understand or define or examine his or her *self,* or when the ordinary interaction process breaks down because other people are not responding to the person in the way he or she expects they should. For example, if a man in a disagreement with his wife tries to see her perspective on the issue and imagines how she sees him and interprets his comments, he is taking the attitude of his wife in an attempt to resolve the argument. Or if a professor is having difficulty explaining a concept to the class, she may try to take the attitude of the students toward the concept and ask them to describe what is confusing, or to imagine herself in their place and seek to guess why they are having difficulty. Similarly, if she wishes to improve her teaching, she may ask for "feedback" from the students' perspective.

The vast majority of social interactions tend to be routine, however, and proceed uneventfully without this kind of process being consciously used. Here are three examples of routine interaction:

"Hi, how are you?" "Fine; and yourself?"
"How much?" "A dollar ninety-five, plus tax."
"A coffee and danish, please." "To go or to stay?"

Nonetheless, even these very routine interactions assume that each person is implicitly taking the attitude of the other. This is clear when the interaction goes amis, or the expected response does not follow:

"Hi, how are you?" "Pretty bad, Kent left last night and took the kids."

Suddenly, one is drawn to take the attitude of the other, and may take the time to find out what is going on from the point of view of the other person. A similar process occurs when one attempts to understand oneself better; this is called self-consciousness.

Self-Consciousness

The middle-aged man on the train in the earlier example was focusing on himself as he thought he appeared through the eyes of the college students. Similarly, the college professor asking for feedback from her students is focusing on herself. These are examples of Mead's concept of **self-consciousness.** It is the process by which an individual becomes aware of his or her *self* and focuses or reflects on it. Thus, when a man has just made a complete mess out of a social interaction, he may spend some time examining himself to try to understand what he did wrong and why his behavior or his words were so misinterpreted by the others. He make take the attitude of the others toward himself and try to see himself as they saw him. He may look at himself in the mirror (in fact, or in his mind's eye) as if he were another person or talk with himself in an introspective fashion about the interaction and the implications it may have for his *self.*

When we are self-conscious, we are taking the attitude of the other toward ourselves. This may occur when we are alone by imagining how we would look to ourselves if we could watch ourselves as if we were another person. We may take the attitude of a particular other toward ourselves when we are interacting with that person by imagining how we look to the person, or by receiving feedback from that person about his or her perception of ourselves. Or we may take the attitude of others in general (the generalized other, or society) by imagining how others would see us if we were to get a divorce or if we were to leave our job and join a farming commune.

In each case, our *I* is experiencing something about our *me*. When we are alone, our *I* is experiencing our *me* as if it were reflected in a mirror. When we are interacting with another person, our *I* is experiencing the other person's *me* (in this case, largely through words and gestures) as that person describes the way his or her *I* experiences our *me*. When we are considering what "society" might think about our behavior, we imagine the reaction of our image of the generalized other to our behavior.

Clearly, Mead used the term self-consciousness in a slightly different way from ordinary usage. It does not necessarily imply any embarrassment, although it might. It does not necessarily imply any insecurity or shyness, although it might. It is a process all persons experience when they wish to understand themselves.

This process is vital for the development of the self in childhood, and is a central process in the continuing evolution of the self during adulthood. It is an important process for one to engage in when choosing a new job, or when seeking to maintain important relationships.

In introspection, the process involves focusing on one's feelings (Gendlin, 1964). This involves attending to one's inner experiencing (*I*), turning those feelings or experiencing into *me*s by forming them into words or thoughts. Since *I* is moment-by-moment experiencing, all *I*s of the past moment may become *me*s of the present moment; each of these *me*s can then be reacted to by the *I* of the present, and so on in an ongoing chain of introspection. Sometimes this process is central to psychotherapy when clients or patients focus on and describe their feelings to the therapist and to themselves. It provides the person an opportunity to examine the *I*–*me* interaction within the self and to practice expressing the subjective *I*-experiencing in words (*me*s) that may be responded to by another person in social interaction as well as by oneself.

The Self and Mind

Mead's concept of the self does not include all of a person's inner functioning. It does not include rational thought, memory, or the kind of unconscious processes that psychoanalysis describes. However, Mead saw a close relationship between the functioning of the mind and the self. Our discussion has certainly assumed that the individual is a rational, thinking person who can reason, understand, and anticipate future consequences. Since an individual's self develops through the process of taking the attitude of the other toward oneself, the rational process of perceiving and understanding the meaning of the attitude of the other is clearly involved in the development of the self. Memory, foresight, and the ability to understand language and to communicate, as well as thinking, planning, and creating, are all processes that are necessary for the self to function to its fullest extent.

It should be noted that Mead's theory deals only with conscious processes. The unconscious self is similar to breathing—one is not ordinarily aware of breathing but from time to time it can be brought to conscious attention, especially if it is important at that moment. Similarly, habits of speech or expression, details of so-called body language, or the precise nature of what makes a statement "joyful" or "sad"—as well as the unconscious processes described by Freud—are not important for Mead unless they become conscious. Also, the psychoanalytic terms—id, ego, and superego—do not fit in Mead's framework, so it is best not to confuse *I* and *me* with the id and ego. The two theories involve very different perspectives of human functioning and, on balance, are more different than they are similar.

The Self in Adulthood

Adults are characterized by a diverse range of attributes that make up the *social self,* which is another term for the objective self, or *me.* During the course of a week, a typical adult may be a mother, daughter, psychologist, politician, wife, and friend; and she may attend concerts or the theater, express herself in writing, counsel a troubled friend, enjoy sex, attend church, become angry, feel joy, teach her children, and repair her car. All these behaviors, feelings, and words can be seen, thought about, or expressed and are, therefore, part of her *me* if she, or another, reacts to them. Clearly, the social self of adults is complex and can change from hour to hour, or from interaction to interaction. Yet, all these characteristics combine to make up the person's *me.*

At the same time, *I* provides adults with a rich and varied range of experiences. Human beings are equipped with the capacity to feel a wide range of emotions and to experience events and social interactions in a variety of ways. For Mead, these inner experiences are as important a part of the complex human self as are the parts of the self that can be observed. Every sunset, every interpersonal experience, every idea or musical sound or human word can bring an inner experience in *I*. All of these are part of the self. The essence of the self in adulthood is the interaction between this immense variety of *I* aspects and the *me* aspects.

Adults also have a range of significant others who influence the person's self. These may include children, spouse, parents, employer, neighbors, close friends, and role models or mentors. Each of these relationships might involve a slightly different set of *mes*—that is, a different facet of oneself may be revealed to each person. Moreover, each significant other may evoke different clusters of inner experiencing in one's *I*. All these relationships, and the *I*s and *me*s associated with them, combine to provide the diversity and complexity of the self in adulthood.

Perhaps the hallmark of the self in adulthood is the person's highly developed ability to take the attitude of a diverse range of others—that is, to attempt to see the world through their eyes. Consider, for example, the young mother who is able to take the attitude of her husband, her children, or her parents; but also able to take the attitudes of teachers toward her children, the attitude of the other parents (and the police and city council) toward the conditions of her neighborhood, and the attitude of federal and state politicians about schools, inflation, unemployment, and so on. She must be able to do this if she is going to participate in these complex social realities.

Likewise, most adults have a well-developed ability to be self-conscious (in the sense of being able to take the attitude of another toward oneself). For example, a successful lawyer self-consciously selects the impression he is conveying in the courtroom and attempts to influence the perceptions of his client held by others in the courtroom. In introspective moments of self-consciousness he may reflect on the morality or the political consequences of his behavior; and he may reflect on the future consequences or past experiences that pertain to the particular case. When he meets with his colleagues or has dinner with his wife, he is also engaging in social behavior that is characterized by the process of social interaction and may involve moments of self-consciousness. If his wife decides to divorce him, or if he enters psychotherapy, he will probably have many moments of self-consciousness when he focuses on himself as others see him and when he seeks to integrate these percep-tions with his own experience of himself. These moments of self-consciousness are one of the main sources of change in the self. They involve the ability to take the attitude of the other, to communicate with oneself and with others using significant symbols, and they involve the interaction of the mind and the self. They may occur in moments of quiet introspection or in extended interactions in which one is attempting to understand a social interaction that has gone awry for some reason. An example from a middle-aged respondent indicates this process clearly:

> I used to think that all of us in the office were contemporaries, for we all had similar career interests. But one day we were talking about old movies and we realized that the younger ones had never seen a Shirley Temple film or an Our Gang comedy. . . . Then it struck me with a blow that I was older than they. I had never been so conscious of it before.[1] (Neugarten, 1967b)

Conclusion

The symbolic interaction perspective calls attention to the interpersonal nature of human life. Since adults usually live in a complex network of social interactions, this perspective seems especially useful for understanding adulthood. At the end of this chapter we use this perspective for an analysis of the central issues in the study of adulthood: the timing or regulation of adult development, the meaning of experi-ence, and the nature of the processes of change and stability in human development. In the next two sections we focus on social norms, status, and roles, and on the process of socialization. These concepts have grown out of Mead's work, but have been modified by other sociologists in many ways. For example, Mead's concept of *I* has largely been lost in these modifications, and it is important for us to remember its central importance in human functioning.

Throughout this book, we must also keep in mind two other significant impli-cations of Mead's approach. First, the self is not a "thing," but is a process. Only the *me* aspect of it exists in any objective sense. *I* is pure process, existing only from moment to moment, as a kind of stream of consciousness, or flow of experiencing.

---

[1]All quotations from Neugarten (1967) are reprinted with permission. Copyright © 1967 by Bernice L. Neugarten.

As soon as we can talk about *I,* it has become a *me,* and *I* of the present moment is reacting to that *me.* Thus the *I – me* interaction is the essence of the self, and this prevents oneself from ever being fully defined, categorized, or measured. Although this may be frustrating to some social scientists, Mead would have argued that this is the essence of humanness.

Second, the self, or the person, is always an active participant in social interactions. In this view, we are not passive creatures shaped by external forces; instead, we are constantly active in social interaction, creating and recreating ourself as the collection of *me*s and the flow of experiencing changes and evolves all the years of our lives.

Social Timing Factors: Norms, Status, and Roles

The discussion of Mead's approach to social interaction focused on the individual in the interaction. To expand this perspective, we shift our focus to the social side of the interaction. This section examines the ways in which society affects individuals in age-related ways.

Age Norms

Norms are a set of expectations about behavior that people carry in their heads and use to regulate their own behavior and to respond to others' behavior. In symbolic interaction terms, norms are the attitudes of the generalized other and affect our behavior as we take the attitude of the generalized other toward ourselves in any social situation. Norms are linked to social *sanctions,* which are the pressures brought to bear on an individual who violates the norms or expectations. Thus, norms exert some degree of *constraint* on behavior so that one usually chooses to do those things that are expected, and not to do those things that violate social expectations. In particular, norms prescribe the expected behavior of persons in such social *positions* as doctor, mother, police officer, and student; those expected behaviors are called *roles* and will be discussed in a later section. There are informal sanctions as well as legalized sanctions that may be used to maintain the expected behavior. These norms, sanctions, and roles differ among various cultures, for men and women, and for persons of different ages.

In general, individuals have expectations for which behavior is appropriate for persons at various points in the life span. These expectations are called **age norms.** We are all aware of these age norms, although we may not think about them consciously; our behavior and our response to others are affected by them frequently. We may note, for example, that we often respond differently to a young person than we do to a middle-aged person or to an elderly individual. We tend to have stereotypes about people based on their age, and respond accordingly, at least to strangers. Consider the following examples:

1. A man quits his job and moves to Florida where he grows vegetables in a small garden and takes life easy. Would you react differently if he was 15? 35? 55? or 75?

2. A woman is shopping and you notice a box of condoms (male contraceptive

devices) in her cart. Would you react differently if she was 15? 35? 55? or 75?

3. You are riding on a crowded bus and a person gets up to offer you a seat. Would you react differently if you were 15? 35? 55? or 75? Would the age of the other person also be important?

Neugarten, Moore, and Lowe (1965) inquired about the expected age for various age-related characteristics among a middle-class, middle-aged sample. For example, 85 percent of the men and 90 percent of the women felt that the 19–24 age range is the best time for a woman to marry (Table 2.1). The same questions were asked of other middle-class respondents age 20–30 who lived in a midwestern city, a group of African-American men and women aged 40–60, and a group of persons aged 70–80 in a New England community. Essentially the same patterns of age norms were found for each group of respondents. This study demonstrated that there was a high degree of consensus about the ages associated with certain age-re-

TABLE 2.1 *Consensus in a Middle-Class, Middle-Aged Sample Regarding Various Age-Related Characteristics*

	Age Range Designated as Appropriate or Expected	Percent Who Concur	
		Men (N = 50)	Women (N = 43)
Best age for a man to marry	20–25	80	90
Best age for a woman to marry	19–24	85	90
When most people should become grandparents	45–50	84	79
Best age for most people to finish school and go to work	20–22	86	82
When most men should be settled on a career	24–26	74	64
When most men hold their top jobs	45–50	71	58
When most people should be ready to retire	60–65	83	86
A young man	18–22	84	83
A middle-aged man	40–50	86	75
An old man	65–75	75	57
A young woman	18–24	89	88
A middle-aged woman	40–50	87	77
An old woman	60–75	83	87
When a man has the most responsibilities	35–50	79	75
When a man accomplishes most	40–50	82	71
The prime of life for a man	35–50	86	80
When a woman has the most responsibilities	25–40	93	91
When a woman accomplishes the most	30–45	94	92
A good-looking woman	20–35	92	82

Source: Neugarten, Moore & Lowe (1965), Table 1. Reprinted with permission from the *American Journal of Sociology*, copyright © 1965 by the University of Chicago.

lated behaviors in the United States in the 1960s. By 1980, however, there was some evidence of lessened consensus about age norms; to cite the same example, only 40 percent of the respondents agreed that the 19–24 age range is the best time for a woman to marry (Passuth & Maines, 1981). Meyrowitz (1985) noted that even the distinction between the roles of children and adults is decreasing today. Neugarten and Neugarten (1986) have also called attention to these changes in our country and suggested that we may be moving toward an *age-irrelevant* society. Such a society would have less rigid age norms about the sort of characteristics listed in Table 2.1.

Since age norms involve the individual's perceptions of what is appropriate and inappropriate behavior at different ages, it is also possible to measure the amount of *constraint* that age norms exert. For example: Is it appropriate for a woman to wear a two-piece bathing suit on the beach (a) when she is 18? (b) when she is 30? (c) when she is 45? (Neugarten, Moore & Lowe, 1965). If the answer is "yes" to all three ages, there is no age constraint reflected. If the answer is "yes" to only one, then the degree of constraint is fairly high. In this manner, age constraint can be measured for individuals of different ages and also for the individuals' perception of "others' views" (i.e., their perception of the generalized other).

The results of three studies, two similar samples in Chicago — one in 1960, the other in 1979 — and one in Japan in 1970, show similar patterns (Figure 2.3).

> First, respondents attributed more age constraints to "other people's opinions" than to their own opinions, and the gap between the two scores [was] the most marked among young adults. Second, personally perceived age constraint was positively related to the age of respondents, but "other people's" views showed somewhat lower constraint scores among old respondents than among young adults. These trends in combination produce a third pattern: a convergence of personal opinion and other people's views among respondents over 65, a pattern that was remarkably similar across the three studies. . . . Fourth, in all three samples, men perceived greater age constraint in

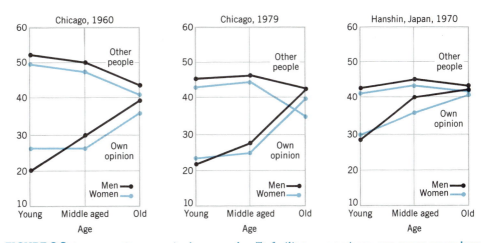

FIGURE 2.3 Age constraint scores in three samples. To facilitate comparisons, raw means scores have been converted to standard ratios (i.e., percentage of total possible scores), a procedure followed by Plath and Ikeda. (*Sources*: Neugarten, Moore & Lowe (1965); Passuth & Maines (1981); Plath & Ikeda (1975). Reprinted from Hagestad & Neugarten (1985), p. 42, with permission.)

themselves as well as in "other people" than did women. The only exception to this trend was young adulthood. (Hagestad & Neugarten, 1985, p. 42)

In general, these findings indicate that although young people felt "others" think age is important, they do not feel much age constraint themselves. However, the older respondents (age 65 and over) felt that age is moderately important in determining appropriate behavior and that "others" placed about the same amount of importance on it as they do themselves. Do these differences reflect a cohort or historical effect, and thus suggest that as younger people grow older, we will have an age-irrelevant society?

Age-Status Systems

In addition to socially defined age norms that indicate appropriate *behavior* on the basis of age, there is also an age-related status system in many cultures whereby one's social *position* and *status* is based at least partly on the person's age. That is, an age-status system in a society awards the rights, duties, and privileges to individuals differentially on the basis of age.

There is some degree of *age grading* in our social structure, so that status and power are awarded to individuals in part because of their age, or their age-related position in the family, but it is not nearly as tight a system as in some other cultures. Some Native American cultures, for example, placed their greatest status on the aged, especially the aged man, who was often their chief or medicine man. There is a certain logic to such a structure, since if a man were to live to an old age he had to be a survivor: strong, healthy, and adept at avoiding the various pitfalls that might have resulted in his earlier death. Other cultures, for example, Japan, base an individual's status directly on age, and the aged are accorded high status (but not so high as children's status; Benedict, 1946). In our society, individuals seldom reach positions of power simply because they are aged; our age-status system tends to favor middle-aged persons who have lived long enough to have some "experience," but not so long as to be "out of date." We discuss the status of old people in other cultures in Chapter 9.

Age-Gender Roles

The concept of social role is related both to the individual's social position and to the norms of the society. A **role** is the *behavior* that is expected from a person occupying a social position. The norms prescribe the expected role behavior. Since many social positions have role behaviors associated with them, the social position is often called a role. For example, the role of "mother" involves some very clear expectations and behaviors for the appropriate enactment of that role. It may be contrasted with the role of "wife" that she plays or with the role of "business executive" that she may also play.

In the symbolic interaction perspective, the role is a *me* that the individual presents in a social interaction. It arises from taking the attitude of the other (or generalized other) toward one's own behavior. A *me* is not always a role, however; it may be any characteristic of the self that can be seen by others (refer back to Figure 2.1). One plays many roles during the day (i.e., presents many *me*s). The *I* selects and integrates these various *me*s into a sense of self.

Perhaps we play roles because it would be much too complicated to work out ordinary behavior self-consciously without being able to rely on the "scripts" that accompany a role. It would be chaotic if teachers, students, bus drivers, and everyone else forgot how to play their roles. Routine interaction would be impossible. Consider a shopper in a large department store playing the role of "customer" greeted by a person playing the role of "salesclerk." As long as both play their roles, they can interact and complete the transition quickly and easily. If the shopper tries to sell a watch to the clerk, however, there will be an abrupt shift and some discomfort. Or if the shopper offers to pay less for the item than the price marked, the clerk may give a response that means: "Get with it; that's not the way to play your role!" If the customer persists in playing the role incorrectly and, for example, pays the clerk $30 for a $50 item and walks out of the store, the store security guard may apply a social sanction.

We are not "programmed" like computers, however. Individuals have a fair amount of latitude in how they ad-lib their roles; and we probably all play our roles in slightly idiosyncratic ways. Nonetheless, if one steps too far out of line, one may feel some degree of social constraint. Moreover, a person does not always yield to this constraint. In extreme situations, this may provoke a confrontation such as the civil disobedience that Mohandas Gandhi and Martin Luther King used successfully.

Roles are often expected to differ for men and women, and for persons of various ages. A particular role may begin or end at specific ages, or when one's social position changes, because roles are defined by social norms. For example, at mar-

Shoplifting is a crime! Social and legal sanctions enforce the proper role of a shopper.

riage there is a shift in role to that of husband or wife; at the birth of the first child there is a new role added, that of parent—mother or father; when one's children have children, one adds the role of grandparent. Such role changes can help us understand the periods of transition and change during the life span. Obviously roles may change in one area of life and not another, or may change suddenly or gradually. In addition, roles change with social change; both age and gender roles are current examples of this process. We discuss role change and transitions in Chapter 3, family roles in Chapter 5, and occupational roles in Chapter 6.

Ageism: Age Norms and Social Bias

Social roles and age norms are clearly important influences on our behavior. They are not always positive influences, however. As noted earlier, persons who deviate from the prescribed behavior may experience social pressure to conform or receive formal sanctions in varying degrees of severity. Moreover, age and other social norms can be used to devalue individuals and to discriminate against groups of people. Similar to *sexism* or *racism*, **ageism** is a form of bias that can be used to stigmatize individuals on the basis of chronological age. It can involve "moderately negative stereotypes about the aged, feelings of superiority among the non-aged, and simple exclusion or avoidance of the aged" (Palmore, 1972). Robert Butler (1969) coined the term to describe the reaction of middle-aged community residents to the establishment of an old age home in their neighborhood; he noted:

> Prejudice of the middle-aged against the old in this instance, and against the young in others, is a serious national problem. Age-ism reflects a deep seated uneasiness on the part of the young and middle-aged—a personal revulsion to and distaste for growing old, disease, disability; and fear of powerlessness, "uselessness," and death. (Butler, 1969, p. 243)

Ageism involves prejudicial attitudes, discriminatory practices, and institutional policies and practices (Butler, 1980). It can be compounded by sexism, since the majority of older people are women (Rodeheaver & Datan, 1988). Likewise, it can interact with racism or any other social bias in complex ways.

In general, there are four important themes that characterize ageism and differentiate it from similar forms of bias. First, ageism can apply to the young as well as to the old. Adolescents are denied privileges that young adults take for granted; middle-aged persons are too young to qualify for Medicare, and also may be too old to be admitted to medical school, for example. Second, stereotypes about the aged may entail both positive attributes (mature, deserving of respect, wise) and negative attributes (old-fashioned, irrelevant, senile). Third, unlike gender or race, one is not born old, but hopes to live long enough to achieve it; thus, everyone is potentially eligible to experience ageism. Fourth, age brings increased status through various seniority systems; this is more pronounced in other cultures than in our own and, in fact, positive age bias is all that ensures care for old people in some cultures such as Japan that do not have extensive social services available for elders (Kimmel, 1988).

Age bias can affect the individual because age is an aspect of the person's *me.* Others react to one's grey hair, appearance, and retired employment status; and

In most cases older individuals cope with the social bias of ageism by relying on their own sense of worth and ignoring the stereotypes.

individuals take the attitude of the other toward themselves. One's *I* must integrate this *me* into the sense of self and, ideally, recognize the inaccuracy of inappropriate stereotypes. At times, there may be a painful recognition that one has entered a period of life that is not highly valued in our society. In most cases, older individuals cope with this social bias by relying on their own sense of worth and ignoring the stereotypes. However, some people attempt to distance themselves from other "old" people who display the characteristics that are stereotypically associated with old age, such as physical impairment or chronic illness. In contrast, people of all ages actively fight the negative stereotypes of old age through organizations such as the Grey Panthers.

The significance of ageism is receiving increased attention in psychological research (Schaie, 1988), in the delivery of psychological services (Gatz & Pearson, 1988), and in the growing trend to consider need as well as age in terms of public policies (Neugarten & Neugarten, 1986, 1987). We discuss legislation that prohibits both age discrimination in employment and mandatory retirement based on age in most occupations in Chapter 6.

In general, ageism and other forms of bias may be reduced if our society recognizes the importance of human diversity in all its forms and we work together to modify social norms.

The Social Clock

The interaction of age norms, age constraints, age-status systems, and age-related roles produces a phenomenon that Bernice Neugarten (1968) called the **social clock.** This is an internal sense of the best time to reach social milestones. The sense of regulation comes from the internalized perception of age-related norms, expectations, and roles. It acts as a *prod* to speed up accomplishment of the task, or as a *brake* to slow one's progress through the social events of the lifeline. This "clock" is sometimes mentioned by middle-aged people themselves as a cue that it is time to take that special trip before they are too old to enjoy it (or too old to think that they *should* take a long trip), or when it is time to go back to school to study painting "now that my children are on their own."

This internalized social clock is one of the major sources of timing in adulthood. It regulates the sequential progression of an individual through the age-related milestones and events of the adult years. The norms and expectations of society (the generalized other) are internalized by taking the attitude of the generalized other toward oneself. One then compares one's own developmental progression with these norms and expectations. An analogy might be to consider the social clock as "Big Ben" (the clock on the tower of the Houses of Parliament in London). We set our individual watches (internalized age norms) to Big Ben. Of course, some of our watches keep better time than others, so there is some variation in the timing of major milestones, but most of us have a reasonably similar sense of the "right time"

Sometimes the social clock reflects the biological clock.

to marry, change jobs, become a parent, and so on. One example of this social clock, here indicating that is is time to change jobs, is given by one of Neugarten's (1967b) middle-aged respondents:

> I moved at age forty-five from a large corporation to a law firm. I got out at the last possible moment, because after forty-five it is too difficult to find the job you want. If you haven't made it by then, you had better make it fast, or you are stuck.

There is some evidence that the social clock is set slightly differently for persons from different socioeconomic classes, for those of different ethnic and racial backgrounds, for persons who suffered economic deprivation during the depression of the 1930s, and for men and women (Neugarten & Hagestad, 1976). For example, Olsen (1969), in a study of a representative sample of persons aged 50–70 in a midwestern city in the 1950s, found that persons from higher socioeconomic classes experienced family-related events later than persons from lower socioeconomic classes (Figure 2.4).

Neugarten and Hagestad (1976) also pointed out that **off-time events** — those that occur unusually early or unusually late, according to the social clock — are particularly difficult, in comparison with **on-time events,** which are likely to be

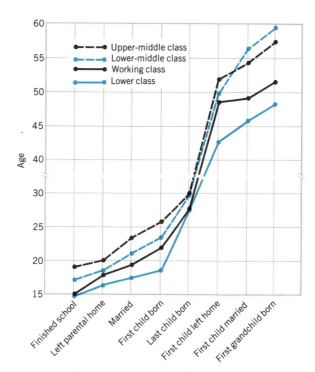

FIGURE 2.4 Median ages at which women of different socioeconomic classes reached successive events in the family cycle. Men showed similar socioeconomic class distinctions. (*Source*: Neugarten & Hagestad (1976), Figure 1; from Olsen (1969). Reprinted with permission.)

less stressful because one may anticipate and prepare for the event. Similarly, early marriage or being off-time in career advancement seems to have significant effects on many measures of satisfaction. Pearlin (1982) likewise noted that "scheduled" transitions do not appear to be associated with psychological change, whereas events that upset the expected sequence may produce major stress.

There may also be events that are more satisfying if they are slightly off-time. For example, Nydegger (1973) found that "late" fathers were more comfortable and effective as fathers than either the "on-time" or "early" fathers. There may also be a kind of "idiosyncracy credit" given to persons who have performed according to the social clock in most areas of life. They are therefore allowed to vary from it in one or more areas, such as for middle-aged women who have raised a family and enroll in college or graduate programs (Neugarten & Hagestad, 1976). As age norms become less compelling, individuals may feel greater freedom to "postpone" marriage or parenthood, as has been the case in recent years, or to "speed up" the age of retirement, as has also been a contemporary pattern.

The process by which these social norms, roles, expectations, and the social clock are learned and translated into behavior is the process of *socialization,* to which we turn our attention in the next section of this chapter.

Socialization: Learning Norms and Roles

Socialization is the process by which an individual learns to perform various social roles adequately; it is the process by which social norms, values, and expectations are transmitted from one generation to the next. In the symbolic interaction framework, socialization involves the basic social process of taking the attitude of the other (or generalized other) toward oneself. In addition, it involves taking the attitude of the other toward the entire range of social objects, including institutions (such as the family, government, and religion), and the entire range of individuals and social positions in one's society. Much of this process, as well as the learning of the significant symbols required for this process to occur, undoubtedly occurs according to principles of learning theory such as reinforcement. However, because of the selective and innovative processes of *I,* this socialization process is not one of passive molding but, instead, a complementary fitting together of two active social processes—the individual and the social community—ideally maximizing the potential of both. Thus, the socialization process is *reciprocal* so that both the person being socialized, the **socializee,** and the person doing the socialization, the **socializing agent,** mutually affect each other. Moreover, the individual is usually quite active in this process and often seeks out the socialization experience.

The Socialization Process

It is sometimes thought that socialization is primarily, if not exclusively, limited to childhood and adolescence. The idea that adults are also socialized by the persons with whom they interact is relatively new. However, the process of socialization does not differ much for children and for adults. It involves a relationship with a *significant other.* As these individuals interact, usually in an emotional relationship of some significance, they influence one another and provide feedback to each other through the symbolic interaction process. This feedback functions to build up a set of mutual expectations for each other's behavior. These mutual expectations contain the role prescriptions, the norms, and the values that the agent attempts to transmit. The agent, in turn, responds to the behavior and to the expectations of the socializee and may modify the expectations or provide corrective feedback to the socializee.

It may be that this interaction occurs whenever two people are interacting in a relationship with some emotional involvement; it is a broad, general view of the socialization process. However, it also pertains to such specific situations as those in which the socializing agent is informally conveying information or formally "teaching." It may involve the transmission of values and moral views, modeling ways of interacting with others, or learning to operate a piece of complicated equipment. That is, the degree of formality or informality varies and the content varies, but the relationship, the mutual influence, and the centrality of a significant relationship between the two interacting individuals do not vary.

As the individual develops from childhood into adulthood, certain parameters of the socialization process may change, however. For example, as adolescents gain the cognitive capacity to think abstractly and to take a more objective view of their own behavior, they also gain the ability to expand their set of significant others from people immediately present (parents, teachers, and peers) to people who are not now living or concretely present (i.e., historical figures, religious deities, or deceased parents and grandparents). This ability continues through adulthood so that individuals may base their central values and expectations for themselves on the remembered or imagined expectations of these significant others.

In addition, the young adult has a wider range of social interactions than was true for the child, and the social world continues to broaden in adulthood. Thus, there is greater freedom to select one's significant others—one's socializing agents—during adulthood than in childhood. However, allowing for the increased intellectual ability of adults and the different kinds of roles that adults are socializing themselves into, the *process* of socialization remains essentially the same as in childhood.

Anticipatory Socialization and Resocialization

The general process of socialization may be subdivided into more specific types of socialization experience. Two of the most common types are anticipatory socialization and resocialization. **Anticipatory socialization** is the process of preparation for a change in role or status. It involves exploring the new norms and expectations that will be associated with the new role or status once the transition is made. It involves an element of practice and of trying out a new role before the actual shift takes place (Clausen, 1968). Examples of this process include the college student choosing a career—imagining what it might be like, talking to persons in that career, and perhaps trying it out in a summer job—or medical students who are given their "black bag," wear a white lab coat, and begin to play the role of "doctor" before they have their M.D. Later in life, a mother may return to school or begin preparing herself in other ways for returning to work several years before her children leave home and she actually enters her field of special interest. Or the family may begin reading different magazines and driving a different kind of car in preparation for the next promotion and a move to another neighborhood. In such cases there is a period of anticipation of the new roles or status and preliminary socialization into them before they are actually achieved. Marshall (1975) noted, however, that: "Socialization for any aspect of aging is not highly programmed within our society. . . . There are few specialized teachers or programs to prepare people for any aspect of old age" (p. 359).

One example of anticipatory socialization during old age focused on preparation for dying among residents in a retirement home and a home for the aged (Marshall, 1975). In one residence, the staff organized the manner in which death was dealt with and the residents had little opportunity to grieve or to prepare themselves for this final "status passage." In the other home, by contrast, the residents "deal with death as a community event."

> They make plans for death, and they have developed informal tacit understandings by which to deal with it. As a result, Glen Brae is a community setting where the residents are remarkably successful in legitimating their impending deaths. Highly important in this respect is the interactional and conversational foundation of community life. Low-keyed and resourceful, the residents have developed community control over the dying status passage. . . .
>
> Death is frequent, visible, and informally dealt with by residents themselves at Glen Brae, where it becomes a focus of mutual status passage control and collective community involvement. (Marshall, 1975, pp. 365–366)

Resocialization, in contrast to anticipatory socialization, takes place when the role or status is actually begun. The amount of resocialization, or reorganization of one's expectations about oneself, depends on the amount of difference between the

Joining a group such as Weight Watchers is an example of resocialization caused by shifting one's reference group.

previous role and the new one. It may involve learning a new skill when one's job is replaced by a machine, or it may involve learning the role of grandparent when one's first grandchild is born. Adulthood involves a series of resocialization experiences. Many of the changes that occur during the adult years involve or reflect these experiences (Brim & Wheeler, 1966).

Socialization in Adulthood

Orville Brim, Jr. (1968), suggested a number of situations in adulthood that typically lead to socialization experiences. In general, individuals seek formal and informal socialization experiences when they feel that a change in their lives is needed. Note that the technical term "socialization" has a somewhat different meaning from the popular term "socializing." Usually other people are required for *socialization,* but having a sociable time with others does not necessarily involve a socialization experience that produces a change in roles or expectations.

Demands of Self or Others

From time to time individuals may feel that they are not living the kind of life they wish to live or not doing the kinds of things they wish to do; conversely, others may feel that way about them. As a result they may change somewhat through informal socialization, or they may seek out a socialization experience to bring about the desired changes.

For some people, this experience may be psychotherapy. For others, it may be a shift in reference group (significant others) to bring about the desired change in roles and expectations; an example would be an urban executive who seeks out new friends in a rural area in preparation for moving from the city to a farm. Insofar as there is change, socialization will be involved since there will be new norms, values, and expectations to learn and internalize. Reading about the new roles, copying role models, talking with informants, and finding significant others to support the new role are usually all involved in this kind of change.

Other individuals may resist the pressure to change, however, and will seek out people who encourage them to remain as they are; an example might be a drug addict who leaves a spouse and family to be with drug-using peers.

The changes that result from the individual's internal social clock (by which age norms exert constraint on a person to behave differently) may also lead the individual to learn the appropriate expectations for "people of that age."

Role or Status Change

Social situations may change as a result of age-related changes, such as the shift in roles from "single" to "husband" to "father." Or they may change with one's growing seniority on the job that brings shifts in role and status. In either case, there would be new expectations and norms to learn that would involve anticipatory socialization and resocialization. Some extreme changes might also be involved, resulting from *radical resocialization,* such as from "junkie" to "ex-addict" where there is a major shift in self-conception and a clear dichotomy between the previous role and the new role.

One characteristic of role or status change is that the conflicts that result between the new role and previous roles must be resolved. The new husband may have to restrict his pattern of socializing after work, for example. Second, the individuals need some support in their new roles. The new wife may receive considerable advice and encouragement from her mother, friends, and co-workers. Third, this process of socialization is likely to take place in informal ways; usually one's colleagues, friends, neighbors, and relatives provide most of the information, support, and encouragement; they usually do so subtly and informally. Only when there are distinct skills to be learned is the socialization formal, requiring education or reading.

Occupational Entry or Change

A frequent occasion for resocialization is change in occupation or occupational role. A major change or even a promotion may bring the need for new skills, for playing new roles, for forming new relationships, and for changing the level of aspiration. A promotion from being a skilled worker to being a manager, for example, requires that the person relate to the previous co-workers and to the other managers in new ways. Often a company with many offices will move the employee from one office to another when major promotions occur to facilitate this resocialization and to reduce conflicts with the previous role. Similarly, a woman who shifts from the role of housewife to novelist will find herself being socialized in many ways as she learns the role and norms that apply for writing and publishing books; if she is very successful she may also have to learn the skills of appearing on TV interviews.

Changes in the Family

During the course of the family cycle there are a number of role shifts that take place. In addition, there are mutual expectations that are set up by the husband and wife about each other's behavior; the spouses function as very important socializing agents for one another. For example, the traditional periods of courtship and engagement provide considerable opportunity for anticipatory socialization; the first years of marriage involve a great deal of mutual socialization as the couple match their expectations with each other and reach working agreement on a great range of behaviors such as housework, sexual behavior, food preferences, entertainment, desire for children, handling of finances, brand of toothpaste, and so on. The birth of the first child brings a shift from previous roles of husband and wife to father and mother. This change not only brings about the socialization into their new roles as parents but also intensifies the mutual socialization for their ongoing relationship. The baby, of course, also has some "expectations" — in the form of immediate and imperative needs — that influence the parents' expectations about their own behavior. As the children grow, they begin exerting an ever-increasing socializing influence on the parents. Although the parents may be the primary socializing agents for the children, the interaction is never only one way, and children's expectations ordinarily influence parents' expectations as well. Finally, as the children begin leaving home and the parents resume a dyadic relationship, additional socialization may be needed to match their expectations about each other once again.

In addition, there may be some changes in physical health that require resocialization. Divorce, if it occurs, brings a marked change in role and status. Grandparenthood, retirement from work, and the death of a spouse each mark a change in role and status that requires resocialization and, if possible, anticipatory socialization to prepare for the change in roles and expectations.

Unmarried, or nontraditional, couples may not have all these socialization experiences, but they are neither constrained nor protected by the roles and norms of society to the same extent as traditional couples. They therefore may seek their own group of significant others to provide support, encouragement, and appropriate role models for their nontraditional life-style.

Geographic Mobility

Physically moving from one community to another brings an obvious need for socialization. Anticipatory socialization might involve reading and talking with others about the new area, and perhaps visiting it. Resocialization involves all that has to be learned once one arrives in the new place.

Relocating for a new job or because of a promotion or to change life-style or to seek better opportunities all require one to learn about the new community. Frequently, one finds some significant others in the new community to ease the process of resocialization; initially these may be members of the same club, or the same religion, or the same ethnic group, or one's family.

Immigration brings an even more dramatic need for socialization because many different norms, values, and expectations will have to be learned, and one's previous cultural norms and roles will need to be suppressed to some degree. Speaking and understanding the language may be a major concern if it is a new or "second" language because socialization requires the use of *significant symbols* such as a shared language.

Downward Mobility

Another change that brings about a need for adult socialization is a decline in status or in the number of roles. Although this is essentially the same process as upward mobility in terms of the demands for socialization, it is a shift in the other direction.

Downward mobility may occur in a period of economic hardship, such as the depression of the 1930s, or may occur as a result of an individual misfortune, such as illness, loss of a job, or disability. It may occur after divorce or widowhood, if the woman's status was dependent on her husband's position. It may also occur after retirement if one's status was defined by one's occupational role, or if there is a marked decline in one's standard of living. Downward mobility may also occur late in life if one survives longer than one's assets.

The process of socialization in these situations is similar to the other examples listed above. If successful, one adds some new roles to offset those that are lost, and

Downward mobility can lead to resocialization as a family learns to cope with being homeless.

one learns how to play one's current roles with meaning and satisfaction and also to find significant others who support and encourage one's performance.

Adult Development: A Social Interaction Perspective

The study of adulthood and aging raises a number of interesting theoretical questions that can be addressed through the social interaction perspective presented in this chapter: (1) the timing or regulation of development during adulthood; (2) the nature of experience as it affects adult development; and (3) the process by which individuals change while they also remain relatively stable during the many years of adulthood.

Timing in Adult Development

Development during adulthood is not regulated primarily by time-dependent biological factors, as is early childhood development. Instead, it appears to be regulated by social processes so that the adult years follow a relatively regular developmental course for most people. Three social processes are involved in regulating adult development and they provide a degree of predictability and order to the sequence of adult life in general. These are: the social timetable of expected events, the social clock, and personal timing events. We discuss each in turn.

Timetable of Life Events

In our society there is an implicit notion that adult development should follow a **timetable of age-related events.** This is a normative expectation that we use to organize our thinking about our own lives and about the lives of others. Age-norms, age-roles, and age-status systems as well as expectations about the usual order of life events all implicitly assume that most people follow a relatively orderly progression through their life. Other societies may have different timetables, or may view timetables in differing ways, of course.

These timetables tend to be closely linked with age — in our own minds, and in social expectations. Thus, a self-made millionaire at age 30, a leader who dies in midlife, or a man in his seventies marrying and beginning a family all attract attention because they violate our shared sense of appropriate timetables.

Not only do we tend to share implicit timetables about family events (marriage, parenthood, grandparenthood, widowhood in that order) and occupational events (first job, serious job, promotion, last chance to change jobs, reaching the peak, retirement), but we even have a timetable for death (the oldest die first). Of course, life does not always follow these timetables, but we have internalized these kinds of ideas about the normative life course through the process of socialization. We, as members of society who share these norms, tend to organize our lives in relation to these timetables, whether they fit us precisely or not.

Adult development, then, may be perceived as more regular and sequential for people in general than it actually is for a particular individual because we are inclined to view development in general within the framework of general socially defined timetables.

On Time or Off Time

In the earlier discussion of the *social clock,* we noted that we internalize the sense of the "right time" to complete events on the social timetable; again, the process of socialization is involved. As Neugarten (1968) phrased it, we know if we are "on time" or "off time"; if we are off-time, the social clock pushes us on faster, or slows us down, whichever is appropriate.

To rephrase the analogy with "Big Ben" (the social clock), we each set our own watches, consult our timetables, and decide whether we must "hurry" or "slow down" to catch the train, boat, or plane that will take us to the next stop in our course of life. We may, however, decide to skip that stop on the itinerary; or to see if we can get an earlier or a later flight. As age becomes somewhat less relevant in our society, more people seem to be willing to take these options.

Personal Timing Events

Although adult development for people in general may be regulated largely by the social clock and socially defined timetables of expected events, individual lives may be affected by **timing events.** These are experiences that cause the person to modify the self in an age-related way. Examples of timing events include a wide range of experiences. Some may be identical with events on the social timetable: graduation, first job, parenthood, retirement, or death of one's spouse. Some might be idiosyncratic events: a son beating his father at tennis, one's daughter being elected to the United States Senate, finding an old packet of "love letters" in the dusty attic, a heart attack, the death of a parent or co-worker, or making the final payment on the home mortgage. They may even be trivial events: noticing grey hair for the first time, trading in an old car, talking with an old friend, or seeing one's grandson going to his first prom.

The crucial characteristic of a timing event is that there is a self-conscious realization that one's *me* has changed in an *age-related* way. It may be triggered by the social clock, social norms, an age-related shift in social roles, physical illness, or any formal event such as becoming a grandparent. It also may occur in a moment of self-conscious introspection, as one of Neugarten's (1967b) respondents illustrates:

> When I see a pretty girl on the stage or in the movies—we used to say "a cute chick"—and when I realize, "My God, she's about the age of my son", it's a real shock. It makes me realize that I'm middle-aged.

It should also be noted that such events are not always timing events, because the individual may not interpret them in a self-conscious age-related way. A young man who is occasionally sexually impotent does not suddenly think of himself as "growing old," although a middle-aged man might interpret it this way if it happens to him. A young person who forgets to take a grocery list to the store does not interpret this as a sign of "senility," although an older person might. And a person who retires does not necessarily feel that this is a sign of impending "old age."

Some of these events may be *milestones,* but not timing events. That is, they may be perceived by the person as an important turning point in their lives, but are not subjectively related to age or growing older. For example, an event such as moving from one house or one city to another may be a trivial event for some; it may be a milestone for others; and it may be a timing event for still others (e.g., selling the "family home" and moving to a retirement home).

This discussion suggests that we need to examine the individual's perception of the event or the change in self-perception in order to determine whether it represents a milestone, a timing event, or an unremarkable occurrence. Although social age norms, age roles, the social clock, and milestones provide good clues to probable timing events in adulthood, the individual's perception of those events (the *I* experience of those events) is the crucial determinant of the meaning of an event for the person in this social interaction perspective.

The Meaning of Experience

It is obvious that as one grows older, one accumulates more and more "experience." The question for the study of adult development is what this means for the individual: What is the nature of this "experience" that accumulates with age?

One of Neugarten's (1967b) successful middle-aged business executives provides a vivid example of at least one kind of experience:

> I know now exactly what I can do best, and how to make the best use of my time. . . . I know how to delegate authority, but also what decisions to make myself. . . . I know how to buffer myself from troublesome people . . . one well-placed telephone call will get me what I need. It takes time to learn how to cut through the red tape and how to get the organization to work for me. . . . All this is what makes the difference between me and a young man, and it's all this that gives me the advantage.

Certainly, this person has learned from past situations, has built up a network of contacts who can be helpful, and has kept track of whom to call and what to do for the ordinary kinds of problems that arise. But we wonder how relevant this "experience" is for the person outside the office — in family relationships, at a concert, or in dealing with close friends. Perhaps some of this "experience" generalizes to other situations; but it might also cause misperceptions, or ineptness in other situations — such as intimate relationships.

Situation Experience

The symbolic interaction perspective described earlier in this chapter suggests that there are at least three different kinds of experience. The first is **situation experience,** where one gains a greater range of past situations from which one can draw possible responses for the present situation. In general, as individuals grow older they gain increased knowledge of what responses lead to which outcomes in a wide variety of situations. Much of this knowledge is reduced to automatic (non-self-conscious) habits, unless something unexpected arises. In that sense, experience consists of habituated reactions and memories of previous *I*s and previous *me*s. In most situations, one can call on such memories and habits to decide on the *me* to present in the situation. This kind of experience is learned through the process of socialization by which one learns how to play the various roles in life and then learns to teach it to others. When something unexpected arises, one may become self-conscious or, in a more general way, take the attitude of the other in an attempt to straighten out the problem or interaction.

In situation experience it is important, however, to distinguish between the *depth* of experience in a particular situation (such as running a business, relating to one's spouse, or skiing) and the *breadth* of experience across a variety of situations. Perhaps the business executive quoted earlier has considerable depth of experience in the business world, but relatively little breadth of experience in other areas of life. Or he may have equally deep experience in a variety of other areas of life (such as tennis, art collecting, and wine making). Thus, if we are to look at situation experience as a measure of development in adulthood, we need to focus on both the deepening and the broadening of experience over time.

Interaction Experience

A second kind of experience suggested by the symbolic interaction approach is **interaction experience.** This refers to the fact that as one interacts with a widening range of different persons over the years, one develops a greater amount of experience in interacting with a variety of other people. For example, a business executive may ''know'' that the best way to deal with subordinates is to be firm and distant because in the past employers were always firm and distant (the effect of socialization). In addition, this executive may once have tried being warm and easy-going and lost control of the office and was nearly fired (the effect of interaction experience).

Similarly, in personal relationships, a man may ''know'' the best *me* to present to his wife, his children, his golf partners, his parents, and his in-laws. These *mes* have been built up over time through interaction experience and generally work well. He knows what to expect from others in the interaction and they know what to expect from him. If he finds that they do not work, he can draw on his interaction experience to find another *me* to try; if he does not have any relevant experience, then he can take the attitude of the other person to develop an appropriate response. In turn, he will learn from this experience and have this new style of responding to use in future interactions. Actual life is not always so tidy, however. When his wife divorces him, he may find that his situation and interaction experience were part of the problem.

In the ideal situation, however, individuals become increasingly adept at taking the attitude of the other, at interpreting the significant symbols (words and gestures) in social interactions, and also develop a repertoire of roles and styles of responding from which they can draw as they experience the wide variety of social interactions that characterize adulthood.

In some cases, older adults may rely on styles of interacting that have proven to be effective in earlier years and thus may appear to be somewhat ''set in their ways.'' However, this does not mean they cannot develop new styles of interacting when the situation calls for it, since they have had experience in creating new patterns of interacting in the past and may, in fact, have also learned from experience that ''if it isn't broken, don't fix it.''

Often, for all of us, familiar responses tend to be used first because they have worked in the past and because taking the attitude of other persons requires a considerable effort and intuitive ability. In addition, although interaction experience typically increases with age, it is obvious that some persons experience a more varied range of interactions than others. Thus, the response repertoires of some older persons will be much wider than those of others.

Self Experience

The third kind of experience suggested by this approach is **self experience:** individuals have the potential to develop greater self-conscious experience of themselves over time. That is, ideally, individuals become increasingly adept at seeing themselves from the point of view of the other and at integrating this awareness in the present moment with the memories of this awareness in past situations. They discover their inner reactions to a variety of persons and situations, so that self experience increases as situation experience expands. Likewise, their self experience grows as their interaction experience increases. They also engage in introspection (self-consciousness) from time to time so that this component of their self experience also may become greater over time.

All older persons do not necessarily have greater insight into themselves, or greater introspective abilities than younger people, of course. The older person would, however, have the potential to benefit from the greater range of experiences in a larger number of situations in comparison with a young person. In addition, there is some evidence that the middle years of adulthood involve an emphasis on self experience. In concluding her report on "The Awareness of Middle Age," from which we have quoted several middle-aged respondents in this chapter, Neugarten (1967b) stated:

> In pondering the data on these men and women, we have been impressed with the central importance of what might be called the executive processes of personality in middle age: self-awareness, selectivity, manipulation and control of the environment, mastery, competence, the wide array of cognitive strategies.
>
> We are impressed, too, with reflection as a striking characteristic of the mental life of middle-aged persons: the stock-taking, the heightened introspection, and above all, the structuring and restructuring of experience—that is, the conscious processing of new information in the light of what one has already learned; and turning one's proficiency to the achievement of desired ends.

In this description of the complex functioning of these economically successful middle-aged men and women, we see the self—*I* and *me*—and self-consciousness very much involved in these "executive processes of personality" and in the process of "reflection" as well. Certainly, the self's ability to profit from experience is also at work.

In summary, situation experience, interaction experience, and self experience reflect three differing, but interrelated, components of experience during adulthood. The processes of socialization, changes in behavior as a result of age roles and age norms, timing events, and the effects of the social clock all combine with personal interactions in a variety of situations to produce these differing kinds of experience.

Stability and Change in Adulthood

The issue of stability and change in adulthood is a complex matter. On one level, we recognize that one man we have not seen for several years is somewhat different (in appearance, in the self and, perhaps, in personality) from when we last saw him; yet he is also similar to our memories of him, and we usually have little difficulty in resuming an old friendship and catching up on the changes that have taken place. On another level, we note that some of the changes we see in him may be the result of actual changes *in him,* but some of them may result from changes *in us.* That is, we may have changed so that our *I* notes and responds to different aspects of him (his *me*) — as when we see something new in a painting or film or play we have not seen for years, but which has remained unchanged. On yet another level, it may be that our friend is presenting a different set of *me*s to us than he did before — possibly *me*s that were present in the past but were never revealed to us.

Nonetheless, we recognize that our friend has had several years of *experience,* and he has probably had some *timing events* since we last saw him. He may have married, published several books, and become a highly respected judge in the intervening years. Each of these events involves changes in roles, socialization, and changes in the self. Thus, not only will we see him differently than we did years ago, but he will also see himself as different than he was when we last knew him. Even with all this change, however, we would expect a reasonable amount of stability as well. That is, we would recognize characteristics about him that are quite similar to the memory we have of him years ago. How do we explain these interrelated processes of stability and change?

We might begin to explore that question by considering the three interacting spheres in which stability and change take place. One of these is the *external environment.* A change in one's social or physical environment is likely to bring some degree of change in oneself. Conversely, a relatively stable environment is likely to promote stability. For example, as long as one lives in the same neighborhood, goes to the same job each day, interacts with the same friends, and so on, one is not likely to feel much push toward change from that relatively consistent environment. In contrast, moving to a new city, developing a new set of friends, or coping with a physical disability that alters one's relationship with the environment is likely to push one to change — in large or small ways. Reacting to these changes in one's social and physical environment will involve the processes of socialization and resocialization. Thus, within a fairly uniform environment, socialization will tend to maintain the relative stability of an individual over time. In a different environment, socialization will bring some change to the individual. Of course, there is always some degree of change within any environment, no matter how consistent. Also, there is always some degree of stability, no matter how different the environment may be, partly because the same individual is responding to the environment.

A second sphere in which stability and change occur is in the *interaction between oneself and others.* Roles change; the social clock brings new norms and expectations as one grows older; socialization brings change; new significant people enter one's life. At the same time, not all roles change; many patterns of interaction do not change very much over time; and not all norms are related to age. Again, the pattern is a mixture of change and stability.

The third arena of stability and change is the self. Changes in a person's experiencing *I* or in the social self *me* may bring change to the individual, even if both the external environment and the pattern of social interactions are fairly constant. For example, one might begin meditating, "come out" as a lesbian, or be "born again" or converted to a different religion. Similarly, a major change in weight or a physical disability may cause one to experience oneself differently (*I*) and to view oneself differently (*me*). Nonetheless, one's experience of oneself is usually fairly constant over time. Changes in the self usually affect only part of

A friend from years ago has changed in some ways, but remains unchanged in other ways. Some of this change may reflect change in oneself as well as with one's friend.

oneself, while other parts remain fairly stable. Again, the pattern is one of simultaneous change and stability over time.

One middle-aged woman in Neugarten's (1967b) study described a change she found in middle age — but she implies that she only came to recognize abilities that were there all along:

> I discovered these last few years that I was old enough to admit to myself the things I could do well and to start doing them. I didn't think like this before. . . . It's a great new feeling.

Another man in the same study described his change in a way that emphasized the stability even more:

> I know what will work in most situations, and what will not. I am well beyond the trial and error stage of youth. I now have a set of guidelines. . . . And I am practised.

In an important sense, these three spheres of change and stability — external environment, interactions with others, and the self — are integrated by the self processes. Just as *I* and *me* are simultaneous aspects of the self, so change and stability are simultaneous processes of the self.

Change in the self occurs when the situation prompts *I* to select a new *me* that is then integrated into the range of *me*s that make up the social self; or when *I* selects a new response in an old situation and that new *me* is integrated into the self; or when one self-consciously modifies the self as in the examples of timing events discussed earlier. Situation experience, interaction experience, and self experience may also bring change to the self. Similarly, socialization and adaptation to changed environmental conditions bring change to the self. And *I* is a continual source of potential change, since one's experience is always somewhat unpredictable and a source of novelty within the self.

Stability of the self results from one's memory of past experiences and past behaviors so that one's present *me*s are usually fairly consistent with past *me*s — for example, in one's behavior, vocabulary, and gestures. Some of these may be habitual patterns that work efficiently in social situations most of the time.

Because repeated social interactions frequently depend on people behaving relatively similarly each time, there is a tendency to perceive oneself as relatively stable and to perceive others as relatively stable, even when this may not be entirely the case. Also, there is a tendency for persons to select social situations that are relatively consistent with past situations, or to perceive the present situation as more consistent with the past than it may actually be. In that sense, stability of the self results partly from our tendency to expect consistency — in ourselves, in others, and in social situations. Only when change is fairly dramatic is it seen as important; otherwise it tends to be shrugged off. For example, one reason stereotypes tend to persist is that often we notice behavior that is consistent with the stereotype but overlook behavior that is inconsistent with it (such as age, gender, or racial stereotypes). We maintain stereotypes about ourselves in the same way.

Thus, the self (the interacting *I* and *me*) is at the core of stability and change during adult development. One may experience conflict between various aspects of oneself — such as between the roles of "good mother" and "good lawyer" — and seek ways to redefine those *me*s in one's experience of oneself to maximize the feeling of a consistent sense of self and to minimize the conflict. Or one may find that a change, such as divorce or other major life transition, brings a period of some distress until one finds a way to reinterpret the self so the sense of conflict is reduced. In some cases, this involves ordinary resocialization and time to integrate the changes into one's sense of self, perhaps with the aid of a self-help group such as Parents Without Partners. In other cases professional help such as psychotherapy may aid in regaining a sense of oneself as a relatively coherent, although evolving, person within a relatively stable social and physical environment.

In the next chapter we focus on these processes of stability and change during the early and middle years of adulthood. We will note that although change and stability are always present, there may be some periods of life that involve greater change than others. Of course, traumatic events may bring change for a particular individual at any point in life. Overall, however, most people remain the same person and do not change in basic ways. Thus, for all of us, the simultaneous processes of change and stability within a social environment, which is also simultaneously changing and remaining stable, are the essence of adulthood.

Chapter Summary

1. Individuals change over time in many respects; yet they also remain relatively stable in other respects. These simultaneous processes of stability and change are brought about by the interaction of social, psychological, and biological factors.

2. George Herbert Mead conceptualized the *self* as made up of the experiencing aspect (*I*), the aspect that can be described to or seen by others (*me*), and the continual interaction of *I* and *me*.

3. *I* is the moment-by-moment awareness of one's experiences, feelings, and thoughts; it is completely subjective or private.

4. The *me* is that aspect of the self others may see or experience when interacting with a person; in that sense it is objective and public. The *me* is also made up of all those characteristics one sees in oneself.

5. According to Mead, the self is not fully present at birth, but develops during childhood through social interaction, through the use of significant symbols (language and gestures that communicate the same meaning to both persons in the interaction), and by taking the attitude of the other toward oneself (seeing oneself from the point of view of the other person).

6. In adulthood the self is very complex, possessing the ability to take the attitude of a diverse range of other people, as well as to be self-conscious (i.e., to reflect on oneself) and to use one's mental powers for the varied patterns of social interactions in which adults engage.

7. Social age norms exert some degree of constraint on social role behavior so that one usually chooses to do those things that are expected at the appropriate ages. Age-status systems award the rights, duties, and privileges to individuals differentially on the basis of age.

8. Ageism is a form of bias that can be used to stigmatize individuals on the basis of chronological age. It involves prejudicial attitudes, discriminatory practices, and institutional policies and practices. It can interact with sexism, racism or any other social bias in complex ways.

9. The *social clock* is the term Neugarten used to describe the influence of social age norms and age roles. It acts as a "prod" to speed up or as a "brake" to slow down an individual's development and thus acts to time or regulate development during adulthood.

10. Socialization is the process by which an individual learns to perform various social roles adequately; it involves learning the norms, values, and expectations of society. In the symbolic interaction framework, it is seen as an active process in which all participants influence each other—not as a kind of programming of a passive individual.

11. Socialization and its two main forms in adulthood—anticipatory socialization and resocialization—continue throughout an individual's life. A variety of different situations are likely to bring about socialization during the adult years.

12. Individual lives are influenced by timing events that may be triggered by the social clock, may be personal age-related events, or may result from a self-conscious realization that one has changed in an age-related way.

13. Experience accumulates with age, but to understand the importance of experience it is useful to distinguish among experience with situations, interaction experience with other people, and self experience. An older person may have greater experience in any or all of these areas than younger persons.

14. The dynamic interplay between change and stability is a central characteristic of development during adulthood. Stable situations, memory, well-rehearsed habitual behavior, and consistent patterns of interaction tend to produce stability of the self over time. Changes in any of these areas, change in the self, and the *I* (a constant potential source of novelty in one's perception of oneself and others) may each bring change.

Key Words

age norms	self
ageism	self-consciousness
anticipatory socialization	self experience
I	significant symbols
interaction	situation experience
interaction experience	social clock
me	socialization
norms	socializee
off-time events	socializing agent
on-time events	symbolic interaction
psychosocial perspective	taking the attitude of the other
resocialization	timetable of age-related events
role	timing events

Review Questions

Symbolic Interaction Approach to Adulthood

1. What are the two aspects of the self that Mead described? Define them.
2. Mead's concept of the *me* is also called the "social self." Why do you think it is called that?
3. Describe how *I* and *me* interact to produce the self.
4. What is the role of significant symbols, significant others, and the generalized other in the development and functioning of the self?
5. Give an example of "taking the role of the other." How does this process affect the self?
6. What is "self-consciousness" as defined by Mead? Give an example.

7. What does the idea that the self is *process* mean?

8. What do you feel is the major shortcoming in Mead's approach?

Social Timing Factors: Norms, Status, and Roles

9. Define and give some examples of age norms in our society (refer to Table 2.1). Describe age norms you have experienced.

10. How are age norms internalized, according to the symbolic interaction framework?

11. Define the concepts of age-status and age-gender roles and give some examples.

12. How does ageism differ from racism and sexism? Give some examples of age bias that may affect older people in negative ways.

13. What is the "social clock"? How does it act as a "prod" or a "brake" in an individual's development?

Socialization: Learning Norms and Roles

14. How does the process of socialization differ from socializing at a party?

15. Give some examples of anticipatory socialization and resocialization that you have experienced.

16. Which of the typical adult socialization situations suggested by Brim have you and your parents experienced?

Adult Development: A Social Interaction Perspective

17. Define "timing events" and give examples of timing events that are: (a) caused by a change in roles; (b) brought about by a moment of self-consciousness, in Mead's sense; and (c) triggered by the social clock.

18. Define the three types of experience suggested by the symbolic interaction perspective. Give examples.

19. What factors tend to bring about consistency in the behavior and personality of an individual over several years? What factors tend to bring about change?

INTERLUDE

George, AGE 43

George was not particularly eager to be interviewed again in 1988, but agreed "if it would help." He had left the dance company and was now working on his own; income and opportunities to perform were much less predictable than at the time of the earlier interview. His relationship with Rick was now of more than 20 years' duration. Acquired immune deficiency syndrome (AIDS) had become an important historical force that affected the life of his community. Although he was not sick, several of his friends had died and he discussed his feelings about the test for antibodies to the virus (HIV) thought to cause the disease.

Viewing a person at two different points in life often reveals both change and stability of characteristics over time. What are some of the aspects of his life that have remained the same since he was interviewed at age 27? What changes do you notice? What effect did the historical event of the AIDS epidemic have, and how does this interact with his relationship with Rick? Is there evidence of increased *experience,* as discussed in Chapter 2? Also, one might note that the interviewer did not focus on milestones this time. Did this make a difference in George's responses? Finally, consider signs of what you think could be a "midlife transition," as this will be the focus of the next chapter.

It's been 15 years since I formally interviewed you and a lot has happened, I'm sure. How has your life been unfolding? What are some of the ways . . . Give me a break! How has my life been unfolding? Oh, yi, yi. The last 15 years. Whew! That's a rough question. Uh. Fifteen years ago. Let's see, I'm 43. Fifteen

years ago, I was . . . 28. I probably still had ideals then; still had hopes and dreams. Well let me see, how can I narrow this down. How is my life unfolding? Since then I think I've developed into a good solid artist. Uh, I don't know how successful. I'm still doing it, so in many people's terms, that's success. I brag to students that I have always, since I first went into dance, since I was invited into————'s Company, I have made my living only doing my art. And that's really true. Of course, my level of living wouldn't be as high as it was without Rick. But I have always supported myself with my art and that's a wonderful thing to have said; I'm really very proud of that. There are very few people who have survived through the arts for as long as that; the average life of a dancer in a company is somewhere around 2 years, 2¼ years, something like that. I was in the Company for 16 years before I quit, which was about . . . I've lost track, I think 3 years ago, maybe it's 4. Another sign of age; the years become less delineated, I guess. So since we have talked on this subject, I truly became a seasoned performer, and we toured everywhere, we've gone everywhere, it seems like everywhere. I don't know where else I would even particularly want to go anymore. It might be fun to see China; I've never seen China. But in general, I've seen the world. A few favorite places I'd like to go back to, but not that much. New York is home. I don't get to see it enough. I truly love the city.

What are you doing now that you're not in the Company? Well, basically I choreograph and dance and teach. I just came back

Friday from five weeks in Northern Europe where I had some good experiences. I've taught in Amsterdam now, this is my eighth year, various times of the year and various amounts. I was also there earlier this year and a group of my students who had taken from me faithfully time and again said to me, "George, we would love to feel like maybe we were advancing, going on, because whenever we take your classes you always have to teach them for everybody, which means you're always going over material that we've done so many times." They literally said to me: "How much would it cost for us to hire you for a week?" I said, "Well, I wouldn't do it for a week; I would do it for two weeks; it wouldn't be worth your money or my time." So I gave them a price, they huddled and said they'd guarantee it. So they hired me then for two weeks. That was kind of fun to have a group of people say, "We want you; we're willing to do what we have to do with our own money to bring you over here." They found a studio and hired it, and me. They're not the greatest students in the world, but they're good people and they learned. It was hard because I think this two weeks showed them how difficult it would be for them. I really taught them advanced classes and they came up to me and said they felt like they were back in the first year of dance again; and it was very hard for them.

I choreograph as much as I can. This year has been a bountiful year. I did a piece in December down at————, a college in North Carolina. They asked me to come back and put on their Spring show. I came back and saw what they thought was a show. I said it was "interesting." I'm not sure what words I really used, but inside I said, I can't believe showing this to people; you just can't do this. I said, "If my name's going to be on that program, there's going to be some big changes." So I took everybody's dance and cut it in half. There were ten dances. Then I proceeded to choreograph ten interludes. Just seeing a recital-like performance, those days are over; maybe still on college campuses some places you can do that. But when you have ten choreographers showing ten dances in an evening, the audience is just going [snoring sound effect]. So I created an evening out of it; I made the show never stop. The moment the curtain came down from a piece, I had one of my interludes already happening in front of the curtain, or out in the house, or in the balcony, running in from the exits, or something. It was fun because I literally got to choreograph ten little dances. That was great fun. They are good people. It's a tiny little campus and you know everybody when you stay there a while. I would stop people on the sidewalks and say, "Could you come to a rehearsal to do so and so?" So, half of the people I used were not dancers. That was great fun.

As soon as I came back from there, the next day, I went up to————, Connecticut, and did a piece up there. Came back and in July I did a piece for myself and showed it in Amsterdam. So I've done a lot. *That was a piece for yourself dancing?* Yeah, just for me; just a little, oh about a seven-minute solo. It was part of a workshop and the teachers got together and said, "So many things we'd like to explain in class we could explain if each one of us performed." So all of the teachers got together and did a small performance for the couple hundred students in the workshop. Which I enjoyed doing. I was nervous! The first time I'd performed in six months. I'd forgotten how nervous I could get. I was absolutely shaking; I was terrified. I'd forgotten how powerful that thing was. That's one of my great regrets about not being in the Company. I just don't get to perform enough. That's been hard. But the fact that a 43-year-old is still performing is great fun.

What's happened in the last 15 years? I've gotten 15 years older. The body's not as supple. I have to be careful and treat it nicely.

Um, bought this house; that's been something. At the right time. In two years the mortgage is paid. Isn't that incredible? *Oh my, a 20-year mortgage?* Fifteen-year mortgage; in two years that's it; it's all paid. So with the rental from the apartment we literally will live house free; because the rental will take care of the taxes and insurance. So that's amazing! A new tenant moves in this weekend. Let me see, what else.

I'm obviously still with Rick. Just a good close, loving relationship. I think we're each other's best friend. It's mellowed a lot in the last five, six years. I think we're a little more considerate of each other's feelings. Partly because at some point when we realized how incompatible we were sexually and we decided that we still really wanted to be together, we started to look for other ways, started to emphasize other ways of showing how we cared. I think that really made a difference. In this day of AIDS, sex is such a bad trip anyway.

Has AIDS affected you very much? In terms of losing people, I've lost some close people, so of course. There was a period about a year and a half ago when Rick and I lost three people within six weeks. By that third one you're punch-drunk with the effect: "Oh, ok, yeah. We just heard another one died." Am I personally affected, oh sure. It's certainly changed my sex life, because it's nonexistent, at least interactive sex life is nonexistent. I've become very good at fantasy and masturbation and that kind of thing. Still like to come at least once a day, sometimes twice. (laughs) *But now it's alone?* Yeah. Well, I've become very attached to [erotic tapes on] my VCR. (laughs) We're very good friends. And I'm looking real seriously at a Sony Watch-Video; it's a Watchman with an 8-millimeter VCR and a color TV. I can take that on tour! (laughs)

I'm still gone 50 percent of my life on the road. I don't know what it would be like not to, at this point. I've been doing this now for—I started touring in '69—that's 19 years I've been on the road. So I don't know what I would do if I didn't travel. This year I've been gone over half the year, so far; but I hope to be in the city now through Christmas, so then it will come out about 50 percent. But the arts being the way they are, that's what enables me to create as much as I have this year. The fact that I've done ten short dances, one medium-length dance, one full act dance and a major solo for myself in one year, that's a heck of a lot. Plus all the music for all of that. *You compose the music as well?* I do all the music for all of the pieces. I've gotten into the habit now. I'll show you my studio upstairs. It's all interacting with the computer now—what a world, what a world that is! The computer now plays my keyboards. It's very good! (laughs) It never hits a wrong note, and if it does, I correct it, and it never does it again. (laughs) It's amazing, just amazing; whole new world.

I think I have higher expectations for myself than I used to even. Quitting the Company was very important, a major step. *Why was that a major step?* Well, there I was, you know, in essence when you work for any employer for a long time, I was taken care of by somebody else for 16 years. Always had that job, always had that income. My motivation, I think, really diminished. And getting away from that, oh it's been really hard. I'm often depressed about where's my next job, when am I going to get to create again, when will I get to show something, when am I going to dance again? But when I look back on the last three or four years, it's really been amazing because the next job has always come. Oh, I've done a new thing. Last year I applied for a per-diem teacher certificate, which enables me now since I finally got it to teach at the High School for the Performing Arts. They use people a lot, she said. So . . . one of my problems is that when I'm in the city I don't make a dime — when I'm in New York I don't make any money at all, it's all out-go. So to be here for long periods of time, to work creatively, to do those kinds of things, I have no source of income. Like I just got back from Europe, so I have a nice amount of money in my bank account. But I have absolutely no prospects on the horizon of another job. So I have to watch that slowly disappear until the next job comes along. But now with this, and if they do use me and if it works successfully, this could be a nice little source of income to have when I'm in the city. So I'm very excited. And those students are fantastic down there, just amazing. Boy those kids are something else. What have I not covered?

Once before when we talked, you mentioned that Rick had a tough time with a drinking problem. What was the outcome of that? Uh, it happened at some point when I was on tour and we were talking on the phone and he said, "Oh, I stopped drinking." I said, "Oh, good." He'd said he'd stopped drinking, or diminished, a thousand times. But when I got home, sure enough he had this time. And he's not taken a drink since — seven years, eight years; he's not had a drink. *Has that made a big difference?* Actually, I didn't think; but you know, thinking, well I talked about our relationship changing; that could very well be connected because that's about when we really started becoming more affectionate towards each other. I never made that connection before. Hum, that's interesting. Less sexual and more affectionate. I'd never made that connection before. I think there is a connection there. *Was there a time when sex between the two of you became less important? When did that happen?* It was never very important. We've always had our own sexual friends outside the relationship. We do both provide something

the other one needs, greatly. Mostly intangible; I'm not even sure I could write it down on a piece of paper. We're both exceedingly tolerant of the other one. People talk about artists being difficult people and it's probably very true. I'm difficult. When I like something, I like it; when I don't, I don't. When I'm happy, I'm happy, when I'm sad, I'm really sad. And I don't hide my emotions; I don't pretend. I seldom do things to be nice. I do what I want to do the way I think it should be done. I don't think I purposely try to hurt, but I'm sure we all do a little of that too. And, speaking of sex, I've had some wonderful sexual friends, F———. That was a wonderful period, a wonderful time. He's moved, he's in California now.

Years ago when we first did an interview, you talked about someone named Bill, and there had been several of them — a kind of fantasy ideal. What's been the outcome of that? Oh, my Bills. All of them, huh. *Was F——— a kind of Bill?* No, F——— wasn't a Bill at all. Let's see, the last Bill, he even lived here with us for a while. Bill lived here for almost a year. That was hard on Rick. *He was really part of that pattern? He was heterosexual?* Basically heterosexual. Nothing before and as far as I know, nothing since. He called me about a year ago———out of the blue. "Hello, George." "Hello?" "Gee, I was thinking about you; how are you?" He had been to some of the funerals I'd been to, friends we'd lost, and I think it really concerned him, how my health was. *He was curious about you?* Yeah, he was really curious. We talked about getting together and everything, but I don't think it will ever happen. Oh, I loved him so much. Look, I love him. If he were to walk in this door right now and say, "Oh, George," I'd throw my arms around him and give him a big fat sloppy, disgusting kiss. I don't know of anyone I've ever fallen out of love with. Someone who I said in my heart that I love, I don't think

I've ever fallen out of love. I find it's really kind of a foreign concept. I don't understand people not loving someone after they've loved them. I really do not understand that. I don't have the opportunity to have an impossible ideal lover quite so much. You have to be careful as a teacher because teachers automatically have certain advantages and so forth that it's not fair to take.

I've become a very good teacher. I wish I loved it enough. You have to love teaching to be a good teacher. I love teaching. How do I say it. I just go crazy because I take my subject so seriously. And even after all these years I still cannot and will not put up with people who don't take it seriously. It matters, dance matters so much to me. When I'm teaching and people aren't responding like I know they're capable of, at whatever level they're capable of, I tell them to get the hell out; I'm not going to waste my time and effort. That's one of the nice things when you're always a guest teacher; you're always a special person; you have that power, that right. That's a reward and it's a responsibility too. I will not go into academia. I've watched too many artists who, because like me they worried about that next paycheck and when they were going to get any money again, and they went to academia and they stopped being artists. I've watched it. I could just name them, draw up lists of people like that. As much as I'd like a nice steady paycheck, I can't, I won't do that; I won't let myself do that because I value what I do.

How would you like things to work out? What are your dreams at this point? I would very much, if we're talking about some grand idea, I would love to be in a position somewhere as, oh, co-artistic director or something — be it a professional school, a dance company that I could get with two or three like-minded creative people, I wouldn't even mind if it was a theater company, and have two or three like-minded people who somehow could work to-

gether. I think it's possible. I'm still looking. I thought I was forming that with one person who succumbed to the need to make money. And I do not blame her one little bit. She got a fantastic offer and she'll have a very creative time. I find it hard to believe it would be as creative as what we were beginning to form will be. She's a beautiful performer, a wonderful creator, and I'm sorry. That was one person. Then I had another person I had worked with twice who I was beginning to have that feeling about, a musician, and that would have been a wonderful core of three people. But it's unlikely to find other people who have living circumstances as easy as I do now [and can take that kind of risk]. And these are easy. I live in a big house and don't have to worry about paying rent, as I told you, basically the tenant pays the rent. The teaching I do is enough for my clothes and my food and that kind of thing. *Rick makes a good salary?* Rick makes a very good salary. *So that helps?* Exactly. A year ago, for my birthday, he gave me a new synthesizer. It was something I wanted and needed for my work desperately, but not something I could have ever afforded to have bought for myself. He bought that. What a beautiful machine that is; it would take your breath away. So, yes, because of what he does for me, it makes my life much, much easier. Beside that, I always have a home; I always have some place to come home to. We were talking about F———. When we would be out on the road, for him it was so much better, because the idea of going home to what he called his "cave" — a little tiny studio apartment — dark; that was not home. That wasn't coming home; he hated that. I have a home to come home to and that's fantastic. I don't think I ever knew how important that was. I wouldn't have been able to guess how important that was.

Talking about home, how are your parents? Very good (laughs). I say that with a stop first because they are not so young anymore. They are 75–76; Dad is 76 this year, so Mom will be 76 in January. In the past Mom had some real serious heart problems. And they went in to do the quadruple bypass and it was all for nought. So she has less than 50 percent of her heart that actually beats in order to get blood through the system. But after an initial period of recovery—she also had a couple of small strokes included in that—after that about two-year recovery, she's doing very, very well. Just amazing. The doctors have started giving her some of the medications that have lots of long-term side effects, meaning that it doesn't matter because she's not going to live long enough for the long-term side effects to be very meaningful. But it has certainly made her life easier. Asthma, which has been a big problem for many years—now she takes a small amount of a drug to keep it under control. You don't do that to a 50-year-old person because eventually the drug will destroy their liver and kidneys; but for a 75-year-old person, it's not going to do it for at least 20 years anyway, so why not make their life pleasant. So asthma, which has been such a problem for so long, has just vanished now as a problem. And that, more than anything else, brought her health back. Because then she was able to do things again. So she's really doing very, very well. *Is she active?* Very active. Oh, she has to be careful. For example, getting up in the morning is tough. After having lain horizontal all night, if she sits right up she blacks out because there's no blood; the heart can't pump the blood fast enough for that kind of a change. So getting out of bed in the morning is a slow, careful process. But she's learned to handle it.

Your father's health is still good? Oh excellent. I mean, he has said to me, "Well, I feel like I'm getting older now." He's slowed down a little bit. Not much. *They're both retired?* Yeah, and they have enough income that they're comfortable. In many ways more than they ever had when they were working; their expenses are so much less. Since all of Mom's trouble that she's recovered from, she's had three great-grandchildren. If she hadn't pulled through, she'd never have seen her great-grandchildren! Now she's seen three of them. (laughs) They love little ones.

How is your relationship with them? Oh, it's as good as ever. I haven't been there in over a year. I've got to get back for Christmas. I've already warned Rick we don't get Christmas together this year. *He can't go, or won't go?* Rick, leave Manhattan? Even the thought of it starts to form withdrawal symptoms. (laughs) It's true. I'm serious. If I even start to talk about him going outside of New York, I see the panic start to set in. I've given up; I don't even ask. Well, that's not true. Just this morning I talked to him—maybe he didn't catch on—I talked to him about how cheap flights were to London.

Obviously, a lot's changed with regard to the gay community and the whole social awareness of gay issues, and the AIDS epidemic. Has any of this had any effect on you personally? We talked about some friends who died, but what about you personally? Well, I implied that it's changed my sexual life, which I discussed, it's changed that completely. Socially, I'm not as active [in gay social/political causes] as I was. Partly that has to do with time and energies. One of the things, you know, as you get older you have to direct your energies; you don't have the time to let them be as spread out as they once were. I don't do many social-active things at all. My art has to speak for me in that case. Rick, we can get this on the record, Rick was elected a District Representative as an openly gay person. He held that for three terms, until I said, "No more!" But I'm not as active as I was. *In terms of social or political causes?* Yeah. It's really hard to be involved in any kind of nonart activity, be it my church, which I still go to, be it political things, social things, because anything I try to get involved in is great, and then off I go on tour for two months. Then I come back and you have to kind of start all over again. That's one of the things that really holds it back. The touring completely destroys that kind of activity. The other thing is my priorities. Not that I don't believe in things, not that I haven't supported them. That includes some of the money I give. But I must concentrate what I do with my art. That has to be my first consideration.

Do you want to say anything about your concerns about your own health, or Rick's health? We're all the walking wounded. Every bruise you're sure is Kaposi's [a rare form of cancer associated with AIDS] and every pimple you're sure is something else. I'm in disgustingly good health. Since I quit the Company and lowered my tension about 46 percent, or more, I stopped having colds. I think I've had two colds in four years. I just don't get sick anymore. I'm in robust good health. But I do think about it; I do worry about it. Everyone I know does. *Have you had the antibody test?* I see no reason to. . . . Doing the test isn't going to change my activity—I'm not going to become more careful, because you can't become more careful than I am—then why should I take the chance of increasing my anxiety level. I see no reason. That's why I haven't done the test.

Do you have a clear sense of who you are these days? I like to think I do. I'd love to think I have an excellent sense of who I am. *Greater than before?* No. I knew what I thought I was then. Was I right, did I really know who I was? Oh dear. We're getting into levels of philosophy that are too deep. . . . I know who I am, I want to be better. I think I still have lots of time to do it. Forty-three seems, when you really think about it, when you're here, seems really young. And I like trying to still be young. I was talking to a friend of mine and we'd just seen the movie "Big"—delightful film. And I turned to her and I said, this movie is somehow about recapturing your innocence, that you really can become innocent again. And I really believe that. That's what I really want to keep as long as I can, my innocence. Not my naiveté, I never had much of that; I want to keep my innocence. People say, "How can you, George, who for many people your name is synonymous with being a very sexual world-weary kind of person, how can you talk about innocence?" I can because I think I still look at each day with a fresh eye. I can see that moon when we came back from running, that white moon and that incredible blue sky and I can still see it with a fresh eye. I was just swept away with how beautiful it was.

CHAPTER 3

Jacob Lawrence, *The Migration Gained Momentum* No. 18 in the series: *Migration of the Negro.* Museum of Modern Art, N.Y., gift of Mrs. David M. Levy.

Transitions in Adult Development

L ike the lobster or the soft-shelled crab, humans seem sometimes to outgrow their "shells" and become more vulnerable as they move from one phase of life into another. This process may be as ordinary as moving from childhood into adolescence and from adolescence into full adulthood, or it may be as traumatic as a divorce or coping with a serious illness. Marriage, becoming a parent, changing jobs, moving to a new city, restructuring one's life-style, reordering one's goals in life, or one's children leaving home may each involve a transition of this kind. Some of these transitions may be positive changes, but others may involve negative changes. Some may be joyous, and others are painful. Some may happen as naturally as graduating from high school, and others may tax one's ability to adapt to major unexpected changes.

This chapter focuses first on the nature of transitions in adult development and then discusses the research on transitions during early and middle adulthood. It provides an overview of the first third of adult development; the remaining two-thirds—from midlife to retirement, and the retirement years—are discussed in detail in later chapters.

Transitions in the Life Cycle

The concept of **transition** refers to a period of change, growth, and disequilibrium that serves as a kind of bridge between one relatively stable point in life and another relatively stable but different point. The study of adult development involves an analysis of these transitions from one pattern of life that no longer "fits" into a new pattern that is different. The difference between the two patterns may be major or relatively minor. The transition may involve some personal turning point or crisis. It does not necessarily involve emotional upset or distress, however.

Thus, the study of transitions focuses on the process of change in adult development. Of course, as discussed in the last chapter, there is always stability along with change; but the study of transitions calls our attention to the patterns of change during adulthood.

There are several different types of transitions in human development that we discuss in this section. It may be noted that a particular transition may fit into more than one of the following categories. The first two are similar, respectively, to *normative age-graded* and *nonnormative* influences on development described by Baltes (see Chapter 1).

1. *Normative* transitions are those that are expected to occur, usually at a particular age, as prescribed by the social traditions of the culture.

2. *Idiosyncratic* transitions, in contrast, occur only to a few individuals, or occur in socially unpredictable ways. Examples include: inheriting a large sum of money, discovering one has cancer, getting divorced, saving a life and becoming a hero, "coming out" as a gay man or lesbian, or experiencing the death of one's child.

3. Some transitions are caused primarily by *internal* causes, such as menopause, romantic love, chronic disease, or mental or emotional disorder.

4. Some transitions are caused primarily by *external* forces, such as retirement, winning a lottery, or experiencing a war.

5. If a transition is normative, then it can occur either *on time* or *off time,* according to the social clock or age norms.

Normative and Idiosyncratic Transitions

Normative transitions are changes that are expected according to the social norms for individuals at particular times of their lives (Lowenthal, Thurnher, Chiriboga & Associates 1975). They include such events as graduation from high school, marriage, grandparenthood, and retirement. Most people in our society expect these events to occur and, as described in Chapter 2, have clear expectations about the age at which they should occur based on their internalized sense of the *social clock.*

Idiosyncratic transitions, in contrast to normative transitions, are those changes in life patterns that are unique to a particular individual. They are not determined by age norms because there are no social expectations about when these unscheduled events should occur. Moreover, it is not expected that most people will experience any of these nonnormative changes. For example, going through a divorce, although not an unusual event today, is not a *normative* or expected or scheduled event. There is no "right time" on the social clock to get divorced. Likewise, experiencing the death of one's child, a major illness, economic setback, or winning a lottery may bring a major transition to those individuals who are affected, but these events may occur at *any* age. In addition, they are not expected to happen in the lives of nearly everyone, as is the case for normative transitions.

Since normative transitions are usually expected events that are anticipated and even planned in detail, they may have less emotional impact on people than the unanticipated idiosyncratic transition. Fiske (1978) studied normative transitions —such as the last child leaving the parents' home or retirement—and found that these transitions are so clearly anticipated by the respondent that they appear to have relatively little impact. In contrast, Chiriboga (1982a) studied divorce as an idiosyncratic transition and found that it brings a major period of upset and reorganization to individuals during the period between the time the divorce papers are filed and the time the divorce becomes final.

Of course, some major transitions—such as remarriage after divorce or widowhood—lie between the two extremes, that is, are neither wholly idiosyncratic nor fully normative. We would expect these transitions to be less unsettling than idiosyncratic transitions, but somewhat less aided by social support than normative transitions.

In general, the study of normative and idiosyncratic transitions—many of which may be described by the individual as *milestones*—provides a useful approach to discovering the patterns of stability and change in a person's life. On one hand, idiosyncratic transitions are likely to have an effect on a unique individual's life; a dramatic event could have a major impact. On the other hand, normative transitions are especially useful for revealing the general pattern of development for groups of individuals.

These idiosyncratic, normative, and mixed types of events are often related to *stress* that is experienced by the individual. For example, research that studies the effect of stress on physical and psychological well-being frequently uses some measure of this kind of normative and idiosyncratic events. We discuss the interrelated issues of stress, health, and psychological functioning in Chapter 8.

Normative transitions serve as one of the principal themes that regulate adult development, as described in Chapter 2, since they are part of the social timetable in the culture and are internalized by individuals through the social clock (Neugarten, 1968; Neugarten & Hagestad, 1976).

> [T]he normal, expectable life events do not themselves constitute crises, nor are they trauma producing. The end of formal schooling, leaving the parents' home, marriage, parenthood, occupational achievement, one's own children growing up and leaving, menopause, grandparenthood, retirement — in our society, these are the normal turning points, the markers or the punctuation marks along the life cycle. They call forth changes in self-concept and in sense of identity, they mark the incorporation of new social roles, and accordingly they are the precipitants of new adaptations. But in themselves they are not, for the vast group of normal persons, traumatic events or crises that trigger mental illness or destroy the continuity of the self. (Neugarten, 1976, p. 18)

These major life events are not the only ones that serve as normative transitions, however. Neugarten found that middle-aged people pay greater attention to their development within their various involvements and concerns — especially in the areas of health, family, and career — than they do to chronological age for "clocking" themselves. For example, respondents often would stop and think before they could state their exact age: "Let's see . . . 51? No, 52. Yes, 52 is right" (Neugarten, 1976, p. 18). In contrast, subtle transitions such as changes in physical health, promotions and other signs of progression in the career, and minor family events, for example, a daughter's first date combine to provide a constant series of cues where one is along the socially defined timetable of normative transitions.

In addition, Neugarten's studies found that respondents also tended to estimate how much time they had left, as least covertly, as they examined their position in the various life contexts: "Now I keep thinking, will I have time enough to finish off some of the things I want to do?" (Neugarten, 1976, p. 18). Implicit in this shift in time perspective to the amount of *time left* is a growing acknowledgment that death is, at least, a real possibility for oneself — if not yet accepted as a personal certainty from which one cannot escape. She also found that a "rehearsal for widowhood" begins among women in middle age and that men tend to emphasize "sponsoring" relationships with their children and younger associates during this midlife period, with an eye toward "the creation of social heirs."

This paper by Bernice Neugarten (1976), first published in 1970, summarized many of the themes found also by more recent studies of adult transitions. Later in this chapter we discuss this research on the stages of adult development. There we will see how precisely these age-related normative transitions seem to regulate development. Not only do people who share a common social environment tend to share similar patterns of transitions and development during adulthood, but also they tend to enter and leave those transitional periods at about the same chronological age.

Internal and External Causes of Transitions

Either normative or idiosyncratic transitions may also be described along a second dimension of whether the changes are brought about by internal changes or by external events. *Internal changes* that may produce a transition involve individual feelings, physical reactions, personal experiences, or other changes in the self reflecting *endogenous* pressures within oneself. These might include puberty, menopause, or a growing dissatisfaction with one's career or life-style. *External events* that can produce transitions reflect social or environmental forces; they may be called *exogenous* causes of transitions. These could include the birth of grandchildren, winning a lottery or a promotion at work.

Most transitions are a mixture of these two types, of course, but theories about transitions tend to emphasize either one or the other. For example, the theories of Erikson, Jung, and Levinson described in Chapter 1 focus on changes in adult development that result primarily from internal factors. Thus, the shift from the issue of Identity versus Identity Confusion to the issue of Intimacy versus Isolation in the Erikson scheme is essentially an *internally motivated* change. In contrast, Neugarten's concept of the social clock as a major factor timing adult development emphasizes *external social norms* as the primary cause of transitions. However, even social norms are internalized; and Erikson's eight ages of life require social interaction. Nonetheless, the distinction is based on the relative importance given to some kind of inner scheme of development in contrast to the significance of external factors for determining an individual's developmental progression.

The internally determined pattern of adult development may be represented by Levinson's (1978) study of development in early and middle adulthood, which we discuss in detail later in this chapter. He portrayed adult development as consisting of stable periods lasting six to eight years alternating with transitional periods lasting four or five years. During the transitional period, individuals reappraise the life structure they had built up during the preceding stable period and prepare for the next stable period. Although the transition may be set off by an external event, Levinson emphasized internal factors in completing the transition:

> [It does not end] when a particular event occurs or when a sequence is completed in one aspect of life. It ends when the tasks of questioning and exploring have lost their urgency, when a man makes his crucial commitments and is ready to start on the tasks of building, living within and enhancing a new life structure. (Levinson, 1978, p. 52)

Similarly, in his model transitions may both begin and end because of internal factors: "A period begins when its major tasks become predominant in a man's life. A period ends when its tasks lose their primacy and new tasks emerge to initiate a new period" (Levinson, 1978, p. 53). In his concluding chapter, he speculated about the universal nature of this developmental progression:

> This sequence of eras and periods exists in all societies, throughout the human species, at the present stage in human evolution. The eras and periods are grounded in the nature of man as a biological, psychological and social organism, and in the nature of society as a complex enterprise extending over many generations. They represent the life cycle of the species. Individuals go through the periods in infinitely varied ways, but the periods themselves are universal. These eras and periods have governed human development for

the past five or ten thousand years—since the beginning of more complex, stable societies. (Levinson, 1978, p. 322)

Thus, his assumptions about the nature of development clearly emphasized internal factors and parallel in many ways the perspective of development proposed by Erikson (cf. Levinson, 1978, p. 323).

In contrast, Neugarten's views of adult development emphasized the individual's internalization of social norms and the adaptation to external social processes (Neugarten & Hagestad, 1976; Neugarten & Neugarten, 1986, 1987). Although she did not view the individual as a passive responder to external events, she did not see any inner developmental scheme that has regulated human development for thousands of years. The perspective she described is an interactive one, similar to our discussion in Chapter 2, in which the interaction between the individual and social processes regulates development.

> Because individuals live in contact with persons of all ages, they learn what to anticipate. There is a never-ending process of socialization by which the child learns what facets of his childhood behavior he must shed as he moves into adolescence; the adolescent learns what is expected of him as he moves from school to job to marriage to parenthood; and the middle-aged learn approved ways of growing old. Thus the social ordering of age-statuses and age-appropriate behavior will continue to provide a large measure of predictability.
>
> There are certain other regularities of the life cycle which may be said to arise more from within the individual than from without. To draw a dichotomy between "inner" and "outer" is, of course, merely a heuristic device, given a transactional view of personality. As the result of accumulative adaptations to both biological and social events, there is a continuously changing basis within the individual for perceiving and responding to new events in the outer world. It is in this sense that orderly and predictable changes occur within the personality as well as in the social environment. (Neugarten, 1976, p. 17)

Both approaches are very attractive. The emphasis on internal factors is fascinating because it implies that there is a regular pattern of human development that may be found for the adult years as has been discovered for the childhood years. Before we can accept the evidence for this view, however, it needs to be examined among both men and women in widely differing cultures and historical periods. This evidence is beginning to accumulate. Levinson's (1978) original data are based on only one cohort of middle-aged men in the United States. Roberts and Newton (1987) reported data from four samples of American women that also show clear evidence of these developmental periods. And Levinson's (1986) more recent summary of his theory cites preliminary cross-cultural evidence for the universality of alternating periods of stability and transition, with one transition around age 30 and another in midlife, around age 40–45.

Neugarten's interactive view is also very compelling. Not only does it emphasize the obvious role of social norms and expectations for creating stability and transition, but also it does allow the possibility that there are some inner factors involved in development interacting with the social influences. It also stresses the individual in interaction with the social environment—a perspective that is central to my own thinking.

On balance, I tend to view the transitions of early and middle adulthood as normative transitions that are caused primarily by external social influences. Later in this chapter, I will argue that the very fact that they occur in the age-stage sequence that Levinson and others found is validation of the subtle and important influence of age norms and the social clock for persons from a similar social environment. Only evidence from cultures with a different social clock than ours will convince me of some inner clock for development in adulthood. Moreover, we recall from Chapter 1 that individuals not only change but also remain fairly stable in basic aspects of their personality during the adult years. Thus, change must be seen against the background of general continuity of the person over time (Costa & McCrae, 1980b).

Transitions and Crises

At the beginning of this chapter we noted that transitions need not involve emotional upset or distress. Erikson, in his theory of the eight ages of life, described each stage as a "crisis" in the sense of a turning point, or critical period; it may or may not involve emotional distress. Levinson's study and reports of adult development by popular writers, however, have emphasized the extent of emotional "crisis" involved in the various transitions. Thus, it is useful to examine this issue.

On one hand, Neugarten's (1976) report on her studies indicated that *normative transitions* that are expected to occur do not bring emotional crises for most people. If a normative event — such as the birth of a grandchild — does *not* occur, however, this **nonevent** may be a cause of stress to the expectant grandparents who are eager for this transition to occur in their lives. Other sources of stress include the minor hassles of daily life and **off-time transitions** (Chiriboga, 1987).

In Neugarten's view it is the unexpected change that is more likely to cause a crisis. On the basis of on her concept of the social clock, she noted also that those events that occur *off-time* — either too early or too late according to social norms — are those that are likely to bring a crisis. Events or transitions that occur *on-time* according to the social age norms are much less likely to involve emotional upset.

> In summary, then, there are two distinctions worth making: first, that it is the unanticipated life event, not the anticipated — divorce, not widowhood in old age; death of a child, not death of a parent — which is likely to represent the traumatic event. Moreover, major stresses are caused by events that upset the sequence and rhythm of the life cycle — as when death of a parent comes in childhood rather than in middle age; when marriage does not come at its desired or appropriate time; when the birth of a child is too early or too late; when occupational achievement is delayed; when the empty nest, grandparenthood, retirement, major illness, or widowhood occur *off-time*. In this sense, then, a psychology of the life cycle is not a psychology of crisis behavior so much as it is a psychology of timing. (Neugarten, 1976, p. 20)

On the other hand, Levinson noted that 62 percent of his respondents experienced a "moderate or severe crisis" during the period he called the "Age 30 Transition," whereas only 18 percent had a smooth transition during that period (Levinson, 1978, p. 87). Similarly, about 80 percent of his respondents experienced "tumultuous struggles within the self and with the external world" during the period he called the "Mid-life Transition" (Levinson, 1978, p. 199). Sheehy

(1976) also called attention to the crises in her book on adult development, *Passages*.

In contrast, however, Roberts and Newton (1987) did not find specific periods of crisis in their review of studies of Levinson's perspective with women. Except for those few who entered early adulthood with a specific occupational goal, "women's lives may be characterized as conflicted and unstable throughout much of early adulthood and into middle age. This appears to differ from Levinson's sequence of alternating stable and transitional periods" (p. 162).

These perspectives are clearly in conflict with each other. Is emotional turmoil a standard aspect of adult transitions (Levinson)? Or is a fairly continual process of inner conflict and turmoil more typical except for those with clear occupational goals (Roberts & Newton)? Or is developmental crisis primarily a matter of being off-time or experiencing an unanticipated event (Neugarten)?

The clearest conclusion we can suggest is that the perspective emphasizing *internal* causes of transitions—Levinson's model—tends to link transitions and emotional crises. Perhaps these crises are, as Neugarten's perspective suggested, *triggered* by external events that are off-time or idiosyncratic, but which, in turn, were set in motion by internal forces. For example, divorce—an idiosyncratic event that causes emotional crisis—might be more likely to occur during a period of transition in Levinson's scheme.

An extended period of conflict and instability that Roberts and Newton (1987) reported for women could, likewise, reflect a sense of being off-time or involved in idiosyncratic transitions—a position not unlikely for women between the ages of 20 and 50 in the 1970s and 1980s when there were few clear norms for timing and integrating women's career and family commitments.

Emotional crises in adult development may also reflect personality and cultural influences. Moreover, stress usually provokes a coping strategy to minimize the emotional distress; the effectiveness of this strategy depends on the individual's personality and culture. For example, as we discuss in Chapter 6, retirement—often thought to be a major crisis in life—does not bring emotional upset and inner turmoil for the vast majority of persons. Similarly, research by Fiske and her colleagues focused on blue-collar men and women who were interviewed when they were about to undergo a normative transition—high school seniors, newlyweds, middle-aged parents whose children were nearing the age to leave home, and preretirees. They were interviewed again five years later when most had completed the transition. The data indicated that they had not experienced emotional crisis as a result of these events. In many cases, the transitions were not even discussed until the interviewer asked about them. Instead, changes that were unexpected and those that were idiosyncratic were more likely to bring an emotional crisis (Fiske, 1978; cf. Lowenthal *et al.*, 1975).

It is still not possible to draw any firm conclusions about the link between transitions and crises until more research has been completed on the nature and causes of emotional crises during the life span, and we should be cautious. For example, early research on adolescence viewed this time as a period of "storm and stress"; many believed this to be universal until Margaret Mead (1928) reported on the smooth transition from childhood to adulthood among the Samoans in the South

Sea Islands. More recent research has found that only a minority of adolescents in the United States actually experience a period of crisis, and when it occurs it reflects the adolescent's personality rather than a period of crisis that is inherent in the human life cycle (Offer & Offer, 1975; Offer, Ostrov & Howard, 1981). Similarly, preliminary studies of persons in their fifties and sixties (Karp, 1988) and seventies and eighties (Shneidman, 1989) suggest developmental patterns that represent stability more than dramatic change.

In the next section we take a close look at research on transitions during early and middle adulthood. In the concluding section of this chapter, we return to this question of the balance between stability and crisis during periods of transition.

Developmental Periods of Early Adulthood

Until a few years ago, development from young adulthood to middle age had been an uncharted area of the life span. Although considerable research had been reported on development in childhood, adolescence, and old age, the period from early adulthood to middle age had been essentially neglected by social science researchers. This was a little curious, since most researchers were, themselves, in that period of the life cycle. Then beginning in the 1970s several studies of this newly discovered period appeared. Some of the books reporting this information became very popular since many people are curious about the two major questions this research addressed: What lies ahead for me in my development? and Is what's happening to me normal? Although no research can answer the first question precisely for any individual, of course, these studies have provided a great deal of new understanding about the transitions, issues, and challenges that many men and women seem to be living through, at least during this period of history in the United States. It should be emphasized that these studies are on firm ground when they *describe* what was happening with their respondents during middle adulthood. They should not be taken as *prescribing* ideal adult development, however. Although one study (by Gould) does state a list of issues that need to be resolved at each successive period of life, even these may best be seen as descriptive rather than prescriptive statements; the study presents no data on whether persons who conform to the descriptions age more successfully than those who do not follow the guidelines.

One of the studies was *longitudinal:* George Vaillant (1977) reported on the developmental progression of a group of 94 male graduates from an elite eastern university in the United States. Each man began the study during college (in 1942–1944) and was studied periodically over the years; the average age of the men was 47 at the latest round of interviews before the study was published.

Three other studies were *cross-sectional.* Roger Gould (1972, 1978) based his reports on three samples: 524 men and women between the ages of 16 and 50 who were not in psychotherapy; approximately 125 psychiatric patients in therapy with residents under his supervision; and 14 groups of psychiatric outpatients that were organized by age. Daniel Levinson (1978), whose study we outlined briefly in Chapter 1 and discussed earlier in this chapter, studied four groups of men who were between the ages of 35 and 45 in 1969 — hourly workers in industry, business executives, novelists, and biologists working in universities. Four other smaller studies by Adams (1983), Droege (1982), Furst (1983), and Stewart (1977) followed Levinson's approach and focused on women (Roberts & Newton, 1987). The sampling and methodological details of these four studies are shown in Box 3.1.

BOX 3.1 *Samples and Research Methods Used in Studies of Adult Development during Early and Middle Adulthood*

GOULD (1972), STUDY 1

Sample: Fourteen outpatient therapy groups, organized by age (16–18, 18–22, 22–28, 29–34, 35–43, 43–50, and 50–60+).

Design: Cross-sectional by age group. Groups observed for several months.

Method: Observation of groups and rating by observers of the characteristics for each age group.

Comments: Age groups, not individual respondents, were studied. Initial age groupings may have determined age differences in concerns expressed by group members. All felt a need for therapy.

GOULD (1972), STUDY 2

Sample: Five hundred twenty-four White, middle-class persons not in psychotherapy. Selected through friendship networks of eight medical students and hospital staff. About half were men and half women. Age range: 16–60.

Design: Cross-sectional by age. Questionnaire administered only once.

Method: Questionnaire based on characteristic statements from the previous "phase of life" groups. It consisted of 160 questions on 10 different areas of life.

Comments: Average scores on each questionnaire statement were used to graph characteristics that were then visually examined to determine "unstable periods." No statistical tests were reported. Age periods identified correspond closely to the original predetermined groups in Study 1.

GOULD (1978)

Comments: Same data used as in the 1972 studies; no information given in this report about sample, design, or methods. The age periods differed somewhat from the 1972 report, however.

LEVINSON (1978)[a]

Sample: Forty men between 35 and 45 years old in 1968–1970; all were from the northeastern United States. Respondents were recruited in each of four groups: 10 hourly workers from two companies (3 were Black); 10 executives from two companies; 10 Ph.D. biologists from two universities; 10 novelists who had published at least two books (2 were Black). Fifty percent Protestant; 70 per-

[a]Also reported in *Counseling Psychologist*, 1976, 6(1),21–25.

BOX 3.1 *(Continued)*

cent completed college; all had married at least once; 80 percent had children; 20 percent were divorced; 42 percent were from "stable working-class or lower-middle-class families"; 32 percent were from "comfortable middle-class Ninety-four male graduates attending one or more of the elite northeastern U.S. colleges between 1942 and 1944. They were part of the original sample of 268

Design: carefully selected college sophomores in the Grant Study begun in 1938; random selection from the 1942–1944 graduates led to 102 respondents, but 2

Method: had dropped out of the study and 6 had died. Initial selection involved likelihood of graduating, sound physical and psychological health, and motivation to continue in the study. Forty-one percent were the oldest child in their families; nearly all served in World War II, often with distinction. At the time of the study (about 1969, average age was 47; average income was $30,000; 71 percent viewed themselves as "liberal"; 95 percent had been married and 15 percent were divorced; 25 percent were lawyers and doctors. Most were "extremely satisfied" with their occupation; their health and mental health was much better than average, although 40 percent had seen psychiatrists (pp. 36–37).

Comments: All male sample. No empirical data or statistical tests reported. Rich biographical information was used to make interpretations that, in the absence of supporting empirical data, are difficult to evaluate.

VAILLANT (1978)

Sample: Ninety-four male graduates attending one or more of the elite northeastern U.S. colleges between 1942 and 1944. They were part of the original sample of 268 carefully selected college sophomores in the Grant Study begun in 1938; random selection from the 1942–1944 graduates led to 102 respondents, but 2 had dropped out of the study and 6 had died. Initial selection involved likelihood of graduating, sound physical and psychological health, and motivation to continue in the study. Forty-one percent were the oldest child in their families; nearly all served in World War II, often with distinction. At the time of the study (about 1969, average age was 47; average income was $30,000; 71 percent viewed themselves as "liberal"; 95 percent had been married and 15 percent were divorced; 25 percent were lawyers and doctors. Most were "extremely satisfied" with their occupation; their health and mental health was much better than average, although 40 percent had seen psychiatrists (pp. 36–37).

Design: Longitudinal. Multiple methods were used, including physical, physiological, and psychological assessments, repeated questionnaires, and periodic interviews by different interviewers. Data were also gathered from the parents.

Method: A "social history" of the respondent's childhood was collected during college from the parents in their home; extensive physical, physiological, and psychological examinations were conducted during the college years. After graduation, each was sent a questionnaire every year until 1955, and every two years after

(continued)

BOX 3.1 (*Continued*)

that. All respondents were interviewed in their homes by a social anthropologist during 1950–1952. In 1969 Vaillant interviewed each of his 94 respondents, usually in their home, and reviewed all previous data. The interview questionnaire was identical for each man (Appendix B); it took a minimum of 2 hours and often much more time was spent, sometimes including an informal meal and conversation. Raters developed empirical data from selected study records, while kept "blind" to other ratings for Adult Adjustment, Childhood Environment, Objective Physical Health, Marital Happiness, Maturity of Psychological Defenses, and Overall Outcome of the Respondent's Children (over age 15).

Comments: Only men from elite educational backgrounds were studied. The focus was on mechanisms of adaptation, especially psychological defenses, and on the patterns of development. Especially rich data because of the longitudinal nature of the study. Report is unusually interesting because it contains Vaillant's personal reactions as well as the respondent's critiques of the study.

ADAMS (1983)

Sample: Eight Black women attorneys between the ages of 28 and 33.
Method: Intensive biographical interviews.

DROEGE (1982)

Sample: Twelve women between the ages of 44 and 53.
Method: Constant comparative method of qualitative analysis in which new samples of respondents are selected to explore themes and patterns presented by initial subsample.

FURST (1983)

Sample: Eight women between the ages of 34 and 44.
Method: Intensive biographical interviews.

STEWART (1977)

Sample: Eleven women between the ages of 31 and 39.
Method: Constant comparative method of qualitative analysis.

Levinson (1978) identified the period from about age 17 to 40 as Early Adulthood; in his scheme, this included "Early Adult Transition," "Entering the Adult World," "Age 30 Transition," and "Settling Down" (Figure 3.1). For Gould (1978), a similar period ranged from age 16 to 34; it included "Leaving Our Parents' World" (age 16–22), "I'm Nobody's Baby Now" (age 22–28), and "Opening Up to What's Inside" (age 28–34). Vaillant described the entire period between adolescence and age 40 as one of "Intimacy and Career Consolidation."

Levinson's study included a range of occupational groups, some respondents

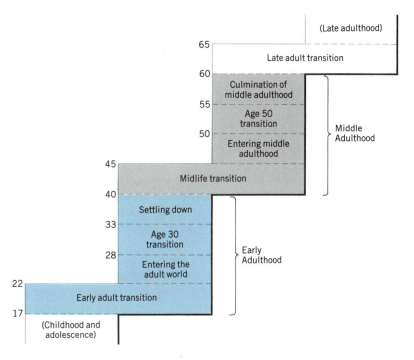

FIGURE 3.1 Developmental periods in early and middle adulthood from the study by Levinson (*Source*: Levinson (1978), p. 57. Copyright © 1978 by Daniel J. Levinson. Reprinted with permission of Alfred A. Knopf.)

who were not college graduates (30 percent of his sample), some African-American men (12 percent), and is the basis for similar studies of women. Therefore, we use his scheme to organize this discussion and integrate the other studies into his framework. We should keep in mind that these studies dealt with very limited samples of men and women so caution should be used in attempting to apply these data to people in general.

Early Adult Transition

The task of the *Early Adult Transition* (age 17–22) in Levinson's scheme is "leaving the pre-adult world," which includes separating from one's parents and becoming more independent, financially and psychologically. He noted that only 18 percent of his respondents maintained close personal relationships with parents or lived geographically near their parents during their twenties. In addition, 20 percent experienced a serious conflict with their parents that often went on for several years. The majority, however, moved away from parents — either geographically or socially — without a major conflict, or to avoid one.

Other preadult aspects of the self are also given up during this period, including important relationships with adolescent groups, teachers, and a range of significant others. Other relationships are modified because the young person is becoming a social adult and the person's self-perceptions are also changing. All these changes may bring a sense of loss and some feelings of fear or insecurity about the future.

Sixty-five percent of his respondents were in military service during this period. Seventy percent completed college. Thus, much of the early adult transition was spent in these settings. During this period, nearly all the men established a life pattern that was very different from their parents. Some moved to a higher social status, and others moved into artistic or academic fields that differed from the business world of their parents. Fifty percent of the men married during this period.

For many of the men, this is the period in which "The Dream" is formed, according to Levinson. **The dream** is the inner sense one has of how one wants life to work out; it is used in the sense of Martin Luther King's famous speech, "I have a dream. . . ." The dream begins as an undefined sense of what one wants to accomplish or move toward. It may include a fantasy such as winning a Nobel Prize or making a million dollars, or it may be simply to pursue a particular career or interest. One-half of the biologists and 7 of the 10 novelists in his sample entered their field as a realization of their dream. Few of the executives and only one of the hourly wage workers had an occupation-related dream or were able to realize it, however. For example, several of the executives had a dream that involved family and community life rather than their occupation; thus they continued living near where they grew up or restricted advancement at work in favor of a stable family life. The hourly workers generally did not form a dream in Levinson's sense, although some had a general vision of what a good life would be.

In contrast, the studies of women using Levinson's perspective found that only a few described a dream in which occupational accomplishment played a major role

The Reverend Martin Luther King Jr. delivered his famous "I have a dream" speech during the march on Washington for Civil Rights in 1968.

(Roberts & Newton, 1987). In a sense, the women resembled the hourly workers in Levinson's study in the absence of an occupation-related dream and the importance of family and community life (Droege, 1982).

Gould (1978), in his analysis, focused on the *false assumptions* that need to be challenged during each phase of development. Note again that these statements are best seen as descriptions of developmental issues, not as prescriptions for successful adulthood since we do not know whether the successful resolution of these issues leads to superior development in later adulthood.

During this young adult phase, the major assumption he felt needed to be challenged was "I'll always belong to my parents and believe in their world." Other misconceptions that he thought needed to be discarded follow from this one: (1) "If I get any more independent, it will be a disaster"; (2) "I can see the world only through my parents' assumptions"; (3) "Only my parents can guarantee my safety"; (4) "My parents must be my only family"; and (5) "I don't own my own body." Gould viewed marriage during this period as an expression of the need for a partner to help the person break away from the parents and gain greater independence; however, he felt that such marriages were likely to fail since they provided greater dependence, not greater independence.

In the longitudinal study by Vaillant (1977), one of the most interesting findings about this period of development was that the research staff could not predict later psychological adjustment from personality traits observed while the men were still in college. That is, the characteristics the staff thought would predict midlife success — such as friendliness and humanism — were later found to be, in fact, unrelated to successful adaptation in middle age. In addition, traits that were thought to predict later emotional problems — shyness, introspection, inhibition, lack of purpose and values — also did not predict male midlife adjustment; instead, they appeared to have been one manifestation of the stress of adolescence for those men. However, looking back from the vantage point of the men at middle age, Vaillant did find that adolescents who had been seen as "well-integrated" and "practical and organized" in college were found to be the "Best Outcomes" in midlife; conversely, those men who were seen as "asocial" in young adulthood were the least likely of the group to be the "Best Outcomes" in middle age.[1]

Entering the Adult World

This period in Levinson's scheme lasts from about age 22 to 28. It is a relatively tranquil period — a pattern he found repeated each decade: a time of transition followed by a more stable period. During this time, a man tests the life structure he has formed during the early adult transition. It is a period of exploration, of making tentative commitments that, the man believes, can always be changed. It is a time of

[1]"Best Outcomes" were 30 men who in middle age were rated highly in career adjustment, social adjustment, psychological adjustment, and self-reported physical health by raters who did not have access to other ratings made on the respondents by Vaillant, staff physicians, or the social workers who interviewed the parents about the respondent's childhood history. Another 30 men were rated very low in adjustment in these areas; they were termed the "Worst Outcomes." Thirty-four men were in between these two extremes (Vaillant, 1977, pp. 261–262, Appendix C).

adventure and wonder. However, there is also a need to make choices, to "grow up" in terms of establishing an occupation or marriage, and to define goals. By this time three-quarters of Levinson's sample had married, and usually the man had made an initial, but serious occupational choice.

The tension between the two contradictory demands—to explore and to commit—was the essence of this period, in his view. Some men, especially the novelists, had made a commitment to their occupation, but had difficult intense relationships with women. Half of the hourly workers felt this time was a "rock bottom" period for them and doubted they would be able to afford marriage. Other men committed themselves to a spouse, but did not settle on an occupation. Still others did make firm commitments in both areas, but wondered if perhaps they had committed themselves prematurely.

In studies of women, the process of establishing an occupation and marriage often extended well beyond this early adult period (Roberts & Newton, 1987). Women who had clear career goals often required more time to enter the occupation because of marriage, children, and other interruptions in their training for the career (Droege, 1982). Those women who followed the traditional pattern focused on marriage and motherhood during this period and occupational issues were not encountered until they were in their thirties (Furst, 1983; Stewart, 1977). However, some women with specific career goals (a sample of successful African-American lawyers) did follow a path that coincided with the one described by Levinson for men during this period (Adams, 1983).

Levinson noted that two unique relationships seemed especially important during this phase: the "mentor" and the "special woman." The **mentor** is a person who is more experienced, typically older, and who functions as a kind of sponsor or guide to lead the person into the field he or she is entering. One of the most important functions of the mentor is to support the person's efforts to realize the dream. Initially, the mentor is superior to the younger person, but gradually they become more equal and the relationship may be relatively intense. Sometimes the younger person surpasses the mentor or threatens the image of superiority; at other times the young person may feel inept or inadequate; frequently the relationship becomes stormy. Eventually the younger person will give up the mentor—as one must separate from one's parents—and perhaps will become a mentor, in turn, to another young person. In Levinson's sample, the mentor is often a boss, editor, senior colleague, or teacher; sometimes a neighbor or a friend. One example of a stormy mentor relationship was given by a novelist:

> Randall gave me tremendous support and encouragement. I was very close to this man—enormously, deeply committed to him in fact. He had a wonderful quality, but I later realized that this quality was good only if you were very young, and once you became a man yourself it almost became a matter of competition. I had to break, and it was too bad because there was a lack of insight on his part, I think. (Levinson, 1978, p. 148)

Levinson suggested that women have more difficulty finding mentors than men do because there are fewer women available for this function; also cross-gender men-

A mentor — someone more experienced, typically older — acts as a guide or sponsor to the person during the phase of Entering the Adult World, according to Levinson.

toring may interject sexual issues that complicate the relationship; moreover, older men may not take younger women's aspirations seriously. The studies of women reviewed by Roberts and Newton (1987) supported these ideas for the 39 respondents:

> It is remarkable that although nearly every woman had a dream, only 4, or perhaps fewer, were able to find a mentor for it. In Levinson's theory, this portends that the highest levels of career or occupational achievement will not be available to them; the chances of these women achieving the level of success that was required of [the biologists, executives, and novelists] . . . for inclusion in Levinson's study, presumably, are small. (p. 158)

The second unique relationship Levinson stressed during this period is the **special woman.** She not only brings out the man's affectionate, romantic, and sexual feelings, but also facilitates his dream in a manner parallel to the mentor. In part, she encourages the development of the man's sense of self by believing in him. She is a critic, guide, and sponsor as he works toward his goal. She helps to shape his dream, shares it with him, and nourishes his aspirations and hopes. As in the mentor relationship, the special woman is a transitional figure helping the man to grow from dependency on his father and mother toward autonomous independence. Thus, if the special woman is the man's wife, their relationship will continue most strongly if each spouse has been able to nourish and support each other's dream.

Otherwise, one partner is likely to feel cheated when only the spouse's dream was nurtured and when the spouse no longer needs this type of support and encouragement. In the Age 30 Transition, or the Midlife Transition, marriages that did not mutually nourish the dreams of the partners may be strained or may break up.

Roberts and Newton (1987) reported that all the women in the studies they reviewed expressed concern about finding a *special man*. By age 30, social and biological factors combine to make this an urgent issue, they noted. This included the African-American attorneys who saw themselves as self-sufficient; whether they were married or not, marriage was their most important concern (Adams, 1983).

> Women's adult development seems to be inextricably bound up in the desire, or in the rejection of the desire, to mate. . . . In many instances, husbands facilitated their wives' entry into the adult world by serving as transitional figures, especially when subjects married during the Early Adult Transition. In this respect, the lover or spouse could be identified as a special man. Few husbands were found to embody the other qualities that Levinson attributed to the special woman, however. . . . Husbands appeared to be the greatest obstacle to the realization of the individualistic components of their wives' dreams. (Roberts & Newton, 1987, p. 159)

Levinson did not indicate the proportion of his male respondents who actually had mentors or special women during this period. Perhaps many persons do not have these intense relationships, or have only one or the other of these supports for their dream. As implied in an earlier quotation from the studies of women, these people without mentors may not achieve as high a level of success as Levinson required for three-fourths of his sample (published novelists, biologists on university faculties, and executives; the fourth group were workers on hourly wages). Vaillant's study, which we discuss next, supported this idea. In addition, some persons may not have a dream in Levinson's sense, or are not able to realize it for a variety of reasons. Also, some married couples may have individual dreams that are not compatible, so one dream may be abandoned, the couple may reach a compromise, abandon both dreams, or split up.

Vaillant (1977) described this period as one that emphasizes **career consolidation.** Adolescent idealism was often given up for "making the grade" among his respondents. Instead of questioning their choice of mate or career, these graduates from prestigious universities were mainly concerned about competition with other men in their field. As a result, "Men who at nineteen had radiated charm now seemed colorless, hard-working, bland young men in 'gray flannel suits'"(p. 217).

Many of these men indicated they had mentors. Although the role models they discussed when they were 19 frequently had been forgotten by the age of 47, they acknowledged the importance of a mentor—often one who served as a kind of "father figure." Although 95 percent of the men felt their actual father had either no influence or a negative influence, the presence of a mentor appeared to facilitate their career consolidation. That is, men who had "relatively unsuccessful careers" had no mentors between adolescence and age 40. Many of the more successful men had mentors who were given up by the age of 40, and later they themselves were serving as mentors for their young apprentices.

Although Vaillant (1977) did not explicitly discuss the "special woman," he pointed out that nearly all the men in his longitudinal study who were seen as "Best Outcomes" at age 47 had married before age 30 and remained married to the same woman. Conversely, three-quarters of the "Worst Outcomes" either married after age 30 or were separated before age 50. Moreover, the majority of "best marriages" were formed between the ages of 23 and 29.

Gould (1978) described this period from 22 to 28 with the phrase "I'm Nobody's Baby Now." Its major false assumption—the misconception that appeared to be most important at this period—was: "Doing things my parents' way, with willpower and perseverance, will bring results. But if I become too frustrated, confused or tired or am simply unable to cope, they will step in and show me the right way" (p. 71). He expanded this major theme into four misconceptions that are often carried from childhood, but need to be discarded during this phase of adulthood: (1) "Rewards will come automatically if we do what we're supposed to do"; (2) "There is only one right way to do things"; (3) "My loved ones can do for me what I haven't been able to do for myself"; and (4) "Rationality, commitment and effort will always prevail over all other forces."

Thus, the young person learns that "trying" is not enough—as in childhood when the statement "At least I tried" was often accepted by the parents, even if the attempt did not succeed. Similarly, working hard does not always bring success. Likewise expecting one's spouse or children to provide one's own fulfillment or sense of success is unrealistic if one cannot do it oneself. Gould described how this unchallenged assumption can turn into a destructive situation:

> When our temporary dependence on others to reassure us becomes a fixed requirement—that is, when we *expect* others to take *responsibility* for us—we form a *conspiracy* to avoid confronting our disguised childhood demons. In this conspiracy, we don't have to do anything; they, our loved ones, will do all that we can't do for ourself. . . .
>
> The conspiracy is a no-win situation. Eventually we feel either hostile or dependent and often both. In any case, our simple pact with our loved one becomes a destructive conspiracy that prevents our developing a fuller, more independent adult consciousness. (Gould, 1978, pp. 110–111)

Age 30 Transition

Levinson identified a period of transition between the ages of about 28 and 33, which he called the *Age 30 Transition*. During this period the person reworks parts of the "life structure" that were tentatively constructed during the period of entering the adult world and creates a second life structure that forms the basis of the next period. The essence of this transition is the growing sense that change must be made soon; otherwise, one will become locked into—and out of—commitments.

For some of the men in his study, this period was one of relatively smooth change—the modification and enrichment of an essentially satisfying life pattern. For others, there was a "crisis" or painful transition with fears of a chaotic disruption, or an inability to achieve a satisfactory future life structure. He reported that 62 percent of the men experienced a moderate or severe crisis during this time. The novelists and hourly workers were more likely to experience a crisis than were the biologists or executives.

One novelist, an African-American writer, experienced a crisis that was similar to many, but was made even more extreme by the effects of all that is involved in being an African-American man in our society. He and his wife divorced when he was 28 because his aspirations were not compatible with hers. This was followed by a long period of guilt about "the corrosive theme of the Black father abandoning his wife and children." The years from 28 to 30 were spent "moving around, often living from hand to mouth, working at transient jobs, hitting 'rock bottom,' nearly succeeding in killing himself, getting psychotherapy, starting a serious love relationship—and through it all finding time to write his novels" (Levinson, 1978, p. 88). By age 34 he had established the beginning of a new life structure—an occupation that brought an adequate income and also allowed him time to write, as well as permitting him an enduring relationship with another woman. It took several more years to establish his writing at the core of his life structure, however.

In contrast, another man had a much smoother transition. Nonetheless, he moved from a secure job in an accounting firm to a middle-management job in a major corporation, left his lower-middle-class, religious-ethnic community and his extended family when he moved to an upwardly mobile, diverse suburban community, and became much more ambitious in his career. Thus, his new life structure was considerably different after the transitional period, but there had been relatively little emotional distress or break in continuity with his previous life structure.

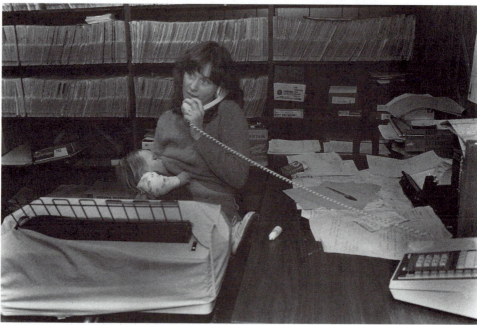

During the Age 30 Transition, women who were unmarried often become married and start a family; women who had no career often add one to their previous life structure.

Studies of women also found clear evidence for the Age 30 Transition (Roberts & Newton, 1987). The pattern is different than in Levinson's study of men, however, where the career remains the dominant priority. Among women the relative importance of family and career were often reversed—those that emphasized family began to stress a career and vice versa—after the decade of the twenties (Adams, 1983; Droege, 1982; Stewart, 1977). Another study reported a different version of this same process: the emergence of self-generated components of the dream among women during this transition. For example, women who were unmarried or had no career added either marriage and family or career to their previous life structure. Stress in existing marriages resulted during this period if the husband did not support these emerging aspirations (Furst, 1983). Adams (1983) also noted the importance of relationships with friends as a newly emerging theme during this transition. In addition, many of her respondents (successful African-American lawyers) felt ambivalent about this shift in attention from her career to her personal life.

Gould (1978) termed the entire period from 28 to 34 as one of "Opening Up to What's Inside." He felt that it involved discovering (or rediscovering) aspects, feelings, goals, interests, and talents that were ignored or hidden during the earlier period. Sometimes these were pushed aside because they interfered with the beliefs or goals of the earlier period. Sometimes they caused inner conflict and were suppressed. Alternatively, they required time that was not available because so much effort was involved in establishing independence and securing a niche for oneself in the social or occupational world.

He focused on a new central misconception for this phase of development: "Life is simple and controllable. There are no significant coexisting contradictory forces within me." It includes four assumptions: (1) "What I know intellectually, I know emotionally"; (2) "I am not like my parents in ways I don't want to be"; (3) "I can see the reality of those close to me quite clearly"; and (4) "Threats to my security aren't real." As in his other periods, these misconceptions should be challenged and discarded.

Gould felt that this stage may begin with a period of depression, but it is followed by a new perspective on the world. It may involve a deeper sense of beauty or the development of a personal philosophy of life. It may also lead to a more realistic understanding of one's strengths and abilities. This period also involves recognizing the contradictory and competing feelings inside oneself and the contradictory and competing pressures outside in the social world.

Settling Down

Following the transitional period of the late twenties and early thirties, Levinson found a calmer period from age 33 to 40 that he called *Settling Down* into a second stable life structure. Not only did Levinson's respondents settle down emotionally from the sometimes turbulent Age 30 Transition, but also they "settled for" a few of their major goals and began building their life structure around those central choices. It tends to be a period of "getting serious," a period in which to decide what is really important in one's life. It is the period of growing beyond the mentor relationship and becoming a full adult instead of an apprentice. Levinson termed this process "Becoming One's Own Man." He found two major tasks of this phase of adulthood: establishing one's niche and working at advancement. Since sometimes advancement involves challenging more senior, established persons, these tasks may be contradictory. The message is often that one should play it safe by not challenging one's superiors, but one cannot advance that way very quickly. Similarly, the man not only seeks affirmation of his worth and advancement up the career ladder, which he now sees clearly ahead of him, but also he becomes vulnerable to the social pressures of superiors who determine his advancement. As Levinson phrased it:

> A man is likely to be rather sensitive, even touchy, about anything in the environment or in himself that interferes with [becoming more senior and expert, and getting affirmed by society]. Since the successful outcome of this period is not assured, he often feels that he has not accomplished enough and that he is not sufficiently his own man. He may have a sense of being held back—of being oppressed by others and restrained by his own conflicts and inhibitions. (Levinson, 1978, p. 145)

The studies of women did not find evidence of this stable period; instead the years following the Age 30 Transition were often quite unsettled. "The addition of either occupational or relational commitments was difficult, if not impossible, to integrate into the life structure at this time" (Roberts & Newton, 1987, p. 161). There is some evidence of "Becoming One's Own Woman" toward the end of the thirties, however, as the women began to become leaders in their community and social groups (Droege, 1982).

Similarly, neither Gould nor Vaillant found this settling down phase to be a distinct period in their studies. In fact, Vaillant described the entire period from 20 to 40 as one of *Intimacy and Career Consolidation*. Gould, in contrast, included the period of the late thirties in the midlife transition, to which we now turn.

The Midlife Transition

Many years before the **midlife crisis** became so widely discussed, Carl Jung (1933) described the important psychological changes that he believed begin between the ages of 35 and 40. As discussed in Chapter 1, Jung considered the period of *youth* to extend from puberty to the middle years. During these middle years he noted a gradual change as some characteristics of the personality reemerge after being dormant for several years; other characteristics become less important and may be replaced by different or opposite personality traits. This period of change ushers in the second half of life that ideally reflects different psychic characteristics than the first half of life. These differences include greater emphasis on inner exploration and a search for meaning and wholeness in life that makes eventual acceptance of death more possible.

Elliott Jaques (1965) appears to have coined the term *midlife crisis* based on his study of the lives of 310 artists, including biographies of composers, painters, poets, sculptors, and writers. He noted that the incidence of death for these creative artists was higher than expected between the ages of 35 and 39 and lower than expected between 40 and 44. He also observed that after age 40 there was often a major change in the person's artistic works that resulted in less "hot-from-the-fire creativity" and more "sculpted" works. In addition, he detected a progression from "lyrical and descriptive" works in young adulthood, through a period of "tragic and philosophical content" during the midlife period, to greater "serenity" later in life; he cited the works of Shakespeare and Dickens as classic examples of this progression. He felt that the middle-aged person's growing awareness of mortality was the main theme of the midlife crisis, and his analysis of the issues of their period relied heavily on the psychoanalytic perspective of Freud and others.

Until recently there has been little empirical research on this midlife period, except for a few studies of menopause in women. Brim (1976) suggested that this lack of research may have reflected the assumption that middle-aged people—at least men—are stable, reliable, stalwart pillars of society and the family; thus, seemingly there would be very little change in their lives to study. As we will see, however, this research suggests that there is a great deal of interesting change taking place in the midlife period of many men and women.

The studies of developmental periods in adulthood we have been discussing focus on the midlife transition. We are also able to include data from a small longitudinal study of women and men by Livson (1976, 1981).

Each study viewed the midlife transition in differing ways. Gould found it to occur between age 35 and 45, similar to both Jung and Jaques. Levinson noted it between age 40 and 45. Vaillant placed it at age 40, "give or take as much as a decade." Levinson reported midlife to be a time of marked crisis, but Vaillant found that the "high drama" often associated with a midlife crisis was relatively rare in his sample. Droege's study of women found a qualitative change at midlife involving relationships, employment, and values: it began with a shift in the relationship between the woman and her aging parents, greater desire for personal expression, and increased awareness of mortality. (The other studies of women did not have respondents who were old enough to describe the midlife transition.) Livson's study examined the decade from 40 to 50 and compared those persons who changed markedly during midlife and those that remained relatively stable.

Later in the chapter we examine the interaction of the family and the midlife transition. Concluding the chapter, we focus on the perspectives introduced in Chapters 1 and 2 to critique studies of the midlife crisis and to place them in historical and social context. In general, these studies should be read with a "grain of salt" provided by the Costa and McCrae (1980b) study cited in Chapter 1: they found no age-related change at midlife and found that those who do experience a midlife crisis also appear to have more evidence of neurotic tendencies both at the time of the study and also 10 years earlier; we return to this point later in the chapter.

Developmental Changes and Issues at Midlife

In Levinson's scheme, the midlife transition begins around age 40 and serves as a link between early and middle adulthood. It has three major tasks:

1. Review and reappraise the early adult era.
2. Modify the unsatisfying aspects of the previous life structure and begin testing elements of a new structure.
3. Resolve major psychological issues introduced by entering the final half of life. These involve forming a new and more realistic picture of oneself and one's world, and exploring the meaning of significant themes such as "young" versus "old" or "masculinity" versus "femininity."

Levinson found that 80 percent of his respondents experienced "tumultuous struggles within the self and with the external world" during this period. They questioned every aspect of their lives and were "horrified" by what they found. They were angry and resentful about themselves and toward others. He noted that the men often were "somewhat irrational," but concluded that this was a normal part of the developmental challenge at this point in their lives. Much of the difficulty, he felt, was caused by the anxiety, dependency, guilt, and vanity the men had

According to Vaillant the 40s, similar to adolescence, can lead the man to feel somewhat uncertain as he reassess his life and relationships. He may seek new experiences and find renewed vigor and excitement during this period.

built up over the earlier years that kept them locked into an oppressive life structure. Thus, in his view, the intense reexamination during this period often brought emotional upset, especially since one is challenging the status quo—the established way one's life structure has been. For example, those aspects of the self that were pushed aside during the earlier Settling Down period reemerged to demand attention once again.

From the perspective of his longitudinal study, Vaillant (1977) focused on this midlife period as the search for a sense of *Generativity versus Stagnation,* Erikson's seventh period of life (discussed in Chapter 1). That is, the men he studied tended to shift away from their earlier emphasis on career achievement and mundane responsibilities at work toward more inner exploration and reassessment of their earlier life. He found several parallels between this period and the earlier developmental transition of adolescence. It is a time of feeling somewhat "gangly and uncertain"; it is a time for reassessing the experiences and relationships of the previous period—childhood and parental relations for the adolescent, and career consolidation and intimacy strivings for men in their forties. It is often a time of breaking out from the restrictions of the earlier period. He disagreed with Jaques' emphasis on the central importance of the fear of death in determining the midlife crisis, but stressed instead the renewed vigor and excitement of this period that seems to result from a sense of liberation after the overconstraint of the thirties. Of course, many of the men had greater contact with the death of persons close to them than they had experienced previously, and this often brought increased feelings of vulnerability; but many also experienced a kind of rebirth. For example, half of the men who had been seen as "unusually bland and colorless" during adolescence had become "vibrant and interesting" by age 45.

> Thus, if men in their forties are depressed, it is because they are confronted by instinctual reawakening and because they are more honestly able to acknowledge their own pain. It is not because they fear death. If they are no longer satisfied with their careers, it may be because they wish to be of more service to those around them. If their marriages are sometimes in disarray and their groping toward love seems adolescent, it may be because they are less inhibited than they were in their thirties. . . .
>
> But always, such transitional periods in life provide a means of seizing one more chance and finding a new solution to old instinctual or interpersonal needs. (Vaillant, 1977, p. 222)

Unlike Levinson, Vaillant found that radical changes during the midlife period were relatively rare. However, one respondent took up deep-sea diving and underwater archaeology in the Mediterranean; another built a "dramatic, shamelessly exhibitionistic" home; and a third had an exciting love affair that surprised the researchers because he had kept his inner life so well controlled when he was younger. The more common, less dramatic changes were also significant. One man who had a secret ambition to travel extensively never did, but he became editor of a travel magazine. Another respondent in an unsatisfactory nonsexual marriage had several discreet affairs and, at the same time, became more satisfied with his marriage, which remained stable. These midlife changes often brought some upset and anxiety, but Vaillant felt they were no more troubling than the similar range of changes during adolescence (which was also not typically a period of crisis for his respondents). Usually these changes involved a sense of vigor and challenge instead of crisis; one 47-year-old stated:

> "I am onto a whole new life, a personal renaissance, which has got me excited most of the time. If I can make it pay adequate to my family responsibility, I will 'really be livin', man.'" (Vaillant, 1977, p. 221)

Vaillant also called attention to the intergenerational nature of this transition. The interaction between middle-aged parents and adolescent children is especially important since each is going through somewhat similar processes; the parents play an important part in the adolescent's transition just as the adolescent plays a part in the parents' transition. In addition, an adolescent daughter or son may rekindle feelings in the parent that had been ignored for years. One striking example of this was a father who disapproved of his son's peace activities; however, the father had forgotten that (as the study records showed) he had been strongly opposed to United States participation in World War II until Pearl Harbor was bombed and he was drafted. Similarly, the changes taking place in the lives of the parents' own parents may be an important influence on these intergenerational midlife issues. We discuss this theme in more detail later in this chapter.

Vaillant's research also pointed out two findings that contradict some popular views of the midlife period. First, for those men who were seen as "Best Outcomes" at age 47, he found that the period from age 35 to the present was reported to have been the happiest of their lives, whereas the period from 21 to 35 was the unhappiest. Only those who were less well adapted at 47 preferred the younger period of adulthood to their more recent years. Second, those businessmen who had the best marriages and richest friendship patterns were the ones who become presidents of their company. This finding was supported in a different study of the men who headed the 100 largest companies in the United States; 95 percent were still married to their first wife (King, 1978).

Levinson and Vaillant focused only on the male midlife transition. The study by Gould (1978) included women and he suggested some issues that differ for men and women. Research by Droege (1982) and Livson (1976, 1981) focused on midlife issues for women.

Gould included the entire decade from 35 to 45 in his description of the midlife transition. The major misconception that he felt should be challenged during this period is: "There is no evil or death in the world. The sinister has been destroyed." This misconception has five components: (1) "The illusion of safety can last forever"; (2) "Death can't happen to me or my loved ones"; (3) "It is impossible to live without a protector" (for women); (4) "There is no life beyond this family"; and (5) "I am an innocent." Each of these is, to some degree, an expansion of the misconceptions that are troublesome during the earlier period in his sequence. The first three deal with coming to terms with one's own mortality and the fact that the death of one's parents or friends is a clear reminder that one also will eventually die. He found the issue of a "protector" to be especially important for women—in contrast to the shock of acknowledging one's own mortality that seems to hit men harder. Thus, whereas men are often badly shaken by the realization that death will come for them, and it may already have come for their parents or co-workers during this midlife period, women often feel a greater drive to strike out on their own, to overcome the notion that they need to be protected, and to expand their lives in new directions. This may include returning to work, striving to realize their own dreams, or simply feeling more independence. Gould noted that earlier in life many women tended to rely on men for protection and to feel that they could exercise their power only through men; but during the middle years, women challenge this assumption as a part of their own increased realization of mortality. Whereas men struggle to recognize that success, hard work, and the family cannot protect them from eventually dying, women must confront their own separateness as well as their mortality.

Droege's (1982) study of middle-aged women reflected many of the themes suggested by Gould.

> Toward the end of the 30s . . ., subjects experienced a shift in their sense of identity, from a member of a family to a sense of self, in a broader context. For example, the women began to take on more leadership and authority in their community—on political committees, in social groups, and as civic leaders. . . .
>
> The majority of women made qualitative changes in life structure that had only a vague connection with children's plans to either remain at home or to leave. The transition to middle age was initiated by more subtle awareness of a shift in role relationships with aging parents, an increasing desire for personal expression in work and family life, and mortality.
>
> A qualitative change occurred . . . at midlife that is correlated with age more than

Women who developed new dreams or risked making changes in their work or family life felt better about themselves during midlife. The departure of children was critical only for those women who were extremely family centered.

any other single factor [such as menopause or the children leaving home]. . . . Those women who formulated a new or an importantly revised dream for the second half of life, or who risked making some real changes in their work or family life, felt better about themselves than did those who declined or failed to build an Entry Structure for middle age. Only for those women who had lived extremely family-oriented lives was the departure of children critical. (Roberts & Newton, 1987, p. 161)

Florine Livson (1976, 1981) provided a very interesting perspective and additional information on this midlife transition for women. She examined a group of 24 women who were part of the original sample of adolescent girls in the longitudinal Oakland Growth Study begun in 1934. When the women were 50 years old, Livson selected those who were in the higher half of the sample on a measure of psychological health.

Looking back over the data collected during earlier years of the study, she determined that 7 of the women had also been high on the measure of psychological health at age 40, and 17 had markedly improved in psychological health between age 40 and 50. She called the stable group "Traditional," because their personalities appeared well suited to the traditional roles of wife and mother. "At fifty the stable women are relatively gregarious and nurturant, placing high value on closeness with others. They are pleased with their appearance and conventional in their outlook" (Livson, 1981, p. 202).

The second group appeared different from the stable group at age 50; not only had their psychological health improved, but also Livson described them as "more ambitious, intellectual, and unconventional in their thinking than Traditionals. They rely on their intellect to cope with the world and to deal with themselves. . . . Nontraditional women, in short, are more autonomous than traditional women and more in touch with their inner life" (Livson, 1981, pp. 202–203).

Examining the two groups when they were adolescents, Livson noted that the *Traditionals* had been more gregarious than the Nontraditionals; they were popular, socially successful, feminine young women who appeared to be establishing a firm sense of Identity in Erikson's terms. The *Nontraditionals* were also establishing an integrated sense of Identity in their own style during the period, but they valued intellectual matters more than the Traditional women; they were also more ambitious and unconventional in their thinking.

By the age of 40, when the women were contacted again after a lapse in the study, the Traditional women were resolving the issue of Intimacy in Erikson's scheme very well — they formed close, trusting relationships, were well liked, and were quite successfully sociable. By age 50, they showed evidence of Erikson's stage of Generativity — they seemed especially nurturant and protective, in addition to remaining gregarious and sociable. Thus, their pattern was essentially stable and consistently feminine from adolescence through midlife, leading to high psychological health within a traditionally feminine life-style.

In contrast, the Nontraditional women showed much more evidence of having experienced a midlife crisis. Their life pattern at age 40 was dramatically different from the pattern of the Traditional women, and different also from what it would be 10 years later. They showed signs of conflict, were relatively low in psychological health, and irritable, and their earlier intellectual strength seemed to have decreased or turned to fantasy and daydreaming. Moreover, there was some evidence that their firm sense of identity had regressed since adolescence. Although they were not studied directly between adolescence and age 40, perhaps they experienced an identity crisis when their child-rearing responsibilities were ending.

By age 50, however, these women showed a dramatic rebound—intellectually and emotionally. They were spontaneous, humorous, intellectual, bright, and open with feelings. They appeared to revive the identity they had been developing earlier.

These data suggest that the Nontraditional group experienced a crisis around age 40 that delayed their psychological development, but did not hamper their psychological health in the long run, since they were among the most well adjusted women at the age of 50. Livson suggested that the fit between the woman's personality and adult life-style may be the key factor in this midlife crisis:

> Women with traditional personalities fit conventional roles for women socialized to value domesticity and a middle-class, feminine life-style. Deriving their basic satisfaction from affiliation with others, they elaborate their interpersonal skills in the mothering role and develop their nurturant side. As wives and mothers, they are able to live out valued aspects of their personalities. They continue to find satisfaction in relationships with others, even as their children grow older and begin to leave home. They are not motivated to change as they move into middle age. (Livson, 1981, p. 216)

> The preferred adaptive skills of nontraditional women—intellectuality and ambition— make them less suited to traditional roles, particularly in a generation socialized to value domesticity and the ''feminine mystique.'' I suggest that their expectations of themselves in these roles induce conflict in these individualistic, achievement-oriented women, requiring them to suppress their ''natural'' adaptive style. . . . By 40, however, when children are growing up, they seem to be confronted with an identity conflict. Having suppressed their intellectual competence, yet moving away from child-care demands, they seem unable for a time to connect with a valued sense of self. I suggest that it is disengaging from the mothering role that stimulates these women to revive their more intellectual, goal-oriented skills. (Livson, 1981, p. 217)

Livson (1981) examined men in the Oakland Growth Study in a parallel fashion and found strikingly similar results. That is, of the 21 men who were in the upper half of the sample on psychological health at age 50, 7 had been relatively stable and 14 had shown a marked improvement between age 40 and 50. The stable men were also Traditional and had followed a consistent life pattern of conventional masculinity—valuing intellectual mastery, self-discipline, and achievement. In contrast, the 14 men whose psychological health had improved from age 40 to 50 were seen as Nontraditionals. They had been emotionally expressive during adolescence and seemed unable to integrate their assertiveness and their emotionality. By age 40 they appeared to have suppressed their feelings under a power-oriented, exploitative, and condescending ''macho'' personality. She noted that ''They emphasize sexuality and seem to engage in a kind of masculine protest—exaggerating stereotyped masculine behavior—but uneasily and at high cost'' (Livson, 1981, p. 214). They appeared to be under considerable stress as middle age appeared. However, perhaps as a result of the midlife transition, these nontraditional men had given up this exaggerated masculinity by age 50. They were more expressive and sensual, less anxious, and seemed to have integrated the emotional aspects with

Some nontraditional men may suppress their feelings under a "macho" personality during young adulthood and develop a more integrated personality after a midlife transition.

their sense of masculinity into a much more comfortable life pattern. The psychological health of both groups was equally high by age 50.

These data suggested that many, but not all, psychologically healthy adults at age 50 may have experienced a distinct reorganization of their life patterns during the decade of their forties. For many, this appeared to involve an acceptance of nontraditional gender role characteristics that had been suppressed earlier in life. Others, about one-third of both the women and men in Livson's study, retained consistent traditional gender-role patterns from adolescence to age 50, with little evidence of a period of emotional crisis during the middle years. These studies do not examine the fate of well-adjusted women and men at age 40, however.

This study suggests an interesting hypothesis about the midlife transition. Perhaps the transition is more disruptive to persons of otherwise high psychological health if the individual's personality characteristics are not readily integrated into the demands of the life patterns they are leading during their thirties and forties. If, let us say, they have played the social roles and followed the age and gender norms that supposedly lead to success and "happiness," but have had to sacrifice a significant portion of their individual uniqueness for the sake of social expectations, the midlife decade may bring an acute awareness that their lives are moving rapidly away from that part of themselves they valued, but had tried to suppress. At the same time, their growing awareness of their own mortality may lead them to question the meaning of the social expectations of "success" and "happiness" for their own lives. Erich Fromm (1941) also observed this phenomenon, although he did not link it specifically with a midlife transition:

All our energy is spent for the purpose of getting what we want, and most people never question the premise of this activity: that they know their true wants. They do not stop to think whether the aims they are pursuing are something they themselves want. In school they want to have good marks, as adults they want to be more and more successful, to make more money, to have more prestige, to buy a better car, to go places, and so on. Yet when they do stop to think in the midst of all this frantic activity, this question may come to their minds: "If I do get this new job, if I get this better car, if I can take this trip—what then? What is the use of it all? Is it really I who wants all this? Am I not running after some goal which is supposed to make me happy and which eludes me as soon as I have reached it?" These questions, when they arise, are frightening, for they question the very basis on which man's whole activity is built, his knowledge of what he wants. (pp. 277–278)

Perhaps this is the essence of the midlife crisis. Levinson found a set of questions that are characteristic of the midlife transition: "What have I done with my life? What do I really get from and give to my wife, children, friends, work, community—and self? What is it I truly want for myself and others?" (Levinson, 1978, p. 60). Thus, it may be that the emotional crisis of the midlife transition often results from a growing awareness that one's life, or style of living one's life, has become more and more out of step with one's inner characteristics, wishes, desires, goals, needs, and feelings. Neulinger (1986) has developed a questionnaire and technique, called "What Am I Doing?" (WAID), that helps assess these characteristics and can be useful for individuals seeking a transition.

In general, perhaps, the midlife transition can be described by a metaphor: It is as if, early in adulthood, one followed the well-worn footpath through the dense forest in pursuit of a distant mountain and for the next 10 or 15 miles (years) the climb was so difficult that one never looked back or paid attention to all that was being ignored along the way. Perhaps not until the summit is reached, or the quest appears no longer meaningful, does one reexamine the path and the mountain that has been selected. Or possibly it is the first cool day of autumn that reminds one to smell the flowers along the path because soon they will be gone.

The Family and the Midlife Transition

Intergenerational relationships between the person in midlife and younger persons (usually one's children) and older persons (especially one's parents) play an important role in this transitional period. In a sense, as Neugarten (1967b) noted, middle-aged persons see the reflection of who they were in their children, and see the reflection of who they will become in their parents. Thus, the dynamic relationship between parents and adolescents and between parents and the adolescents' grandparents may be crucial for triggering the midlife transition.

For example, the fresh sexuality of the adolescent may pose issues for middle-aged parents. Gould (1978) described this very candidly:

As mothers, we are attracted to our sons and their friends. After reading a magazine article about older women with younger men, we may wonder what it would be like. We find that our husbands are slightly aware of what's going on and are reacting competitively with the boys. One of the young girls comes into the room in tight shirt and without a bra, and we feel a flash of hatred and envy of her firm breasts as the young boys turn to her.

As fathers, we do what we can to avoid staring at our daughters' curves or their friends who make a game out of seducing us; we do what we can to keep our wives from knowing. Our sons' girls are awfully appealing, and sometimes we day dream about being in their place during this sexual revolution. It was never like this in our day. From time to time we wonder whether our anger at our sons is really jealousy. (pp. 269–270)

As the children become more sexually informed and aware, conversations about sex may become more frequent in the family. At the same time, as the parents begin having more time alone (when the children are out on dates, away for the weekend, or off at college), opportunities for relaxed sex between the parents become more frequent than during the child-rearing years.

All these factors are likely to increase the importance of sexuality in the lives of middle-aged persons. In addition, the "second adolescence" that Vaillant (1977) described as occurring during the forties — which brings a reawakening of instinctual urges or, at least, the inner exploration and reevaluation of one's life pattern — could focus renewed attention on matters related to sexuality. At the same time, marital satisfaction may be at a low point (cf. Rollins & Feldman, 1970); intact marriages can be 20 years old at midlife. Thus, the relationship with one's spouse is likely to be very much involved in the midlife transition.

Menopause, the ending of the menstrual cycle in women, may occur during this period. Of course, it might be produced earlier for medical reasons by a surgical hysterectomy; and other women may experience this midlife period before experiencing menopause. In any event, it does not seem to be a critical aspect of the midlife transition among the women in the study by Droege (1982). Likewise, the classic study by Neugarten, Wood, Kraines, and Loomis (1963) found that most women reported that menopause does not change a woman in any important way. (We discuss menopause in Chapter 5.)

Similarly, the change in male sex hormones appears to have little relation to the midlife transition. The inability to have an erection of the penis when desired is often caused by nonphysiological factors such as overindulgence in food or drink, stress, or boredom with the partner (Masters & Johnson, 1970); certain medications, diseases, and surgery may also produce erectile dysfunction (impotence). Periodic episodes of impotence might be misinterpreted by the man as a sign of declining biological potency and advancing age, however, and thus increase the stress of his midlife period. Such a connection, based on the man's own misinterpretation, is only an indirect link between biological changes and his midlife transition. For both genders, there is a more direct connection between a midlife crisis and other idiosyncratic factors related to physical health or vigor, such as an injury during a game of tennis, a sudden chest pain, or reduced activity because of high blood pressure, excess weight, or chronic disease. These changes are not caused by aging, however; they may occur during midlife, or not until the seventies, or not at all.

Often, the family element that is most involved in the midlife transition is the relationship with one's own parents or with the parents of one's spouse. Concern over the elder parents' health, their ability to live independently, or their death may bring the middle-aged person's growing awareness of aging into sharp focus. There is sometimes a shift in the relationship toward greater dependence of the elder parents on oneself, unlike the previous dependency of oneself on them. Also the parent is likely to be caught *in between* the generations, feeling a conflict between

The illness or disability of a parent can place particular strain on a person during midlife.

independence and dependence on the part of both the adolescent children and the elder parents. Today, with our longer life span, this concern about one's parents will become less frequently a midlife issue and more typically an issue during retirement.

Nonetheless, the illness of a parent may drain a person in midlife emotionally and financially; it may require a large expenditure of time and effort; it may cause a woman to divert her career to care for her parents, or her spouse's parents; and it destroys the illusion of always being able to rely on one's parents. At the same time, the costs of children's college education, emotional concerns about them, and their visits home can also be stressful. Combined with pressures to reach one's peak at work, critical reexamination of one's goals, and evolving relations with one's spouse, these concerns about one's parents may make the midlife period a difficult thicket indeed. Add the increased awareness of one's own mortality, brought on in part by the aging of one's parents, plus concerns about one's own health and the health of one's spouse. We can see many of the threads that can combine to create this midlife transition.

Themes and Variations in Middle Age

The midlife transition demonstrates a number of important themes we discussed in the first two chapters, so it will be useful to conclude this chapter by examining the problems and shortcomings of the research and theoretical assumptions that underlie the idea of a midlife transition. Let us begin with some of the central theoretical assumptions.

As discussed in Chapter 1, it is important to be aware of differing perspectives on adult development. The theories described in this chapter regarding the midlife transition represent one type of perspective that focuses on ages and stages of development; this is similar to the views of Bühler, Jung, and Erikson. In contrast, Costa and McCrae (1980b) emphasized the importance of *stability* in adult development. They reported data from two samples of men ranging in age from the thirties to the seventies who responded to a questionnaire that measured the extent of various symptoms of a midlife crisis. These symptoms included feelings of inner turmoil, sense of failing power, and viewing life as boring. The resulting data showed no differences between age groups. Thus, Costa and McCrae (1980b) concluded: "The midlife crisis, whatever it was, did not appear to be confined to the midlife" (p. 83). Similarly, in another study they measured personality traits by questionnaire in a large national sample and found no evidence of any difference in the traits measured from one age to another during the thirties and forties for either men or women (Costa et al., 1986).

As noted earlier, Vaillant (1977) found no evidence of a midlife crisis among the men in his study; there was evidence of change and growth, but not of a general crisis. Similarly, Haan (1981) found no clear evidence of a midlife crisis among the men and women in two longitudinal samples she studied that followed respondents from adolescence to their forties: "Instead, adaptation at mid-life appears to reflect the accrued wisdom of people who have grown tolerant and become instructed, socially and psychologically" (p. 150). Of course, some respondents in her study

Adaptation in midlife does not necessarily involve a crisis or transition. It often reflects a greater tolerance, wisdom from experience, and an ability to enjoy oneself.

experienced unexpected positive and negative life events. Nonetheless, she concluded: "Despite the unpredictable traumas and dramas visited on some person's lives, the 'generalized' middle-aged persons described here appear to be equipped by reason of past experiences both to savor and deal with themselves effectively and comfortably" (p. 157).

Costa and his colleagues reached a similar conclusion about the midlife crisis:

> It is also possible that the timing of the crisis varies with the individual, or that the experience of a crisis is limited to certain segments of the population (e.g., professional men). However, the present study does add to the growing body of evidence against the idea that there is a universal, age-related mid-life crisis. Individuals do sometimes experience crises, but these seem to be more a function of enduring levels of neuroticism than of chronological age. (Costa et al., 1986, p. 148)

As noted in Chapter 1, Costa and McCrae's (1980b) earlier study found that the men who experienced a midlife crisis according to their answers on a questionnaire also showed evidence of neurotic tendencies on a personality questionnaire both at the time of the study and also 10 years prior to their answering the midlife crisis questionnaire.

A different perspective is suggested by the *dialectical view* proposed by Riegel, described in Chapter 1. That is, instead of Levinson's perspective of alternating periods of stability and crisis, the dialectical model suggests a focus on the continual process of change. Unlike Costa's perspective on general patterns of personality stability across large samples, Riegel's view focuses on individual patterns of change—similar to Livson's (1981) study of nontraditional men and women described earlier. Likewise, Chiriboga (1987) suggested that *random events* can drastically affect an individual's life and the effects of these changes can last for varying periods of time, including for the long term. Some of these events can cause idiosyncratic transitions, such as divorce, and also can lead to a **chaining of life events** in which one change precipitates another, and another in turn. Thus, Chiriboga (1987) argued that we should focus on the "melding of the three underlying models of personality, those involving stability, orderly change, and random change" (p. 157).

It should also be noted that many of the studies described in this chapter involve relatively small numbers of respondents who are not representative of the general population. Thus, we cannot base a general model of adult development on such limited samples as those that have described adult development as a sequence of stages.

Moreover, it is useful to consider the pluralistic perspective of Baltes and his colleagues, described in Chapter 1. We need to consider the interaction between *normative history-graded* influences such as cohort factors and *normative age-graded* influences such as the social clock.

Cohort and Historical Influences

Looking first at historical forces, it is clear that the cohort of middle-aged people who have been studied (as well as those conducting the research) lived during a time of growing economic affluence, greater education, more emphasis on self-realization, and a change in gender roles (especially as related to work). For example, greater affluence among the middle class in our society has allowed many persons more freedom to explore experiences that once were reserved only for the very wealthy, such as European vacations, second homes, greater "leisure" time, and countless "labor-saving" devices and technology. No longer do we feel that fulfillment in life can come only through hard work, sacrifice, child-rearing, and a few community activities. Instead, our society now encourages the pursuit of individual happiness and self-fulfillment.

This change has been especially dramatic for those persons who were raised during the Great Depression and World War II when the opportunities that are now available for many were quite foreign to the vast majority. Whereas the greatest personal fulfillment for many of their parents was to keep body and soul together and to raise their children to achieve the goals that were impossible for the parents, today's middle-aged men and women are frequently achieving those dreams and are wondering what else there is, since many of those dreams do not automatically provide fulfillment.

In contrast, the so-called "baby boom" generation (born between 1945 and the mid-1960s) is nearing middle age and is finding that often they are not able to live as well as they would like — or as their parents did (Easterlin, 1980). Clearly, this next generation of middle-aged persons will differ from the one reported in this chapter in the effects of their cohort-specific historical experiences. Moreover, many other sociocultural factors may also affect midlife development, including the effects of television, increased life span, and reduced emphasis on age and gender roles. Thus, historical forces probably play an important part in creating the meaning and intensity of any individual's experience of a midlife transition.

Another central question raised by this discussion is whether *all* persons experience these developmental transitions. Instead, are they limited to a particular cohort that experienced specific historical conditions? Likewise, are they limited primarily to one segment of our society — such as urban, middle-class, married persons? Are they experienced by lobster fishers in Maine, farmers in Iowa, Hispanics in Miami, Chinese-Americans, homeless people, and a wide variety of other groups who have not generally been represented in these studies? Vaillant (1977), for example, devoted an entire chapter to a gay man in his study who did not fit the general patterns. Moreover, are developmental transitions different in our culture than in other cultures? Anthropological research clearly answers, yes! (See Chapter 9; cf. Fry, 1985; Keith, 1985.)

Obviously, much further research with more diverse samples, including cohorts and cultures other than those studied so far, will be required before we can discount the following hypothesis: The developmental transitions of early and middle adulthood are largely a historical phenomenon confined to a particular group of persons in the United States in the 1970s and 1980s.

Psychosocial Issues

Turning next to normative age-graded influences that may affect transitions during adulthood, we recall from Chapter 2 the discussion of age norms, age roles, and the social clock. As suggested earlier, the relatively rigid age-related patterns found in some studies of adult development may result from the age-related social norms in our society about the "right" time to accomplish the various expected tasks of adulthood. Thus, if developmental transitions in adulthood occur at a particular age in our society it may be because of the social expectations about the tasks adults should face at particular points in their lives.

Since the respondents in these studies generally are drawn from a single historical cohort and from similar social backgrounds, the uniformity of their "ages and stages" is not as surprising as it might at first appear. For example, the age at which the respondents in Levinson's study finished college, got married, had children, bought houses, received promotions, and had a midlife transition all tended to be fairly similar. This would be likely for "successful" or "well-adjusted" persons whose very success and adjustment may reflect the fact that the timing of their adult tasks is in step with social expectations. The pattern may not be so neat for persons who are less "successful," however. Moreover, these ages would likely differ for men and for women, and for persons from different socioeconomic backgrounds in society. Again, this pattern would not occur in all cultures, since social expectations are not the same in all societies.

Even within a society, some persons may lessen the impact of these transitions by anticipating and preparing for them. Others may be largely exempt from them because their life pattern is to some degree outside the social mainstream—such as members of tight-knit ethnic groups (Datan, Antonovsky & Maoz, 1981), never-married persons (Rubinstein, 1986), or lesbian and gay adults (Adelman, 1986; Kimmel, 1978). Moreover, as the studies by Livson suggested, personality factors—or the fit between the individual and social expectations—may play a major role in causing a period of crisis at particular points during the life span, such as during midlife.

Since the many questions raised by the studies we have discussed will be answered only after much more research, with more diverse samples, let us conclude with a brief critique of the research, drawing again from the discussion in Chapter 1.

Research Issues

The longitudinal studies (Livson, 1976, 1981; Vaillant, 1977) were especially helpful in pointing out the stability of life over several decades of adulthood. Both, but especially Livson, described the characteristics of those persons who did undergo a major change in midlife, compared with those who did not. These studies suggested that a midlife transition may occur for many, but not all, respondents. In addition, a dramatic midlife crisis was rare in the Vaillant study. This long-term perspective is obviously not possible in a short-term study, since the later is limited to data gathered within a relatively brief period of time and relies on the respondents' retrospective report of their earlier years. Therefore, it is impossible to determine the actual characteristics of the respondents in the Levinson study before the midlife period began. We cannot tell, for example, whether the 80 percent of respondents who had major midlife crises might also have been "crisis prone" all their lives (cf. Costa & McCrae, 1980b).

Similarly, retrospective studies are more likely to find evidence of change, whereas longitudinal studies are more likely to find evidence of stability. This bias is inherent in the methodology, since retrospective studies combine developmental and cohort changes, longitudinal studies tend to lose those respondents over time who change the most, and persons typically perceive that they have changed more than they actually have (cf. Woodruff & Birren, 1972). Thus, as in the example of cross-sectional and longitudinal changes in intelligence discussed in Chapter 1, the "truth" probably lies somewhere in between the relative stability found in longitudinal studies and the considerable change found in the retrospective studies.

An additional problem is that these studies have focused on essentially the same cohort, so that these data—both short term and longitudinal—are based on a limited segment of the population in the United States. Nonetheless, the studies of women suggest that, even within this cohort, there are differences between women and men.

Future studies of adult development should ideally follow a more complex approach by following each of several different cohorts over this period (Schaie, 1977). Of course, they should also select respondents from a wide variety of social and ethnic backgrounds and life patterns, or compare respondents from markedly different cultures. Differences between women and men are important, but should be linked with relevant social and ethnic differences since biological sex is not necessarily the cause of complex developmental differences. This approach is likely to provide a picture of the transitions in adulthood that uncovers much more diversity than the present data suggest.

The next interlude provides one example of a woman's development during early and middle adulthood. The next chapter focuses on the stability and change in a different kind of functioning during adulthood—cognitive and intellectual development. That chapter also expands our focus to older adults and the possible development of wisdom as one ages.

Chapter Summary

1. Throughout the life cycle, changes or transitions are made from one pattern of life to another. These transitions may be caused by internal factors, such as biological changes, or by external influences, such as social expectations.

2. Normative transitions are changes that are expected by social norms, such as graduation from high school, marriage, and retirement. Normative transitions that occur "off time" (compared with "on time") may produce emotional upset.

3. Idiosyncratic transitions are changes that are unexpected, that do not occur in everyone's life, and that cannot be predicted by social norms; examples include divorce, serious illness, or winning a lottery. Idiosyncratic transitions often have more impact on the individual than normative transitions and may involve an emotional crisis.

4. Levinson described four phases of development during early adulthood (about age 17 to 40), alternating between relatively stressful periods of transition and relatively stable periods. Women and men differ in the issues faced during these periods.

5. Vaillant followed respondents from college to age 47 in a longitudinal study. He viewed this period of early adulthood as one of striving for intimacy and career consolidation; he did not find as much emotional crisis during this period as Levinson reported.

6. Gould emphasized the misconceptions that individuals need to discard as they progress through a series of stages similar to those Levinson described. He stressed the importance of examining the meaning of interpersonal relationships and beliefs about oneself.

7. A "midlife transition" was observed among many of the respondents in all these studies around the age of 40. It often involved the issue of one's own mortality, the search for meaning and wholeness in life, increased desire for personal expression, and an inner search and examination of one's goals for the future.

8. Livson, in a longitudinal study, found that those well-adjusted men and women at age 50 who had been traditional in their gender role earlier in life showed less evidence of a difficult midlife transition than nontraditional men and women. This suggests that the congruence between one's personality and one's life-style may affect whether the transition is quiet or stormy.

9. The influence of intergenerational family relationships appears to be central to many of the issues of the midlife period. Relationships with one's aging parents and one's maturing children, reevaluation of the importance of sexuality, inner exploration, and concerns about the physical health of oneself and one's spouse combine to provide major themes of the midlife period.

10. Stability of personality, historical changes, random influences on individual development, and inner psychological changes each may contribute to the developmental patterns during midlife.

11. A close relationship between chronological age and developmental changes may reflect the direct and indirect influence of social age norms and the social clock, although individuals outside of the social mainstream may not be affected in the same ways.

12. More diverse samples of middle-aged men and women are needed to determine whether these developmental themes apply to all people in our society. Data from other cultures would indicate whether these changes are limited to our society.

Key Words

career consolidation	midlife crisis
chaining of life events	nonevent
dream	normative transition
idiosyncratic transition	off-time transition
menopause	special woman/man
mentor	transition

Review Questions

Transitions in the Life Cycle

1. How do normative and idiosyncratic transitions differ? Give an example of each type.

2. Describe and contrast internal and external causes of transitions.

3. What are your conclusions about the link between transitions and crises in adult development?

Developmental Periods of Early Adulthood

4. Describe the strengths and weaknesses in the studies by Levinson, Gould, Vaillant, Droege, and Adams.

5. According to Levinson, what are the major issues in each of the following developmental periods: (a) Early Adult Transition; (b) Entering the Adult World; (c) Age 30 Transition; and (d) Settling Down?

6. What issues did Vaillant's study find during the period corresponding to Levinson's Early Adult Era (age 17 to 40)?

7. In what ways do men and women differ during this period, based on the studies reported?

8. What does Levinson mean by his concepts of the "mentor," the "special woman," and the "dream"? Do you think these concepts apply to both men and women, and to persons in all socioeconomic levels?

9. In your opinion, why do these transitions seem to be so closely linked to chronological age?

The Midlife Transition

10. Describe the major issues that appear to be involved in the midlife transition. Is this a period of emotional crisis?

11. What do the studies of Livson add to the other studies of the midlife period?

12. What role does the family play in the midlife transition?

13. Which of Erikson's stages of development are involved in the Early Adult Era and the Midlife Transition?

Themes and Variations in Middle Age

14. Some studies find no evidence of a general midlife transition or crisis, others find it among only some of the respondents, and still others find a severe emotional upset for most of the respondents. How can we explain these divergent findings?

15. What considerations would you be sure to include if you were designing a study to explore development during early and middle adulthood?

INTERLUDE

Theresa, AGE 34

Theresa is a 34-year-old woman who moved to New York to pursue a career as a laboratory technician. She worked for nine years until her first son was born; when he was five she returned to work and is doing what seems to be important research. However, she returned to her career almost accidentally and is now thinking of eventually having a second child and working for her husband (Al) in his free-lance business. She seemed rather unsatisfied staying home when her son (Jan) was young, but even now does not seem entirely clear about how to be a mother, a wife, and also to have a satisfying career.

Several questions are raised in this case example. How important is her career to her? What are the important satisfactions in her life? In what ways does it make a difference that she is a woman in terms of her milestones, satisfactions, and goals in life? What would her life have been if she had not returned to work? Is she different from other women in that way? In what ways has she changed in the last few years? Is there evidence of an ''Age 30 Transition'' and a ''Settling Down'' period in her life?

What are some of the milestones that stand out in your memory as you look back over your life? Well, the first thing that I think of . . . when I was in fourth grade we were asked to write a theme on my ambition. I had no idea what I wanted to be. And my mother first brought up the subject of what I eventually ended up doing—medical technology. And she told me when she was young she wanted to work in a laboratory and work with animals and work in a health field. And so I wrote my theme about being a laboratory tech-

nician and from that time on every time somebody asked me what I was going to be, this was it. And I did, I just went right on.

Another milestone was . . . well, I guess that's not really a milestone . . . my mother has a blood disease, and because of her connections with a blood specialist I eventually got into the field of hematology and that's something I enjoy doing. When I returned to work this time I didn't go into hematology, though; I went into cancer research. It's also very interesting. In a way it's allied to hematology, blood diseases like leukemia are cancer. *Were there any particular reasons you changed?* Only because there was an availability. In fact, I wasn't even going to go back to work. A friend of mine heard about an opening—some doctors needed a technician very badly, so she called me up and asked me if I wanted to come in. And, Jan is getting on three-and-a-half and he's going to start nursery school and I've a pretty easy routine around here; I thought it might be stimulating; and I'm glad it worked out. I was getting pretty bored, I think—addicted to the afternoon movies, the soap operas, you know, that rut that I didn't want to be in. *How long ago was it that you went back?* Last October [five months ago].

Are there any other milestones that stand out to you? I guess another milestone was moving to New York, because I met my husband. *You met him in New York?* Right. A mutual friend, who was our best man, came to New York and visited me and asked if I'd like to come with him. He had to visit a friend of his, and then I met Al. We didn't start dating right away. We eventually had our first date back in Hartford when we were both home for Thanksgiving. Another milestone? It's hard, you know, when you think back for milestones you can't think. *Anything more recently?* More recently. Not really. I guess my husband's business probably is a milestone. I'm getting . . . I feel like I'm getting out of the sciences and into the arts, because I do work with him. I help him with some editing, and practically every aspect of his business we consult together, and I find that very interesting. *Are there any milestones in terms of your career? Your occupation?* I guess so. I went from an $80-a-week technician when I started out in my home town to a research assistant for my mother's blood specialist and then I came to New York and became supervisor of hematology at _____. And when I got married and we moved to _____, I started to work at _____ because it was more convenient, and I did some pediatric hematology, and now I'm back in the research field. It's been a progressive rise up the ladder, so to speak.

Would you say that being married or the birth of your child was a milestone? Oh, yes. It was. Getting married for me was especially a milestone. We have a mixed marriage [religions], and, you know, we had so many hurdles to overcome before we actually got to say "I do," so to speak; that was a big accomplishment. And our son was a big thing too. He was a planned child, and we looked forward with great anticipation. My husband took some courses [in natural childbirth] with me. We went through the Lamaze Method. He was present when Jan was delivered, and he was present in the labor room and everything. At first he didn't want any part of it. He didn't want to look at blood or anything and can't stand hospitals. But he rallied and really came through very nicely and I think he was glad to have been there. This was something very big. It's a long wait, you know, to have a child. You

build up to a certain point. We were delighted with him. He's shaping up.

What about crisis points? Have there been any crises? Oh, yeah. There have been crises. Well, I guess we had a crisis over our marriage. When I moved to New York there was a crisis. When I left home [in a nearby suburb] and moved to Hartford there was another crisis with my family. As far as personal crises — I like to think of myself as a fairly stable, fairly calm, fairly relaxed, easy-going individual, so I usually don't get too upset about things. My parents are both alive, so there have been no crises over death. I did lose my grandmother when I was living in Hartford, and although this didn't really wreak havoc with my life, you know, it left a fairly marked scar, 'cause I was very close to her. She's the only grandparent I knew. All the others died before I knew them. I got through college pretty easily, there was no problem there. I guess there weren't too many crises.

No real crisis points in your marriage? No, no, we have a pretty good life. Of course, occasionally, we have a little blow-up, but we get along well, I think.

What about in terms of your job? Any crisis points there? There was a crisis with Jan. When I first returned to work; actually I started working on a part-time basis before October — Saturdays and Sundays from four to midnight. I was getting a little bit bored around the house and I thought maybe I'll try working part-time and see what happens, because I didn't know if I could handle everything. At first, Jan didn't really understand what was happening, Mommy was going to work. But when he got to realize that on certain nights I wasn't putting him to bed, he got very upset about this, and the days that I had to go to work would reach an absolute tantrum on his part. And especially if my husband was working on the same night. So, eventually, I got to bribing

Jan with certain things. "When Mommy goes to work I'll bring you something back." Sometimes it would be a candy bar, a package of M & Ms, or something. And he got to associate my going to work with something nice that would come to him the next day, so that's a pacifier. And then, when I found out about the full-time job, we enrolled him in nursery school and he was ecstatic. He was going to go to school like the big kids. It was just wonderful, until the first week. The second week of putting him on the bus was such an emotional thing. I'd put him on the bus and he'd cry, cry, cry. So I talked to the teachers at school and they said that's very strange because when he gets to school, he's very happy; he's a very well-adjusted child; he mixes with the other children; he loves being there; he loves to do things; he does whatever they tell him. So we had another period the second week of school where he went from this real enthusiasm about going to this reluctance to go; finally in the third week he got on the bus with a smile and a wave again. There were times when he did not want me to go to work, he wanted me to come to school with him, or he did not want to go to school, he wanted to stay home with me, and I'd explain that mommy wasn't going to be home, "Mommy's going to work." And "Why do you have to work? Why can't you stay with me?" Finally now he's pretty well over this. Saturdays and Sundays come and he says, "Why can't I go to school today?" Occasionally he'll ask me if I can be home to meet his bus. My husband usually meets his bus about four-thirty and then they come and pick me up. I try to get out once in a while early so that I can be there. It seems to please him. And, another thing that makes him happy is that my husband or I will go to school at four o'clock and pick him up instead of letting him take the bus home. *What were your feelings about leaving him like that?* It tore the heart out of me when he started to cry. It was very important that he did have some contact with other children because right now he is our only child and there are no other children in the building his age. There's one little boy but he doesn't really enjoy playing with him. Most of his contact has been with older children. Now he does have children of his own age and he refers to his friends at school as "my friends."

How do you feel about working? Very good. For sanity reasons I wanted to go back. I think I was getting in a terrible rut. I feel I'm now being stimulated again. We talk about someday having another child. I just have this feeling, you know, how soon after we have this second child can I go back to work again? Because I just don't want to get into the same rut, but I have a feeling that I probably won't go back to work again, that I'll do work at home with my husband, which is all right, as long as I'm not with that boob tube [TV] on all the day. That gets very bad. I guess I have always looked forward to the day I'd be married and home with a child and I didn't have to do anything. Well, I had three years of this and, you know, it was just too much. You don't need that. *You couldn't stand that any longer.* Right. I think that I could probably have filled my days more efficiently, but, you know, you grow up in the middle American society thinking the epitome of life is to get married, have a family and stay home, and take care of your family. But that's just not it. You've got to have other things to fill your days. Before I went to work I started to do some paintings and some crewel. I do sew, so I've always done a bit of that, but I find now working with my husband, working, and helping my son, I'm doing more things now than I ever did and I seem to have just as much free time. You know, just on the go, I don't watch television as much; I don't get to read much either. I'm out every day. I get out early in the morning. When you're home you . . . well, maybe I'll get the house picked up and get dressed, then you find that it's eleven o'clock before you're dressed. You know, we have another cup of coffee, and then you get a phone call, and don't get dressed until one, and if it's summertime you don't get out to the park until two, then the baby has to have a nap, and you're in until four. It's really bad.

How did you happen to take the career route rather than just be the mother that middle America entices you to be? I don't know. I guess . . . well, probably it was financial. We had just started a business, and my husband's brother is a Ph.D. in finances and he came over from Chicago on his way to Hartford last summer and Al says please look at the books and tell me what's happening here; and he said "Believe it or not, your trouble isn't financial." It was just that we're having growing pains. So he said the best thing you could do is send Theresa out to work. So I said, "I don't want to go out to work. Are you kidding? I've got things to do here." And, finally, I started to think about it and I said, well, maybe that wouldn't be such a bad idea. So, all things considered, the best thing is to find something suitable. And a friend of mine had heard about this opening. So I guess if the need had not been financial, I probably would still be sitting home. *So in a sense it's almost accidental.* It's accidental, but it's probably the best thing that ever happened. *Yet you had a career before Jan was born.* Right. Well, I had worked. I graduated in 1960 and Jan was born in '69, so I had been working for nine years already. You know, I felt that this is almost a decade of work and that's enough. I had also worked while I was in college because I lived right near a hospital and I was doing weekend technology work, which was good because it pointed out to me that I was on the right track. I was getting into something that I would enjoy doing later. This was something my mother encouraged me to do, because I guess she knew a lot of people that graduated, and then they found when they went into their field they finally hated it. So, she said . . . even in high school: "If you think

you're going to want to work in a hospital you should go down and see if you can get a job there to try the atmosphere." So I did. I started in my senior year and kept the job all through college. *Did you do graduate work in this?* No, I didn't. I didn't feel it was necessary because you know, that middle America bit, I said some day I'm going to be home—I didn't want to make a full-time career for the rest of my life. *How does it look to you now? Do you think that you will?* No. I think I'll be working, but . . . I think there's more of a need here. I do his [Al's] bookkeeping, I write out all the checks for the employees. I do all his typing. You know, I never meant to be a secretary or bookkeeper, but I think it's better. He really can't afford to hire anybody right now and we're in at the beginning of it together so that as it grows I can grow with it. And I think in a way I like this. I don't want to feel too much apart from my husband; I don't want to feel that I don't really know what he's talking about. I just want to be able to communicate with him. I was in the sciences and he's in the arts; you know, I just don't want there to be a distance there. The other nice thing about working for him is that I guess it is not quite as regimented as being some place at nine o'clock and being there 'til five. You know, if my husband is my boss, then he's not really. I don't have to impress him.

I guess it's almost obvious in the way you've answered the questions so far, about how he feels about your working. He was negative also. He didn't want me to have to go to work. In fact, just the other day he said, "I wish you didn't have to go to work." I guess he's seeing that I'm enjoying it. He always felt that, you know, it was his place to support the family, and by the fact of my working, he gets a little feeling that he is not quite able to do it, which isn't right at all, because he's always been able to do it, and it's just been that, you know, he started a business and he's got to work very hard to have it grow. If I can help out, well, I'm glad to.

I'm curious what your feelings are about women's liberation. Well, I've been liberated, I guess. I've never run into any discrimination problems, so I can't feel very sympathetic towards women's liberation. I feel, however, that they're doing something very good and that's equality in wages. . . . I believe that this should be—equal money for equal work. However, I feel some of their, well, getting into a men's bar, is absolutely ridiculous! I believe that there should be places where men can go and women can go. Why does it always have to be integrated? I don't really approve of that. I think the work they're trying to do for the overpopulation is very good. I think the work they're trying to do for day care is very good. They've got some very good things. I think that if women want to work, they should be able to have good care for their children. A lot can go out and do what they want to do, but I can't agree with everything. *I get the feeling from you that you don't feel that either motherhood or having a career is the necessary way of life for a woman.* Well, some people are just not meant to be mothers. Some people are getting married today, and just not having children, which is very fine, if they don't feel cut out to have children. I think they should do what's best for them. *The two can merge and being a career person doesn't necessarily mean being full time in some occupation completely separate from the husband, it can be almost like a partner.* Right. Another thing about work too, when I first started to go back my feeling was that I didn't want anything that was going to take too much time away from me at home. I didn't want to have to come home and think about the work that I was doing. I felt that I don't want to have anything that is going to infringe on my time with my family. And so,

that's why I took this weekend evening job, because it was purely routine—absolutely nothing to think about when I got home. And yet, now that I'm in research, I do come home and, you know, there'll probably be a time during the evening when I'll think I know a way to do something and I'll go in the next day and try it out. So, I do think about it . . . it's not really infringing as much as I thought it would be. I think the thing that I had feared was when I was supervisor at _____, I used to have to often come home with paperwork that I couldn't get to; and absolutely none of that I wanted here. Now whatever I take home is up here [gesturing toward head].

If I would ask you who you are, how would you answer? Who I am? I don't like to think of myself as a woman, because a woman has always been to me an older person and I like to think of myself as young. I'm 34 and somebody asked me the other day how old I was and I said "[19]38 from [19]72. . . ." I don't think in terms of age. I feel young and I like to think of myself as young. I don't think numbers are significant. Who I am? I guess primarily I'm a mother because I can feel so much emotion for my son. I also feel emotion for other parents, you know when you see something on television in the news about some tragedy—I never used to feel this way before—I feel emotional. I'm a wife. I care about my home and care about my family. I want to do things for my husband and child. And I guess, naturally, I'm in a career which I care very much about also. It's something that means a lot to me also—cancer research. I feel that I can probably make a significant contribution. Cancer means—to me—something that will probably strike in our family, because it's been coming from all angles in our family. My grandfather died of it. My husband's mother had a form of cancer. My mother's blood disease was a benign type of cancer. I just feel that, you know, it's doomed that it's going to happen to us; if I can help by working now, maybe help science discover more about, not how to cure it, but how to prevent it and treat it, maybe I can be doing something for my family, which makes it all worthwhile. *It sounds like very exciting work for you. Very meaningful.* I'm happy doing this. I find it stimulating, challenging, rewarding.

Do you feel you have a firmer sense of identity now than you had before? Oh, yes, much so. *How has that changed? How has that firmer sense come about?* Well, it's come about by my life being full again. By being very active, getting me out of the house, getting me to do more things. I guess I'm stronger emotionally; stronger about wanting to get things done. Before I might have said well, I have this and this to do, I'm home ad infinitum and so I'll get it done, some day, but now I say I have these things to do and I assign a day to them in order to get them done. I make up a little schedule. I really live by a schedule. It's the only way you can fit everything in when you're so busy. We're working now to move out of an apartment into a house, because one little room for my husband's business is not adequate, so we're considering getting a two-family house where we can have some help on some income coming in, to help pay off the mortgage, where he can have an entire basement to set up as his studio. We have goals.

Would you say that you've changed very much over the past few years? I don't know if I've changed *very* much. I've probably become more mature. I probably worry a lot more. I think mothers do. *What do you mean, "more mature"?* I always used to think of myself as—not really silly, but I used to take things lightly. I was probably more daring. You know, now I worry about going too fast in a car. Before, I would speed to get there faster. I think I take the business of running a house a lot more seriously, more maturely. Certainly, when you have a child you have to become

more mature. I think one thing is I can probably handle situations better now. My husband would sometimes say, "I guess I'm not a good father. I don't know the proper things to do." But this is something you learn, you know; I've learned. When my son doesn't want to do something that I feel he has to do, what is the best way of getting him to do it? And so I've learned these little tricks to get him to do what I want him to do. My husband hasn't learned them because, you know, he hasn't had to deal with him as much. And so, I've been passing these little tricks along to him. I guess that's maturity too.

What other ways have you changed? I think in my relationship with my husband too, I've become more mature. I know that in our early courtship and marriage, if he were away from me, it really bothered me a lot. It's just growing used to each other a little bit. If I have to go to Hartford for a weekend, you know, I don't feel falling apart as we leave one another. I can take it easier. *Any other ways that you've changed in the last few years?* Not really; I guess the biggest change in our lives in the last few years is having a child, and trying to do what's best for our son. Seeing that he gets a liberal enough upbringing. You know, just enough discipline.

Was giving birth to him a big event for you? Oh, yes. It really was. I don't know how old I was—I must have been a teenager probably—sixteen or seventeen. I had seen a movie and I believe it was called "The Case of Dr. Laurent." And for some reason the interpretation from the French, the word "strange" was put before "case" . . . "The Strange Case of Dr. Laurent." And a couple of girlfriends and I had gone to see this movie. We knew nothing about it, and we got there and found out that it was a movie on natural childbirth. It was playing at the local cinema, so it wasn't anything educational at all. This girl had, through breathing, delivered her child without pain, and I'd never forgotten this. I guess it must have made some impression on me. And when I did become pregnant, I had since been hearing more things about what they call the Lamaze Method and I started to investigate. We got involved in a course on breathing. And the big thing was that I had heard from so many people that childbirth is the most terrifying of all pains, and that what you go through—you curse your husband, you say that you're not going to have any more children, and then, you know, a couple years later you have another child. So, it can't be all that bad, but everybody says, "Well, you forget pain. You don't remember pain." Well, I just did not want to be in this position of coming to pain. I wanted to be in control, so we took this course, and were very pleased with the outcome of it. You know, I felt on top of everything. We had a very good experience. Now, everybody that I find out is pregnant I recommend the Lamaze Method to. It worked for us. We were both there and we saw our son being born and it was a very rich experience.

Has your outlook on life in general changed in the last few years? Yes, it has. Again, I think because of our child. I have this overwhelming drive to preserve myself. Before, I didn't care if . . . I didn't care when death came. I never thought about it, you know . . . death, it has to be part of life, so when it comes it comes. Now . . . I think part of it may be the violence that is so prevalent. You hear about it constantly. I worry more about living. I'm very happy; I don't want to die and I want to protect myself.

Has your marriage changed in any way? Your relation with your husband in the last few years? We've been married five years. I think the only way it possibly has changed is for the better. I think that it's nurturing. I think we're helping each other a lot. We had been dating for over three years before we got mar-ried and so we didn't enter a marriage as strangers. We knew each other very well. And, in spite of it, the first year was a big adjustment. Some friends of ours had said that the first year of marriage the word "divorce" flies around so much because there is such an adjustment. You have two virtual strangers coming together—you know, he puts his dirty socks by the bed, she hangs her stockings in the bath tub—all these things that you have to work out and adjust to. It's a big thing. *So the first year was pretty difficult.* The first year, I don't think was as difficult for us as it was for some of our friends. We'd lived together for a while before we were married. We sort of got some of the wrinkles ironed out. We also knew each other for three years. I knew his hangups and he knew mine before we got married. Knowing them we went into marriage not wanting to change one another, but willing to accept each other's idiosyncracies. You know, you cope—you just have to understand. Somebody wise made the best statement I ever heard: "If you are willing to each give into your marriage, feel that you're giving more; if you can always go through your marriage giving the most of yourself; if each one does that, you're always giving and you're not wanting to take all the time, you'll have a good marriage," and I think we give a lot.

Has sex become more important, less important, or about the same in your marriage? I think it's less important. I think that probably in the beginning it's something new; it's probably the thing that brings you closer together. As your marriage gets older, it becomes less important because there's other things that you do together. Unfortunately we don't get to do too many social things because we're too busy. But whenever we do it [sex], it seems to be enough. It's not that driving need that there used to be in our early marriage. I guess it's still fairly important, but I guess it's not quite as imperative, so to speak.

Have your relations with your parents changed in the last few years? Yeah, I guess. I feel that I'm not quite as close to my father as I used to be and would like to be. It's probably that we don't get to see each other too often. You know, when you think about going home once a month for a weekend after I've spent a lifetime with people, you only see them for . . . 24 days a year. I find that I don't know what to say to him any more, outside of his work. . . . What do you talk about? I think that I'm in a different world now. I feel that they're not really into our world. It's just, you know, we have this gap. I can talk to them about Jan. They can talk to me about the other grandchildren. My mother and I talk about what's going on in the family—who's doing what. It's not that I have trouble talking. I just feel that I don't have as much to say as I would like to. I'd like to be able to talk more to him [father]. *Is your relationship now different from, say, when you were a teenager?* Oh, yes. Heavens! There's a great deal of difference. My mother was very strict and my father tended to be more liberal. As a teenager growing up I hated to ask my mother for permission to do anything. I'd much rather ask my father. I resented very much that lack of freedom that I grew up with. A lot of my friends had a lot more freedom, and this was, you know, [a source of] . . . good arguments; [I was] really rebellious. *I take it that there was a fair amount of tension between you and at least your mother then?* Yes, terrific tension when I was a teenager. As I grew older, when I left home to go to Hartford —I don't know how I got away. I really don't know how I got away. I must have been very strong. I'm sure there must have been arguments, but I must have mentally blocked them out. When I moved to New York I came home and announced . . . I think this is what I said, "They need me in New York!" (laughter) You know, I don't know how they ever fell for this stuff. "There's a job and they need a hematology supervisor and I must go." I drove off in my Volkswagen into the sunset; my mother's standing at the door saying, "This is terrible! This is a terrible way to go!" But I went and I got there. It was always my mother I had to work the hardest to get to do what I wanted to do, but we're very good friends now. And once we got married, once all the hurdles were over, you know, and I finally settled down—after she came to New York and saw where we were living and saw our furniture and saw that we did have substantial material things—she stopped pressuring me. We're very close now.

Has the way other people think of you changed over the years? The way other people think of me? I guess I care about what people think of me. Some people can just go on in life. It bothers me. It bothers me if I'm not well-accepted. That doesn't bother me as much now, where as a child in grammar school . . . I was part of a popular group, but I never felt that I was completely accepted. But today I am more accepted for myself. I still worry what the neighbors think—that sort of thing. I try to keep up appearances.

Would you say that you married at about the right time? Or early or late? No, we married about the right time. I was 29, I think, I'm not sure any more. I had traveled what I thought was fairly extensively. Probably not as extensively as some people, but I had gone to Europe once. I've gone cross-country. I went to a couple of islands. And, you know, I enjoyed being single. I worked what I thought was sufficiently. There was nothing left that I wanted to do. Like a lot of kids get married at 17 and 18 and that's it. They get nowhere. I think I got married at the right age. Maybe a year or two years earlier would have been okay, too. But I don't feel that it was too late. Certainly not too early. *Did you feel much pressure to get married earlier?* Oh, yes. My mother was always urging a little bit. She didn't like the fact that I was single and living in an apartment. That's not the way she was brought up. She probably would have been happy if I had stayed at home and gotten married a couple of years after I got out of college, but I enjoyed it very much.

Would you say that you have a pretty firm sense of who you are? Yes. I'm not confused about my personality. I don't try to fool myself in being something I'm not. The only thing that I hope is that I can "grow up" to be as gracious as some of the more mature women I see today. You know, you learn things as you go through life. You learn things like tact; you learn things about being kind to people, which, I think, as a teenager . . . you just don't consider. I think about them more now. You know, I feel it's important to be charitable. I think if every woman could learn to be gracious, if every person could be gracious, if every man. . . . Graciousness is a composite of everything I'd like to be. *How long have you felt that you had a firm sense of who you were?* I guess most of my life. Maybe not most of my life; well, at least since probably the middle of college. I guess in high school you don't think about that too much. Maybe it's become more important that I was aware of who I was since maybe the last five years or so. So much of your youth is finding out where you're going, what you're going to do and getting there. I think once you get there — like, I probably got there after I got married — the rest of your life becomes pretty much a straight course. You find your mate and start your family and you go in one direction. I guess, getting married [was the point] now that I think about it.

Do you sometimes look back over your life and review what's happened? Yes. I think about things I would have done differently . . . ways I would have handled situations differently. I think if my mother had been different, probably things would have been a lot different too. Maybe not, maybe I don't resent the strictness as much now as I did then. You know . . . when you want to do something and you can't do it you're very upset about it. It's probably very good for you.

Do you sometimes think about death? I think I mentioned that I think about it with great trepidation. I didn't mind it before, but I mind it now. I don't want my husband to die, I don't want my son to die, I don't want me to die. As far as my parents now, I love them very much; I know they are getting older, you know; I'm more willing to accept the fact that maybe in this decade, maybe in the next decade, they'll go. This is a fact that I can accept, whereas — this is something too when I was not married and I didn't have a child — I just couldn't conceive of my parents dying. I didn't want them to die. I knew that I'd get very, very upset if they died. Now, I feel that I could accept it. So, I guess I've got my own family too — it's not as important.

How does the future look to you in terms of your life? It's good. We have dreams. We have dreams about a home in the country and a prosperous business. I think the business is getting good. As far as a dream house in the country, I don't know. We obviously dream too hard. But if you don't have something to aim for, what are you going to work for?

I gather that you'd say that you have a very intimate relationship. Yeah, we do. We have a good understanding of one another. It's good. If lovers can be friends, that's important; and I think we're friends. Anybody can be a relation, but to be a friend is to know somebody, and we know each other. It's nice. *Do you feel pretty productive in your life now?* Yeah, I do. And again, it's all since I returned to work. I'm doing a lot; I'm doing a lot more and I enjoy it. I enjoy being busy. I thought I was going to enjoy just having lots of leisure time, but I don't. I'm not cut from that mold, and the busier I can be, it seems, the better I function.

Do you have any sense of leaving your mark? I guess I'm leaving my mark. I'm not a radical. I don't feel that I've got to go around and change everything, leave my mark in that way, but I guess, you know, in very quiet, subtle ways I do leave my mark. *Is that important to you?* No, no. Not especially. I just get along and get things done. I know that . . . maybe it sounds vain but once I've been somewhere, like once I've worked somewhere, I must have left some impressions there. One thing my boss said to me a couple of weeks ago: ''Whenever you take your vacation, I'm going to take mine,'' because . . . you know, I'm getting so much work done that if he stays and I'm away, that he's going to have all the work to do and he'll never get it done. I just feel that after I'm gone I think he's going to have a difficult time finding someone as efficient, as vain as it may sound. You know, I think this is how I leave my mark, but it's not important.

What kind of things are important for right now? I guess they're all material things. Getting a flourishing business, getting a house, having one more child. I think those would have to be the three important things. Getting my son into a good school is really important, too. That's just about it. As far as material possessions, the house is the only real thing.

Would you say that your life has been a meaningful adventure? Yes. I think so. I feel sorry that it didn't start becoming more meaningful earlier. But, I guess . . . you just can't have a more meaningful life too early. I'd say

that my life has probably become more meaningful again in the last five years. It seems to me, since I've been married that things have had a definite purpose. Before that, you know, you're just running from here to there; you're unsettled. Now I feel this is home, because for many years I would always refer to home as my parent's house, and now I refer to my own home as home. And like, thoughts are channeled here.

Are you looking toward the future mostly, or thinking about the past, or just concerned with the present? I'm more concerned with the future. Well, I guess I'm concerned with the present in order to get to the future. Yeah, I don't really think about what's gone past. I never cry over spilt milk, but I care about the present—whether we're going to survive in the jungle long enough to get to the future. *But the future is important for you now.* Yes, it's important. I guess it's important that I get my home in the country and I get my children, well, raised without getting them hung up on drugs and, you know, without having them travel with some wild crowd—protecting them in this world is important.

In 1979, Theresa had moved and was no longer working at the medical center. I was unable to locate her through the personnel office or to contact her husband's business. Thus, we do not know what happened in her life during the years following this interview.

C H A P T E R 4

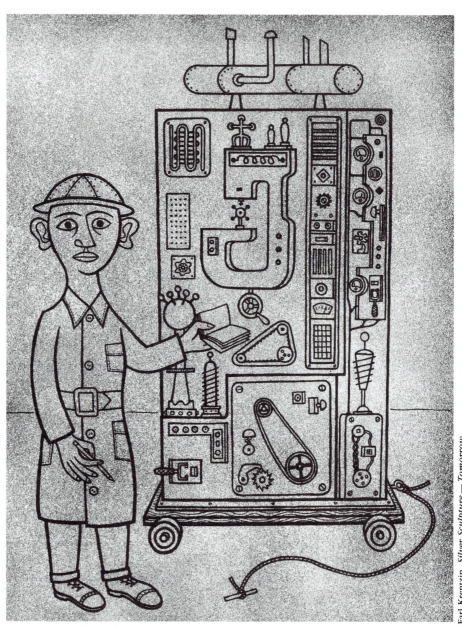

Earl Krentzin, *Silver Sculpture — Tomorrow.*

Cognition, Memory, Intelligence, and Wisdom in Adulthood

*I*n Chapter 2 we described how the self develops through social interaction and functions as a complex process that allows adults to interact effectively with others in our complex society. The model proposed by G.H. Mead assumes that the individual has an active mind and agile memory. For example: "The faces of our acquaintances are largely filled in by our memories of them" (Mead, 1936/1964, p. 76). Likewise, his use of concepts such as "self-consciousness," "reflection," "introspection," and "attention" clearly imply mental processes. Mead viewed the individual as an active participant in these mental activities, not a passive organism, as is also the case in social interaction. Three brief quotations from Mead illustrate his perspective on human intelligence. Although these statements were made over 50 years ago, they provide an introduction to the contemporary study of intelligence in adulthood.

> Our whole intelligent process seems to lie in the attention which is selective of certain types of stimuli. Other stimuli which are bombarding the system are in some fashion shunted off. We give our attention to one particular thing. Not only do we open the door to certain stimuli and close it to others, but our attention is an organizing process as well as a selective process. When giving attention to what we are going to do, we are picking out the whole group of stimuli which represent successive activity. Our attention enables us to organize the field in which we are going to act. Here we have the organism as acting and determining its environment. It is not simply a set of passive senses played upon by the stimuli that come from without. The organism goes out and determines what it is going to respond to and organizes that world. (Mead, 1934/1964, pp. 138–139)
>
> Human intelligence, by means of the psychological mechanism of the human central nervous system, deliberately selects one from among the several alternative responses which are possible in the given problematic environmental situation. (p. 176)
> Intelligence is essentially the ability to solve the problems of present behavior in terms of its possible future consequences as implicated on the basis of past experience. (p. 178)

This collection of psychological processes that Mead called "mind" or "intelligence" is often termed "cognition" today. **Cognition** may be defined as the way we think about and know things. *Cognitive processes* include paying attention to particular stimuli, recalling previous experiences from memory, solving problems, and understanding the physical and social world, including oneself.

In this chapter we explore the process of cognitive development, especially in terms of adult thinking abilities. We consider, first, whether the stages of cognitive development described by Piaget during childhood and adolescence continue on into more advanced styles of thinking in adulthood. Next, we examine the adult's cognitive abilities as if the mind were a very sophisticated computer that is engaged in elaborate *information processing*. Then, we describe changes in these processes that are sometimes associated with aging — specifically memory and intelligence — and ask if these changes are important or relevant for ordinary activities. We conclude the chapter by considering whether cognitive development during adulthood perhaps culminates in *wisdom*.

Cognitive Development in Adulthood

Students of child development are familiar with the work of Jean Piaget. Discussions of his theory usually end with adolescence and the stage of *formal operations* that is associated with the beginning of adult styles of logical thought. We begin this section with a brief overview of Piaget's general theory and the major characteristics of the stage of formal operations. Then we describe styles of thinking that other researchers have suggested may actually follow from and build upon the stage of formal operations; these are called *postformal operations.*

It should be noted at the beginning of this discussion that some of these topics are relatively new in developmental psychology and the evidence to support them has been criticized. For example, not all adolescents, or even adults, seem to reach the more advanced stages of formal operations; moreover, a young adult who does not demonstrate this stage of cognitive development in a psychological study might be capable of this style of thinking when working on a topic of special expertise, whether it be as an auto mechanic or as a lawyer. In any case, we cannot simply assume that formal operations, or postformal operations, characterize adults across the board. Researchers need to look closely at where these appear and why.

A young adult may show formal operations in an area of special expertise, but not in less familiar areas such as those tested on Piaget's experiments.

Piaget's Theory of Cognitive Development: Formal Operations

Jean Piaget described the general process by which the active human organism, in interaction with a stimulating environment, progresses through the stages of cognitive development. This succession of stages is the same for all children, although the ages at which each is attained may vary. The sequence of periods in Piaget's theory of cognitive development is shown in Box 4.1.

BOX 4.1 *Periods of Development in Piaget's Theory of Cognitive Development*

Period I. Sensorimotor Intelligence: Intelligence of action, consisting of six stages beginning with the use of reflexes at birth and concluding with the advent of thought using mental symbols (at approximately age 2).

Period II. Preoperational Thought: Period of organization and preparation for concrete operations. Thinking differs from adult thinking (approximately from ages 2 to 7).

Period III. Concrete Operations: Logical and systematic thought about objects and activities (approximately from ages 7 to 11).

Period IV. Formal Operations: Ability to think about thinking and other abstract and hypothetical ideas (begins about age 11).

Source: Kimmel & Weiner (1985), Box 3.2, p. 120. Reprinted with permission.

Four general principles are involved in this progressive sequence of cognitive development (Piaget & Inhelder, 1969).

1. Maturation of the nervous system creates opportunities for mental growth, but is not sufficient to cause it.
2. Exercise through physical practice and mental experience involves the child actively in the development of understanding of the external world.
3. Social interaction and teaching is necessary, but also is insufficient by itself.
4. An internal process of self-regulation, called *equilibration*, functions as a kind of feedback system of active adjustment to new information.

Since our goal is to understand adult styles of thinking, we focus our discussion on the period of formal operations. The term **operation** refers to those actions that a person performs mentally that form a coherent and reversible system. For example, the union of two classes (mothers and fathers are parents), or addition, or subtraction of two numbers is an operation. All operations are mentally reversible; that is, the union of two classes can be separated, or numbers added together can be subtracted. In the stage of *concrete operations* the child is able to perform a variety of operations on objects that are physically present and on thoughts about such objects. The operations in this stage are called "concrete" because they involve objects; they do not involve hypotheses or reasoning about the nonpresent or future.

The period of **formal operations** involves the mental ability to perform logical operations on the operations of the concrete period. It involves an ability to think about nonpresent objects and the future, about possibilities, and about hypotheses that are not concrete and present. It allows one to think about things that one does not believe in, or to draw conclusions from things that are only possible. Thus, it marks the beginning of the sort of logic that is involved in scientific experimentation. Two examples of formal operational thinking are the *pendulum problem* and the *combination of liquids problem;* these are described in Box 4.2 on p. 160.

> To summarize, the adolescent begins in the realm of the hypothetical and imagines all of the possible determinants of the results. To test hypotheses, the adolescent devises experiments which are well-ordered and designed to isolate the critical factors by systematically holding all factors but one constant. She observes the results correctly, and from them proceeds to draw conclusions. Since the experiments have been designed properly, the adolescent's conclusions are certain and necessary. (Ginsburg & Opper, 1979, p. 185)

It is important to note that these changes do not occur all at once; instead, adolescents gradually apply these cognitive abilities to a greater range of thoughts and situations.

Many important aspects of this theory continue to be debated and subjected to empirical study. In particular, there is disagreement about whether formal operations is a form of thinking that characterizes only some adolescents, or whether it is generally attained during adolescence, but is difficult to measure accurately. Nonetheless, the basic characteristics of adolescent thought that Piaget observed are widely accepted as useful for understanding adolescents. Although the reasons for these differences in cognitive ability between young children, older children, and adolescents have been debated extensively, there is no debate that these differences are typically observed.

Keating (1980), in a review of adolescent thinking abilities, noted that there are five major characteristics that mark the difference between the thinking of adolescents and younger children.

1. Thinking about possibilities that are not concretely present, or even implausible or impossible ideas.

2. Thinking through hypotheses, in a kind of scientific process of accepting and discarding alternative possible explanations, the use of accurate observations, and systematic testing of hypotheses.

3. Thinking ahead, planning in advance, and designing appropriate strategies before the experience—this might include a scientific experiment or even the purchase of contraceptive supplies before the person goes out on a date.

4. **Metacognition,** thinking about thinking—this may include introspection, keeping a diary of one's thinking, or "deep" discussions with friends.

5. Thinking beyond old limits; no longer bound by things as they are, the adolescent can question politics, religious beliefs, moral issues, and personal relationships; old ideas may be challenged because of a sense of excitement and intellectual pleasure; this can also provide an important source of intellectual ferment and even political or social change.

BOX 4.2   *Examples of Piaget's Stage of Formal Operations*

The Pendulum Problem: A pendulum, consisting of a weight hanging on a string, is shown to the children and they are asked to determine what affects how rapidly the pendulum swings from one side of its arc to the other. They are shown how to vary the weight, change the length of the string, release it from different heights, and push it with different amounts of force. The children are allowed to experiment with the pendulum in any way they please.

Concrete operational children approach the problem in a haphazard manner, varying several factors at once. They use no pattern to test the influence of weight, length of the string, height from which it is released, or force of the push it may be given to start the swing. Thus, young children's conclusions are not accurate; for example, they may conclude that weight influences the rate of swinging because a heavy weight on a short string swings faster than a light weight on a long string.

To solve this problem, children need to be able to perform the mental processes involved in conducting a scientific experiment. They must separate each variable from the others—weight, length, height of the swing, and force of the push. Then they must hold all possible factors constant while they change one variable at a time. Consider the following observations by Inhelder and Piaget (1958):

EME [child's code name, aged 15 years, 1 month], after having selected 100 grams with a long string and a medium length string, then 20 grams with a long and a short string, and finally 200 grams with a long and a short concludes: *"It's the length of the string that makes it go faster or slower; the weight doesn't play any role."* She discounts likewise the height of the drop and the force of her push (p. 75).

Thus, this task requires the ability to separate the relevant variables and to think systematically in order to perform an experimental analysis of the problem. These are characteristics of formal operational thinking.

Combination of Liquids: In another classic demonstration of formal operational thinking, five containers of clear liquids are presented that, when combined in a particular way, produce a yellow liquid. In reality, three of the liquids together are required to produce the color; one bleaches it out; and one is neutral (pure water). The task is to discover the combination of liquids that produces the color and the roles of the other two. The younger child (approximately age 7 to 11) usually combines the liquids two at a time and then puts all five together, neither producing the appropriate color nor determining the influence of each. However, "after the age of twelve he proceeds methodically, testing all possible combinations of one, two, three, four, and five elements, and thus solves the problem" (Piaget & Inhelder, 1969, p. 134).

Thus, the adolescent is able to imagine all these possible combinations and then systematically proceeds to test all these possibilities. That is, chemicals 1 and 2 are combined; then 1 and 3 and so on; then 1, 2, and 3 and so on; then 1, 2, 3, and 4; and eventually all five in a well-planned series of all possible combinations. This mental process of considering, in the abstract, all conceivable combinations is a demonstration of the formal operational ability to think about possibilities in a way that younger children do not.

Source: Kimmel & Weiner (1985), pp. 125–126. Reprinted with permission.

Postformal Styles of Thinking

Do adults develop styles of thinking that are more advanced than those described by Piaget as formal operations? This seemingly simple question is very complex, and involves a number of interrelated issues. For example, as noted in the previous discussion, there is not universal agreement that formal operational thinking is the best way to describe thinking processes during adolescence; therefore, there will be considerable debate about an even more advanced stage of thinking in adulthood. In addition, there are those, including Piaget, who argue that the more advanced styles of thinking during adulthood — such as that engaged in by Piaget himself — are only elaborations on the basic stage described by formal operations. Moreover, since only some adults seem to be capable of using formal operations, as measured by Piaget, at most only a fraction of those would be likely to develop higher forms of thinking ability — unless, of course, an adult's ability to solve everyday problems utilizes more advanced thinking than the same adult demonstrates in the kinds of tests Piaget developed.

Nonetheless, the revolution in thinking about physical objects, space, and time that resulted from Einstein's theory of relativity has led to vastly more advanced ways of scientific thinking; so, it is felt, humans may now be capable of thinking that goes beyond the mechanistic style of thinking that Piaget described. Sinnott (1981) used this idea to develop her argument for a kind of *relativistic* thinking that might be more advanced than formal operations. She cited Einstein's (1961) famous example of the observer taking measurements out of the window of a speeding train, but unaware of its movement; the observations would be accurate from the perspective of the observer, but some would be drastically incorrect if the train were suddenly to come to a stop. The measurements, clearly, would not be the entire picture of reality. Using this analogy, the scientific world of pre-Einstein thinking was similar to that of the observer on the train who was unaware of the motion. She suggested that the study of life span development may likewise be in transition from an earlier "pre-relativistic" conception to "relativistic" concepts. Such concepts might include focusing on the meaning of events not in an "objective" sense, but *from the viewpoint of the individuals who participate in them;* studying the direction, rate, and quality of developmental change instead of ages and stages of development; recognizing that the subject and experimenter are affecting each other in the experiment; and acknowledging that interpersonal and social dimensions are always relevant in developmental processes.

Few life span developmental researchers would disagree with this viewpoint today, at least in general terms. It is often described by the term **contextualism,** by which we mean that the multifaceted context of the observations must be considered. For example, age, gender, ethnic and cultural background, socioeconomic status of the participants in a research study, characteristics of the experimenter, setting of the study, and similar aspects of a research project are now routinely considered to be potentially relevant to the study.

However, this contextual perspective does not necessarily imply postformal styles of thinking. Instead, this emerging perspective may reflect historical development including greater understanding of the social influences on human development and more sensitivity to ethnic and racial diversity. Moreover, a variety of political and intellectual developments since the 1940s have focused attention on the interaction of the individual with the physical or social environment. Examples include the atomic bomb, the Civil Rights movement, and growing recognition of the effects of air and water pollution on human life. The term *zeitgeist* refers to the influential ideas of the times that define how issues are characterized in particular historical periods. One might observe that the *zeitgeist* among liberal scholars, scientists, and theologians in the United States from at least the mid-1960s to the mid-1980s has been one of relativism and contextualism. Thus, contextualism may be a manifestation of formal operational thinking in the contemporary *zeitgeist*. Alternatively, the *zeitgeist* itself might reflect the impact of Einstein's insights about relativity and indicate the emergence of a new level of cognitive development among the intellectual leaders of our time. Perhaps, as Piaget (1972) suggested, the development of human cognition goes hand in hand with the evolution of social and scientific thought.

In addition to relativistic and contextual thinking, another form of thinking more advanced than formal operations has been suggested by *dialectical analysis* (Riegel, 1973). This approach was developed in sociology by Karl Marx and also has been part of the *zeitgeist* of the twentieth century. We discuss relativistic thinking and dialectical analysis in detail in later sections.

In general, the various models of **postformal operations** in cognitive development have three characteristics in common (Kramer, 1983): (1) recognition that knowledge is relativistic and not absolute; (2) acceptance of contradiction between differing viewpoints; and (3) integration or synthesis of the contradictions into a more inclusive system. We examine three examples of these models of postformal development in the remainder of this section.

The analysis by Rybash, Hoyer, and Roodin (1986) provides a useful introductory perspective for this discussion:

> The postformal research is limited, because the quality of studies has *not* kept pace with the level of theorizing that has surrounded the topic of postformal development. This may be because of the inherent difficulty in constructing and scoring sound measures of postformal thinking. . . . Despite this problem, there is tentative empirical support for the existence of postformal modes of thought. Some psychologists support the existence of cognitive structural stages extending well beyond formal operations. . . . Other developmentalists, however, suggest that changes in thought beyond formal operations do not meet the criteria that define true structural stages. . . . Therefore, our position is that postformal cognitive development should be regarded as a set of *styles* of thinking that emerge during adulthood . . . , not as a true structural stage of thought. (pp. 55–56)

The three styles of postformal thinking that we describe in turn are: problem finding, relativistic thinking, and dialectical analysis.

Problem Finding

Patricia Arlin (1975) suggested that the stage of formal operations in Piaget's theory of cognitive development is a building block for a possible fifth stage of development. In her view, the period of formal operations may be seen as a *problem-solving* stage and the new stage she proposed is called the **problem-finding** stage. This latter stage involves creative thought with respect to discovering problems, formulating problems, raising questions about poorly defined problems, and the process of cognitive growth reflected in significant scientific inquiry.

Identifying and defining problems is an important aspect of problem resolution (Bransford & Stein, 1984). Figure 4.1 shows a few inventions that are available to solve some common problems. To create these solutions, the inventor first had to find the problem. In looking at these inventions, can you identify the problems they were designed to solve? How do you think the inventor found these problems?

Likewise, in social science we often have to find problems in research that is reported in various studies. Bransford and Stein (1984) gave a typical example:

> At a meeting of educators, a committee chairman reported on a study that had just been completed. Questionnaires had been sent to teachers; two of the questions asked were: (a) How much do you like computers? and (b) How much experience have you had with computers? The data showed that people who said that they had had more experience with computers were the ones who liked them better. Based on these data, the chairman made the following conclusion: "We can therefore see that the more that people are exposed to computers the more that they will like them." Do the data support this factual claim? (p. 77)

In fact, an alternative conclusion is also supported by these data: the more one likes computers, the greater contact one is likely to have with them. Therefore, we have found a problem that the chairman did not see.

Arlin (1975) studied the relationship between formal operations and problem finding in a study of 60 women who were seniors in a "middle-size southern state

Medicine clock. Set this little pill-box alarm to ring every ½, 1, 2, 4, 8, or 12 hours, and it plays a little song to remind you to take your medicine.

Don't lock yourself out of house, car! Magnetic cases hide spare keys safely.

A quick twist opens the most stubborn jars and bottles.

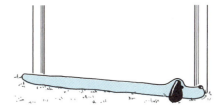

Wage war on energy costs. Dog sleeps in front of drafty doors and windows.

FIGURE 4.1 Inventions designed to solve some common problems. (*Source: The Ideal Problem Solver* by John D. Bransford and Barry S. Stein. Copyright © 1984 by W. H. Freeman and Company. Figure 2.3, p. 14. Reprinted with permission.)

university." Her research technique involved giving the respondents 12 objects (such as a C-clamp, 3 candles, a black wooden cube, a pair of scissors, 10 thumb tacks, and a quarter) and asking the person to write several questions about these objects during a 10-minute period. Their responses subsequently were coded by the degree of abstract thinking. About half of the participants in her study showed evidence of formal operations on traditional Piaget tasks (the problem-solving stage). Of these, 12 also showed a high degree of skill in problem finding, and 18 showed a medium degree of skill (Table 4.1). The critical finding, however, was that those who did *not* show formal thinking also did not demonstrate a high degree of problem finding skill; this suggested that formal operations is necessary for problem finding. Moreover, since several of the participants showed evidence of formal operational thinking, but low or medium skill in problem finding, formal operations did not appear to be sufficient to produce problem finding skills by itself.

Arlin (1977) thought that problem finding was a link between Piagetian operations and creative production. For example, she studied problem finding in a group of young adult artists and reported that those who were judged to have produced highly creative and original works of art scored higher than those whose creative work was rated lower (Arlin, 1984).

Thus, problem finding may be a characteristic of postformal cognitive development that is reached by some creative or inventive people who have developed formal operations.

Relativistic Thinking

A relativistic perspective in thinking about complex issues has been suggested as another likely aspect of advanced adult thought. This theme has been adopted by several researchers in this field.

Relativistic thinking, as defined by Jan Sinnott (1984c), is a set of information-processing skills that involve an element of subjectivity and self-reference; they are the kind of skills that are involved in analyzing complex interpersonal relationships that may evolve on a moment-to-moment basis. Although she noted that individuals may have styles of thinking that are unique combinations of relativistic thinking and formal operations, this style of thinking is proposed as a set of skills that are postformal in Piagetian terms.

TABLE 4.1 *Number of Respondents Who Demonstrated Formal Operational Thinking and Problem Finding (N = 60 Female College Seniors)*

Formal Thought	*Problem Finding*			
	High	*Medium*	*Low*	*Total*
Formal thinking	12	18	1	31
Nonformal thinking	0	20	9	29
Total	12	38	10	60

Source: Arlin (1975), Table 1. © American Psychological Association. Reprinted with permission.

Problems involving people often stimulate the use of relativistic thinking. Thus, this style of thinking can provide a link between research on cognitive processes in the laboratory and "everyday problem solving"; it calls attention to the potential importance of emotions and other psychosocial factors. It also often considers the importance of feelings and interpersonal interactions in its logic (Cavanaugh, Kramer, Sinnott, Camp & Markley, 1985).

One of the more widely used models of relativistic thinking has been the Reflective Judgment model proposed by Kitchener and King (1981). It is based on seven different developmental levels of assumptions or beliefs about reality and knowledge, with corresponding concepts of intellectual justification for these beliefs (Box 4.3). It is assumed that the higher the stage, the greater the degree of relativistic thinking.

Two studies suggest the type of research that has been stimulated by this perspective on postformal thinking styles; we discuss each in turn. The first study (King, Kitchener, Davison, Parker & Wood, 1983) suggested that relativistic thinking does seem to require formal operations, and that some people display it whereas others do not. It is unclear, however, whether they do not display it because their cognitive ability has not advanced to that stage or because of some other factors. The second study (Blanchard-Fields, 1986) suggested that emotional involvement in one issue may hinder some forms of postformal thinking. Perhaps other factors similarly hamper, or encourage, these styles of thinking. Neither study provided convincing evidence that this pattern of thinking is more advanced than formal operations, however.

King and colleagues (1983) used this model to study the characteristics of young adult thinking as it developed over the course of two years. The participants were high school juniors, college juniors, and doctoral-level graduate students in 1977 who were tested then and again in 1979. The three groups were matched on the basis of high school Scholastic Aptitude Test (SAT) score, size of hometown (when in high school), and gender. Verbal ability was measured in addition to the reflective judgment scores. The measurement of relativistic thinking was described as follows:

> The Reflective Judgment Interview consists of four dilemmas and a set of standardized probe questions administered by a trained interviewer. Each dilemma is defined by two contradictory points of view, and subjects are asked to state and justify their points of view about the issues. The four dilemmas were chosen to represent different intellectual domains: scientific, current events, religion, and history, with the breadth of topics intended to assure some generality. . . . Two trained raters independently score each subject's response to each dilemma using the Reflective Judgment Scoring Manual. (p. 110)

Over the two-year interval, there was a significant increase in the measures of both verbal ability and reflective judgment (Table 4.2). Although both verbal ability and reflective judgment were correlated with each other to a significant extent, an analysis of covariance indicated that, even when the effect of verbal ability was statistically eliminated, the increase in reflective judgment over the two-year period remained significant. It differed also between the three groups. This study suggested that reflective judgment, as measured by this interview, increased with age, as predicted; that the stages described in Box 4.3 appeared to follow a sequential order of development; and that verbal ability, although related to reflective judgment, was not responsible for the increases that were found. It should also be noted that the sample is obviously highly selected (graduate students and those with similar SAT scores). Also they reported that the amount of actual change among the graduate students was only one-quarter stage, on average; thus, the model may have a "ceiling" that is too low to measure the highest levels of development in adult thinking styles on this dimension.

BOX 4.3   *Reflective Judgment Model*

Stage 1: Belief that there is an absolute correspondence between one's perception and reality; one must only observe in order to know the truth.

Stage 2: Belief that an objective reality exists and it can be known with certainty. Authorities (e.g., scientists, religious leaders, or professors) know the truth, which is not known by everyone. When simple observation does not reveal the truth, then the authority's view is accepted as the true belief.

Stage 3: Truth is temporarily inaccessible, but will become manifest at some future point. Evidence is incomplete and no one can know more than is revealed by personal feelings and impressions. Alternate viewpoints and different theories indicate areas of uncertain knowledge.

Stage 4: Although an objective reality exists, it can never be known with certainty. The reason it can never be known is concrete and specific (e.g., it happened too far in the past). The belief is that each person sees reality differently, so there is no way to determine which answer is right, and knowledge is idiosyncratic to the individual.

Stage 5: Since knowledge is uncertain, objective knowledge does not exist and reality can be understood only through subjective perspectives. Beliefs are always relative to the context, which in turn may have different rules and perspectives from an alternate context. For example, a nuclear plant may be "safe" from the perspective of a nuclear engineer, but "dangerous" from the perspective of an ecologist. The advance from stage 4 is a recognition that the perspective needs to be considered when interpreting an individual's perceptions.

Stage 6: Belief that knowledge is based on subjective interpretations of data, so that objective knowledge is impossible to obtain. There are established principles of inquiry, however, that apply across various contexts. These principles provide a kind of superordinate perspective so that, for example, nuclear and ecological scientists can agree on certain principles of data collection and analysis as providing a rational and reasonable basis for interpreting data and evaluating hypotheses.

Stage 7: Recognition that the search for truth is an ongoing process of inquiry that involves many individuals' contributions over the course of time. Thus, knowledge is always subject to revision based on future inquiry, but one can make definitive statements based on the best current understanding, which relies on the accepted process of critical inquiry.

Source: Adapted from King, Kitchener, Davison, Parker & Wood (1983), pp. 107–109.

TABLE 4.2 *Reflective Judgment and Verbal Ability in 1977 and 1979 for Three Samples (Means ± SD)*

	Year	Group 1: High School Juniors in 1977 (N = 17)	Group 2: College Juniors in 1977 (N = 27)	Group 3: Graduate Students in 1977 (N = 14/15[a])
Reflective judgment	1977	2.79±0.51	3.75±0.72	6.03±0.63
	1979	3.61±0.46	4.18±0.80	6.26±0.48
Verbal ability	1977	40.06±18.71	73.70±28.58	121.43±29.59
	1979	88.35±29.79	104.78±29.57	141.57±24.94

[a]$N = 14$ for reflective judgment; $N = 15$ for verbal ability.
Source: King, Kitchener, Davison, Parker & Wood (1983), Table 1. Reprinted from *Human Development* with permission of S. Karger AG, Basel.

A study by Blanchard-Fields (1986) also found support for a similar model of cognitive maturity. This study used ''college-track'' high school students, undergraduate college students, and highly educated adults (mean of 18.3 years education). They were presented with three dilemmas, similar to those used by King et al. (1983), but with an interesting variation. One dilemma was selected to have low emotional involvement—conflicting accounts of a ''war'' between two fictitious countries, ''North and South Livia,'' each written by a partisan of one country. Two other dilemmas were selected to have high emotional involvement for the respondents:

> The first of these tasks was the *visit to the grandparents conflict.* Again, two conflicting perspectives, that of the parents and that of their adolescent son, were presented, describing a trip to the grandparents' house. The adolescent was unwilling to attend, and the resolution that followed was described from the differing perspectives of coercion and compromise. . . . The final task consisted of the *pregnancy dilemma,* involving the decisions of a man and a woman about an unintentional pregnancy. Again, differing perspectives were presented: a woman's proabortion stance and a man's antiabortion stance. (Blanchard-Fields, 1986, p. 326)

Responses to these dilemmas were assigned numerical values based on a coding scheme consisting of six levels similar to the seven-stage model described in Box 4.3. Results are shown in Figure 4.2.

Two findings stand out from these data. First, there was a significant difference in reasoning level across the three age groups, with the older respondents scoring higher than the younger ones. Second, the high school students did not differ from the college students on the dilemma involving the fictitious war between North and South Livia, but they scored significantly lower on the visit to the grandparents and the pregnancy dilemmas. This suggested that adolescents (and perhaps others as well) reason at less advanced levels when the topic is especially emotionally salient to them.

Measures of formal operational reasoning, verbal ability, and ego development were given to participants in the study. Ego development level (Loevinger, 1979)

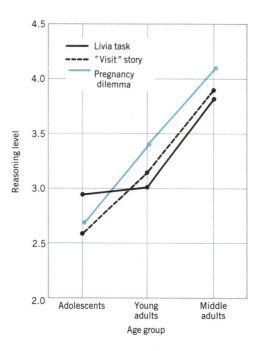

FIGURE 4.2 Reasoning level for three age groups and three different dilemmas. (*Source*: Blanchard-Fields (1986), Figure 1. © American Psychological Association. Reprinted with permission.)

was related to reasoning scores, with higher levels associated with higher scores. Verbal ability was also significantly related to reasoning scores. Formal operational performance was not strongly related to reasoning scores, perhaps because most of the participants were rated as either "early" or "late" formal operational, so there was little variation on this variable.

These data may help to explain such puzzling phenomena as adolescents' frequent lack of planning for birth control the first time they had sexual relations, despite their supposed formal operations ability to "plan ahead"—such an issue is too emotionally salient for them to use their highest level of cognitive ability. However, the data do not shed much light on the relation of this type of thinking to postformal thinking ability, since age and emotional salience were more significant than level of cognitive development. That is, "maturity"—measured by ego development level or by age—may allow persons to think in relativistic ways if they are capable of formal operations; this does not imply that this thinking is "postformal" in structure.

Kramer and Woodruff (1986) examined whether relativistic thinking represents development beyond formal operations and concluded that it does not. On the basis of their study of adults ranging in age from 17 to 75, they concluded: "The evidence did not support the hypothesis that awareness of relativity represents a postformal development" (p. 288). In fact, in their data it appeared that formal operational reasoning was not required for awareness of relativity, but that, con-

Adolescents may not use their cognitive ability to plan ahead in areas of emotional significance.

versely, awareness of relativity was necessary but not sufficient for the achievement of formal operational thinking (p. 286).

This does not invalidate the importance of relativistic thinking in adulthood; it simply implies that the evidence for its being a more complex logical system than formal operations is doubtful. Therefore, it appears that another style, called dialectical thinking, may represent a more promising candidate for postformal cognitive development (Cavanaugh et al., 1985, p. 159). We turn next to this perspective.

Dialectical Analysis

Dialectical thinking, as one might expect, is highly complex. Klaus Riegel (1973) proposed this model of postformal thinking as transcending the limits of formal logic associated with Piaget's concept of formal operations. We discussed a version of his model in Chapter 1, in which four dimensions of development interact: individual-psychological, individual-biological, cultural-sociological, and outer-physical. In general, this model focuses on the conflict between interacting forces that are always changing. It also emphasizes the conflict between an idea (thesis) and its opposite (antithesis). The resolution of the conflict (synthesis) is always temporary because the interacting forces are constantly changing.

Riegel (1977) summarized the possibilities of dialectical thinking as a postformal style of thinking by noting that it includes, but transcends, formal logic.

> Dialectical logic recognizes that it cannot exist without formal logic. This recognition provides a more general basis to dialectical logic than is available to formal logic. Formal logic fails to recognize such mutuality and is bound to consider itself immutable. Dialectical logic represents an open system of thinking that can always be extended to incorporate more restricted systems. Formal logic aims at a single universal analysis. As a consequence it is inflexible and primarily concerned with static conditions. Formal logic cannot apprehend itself. In particular, it cannot apprehend itself in the developmental and historical process. (p. 41).

An example of thesis-antithesis-synthesis movement can be seen in the conflict between those who oppose abortion and those who favor women's freedom of choice. It is not yet possible to know what the synthesis of these opposing views will be.

Sinnott and Guttmann (1978) applied Riegel's concepts to an analysis of the decision making reported by a sample of 447 persons aged 60 years or older. They defined the dialectical analysis of decision making as follows:

> (1) The alternative choices may be in conflict, creating a thesis/antithesis situation; (2) the choice may resolve the conflict, and (3) resolution of the conflict may proceed so that a synthesis of several alternatives takes place. (p. 192)

Inquiring about decisions regarding a recent real-life major event, they found that the dialectical model provided a useful framework of analysis. The psychological and social dimensions were the ones most frequently mentioned by the respondents; the environmental dimension was seldom mentioned. For those who reported a conflict between more than one dimension, 38 percent of those who had resolved the conflict in some manner indicated that they used dialectical operations.

Another study of dialectical thinking was done by Basseches (1980). He defined several dialectical schemata that may characterize thinking. For example, "Thesis – antithesis – synthesis movement" is one most often associated with dialectical thinking:

> In a thesis – antithesis – synthesis movement, the confrontation of a thesis with an antithesis (which may have been generated by the thesis) leads to the formation of a synthesis in which components or aspects of the thesis and the antithesis are both included and related to each other. (p. 409)

This style of thinking was present in the interview with George, Age 27 (the Interlude following Chapter 1). Some readers may have thought that George was "confused" by these conflicts; but one can also see them as an example of postformal logic in the form of dialectical analysis. For example, he described the conflict between being gay (thesis) and his Christian background (antithesis). The synthesis appeared to be his feeling that he is no more proud or ashamed of being homosexual than a heterosexual is proud or ashamed of being heterosexual. He described a similar dialectical conflict regarding abortion. Likewise, it is possible to find examples in the interview of relativistic thinking (e.g., the "great crystal" that appears green no matter what color it is when green light is shining on it) and problem finding (e.g., considering the importance of children in one's life and wondering about adoption and his ability to "father" young people through teaching). These forms of thinking would be expected from a creative person, such as George.

In his study, Basseches (1980) interviewed freshmen, seniors, and faculty members in a college about issues related to college education. He recorded and coded the interviews for the presence of dialectical schemata. The faculty showed more frequent use of dialectical thinking, the freshmen the least, with college seniors in between. Thus, he concluded that academic level appeared to account for a significant proportion of the findings, and is consistent with the idea that dialectical thinking develops as a postformal stage of cognitive organization. It is unclear from these data whether this style of thinking results from educational experience or from maturation.

Kramer and Woodruff (1986) found evidence in their research that dialectical thinking may be a form of postformal thinking (in contrast to the findings about relativistic thinking noted in the preceding section). Their study involved three groups of 20 adults each, age 17–25, age 40–55, and age 60–75, roughly matched for educational level. They were given tests of formal operational thinking. Two "dilemmas" were devised to assess relativistic and dialectical thinking. One dilemma was related to a hypothetical hostage situation where there were potentially constructive and destructive intentions, and one was related to a wife entering a career (involving elements similar to those described by Theresa, Age 34 — the Interlude following Chapter 3). They found that older adults showed significantly higher levels of those characteristics that are associated with dialectical thinking: acceptance of contradiction and dialectical syntheses. Also, formal operational thinking was found to be similar across the three age groups. Thus, they concluded:

> Formal operations were necessary but not sufficient for acceptance of contradiction and dialectical syntheses, for both the career and hostage dilemmas. This lends empirical support to the hypothesis that acceptance of contradiction and dialectical syntheses represent structural development beyond the level of formal operations. (Kramer & Woodruff, 1986, pp. 288–289)

Conclusion

Although the evidence for the existence of postformal thinking styles is compelling, there is no convincing evidence that their precise form has been identified. Moreover, we are left with a question about the implications of postformal thinking for the study of adulthood and aging. However, three points do seem clear. First, postformal thinking is a very interesting topic for further research and certainly will receive considerable attention in the future. Second, those who find the perspective of G.H. Mead in Chapter 2 to be a useful perspective may note that the logic involved in his concepts contains many elements of both relativistic and dialectical thinking; this suggests that these forms of cognitive development are important for understanding adulthood and the complex patterns of social interactions we have described. And third, since we sometimes believe that intellectual functioning in adulthood is a pattern of decline and loss, this perspective of increasing cognitive abilities with age provides a useful and positive view. We expand on this idea in the next section, and also discuss the declines that do occur in some aspects of cognitive functioning. We return to it in the final section of the chapter in a discussion of the concept of wisdom.

Information Processing and Aging

The conception of adult cognitive development presented in the preceding section on postformal thinking may be seen as one of increasing potential with age. There are also declines in some aspects of cognitive functioning with aging. In this section we examine **information processing,** which can be defined as the perception, understanding, reaction, and response to a stimulus — such as a colored light, or a symbol on a computer screen. Two aspects of information processing are related to age. The first is slowing in *response time* — that is, the time it takes for new information to be processed. The second is experimental research that deals with changes in **memory** — that is, the learning, storage, and retrieval of information.

Speed of Response and Aging

The most general change in information-processing ability is that the speed with which information is processed is slower for an older person than for a younger person. This difference is not very great in practical terms — less than half a second —but it is a significant difference in terms of statistical analysis. Moreover, when complex or unexpected circumstances are encountered, this slowing of reaction time may be important — for example, when crossing a street, when driving, or in accidents at home.

However, in ordinary circumstances, an individual can often compensate for the slower processing speed and perform as well as a younger person, especially if one is an expert in a particular skill. For example, Salthouse (1984, 1987) found that older typists did not show any difference in their rate of typing, despite slower responses on other measures; they compensated for the slowing by looking farther ahead in the material to be typed and so gave themselves a little more time to process the information, and their typing speed remained high.

The slowing in response time with age was identified in a classic study carried out by Birren, Butler, Greenhouse, Sokoloff, and Yarrow (1963). They obtained a sample of 47 men between the ages of 65 and 91 who were extremely healthy on the basis of clinical examination. These subjects were found to consist of two different groups: Group 1, who were in optimal health in every regard; and Group

Older expert typists read farther ahead and thus compensate for the slower reaction time accompanying aging so that their typing rate does not decline.

2, who were without obvious symptoms of disease, but who were found to have mild diseases that were discovered only through intensive medical examination. This subtle difference in health turned out to be important in understanding changes in information processing with aging. For example, scores obtained by the subjects in Group 2 were poorer than scores obtained by the optimally healthy group on 21 out of 23 tests of intellectual performance. Thus, one central finding is the negative effect of even mild disease on cognitive performance, particularly on the processes involved in the retrieval of stored information. However, the performance of the elderly subjects (both groups) was superior to the norms for young subjects on measures of verbal intelligence (such as vocabulary) and was also superior to previously studied elderly samples (perhaps related to the superior health of both groups of subjects in this study).

Both groups were significantly slower in psychomotor speed than young adults, and intelligence measures that involved fast responses were impaired for both groups. Thus, *age* was found to be most important in measures of the **speed of response**, such as reaction time, whereas *health* was more important than age on verbal measures that involved the retrieval of stored information. These data indicate that one effect of aging (in the absence of disease) is a *slowing down* of reaction time, regardless of the sensory modality (auditory or visual) and regardless of the muscle used for the response (foot, jaw, finger, speech, and so on). This change, since it occurred equally in both Group 1 and 2, seemed to be related to aging rather than to disease (and it may be related to the slowing down of the EEG measure of brain activity pattern that was also found in the study; see Chapter 7). This general slowing down was also found to be greater when there was a history of greater social and environmental losses, and it was more marked for respondents who were rated as "depressed" in psychiatric terms. Thus, this age-related change is apparently independent of mild disease but is modulated by social and psychological factors.

Surprisingly, neither the cause of this slowing, nor precisely where in the central nervous system it occurs is known. Some think it lies in the central processing functions of the brain and give as evidence that the more *complexity* in the problem, the greater the slowing. Others, using measures of brain waves, argue that particular electrical impulses measured in the brain during problem solving do not show any age difference, so the slowing must be outside the brain, perhaps in peripheral nerves. Still others think that younger people could function as slowly as older people if younger people were as concerned with making accurate responses as older people have been found to be; perhaps older people could also be trained to respond as fast as younger people if they gave up their preference for accuracy. This latter phenomenon is called a **speed–accuracy trade-off;** it involves participants selecting a strategy in which they emphasize responding quickly versus waiting a short time before responding to be sure the response is accurate. Thus, they "trade off" speed for accuracy, or vice versa in responding to specified cues in laboratory experiments.

The slowing in the rate of information processing naturally affects all aspects of cognition: for example, memory and intelligence. It is interesting, however, that not all areas of knowledge are affected the same way in healthy older persons. Those areas in which one has considerable experience and *expertise*—like the expert typists noted above—show little or no change decline with age. In contrast, ***unfamiliar*** tasks do not become so well learned that they become "automatic" in older persons (as they do in younger persons with lots of practice); and they are affected by this slowing in the rate of information processing. The situation is different with Alzheimer's disease, of course (see Chapter 8); this disease causes unusual slowing in reaction time tasks (Nebes & Madden, 1988).

We discuss memory and intelligence as examples of information processing in the next two sections. The chapter concludes with a focus on the practical effects these changes have for everyday functioning, and with a look at the concept of *wisdom*.

Memory and Aging

A great deal of research on the psychology of aging has focused on memory (Poon, 1985). This research has succeeded in disproving many myths. As an introduction to this topic, let us briefly state the major general conclusions that research about memory and aging has supplied to replace some of the myths. We discuss each in greater detail later in this section.

1. Memory decline does not affect all old people; under similar conditions, some elderly people perform as well on memory tests as younger people and there is great variability in memory performance.

2. Exercises to improve memory can have as great an effect on older people as on younger people, sometimes increasing memory functions to levels of extreme skill.

3. Older people usually compensate for any loss of efficiency in memory in areas where they are competent or expert, so that they can perform as well—or better—than younger people in these areas.

4. Unusual factors, such as Alzheimer's disease, psychiatric depression, or even general inactivity and boredom, can impair memory functions in ways that are not typical of other older persons.

5. Memory of distant events is not necessarily better than memory of recent events at any age. Likewise, retelling stories from one's past does not necessarily indicate that one's memory is accurate or better than one's memory of current events.

6. As an important component of information processing, memory is affected by the same processes that affect other components, such as expertise, speed of response, and motivation.

7. Tests of memory that one engages in during ordinary daily life often show no decline with age, for example, remembering to make telephone calls at certain times.

It may be apparent that many complex issues are interrelated in the seemingly simple issue of memory change with age. In addition, research has not been very helpful in clarifying the nature of memory and the effect of aging on different aspects of it. We cannot review or describe all the issues that have been studied, but we will summarize three of the major themes in studies of normal aging: declines in some aspects of memory efficiency; memory for distant events; and continued high levels of competence. (We discuss Alzheimer's disease and depression in Chapter 8.)

Decline in Memory Efficiency

Current views of memory typically adopt an *information-processing* model, that is, they emphasize the active encoding, storage, transformation (e.g., integration, synthesis), and retrieval of information (Rybash, Hoyer & Roodin, 1986, p. 93). It is also assumed that there are different stages or types of storage for memories: sensory memory (i.e., auditory, visual, olfactory), short-term primary memory (where the information is still "in mind"—similar to the "RAM buffer" in a computer), secondary memory (for newly learned information), and tertiary memory (for permanent storage and the repository of remote memories). Of these, age-related changes have been shown primarily in *secondary memory* (Poon, 1985).

Figure 4.3 illustrates typical declines in a variety of measures of newly learned information in the psychological laboratory for persons of different ages. The tasks involve learning a paragraph of prose, recognizing two words presented together (paired associates), remembering a string of numbers (digits), and recalling specific designs shown on cards. In studies such as this, however, it is not clear whether the decline reflects a deficit in learning new information or in retrieving the newly learned information (Kausler, 1970). Moreover, if the information has to be transformed in some way—such as repeating the digits *backwards*—the relative proficiency of elderly subjects shown in the top line of Figure 4.3 declines significantly (Gilbert & Levee, 1971).

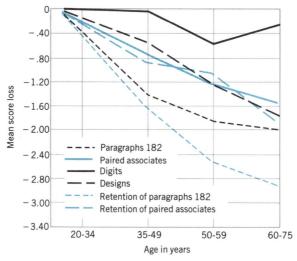

FIGURE 4.3 Decline on memory tests of different types by age group. (*Source:* Gilbert & Levee (1971). Reprinted with permission from the *Journal of Gerontology*, Vol. 26, p. 73.)

Another aspect of memory decline is the slower speed with which older adults search the *short-term primary memory.* "The time needed to activate information from memory increases by over 60% between the ages of 20 and 50," according to Salthouse (1982, p. 113). Retrieval of information stored in the secondary memory is also slower for older adults (Poon & Fozard, 1978, 1980). The reason for this slower access to memory is unclear. It may reflect any of the following theories: slower processing rate, neural "noise" that interferes with efficient processing of information by the central nervous system, limited capacity of the memory storage system that is nearly "full" in old age, or the speed–accuracy trade-off.

In an attempt to determine the cause of slower access to memory with age, Strayer, Wickens, and Braune (1987) examined several possible sources of this widely reported slowing:

1. All processing stages slow with age (Salthouse, 1982).

2. Central-cognitive processes are more affected than perceptual-motor ones; thus, more complex tasks should be slowed more than simpler ones (Cerella, 1985).

3. Older persons have a higher motivation to give accurate responses which takes precedence over fast responses—the speed–accuracy trade-off (Pachella, 1974).

They used a methodology called **Event Related Potentials** (ERP), which measures electrical responses of the brain to specific stimuli. Electrodes are placed on the subject's head and a computer is used to collect the data and to separate the particular ERP component of interest from other electrical responses (such as the background EEG waves). Previous research had demonstrated that one component of the ERP, called the P300, is sensitive to cognitive processing, that it slows with age, and that it is not influenced by processes related to the individual's response to the event. Thus, *reaction time,* which includes encoding, searching memory, and responding, can be compared with the P300 component. Their study involved 60 subjects ranging in age from 20 to 65 who were presented information to memorize on a graphics display and had a hand-held button to press to indicate when a stimulus was part of the set they had memorized previously. At predetermined points they were given verbal instructions to emphasize speed, speed and accuracy, or only accuracy.

The study led to the finding that there are three approximately equal contributing sources for the slowing of reaction time. About one-third of the effect was attributed to a delay in encoding information. Another third was accounted for by the speed–accuracy trade-off; older respondents tended to emphasize accurate responses more than fast responses. And the size of the memory set that was to be learned accounted for the remaining one-third of the difference in processing speed. The investigators noted:

> Traditional interpretations of these data would have concluded that memory search rate was slowed with age, *but* the P300 slope (the increase in latency with set size) was equivalent for all age groups. This suggests that the locus of this age effect is not related to memory search; rather the slowing appears to be response related. . . .

> Taken together, the . . . experiments suggest that central-processing speed and capacity are no different between young and elderly subjects. The difference in performance lies predominately in the perceptual-motor systems. Thus, input output processes seem to be the locus of the large decrements in response performance related to age. (Strayer, Wickens & Braune, 1987, p. 109)

Research has also begun to emphasize the diversity of these changes in memory with aging. For example, Craik, Byrd, and Swanson (1987) compared three different groups of older people with a younger sample on a variety of memory tasks and concluded:

> We argue that age deficits should not be viewed as all-or-none effects, but rather that the age differences observed will be large, small, or nonexistent depending on the tasks and materials. Further, the same patterns of differential losses appear within a large sample of elderly people, with higher performance shown by more active and highly verbal participants. (p. 83)

Another line of research has focused on those memory tasks that show little or no age difference in performance between elderly and young people. We discuss this later in terms of "everyday memory," but it also occurs in laboratory experiments. For instance, Park, Puglisi, and Smith (1986) found that there was no age difference in the immediate recall of pictures. In addition, adding details to photographs presented to old and young adults enhanced recall for both groups.

Memory of Events from Long Ago

Suppose a person born in 1970 and one born in 1920 were given the following questions to test their long-term memory (Salthouse, 1982, p. 118):

1. What happened on December 7, 1941?
2. Which baseball team won the World Series in 1955?

It is likely that both persons would be able to "remember" the attack on Pearl Harbor that brought the United States into World War II (event 1); but only one was alive at the time. It is unlikely that either person would be able to answer the second question, unless the older person lived in New York City, or either person was a fan of baseball or the Brooklyn Dodgers. This example alerts us at once to the problems of assessing long-term memory, sometimes called *remote* memory or tertiary memory.

Another less obvious problem is that the individual may have told and retold the memory so that it is relatively "fresh" even if the original incident happened many years ago. Moreover, each time one recalls the memory, one may change it. The "Interludes" in this book are a convenient example of this process. As the person describes memories of the past, they are likely to be reinterpreted in the context of more recent events, and perhaps selected and modified to fit the image the person is presenting in the interview (cf. Cohler, 1982; Whitbourne, 1985).

Conversely, "forgetting" past events may be deliberate and selective (Rybash, Hoyer & Roodin, 1986, p. 96). The Watergate and Iran–Contra hearings featured key actors in the events who were unable to remember important events. It is likely that most people selectively forget events that are inconsistent with their personal views: a depressed person may remember the "bad" things that happened and the "failures" in life; angry persons may remember the "injustices" they experienced; optimistic persons may remember the "successes" in their lives; and so on. Not surprisingly, no clear patterns have been found in age differences for the memory of personal events (Rybash, Hoyer & Roodin, 1986, p.97).

Methodological problems make it impossible to reach any conclusions about the influence of age on "old" memories. The decline in the ability to remember specific facts is probably a result of both the age of the memory and the age of the respondent and it is impossible to separate these effects (Salthouse, 1982). For example, one study found that high school graduates (aged 17 to 74) were able to recognize names and faces of classmates in yearbook pictures at consistently high levels up to 15 years after graduation; even up to 48 years after graduation, a surprisingly high percentage could recall names when shown the pictures, but it was much lower than for younger samples — 60 percent compared with 90 percent (Bahrick, Bahrick & Wittlinger, 1975). Another study found that middle-aged persons had better memory of songs than older adults, despite the fact that some of the songs had been popular before the middle-aged sample was born (Bartlett & Snelus, 1980)!

Thus, we are left with the impression that "old" memories are an unreliable guide to the efficiency of memory processes in old persons. There is no reason to

One study found that 60 percent of the participants could recall the names of classmates in the school yearbook 48 years after graduation from high school.

think that long-term memory is either more or less affected by aging than other types of memory processes.

Everyday Memory and Expert Memory Skills

Margaret Mead (1970) once speculated that the reason humans have such a long life span compared with other mammals is that the memory old people maintained for coping with rare environmental crises — such as remembering where the tribe got water during the last period of severe drought — provided a survival advantage to groups that had long-living members. Certainly, memory was vital for passing on traditions and other dimensions of oral history before writing was invented and became widespread. Moreover, many of today's leaders in business, education, government, and religion are relatively old men and women. One can only be struck by the contrast between studies showing dramatic declines of memory in the laboratory (recall Figure 4.3) and the highly competent demonstrations of skilled memory by many older people (excluding, of course, those affected by Alzheimer's, cerebrovascular, or other diseases). Clearly, psychology needs to focus attention also on everyday memory performance — not just on memory experiments in the laboratory.

Sinnott (1986) noted that *motivation* to remember may be especially important. An older person may find the task less interesting than a younger person, or feel that it is not worth the expenditure of a more limited store of energy to remember the task. It is not a simple matter of "ecological validity" — a city map may be no more interesting than a string of digits for an older person. She suggested that memory for relevant information when the person is actually trying to accomplish an activity or to reach a goal may be nearly as good, or even better, among older persons as among younger persons. For example, Poon and Schaffer (1982) found that older adults (mean age 73) remembered to make telephone calls at specified times more often than younger adults (mean age 25) and they called closer to the specified time than the younger adults. Sinnott (1984a, 1986) provided additional support for this idea, finding that memory for "incidental" items was lower for older persons, but that age was not related to memory for "prospective/intentional" items. **Prospective memory** involves those situations where one is remembering something in order to reach a goal or to accomplish an activity that requires planning. *Incidental memory* is not related to planned action or to experiences that focused the attention of the participant, such as remembering the articles present in a room where the testing took place. She concluded:

> Selecting to remember salient, contextually meaningful information rather than less meaningful information may be a compensatory mechanism useful in older age. . . . It might be expected that as memory abilities decline, strategies change within the overall information-processing system. . . . The person (and frequently an old person) with limited memory ability may choose to use that ability to keep his or her commitments as a social being, above all. . . . It makes sense that busy, functioning adults of all ages usually do remember meaningful events that they need to remember in order to get through life. By contrast, they remember less often details that have little meaning or utility to them. (Sinnott, 1986, p. 114)

Rybash, Hoyer, and Roodin (1986) reached a similar conclusion in their review of research on memory and aging.

> Older adults frequently exhibit a reduced speed and efficiency in information *processing* and in the mechanics of cognition, but such age-related losses may not interfere with cognitive effectiveness in real-world contexts. (p. 99)

Moreover, some adults become *expert* in a particular area and are able to perform at higher levels in old age than young adults who are not experts in that area. For example, studies of chess experts (Charness, 1988) and physicians (Elstein, Shulman & Sprafka, 1978; Kuipers & Kassirer, 1984) suggested that their use of memory tends to be different from that of novices. *Expert memory* appears to be more intuitive, less bound by formal rules; it integrates information into a reservoir of experience; it is often rapid and efficient, and defies explanation to persons who are less expert (Rybash, Hoyer & Roodin, 1986, p. 111).

This type of expertise can be taught in specific memory tasks, so the person can perform at levels far above the ordinary untrained person. For example, Kliegl, Smith, and Baltes (1986) developed a scheme to teach persons to remember a list of digits by combining them into groups of three, adding an initial digit "1", and

Memory decline does not affect all old people, especially in areas of expertise.

associating the resulting number with a historical date. Thus, 492789945 becomes 492-789-945, and then 1492 (Columbus sails to America), 1789 (French Revolution), and 1945 (end of World War II). Each event then becomes associated with a particular landmark in their city, and the memory task then is transformed into an imaginary walk to each landmark in turn. Alternatively, each number can be changed into a consonant that sounds similar to the digit; pairs of digits can be turned into words by inserting vowels; the resulting words are then associated with places in the city. The three-digit method requires a maximum of 1000 historical dates; the two-digit method requires 100 words. In their laboratory, the best performance was achieved by a 69-year-old woman, who "after 13 practice trials of the History-Dates model and 38 sessions of memory training—is able to recall strings of 120 digits . . . presented once at a fixed rate of eight seconds per digit. Note that presentation of such a long digit string takes 16 minutes" (Kliegl, Smith & Baltes, 1986, p. 402). It is unclear, however, whether this type of strategy can increase short-term memory capacity for other kinds of memories, or whether it only enhances the efficiency of memory for the specific task.

Conclusion

Older people often say that they have more difficulty remembering things than they did when they were younger. A frequent complaint of older persons is that they were in the middle of a task and left to get something, but forgot what it was they were about to do, and have to return to the task to remember it. For example, if they are repairing something and put down the hammer to go get a tube of glue, when they get to the kitchen they forgot what they wanted to get (glue) and have to go back and then hunt for the hammer, and only then remember the glue.

The noted psychologist B. F. Skinner described his own experience of memory changes with aging in a good-humored and practical book titled *Enjoy Old Age*. A sample of his comments and suggestions provides concrete illustrations of the everyday memory problems that some older people experience.

Ten minutes before you leave your house for the day you hear a weather report: it will probably rain before you return. It occurs to you to take an umbrella. (The sentence means exactly what it says: the act of taking an umbrella occurs to you.) But you are not yet ready to execute it, and ten minutes later you leave without the umbrella. You can solve that kind of problem by doing as much as possible at the moment the act occurs to you. Hang the umbrella on the doorknob, or put it through the handle of your bag or briefcase, or in some other way start the process of taking it with you. (Skinner & Vaughan, 1983, pp. 55–56)

Proper names are especially easy to forget, and it is especially obvious that you have forgotten them. . . .

Failure to recall a name in making an introduction is embarrassing, and the embarrassment is part of the problem. (p. 51)

If you know in advance that you are going to have to call people by name, you can improve your chances of doing so in various ways. Before taking a friend to a club meeting, for example, review the names you will need by reading a list of the members. Or start recalling the names of people you see as soon as you arrive, before introductions must be made. . . .

Another useful strategy is to give your own name as you extend your hand to someone you have not seen for a long time. This is an act of courtesy, and you may be rewarded by having the courtesy returned. (pp. 52–53)

"Where are my glasses?" "Where are the extra keys to the car?" There are a thousand places where you may have put them, and they will be all the harder to find if you cannot see as well as you used to. You need your glasses to find your glasses, and even when wearing them you will have trouble spotting the keys. Your fingers, too, reaching into a dark space, will not recognize objects as quickly as they once did. Learn your lesson from blind people: the only solution is "a place for everything and everything in its place." (pp. 58–59)

Young people also forget, and if they develop corrective strategies while still young, they will have taken a big step toward an enjoyable old age. (p. 61)

In the next two sections we examine other important aspects of cognitive functioning that involve information processing: intelligence and wisdom.

Intelligence and Aging

Intelligence may be thought of as a characteristic of an individual that affects the ability to solve problems. It involves information encoding, cognitive processing, memory, and communicating the solution of the problem. Piaget's study of cognitive development focused on the ways in which intelligence, measured by tests of logical thinking ability, differed between individuals of differing ages, and the process by which it developed from infancy to adulthood. A second approach involves a focus on an individual's relative amount of intellectual ability, compared with other persons of the same age — for example, as measured by an IQ test. A third approach considers the person's ability to solve the kind of problems one typically encounters in daily life, such as getting the landlord to make expensive repairs that one wants done.

Obviously, the way in which intelligence is defined determines the type of measures that are used to measure it. In the first section of this chapter, we described formal and postformal operations, which may be considered to be styles of intelligence. We noted that they differ between individuals and across situations, and may develop toward greater intellectual power to solve problems during adulthood. That view is both an idealized and optimistic conception of intelligence in adulthood. Although it is likely that some people develop greater and greater skills in solving certain types of problems in which they are expert, it is not likely that most people develop increased ability to solve all types of problems as they grow older. Moreover, as we discussed earlier in this chapter, there is too little information available to reach any firm conclusions about this conception of intelligence and its changes with aging.

In contrast, a great amount of data has been collected about the second conception of intelligence — the relative amount of intellectual ability — which may be called *psychometric* measures of intelligence. As noted briefly in Chapter 1, various forms of intelligence tests have been given to persons of differing ages, or to the same individuals as they grew older, and the results are very difficult to interpret. If

The meaning of wisdom or intelligence may differ during young, middle, and late adulthood; it also differs among various cultures.

the scores decline with advancing age, it may reflect: (1) age-biased instruments; (2) slower processing speed; (3) lower motivation to pay attention to trivial questions; (4) greater length of time since formal schooling ended; or (5) more interest in the context and meaning of the problem than in a "textbook" answer. Also, as noted in Chapter 1, cross-sectional studies are likely to show declines in psychometric intelligence because of *cohort* factors.

If the scores increase with advancing age, then we must consider *selective dropout* effects in which the older samples are more selective than the younger samples—especially in longitudinal studies—but also when only a select portion of the older population is included, such as "healthy" or "college-educated" persons. Even in the general population, since all samples of older persons are, by definition, survivors, it is not possible to be certain whether some bias has been introduced into the sample as a result of less intelligent persons dying earlier, or being unwilling to participate.

One general pattern in studies of psychometric intelligence is that some abilities decrease with age during adulthood; these are called **fluid intelligence** and consist of skills such as seeing relationships among stimulus patterns, drawing inferences from relationships, and comprehending implications (Horn, 1982, p. 850). Fluid intelligence is thought to reflect cognitive processes and to be highly dependent on the speed of processing (Dittmann-Kohli & Baltes, in press). These data have been widely reported and are generally accepted. Age-related neurological change, or injury and disease, may be the cause of much of the change (Horn, 1982, p. 853). Schaie (1987) reported preliminary data suggesting that these fluid abilities may be strongly associated with the ability to perform everyday activities. It is important to note these age-related declines in intellectual functioning and to study the changes in "the aging brain" so that the precise causes can be discovered; this may lead to interventions that can reduce the declines (Jarvik, 1988).

Another general pattern is that some intellectual abilities do not decline, or may increase with age. Horn (1970, 1982) called these **crystallized intelligence** and suggested that the cumulative effects of experience may be responsible for this pattern (Horn & Donaldson, 1976).

> This form of intelligence is indicated by a very large number of performances indicating breadth of knowledge and experience, sophistication, comprehension of communications, judgment, understanding conventions, and reasonable thinking . . . such as verbal comprehension, concept formation, logical reasoning, and general reasoning. (Horn, 1982, p. 850)

Dittmann-Kohli and Baltes (in press) call these abilities **synthesized intelligence;** this term refers to contextual and knowledge-based intelligence, emphasizes problem-solving strategies, and reflects the ability to deal with complex and important life tasks. It is based on the basic cognitive skills developed earlier in life (i.e. fluid intelligence), but is an active transformation of those skills through the acquisition of cultural and individual knowledge. As such it is not "crystallized," but rather it is synthesized in a dynamic ongoing fashion. Moreover, they argued that it is of no less importance than fluid intelligence. Thus, Dittmann-Kohli and Baltes suggested a "dual-process" model of adult intelligence that gives equal significance to fluid and synthesized intelligence. For example, synthesized intelligence provides the "potential for problem-solving dealing with important (existential) aspects of real-life situations which must be confronted after decades or even throughout adult life. . . . In contrast, fluid abilities involve solving clearly limited, decontextualized problems with clear-cut answers" (Dittmann-Kohli & Baltes, in press).

To summarize, the concept of intelligence is complex and has been studied in many different ways. The psychometric approach to measuring "how much" intelligence a person displays may be characterized by four general conclusions (Dittmann-Kohli & Baltes, in press; Willis & Baltes, 1980):

1. *Intelligence is multidimensional.* It consists of a multitude of differing abilities. For example, in the theory of Horn and Cattell (1967), crystallized intelligence refers to knowledge such as the definition of vocabulary words or general informational questions; this dimension may continue to increase up to late adulthood. In contrast, fluid intelligence refers to a type of intelligence that is defined as: "relatively independent of any systematic educational or accultura-

tion experiences and that increases through adolescence and then declines in middle and later adulthood" (Rebok, 1987, p. 536).

2. *Multidirectionality of age trends.* These intellectual abilities follow varying age trends. As noted above, some increase whereas others decline.

3. *Interindividual variability.* Individuals differ in both the level and the pattern of their intellectual abilities. This means that some persons decline in measures of intellectual abilities as early as their forties or fifties; others show no change, and others increase in intellectual abilities into the seventies or eighties (Schaie, 1979). One possible factor in this variability from one individual to another is that scores may decline a few months before death; see the discussion of "terminal decline" in Chapter 10.

4. *Intraindividual plasticity.* Intellectual abilities differ in the extent to which they can be modified by attempts to improve performance. Although there is clear evidence that intellectual abilities are stable over many years for the same individuals (Hertzog & Schaie, 1986), there is also evidence that scores on some abilities can be increased by training for a substantial number of older adults (Schaie & Willis, 1986).

Age Changes in Intelligence: Seattle Longitudinal Study

Beginning in 1956, K. Warner Schaie and his associates have studied the intellectual performance of participants in a Seattle, Washington, health maintenance organization (HMO). The research strategy was carefully designed as a sequential study, as described in Chapter 1. At seven-year intervals a new cross-sectional sample was drawn from the same population, and all previously tested participants were invited to be retested. Thus, the design is a multiple-cohort longitudinal sequence (Baltes, Reese & Nesselrode, 1977). The study used five scales from the Primary Mental Abilities (PMA) test developed by Thurstone and Thurstone (1949). They are described as follows:

1. *Verbal meaning* — the ability to recognize vocabulary words.

2. *Space* — a test of spatial orientation requiring visualization of objects in a two-dimensional plane, and the ability to rotate the orientation (as in visualizing one's place on a map and determining which direction is which).

3. *Reasoning* — requires recognition of patterns of letter sequences and extrapolating from the pattern to add additional letters.

4. *Number* — accuracy and speed in performing simple two-column addition problems.

5. *Word fluency* — ability to retrieve words from memory according to an arbitrary syntactic rule (Hertzog & Schaie, 1986, p. 161).

Figure 4.4 shows these five scales at two of the testing points, 1963 and 1970. Similar findings were reported for earlier (Schaie & Strother, 1968) and later comparisons (Schaie, 1983). Note first the general decline in each solid line, representing cross-sectional data. Recall that *cohort* factors are likely to affect

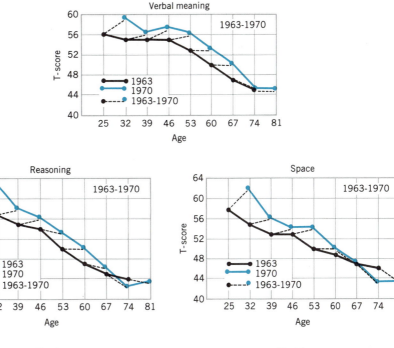

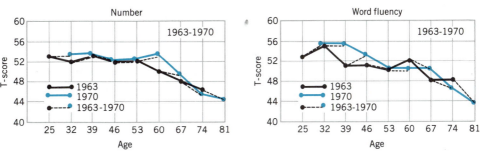

FIGURE 4.4 Comparison of cross-sectional with longitudinal gradients (dotted lines) in Schaie's cohort-sequential research on adult intelligence. (From "Generational versus Ontogenetic Components of Change in Adult Cognitive Behavior: A Fourteen-Year Cross-Sequential Study" by K. W. Schaie and G. Labouvie-Vief. *Developmental Psychology*, 1974, *10*, 305–320. © 1974 American Psychological Association. Reprinted with permission.)

cross-sectional data; these are shown by two points at the same chronological age. The data analysis indicated that these cohort effects equaled or exceeded the age differences, up to ages 60 – 70 (Schaie & Parham, 1977). These data also reflect the specific historic period in which they were collected, and the cohort effects were seldom linear — that is, could be described by a simple straight line (Schaie, 1979).

Next, note the frequent increase, or stability, of the dotted lines, which represent the average scores for the same individuals seven years later (in 1963 and 1970). No significant decline in performance was found before the late sixties. Of course, as noted in Chapter 1, longitudinal studies tend to become less representative of the original population as the study progresses because some respondents do not return for testing at later points. In this study, the longitudinal sample differed somewhat from the new comparison sample that was recruited for each age group. That is, the longitudinal sample "appears more representative of a stable population of healthy, well-educated, middle-class individuals, whereas the independent sample appears to be more representative of less well-educated, lower-middle-class populations" (Willis & Baltes, 1980, p. 263).

Botwinick (1977) reviewed these data as well as other research and concluded that, although longitudinal studies show more stability and cross-sectional studies show more decline in intelligence with age, when cohort factors and selective dropout effects are considered, a pattern described as the "classic aging pattern" of IQ test performance is found. This pattern consists of a decline on tests that measure *performance* aspects of intelligence, and little or no change with age on tests that measure *verbal* abilities before ages 50–60. This is similar to the findings discussed earlier regarding "fluid" and "crystallized" intelligence. "Performance" scores are based on those tests in which the person is asked, for example, to demonstrate psychomotor skill by filling in symbols that correspond to numbers or to perform perceptual integrative tasks. Slowing of the rate of information processing, which is associated with aging, would affect scores on this kind of test. "Verbal" scores are based on tests such as defining a series of words, solving arithmetic story problems, or determining elements that objects have in common.

The issue that emerges is whether these declines are important. Put another way: Is the question of whether intelligence declines with age the most useful one to pose (Labouvie-Vief, 1985)? Three points need to be addressed: (1) How much difference in real-life functioning does a difference on these tests make? (2) Do people compensate for declines in areas of expertise so that they perform as well or better than persons who are younger? (3) Do adult styles of thinking, of the sort suggested in the first section of this chapter, play a role in producing *both* the decline, especially in fluid intelligence, and the characteristic that one could describe as wisdom?

How Much Difference Does a Difference Make?

Schaie (1988) pointed out that the actual change in measures of processing rate and other aspects of cognitive and intellectual functioning is very small. They may be statistically significant changes, but their practical importance is debatable. Moreover, *average* changes do not reflect the important aspects of interindividual variability. Although the average score for the group may show a statistically significant decline with age, the individual's score may show no decline, or even an improvement. This point is especially important in terms of employment criteria. For example, individual performance would be a better measure than chronological age of ability to continue working or to perform other complex tasks.

Rybash, Hoyer, and Roodin (1986) made a similar point from a different perspective:

It seems as if many assessments of fluid intelligence are artificial, because they do not take into account the actual contexts in which adults think. Thus, the significance of the robust finding that fluid mental abilities decline may *not* be that intelligence declines, but that with age much of everyday cognitive performance depends . . . increasingly more on contextual and domain-related factors. (p. 103)

By "domain-related" factors, Rybash, Hoyer, and Roodin refer to those areas of knowledge and performance that make up a coherent *domain* of skill; music, developmental psychology, politics, chess, or bowling are examples of plausible domains. We expand on this point in the next section.

Expertise and Encapsulation

Earlier we mentioned a study of expert typists by Salthouse (1984). He conducted this complex study to assess the characteristics of skilled typing performance among expert secretaries and to determine whether the skills and performance differed between younger and older expert typists. Using a computer to display and record characters, experienced typists who ranged in age from 19 to 72 years were instructed to type material in a variety of different tasks. In one task they were asked to press the leftmost or the rightmost keys on one row of the keyboard when the letter "L" or "R" appeared on the screen, respectively; this was called a choice RT (reaction time) test. In another task they were to use the right and left index fingers and alternately tap the "f" and "j" keys as rapidly as possible for 15 seconds. In a second study, they were also asked to tap a finger as rapidly as possible for 15 seconds. As shown in Figure 4.5, there is a clear difference between the speed with which the typists performed the choice reaction time task and normal typing. In

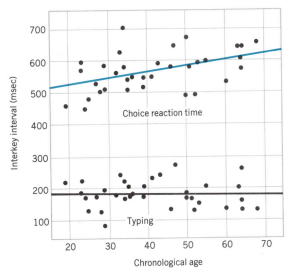

FIGURE 4.5 Median interkey interval in milliseconds for the normal typing and choice reaction time tasks as a function of typist age. Each point represents a single typist, and the solid lines illustrate the regression equations relating interkey interval to age. (*Source*: Salthouse (1984), p. 354. © American Psychological Association. Reprinted with permission.)

addition, the choice reaction time measure increases (thus, reaction time slows) with age, but the rate of typing remains stable. Similar findings were obtained in both studies.

To discover why older typists were able to type as rapidly as younger typists, although they had slower reaction time, Salthouse noted that when typists were allowed to see fewer than seven characters in advance of their keystroke (called the eye–hand span), the typing rate was much slower. In general, the greater the skill in typing, the greater the eye–hand span between the keystroke and the characters on the screen. Moreover, the older typists typically had a greater eye–hand span so that, on average, typists in their sixties had about 300 additional milliseconds of preparation time between seeing the letter and making the keystroke compared with typists in their twenties (Salthouse, 1984, p. 356).

As might be expected, older typists also were slower in the tapping tests, and there were other age-related changes that indicated the older typists were slower in those ways we would expect older subjects to show declines in speed. However, their typing speed was not affected. Apparently they compensated for their slower reaction time by giving themselves more time by looking farther ahead when they typed (the eye–hand span). "A dramatic discrepancy therefore clearly exists between the results of traditional laboratory tasks and the performance of the real-life activity of typing" (p. 369).

Rybash, Hoyer, and Roodin (1986) proposed that this process of compensating through expertise for age-related declines in intellectual or cognitive functioning is a general phenomenon. It is, in their view, an explanation of the fact that older people continue to perform competently in those areas where they have developed relatively high levels of expertise. Their model suggests that "knowledge becomes increasingly expert during the adult years" (p. 108), by which they mean that it becomes more "intuitive," "automatized," and specific to the particular "domain" of the knowledge. Skill in these areas of **expertise** is based more on the organization of information in long-term memory than on measures of logical thinking or general problem solving (p. 112). Comparing chess experts with novices, for example, they noted that experts could recall the positions of a larger number of chess pieces after viewing the arrangement for 5 seconds, focused less on exploring poor moves, spent more time considering good moves, and generally could recall more specialized information. They cited similar differences between experts and novices in the domains of bridge, computer programming, music, and physics.

This reasoning led Rybash, Hoyer, and Roodin (1986) to propose a model of adult cognition that they termed **encapsulation.** The basic idea is that *processes* of cognition (such as attention, memory, and reasoning) become linked with the *products* of cognition (such as knowledge within a specific domain). As a result of this linkage, or encapsulation, performance in the domain of expertise is relatively unrelated to declines in fluid intelligence or in processing rate because the knowledge base compensates, or enhances, the performance. Thus, expert typists, or experts in any domain, have the ability to draw upon their expertise to offset modest age-related declines. Therefore, they can perform as well as younger experts, and better than younger novices.

Given the tenets of the Encapsulation Model, it is futile to continue to examine the cognitive performance of older adults via a singular assessment of their fluid or unencapsulated mental abilities. Assessments of cognitive functioning should emphasize the forms of *knowing* and the style of *thinking* that a person uses to create and resolve the problems of everyday life. The frequently reported age-related declines in fluid abilities may, to a large extent, be due to the practice of assessing mental processes apart from the domains in which they have become encapsulated. (Rybash, Hoyer & Roodin, 1986, p. 122)

In a similar vein, Labouvie-Vief (1985) argued that most research on adult intelligence and cognition has focused on variables that have been used to study young persons and that emphasize the acquisition of new information and adaptation to new situations. In contrast, adult intelligence needs to be redefined within the context of successful application of one's experience to ambiguous situations. Likewise, Sternberg and Berg (1987) compared the importance of various behaviors individuals felt was important in defining intelligent individuals at differing ages. They found that greater emphasis was given to novelty in solving problems for young adults, and to competence in everyday intellectual abilities at older ages. This latter dimension included: "displays wisdom in action and thoughts"; "is perceptive about people and things"; and "thinks before acting or speaking" (pp. 17–18).

These views of intelligence in older adults suggest the potential development of a style of thinking that may be termed wisdom, which is the topic of the final section of this chapter.

Wisdom

In traditional societies where the elders hold power and receive respect because of their age, the "wisdom" of older adults may be regarded as a natural sign of their survival and of the nearness to the spirit world they will soon enter. Conversely, in youth-oriented societies, the "wisdom" of older adults may be regarded as "old-fashioned," "feudalistic," or otherwise irrelevant to modern life (Gutmann, 1977, p. 314; 1987, p. 238). If we are to consider wisdom as an aspect of adult intelligence, we must avoid both of these myths. We should examine *wisdom* as if it were on the same order of neutral terminology as *fluid intelligence*. Current thinking, in fact, suggests that wisdom may play a role in later adulthood similar to that played by fluid intelligence in earlier life.

Clayton (1982) defined **wisdom** and differentiated between wisdom and intelligence. In her view, "Intelligence is defined as the ability that allows the individual to think logically, to conceptualize, and to abstract from reality." Wisdom, in contrast, is "the ability that enables the individual to grasp human nature, which operates on the principles of contradiction, paradox, and change" (p. 316). She suggested that intelligence refers to areas that are essentially nonsocial and impersonal, whereas wisdom deals with topics that are social, those that involve self-knowledge, and interpersonal issues (p. 317).

Moreover, Clayton and Birren (1980) suggested that conceptions of wisdom differ between Eastern and Western philosophies. Although both views stress knowledge that focuses on understanding the meaning of life, God, and the relation of human life to the universe, the Western approach emphasizes the role of intellect and reason; Eastern approaches view the wise person as one who has direct experiential knowledge of the meaning of life.

Western psychology and research on cognitive development have only recently begun to focus on wisdom as a characteristic that may be relevant to understanding adult intelligence. In an exploratory study of conceptions of wisdom among a sample of well-educated professionals in the United States, Clayton and Birren (1980) found that it was seen as multidimensional, representing an integration of affective, cognitive, and reflective qualities such as introspection, intuition, understanding, empathy, peacefulness, and gentleness. Also, the older respondents saw the qualities of empathy and understanding as more identified with wisdom than chronological age, per se; they also perceived *less* connection between wisdom and old age than either the younger or middle-aged respondents (pp. 118–119). Likewise, older respondents saw themselves as neither more nor less "wise" than younger respondents (p. 130).

Another systematic analysis of wisdom as a possible form of progressive intellectual growth during adulthood was provided by Dittmann-Kohli and Baltes (in press). They suggested a useful working definition of *wisdom:*

> In general, we view wisdom as an individual's ability to exercise good judgment about important but uncertain matters of life. It is a highly developed aspect of synthesized intelligence in a particular domain accessible to everybody, i.e., human life and the conditions of existence. (p. 25)

They proposed five aspects that constitute wisdom as an ability or as perspectives that are related to wisdom:

1. Wise persons are judged by others to demonstrate good judgment and are sought out as advisors in particular areas of their expertise.

2. Problems and crisis situations in major life events and those that have lifelong significance for human existence are likely to call for wisdom. Wise persons are able to identify important dimensions, alternatives, and solutions using an integration of affective, cognitive, and reflective skills.

3. Wisdom demands a contextual perspective for the definition and solution of the problem. It involves a focus on the ecological, social, and human relevance of the problem.

4. Uncertainty, ambiguity, and complexity of the problem are acknowledged; the issues are interdependent and not well defined.

5. Relativistic and reflective thinking are involved in recognizing variability among individuals and in accepting different steps toward a solution or different solutions to real-life problems.

These characteristics are similar to some of the ideas in the discussion of postformal thinking and in the discussion of synthesized intelligence earlier in this chapter. It should also be noted that these attributes are not necessarily restricted to older adults or to highly educated persons. Since the relevant domain of knowledge is human life, it is theoretically accessible to anyone. Moreover, the essence of "wise judgment" is likely to differ among cultures, social strata, and historical periods. Thus, the empirical study of wisdom may be very difficult because "its tasks do not have clear solutions and the problem definition itself is part of the task solution" (Dittmann-Kohli & Baltes, in press). Potentially useful approaches to the study of wisdom include social intelligence that focuses on interpersonal relationships and practical or everyday intelligence that emphasizes synthesized intelligence (rather than fluid intelligence).

Dittmann-Kohli and Baltes (in press) also distinguished between *practical wisdom* that focuses on personally relevant situations and *philosophical wisdom* that includes the meaning of life and the relationship of oneself and others with the universe. The former may apply to traditional psychological issues such as the midlife crisis (Chapter 3); the latter may be especially relevant to theological and philosophical issues that are difficult for psychology to grasp (e.g., death; see Chapter 10).

It is interesting to consider in this context the study by Blanchard-Fields (1986), described earlier in this chapter. The study involved reasoning on social dilemmas that might be seen as involving "practical wisdom." Recall that the adolescents performed less well than young and middle-aged adults on topics that were presumed to be emotionally salient to them (Figure 4.2, p. 168). Middle-aged adults performed at a higher level than the young adults on all the tasks. Could this reflect increased wisdom among the older persons?

Additional studies based on the perspective suggested by Dittmann-Kohli and Baltes will shift the discussion of wisdom from its present speculative position toward one that is based on, or refuted by, empirical data. For now, we can only describe this approach as a compelling perspective that is consistent with current thinking about adult cognition.

Conclusion

This chapter has sought a balance between two contrasting themes of adult cognition. On one hand, there are clear and important *declines* in reaction time, processing rate, and fluid intelligence. These declines occur at different ages for different individuals, but on the average they are age-related. The importance of these laboratory-experimental findings is probably not significant for daily life until very old age, or if the age-related changes are magnified by disease (e.g., Alzheimer's). The precise cause and exact nature of these changes are not known. Reduced speed and efficiency with which messages are transmitted through the nervous system, motivation to respond accurately (rather than quickly), and physical damage to components of the central nervous system are plausible explanations for these declines.

On the other hand, older persons are able to *compensate* for many of the declines that occur by adopting specific strategies (such as looking farther ahead when typing) or by drawing upon past experience (e.g., in a game of chess). An individual's memory, intelligence, and performance are especially likely to remain competent in areas or domains of expertise. Competent older persons can be trained in memory skills so that extraordinary feats of memory are possible.

Striking a balance between these two perspectives is very difficult when thinking about these issues. On one hand, one seeks to avoid promoting the stereotype that being old means being "senile" so there is a tendency to underemphasize the importance of cognitive declines in old age. This underemphasis, however, precludes continued research on the nature and cause of these declines; thus it is, itself, a manifestation of age bias, and could interfere with discovering ways to reverse the age-related changes (Jarvik, 1988). On the other hand, one also seeks to avoid a "rosy" distortion of aging, because that perpetuates the opposite stereotype — of the wise, highly experienced sage. This positive age bias is the danger in an overemphasis on wisdom or on the postformal operations perspective.

In fact, most older people are neither "senile" nor "sages"; they are a very diverse group of people seeking to maintain a variety of competent skills and behaviors in various intellectual, artistic, social, and personal domains of their lives. This occurs often in spite of some degree of physical disease (e.g., arthritis, hypertension), chronic conditions (e.g., needing bifocal glasses or a hearing aid), and personal-social losses (e.g., retired from work, children away, widowed). The importance of reduced intellectual stimulation, social interaction, and physical exercise on cognitive function also cannot be ignored. We discuss these various influences — which by no means affect all old persons, or affect all persons the same ways — in later chapters.

Chapter Summary

1. Cognitive processes include paying attention to particular stimuli, recalling previous experiences from memory, solving problems, and understanding the physical and social world, including oneself. The individual is an active participant in these mental activities, not a passive organism.

2. Five major characteristics mark the difference between the thinking of adolescents and younger children: thinking about possibilities, thinking through hypotheses, planning in advance, thinking about thinking, and thinking beyond old limits such as questioning politics, religious beliefs, moral issues, and personal relationships.

3. Problem finding may be a characteristic of postformal cognitive development that is reached by some creative or inventive people who have developed formal operations. It involves creative thought with respect to discovering problems, formulating problems, raising questions about poorly defined problems, and the process of cognitive thinking reflected in significant scientific inquiry.

4. Relativistic thinking is a set of information-processing skills that are involved in analyzing complex interpersonal relationships; they involve subjectivity and self-reference and call attention to emotions, feelings, and interpersonal interactions. This style of thinking is complex, but does not require more advanced logic than formal operations.

5. Dialectical thinking focuses on the conflict between interacting forces that are always changing. It emphasizes the conflict between an idea (thesis) and its opposite (antithesis). The resolution of the conflict (synthesis) is always temporary because the interacting forces are constantly changing. Dialectical thinking may be a form of postformal thinking.

6. Information processing can be defined as the perception, understanding, reaction, and response to a stimulus. Two aspects of information processing are related to age: slowing in response time and memory—the learning, storage, and retrieval of information.

7. The slowing in information-processing speed with aging is not very great in practical terms. When complex or unexpected circumstances are encountered, however, this slowing of reaction time may be important. In ordinary circumstances, an individual can often compensate for the slower processing speed and perform as well as a younger person, especially if one is an expert in a particular skill.

8. There are three approximately equal contributing sources for the slowing of reaction time on tasks involving memory: delay in encoding information, size of the memory set to be learned, and the speed–accuracy trade-off—emphasizing accurate responses more than fast responses. Input–output processes, rather than memory search rate, seem to account for the largest decrements in response performance related to age.

9. The decline in the ability to remember specific facts is probably a result of both the age of the memory and the age of the respondent. In general, "old" memories are an unreliable guide to the efficiency of memory processes in old persons. There is no reason to think that long-term memory is either more or less affected by aging than other types of memory processes.

10. Highly competent demonstrations of skilled memory are shown by many older people. In everyday memory performance, motivation to remember—to reach a goal or to accomplish an activity that requires planning—improves memory performance. Expert memory performance involves information integrated within a reservoir of experience; it can be taught in specific memory tasks.

11. Various forms of intelligence tests have been given to persons of differing ages, or to the same individuals at different ages; but the results are very difficult to interpret. One general pattern is that some abilities decrease with age during adulthood; these are called fluid intelligence. Some intellectual abilities do not decline, or may increase with age; these are called crystallized intelligence, or synthesized intelligence.

12. Individuals differ in both the level and the pattern of their intellectual abilities. This means that some persons decline in measures of intellectual abilities as early as their forties or fifties; others show no change; and others increase in intellectual abilities into the seventies or eighties. Scores on some abilities can be increased by training for a substantial number of older adults.

13. In the Seattle longitudinal study of mental abilities, which used a sequential research design, cohort effects equaled or exceeded the age differences, up to ages 60–70, similar to the example reported in Chapter 1. No significant decline in

performance was found before the late sixties in this relatively stable, middle-class, well-educated sample.

14. On a measure of cognitive functioning, the average score for a group may show a statistically significant decline with age, but an individual's score may show no decline, or even an improvement. Therefore, individual performance is a better measure than chronological age of ability to continue working or to perform other complex tasks.

15. Older people continue to perform competently in those areas where they have developed relatively high levels of expertise. Skill in these areas of expertise is based more on the organization of information in long-term memory than on measures of logical thinking or general problem solving. This process is termed encapsulation.

16. Wisdom may be seen as representing an integration of affective, cognitive, and reflective qualities such as introspection, intuition, understanding, empathy, peacefulness, and gentleness. It involves an individual's ability to exercise good judgment about important but uncertain matters of life. Since the relevant domain of knowledge is human life, it is theoretically accessible to anyone.

17. The importance of declines in reaction time, processing rate, and fluid intelligence is probably not significant for daily life until very old age, or if the age-related changes are magnified by disease (e.g., Alzheimer's). Older persons are able to compensate for many of the declines that occur by adopting specific strategies or by drawing upon past experience.

Key Words

cognition	memory
contextualism	metacognition
crystallized intelligence	operation
dialectical thinking	postformal operations
encapsulation	problem finding
event related potentials (ERP)	prospective memory
expertise	relativistic thinking
fluid intelligence	speed–accuracy trade-off
formal operations	speed of response
information processing	synthesized intelligence
intelligence	wisdom

Review Questions

Cognitive Development in Adulthood

1. Define the term operation. How do concrete and formal operations differ, according to Piaget's theory? Give an example.

2. Some young adults do not show formal operations on Piaget's tasks. Why do you think this happens?

3. Do you see a link between historical events, such as the Civil Rights movement, and the subsequent emphasis on contextualism in developmental psychology?

4. What is the difference between the problem-solving stage (formal operations) and problem finding?

5. Why is relativistic thinking a link between laboratory research on cognitive processes and everyday problem solving?

6. Give an example of dialectical analysis.

Information Processing and Aging

7. What did the study by Birren and colleagues of healthy older men conclude about the effect of aging in the absence of disease?

8. What are three explanations of the cause for the age-related slowing of response speed? What is the relative contribution of each to slower access to memory with age?

9. Why are "old" memories an unreliable indication of the efficiency of memory processes in an old person?

10. Give an example of each: everyday memory, prospective memory, incidental memory, expert memory.

11. Why does reduced speed and efficiency in information processing not interfere with some types of everyday memory?

12. What memory aids do you use to reduce forgetting?

Intelligence and Aging

13. Why are results of intelligence tests for people of varying ages very difficult to interpret?

14. How do fluid intelligence, crystallized intelligence, and synthesized intelligence differ? How does each change with age?

15. What explanation does Salthouse give for older expert typists performing as well as younger expert typists?

16. Do you think that "intelligence" means something different for younger people than for older people? What is the difference?

Wisdom

17. What is the difference between intelligence and wisdom?

18. How do "wise judgment," "practical wisdom," and "philosophical wisdom" differ?

Conclusion

19. Describe the two contrasting themes that need to be balanced in understanding changes in cognition during adulthood and aging.

Murray, AGE 48

> The serious problems in life . . . are never fully solved. If ever they should appear to be so it is a sure sign that something has been lost. The meaning and purpose of a problem seem to lie not in its solution but in our working at it incessantly. (Jung, 1933/1971, p. 11.)

Murray was a 48-year-old successful vice-president in a large organization at the time of this interview. As he quickly points out, he has just published a book, teaches in a university, and lectures around the country. He is a man of many abilities and much energy; yet there is a sense in which he feels insecure and unfulfilled. Although George said it explicitly and Theresa implied it, Murray seems to be the person who is most clearly working at a problem that perhaps will never be fully solved. He has had serious problems with his marriage, problems with his son, and leaves the impression of having escaped into his work where he feels confident and secure, yet also strangely vulnerable.

Several intriguing questions are raised by this case example. How satisfied is he (actually) in his job? Why does the need for security remain so important? What is happening in his relationship with his son? Why did so many turning points occur when he was 28 (a major milestone for him)? How did his work life become so separate from the rest or his life? Are his future goals and plans for retirement realistic, or are they typical for a middle-aged person? Is he leaving his mark (in Erikson's sense of generativity)? Are his feelings about death realistic, or is the thought rather frightening to him? Why?

What are some of the milestones in your life? As you look back over it, what are some of the events that stand out? Let me start from the present and go backwards. I wrote a book which came out last week. That probably is one of the most important things that's happened to me in my life. Going back from there, I was given an award this last year for outstanding contributions to literature in my field. That was an important milestone; one coming on top of the other. Over the last five years, I have been the president of _____. That was a milestone. One of the more important things that happened to me was finally getting the recognition in the company and becoming vice-president. That's a milestone for several reasons. I'll never forget that day, when the board passed on that. *Was it celebrated in some way, that event?* Yes, it was celebrated. My wife and I celebrated it. It was celebrated with friends as well; it was important. It really didn't change my role in the company, but it meant something to me. I can't really document what it meant, because it didn't change my salary; it didn't change the respect I receive from my peers; it didn't change my national reputation or my business reputation, but it had some effect on me. I considered it quite a moment. I suppose these are the most important things in my work career.

My social life, my life as a husband and a father, has had many milestones, some good and some bad. I'm going through a very important trying time now. My son left college after two years, settled in Europe for a while, and is trying to get himself out of Casablanca today. My son is my only child, so a great deal of my life has been affected by my son. My life with my wife has had many milestones, most of them not happy ones; so, that is another area. There are pockets. The third pocket of my life is my academic life, which I find probably the most rewarding of all my pockets. I'm an associate professor at————College in the Graduate Program. This has been the unique part of my life, because it's almost without any relationship to superiors. It's a very independent kind of existence. I find my life very free in the school. Another part of my life, which is really tied into my academic life, is the lectures I give around the country, and that's probably—with the lectures in the classroom—the most rewarding of all my endeavors.

Let me go back a minute and pick up on some of these. You mentioned the book that you've just published. I had published 50 articles before that, and I started together with a young member of the faculty to get this book out and we got it out in a year's time. It's being well received, and it's a damn good book. I think basically the real rewards I get out of life are tied in to the recognition I get outside in the field. Inside it's a real fight. It's a very, very complicated environment. . . . . It's trying.

Probably the turning point of my life has been not to be an entrepreneur and work for a living. I love to live well, and I'm always tempted to parlay my success into something other than working for a living; but I do not do it. Probably because I'm a Depression child. And that's another part of my life, a milestone in my life, growing up as a young boy in the Depression years in more or less a limited-income family. I wouldn't say poverty, but a limited-income family. The second milestone in my life was the war, World War II, which was the first time I was away from home; and the constant knowledge that you might be killed. I got married when I was very young—21— right after I was discharged from the service. Another milestone was deciding that I didn't want to be an accountant after graduating as an accountant and starting a career in my present field. So these are the milestones; I never put them together.

What was it about the Depression that made that a milestone for you? Well, the struggle, to see my parents struggling, my father being out of work for almost two years; my mother having to work and be away. The whole era where . . . and it's very vivid . . . where small things were important. Where certainly no one ever thought of luxuries. I think while I was living through it I didn't realize how my parents were sheltering me from it. The impact was later. It became more obvious as I got more affluent. We talked about it and reflected upon the little things that were so important then, that are so unimportant now. I never, never took a train or a trolley to school. I walked to school and that was several miles. One would never spend a nickel to do that. That was no sacrifice. Based upon that experience during the Depression, I find money to be very important as a base of security, and I'm not willing to gamble with it. That's what I came out of the Depression with. *That's what you meant earlier when instead of an entrepreneur, you don't risk?* That's right. No risk. I have to know what's going to be ahead for me in the next year, and that's why the relationship, employee to employer, is more satisfactory in that area. The more interesting facet of that is that it's probably the most unsatisfactory part of my life, inasmuch as I have a hard time accepting the superiors who are not really my superior intellectually or otherwise. And I find that in order to exist you must suppress that feeling, and in an organization such as ours you deal with many powerful people. And you walk a tightrope.

Let me tell you something that just, you know, popped in and out of my head. I never had this feeling of desire for security until in the midst of my career there was a milestone. I was 28 years old. I had a fairly nice job, and I lost the job because the place was in deep financial trouble. At the very moment my wife gave birth to our first and only child after six years of marriage where both of us worked and made comfortable salaries we found ourselves —she not working—with the child; me not working with no savings, and I did not handle that situation well. I was out of work for eight weeks and it seemed like eight years. [I was] very frightened, extremely frightened. And that fear has really permeated the years subsequent to that. Up to that time I don't think I really thought about the Depression. I didn't think about security. I was happy-go-lucky. That changed my life, and that made me want to be in a very secure situation, and altered my later life. Now, 20 years later, where I have a national reputation, and I probably would have a job the day I was fired from this job or quit this job, that still gnaws at me. That has affected my ability to gamble, and yet I'm certainly not famous for my reserved attitude. I'm very outspoken, and that's a form of gambling. So, I don't know how you put it together. I haven't thought about it enough.

It sounds like there are some ways in which you are reserved in the sense of not taking financial risks, but other kinds of ways in which you really let it hang out. You're on an interesting point in this interview—many milestones all within the same week span—book coming out, my son on his way back from Europe, and I just decided to buy a country home. I've never been a homeowner. I've committed myself to a country home, an economic commitment I've never made in my life. I've been very cautious. For a man in my income level, as of this moment I have no, well, minor outstanding debt . . . minor. That's how cautious I am about that. And yet, I've taken that step. I thought that that's a major commitment, financial commitment. So, I don't know, that's certainly a milestone. *What brought about that shift in terms of buying a country home?* I suppose there are several things. One, I would like to have the comfort of a retreat like that. Two, I hope it will affect my son's desire to stay home,

rather than float around the world; it might be this country home which is a little remoter than living in the city would help that. Third, economically I feel that it is feasible, and that I've been too cautious, and fourth, I think it's a good investment. [Telephone rings; call about son's arriving flight from Casablanca.]

I gather that was about your son. Yeah. That has dominated much of my life in the last 20 years. *You mentioned him earlier as a milestone.* Oh yeah. *In what sense? Can you say more about him?* Our whole relationship, my wife's and mine, is built around a deep concern about our son and investment in our son, emotionally an investment, probably far beyond what a psychiatrist would permit as normal. It's not unusual. It's not unusual in a Jewish family, okay. It's not unusual with an only son, an only child, and it's not unusual based upon my wife's background, which was abject poverty, an orphan at 13; and not unusual since we were both planning on not having a family when we had a family, although we were married six years without one. So we are . . . our son has a great deal to do with our moods, and with our satisfactions. We're highly protective . . . so when I consider it a milestone, it is a very important part of my life. I define milestones as important parts . . . negative, positive, or anything that changes your life. I consider my son as something that has had a deep effect on my life. *I gather both positive and negative?* Yeah. Yeah, both.

Have there been some crisis points in that relationship? Very, very many. And crisis points in my marriage as well. Crisis points, which anyone who has had a 20-year-old son, of the same type—directionless kind of existence, under-achiever. I don't like the word, but basically what I'm saying is a lack of motivation . . . the drug scene . . . terrible crisis one time. We got a call from Canada that he was in jail; and going up there to get him out. *How did you feel about that?* I was . . . first of all, my wife almost cracked up. She's very . . . she gets very uptight. She's having a tough day today. She doesn't know . . . because he called us yesterday saying he couldn't get out of Casablanca and now we're hoping he's on one of these two planes. Ah, I felt the way I usually feel when there's a crisis with my son; I get very, very worried, but basically I attempt to handle it the same way I have success with handling my business life. I tend to get overpowering at that point with my wife, and that may be a mistake. I take charge, which I normally don't do. My wife is in charge in the house. My wife is in charge with my son. I quickly started the checklist and within hours I had a lawyer specializing in this, who I picked up at three in the morning; went down to the airport, had the tickets arranged, had several thousand dollars in cash in my pocket, got on the plane, got there; he got back on the plane with us within two hours. It's very interesting as I reflect back. I never was that kind of individual while my father was alive. And my relationship with my father was interesting. My father used to be an arranger. He was a bright guy but he wasn't an intelligent guy, and he was the arranger. And I did very well as a young man, everything was arranged. When I was in trouble, he would arrange things. I wasn't famous for being an arranger; in fact, most of my life 'til the last 10 years, I avoided problems. Now I've become an arranger. You asked me how I felt and I felt very troubled, deeply disturbed, but didn't get my mind off of what I had to do. I knew what I had to do. And nothing would stop me from doing it. Without a doubt, nothing would stop me, and it didn't stop me. *It sounds like a lot of the skills you use here on your job are relevant there.* Exactly. Exactly. That's the way I operate. It's successful in my job. I have not been successful in my marriage, so that . . . that's another area. At times I get too short-tempered about that kind of problem and I may operate too quickly, because basically I

tend to want to do it myself. *I'm getting a sense that you would like a lot more out of this relationship with your son than you're getting.* Oh, sure I would. Sure. But I think every father would. My son's not going to follow in my foot steps and that's good. I didn't want him to. And he's not going to do what I want him to do. I have to come to accept that. Certainly I have disappointments, but I have a lot of satisfactions. He's a brilliant boy. He's starting to challenge my own sense of intelligence and that I like. I would like to see him less concerned with the occult and more concerned with day-to-day happenings. I am not a father who is interested in seeing him join the establishment as it's defined, but in some ways . . . yes, compromise. I don't think he has a sense of compromise yet, but he's only 20. I not sure I had it. At 20 I was dodging bullets. *You were doing what?* Dodging bullets. It was a favorite pastime of my generation.

You fought in the Second War? Yeah, I was in the Navy. It wasn't really that bad. *But you indicated that it was one of the milestones for you.* Oh, yes . . . it was a milestone, being away from the protected environment very young, naive, traveling around the world for better or worse. That's certainly a milestone. And, wondering if your ship is going to get hit or not by a submarine. That's a milestone. Getting by it was a milestone also.

I think I changed the direction of my life, and I did it rather than having it done for me. I decided that I didn't want to go on to accounting. I went on to evening school to do my graduate work in education, which I thought I wanted to do, and then got involved in industry and decided that the   field was a good field, and just by making the decision got into the field, which is very interesting. That I did myself. I had no preparation for it, and made a career out of it, and reached the point where I am considered the dean of my field; so that was an important turn in my life. Much has come from that decision. *It took you several years to reach that decision?* Oh, yeah, I didn't know what I wanted to do. I was just floating around, doing the best I could, like most people do, until I was 28. You do the best you can. *That was the time when you lost the job?* Right. *And your son was born?* Yeah. *And you made the decision to get into your present field?* Right. And I did it. I was in industry for many years and moved into my present specialty. That's another milestone. It afforded me an opportunity to make out of myself what I am now. It was a burgeoning industry, as far as my field of specialty. That was a little fortuitous also. After being with a firm for a long time, I took a job in Illinois because I had that feeling from the last time of being out of work, and I didn't want to go through it again, so I took the first job that was offered to me, and it was offered to me before my last check, and I made sure that I was set. And I moved to Chicago and my wife didn't want to move there. And we had a very difficult six months. She insisted that we come back to New York and, fortuitously, there was a job opening at this company. It changed my whole life. That was not planned. It was still in my same field that I planned on staying in, but not in the same industry, and that changed everything. *It was almost accidental that you wound up in this position?* Oh, very, very much so. But in reviewing it, it wasn't accidental that I made out of it what it turned out to be. That was me. No one could take that away from me. I had come to the company knowing that they had very little here, and it was not very difficult for me to look like a genius by rediscovering the wheel. I'll be very, very frank about it. Here I am with a bag of tricks . . . really a great magician . . . coming into a situation where all the tricks were perfect, useful. That was magnificent . . . unbelievable! I don't know how many men get that opportunity in their lifetime. That was unbelievable! Before I knew it, there was an in-

dustry-wide problem and I was an industry spokesman, and from there on in it was all very easy, to the point where anything I wrote would be published. It was just great! Not very many people find themselves.

That didn't make me happy, though. . . . Satisfaction with your job and overall happiness with your life are usually two different departments. One may have an effect on the other. I have an extreme satisfaction . . . I *had* extreme satisfaction from my job, tremendous recognition. I did not have that kind of satisfaction from my life, in the main. I've come to grips with that in the last two years. I think I have more of an understanding of the satisfaction I've had in the past, but during that time my life was work oriented. This was my total satisfaction. Certainly not satisfaction in my social life.

So your personal life was very different, very much less satisfying? Yes. *What was happening there?* Marital problems that are not untypical of affluent, middle-class people who have some satisfaction in their life and tremendous exposure to a different world. *Exposure to a different world?* Yeah, rather than the limited world of your home and your neighborhood. Yeah, my wife is in a terrible disadvantage. Women's lib . . . there's a lot of nonsense in it, but there's a lot of meat, and the whole business of being tied down to the home, although I think that's also a choice a person makes. Geographic exposure . . . a man's a successful executive like myself who travels around and is exposed to the academic world, is exposed to a work area that's large and interesting, has so many more contacts and so many more opportunities for satisfaction and for exploration, that it's definitely a threat when the woman is not exposed to anything other than the family and the home. And that caused a great deal of difficulty in my marriage.

What was some of that difficulty about? Women. My exposure to many women, who happen to have the same drive I have. My feeling of lack of freedom, which has always been a pervasive feeling, that I was always tied down economically. You see that business from the Depression—although I didn't want to be tied down economically. I was frightened of economic responsibility. I always had it. So my hedge against it was a secure job, and yet innately what I wanted was freedom. I didn't want a secure job. I wanted to be able to not worry about economic pressures that most men do. When women's lib talks about exchanging roles with men, I wonder if they talk about or consider the economic pressures that are on most men in our society. Some real and some not real; but they are just as real if the person thinks the pressure is upon him. And most men do think that the economic pressure is upon them. *Were there other ways you felt tied down?* Oh, sure. I wanted to be a jet-setter. I always had that feeling of being able to enjoy, always wanting to enjoy. I suppose you kind of do that as a couple as well, so a lot of it is rationalization. An individual says he is tied down, but most people tie themselves down. I realized that a couple of years ago. It was not in my stars, but in myself that the problem lay. I'm coming to peace with myself on that.

Did you always feel this way in your marriage, or was there some point when it became a really definite feeling? When I was 28 and my son was born. That's probably the single most important milestone in my life. Because a lot turns on that. The feeling of the pressure of the responsibility of a child. My wife's own feeling about this. She was very, very hysterical about being a mother. Once it happened she became the ultra mother, the most mother. I suppose that was a guilt reaction, but all this happened then—the feeling of being tied in. That eight-week period of being unemployed had a tremendous . . . this

is where . . . see, look at the economic responsibility that's on my shoulders, that I didn't want. My parents shielded me from the economic responsibility during the whole Depression. This is a direct relationship, my feeling about the need for freedom. How did I define that? Was I talking about girls? Yes I was talking about girls. Was I talking about traveling? Yes, I was talking about traveling. But when you got to the core of it I was talking about no need to provide for anybody but myself. That's what I wanted when all this pressed in on me, and had an effect on me for a period of 10 years, 15 years. *What kind of an effect?* That I tended to run away from the responsibilities at home. And became more responsible on the job, but less responsible at home. That business that happened with my son was atypical. The pressure was on me, and I had to deal with it. Usually I walked away from those problems. Those were my wife's problems . . . taking care of my son.

How did she feel about this? Terrible. We had a terrible relationship. It culminated in our splitting up and going back together again. But it was all a function of my feeling of wanting less responsibility at home and more responsibilities at work. I never ran away from responsibilities at work. Figure that out. *So you did split up at one point.* Yeah. *How long ago was that?* Two years ago. *And you've recently gotten back together?* No, right away. It was a very short split. It was only two weeks that I was away, and we've restructured our lives since then. It's been satisfactory. *What do you mean you restructured your lives?* Well, there are a lot of things that bothered me in our relationship. We moved into the city. We started to do more things together. I made an investment which I hadn't done in the past. Let me give you a mind picture. I'm like a balloon. I tend to fly with the air currents. That's been the opposite of my life in the business world. There I'm like a lead balloon—really anchored. And I tend to fly around from experience to experience and not make an investment; and you could be married a long time and never make an investment, you know. The fact that you see people celebrating their fiftieth anniversary together, their twenty-fifth anniversary together, doesn't tell you whether they've been together, really together. I find that many marriages are two separate lives that meet in the night. On the other hand, one of the problems I've had with marriage is that I find it didn't afford enough freedom, and I'm more and more enchanted with the writings on the open marriage concept . . . not that I practice it. I practiced a one-way open marriage for 15 years, 10 years, I should say. So we start to restructure our lives. I did, it's never too late.

It sounds like you've decided to stay together. Yeah. Without a doubt. *Why is that?* Well, there are many factors. One is that I, for some reason, find divorce impossible to think of, and that deep-seated problem that I went through with a psychiatrist when we broke up for a period of time after that. It's my own feeling that I don't want to hurt people. That's interesting, because I'm in a business where you have to be real rough sometimes. But I don't see it the same way. I have a strong feeling of my responsibility for other people, and yet I don't. It's really a contradiction . . . that I really want to escape that. I've always felt I didn't want the responsibility . . . I always take on the responsibility. Being the arranger is part of that. I find this drive that I can't stop—to be the responsible person. That's the way we even manage the house. I take care of the complete finances. I pay all the bills. You know, it's the kind of thing . . . it's almost male chauvinism. But it's this . . . the two forces that are constantly at fight with each other. One is the force that gnaws at me . . . that I don't want responsibility. The other is constantly taking responsibility . . . feeling responsible.

Therefore, divorce is something that I can advise other people about if I think it's appropriate, but I could never take it into my own life. *You could never take that step.* Yes, it's impossible. You can't kid yourself about it. You can pretend about it, but it's just not my makeup. I feel like I would be deserting my family, and you always, there's always a rationalization for it, but . . . there's always a good reason why you do it, but basically it's that sense of responsibility that I'm driven to. I always feel that I don't want to hurt anybody.

Have there been any crisis points in your relations with your parents? No. My parents were my children for a long time. Again I took the responsibility. My father always arranged things when I was younger, then, as soon as I got out and made something of myself in the business world, I became the arranger for my parents, and they depended on me. And I did it with great relish. When my father died I had my mother still alive, and I take care of her. I arrange everything for her. So, there have been no crisis points with my parents. My mother tends to be irresponsible. When you're 75 you can be irresponsible, too. I don't mind it. I don't mind taking that responsibility. *Was it a crisis point at all when your father died?* No . . . a very sad point. It becomes sadder by the year because I reflect back more and more on it. It's funny about sons . . . although if my son treated me like I treated my father I would be ecstatic but, in reflecting back, I think I should have been closer to my father. *How long ago did he die?* Seven years now. Seven years.

Have your relations with your parents changed over the years? No! They were always childlike, whoever assumed the role of the child in the relationship. It was always me the child and then, finally, they became the child. No, it didn't change. I never discussed important matters with my parents . . . of intellectual or philosophical importance that my son discusses with me now . . . challenges me on. My father and mother thought that the sun rose on me, the sun set around me, and that I could do no wrong. They were very good to me. Whether it was because I never rocked the boat in exchange or not, I don't want to challenge. I closet that. It has been suggested to me that it was easier for them to be good to me than to face up to the problems. I can't deal with that. I had a good relationship with my parents.

Have there been any crisis points in your job? Oh, many. I have a terrible, terrible reaction to doing something wrong. And there's a depression that comes over me when I think I made a mistake. At my company I took on . . . or someone took me on, in a fight that I was unequal to. Now I'm the middle-weight champion, not the heavy-weight champion, and the heavy-weight champion took me on, and I didn't talk for two days . . . I couldn't speak. I ran away and didn't want to speak to anybody about it. That was a real crisis. *I take it you lost the battle.* No, I won the battle. *You won the battle?* Yeah, isn't that funny? I won the battle, but inside I had the feeling of having lost, of having been bested. In fact I not only won, I won the battle for the industry, inasmuch as what came out of it was very important for the industry. And that guy became a very close friend of mine, a very close backer. I won the battle, but it was very, very traumatic for me. *Traumatic in what sense?* I felt crushed that I was being singled out individually, and singled out for making an error. By the way, I didn't make an error then . . . you see, I started the story off by telling you that there are times I made errors. This was not an error, but it was considered as an error by some. I have a hard time when people criticize me. . . . It's strange. I would love to have the ability to be thick skinned. People think I am, but I'm very thin skinned, extremely thin skinned. That was the time where I needed a thick skin, and I was very thin skinned. He hit me hard and I thought he was unfair. I didn't do well emotionally. I've

reached a level of acceptance and respect that when somebody doesn't give me acceptance and respect, I get childish about it. I sulk. I've got to be able to be like an actor who's got to be able to take a bad review. I haven't been able to take bad reviews too well, even when they were deserved.

In what ways have you changed on the job? What effect has the experience that you've had made? Well, let's first get out of the way the fact that I've become a true expert rather than a magician based upon a bag of tricks. After the years of dealing with the problems, I'm an expert in them. I have the confidence. I know my job. I am the best person I know in my job! So, that gives me a lot of confidence. That's how I've changed, and I've developed that over the years. Number two, I suppose the feeling of that whole thing about the outside of the organization. I've changed inasmuch as I expect less from the inside of the company and expect more and get more outside, again within the parameter of my business life. I'm talking about the respect of my peers outside. That's not a new change, but it's something that has developed over the years. I think I'm less defensive than I was. With all I told you, I think I do better at taking a bad review. I'm willing to say, "That's the way the cookie crumbles." I get a lot of comfort when I'm able to do that, because I know that that's a different person than the person I've been all my life. I think I churn up inside less—that's another thing—because I have so many outlets now. If I'm unhappy over what happened today at the job, tonight I'll be writing something; the next day I'm lecturing at   . I've got that. So I have a lot of escape valves. And maybe they're not as haphazard as one may think. Maybe I put them there, because I'm worried about the repetition of that time when I had no escape valves. I've got lots of escape valves! The final escape valve for me is when I'll have enough money where I won't even need an escape valve. But I've never done anything about that. *In terms of building up money faster or something?* Yeah. We live extremely well! We live an upper-middle-class existence . . . within our means, but right up to the extent of our means. We never want for anything. We're opera goers, ballet goers, concert goers, Europe goers . . . we've done well by ourselves in that area.

How does your job future look to you? What do you see ahead for yourself? I see myself retiring in this job. Normal retiring age is 65 and I'm 48 now, so I see myself retiring in 17 years. I see myself continuing to teach during this period of time, continuing to write, and continuing to have outside activities. So, it's really a repetition of what I've had in the last few years, only with new challenges, variations on the challenge. I don't see myself outside of this job. *Does that mean after retirement?* Oh, after retirement? No. I want to get to retirement. I hope that within this period of time I'll be able to manage an early retirement. I would love to retire at age 55. I don't think its realistic, but certainly no later than age 60. If I could manage a reduced retirement at age 55, I would certainly grab it. What do I see myself doing? Just what I told you . . . teaching, consulting, lecturing . . . that's my life . . . and writing more. *So it would be retirement from the job and not from all your other activities?* That's right. That would be the only retirement. The activities that I have outside the job are great, and I would love to be freed from the job with the same nice salary and be able to do the others. *Do you see yourself retiring from your other activities of teaching or writing?* Oh, yeah . . . I could . . . in fact I would see probably the first year that I retire, traveling around the world. I could do that. I would have no trouble, because I could keep myself busy; I would not be moping around. I would love the freedom. I would retire to my country home and retire on and off. When I say I would con-

tinue to do the other things, I would continue them, but not on a full-time basis. I want the freedom of retirement. I want the freedom of not having to work this week, you see. I look towards that. I don't look towards it to play golf or to settle in some retirement community . . . God I wouldn't . . . I would die . . . I look to it, towards the freedom it affords me to do whatever I want to do.

How do you see your personal life developing in the future? Do you think there will be more satisfaction there? Yeah, I think so. I'm optimistic. I think there is a . . . my friends would say a . . . good prognosis for my marriage. That's an area I've changed sharply in the last two years. Every problem doesn't make me say, "Let's fly away."

Has your outlook on life changed much over the years? Yeah, I think it has. I've been what might be considered a radical-liberal all my life and I think I am as close to being a conservative as possible now, so I would say that was a sharp change, and that's recently. *What brought that about?* I'm tired of violence. I'm tired of rationalizing the act on the basis of a cause. I think they're two separate things. I think the cause is important, and that causes, the root causes, should be remedied, but, on the other hand, that's where my former philosophy stopped, and my new philosophy incorporates dealing with the acts as well. A crime is a crime no matter what the cause. I'm tired of violence. So, that . . . and I suppose, now your getting to a more basic cause . . . my affluence is threatened by the radicalism, so I'm not going to kid myself about it. I've got it. I got it the hard way.

Would you say that you have a pretty firm sense of who you are? I've always had a firm sense of who I am. My problem was, was I happy with who I am? I'm getting a lot happier with it. But I knew who I was and what my limitations were, what my strong suit was for a long time. When I say a long time, I mean for 10 years or so. That's a long time. *Before then you didn't have quite a . . . .* No, I wasn't sure, I wasn't sure. I also think I have a firm understanding and realization of where I'm going, and where I'm not going. I've got a good thing going. I don't use the word "happiness." That's from my other life. Happiness equals good times equals excitement.

Do you sometimes look back over your life and kind of review it? Yes, I sometimes do that. I don't dwell on it. I like to review my life. I like to go back and think about things that happened to me, both pleasant and unpleasant. I do it every so often. I'm not afraid of doing it, but I don't dwell on it, and . . . I rarely have the feeling I would like to be 17 or 18 again.

I must say that I don't think of myself as destructible. I think I'm going to live forever. That's a nice feeling. I'm not worried. Maybe in about 10 years from now I'll start worrying about dying. I'm still not at the point where I'm worried about dying. Then, when you worry about that, you look back on your life more. No, I'm still looking ahead. I really think I have 20 productive years ahead of doing something and then maybe the kind of retirement where you sit around and contemplate your navel. I've got 20 years. I've got a lifetime ahead of me. *Do you sometimes think about death?* Death? Yeah, I think about it sometimes. In fact, recently I have prepared my will. I never had one. I think about it — not oppressively. When I say I think I'm indestructible, that's nonsense. I mean, I don't think about death as imminent. I think of it as a possibility, and it's not a . . . it's not within the context of my life right now. As I said before, it may be five years from now or 10 years from now. On and off it appears, I was thinking of death a great deal two years ago when I had this great difficulty at home. *You mean in terms of possible suicide?*

Just about death. Just about it being an easy way. Now I don't. I think of life more than I think about death. Much more. There's so much more of life right now. I'm very excited about what's ahead of me, you know, in the next year, with my country home, my son coming home, my book. There's a lot of exciting things ahead, so I've got a lot . . . it's not going to be a dull year. I say it's more of the same of what I'm doing, but it's always a variation on a theme. So it's a very exciting period ahead, very exciting.

Is sex as important to you now as it used to be? No. *In what way?* Well, it was very important to me. I don't know if you decide this or it happens to you, but it's just something that takes a back seat in my life now. It took a front seat for much of my life. *What do you mean that it takes a back seat now?* Oh, I'm not as hung up about the whole thing. Which I was in the past. Hung up inasmuch as I used to sleep around a great deal. I think I've come to some kind of understanding of that. Maybe it's accepting less. But in any case, it's an acceptance, and I'm not willing to rock the boat. I'm accepting it, and I'm not willing to go into the psychological roots of my acceptance. There's no question about it. It's a compromise. *What about sex with your wife?* That's what I'm talking about as well. It's a compromise. *A compromise in what sense?* I expect less. I give less too. I've always given less at home, but now every time I'm unhappy about my sex life, I don't run out and satisfy myself in a relationship. My relationships were always permanent relationships. When I say "sleep around," that's a very poor term. Always that sense of responsibility. They were long-term relationships — a strange phenomenon — my analyst enjoyed that. You see, I see a difference between a guy who sleeps around, and a guy who has a permanent mistress. Within the context of my stupid kind of morality, one is quite different from the other.

Would you say that you're having a close, intimate relationship now with someone? No. Other than my wife. *With your wife?* Yeah. I think we're close now. Closer than we've ever been. Extremely close now. More understanding on my part. *Was it very intimate earlier; for example, after your marriage?* No, we were children . . . absolute children . . . playing house. There should be a law. One big game. No responsibilities. *From the very beginning?* From the very beginning. Until my son was born. Then all of a sudden we found ourselves with responsibilities. It was a very free life. That's what it was. It was just an extension of our childhood. I came right out of the service . . . not even finished with college . . . and got married. My wife worked while I went to college. It was like being home with mama. The same thing, no difference. Just moved from one place to the other; in fact, we lived at home for a while, at my house for a while. No difference. Same kind of life. No responsibilities. My only responsibilities were getting good marks at school. That was very important. That had carried over from being at home with my mother and then later with my wife.

Would you say that you are different now than you were a few years ago? Oh, it's like day and night. Oh sure. *In what ways?* I tend, as I said before, and I'm very happy when it happens, to be reserved at times where I never was reserved, number one. Number two, I tend to accept more often than I have in the past, a bad review. Number three, I'm not look-ing for the excitement of the good life, the jet-set life, as I did in the past. And I could find happiness in a very comfortable relationship at home. That's very important. That's really the one thing that I needed to stabilize my life.

Do you have a sense now of leaving your mark: somehow being productive? Yeah. I think my obituary would interest me if I was reading it to someone else. Let me put it that dramatically. Yeah, my obituary would interest me now, if I read it in today's paper to somebody else. I think I will have left my mark. I will have left my mark with this book [I've just written]. This book will be around long after I expire, and with all I'm going to do after this. I set the standards. I've legitimized my profession in this industry. That's a deep mark. And in teaching I've left my . . . we didn't talk about it much, but of all the things I do, I teach with the best. I'm just alive in that classroom. I didn't even talk about it; that really is the thing that I do well. So, I've left my mark. I've left my mark now if I stop now. I'm not going to stop now. There's a lot more to do. Yeah, I'll leave my mark. They won't say, "He was a nice guy," like they did when my father died, with all of the accomplishments and say he was a nice guy. A lot of people will say I was a nice guy, but that won't be my accomplishment. I will have accomplished something.

Murray was interviewed again after six years and once again 10 years later; those interviews are the next Interlude, following Chapter 5.

CHAPTER 5

Fernando Botero, *La Familia Pinzon*, 1932. Museum of Art, Rhode Island School of Design Nancy Sayles Day Collection of Modern Latin American Art.

Families, Menopause, Sexuality, and Singles

dults in the United States live in a diverse society that includes a range of life-styles and interpersonal relationships. Most men and women marry and form a new family unit. They rear their children, launch them into their own families, and grow old along with their mate. Even with the high divorce rate in the United States, most adults remain married to their spouse and, because of longer life span, are more likely to celebrate their golden wedding anniversary than was true for past generations (even though divorce rates were lower then). Some adults do not marry, and others do not remain married, however; but they may have children they are rearing, and they usually maintain family ties to parents, siblings, and other relatives as they grow older.

Whether one is a man or a woman is very important in these adult life-styles and relationships, obviously. For example, women are likely to outlive men, so they are more likely than men to be widowed; they are more likely to be caring for children, if divorced, and to be responsible for child care in any event; they are more likely to be involved in caring for elder parents; and they experience the physical changes known as menopause.

In differing ways, nearly all women and men invest a great deal of time and emotional energy in the family. Sometimes families provide deeply meaningful intimate relationships and significant opportunities for personal growth and fulfillment. Occasionally they provide some of the greatest emotional upsets and potentials for violence. For instance, homicide rates indicate that most people are killed by family members; spouse abuse, elder abuse, and child abuse are also well-known examples of family violence; and police approach all family disputes with great caution. Obviously, there is a great range between these two extremes and some families provide little more than comfortable bedrooms and dining facilities. Some aspects of family life are especially important for students of adulthood and aging; these include intergenerational kinship ties and mutual support, grandparents, widowhood, and ethnic differences.

This chapter begins with an exploration of the characteristics of families in the United States and describes the family cycle in the lives of adults. The second section focuses on the physical and psychological effects of menopause. The third section focuses on sexuality during the adult and aging years. We conclude the chapter with a discussion of three groups of unmarried adults: those who are divorced or separated, those who are gay or lesbian, and heterosexual persons who are living unmarried life-styles.

Families

There is much controversy about the family. Some feel that the relatively high divorce rate indicates a decline in the stability of family life. Indeed, beginning in the mid-1970s a majority of first marriages ended in divorce and the rate of remarriage after divorce declined sharply during the 1970s and more moderately during the 1980s. By 1987, about 1 in 5 married-couple families were remarried families (Glick, 1988, 1989a). Conversely, 4 in 5 married-couple families were in their first marriage.

The rate of divorce peaked around 1980 and remained relatively stable during the 1980s. It is estimated that of those who divorced, about 2 out of 3 will remarry while they have young children living with them (Glick & Lin, 1987). It is too early to tell whether the remaining third of divorced young adults will remarry later in life, or whether those who do remarry will divorce again. However, since more adults are living into old age today than in the past, in general marriages are also lasting longer today. For those married in the first decade of the 1900s, the average marriage lasted 35.6 years; for those married in the 1980s, the average marriage was expected to last 44.4 years if not cut short by divorce (Glick, 1989b). Thus, a person could spend more time in a second marriage today than his or her grandparents spent in their single marriage.

It has also been argued that the contemporary family is losing much of its function because society has become so complex, family members are living apart from each other, and many of the functions once left to the family — such as caring for aged members — are being taken over by institutions. However, Shanas (1979) suggested that the family is instead gaining greater importance as the place where one can relax, be appreciated as a unique person, and find support and interpersonal warmth as society becomes more technological and impersonal. In her 25 years of research on the family, Shanas found no evidence that the family is becoming irrelevant.

> It is still the family, that group of individuals related by blood or marriage, that is the first resource of both its older and younger members for emotional and social support, crisis intervention, and bureaucratic linkages. (Shanas, 1979, p. 5)

We discuss this issue in detail when we focus on the aging family, but now we begin with an examination of the structure and diversity of families in the United States.

Extended, Nuclear, and Modified Extended Families

Most families in our society seem to be **nuclear families** since they are made up of a mother, a father, and their children sharing a household. However, these nuclear family units have a variety of ties with other members of their family — that is, with their extended family. An **extended family** is made up of those individuals one is related to through blood or marriage, as well as "fictive kin" who are treated as family members even though they are not actual relatives. Although the young couple typically establishes a home separate from their parents, family ties generally remain intact. Even if the family units are separated by a considerable distance, they keep in contact by telephone, airplane, and automobile. In general, nuclear family units retain close ties with other family units in a kin network; mutual aid and social interaction are frequent (Aizenberg & Treas, 1985; Shanas, 1979; Shanas & Sussman, 1981; Sussman & Burchinal, 1962). Financial help, as well as help by providing services (e.g., house cleaning, baby sitting, and shopping), frequently occurs between generations of the family, so that parents help the newly married couple, and later the younger couple and elder couple provide a variety of services to each other as needed. This interconnected family structure is termed the **modified extended family** (Sussman & Burchinal, 1962, after Litwak, 1960). It differs from the isolated

Multigenerational households have been romanticized as representative of "the good old days"; in fact they were common only during periods of economic hardship. In Western cultures families prefer to live separately if they can afford to.

nuclear family since the family units maintain interrelations across generations and among siblings while also maintaining much autonomy and mobility. It differs also from the extended family household in which three or more generations live together.

Although it has been thought that **multigenerational households** were very common during earlier periods, historical research has challenged this notion. It now seems clear that this form of family was not prevalent in Western society, except during periods of economic adversity or family disruption. For example, Back (1974) examined census records in England from 1574 to 1821. He found that only 6 percent of households contained three or more generations of family members, and these nearly always appeared to result from a family calamity such as widowhood or a broken household. He concluded that there is no evidence that three-generation households were the preferred family pattern before the industrial revolution, or that industrialization led to a decline of multigenerational households. Similarly, van de Walle (1976) examined census records for a small community in Belgium for the period 1847–1866. He found that, at any given time, about two-thirds of the households were nuclear families, compared with about 10 percent extended households and 11 percent multiple households (consisting of more than one nuclear family living together). The nuclear families were also more lasting than the other forms, suggesting that multiple and extended households were transitional patterns that resulted from family disruption. Thus, there is no evidence in these studies that multigenerational households were prevalent in rural areas or before the industrial revolution in Western society.

Other cultures have emphasized extended family households, however. In the United States, for example, Rogers and Gallion (1978) found that about two-thirds of older Pueblo Indians living in New Mexico were in extended households. Similarly, Murdock and Schwartz (1978) found that over half of the older Sioux Indians living on a reservation in North and South Dakota were living in a multigenerational household. Also, Staples (1976) pointed out the importance of the extended family in African cultures that is carried on today in many African-American families. One illustration is that 48 percent of Black families headed by elderly women have relatives under 18 in the household, compared with only 10 percent among White families.

In Asian countries, such as Japan and Thailand, much higher proportions of persons over age 65 live with their children than is true in the United States and other Western countries, such as Denmark and Italy (Table 5.1). To understand these national differences, one must consider cultural values and the nature of housing arrangements. In Japan, for example, this does not imply that the younger generation provides housing for the elderly; in reality, the elder generation provides housing for the oldest son and his family in exchange for lifelong care by the daughter-in-law. Housing is scarce, as are community services for infirm old people, so both generations benefit. In Denmark, to take the opposite example, elders value their independence; a close friendship network and community involvement and support are highly valued and elders prefer not to depend on their children for housing. Thus, family structure reflects cultural values and cannot be understood apart from its larger cultural context. Moreover, there are advantages and disadvan-

TABLE 5.1 Family Composition of Persons over Age 65 by Sex in Five Countries (Percentages), 1986

	Japan		Thailand		Italy		U.S.A.		Denmark	
Composition	M	F	M	F	M	F	M	F	M	F
Aged living alone	2.8	10.3	2.6	6.1	8.8	25.6	19.0	54.7	27.2	57.3
Husband and wife living alone	36.0	19.3	9.1	2.6	39.0	22.8	60.8	25.5	62.9	33.7
Aged, married children and unmarried grandchildren living together	16.0	9.2	15.2	8.7	27.5	18.4	11.0	9.0	6.7	3.4
Three generations of married adults living together, possibly with unmarried great-grandchildren	31.7	42.4	44.1	51.7	9.6	17.1	0.5	0.5	—	0.3
Others	13.5	18.6	29.1	30.8	15.2	16.1	8.7	10.3	3.2	5.3

Source: Life and opinions of the elderly: Report of an international comparative study. Office for the Elderly, Director's Secretariat, General Executive Office of the Japanese Government. Tokyo, Japan, 1987, p. 59. (Translated by Kumiko Kawamura.)

tages to either pattern. For example, Japanese elders without children, or who were relocated to urban apartments as their children moved from the farm to the city, may be as isolated as any old person could be (Stanaway, 1987). Conversely, elders in the United States may choose to move to the "sun belt" away from their children and return only when their health fails and expect their children to provide the necessary care and support.

Within the modified extended family structure that is prevalent in the United States today, there are a variety of family structures. These are crafted by individual families to meet a diversity of individual needs and circumstances. For example, some families have one parent living with the children because of divorce, separation, widowhood, or the children were conceived before the parent married. Other families have "extra" people in the family—an aged parent, a housekeeper, or an unmarried relative, and so on. Some families may be very complex since they reflect the effects of divorce and remarriage. Thus, one "nuclear" family may consist of parts of two previous families living together during the week as a single family; on weekends the members may shift as the children visit their parents in their own reconstituted families, or visit their various sets of grandparents.

Ethnic Variations among Families

Frequently it is assumed that all families are, or should be, basically similar. This overlooks the considerable variations within families, especially among the diverse ethnic groups that make up family life in the United States (Mindel & Habenstein, 1976). Gradually through the mutual process of retaining their heritage and traditions while being assimilated into mainstream culture—often with the burden of social stereotypes and oppression—families have evolved in differing ways. In attempting to understand families, we need to avoid stereotyped descriptions of the variation between ethnic groups and to be especially careful about the tendency to see ethnic variations as abnormal or deviant family forms. Instead, they should be seen as cultural variations that exist in different cultural and social environments (Allen, 1978).

Woehrer (1978) summarized research on some ethnic families with a particular focus on the elderly, pointing out a number of interesting observations that may provide us with a flavor of the rich diversity among ethnic families in the United States. For example, Greeley (1971) found striking ethnic differences in the proportion of persons who visited their parents weekly: 79 percent for Italian Americans, 65 percent for Polish Americans, 61 percent for French Americans, and 39 percent for English and Scandinavian Americans. Moreover, Italian and Polish Americans tend to emphasize family ties and to have fewer nonfamily friends, to value friends less than kin, and to belong to fewer organizations than other ethnic groups. Scandinavian Americans, in contrast, are likely to belong to organizations. African Americans and Irish Americans are likely to have close ties with siblings and also to value friendships very highly. For African Americans, friends who are very close often have a kinshiplike bond in which they are regarded as family members. Thus, in some ethnic groups—such as Italian, Mexican, Polish, and Jewish Americans— the family is the major source of emotional and financial support. Others—such as

Irish and African Americans—rely on friendship to a higher degree than other ethnic groups. Still others—such as Scandinavians—count on social organizations for an important part of their daily life (Woehrer, 1978). These differences are important to understand, since the pattern of behavior or social environment that is meaningful for one group may be different for another group.

> The Scandinavian senior in the high rise who sees her children only occasionally and the Polish grandfather who has no close friends outside the family and belongs to no organizations may both be socially integrated within the context of their own cultural values and expectations. Likewise, the German grandmother who sits alone at her sewing machine stitching together doll clothes for her granddaughters and patch quilts for the missions and the Irish grandmother employed at the information booth when the state legislature is in session may both find meaning and happiness in their work. Make them switch roles, however, and you may have two unhappy and alienated seniors. (Woehrer, 1978, p. 335)

Whether the parents have a college education or finished only eighth grade, immigrated from another country, or were born in, or currently live in, an urban or rural county may make a considerable difference in family patterns and characteristics. This is as true for African–American or Hispanic families as for American families of Anglo-European descent. For example, Willie (1988) described general family styles of middle-class, working-class, and low-income African-American families. He summarized some of the differences between these groups:

> Middle-class black families in the United States manifest probably better than any other population group the Puritan orientation toward work, success, and self-reliance so characteristic of the basic values of this nation. For them, work is a consuming experience. Little time is left for recreation and other kinds of social activities except perhaps regular involvement in church affairs. . . .
>
> Family life in the black working class is a struggle for survival that requires the cooperative efforts of all. . . .
>
> The bearing and rearing of children is considered to be an important citizenship responsibility, so much so that black working-class parents make great personal sacrifices for their families. They tend to look upon children as their unique contribution to society, a creative contribution they are unable to make through their work roles, which at best are semiskilled. (pp. 50–51)
>
> The most important fact about poor black families is their low-income status. They therefore are forced to make a number of necessary, clever, and sometimes foolish arrangements to exist. . . .
>
> The struggle is severe and there is no margin for error. Poor black families learn to live with contingency. They hope for little and expect less. (Willie, 1988, pp. 55–56)

Extensive patterns of kin involvement are often maintained among three-generation African-American families (McAdoo, 1978). Thus, the older African-American person usually has a kinship network for support and, in addition, a friendship network to call upon for aid (Woehrer, 1978). Gibson (1986) noted that the role of religion, and the use of informal support networks during times of distress, provides many African-Americans with a versatile array of resources to cope with problems of aging. "Whites, in contrast, were more likely to limit help-seeking to their spouses in middle life, and when their spouses were no longer available for this support, to confine their attempts to replace it by calling only on single family members as they approached old age" (Gibson, 1986, p. 195).

To take another example, in a study of low-income persons over age 65, Lubben and Becerra (1987) noted that Chinese- and Mexican-American elderly were more likely to share housing or to receive help from an adult child than either African-American or Anglo-American elderly. In general, those elders who did not speak English and had values closer to their traditional culture were more likely to receive aid from their adult children. However, language barriers and recency of immigration might have produced their economic circumstances, so these findings may not apply to more affluent ethnic elderly persons.

In summary, we may note that the family remains very important in the lives of a vast majority of adults in our society. Despite divorce, and other changes in the structure of families, there is no evidence that the family is losing its function as the most flexible and most significant source of support. In addition, the modified extended family pattern prevalent in the United States today seems to have been the preferred family form in Western society for at least several generations, when economic conditions allowed it to exist. Different ethnic groups emphasize family ties to varying degrees, and all families reflect cultural, socioeconomic, and demographic conditions.

The Family Cycle

Just as each individual goes through a life cycle with developmental stages marked by milestones, so also there is a **family cycle** with milestones that mark its stages of development. These major family milestones are: marriage, birth of the first child, birth of the last child, the last child leaving home (the "empty nest"), and widowhood.

As with individual development, the events that make up this family cycle reflect cultural and historical change. For example, the average age at marriage has increased in recent years. In addition, the average length of time between the family events of marriage and the last child leaving home has decreased since the turn of the century because of the preference for fewer children. The average age of widowhood has increased because of greater longevity. Thus, the parental years of the family cycle have "speeded up" whereas the postparental years (after the children have left home) have lengthened dramatically.

These changes have affected the family cycle to a great extent. They have brought about middle-aged grandparents who are also caring for their elderly parents. Four- and five-generation families are now more common than in the past. One person may have a large number of children, grandchildren, and great-grandchildren spread across the country in a complex extended family network.

The milestones of the family cycle suggest a progressive development of the family through a series of sequential phases. They also call our attention to the social and psychological effects of these family events on the individual. For example, the birth of the first child not only brings a shift in role from "spouse" to "parent" (with the consequent shift in norms and expectations), but may also bring a shift in self-conception and motivation as well as a possible reawakening of unresolved childhood conflicts in the parents.

It may be noted that the events of the family cycle are more varied today than previously because of greater diversity in family patterns, and more intertwined with work and career cycles for both parents than in the past (see Chapter 6). Ethnic differences, geographic mobility, socioeconomic variations, and urban–rural contrasts call into question any general statements about the family cycle. Thus, we can select only a few topics for discussion here. In the next section, we take a closer look inside the family by using the developmental perspective. We discuss the family in each of the following phases: establishment, new parents, child-rearing family, and postparental family.

Establishment

The **establishment phase** begins at marriage (or when the partners begin living together as a couple) and continues through the initial period of settling into the relationship. It is characterized by the couple functioning as a dyad and may last until the first child is born. The process of mutual socialization is undoubtedly of great importance during this phase as the partners seek to fulfill their new roles with one another, with parents, and with society in general. To aid in this respect, the event of *marriage* serves as a rite of passage between past roles and future roles. It represents a normative transition and serves as a milestone for many couples. Of course, couples who live together before marriage do not have as clear a shift in roles as couples who follow a more traditional pattern, but the event of marriage may mark a subtle transition for those couples as well.

One of the early tasks in this phase is to develop mutually satisfying patterns of sexual interactions and patterns of living intimately with another person. Carl Rogers (1972) studied several couples who had been together from 3 to 15 years in order to understand those relationships that appeared to be satisfying, growth-oriented, and possibly enduring; he also included his own 47-year marriage in the analysis—he and Helen were in their seventies at the time. Four themes stood out for him in his analysis of these couples. The first was dedication or commitment to the relationship and to working together on the relationship as it changed and evolved over time. A second theme was communication of persisting feelings and understanding the response of the partner whether the feelings or responses are positive, negative, critical, or self-revealing. The third theme was the dissolution of roles in the sense that one does not perform specific roles, or expect the partner to perform specific roles, simply because they are prescribed by one's parents, culture, or religion. As the relationship grows and becomes more uniquely suited to the couple, new roles evolve that fit the partners more fully than those externally prescribed roles. The fourth theme was becoming a separate self and finding greater acceptance of oneself as a unique person while one's partner also grows to greater self-awareness and acceptance. During the early months of marriage or a committed relationship, many of these themes are likely to involve the resolution of specific conflicts between the couple (such as whether to squeeze or roll the toothpaste tube, as well as more serious conflicts); the development of styles of conflict resolution, decision making, and social interaction; the development of role patterns within the family; and the division of responsibilities. As the relationship grows and matures, the four themes Rogers noted are likely to be important as ideal goals toward which enduring and satisfying relationships strive.

New Parents

The **new parents phase** begins with pregnancy and the birth of the first child. It involves a major shift in roles from wife and husband to mother and father. In addition to the resocialization involved in that role shift (or addition of a new role to one's set of roles), the couple needs to adjust to the presence of a third family member. Up to this point the couple has probably established a fairly stable relationship. The addition of a third person, who is also a demanding, dependent infant, may bring considerable change to the couple's relationship.

An exploratory study by LeMasters (1957) found that the birth of a first child had been a "severe" or "extensive" crisis for 83 percent of the 48 couples he interviewed. He found that those couples who experienced a major crisis had "romanticized" parenthood and had little preparation for their new roles as parents —little anticipatory socialization. Their expectations about parenthood were disconfirmed when the child turned out to be demanding and to upset their routine. In addition, all the mothers with professional training and extensive work experience

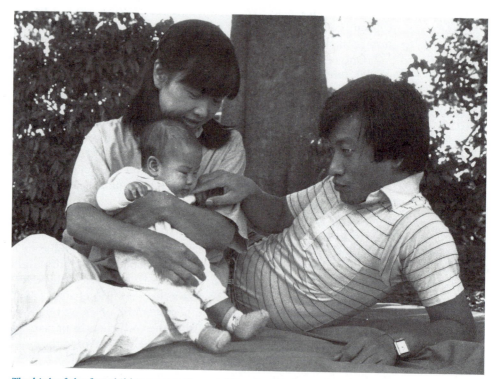

The birth of the first child is a normative transition that involves a shift in roles for the new parents. It may bring a period of emotional stress for the couple.

suffered "extensive" or "severe" crises. Since they had given up their work, this probably intensified the role shift and brought about an even greater change in self-concept that added to the severity of the transition. Three considerations must be considered in interpreting this study, however. First, these parents were not drawn from a representative sample: all were middle class, the husbands were college graduates, none was divorced, and the wife did not work after the child was born. Second, the couple was interviewed together and the degree of crisis was determined jointly by the parents and the interviewer, not by some objective measure of "crisis." Third, although all the parents had their first child within five years of the interview, many were looking back on this period from the perspective of having resolved whatever degree of crisis may have occurred.

Other studies of new parents found much lower levels of crisis. For example, Hobbs and his colleagues found that over 75 percent reported no crisis or only a slight crisis in two studies of White parents randomly selected from public birth records a decade apart and one study of Black parents randomly selected from family planning and prenatal clinics (Hobbs, 1965; Hobbs & Cole, 1976; Hobbs & Wimbish, 1977). These studies differed from the LeMasters study not only because their samples were much more representative of all new parents, but also because the respondents reported their degree of crisis by checking the extent to which each of 23 items on a standard questionnaire was felt to have been bothersome. On the basis of these studies, Hobbs and Cole (1976) concluded: "It is more accurate to think of beginning parenthood as a transition, accompanied by some difficulty, than a crisis of severe proportions" (p. 730).

These studies are limited, however, by the consideration that the respondents may have tended to conceal, even from themselves, the extent of the crisis they were experiencing. In contrast, the respondents in the LeMasters study may have been more willing to describe, and perhaps exaggerate, their extent of crisis, since many of them were looking back on a period of transition that they had successfully completed.

A third approach to studying this issue was taken by Entwisle and Doering (1981). They gathered a sample of 120 White couples in stable relationships (3 were unmarried) where the woman was expecting her first child. Socioeconomic status was considered such that half were middle and half were lower; approximately equal proportions of Catholics, Jews, and Protestants were included. The women were interviewed twice before the birth and once after; they also were contacted by telephone for short interviews when the baby was six months old. This provided longitudinal data and allowed a more detailed analysis than either the LeMasters or Hobbs et al. studies. The findings may be seen as indicating somewhat of a compromise between the two extremes represented by those earlier studies, and portions of both are supported. Their major findings were:

1. Early days at home after childbirth are stressful, especially for mothers. Many experienced a period of depression (81% at some time during the first few weeks; p. 254). The severity of the depression reflected the stress of the birth more than the baby's behavior or the husband's reaction (p. 163). In particular, pain of birth was greater than either the wife or husband anticipated. More medication was given than had been desired. More obstetrical procedures were

performed than had been expected and their effects lasted for several weeks. The preparation the women had received before birth provided little protection against this stress (p. 192). Twenty of the 120 women had cesarean deliveries and 14 others experienced a variety of serious complications (p. 253).

2. The couples were generally unprepared for the extent of work involved in infant care. Childbirth preparation classes did not focus on this topic, and few had previous exposure to baby care; they did not seek information during pregnancy about infant care (p. 192). 3. Those who were most successful were those who were more flexible in the division of tasks between the parents. This did not prevent depression, however, which was related to the stress of birth. Informal family supports were helpful, but many mothers became depressed afterward when left on their own (p. 192).

4. The new parents tended to see each other in an idealized manner during this period ("the postpartum honeymoon"). This "may signify stress so intense that most couples do not face it; put simply, the honeymoon may be an unconscious cover-up" that may postpone resolving problems (p. 255). It is unclear whether this is adaptive or maladaptive as a coping style on a short-term basis, however. (Nonetheless, it may explain the findings in the Hobbs et al. studies.)

5. The parents were not emotionally prepared for the tasks after childbirth. For example, some women felt the baby was ugly or otherwise distasteful. This apparently resulted from the fact that couples tended to be overly confident about their ability to cope with an infant and men often had unrealistic ideas about their wives' skills. Also, childbirth classes did not stress parenting. It often required one or two months to develop parenting skills (pp. 256–258). This is consistent with the finding in the LeMasters study that parents tend to "romanticize" parenthood and are unprepared for the reality of it.

6. One-third of the women planned to return to work by the time the baby was six months old; only 6 percent did so (pp. 255–256). Most were working part-time, regardless of social class. As many women tried working and stopped as continued to work (p. 261). This probably produced financial strain for many families, and added to the cost of childbirth.

7. Division of labor between wife and husband in the home resulted in women assuming almost all the responsibility for the infant. "No husband stayed home longer than two weeks after the birth, and none took his infant to his workplace. Even though fathers held infants for 1½ hours daily, the lion's share of infant care was assumed by *all* mothers" (p. 261).

8. Increased education about parenthood would be helpful. However, new parents appear unaware that they need help, or are reluctant to seek it. Visits to the home by nurses or child-care counselors during the first two weeks might be especially beneficial (p. 265).

In the light of these data it is clear that the birth of a first child may be a time of both "crisis" and "transition." New parents may expect a period of stress, especially for the mother. Prospective parents may benefit from greater education about infant care and the potential difficulties and realistic changes they may expect with the birth of their first child. Moreover, new parents should not feel "guilty" about experiencing some degree of emotional stress during this period, and they should ask for help if they find it difficult to cope with the stress.

Child-Rearing Family

Some of the central tasks of the **child-rearing phase** of the family cycle include maintaining an intimate relationship with one's spouse, providing space and financial resources for the expanding family, and rearing the children. The task of child-rearing involves nurturing, socialization, and providing opportunities for the child's maximum emotional, intellectual, and psychological development. According to psychoanalytic theory, the child is developing rapidly and progressing through a series of psychosexual stages such as those described by Erikson (Box 1.2, p. 14). Benedek (1952) suggested that the child's development may also cause parents to rework their resolution of these psychosexual stages at the same time. In addition, parents need to develop effective and comfortable styles of parenting and to allow for themselves to change at the same time their children are growing and changing. For example, the process of socialization—by which the parents teach their children the norms, values, and expectations of society—is a mutual process that also allows the parents to be socialized by their children (Zeits & Prince, 1982). This mutual socialization process is especially clear when the children become adolescents (Kimmel & Weiner, 1985). Throughout this complex process of learning how to be a parent for this particular child, and fitting that *me* as a parent together with one's other *me*s into a coherent sense of self, both the children and the parents ideally grow in their own ways.

Sometimes parents become anxious about how to raise their children "correctly." Of course, this is a realistic concern and there are ways that are "better" in some sense than others. But, in general, children are relatively hardy creatures and manage to grow and develop surprisingly well, even in relatively difficult circumstances. After all, if children had to have perfect parents, few of us would be functioning today! Perhaps the best guide is for parents to develop a style of parenting that is comfortable for them and comfortable and realistic for the child. Yet, the more one knows about child development, the more comfortable and realistic one can be.

The child-rearing period of the family cycle includes the overlapping phases of the family with preschool children, the family with school-age children, and the family with adolescents. It begins with the birth of the first child and ends when the children begin leaving home. Obviously, this area involves an enormous range of important topics. We can only suggest a few of those most related to adulthood. Students interested in family development may find entire books devoted to this field. In Chapter 6, we also discuss another relevant topic, maternal employment.

Understanding this period involves consideration of the father's and mother's role in the family (cf. Biller, 1982; Field & Widmayer, 1982). Moreover, these roles may change as the children grow older, such that the father and mother are more similar in roles when their children are 15 compared to when they are infants, regardless of the age of the parents (cf. Turner, 1982, p. 925).

Single-parent families also must be acknowledged: in 1986, 24 percent of children under age 18 were living in one-parent families (Glick, 1988). One issue in these families that is often overlooked is the "parental deprivation" experienced by the father or mother who is absent and not able to be a parent (Hagestad, 1982b, p. 495). Likewise, in single-parent families, the mother (usually the single parent) may also experience "maternal deprivation" because she is deprived of the support of a spouse (Skard, 1965).

In addition, attention needs to be given to the fact that many families are "reconstituted" after remarriage of the parents (Furstenberg & Spanier, 1984). An aspect of this that is not always recognized was noted by Lillian Troll:

> Most writers refer only to the in-law adjustment problems of young married couples; few note the adjustment problems of middle-aged parents and even older grandparents to the new families introduced into kin networks upon each new marriage in the family. (Troll, Miller & Atchley, 1979, pp. 126–127).

Finally, the intergenerational nature of the family is important to note. One specific manifestation of this is the concept of the **generational stake** (Bengtson & Kuypers, 1971):

> The effort and commitment now middle-aged parents have invested in raising their children combined with their present diminished influence on them, as well as the shortening of their own future, make it important to them that the next generation "carry on." Their children, on the other hand, look forward to a whole life ahead and need to express their uniqueness at least with respect to their parents. The parents' tendency will be to exaggerate similarities between themselves and their children. Their children's tendency will be to exaggerate differences. (Troll & Bengtson, 1982, p. 893)

This generational stake may manifest itself in a belief that there is a "generation gap," when, in fact, there is usually relatively little difference in *basic values* within families, especially with regard to religious and political views; there is generally less parent–child similarity with regard to gender roles, life-style, and orientation toward work, however. Surprisingly, the quality of the family relationship, such as "closeness," does not seem to affect the transmission of values across the generations (Troll & Bengtson, 1982, p. 907). In fact, parents appear to be used by adults of all ages as important reference persons, even if the parent has been dead for many years (Hagestad, 1982b, p. 492; Troll, 1972).

Postparental Family

The average length of the **postparental phase** of the family cycle has grown far longer during the 1900s (Figure 5.1). The last child leaves home earlier today than 90 years ago since families are smaller. Also more people are living into old age today than in the past. This period of the family cycle involves several phases: (1) "launching" the children from the nuclear family; (2) preretirement, when plans and preparations are made for the couple to spend their days together after retiring from work; (3) aging family after retirement until the death of a spouse; and (4) widowhood. Many parents become grandparents during this period, as well.

These postparental years often involve responsibility for the care of aging

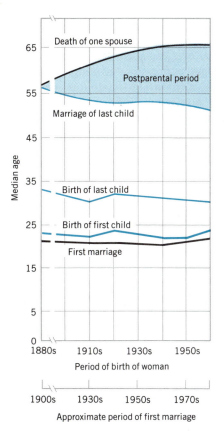

FIGURE 5.1 Median age of mothers at selected milestones in the family life cycle. (*Source*: Glick (1977). Figure 1. Copyright © 1977 by the National Council on Family Relations. Reprinted with permission.)

parents. Thus, many women find their focus shifts from care of children to care of their parents, or their husband's parents (Neugarten, 1976). As a result, families may experience a "re-empty nest" transition after the death of the parents (Aizenberg & Treas, 1985, p. 174).

As with the earlier periods of the family cycle, we can only highlight some of the most relevant aspects of this phase in the family cycle; other reviews are available elsewhere (cf. Aizenberg & Treas, 1985; Sussman, 1985; Troll, 1986).

As the children near the end of the teenage years, they begin departing from the family into other living arrangements or their own nuclear families. This phase of the family has been described as the *launching center,* but it is seldom as clear-cut as the term implies since ties between the parents and children often remain very close, with frequent visits, financial support, and other forms of assistance from the parents to the children. Turner (1982) also noted that often children return home. In many cases it is this return, or a reluctance to leave, that is more distressing to mothers than the timely departure of the adolescents (Troll, 1975).

Although the effect on the parents of launching their children would seem to involve a transition and a potential for some degree of upset and conflict, it seems to depend on cultural and ethnic factors related to the meaning of motherhood. For example, Bart (1971) conducted an extensive study of depression in middle-aged women and found that, in general, it was related to a lack of important roles and a recent loss of maternal roles. However, according to Bart, in cultures where women's status increased with age, depression in middle age was rare compared with societies such as ours where, in the traditional view, women's status declines with age.

Thus, for some women, the launching of their children may involve a considerable role shift that occasionally may bring on an emotional crisis. For other women, it may bring a sense of freedom from the career of child-rearing and, possibly, the opportunity for a "second career" of their choosing. Deutscher (1964) interviewed 49 men and women between 40 and 65 whose children were no longer living at home. Nearly half felt this postparental period was better than any earlier period of the family cycle, and wives were almost twice as likely as husbands to feel this way. A typical response from a mother was:

> There's not as much physical labor. There's not as much cooking and there's not as much mending, and, well, I remarked not long ago that for the first time since I can remember my evenings are free. And we had to be very economical to get the three children through college. We're over the hurdle now; we've completed it. Last fall was the first time in 27 years that I haven't gotten a child ready to go to school. That was very relaxing. (Deutscher, 1964, p. 265)

Cassandra had been given the power to foretell the future by Apollo but no one ever believed her, according to ancient Greek legend. When the giant Wooden Horse was brought through the gate of the city of Troy, Cassandra predicted that the enemy was hiding inside. Her warning was ignored and Troy was destroyed after those inside the horse succeeded in opening the city gates to their army in the middle of the night.

It is not a period that is free of stress, however, especially for women (Turner, 1982, p. 929). Concerns about others are frequently mentioned as sources of stress for women. In one study (Lowenthal et al., 1975), women at the "launching center" phase were concerned with their children's problems such as educational and occupational difficulties, health, divorce, or friction with relatives. Many in the "preretirement" phase were concerned about the health of their husbands; but only two preretirement husbands mentioned a stress centered on their wives.

In another study, women saw themselves as **kinkeepers** who sought to maintain relationships among multiple generations of family (Huyck, 1977). This may involve the "Cassandra" role of being worried about all that can go wrong and the feelings of attachment and irritation that often go along with this role (Troll & Turner, 1976). According to legend, Cassandra was a prophet who was able to foretell that disaster was coming, but no one believed her; for example, she warned about the enemy hiding inside the wooden horse that was allowed inside the city gates of Troy (Hamilton, 1940).

> The Cassandra function of middle-aged women increases their own vulnerability to stress but has a generally beneficent effect upon others. Middle-aged wives' concern with their husbands' health, for example, probably functions to enhance the longevity of many husbands. (Turner, 1982, p. 931)

The man's longevity is a critical concern, since many women live much longer than their husbands; we suggest some reasons for this in Chapter 8. Moreover, women tend to marry men who are a few years older. Thus, one of the most dramatic sex-related differences in the aging family is the preponderance of women. This is shown in terms of the ratio of men to women in Figure 5.2. The sex ratio is

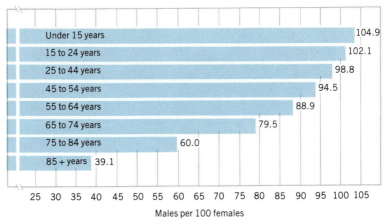

FIGURE 5.2 Sex ratio by age in the United States, 1987 (males per 100 females). (*Source*: U.S. Bureau of the Census. United States population estimates, by age, sex, and race, 1980 to 1987, *Current Population Reports*, Series P-25, No. 1022. Washington, D.C.: U.S. Government Printing Office, 1988, Table 2.)

approximately equal during the childbearing years, but thereafter the number of women is greater than men of the same age; in later life the difference is dramatic, with over twice as many women alive compared to men after age 85.

Two of the major changes during the postparental period of the family cycle involve the oldest and the youngest generations in the extended family. On one hand, sometime during these middle years the couple is likely to be faced with providing some form of care for one or more of their aging parents, and eventually they will have to deal with the grief and mourning upon the death of their parents. Certainly the death of one's parents and of one's siblings would seem to be events of importance during middle and late adulthood. Hagestad (1987) noted that this transition is becoming a more predictable transition than it was in the past: "It most likely occurs during the empty nest phase, after the period of active day-to-day parenting, but before widowhood. It is also, at least for women, likely to occur after the birth of the first grandchild" (p. 155). The impact of the death of an adult's parents is thought to reflect the fact that one is now "next in line" for death and that one is no longer anyone's child; however, it seems to be less stressful than the death of a child or the death of a spouse. The age of the bereaved, other losses at about the same time, and the extent of the parent's preparation for death may affect the severity of the bereavement (Sanders, 1989; cf. Moss & Moss, 1989).

Grandparents fulfill a number of important functions in the family, such as being a resource when help is needed.

On the other hand, and at the opposite end of the generational continuum, the parents probably will become grandparents and, in growing numbers, great-grandparents. Indeed, one of the most apparent effects of the lengthening of the life span has been the increased prevalence of grandparenthood as a phase in the family cycle. Today, in contrast to the past when the average life span was shorter, children not only are more likely to have several living grandparents, but also can expect to have grandparents present long enough to attend their wedding (Hagestad, 1987, p. 154). We discuss the characteristics of grandparents in the next section.

Grandparenthood

Two themes stand out in studies of grandparents. First, there is wide diversity across individual styles of being a grandparent. This reflects age of the grandparent, with older persons tending to be more formal; it also reflects ethnic background, with some groups tending to be more involved with the parents and grandchildren than other groups; and it reflects gender, with men tending to emphasize different aspects of the grandparent role than those stressed by women. Second, there are a variety of symbolic functions that the grandparents fulfill within the family; these include providing stability, being an emergency resource, negotiating between generations in the family, and constructing the family biography (Bengtson, 1985). In addition, the study of grandparents calls attention to the lifelong "bumping and grinding" of generations within families, considered as "bundles of interacting lives" (Hagestad, 1981, 1987, p. 158). That is, the pattern of interaction among grandparents, parents, and grandchildren may be idiosyncratic and reflect personal relationships, rather than normative expectations. Moreover, the "generational stake" may be more significant for the grandparents than for the other generations (Troll, 1980). Let us examine each of these points in turn.

In a classic study, Neugarten and Weinstein (1964) explored the satisfactions and styles of grandparenthood among middle-class respondents in their fifties and sixties. They found that the majority of grandparents felt comfort, satisfaction, and pleasure in the role; but about one-third felt some discomfort or disappointment in the role of grandparent (Table 5.2). The meaning of the role varied considerably among the respondents. Some felt it provided a sense of biological renewal ("It's through my grandchildren that I feel young again") or biological continuity ("It's carrying on the family line"). Others felt it provided a source of emotional self-fulfillment ("I can do for my grandchildren things I could never do for my own kids. I was too busy with my business to enjoy my kids, but my grandchildren are different. Now I have the time to be with them"). Others felt they served as a resource person to their grandchildren, and still others felt they were able to achieve something through their grandchildren that they (and their children) were not able to achieve. In addition, a substantial number felt remote from their grandchildren ("It's great to be a grandmother, of course—but I don't have much time").

Neugarten and Weinstein also identified five different styles of grandparenting. Three are fairly traditional grandparent roles: the *formal,* who leave parenting to the parent but like to offer special favors to the grandchild; the *surrogate parent,* usually the grandmother, who assumes parental responsibility for the child at the

TABLE 5.2 *Ease of Role Performance, Significance of Role, and Style of Grandparenting*

	Grandmothers (N = 70) N	Grandfathers (N = 70) N
A. Ease of role performance:		
1) Comfortable-pleasant	41	43
2) Difficulty-discomfort	25	20
(Insufficient data)	4	7
Total	70	70
B. Significance of the grandparent role:		
1) Biological renewal and/or continuity	29	16
2) Emotional self-fulfillment	13	19
3) Resource person to child	3	8
4) Vicarious achievement through child	3	3
5) Remote: little effect on the self	19	20
(Insufficient data)	3	4
Total	70	70
C. Style of grandparenting:		
1) The formal	22	23
2) The fun-seeking	20	17
3) The parent surrogate	10	0
4) The reservoir of family wisdom	1	4
5) The distant figure	13	20
(Insufficient data)	4	6
Total	70	70

Source: Neugarten and Weinstein (1964), Table 1. Copyright © 1964 by the National Council on Family Relations. Reprinted with permission.

invitation of the parent; and the *reservoir of family wisdom,* who maintains his authority and sees himself as the dispenser of special wisdom or skills (it was usually the grandfather, but this type was not very frequent). The two other styles of grandparenting seemed to be emerging as new roles for grandparents: the *fun seeker,* who joins the child in activities to have fun and to enjoy leisure and tends to ignore authority issues; and the *distant figure,* who is present only on special occasions and has only fleeting contact with the grandchild. These two new roles were significantly more common among younger grandparents (under age 65), whereas the most traditional role (formal) was more frequent among older grandparents. Similar age differences in styles of grandparenting have been reported in more recent studies (Cherlin & Furstenberg, 1985; Hagestad, 1985). Parallel differences also have been found in the child's perception of grandparents: young children (age 4–5) tended to see grandparents as indulging them, for example, by buying gifts and treats; school-age children (age 8–9) enjoyed grandparents who were active and fun to be with; older children (11–12) appeared most comfortable with relatively distant relations with their grandparents (Kahana & Kahana, 1970).

These data suggest that perhaps grandparents' roles reflect not only their own age, but also the age of their grandchildren.

Diversity is also shown in those families where grandparenthood may come "too early" ("off time," as discussed in Chapter 2). Burton (1985) studied the effects of early versus on-time grandmotherhood among a group of African-American grandmothers between the ages of 25 and 57. As we might expect, the "on-time" grandmothers expressed greater comfort with the role, and had "learned a great deal" from friends about being a grandmother; they also learned about their daughter's pregnancy earlier, compared with the "off-time" group who, it appeared, were largely caught unprepared. Some of these "early" grandmothers reported discomfort with the role:

> "I am 38, footloose, and fancy free. I love my grandbaby, but I don't have time for knitting booties and babysitting. I have done my part. Now it is my turn and I could care less who doesn't like it." Another woman said:
> "I really am a grandmother in name only. I don't have time to do what I would like to do as a grandmother. I work every day. I have young children. Right now I'm just too busy." (Hagestad & Burton, 1986, p. 480)

In contrast, an *on-time* grandmother commented:

> "This is the best time for me to become a grandma. I'm not too young to regret it and I'm not so old that I can't enjoy it. . . . I have the time, the money, and the knowledge to deal with my grandchild. I have no commitments to anyone except Anthony (her grandchild). . . . My daughter's grown, she can take care of herself. . . . My mother takes care of herself . . . I spend quite a bit of time with Anthony. . . . On the weekends I take him so that my daughter and her husband can have respite time." (Burton & Bengtson, 1985, p. 73)

In some families, the grandchild produced great-grandparenthood — a kind of domino effect that cascaded through the generations in the family — and produced frustrations or satisfactions for this elder generation as well. One 91-year-old great-great-great grandmother said:

> "My ma say women are 'post to have babies. That why God put us here. I say have um while you young. Then you have mo' people to look out behind you when you old like me." (Burton & Bengtson, 1985, p. 74)

Ethnic background may also influence styles of grandparenting. Wood and Robertson (1976) studied a representative sample of 257 grandparents in a working-class area of Madison, Wisconsin; they were predominately of Germanic and Scandinavian backgrounds. For this sample, a good grandparent was nearly always described as "someone who loves and enjoys their grandchildren and helps them out when they can" (p. 301). Although the grandparents felt their role was significant, there was very little they actually did as grandparents — some baby-sitting, trips to the zoo, movies, giving gifts, and remembering birthdays — and these happened only a few times a year. "Less than half the grandparents reported that they had told their grandchildren about family and customs, or had taught them a special skill such as sewing, cooking, fishing, or a craft" (pp. 301–302). Interestingly, there was no significant relationship between the grandparents' life satisfaction and their grandparenting activities; their life satisfaction depended on friendships and activities in organizations. They seemed content to boast about their grandchildren when they achieved success and to ignore them when they did not. They expected nothing tangible from them and were satisfied if their grandchildren showed some interest and concern. Although we might conclude from this study that the grandparent role is not very significant, instead, it is likely that these grandparents were displaying the influence of ethnic differences discussed earlier in this chapter. We may recall that Scandinavian Americans have the lowest frequency of kin visiting and the highest rate of membership in organizations (Woehrer, 1978). Thus, the importance of organizational activities and friendships for these grandparents is not surprising.

In contrast, Bengtson (1985) noted that a study he and several colleagues conducted found that Mexican-American grandparents reported greater amounts of contact with grandchildren, higher levels of satisfaction in this contact, and greater expectations of intergenerational assistance than either African-American or Anglo-American grandparents. One of the most striking ethnic contrasts among African Americans was the importance of "fictive kin": 47 percent of the sample over age 60 had reared children other than their own and the same number reported having "fictive" grandchildren (pp. 18–19).

Woehrer (1978) summarized several relevant cultural differences:

> Mutual sharing and exchange of help and resources takes place within a family context with culturally defined expectations. Whereas a German or Scandinavian American may perceive carefully defined boundaries around the nuclear families of her children, those boundaries may be much more vague for a black grandmother. Thus, while the German grandmother may not view it as in her place to give advice or rear her grandchildren, the black grandmother may very well perceive it as her responsibility to rear a grandchild, or a niece or nephew, or to give advice and assistance in rearing the children of her kin. The ways in which people of different ethnic backgrounds perceive family boundaries, responsibilities, and expectations varies greatly and affects the patterns of help and social and emotional support across generations and between kin. (Woehrer, 1978, p. 333)

Since grandparents are an integral part of the family lineage, they also provide a number of *symbolic functions* (Bengtson, 1985). These involve:

1. Simply "being there" to protect the next generation from the fear of mortality and the threat of being the next to die (Hagestad, 1984).

2. Providing a calming influence—an anchor of stability—during upsetting transitions, such as divorce (Hagestad, 1982a).

3. Serving as a "national guard" (Hagestad, 1985) or "family watchdog" (Troll, 1983) to protect against disaster and to provide help if needed.

4. Facilitating the active negotiation of values and behaviors between parents and children, with the goal of maintaining family continuity and individual growth. This may involve attending to "conversational demilitarized zones" (Hagestad, 1981) that make certain topics that are disruptive, such as those that reflect "cohort gaps" between generations, "off limits" so that they do not split the generations of the family.

5. The autobiographical interpretation of the continuity of the past, present, and future for the family. Grandparents have a "stake" in the grandchild's continuity with the past that may distort reality, but is also a source of identity (Bengtson & Kuypers, 1971)

Moreover, there may be sex-related differences between grandmothers and grandfathers. On one hand, their actual role behavior may differ much less than the role behavior of parents, and thus approach a unisex role (Turner, 1982, p. 931). On the other hand, women are often "kinkeepers" and grandmothers may function as "ministers of the interior" of the family by focusing on the interconnectedness of interpersonal relations within the family (Hagestad, 1985). Grandfathers, in contrast, may often function more as "ministers of state" or "head of the family" (Bengtson, 1985).

Of course, each grandparent may have different relations with each grandchild (Cherlin & Furstenberg, 1985), and this relationship may differ depending on the age of the grandchild (Kahana & Kahana, 1970).

Kinship Ties and Caregiving

Contrary to the myth that older persons in the United States are isolated and neglected by their family, there are close ties within the kinship network between most older people and their children. Using data from three national surveys of noninstitutionalized persons over age 65 in 1957, 1962, and 1975, Shanas (1979) concluded:

> In contemporary American society, old people are not rejected by their families nor are they alienated from their children. Further, where old people have no children, a principle of family substitution seems to operate and brothers, sisters, nephews and nieces often fulfill the roles and assume the obligations of children. The truly isolated old person, despite his or her prominence in the media, is a rarity in the United States. (pp. 3–4)

She found that about 80 percent of persons over 65 have living children. Of these, slightly over one-half have a child within 10 minutes of their home; three-quarters live within one-half hour of their children. Although the proportion of older persons living in the same household as their child declined from 36 percent in 1957 to 18 percent in 1975, the proportion of older persons either living with a child or who had a child within 10 minutes remained fairly constant: 59 percent in 1957 and 52 percent in 1975. Apparently both older people and their children typically prefer separate households that provide both generations with independence and privacy; as economic conditions improved from 1957 to 1975, greater numbers of older people were able to live in separate households, but did not lose close contact with their children. In fact, there was frequent contact. About 80 percent saw one of their children during the week before the interview, and over half had a visit the day of the interview or the day before. Only 1 out of 10 older persons with living children had not seen at least one of their children for a month or more. Of course, in individual cases it may be family friction or personality conflicts rather than old age that reduces the amount of contact. The frequency of

Divorce and remarriage complicate the relationship of grandparents and grandchildren; visitation rights after remarriage are problematic, especially during family holidays.

contact is about the same for White and Black grandparents and grandchildren, based on a national survey; the only difference was a slightly greater likelihood that the Black grandparents lived with their grandchildren, or if they lived apart, visited less frequently than White grandparents (Mitchell & Register, 1984).

Brothers and sisters are also important kin for older people. One-third of the respondents with living siblings had seen at least one during the week before the interview, and one-half had seen one during the month before the interview. Contact with siblings was especially important for widowed persons and older persons who had never married. In addition, 30 percent of the older persons in 1975 had seen some relative other than a brother, sister, child, or grandchild during the week before the interview; for older persons without children, this relative was often a niece or nephew.

There is also no evidence to support the myth that families refuse to care for their older relatives. Shanas (1979) noted that in both 1962 and 1975 about twice as many older persons were homebound and cared for by relatives as were living in nursing homes and other institutions (10% and 5% in 1975, respectively). Those persons in nursing homes were three times as likely to have never married than those older persons who lived in the community. Older persons in nursing homes tend to be those who have outlived their families and are the sole survivor of the kinship network, those never-married persons who have no younger family members to care for them, or those in such need for care that the family had no other alternative. Brody (1977) reported that:

> Studies of the paths leading to institutional care have shown that placing an elderly relative is the last, rather than the first, resort of families. In general, they have exhausted all other alternatives, endured severe personal, social and economic stress in the process, and made the final decision with the utmost reluctance.

Nonetheless, the myth persists that we do not provide enough care for our aged. Even among respondents in a study of women who were the principal caregivers of their widowed mothers (and often of their fathers before), 3 out of 5 felt guilty "somehow" about not doing enough for their mothers (Brody, 1985). Three out of 4 felt that children today did not take as good care of their parents as was true in the "good old days." Perhaps, Brody suggested, the persistence of this myth reflects the fact that we use as a standard the care we received as infants from our parents, and can never repay them:

> *The "truth" to which the myth speaks is that adult children cannot and do not provide the same total care to their elderly parents that those parents gave to them in the good old days of their infancy and childhood.* The roles of parent and child cannot be reversed in that sense. The good old days, then, may not be earlier periods in our social history (after all, the myth existed then too), but an earlier period in each individual's and family's history to which there can be no return. (Brody, 1985, p. 26)

A variety of studies have found that family supports are vital for maintaining older people in the community. For example, Johnson and Catalano (1983) interviewed the families of a sample of 115 patients age 65 and over 2–4 weeks after discharge from an acute hospital and 8 months after. They found that most patients were cared for by a primary caregiver (rather than by the family as a unit). The caregivers reported a high degree of strain, but few of the patients had their needs unmet. Only 17 percent of the patients were institutionalized within this period, although 22 percent had been rehospitalized at least once. Over time, spouses tended to become more interdependent as a result of the need for caregiving, sometimes to the exclusion of other interests. Of particular importance, caregiving may affect the health of the spouse; 17 percent of the spouse caregivers developed health problems. Adult children often used "distancing techniques" in an effort to cope; this included involving others in the care by enlarging the family network's responsibility or finding outside help such as a homemaker; others attempted to establish psychological distance, sometimes with the aid of psychotherapy.

Troll (1986, p. 11) suggested that the degree of intimacy required in caring for an infirm person may be more acceptable for a spouse who has shared an intimate relationship for many years than for an adult daughter or son. When there is no spouse, however, responsibility for parent care is frequently assumed by the daughter or daughter-in-law (Turner, 1982, p. 930). Since many of these women work, this responsibility often is added to other family and work-related demands.

Brody and Schoonover (1986) interviewed 150 families that included an elderly widowed woman who had the following characteristics: she was a community resident, needed some supportive services, and her primary caregiver was a married daughter. Those daughters who worked provided the same amount of help with household tasks, shopping and transportation, and arranging money and services as daughters who did not work; they also provided the same amount of general emotional support. Daughters who worked provided less help with personal care and cooking; however, they often paid others to provide these services.

Thus, families assume the major burden for giving care, and this is a major theme in the postparental family. Often the caregivers themselves are advanced in age, and may be giving care to their aged parents, or even to their adult children during a health crisis. We return to the topic of caregiving in Chapter 9, where we consider also the role of formal supports such as nursing homes, which may actually enhance the family relations by relieving the burden of daily care for an infirm person (Aizenberg & Treas, 1985, p. 182).

We conclude our discussion of the family cycle by focusing on widowhood.

Widowhood

Women have longer life spans than men, on the average, but this also means they are more likely to be widowed than men. Widowed women outnumber widowed men by more than five to one because of this difference in life span, the tendency of women to marry older men, and the higher remarriage rate of widowed men. There appears to be little sex-related difference in the adjustment of widowed women or men in terms of morale, loneliness, life satisfaction, or well-being; the majority of both sexes cope well (Turner, 1982, p. 929). In general, poverty is one of the greatest problems for widows, as the majority are living with very low income (Troll & Seltzer, 1985). Because of higher mortality rates and lower remarriage rates, widowed persons constitute a larger proportion of Black adults than of White adults and Black women who are widows are particularly likely to have very low income.

Widowed persons also frequently have the ordeal of caring for a terminally ill spouse, which often places a severe strain on the health of the caregiver. Troll (1986) noted that men tend to die shortly after being widowed more frequently than do women, but this probably reflects men's generally higher rate of mortality. We discuss bereavement in detail in Chapter 10. In this chapter we focus on the transition experienced by women as they enter this phase of life and the process of resocialization into this new role. We also consider some of the most important aspects of the widowed life-style.

Lopata (1973) interviewed a random sample of 301 widows in Chicago over age 50 who had not remarried; they had been widowed an average of 11½ years. Most were between 45 and 65 when they were widowed. Many had cared for their husband at home for over a year during his last illness, thus they had some opportunity to "rehearse" for widowhood—a process that is frequently reported by middle-aged women (Neugarten, 1967b). Nevertheless, four out of five women reported that their grief lasted longer than one year, and 20 percent felt that one never gets over it.

Lopata found three general patterns of adaptation to widowhood among the women she interviewed. One pattern was the "self-initiating woman." Although she experienced much disorganization in her life when her husband died, she modified her social relations with friends and children in realistic ways, built a new life-style that was relatively flexible to accommodate future changes, and did not try to hang on to unrealistic aspects of her previous life-style that were impossible to maintain. She continued relationships with her children, developed relationships that provided personal intimacy, created a life-style that suited her needs and potential, and, in general, attempted to match the resources available to her own needs and goals. A second pattern was the widow living in an ethnic community that paralleled a traditional village life-style. She did not experience much change, was involved in relationships with relatives, friends, and neighbors, and generally lived out her life as her earlier socialization had taught her. A third group were "social isolates." These women, in general, had never been highly involved in social relationships and were unable to maintain their few previous relationships because the friends had died or moved away and were not replaced. Often, poor finances increased their difficulty in maintaining contact with old friends or making new ones. In a later study of widows in Chicago, Lopata (1988a) found that relatively few received economic, social, or service support from social or community resources (with the exception of Social Security); as a result, some widows were destitute and isolated, and others were very dependent on their children, usually a daughter. Lopata recommended greater community efforts to reach out to widows with information and links to available services.

Another study of 245 women who had been widowed for three years or less found that different types of social support were helpful at different phases of the transition to widowhood. Elizabeth Bankoff (1983) mailed a questionnaire to a nationwide group of widows, 98 of whom had been widowed 18 months or less (termed the "crisis-loss" phase) and 147 who had been widowed between 19 and 35 months (termed the "transition" phase). Their average age was 52 years. She found that social support has relatively little effect during the crisis-loss phase when the women were in the midst of intense grief and may have been apathetic about the world in general. Of all sources of social support asked about, support from the parents—most likely a widowed mother—helped most during this phase. Bankoff speculated that the nurturance of a parent, combined with the role model provided by a woman who has been through widowhood, was the major reason that this source of support was helpful. Support from widowed friends was also somewhat helpful during this phase. During the transition phase, support from widowed or unmarried friends appeared to be most helpful. In contrast, support from married friends was associated with lower levels of well-being. Children provided high levels of support during both phases, but this did not appear to have much effect on the widow's sense of well-being. Thus, although social support is important, it depends on *who* is providing the support, and which phase of widowhood the recipient of the support is coping with, according to her data.

Shuchter (1986) studied 70 widowed persons for up to five years as a part of the San Diego Widowhood Project. He found that six psychosocial traits were important aspects of grief that may also focus the kind of help that can benefit a widowed person.

1. Experiencing, expressing, and integrating the painful emotional reactions of grief.

2. Finding ways to ward off the pain so it is not overwhelming.

3. Integrating a continuing relationship with the deceased spouse into ongoing life without interfering with daily living.

4. Maintaining health and finding help with practical matters from medical, legal, financial, and social support services.

5. Adjusting to altered relationships and forming new emotional involvements, perhaps with the help of a support group.

6. Developing an integrated and positive self-concept and view of the world (Shuchter, 1986, pp. 12–15).

Many older widowed women grow accustomed to living alone and prefer to do so. They often develop a social life with friends, especially if they live in an area with many other widows. They may even have higher rates of social involvement outside the home than married women of the same age do. Widowed men, in contrast, usually have fewer friends than women do and their wife was often their primary friend. Men usually remarry soon (Troll, 1986, p. 51).

Remarriage for older widows is statistically unlikely—there are few unmarried men in their age group. In addition, it may be discouraged by the family, who fear loss of control over inheritance. Moreover, in some cases, widowed persons may lose payments from the deceased spouse's pension if they remarry. Some widows cope with the loss of their spouse by a process Lopata (1981, 1988b) described as "husband sanctification" by which they idealize the deceased husband; this further reduces their availability to another relationship since no real person could compete with the sanctified spouse.

The special concerns of men who are widowed are also important since there is some evidence that the death of a spouse may be even more traumatic for men than for women. Social isolation, loneliness, depression, issues about dating and sex, remarriage, and financial problems are often important issues for widowers (Burgess, 1988).

Likewise, loneliness, health problems, and maintaining an adequate income may be major challenges for older widows. Morgan (1976) compared over 500 widowed and married women between the ages of 45 and 74. African-American, Mexican-American, and Anglo-American women were selected in representative samples from Los Angeles County. She found that poor health had a greater impact on morale among the widowed women than it did among the married women, and greater family interaction had positive effects on morale among all the women. However, this difference in morale was not found when the level of income was considered. That is, across all three ethnic groups, the lower morale of widows appeared to result more from their social situation (lower income) than from bereavement and grief, or from the loss of social roles associated with widowhood. Thus, Morgan suggested that the problems of widows, not widowhood as a problem, should be the focus of future research on widowhood.

Menopause

The term *menopause* refers to the cessation of the menses. Since men do not menstruate, they do not experience menopause. The term *climacterium* refers to the loss of reproductive ability. In women these events are two sides of the same coin since, when the menstrual cycle ends, reproductive ability also comes to an end. In men there may be a climacterium late in life when fertile sperm are no longer produced. Some men retain the ability to produce offspring into extreme old age, however (Harman & Talbert, 1985, p. 478).

Menopause typically occurs between the ages of 48 and 51 in a wide variety of populations (Talbert, 1977). For example, the age of menopause in Japanese, Caucasian, Chinese, and Hawaiian women in Hawaii was between 49 and 50 and was unrelated to the age at which the women began menstruating (Goodman, Grove & Gilbert, 1978). The onset of menopause may not be sudden, but may be preceded by some irregular cycles and menses. Once it has stopped, however, it does not begin again and any renewed "menstrual" flow should be checked by a physician to determine the cause (Comfort, 1976).

Although it is not clear why menopause occurs, it appears that the ovaries stop responding to the gonadotropic stimulation from the pituitary, which had regulated the menstrual cycle since puberty. Only a small fraction of the number of *oocytes* that are present at birth are ovulated during the woman's reproductive years; about half appear to be lost by the age of puberty, and those that do not become ova are lost by the process of atresia (atrophy of follicles) by the age menopause begins (Harman & Talbert, 1985). When the ovaries no longer respond by bringing an ova to maturity and do not produce estrogens and progestins, menopause occurs and the menstrual cycle ends.

Surgical removal of the uterus (hysterectomy) also brings an end to menstruation. This operation may be performed to remove abnormal tissues that can enlarge and produce discomfort or for other serious medical reasons. If the ovaries are not removed, estrogens and progestins are still produced up to the normal time of menopause, even if the uterus has been removed.

Hormone production is an important change during menopause. There is a marked drop in levels of estrogens and progestins that are produced by the ovaries and a related increase in the gonadotropic hormones (FSH and LH) that are produced by the pituitary to stimulate the ovary (Figure 5.3), which, after menopause, does not respond. Small amounts of estrogens continue to be produced in other parts of the body; for example, body fat converts androgens into estrogens and this appears to increase after menopause. There is little decline in the level of androgens in women after menopause, unless the ovaries have been removed (Harman & Talbert, 1985, p. 467). Thus, there is a shift in the relative amounts of estrogens and progestins (the predominant hormones in women) and androgens (the predominant hormone in men).

In contrast to women's menopause, men do not experience a sudden decline in hormone production during adulthood. Some studies have found a gradual decline in testosterone (an androgen) beginning about age 50, although there was consider-

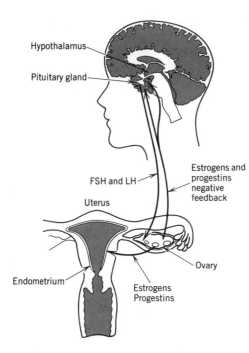

Hypothalamus

Pituitary gland

FSH and LH

Uterus

Estrogens and
progestins
negative
feedback

Endometrium

Estrogens
Progestins

Ovary

FIGURE 5.3 The hypothalamus-pituitary-gonad feedback loop of hormone response and production, which regulates the menstrual cycle in women, involves FSH and LH produced by the pituitary and estrogens and progestins produced by the ovaries. (*Source*: Hyde, Janet Shibley. *Understanding human sexuality* (3 ed). New York, NY: McGraw-Hill, 1986, Figure 4.1, p. 69. Reprinted with permission.)

able individual variation: some men between the ages of 70 to 90 had very low levels but others had normal or even higher levels of testosterone. Physical health may be a factor since some studies that selected older men on the basis of good health found no age difference in levels of testosterone between younger and older men (Harman & Talbert, 1985, pp. 481–482).

Physical Effects of Menopause

Many women experience a sensation known as a **hot flash** or *hot flush* from time to time after menopause. It is the most frequent symptom attributed to menopause, reported by about 70 percent of women in a number of different studies (e.g., Polit & LaRocco, 1980). It appears to be related to the release of a pulse of the gonadotropic hormone associated with ovulation (LH) from the pituitary (Harman & Talbert, 1985, p. 476).

> The hot flush is a brief episode of feelings of warmth and flushing, accompanied by perspiration. Its frequency and duration are quite variable. Some women report great discomfort and others none at all. (Williams, 1977, p. 118)

The reaction, characterized by measurable increases in skin temperature and heart rate, can be stimulated in laboratory experiments in postmenopausal women (but not premenopausal women) by placing pads of heated water against the body (Germaine & Freedman, 1984, pp. 1072–1073). In this experiment, a technique of systematic relaxation using biofeedback was found to reduce the reported symptoms significantly, suggesting that this method might be useful in treating women who are severely affected by ordinary hot flashes.

The decline in estrogen at menopause is also implicated in the loss of bone mass with aging, known as **osteoporosis.** This condition is related to calcium intake in the diet, with postmenopausal women requiring greater amounts than premenopausal women. Supplementing the calcium intake, providing low dosages of synthetic estrogens and progestins, or combining estrogen replacement with calcium and fluoride supplements have been reported to reduce or prevent bone loss and the increased risk of fractures after menopause (Exton-Smith, 1985, pp. 529–532). Adequate levels of vitamin D and regular exercise are also important preventative measures (Jarvik & Small, 1988).

Estrogen replacement therapy (ERT) involves receiving a low dosage of estrogens and progestins (the hormones that are produced by the ovaries before menopause) so that the body has hormonal levels similar to those before menopause; the levels are not high enough to produce menstruation, however; and no egg is released from the ovary after menopause. ERT may reduce the severity of hot flashes and increase vaginal lubrication during sexual excitement. Although this therapeutic use of estrogen is controversial because some studies found it associated with increased risk of breast and cervical cancer, some feel that the risk of cancer is reduced when progestins are also provided. Thus, for some women, the benefits of therapy outweigh the risks, especially when the increased protection against osteoporosis is considered (Harman & Talbert, 1985, pp. 477–478). However, estrogen replacement has been criticized as both sexist and ageist—as a "magic pill" intended to retain a woman's youthfulness in a male-oriented society (Unger, 1979, p. 406). Thus, a woman in her forties should consult her physician about tests to measure bone mass and discuss the risks and benefits of estrogen replacement therapy in her individual case (Jarvik & Small, 1988).

Psychological Symptoms and Menopause

The frequency of psychological and psychosomatic symptoms of menopause appears to be significantly lower if we accept the reports of menopausal women than if we believe reports by medical professionals. One study, for example, found that menopausal women rated their symptoms less frequent and less severe than did either nurses or physicians who were asked to rate symptoms of "menopausal women" in general (Cowan, Warren & Young, 1985). This study also found that physicians were more likely to regard menopausal symptoms as pathological than did either nurses or menopausal women themselves. Similarly, physicians were more favorable toward estrogen replacement than either nurses or menopausal women.

Another study found that three out of four menopausal women reported *none* of the symptoms usually associated with menopause (Goodman, Grove & Gilbert, 1978). This study examined the medical records of 332 Caucasian and 346 Japanese women living in Hawaii who came to a clinic for health screening; they were generally representative of their ethnic groups in terms of biomedical profiles and health problems. In comparing women who had not menstruated within the past 12 months with those who had menstruated within 2 months, they found that 28 percent of the Caucasian women and 24 percent of the Japanese women who were menopausal reported traditional symptoms of menopause such as hot flashes, irritability, insomnia, sweats, nervousness, depression, and crying spells. However, 16 percent of the Caucasian women and 10 percent of the Japanese women who were not menopausal also reported these symptoms.

These studies suggest that the stereotypic symptoms of menopause may be biased by the fact that women who are experiencing severe problems would be the ones most likely to come to a physician's attention, whereas the majority of women may experience few or no symptoms and view menopause from a different perspective.

Another study of 135 menopausal and postmenopausal women from a general urban population found that those women who reported a greater number of symptoms also tended to be less well educated, were less likely to be working, and reported poorer physical health than women with few or no symptoms. Symptoms such as depression, headaches, irritability, and nervousness were found to be related to personality characteristics such as lower self-confidence and personal adjustment (Polit & LaRocco, 1980). This suggests that these symptoms may not be caused by menopause, but by other factors reflecting economic, family, health, and psychological concerns. Some of these symptoms may, in fact, reflect our cultural view that women are expected to have difficulty at this period of life.

Unger (1979) noted that several studies suggested that the "menopausal syndrome" may be culturally determined and that it appears limited primarily to Western European and American women (p. 407). In our culture, one aspect of this syndrome is the presumed importance of the loss of ability to conceive additional children. Helena Deutsch (1945) termed menopause "the closing of the gates," an "omen of aging and death" (p. 478). Nancy Datan (1986) described how, as a younger woman, she accepted this idea and therefore had been greatly surprised by her findings in a cross-cultural study on this point (Datan, Antonovsky & Maoz, 1981). She and her colleagues studied North African, Arab, European, Persian, and Turkish middle-aged women living in Israel and found that they did not regret the loss of fertility that is related to menopause. "On the contrary, whether a woman had planned and restricted childbearing to only one or two children, or had been bearing children over most of her fertile years, the response to the cessation of fertility was positive" (Datan, Antonovsky & Maoz, 1981, p. 112).

Even with the Western cultural view of the importance of childbearing for women, menopause did not rank very high among all the changes and fears of middle age in the United States (Neugarten, Wood, Kraines & Loomis, 1963). The greatest concern was widowhood (Table 5.3). About one-half of the middle-class women who were interviewed in this pioneering study felt that menopause was a disagreeable event, and one-half disagreed. However, those women over age 45 were more likely than younger women to see positive changes after menopause had passed. They were also more likely than younger women to feel that menopause created no major change in life, that women have a relative degree of control over the symptoms, and that they need not inevitably experience a crisis. The most common complaints about being middle-aged were "getting older," "lack of en-

TABLE 5.3 *Attitudes toward Menopause Among White Mothers of Age 45–55 (N = 100)*

	Percent
The worst thing about middle age	
Losing your husband	52
Getting older	18
Cancer	16
Children leaving home	9
Menopause	4
Change in sexual feelings and behavior	1
What I dislike most about being middle-aged	
Getting older	35
Lack of energy	21
Poor health or illness	15
Feeling useless	2
None of these	27
The best thing about the menopause	
Not having to worry about getting pregnant	30
Not having to bother with menstruation	44
Better relationship with husband	11
Greater enjoyment of sex life	3
None of these	12
The worst thing about the menopause	
Not knowing what to expect	26
The discomfort and pain	19
Sign of getting older	17
Loss of enjoyment in sexual relations	4
Not being able to have more children	4
None of these	30
How menopause affects a woman's appearance	
Negative changes	50
No effect	43
Positive changes	1
No response	6
How menopause affects a woman's physical and emotional health	
Negative changes	32
No effect	58
Positive change or improvement	10
How menopause affects a woman's sexual relations	
Sexual relations become more important	18
No effect	65
Sexual relations become less important	17

Source: Neugarten (1967a), p. 44. Reprinted with permission.

ergy," and "poor health or illness"; only a few women related these changes to menopause. Three-fourths of the women reported the "best thing" about menopause was either not worrying about pregnancy or not having to bother with menstruation. The worst things were not knowing what to expect, the pain and discomfort, and the indication of getting older. Most felt menopause had no effect on sexual relations or on physical and mental health; however, one-half felt that it had a negative effect on a woman's appearance. Individual differences in coping ability were also evident, since some respondents indicated great discomfort but discounted the importance of menopause and others did the opposite. In general, the respondents were eager to discuss menopause since there were apparently few social supports for menopausal women (as compared with many such supports for pregnant women), and they frequently indicated an interest in more information about this topic. These respondents also indicated that there was a social expectation for a crisis at menopause, since they generally felt that "other women" saw it more negatively than they viewed it themselves (Neugarten, 1967a).

In general, it appears that menopause is similar to other transitions women experience. The impact of this biological change is affected by sociocultural factors, by individual personality, and by external influences such as whether the woman is working full time. Women appear to cope with it in much the same way they cope with other transitions. Women with children do not cease being mothers; wives continue relations with their spouse; and other important roles also provide considerable stability. The severity of physical and psychological symptoms seems to depend on who is reporting them—the woman herself or medical professionals. Some women may benefit from estrogen replacement, but this is a decision she must make in consultation with her physician.

Similarities and Differences in Sexual Response

Perhaps genital anatomy is the most apparent difference between men and women. Certainly, the complementarity of sexual organs and the insertion of the penis into the vagina has been necessary for producing children (until techniques of artificial insemination and *in vivo* fertilization were developed). Surprisingly, however, until a few years ago little was known about the precise similarity and differences in the functioning of male and female sexual organs. Of course, the physical structure of the genitals and the male's pattern of sexual arousal and ejaculation have been known for centuries. But the physiology of the female's orgasm—what causes it, how it is similar to and different from the male's orgasm, and the connection between vaginal and clitoral aspects of orgasm—were little understood until the studies by Masters and Johnson (1966, 1970).

Masters and Johnson reported that male and female orgasms are physiologically similar, disregarding (of course) the anatomic differences. That is, the orgasm is initiated by similar muscles and involves a similar reflex mechanism in the responding muscles for both men and women. The muscle contractions act on the erectile chambers that fill with blood during sexual excitation. In men, there are three such chambers; two produce an erection of the penis and the third is involved in the orgasm and expulsion of the semen during ejaculation. In women, there are five such chambers; one surrounds the vagina and is involved in the contractions in the lower vagina during orgasm (Sherfey, 1972, p. 94).

Two of the most important findings of the Masters and Johnson research are that there is no physiological difference between an orgasm reached through vaginal or clitoral stimulation and that, indeed, some clitoral stimulation is always achieved during intercourse. That is, there is no vaginal orgasm without a clitoral orgasm since the orgasmic reaction includes all the pelvic sex organs and is identical regardless of the mode or area of stimulation. Although the lower third of the vagina is an erotic zone during intercourse, its sensitivity is about equal to that of the clitoral shaft; but the clitoral glans is much more sensitive. During intercourse, the vaginal passageway narrows because of the increased accumulation of blood in the many veins surrounding the vagina. This leads to greater stimulation of the partner's penis, and further increases the stimulation on the tighter vaginal walls. The thrusting of the penis produces simultaneous stimulation of the labia minor, the clitoral shaft, and clitoral glans as an integrated unit. The clitoral glans seems to be the most important source of stimulation. Thus, some women may prefer more direct stimulation of the clitoral area than is provided by vaginal intercourse if they are to reach highly satisfying levels of orgasm. Research on the presence of a so-called "G-spot" in the vagina that produces orgasm without clitoral stimulation has indicated that this response is very rare (Masters, Johnson & Kolodny, 1988).

The Sexual Response Cycle

In both men and women the sexual response cycle may be divided into four phases (somewhat less well defined in men than in women). *Phase I* (excitation) occurs more rapidly in men than women and is characterized by the erection in men and by the rapid production of lubricating fluid in the vagina, increased diameter of the clitoris, and increased blood congestion in the labia major and labia minor in women. Nipple erection occurs in all women and in about one-third of the men studied. *Phase II* (plateau) is marked by a high degree of blood congestion and sexual tension in the entire pelvic area for both men and women. There is a sexual flush of the chest, neck, and forehead in both sexes and, in women, it frequently includes the lower abdomen, thighs, and lower back. It was noted in about 75 percent of the women and 25 percent of the men studied. The orgasm, *Phase III,* occurs in two stages for men—the first part involves slight contractions of all the involved organs and is experienced as a sign of imminent ejaculation. The second part is the actual ejaculation produced by the same contracting muscles as are involved in the woman's orgasm. The initial contractions occur at intervals of 8/10 of a second (the same as in women) for two or three expulsive efforts and then slow in spacing and in expulsive force. The woman's orgasm occurs in one longer stage. It is characterized by contractions of the uterus, vagina, and labia minor, producing the sensation of pelvic visceral contractions associated with the orgasm. In both sexes there are contractions of the rectal sphincter muscles (at intervals of 8/10 of a second), contractions of other body (skeletal) muscles, rapid and shallow breathing (hyperventilation), and rapid heart rates (100 to 160 beats per minute); a sweating reaction develops in 30–40 percent of either sex—usually on the soles of the feet and palms of the hands for men, but more widely distributed over the back, thighs, and chest for women. *Phase IV* (resolution) is a lengthy process of decreasing congestion of the many blood vessels involved in the sexual response cycle; this usually proceeds more slowly in women than in men.

Despite the many similarities in the sexual response cycle of men and women, there are marked differences as well. Most notable are the ability of many women to have repeated orgasms (Figure 5.4, pattern A) and the *refractory period* characteristics of the man's cycle (Figure 5.5). That is, after completing the orgasm, the male requires a period of return to the plateau stage before another orgasm can be achieved. This period is relatively short in young men (the highest frequency was three orgasms in a 10-minute period) but typically requires complete resolution and a new response cycle in men over the age of 30. Women, however, are usually able to experience successive (or multiple) orgasms without loss of sexual tension below the plateau level, if they continue effective stimulation; more than 50 percent of the female sample was capable of immediate return to the orgasmic experience.

The implications of these findings about the sexual functioning of men and women are currently having important theoretical and practical influences—such as the development of clinics dealing with practical techniques of therapy with persons experiencing some kind of sexual dysfunction. For our purposes, however, one of the important implications is that men and women are both physiologically similar and different in terms of sexual functioning. Certainly, an understanding of the differences may enhance sexual relations, but the striking data on the similarities clearly suggest that adult men and women have a great deal in common that may aid in understanding and communicating with one's partner. Neither men nor women can ever really know what the experience of the other is like, but they can discuss it, if they will, so that the sexual relationship is a fully integrated aspect of their total relationship.

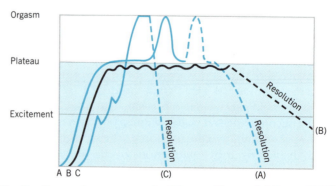

FIGURE 5.4 The female sexual response cycle. (*Source*: Masters & Johnson (1966), Figure 1–2. Copyright © 1966 by William H. Masters and Virginia E. Johnson. Reprinted with permission.)

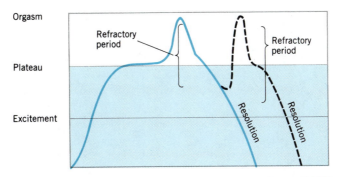

FIGURE 5.5 The male sexual response cycle. (*Source*: Masters & Johnson (1966), Figure 1-1. Copyright © 1966 by William H. Masters and Virginia E. Johnson. Reprinted with permission.)

Sexuality and Aging

The capacity for satisfying sexual relations continues into the decades of (at least) the seventies and eighties for healthy persons. Masters and Johnson (1966) reported:

> The most important factor in the maintenance of effective sexuality for the aging male is consistency of active sexual expression. When the male is stimulated to high sexual output during his formative years and a similar tenor of activity is established for the 31–40-year age range, his middle-aged and involutional years usually are marked by constantly recurring physiologic evidence of maintained sexuality. Certainly it is true for the male geriatric sample that those men currently interested in relatively high levels of sexual expression report similar activity levels from their formative years. It does not appear to matter what manner of sexual expression has been employed, as long as high levels of activity were maintained. (pp. 262–263)

They report a similar indefinite ability for sexual expression among women.

> In brief, significant sexual capacity and effective sexual performance are not confined to the human female's premenopausal years. Generally, the intensity of physiologic reaction and duration of anatomic response to effective sexual stimulation are reduced . . . with the advancing years. . . . Regardless of involutional changes in the reproductive organs, the aging human female is fully capable of sexual performance at orgasmic response levels, particularly if she is exposed to regularity of effective sexual stimulation. (p. 238).
>
> In short, there is no time limit drawn by the advancing years to female sexuality. (p. 247)

During the early years of the postparental period, many women report an increase in sexual interest, perhaps because they no longer have to worry about pregnancy after menopause and because children are out of the home so the couple can spend much more time alone in privacy. However, their husbands may feel less interest in sexual intimacy at this time because of their preoccupation with vocational goals as they deal with the threat of younger competitors and possible retirement on the horizon. Other factors that may be involved are youth-oriented standards of beauty and sexual attractiveness.

Most people can expect to be able to have sex long after they no longer wish to ride bicycles.

Studies of sexuality among a randomly selected sample of White men and women between age 46 and 70 who were members of a medical group insurance plan found that sexuality remained important for most of the respondents (Table 5.4). Only 6 percent of the men said they were no longer interested in sex, and only 12 percent reported they no longer had sexual relations; one-third of the women said they were no longer interested, and 44 percent said they no longer had sexual relations (Pfeiffer, Verwoerdt & Davis, 1974). Nearly all the respondents reported a decline in their sexual interest and activity. Women typically attributed the ending of sexual relations to their husbands (because of death, divorce, illness, or inability to perform sexually). Men who felt they were responsible for ending sexual relations attributed it to inability to perform sexually, illness, or loss of interest in sex. A second study found that past enjoyment of sexuality was the most significant factor in the level of present sexual activity (Pfeiffer & Davis, 1974). Both studies supported the important conclusion that "an aging woman's sexual activity and interest depends heavily upon the availability to her of a societally sanctioned, sexually capable partner" (Pfeiffer & Davis, 1974, p. 261).

A third analysis of these respondents over a period of six years by George and

TABLE 5.4 *Frequency of Sexual Intercourse Reported by White Participants in a Medical Group Insurance Plan*

Group	Number	Percent Reporting Intercourse				
		Not at all	Once a month	Once a week	2–3 times a week	More than 3 times a week
Men, age						
46–50	43	0	5	62	26	7
51–55	41	5	29	49	17	0
56–60	61	7	38	44	11	0
61–65	54	20	43	30	7	0
66–70	62	24	48	26	2	0
Total	261	12	34	41	12	1
Women, age						
46–50	43	14	26	39	21	0
51–55	41	20	41	32	5	2
56–60	48	42	27	25	4	2
61–65	44	61	29	5	5	0
66–70	55	73	16	11	0	0
Total	231	44	27	22	6	1

Source: Pfeiffer et al. (1974), Table 7-9. Copyright © 1974 by Duke University Press. Reprinted with permission.

Weiler (1981) concluded that sexual activity generally remained stable (Table 5.5). If it declined, it did not diminish gradually, but ceased abruptly. Thus, it appears to be more dependent on changes in health than on more gradual changes in appearance or attractiveness. Moreover, they found that *cohort* differences were significant: when compared at the same age, cohorts born more recently reported higher frequencies of sexual intercourse than cohorts born earlier. This suggests that sexual activity among older persons will probably increase as persons who began sexual activity during more sexually permissive periods grow old.

These findings point out the inaccuracy of the perceptions many young people have about sexuality during adulthood. A study of 646 college students revealed that over half thought their parents had sex only once a month or less; one-quarter of them thought their parents no longer had intercourse, or had it less than once a year (Pocs, Godow, Tolone & Walsh, 1977). In contrast, the data in Table 5.4 show that most of the men and a plurality of the women in the 46–50 age group said they had intercourse once a week. Perhaps, as Comfort (1974) noted, ''Freudian anxieties about parental intercourse'' are involved in the myth that older persons are no longer sexual, but the reality is that ''most people can and should expect to have sex long after they no longer wish to ride bicycles'' (p. 442).

Nonetheless, Masters and Johnson (1970) reported an increase in the incidence of sexual dysfunction after age 50 for men. This is not caused by age, however. They cite six reasons for this increase:

TABLE 5.5 Distribution of Sexual Activity Patterns over Six Years of Study[a]

	Age at Start of Study (years)		
	<56	56–65	>65
	Men		
Stable activity	66.6	63.5	42.4
No activity to some activity	1.6	2.7	9.1
Increasing activity	3.2	1.4	0.0
Some activity to no activity	4.8	6.8	18.2
Decreasing activity	11.1	8.1	3.0
Continuously absent	0.0	9.5	12.1
Other	12.7	8.1	15.2
	Women		
Stable activity	61.4	55.6	33.3
No activity to some activity	1.8	2.8	0.0
Increasing activity	1.8	0.0	0.0
Some activity to no activity	5.3	22.2	33.3
Decreasing activity	10.5	8.3	0.0
Continuously absent	5.3	5.5	33.3
Other	14.0	5.5	0.0

[a]The values are percentages of gender groups. The percentages are rounded to one decimal place; consequently the column totals may depart slightly from 100%.
Source: George & Weiler (1981), Table 3. Reprinted with permission from *Archives of General Psychiatry, 38*, p. 922. Copyright 1981, American Medical Association.

1. Monotony of a repetitious sexual relationship
2. Preoccupation with the career or economic pursuits
3. Mental or physical fatigue
4. Overindulgence in food or drink
5. Physical and mental infirmities of either the individual or his spouse
6. Fear of performance associated with, or resulting from, any of the other categories

Erectile dysfunction, sometimes called *impotence,* is the inability to have an erection; it may be caused by any of these six factors and is often successfully treated by a qualified sex therapist. It can also result from physical causes such as blocked arteries and medications, or by certain types of surgery on the prostate. Accurate diagnosis of the cause of erectile dysfunction is necessary to determine if there is a physical cause. Treatment might require surgical procedures or the use of devices that are implanted in the penis so that the man can make his penis erect at will.

Although the older man may note some physiological changes in sexual response, such as slower and less firm erections, less quantity and power of the ejaculation, less awareness of an impending orgasm, a need for more stimulation for orgasm, and a longer delay between successive erections, these changes do not alter his ability to have highly satisfying sexual relations. In fact, they may allow him to delay ejaculation and to enhance both his own and his partner's enjoyment (Butler & Lewis, 1976). An older man may find that he does not experience orgasm with each sexual encounter: "It occurs in every second act of intercourse, or in one act in three, rather than every time" (Comfort, 1976, p. 192). It is possible that even these changes do not reflect age as much as one of the manifestations of other changes such as arteriosclerosis, which reduces the efficiency of blood flow in the veins and arteries. In addition, contrary to popular myth, sexual activity is not likely to cause heart attacks.

> The incidence of death during intercourse is estimated at less than one percent of sudden coronary deaths. (In one major study the rate was less than 0.3 percent!) Of this small percentage, seven out of ten deaths occur in extramarital relations, suggesting that the stressful aspects associated with such affairs, such as hurry, guilt and anxiety, are a factor. (Butler & Lewis, 1976, p. 29)

Men who have suffered heart attacks are usually able to resume sexual activities as soon as they are able to walk around the room. One risk to a man's sexuality in the later years is abstinence; thus, if one's partner is hospitalized or unavailable for several weeks, masturbation or some other sexual activity is important to retain sexual ability. Another threat to an older man's sexuality is medication or surgery of the prostate; the physician should be informed if sexuality is important, and if the ability to have an erection is diminished when a new prescription is begun (Comfort, 1976, pp. 194–195).

Women's sexual capacity is less affected by age, although maintaining one's accustomed level of sexual activity can be important for retaining the capability for satisfying sexual relations in women as well as in men. The decline in estrogens and progestins in women after menopause typically causes some thinning of the lining of the vagina wall that may make it more easily irritated during intercourse. The bladder and urethra may also be more easily irritated during sex and it may be helpful to urinate before sex. The vaginal secretions become less acid so vaginal infections are more likely. Vaginal itching and discharge should not be assumed to be caused by age, but suggest the need for a medical examination, including a Pap test to be certain of the cause. The clitoris remains the source of sexual arousal, and women who are healthy and had experienced orgasms earlier in life can continue high levels of sexual satisfaction well into the eighties (Butler & Lewis, 1976).

> Women who have had patterns of regular sexual intercourse once or twice a week over the years seem to experience fewer symptoms of sexual dysfunction than women with patterns of irregular and infrequent intercourse. Even though older women with regular patterns may show physical signs of steroid insufficiency [decline in estrogens and progestins], their lubricating capacity continues unimpaired, while regular contractions during intercourse and orgasm maintain vaginal muscle tone. Contact with a penis also helps preserve the shape and size of the vaginal space.
>
> It is, of course, impossible for numbers of older women to continue sexual contact after the illness or death of their partners. Many other women have never married or are divorced or separated. For them, self-stimulation (masturbation) can be effective in preserving lubricating ability and the muscle tone which maintains the size and the shape of the vagina. In addition, it can release tensions, stimulate sexual appetite and contribute to general well-being. (Butler & Lewis, 1976, pp. 14–15)

A water-based lubricant (such as K-Y) can reduce irritation of the vagina that may result from decreased vaginal secretions; however, lubricants that are petroleum-based (e.g., Vaseline) may increase the risk of infection. Low-dosage estrogen and progestin replacement therapy may also be prescribed by a physician and can enhance lubrication of the vagina (see the discussion of this therapy in the section on menopause earlier in this chapter).

Of course, sexuality need not always involve intercourse. Touching, caressing, noncoital sex, and being close to a loved partner are important aspects of sexuality, especially during the aging years (Starr, 1985). Moreover, there are wide variations in individual frequencies of sexual activity throughout the life span. One person's sexual behavior may be regarded as normal whether it is relatively high, moderate, or low. In general, sex becomes less frequent with advancing age; this can actually enhance the pleasure, however, as reduced frequency may make the experience more special and satisfying.

In general, the chief factor involved in limiting sexual activity for older persons is the shorter life span for men than women combined with women's tendency to marry men who are a few years older. This leaves many women without a sexual partner when their husband dies and they have little chance of finding another male partner for the same reasons (Newman & Nichols, 1960). In addition, social norms imply that sexuality is only for the "young" and that older persons who have sexual interest are "dirty" old men and women. This myth is prevalent in many nursing homes, and may even arise when a widowed parent seeks to remarry or live with someone in a sexual relationship.

Singles: The Unmarried and the Previously Married

Although marriage is typical in our society, a sizable minority of the population are not married. We would expect that there is at least as much diversity among these single and previously married adults as there is among their married counterparts. Ethnic differences and the nature of their unmarried life-style would be expected to be important. For example, a gay man or lesbian may differ in life-style from a heterosexually married person more because of sexual orientation than because of the absence of marriage. Similarly, widowed persons differ from divorced persons, and both differ from never-married persons.

Divorced and Separated Persons

Just as marriage involves a change in social role and status from "single" to "married," so does the process of divorce—which is often a lengthy one—involve a marked change in role and status. This change is an example of the *idiosyncratic transition* described in Chapter 3. That is, unlike marriage, divorce is not an institutionalized status passage in which the new roles are prescribed by social norms. Instead, one has to find one's own way through this change in roles with little outside support and few normative guidelines.

The transition of divorce involves not only shifting to a single life again, but also reformulating a range of social ties — to the ex-spouse, to children, to relatives, and to friends. Often there is a feeling of failure involved in terminating a marriage, and one's married friends are apt to feel somewhat divided and threatened in their loyalties to the divorced couple. The process usually involves a complex tangle of emotions and adjustments to new situations. Feelings of love and hate, of mourning and relief, of failure and a new beginning, all alternate while one attempts to adjust to sleeping alone, eating alone, managing a household, and dividing up treasured joint possessions. Loneliness is a major reaction. If children are involved, they frequently also experience a period of upset and provide an added dimension of complexity to the resocialization process for the parents, as well as one major responsibility for the parent who retains custody. Legal aspects of the process are often difficult and may provide more opportunity for expressing anger than for smoothly meeting responsibilities and dividing up joint possessions. The emotional distress that usually precedes divorce increases the difficulty.

Termination of a marriage, either by divorce or by separation, results from a variety of causes both personal and social. On one hand, divorce is more common among persons poorly prepared for marriage, among those who married to escape their parents, and among couples who cannot tolerate differences; it is more common among children of divorced or unhappy parents, among childless marriages, and among pregnant brides (Duvall, 1971; see also Glick, 1980). It is also much more common among couples who married early — before the age of 20 — and during the early years of marriage (U.S. Bureau of the Census, 1973, 1977). As social barriers that inhibited divorce diminished during the 1970s, marriages that were unsatisfying and might have broken up eventually probably were ended by divorce sooner rather than later, contributing to the increased divorce rate (Norton & Glick, 1981). The high divorce rate may also reflect the stress and competition experienced by the "baby boom" generation (Easterlin, 1980). During the 1980s the divorce rate stabilized and then began to decline slightly, although the number of divorced persons (who did not remarry) continued to increase (U.S. Bureau of the Census, 1988).

Divorce appears to be more difficult for older, compared with younger, men and women. Chiriboga (1982a) interviewed 310 recently separated persons ranging in age from 20 to 79 in the San Francisco-Oakland area of California. Names of potential respondents were drawn at random from county records and half agreed to the interview; 18 percent of the men and 25 percent of the women identified themselves as belonging to some ethnic or minority group. The study focused on differences between younger and older respondents and between women and men. In general, separation or divorce was a period of crisis for most of the respondents, but older persons appeared to be more vulnerable than younger persons: the older respondents were more likely to be unhappy, expressed more personal discomfort, appeared more "tortured," and indicated greater pessimism and long-term dissatisfaction than the younger group. In particular, persons over age 50 seemed to be the most maladapted group, whereas those in their 40s were more similar to younger age groups. The reason for the greater disturbance for the older respondents was not clear. It appeared that there were different areas of vulnerability between the sexes. For example, the older men were especially vulnerable with regard to uncertainty about what to do next. They also reported being less happy and were more troubled by the separation than the older women. Older women, in contrast, showed a greater amount of emotional tension and a greater number of psychological symptoms and tended to be more disorganized and more distrustful than the men. Nonetheless, both groups expressed equal optimism about the future (p. 113). The results in this study were also consistent with previous research that found men to be relatively unaware of marital problems prior to divorce, whereas women were more likely to feel that life before divorce was particularly difficult and divorce provided some relief (Chiriboga & Cutler, 1977).

Following divorce, most persons eventually remarry. As divorce rates increased in the 1970s, 3 out of 4 women and 5 out of 6 men who divorced eventually remarried—within three years, on the average. Between one-half and two-thirds of remarriages were estimated to last until one of the partners died (U.S. Bureau of the Census, 1976b). During the 1980s remarriage rates were somewhat lower—about 70 percent of the divorced women in their thirties were expected to remarry (Glick & Lin, 1986). Since the divorce rate also declined in the mid-1980s, the number of remarried families and stepfamilies in the United States did not change significantly. In 1987, 21.3 percent of all married-couple families were remarried and 8.3 percent of all married-couple families were stepfamilies—that is, with a child under age 18 who was the biological child of one of the parents and born before the remarriage (Glick, 1989a).

Remarried families have been termed "reconstituted families" (Furstenberg & Spanier, 1984). However, one remarried mother commented:

> There is an unfortunate term—"the reconstituted family"—currently in vogue to describe the more than 500,000 new family groups formed each year in this country as a result of divorce and remarriage. Implicit in this phrase is the misguided notion that stepfamilies are like frozen orange juice: what was taken away has been replaced, but the resulting new family is the same as the original. As any stepparent and stepchild can tell you, this is an absurd idea; the painful loss of a parent and the addition of one or more unfamiliar adults does not reconstitute anything. It creates an awkward, new system called a stepfamily which, in fact, is not at all a stable family. It has to learn to be one, over time, drawing on the creativity, flexibility, strength, and courage of all its members. This is not an easy process. (Raine, 1989, p. 13)

Stepfamilies also involve stepgrandparents. For example, Johnson and Barer (1987) found that a middle-class White sample of paternal grandmothers were likely to maintain relationships with their former daughter-in-law because she is the mother of her grandchildren, even despite remarriage of the daughter-in-law. Thus, the "kinkeeper" function of women appears to expand to include the new parents of her grandchildren, at least for this sample of grandmothers. Likewise, maternal grandmothers usually maintained contact with their grandchildren because their daughter generally had custody of the children after a divorce; a new stepfather is included in the expanded family network, and the grandchildren's father may remain part of the family network if he is involved with the children. In some families, however, the grandparents have had to seek assistance from a court of law to obtain visitation rights with their grandchildren (Wilson & DeShane, 1982).

Gay and Lesbian Persons

Another type of unmarried life-style is represented by **gay men** and **lesbians** (gay women), who are sexually attracted to persons of their own gender. It is not known why some adults are homosexual and others are heterosexual. The origins of sexual orientation appear to develop in stages beginning during the prenatal period when hormones influence the development of the brain before the person is born. Early childhood experiences also may play a role, but the formative years seem to be before puberty. An individual may not begin homosexual or heterosexual behavior until after puberty or even several years later, however (Money, 1988, pp. 123–124).

The diversity of gay men and lesbians is often overlooked. There are many different kinds of homosexualities and so knowing that a person is homosexual tells one little more than knowing a person is heterosexual. For example, one study (Bell & Weinberg, 1978) found that 20 percent of the gay men had been married heterosexually, and over half of them had children (this was the case for 71 percent of the Black gay men who had been married). Over one-third of the White lesbians and almost half of the Black lesbians in the study had been married, and most who had been married also had children.

Lesbians and gay men live a variety of different life-styles, including monogamous couples and sexually active noncoupled individuals. Some are rearing children, and many have formed family-style relationships within the lesbian and gay community. One study of lesbian couples and nonmarried living-together heterosexual couples found that the lesbian partners tended to be more equal in the division of labor and showed less gender role stereotyping, but were somewhat less financially interdependent than the heterosexual partners (Schneider, 1986). A study by Harris and Turner (1986) compared 10 gay male and 13 lesbian parents (15 of whom had custody of the children) with 16 heterosexual single parents (14 female, 2 male). They found few differences between the gay/lesbian parents and the heterosexual parents; although the sample was obviously small and nonrandom, they were able to conclude that "being homosexual is clearly compatible with effective parenting and is not a major issue in parents' relationships with their children" (p. 101). However, the heterosexual parents were more likely than the gay and lesbian parents to feel that role models of the other gender from themselves should be provided for the child. In addition, they found gender differences between gay men and lesbians: the gay men reported more satisfaction with their child, mentioned fewer disagreements with their partner about discipline, were more likely to encourage the child to play with sex-typed toys, and had higher incomes; the lesbians were more likely than the gay men to perceive that their homosexuality could benefit their children.

A variety of special concerns and issues are involved in living as a lesbian or gay person. These may include problems in dealing with parents, discomfort in relations with neighbors and friends in the community, and discrimination in employment or housing. There may also be unique issues with regard to decision making, division of household tasks, and sexual exclusiveness in committed couple relationships. Moreover, the courts are a common threat to gay and lesbian households with children because they often are reluctant to grant custody or even visiting rights if sexual orientation is made an issue, despite evidence that homosexual parents have no negative effect on the sexual orientation or social adaptation of their children (Harry, 1988).

Some gay and lesbian couples are deciding to adopt children or to have children through artificial insemination; for example, a lesbian couple might choose to produce a child using sperm donated by one partner's brother or by a gay male friend. Useful guidebooks are available for help with some of the concerns faced by lesbian and gay parents (e.g., Schulenburg, 1985) and most urban areas have support groups for lesbian mothers and gay fathers.

The epidemic of Acquired Immune Deficiency Syndrome (AIDS) dramatically affected the gay male community during the 1980s, and sexual behavior has been altered significantly especially in urban areas (Stall, Coates & Hoff, 1988). Many gay men lost a significant number of friends and some lost long-term partners to the disease. The community also mobilized its resources to support those affected by the disease, and in many ways grew stronger. It also became more visible to the general public as a result of the vast publicity the disease received. Self-help books on lesbian and gay couples also became more widely available during the 1980s (e.g., Berzon, 1988; Clark, 1988; Marcus, 1988).

Very little was known about older gay men and women until the mid-1970s. Their life-styles and patterns of coping with the social stigma of homosexuality earlier in this century have been found to be quite diverse (Adelman, 1986; Almvig, 1982; Berger, 1982; Gray & Dressel, 1985; Kehoe, 1988; Kelly, 1977; Kimmel, 1979). Long-term partnerships are not uncommon, some lasting over 50 years.

Long-term partnerships among gay persons is not uncommon. Bruhs and Gean have been together for over 50 years and their aging years have been enriched by a program in New York City called SAGE that provides volunteer social support and services.

Relations with family and children, developing self-acceptance, and conscious attempts to build friendship networks to provide support are some frequent themes in many of their lives. Special problems faced by older gays include discriminatory visiting regulations in hospitals where only "family" may be allowed in intensive care units and in nursing homes where a gay partner may not be welcome, problems in inheritance, and general issues involving "openness" about sexual orientation with family, "in-laws," physicians, nursing home staff, and funeral directors. For example, a bereaved partner may find little support during bereavement since his or her relationship may not be seen as valid. The AIDS epidemic has called attention to many of these issues and to the importance of wills, power-of-attorney arrangements to replace family control over health care decisions, and the support of lesbian and gay friends during times of crisis. Programs to provide opportunity for social support and interaction for older lesbians and gays have been developed, such as SAGE in New York City. It offers assistance to persons who are homebound because of illness, a variety of activities at a community center, and monthly socials for an intergenerational community of gay men and lesbians.

Masters and Johnson (1979) reported on the sexual differences and similarities between heterosexual and homosexual men and women. Not surprisingly, they found no physiological difference in sexual response patterns between the two groups of men or between the two groups of women. However, they did find striking differences in the degree of verbal and nonverbal communication between the partners during sex, and between the extent to which the partners focused on providing pleasure to the partner or simply focused on achieving orgasm. Interestingly, the homosexual couples communicated better; they shared information about sexual wishes, level of excitement, preferences, and dislikes freely and openly. In contrast, married heterosexual couples seldom exchanged this kind of information during the study; frequently the man acted as the "sex expert" who seldom indicated any curiosity about what might please or displease his partner, and she rarely told him or asked his preferences. Also, the homosexual couples were more relaxed about sex, whereas the heterosexual couples typically focused on achieving orgasm.

Homosexuality was officially removed from the American Psychiatric Association list of mental disorders in 1973 and, in 1975, the governing body of the American Psychological Association urged "all mental health professionals to take the lead in removing the stigma that has long been associated with homosexual orientations" (Conger, 1975, p. 633). However, antihomosexual attitudes and stereotypes continue to be widespread in our society and violence and discrimination against lesbians and gay men are a serious concern.

Unmarried Heterosexuals

For some, singlehood is a stage before marriage, or between marriage and remarriage. For others, it is a life-style over a long period of time. One study of single persons between the ages of 60 and 94 found that they see nothing special about being unmarried: it's "just another way of life" (Gubrium, 1976, p. 190). They valued being independent, tended to be relatively isolated but not lonely, and were generally satisfied with their solitary activities. They felt a continuity to their lives

Older persons may remarry after widowhood or divorce, or live together for a variety of economic, family, or personal reasons.

and found nothing particularly different about being old—unlike married persons, they did not have to face widowhood or divorce and tended to take their life-style for granted. Thus, they conveyed a sense of being unique persons—not misfits, but persons who tended to see things differently than the majority of others do.

There is considerable variation among unmarried adults. The range of singlehood includes those who have chosen to remain single (''creative singlehood''), those for whom singlehood is a stage before marriage or remarriage, and those for whom it is a stage involving **cohabitation** (e.g., living with a person of the other gender in a sexually intimate relationship) that may lead to marriage (Libby, 1978).

For a variety of reasons, a growing proportion of adults have postponed marriage and lived for a longer period of time in singlehood. The average age of marriage rose to 26 for men and 24 for women during the 1980s, the highest it has been since 1900 (Cowan, 1989). Many of the reasons for later marriage reflected demographic and economic factors, that is, the ''baby boom'' generation tended to delay marriage perhaps because of the great competition among this cohort for all of life's opportunities, including education, jobs, and marriage partners (Easterlin, 1980).

Among the variety of single life-styles are single parents, usually single mothers, who are rearing one or more children, sometimes in the context of an extended family. Some of these parents began this life-style early in adolescence. It is often associated with having dropped out of school, low income, and less available health care. As a result, they tend to be burdened with social, economic, psychological, and family problems that existed before they became parents (Chilman, 1983, 1988).

Obviously, social class affects single life-styles. For example, in contrast to low-income single parents, Starr and Carns (1972) studied a sample of college graduates in their early to mid-twenties in Chicago. They noted the role of singles bars and work for meeting dates. Singles bars may recreate the college-type environment for casual evenings and for meeting friends and dates (Kaplan, 1974), but most singles probably go to such bars infrequently. Starr and Carns (1972) reported that most of their sample did not establish dating relationships in bars, in their apartment buildings, in organizations, or in "singles only" dances. Instead, most dates arose from contact at work; usually co-workers were not dated, but they arranged dates in a friend-of-a-friend pattern. In fact, they concluded, the popular image of "swinging singles" is a misnomer, for these singles are coping with the same kinds of problems everyone else is and are generally not living lives of "wild abandon."

Heterosexual dating patterns and sexual behavior were affected by the AIDS epidemic beginning in the 1980s because the disease can be transmitted by the exchange of semen or vaginal secretions during sexual intercourse with an infected partner. Public education campaigns were begun to provide relevant information on prevention and control of the disease. In general, they stressed that if one does not know whether one's partner or oneself might have become exposed to the disease by the use of intravenous drugs or by engaging in sex with someone who could have been infected, condoms should be used to reduce the risk of transmitting the disease. Couples in committed monogamous relationships can have their blood tested anonymously to determine if either partner has been infected. Counseling is required to interpret the results of the test and to help the individual determine appropriate sexual behavior and to decide whether to avoid having children.

Ethnicity and gender interact with socioeconomic status to affect single life-styles. For example, Higginbotham (1981) noted that some lower-middle-class African-American women have postponed marriage to seek education and career opportunities. As a result, many of these women remained single into their twenties and thirties and it is likely these women will find considerable competition for marital partners, as men of similar or greater education may have already married.

Age may also affect singlehood, since not all singles are young, or are parenting young children. One study of 47 men over 65 years of age living alone called attention to the diversity of their past lives and current life-style (Rubinstein, 1986). Of the 47, 30 had been widowed, 6 divorced, and 11 had never married. Many of the never-married men had lived with their parents until the parent died. The present life-style of these never-married men followed three general patterns. One group had a high level of social contact and interaction; they were outgoing and interested in people and world events. Members of a second group were relatively isolated on a daily basis, had little family interaction, but were able to recognize and satisfy their minimal social needs; they were the only group to report feeling lonely, however. A third group, although not exactly loners, tended to be on the periphery of social interaction; none had a close friend, but a few did name some acquaintances and most attended senior center programs from time to time.

One aspect of single life-styles that has received considerable research attention is *cohabitation* (Macklin, 1978, 1988). In many states, nonmarital cohabitation is considered to be a crime; at the same time, if the partners present themselves as a married couple, their relationship eventually becomes regarded legally as a common-law marriage in some states. Also, if they break up, one partner may be able to force the other to pay a financial settlement similar to alimony under some conditions. This confusion about the social and legal definition of these relationships is also reflected in the term used to describe one's partner; housemate, partner, significant other, and friend were among the terms commonly used in the 1980s. Macklin noted five general styles that reflect the range of cohabitation relationships:

1. *Temporary casual convenience.*   Two persons live together because of the practical advantages of sharing the same living quarters. The interaction ranges from friendly companionship to little or no interaction.

2. *Affectionate, going-together relationship.*   The couple enjoys living together and will continue to do so as long as this is true.

3. *Trial marriage.*   The partners are considering a serious commitment and wish to test its feasibility.

4. *Temporary alternative to marriage.*   The couple has made a commitment to marry each other and are living together until it is convenient to do so.

5. *Permanent alternative to marriage.*   The couple is living together without legal and religious vows in a long-term committed relationship (Macklin, 1988, p. 58).

In her review of the research on cohabitation, Macklin (1988) noted that few couples choose to live together in a permanent or semipermanent long-term relationship; most cohabiting relationships either result in marriage or terminate, usually within a year. Thus, cohabitation appears to serve as a stage in the process of courtship and mate selection leading to marriage and is generally not an alternative to marriage. In addition, whether a couple has lived together or not has little effect on the quality of the later marital relationship. Similarly, persons who have lived together are just as likely to divorce as those who did not live together before marriage.

A study by Blumstein and Schwartz (1983) of 642 cohabiting couples, 3574 married couples, 957 gay male couples, and 772 lesbian couples across the United States noted that:

> Of all four kinds of couples, cohabitors have the clearest sense of a need for personal time. Not only do they consider it a central value in their lives, but their day-to-day activities reflect this belief. They are more likely to see friends separately, go to movies and other leisure activities separately — not even have dinner together. When we asked them whether they would like more time together, they were less apt to say yes than married couples. This response, we feel, is rooted in a complex set of causes. Many cohabitors are tentative about their relationships: The partners may not have developed a

commitment to each other, only in rare cases have they pooled their incomes or created joint property, and they have not subordinated their individual needs to their future together. This lack of focus on their life as a couple allows them to go their separate ways. Their belief in personal independence further encourages them to maintain separate lives. These factors combine to direct them away from the relationship, whereas developing a need for one another would sustain their commitment through bad as well as good times. (p. 186)

Those cohabiting couples who became married during the two-year follow-up in the study tended to be those who were more traditional. They were likely to combine financial resources early in the relationship, preferred to spend more time with each other, were more possessive, and did not have an ''open'' sexual relationship (pp. 315–316). A smaller proportion of couples broke up than got married over the two-year period. There was not much difference in break-up rates among the cohabiting, gay male, and lesbian couples; married couples had the lowest rate of breaking up.

Older persons also may choose cohabitation, for example, after divorce or widowhood. They may not wish to remarry late in life for several reasons, including the loss of the deceased spouse's pension, the wish to preserve the rights of one's children to an inheritance, unwillingness to provide nursing care in the event of chronic illness, and pressure from children not to remarry.

Conclusion

It has been possible to sketch only the outlines of the diverse life-styles of adults in our heterogeneous society today. The need for intimate relationships and family ties is very strong for most people and a variety of complex factors influence the nature of those loving relationships. Rearing children, caring for aging parents, supporting one's spouse or ''life partner,'' and satisfying one's sexual and affectional desires are significant aspects of adulthood and aging. The next interlude includes each of these points as we reinterview Murray at two different points in his life: age 54 and 64.

Chapter Summary

1. Contrary to popular belief, 4 out of 5 American families consist of a husband and wife in their first marriage and their children, if any. Of those who do divorce, most remarry and, because of longer life spans today, marriages often last longer than in earlier generations.

2. In the United States, the modified extended family is predominant; it consists of nuclear family units that maintain close ties with other family units in a kin network. In Western societies, multigenerational households have been prevalent in the past only during periods of economic hardship or family disruption. Multigenerational households are the typical pattern in some other cultures.

3. Ethnic background influences family structure, patterns of family interaction, and the relative value placed on friendship, community activity, and family ties. Socioeconomic status also affects the values and life-style of families. The pattern of behavior or social environment that is meaningful for one group may be different for another group.

4. Just as each individual goes through a life cycle, so families have a cycle with milestones that mark stages in the family cycle. There is more diversity of timing in these events today than in the past and, with fewer children and longer parental life span, the pattern of the family cycle is also somewhat different.

5. During the *establishment* phase of the family cycle, the partners function as a dyad and develop styles of interaction through the process of mutual socialization, including patterns of decision making, division of household responsibilities and roles, styles of sexual interaction, and planning for children if they are desired.

6. The birth of a child begins the *new parents* phase of the family cycle. Although some studies find less emotional upset during this period than other studies, the transition into parenthood may be a time of stress, especially for parents who are unprepared for the amount of work involved in childcare.

7. The task of a *child-rearing family* involves nurturing, mutual socialization, and providing opportunities for the child's maximum emotional, intellectual, and psychological development. Single-parent and stepparent families face special issues. Parents and adolescent children often are invested in different "developmental stakes."

8. The *postparental* phase of the family has grown longer in recent years and can bring new satisfaction and opportunity. However, some children return home after divorce or for other reasons; also care of aging parents, especially for women who function as "kinkeepers" in the family, often brings stress.

9. Style of grandparenthood differs among ethnic groups and reflects the age of the grandparents, gender differences, and the age of the grandchildren. Grandparents provide stability, serve as emergency resources, and help to construct the family biography.

10. There is no evidence to support the myth that families generally refuse to care for their older relatives. Perhaps the persistence of this myth reflects the fact that we use as a standard the care we received as infants from our parents, and can never repay them.

11. Widowed women outnumber widowed men by more than 5 to 1. There appears to be little sex-related difference in the adjustment of widowed women or men in terms of morale, loneliness, life satisfaction, or well-being; the majority of both sexes cope well. In general, poverty is one of the greatest problems for widowed women, as the majority are living with very low income.

12. Menopause refers to the cessation of the menses; it typically occurs between the ages of 48 and 51. Many women experience a sensation known as a hot flash from time to time after menopause. The frequency of psychological and psychosomatic symptoms of menopause appears to be significantly lower if we accept the reports of menopausal women than if we believe reports by medical professionals.

13. Men and women have considerable similarity in sexual response that can provide the basis for improved communication between heterosexual partners. Older men and women usually continue to engage in sexual relations as long as they have an interested partner. Age is associated with changes in sexual response, but does not set any limit to sexuality for healthy persons.

14. Divorced persons experience a major transition that has few social expectations or sources of support to ease its impact. It often leads to remarriage and stepparents and affects relations with grandparents. The effect on older persons who divorce appears to be greater than for younger persons.

15. Gay men and lesbians lead a diverse range of life-styles, including long-term couple relationships and rearing children. The social stigma of homosexuality has caused some unique problems with custody of children, visitation rights in hospitals and nursing homes, and relationships with family members. Programs to provide social support for older lesbians and gays have been developed.

16. Singlehood is a life-style with many variations. It may involve cohabitation, sometimes as a prelude to marriage, or single parenthood, or a lifelong pattern that is simply another way of life. Some older persons choose cohabitation after divorce or widowhood as preferable to remarriage.

Key Words

child-rearing phase	hot flash
cohabitation	kinkeeper
erectile dysfunction	lesbians
establishment phase	modified extended family
estrogen replacement therapy	multigenerational household
extended family	new parents phase
family cycle	nuclear family
gay men	osteoporosis
generational stake	postparental phase

Review Questions

Families

1. Define each of the following types of families: extended, nuclear, and modified extended. Which type of family is most prevalent in the United States?

2. Give some examples of differences in patterns of family relations among various ethnic groups.

3. Define the concept of the family cycle. In what ways has the family cycle changed since the 1880s (refer to Figure 5.1)?

4. What are the major tasks of the establishment phase of the family cycle?

5. Describe the transitions that occur during the new parents phase of the

family cycle. What are some of the reasons that the birth of the first child may bring a period of crisis for some couples?

6. Give some examples of the "generational stake" held by the different generations in the child-rearing family.

7. Describe the transitions that occur during the postparental period. Why is this period in the family cycle receiving more attention today than earlier in this century?

8. List some of the functions grandparents may play in the family. What factors affect the style of grandparenting?

9. Cite evidence that disproves the myth that old people are isolated from and neglected by their family. Do you believe the evidence? Why or why not?

10. Describe some of the issues typically faced by widowed persons.

Menopause

11. When does menopause occur and what changes does it involve? What is your feeling about estrogen replacement therapy?

12. How does menopause affect the sexual functioning and emotional health of women? Is menopause one of the problems that women worry most about during middle age?

Similarities and Differences in Sexual Response

13. What are the characteristics of the four stages of sexual excitation in men and women?

14. What did Masters and Johnson conclude about sexuality and aging? List several factors that affect sexual functioning in older men and in older women.

Singles: The Unmarried and the Previously Married

15. What are some of the issues dealt with during the period of resocialization after divorce?

16. Cite several life-styles of gay and lesbian adults. What special problems are faced by older gay men and women?

17. What are some of the reasons that younger and older heterosexual couples live together without being married?

INTERLUDE

Murray, AGE 54 and AGE 64

Murray responded quickly and eagerly to the request for an interview in 1979 and 1989. At the age of 54, family issues seem less troubling for him, and his son appears to have changed dramatically, at least from Murray's perspective. But he is still working on many of the issues he discussed in the earlier interview, with the added problem of being unhappy in his job. He appears to be facing a major decision about his career, although the idea of making a change is disturbing to him. Much of his life seems to him like it's following a "railroad track." He feels that he must have chosen to follow it but, at the same time, he thinks that there must be more to life than he is experiencing. At age 64, both the job and the family concerns seem to have been resolved and he is planning for retirement.

Viewing a person at different points often reveals both change and continuity. Does Murray seem different in some ways than he did in the first interview? How much of this change has been brought about by growing older? What else has affected it? Is there any evidence of a midlife transition (as discussed in Chapter 3)? What has remained fairly continuous in his outlook on life and his view of himself over these years? Has his attitude about death changed during this period? Why? How do you think things will work out for him in the future?

Murray, Age 54

When we last talked in 1973, you told me that you had just bought a house and that your son was at that moment expected to be arriving back from Casablanca. My oh my. So much has happened. That was a country house I bought; we had that for about three years. We sold it when my wife decided to go back to work, which she did. . . . My son has turned out to be a great joy. He came back from Casablanca and decided that he would go back to school and stay in the city. Moved away from the nebulous involvement he had in school before, which was actually majoring in nothing, and decided that he was interested in political science and graduated magna cum laude. An amazing turnabout. Not amazing from the point of his intelligence but rather his motivation. *What brought about the change?* It is very difficult to say, except maybe our apprehension was the misguided apprehension that parents have when their offspring are not "straight" about the mores that we accept — you know, the traditional mores — you have to be a professional, which is part of our own misconception about work and its place in a person's life. He was always interested in politics — less so from the direction that finally developed, which was an intense interest in political systems, but more from a humanistic point of view. He did so well, and of course the interesting thing is . . . if you are fortunate enough to find a professor who's interested, your whole direction can change. I've been on university faculties — I'm on three now, I cut back from five to three — for over 20 years and I know that the professor can really be instrumental in guiding, motivating the direction that some of the students that they have will take. In his case, he found a professor who related to him. He was extremely verbal, my son, and of course that's always a joy to a professor and he became very interested.

He did not come to live with us, which is

very interesting. We took the house out in the country; we thought that way he might want to settle down because we had no hopes of his settling down, *per se.* But instead, he took a little apartment downtown and part-time jobs here and there and finished his baccalaureate and then finished his master's. He got married. He married an older woman; older than he . . . maybe seven or eight years older, I think, with two children. Real joys. I had my first grandchild—although I consider both of those my grandchilden, both her children by her former marriage—about three years ago. Of course, my wife is ecstatic about it. My wife is the consummate mother, consummate grandmother. My wife's life is filled with concern and love for my son, as mine is. But with the grandchild it's a joy. I think if you go back over the six years, the highlights of our life have been the direction my son has gone. He has taken a job and has done very well. Not a job in an area he likes but of course, when you're a married man you have responsibilities. He is doing it because his wife's going for her Ph.D. They made a decision—she's finishing her Ph.D. and then he'll go back. So that has turned out to be a real joy for me. . . . My son— amazing turnabout from the Casablanca days, if you will—great father, a wonderful son, a caring son, and a joy.

As far as my career is concerned, I published my fifth book about six months ago and it's a raging success, which is of course, great —because most of my success comes outside of my institution, and that's sad. The institution has changed as I approach my fifty-fifth birthday and I'm finishing my twentieth year at the end of this year. I have to start looking towards critical decisions—what I'm going to do, whether I'm going to stay here or do something else. A sixth book of mine will be out within about two months and I've just received a contract to edit a magnum opus, a collection of writings, which is an unusual undertaking because I like to write myself. I'm not so sure I'm going to enjoy editing other people's material. But that part of my life has been very successful; but that's outside the institution. In the institution itself there's been a revolutionary change in management style. I'm the oldest surviving senior person in the institution, in the administration, and it's a burden. Things have changed so dramatically in the last three years as far as my position in the institution that I have major problems dealing with it— personal problems dealing with it. I'm so used to being accepted that it's hard to fight my way through this new political and managerial environment and that brings me to a very difficult point in my life because I'm unhappy. It's hard [for others] to tell because I don't like to share discontent. It's a major problem I have. I think if I could share my discontent with my wife it would be a lot better, but I guard her from it—and that puts a burden on these days which are filled with thoughts of what else I should be doing with myself as far as my work is concerned. *But you can't discuss the problems.* I do, I do, but I temper my discontent which is basically a role I've played all my life. I've always been a pillar of strength, at least that's the role I play. Not that I've been a pillar of strength. So I've come to a critical point in my life; I'm 55, I'll be 55, I had an amazingly successful career, I'm extremely well paid, I have a national reputation, I'm a prolific writer, and I'm unhappy. Not unhappy about those things, but unhappy because I'm unhappy here on a day-to-day situation; that's more real than what's outside. I'm very proud about what I've accomplished, and it gets shot down now because there are new boys on the block. I never resent new boys, I can usually deal very well, but this is a completely different environment. What I am talking about is a revisionist environment. I'm a historian. I know why things developed in my particular industry in 20 years, and it's just a burden to go back in each case and explain why we're where we are now and what happened then—that was quite different from what is now—and try to rationalize it. I find it very, very debilitating.

My life is very much, unfortunately, on a railroad track; nothing changes. I've given up on the part of my life that led to the crisis that I had many years ago—outside interests from my home. I've been very attentive at home. It's a very even plane and I'm wondering whether that isn't a source of my unhappiness. I doubt it. I like stability. . . . But I often think of that. Am I letting things just roll down that track—there's a lot of track ahead of me, I don't think I am going to die in 5 years, 10 years; I think I have a lot of track; I'm in very good physical condition—deeply concerned about "Should I be on that track or should I be really going over hills? Shouldn't I be going into valleys?" and things like that. . . . *Maybe there should be more?* Maybe there should be more, that's better. You stop to think about it, you know; 55 years are behind you, you look forward to 20, so the major part of your years on earth are behind you. Is this the time to be thinking about exciting things or not? And that's the dilemma. I have discussed options with my wife; she would like me to take the burden off my back. She believes we can do anything we want to do. . . . *She is kind of supporting . . . ?* Very supportive as far as my happiness is concerned. Extremely supporting. *So, she feels that even if you left your job, that if that made you happy, that would be fine?* Fine. No problem. Of course, she doesn't want to leave the city, she doesn't want to leave her son, my grandchild. So there are limits to my seeking out happiness, whatever that means.

You said she'd gone back to work. Yes, she did. She works and she enjoys what she is doing. . . . *What kind of work does she do?* She does the same kind of work that I do. Not in my industry. Same kind of work I do, which is interesting. So does my son. My son has a position in a major institution. He's just 26. Same position I have here . . . I'm a vice-president, but that doesn't mean anything. I run the department, my son runs a [similar] department for a very large institution. He doesn't like it. It's very interesting; and it's fortuitous. Well my son, the first job he got when he got married and he needed a job, I got him in the field through an associate of mine. But he got [his present] job on his own. But he doesn't like it. He is doing very well as far as his finances are concerned at that job, but that's not his life's work. I'd hate to see him buried in something. . . .

How have sexual relations been between you and your wife? For a period of, I would say about two years, there have been no sexual relations. They always have been very bumpy. It's always been a major problem. A problem that, I don't know, cause and effect. You know, I'm not as willing to say that she was the cause of it—of my philandering. By the way, my definition of philanderer is probably what the normal person does now in society—looking outside the marriage for sexual satisfaction. . . . When I say outside relationships, given my situation of getting around the country and being out of town, I meet ladies and have relationships, but I'm talking about the kind of relationship I had, which was a decade, that relationship. Let me put it this way, I don't have a mistress. I get my sexual satisfaction on an ad hoc basis outside the house. It's almost as if it's an unspoken agreement. One never knows how that happens. I really don't know how [sex] stops. *An unspoken agreement between you and your wife?* That's right. How it stops. It's a difficult thing to discuss. It's very difficult. I don't know how it happens. I know that I have a view of sexuality that may be too youthful for my age. *In what way too youthful?* Talking about what an attractive woman should look like, sexually attractive; slim, young, et cetera. Now that may be a rationalization for the lack of drive in the marriage but it's mutual. . . . none of these things happens on their own. Sexual problems in marriage very rarely happen because of one partner. So, I point no fingers; it is not a predominate concern of my mine. *Do you share the same bedroom or . . .?* Yes. Absolutely. We're loving. . . . *So there is a great deal of physical affection?* Well there is physical affection, certainly. Yes. *So there hasn't been a point when separate beds . . .?* No. No. That hasn't come up, although we have enough room. No. We don't talk about it. We've accepted it. Maybe we've rationalized it. It is not a bone of contention as such. Again, I'm not sure whether it's because we both sublimated, or whether we're both on that track together, or we're comfortable on that track. *Do you think that she has outside relationships also?* I used to say no, never. Very possible. Very possible, now that she is in the working world. Knowing her own feeling about sex, it's not a predominate concern of hers. She's an attractive woman, extremely attractive. She's a beautiful woman, so it's very possible. You always think that you are the only one who makes out on the outside. I think maybe I am giving you the wrong impression; I have very few liaisons on the outside. It hasn't become, or it's not an obsession, I should say. At one time it was an obsession. *Having outside liaisons?* Oh, yes, very important. It's being loved. Besides the sexual gratification, a lot of it is being loved as well, being accepted. *Was that during the period that you had a mistress?* Oh, sure. *And liaisons as well?* Oh, sure. Absolutely. Which should have told me a little about the seriousness of my commitment to this other woman. That was a sad part of my life. Then, I was not a good guy. *You were not a good guy?* I should not have continued it. It was with a young woman who became old. Any man who has a relationship with a woman for a long time outside his marriage cannot be a good guy, because he knows what he's doing. If you know what you're doing, even if the woman says it's

okay, you know that you are not available to that woman; and you're holding out the possibility of the availability no matter how much you deny it. And that was a sad, sad conclusion that I have to come to in reviewing that part of my life. I used to absolutely condemn people who were philanderers and I didn't consider myself a philanderer, you see, because I had a permanent relationship outside the marriage. That's to be condemned. Not the guy who has one-night stands or the woman who has one-night stands, to satisfy some sexual needs—I'm not talking about bordellos—I'm talking about just meeting a woman—smiles at you, friendly with her—and then going to bed with her. That's not, within the context of my morality, to be condemned anymore. But having a long permanent relationship with a woman outside the marriage can't be rationalized. *That was a pretty painful ending for you?* The ending was probably the most painful thing that ever happened to me in my life. Not from having to end it, but from knowing what I had done. Leaving my wife. Holding out again right there. Okay, now it's going to be something between this other woman and myself. And then, within a short time saying, "I can't do it, I'm going back." It's funny I think of myself as a good guy. No one can say they are a good guy who did that. No one. No one. There is no way to rationalize it. Even though I'd try to break off year after year and she always wanted me to stay in the other relationship. That has nothing to do with whether it is right or wrong. I wanted to break off. I still get back to my theory, you do what you want to do. And that was a horrible thing.

How has your health been? I am very, very committed towards being in good shape, and not by exercise; I will it. I have a feeling about obese people, a negative feeling, and about the need to stay slim and to be in good shape. I have a picture of myself which will not permit me to let my body to go to hell. I have the same body I had when I was a young man. Very good shape, and I'm not a golfer or a tennis player. I just keep in shape, I walk a lot . . . I am not anxious to jog or to get into those kinds of things. But my health is good. *No health problems?* Nothing that would shorten my life. In fact my numbers are such that I'll probably live to a ripe old age—not having high blood pressure; I'm very careful about my cholesterol; I see my doctor regularly; and if I have problems they take care of them right away. So, physically I'm in very good shape. And my sex life is not over in my marriage because I'm impotent, so that physically I'm in real good shape. Real good shape. . . . I don't think that I will have any physical problems, that I can foresee, that will debilitate me in my later life. The one that you have to think about is cancer, you can never know by the way you look now, and by the way you feel now, whether you are going to get cancer or not. I'm very sure I'm not going to have a heart attack. . . .

Does death seem any more . . . real? Yes. Yes, it seems more real. *In what way?* In that even though I will live, I imagine, more than the—what is it six score and ten, no, no, three score and ten in the Bible—I'm not going to live another 55 years. Okay? So you know you're more than halfway through. Right? If you are realistic about it, then you expect to live to 75–80; then I'm a good two-thirds through my life. So, death becomes real. Since I don't believe in an afterlife, nor do I believe in judgment day, I know that this is it. So death is real. The only concern I would have is dying of something like cancer or something where you're lingering and debilitating, which would be terrible; I see too many people in that situation. I see my mother debilitating, a very active woman, and that's why death is real to me. *Because of her?* Yeah. Because being so close to her. She was close and seeing her going downhill and knowing that she lives from year-

to-year, makes death real. It's not an obsession. *Her health is failing but she's not terminally ill yet?* No. It's just that the machine is breaking down. Which would bother me if my machine broke down. That would bother me. That's the only concern I have about death, that it's not [going to be] the kind of death I've seen too many people go through. *But there is a kind of different time perspective?* Oh, very much. I'm very realistic. I don't look as youthful as I feel and I'm not 25 any more. Therefore death is real. . . . I am going to die. I'm not going to live forever and I'm getting closer to that, but not that close. I don't have to get my things in order. Although every so often I tell my wife where all the things are. *Have you written a will?* Yes, Yes. Oh, I'm a very responsible person. I told you that. Everything is in order. I have to do everything right. I have to take care of those after me. I have written a will. I'm very careful about making sure my son is provided for, my grandchildren are provided for. My wife knows there's a drawer; she doesn't like to deal with that. But there is a drawer where you go —everything is clear. *How long ago did you do that?* I've had a will for about, less than 10 years, somewhere between 5 and 10 years. My wife didn't want to hear about it at first; now she says it's very realstic. The thought of death doesn't bother me at all. It's the thought of dying a slow death that would bother me. So, I've got everything in order as far as that's concerned. I'm a very orderly person.

I guess the major question is where do you go from here to there. That's it! And how you do it. And how about doing it with a little less pressure on yourself. How about not being as . . . well known, as out front. How about relaxing? How about walking a nice pace toward there rather than jogging towards there? Or rather than running as I did for a long time towards bigger and better conquests. It almost sounds like I'm getting old (laughter). *Thank you very much.* It's a pleasure. You give me an opportunity I don't permit myself to take. And doing it every 6 years is cleansing. I just cannot relate—often when I have major problems, I thought of going to psychiatrists. . . . I can't do that because I find myself in a position very often of sounding too mature and saying to myself what the hell am I doing here. So you give me the opportunity of being on a couch once every 6 years, and I thank you for that opportunity.

Murray, Age 64

Murray was interviewed for a third time in 1989 at the age of 64. His son had divorced and remarried; his mother had entered a nursing home; and Murray was planning the twilight of his career. What are some of the aging family issues that Murray describes? Is his pattern of friends typical for men in our society? What problems will retirement pose for Murray and his wife? In what ways has he changed since the age of 48? Has his relationship with his wife and son changed? Why?

The last time we talked you had just become a grandfather, and that was almost 10 years ago. That's true. Actually I became a grandfather 11 years ago.

How has your life been unfolding this past decade? Very interesting as far as the twilight of my career, which I like to refer to it as, since I am near retirement. I put "retirement" in quotation marks because it won't be the normal retirement. I just reached my sixty-fourth birthday and will be finishing up for all intents and purposes in the middle of this year and then going on a sabbatical, where I will be a visiting professor at a graduate program in my discipline. And that six-month period should be very enjoyable. I'll be in and out of the city and indeed I am looking forward to that. All my life I had been directed towards the academic side, but I had to make a living. One doesn't make a living on the academic side, so I became a practitioner in my field and taught while I was practicing. The combination of both was

very rewarding. . . . My wife still has been supportive; she has her career. In fact, it's very interesting, she doesn't intend to give it up and I may have to travel back and forth from city to city while I am doing my visiting professorship because, I don't blame her, she has her job and she is enjoying it, which I think is to her credit. *Is she still in the same field?* Yeah. Of course, the economic situation in general is not a healthy one in her particular industry, but she seems to survive, that's fine.

My son is doing very well. Except a great deal has happened. You ask about the last 10 years. My son is divorced and remarried. That's the trauma in our lives. Our granddaughter is in one state; our son is in another state. He travels to see her on a regular basis. But it's quite a problem as far as logistics—and the effect it has on a young girl. But my son has found happiness and one doesn't stare a gift horse in the face. He's found a lovely woman, and we're happy for him. He is a fine, fine human being. Whatever I did and whatever my wife did— and I can step back and be critical of it—he turned out a fine product. He is pursuing his career in a world that he didn't want to be in; he'd rather be the academician—maybe someday he will be. But he is doing o.k. We see him several times a month and his career is certainly developing. The problem is whether it will be fulfilling and meaningful work for him, and he will have to make that choice. *Is he still in the same field?* Same field; different employer because he left the city. But he is a brilliant young man who has his feet on the ground. I think back in our first interview—my concern was his traveling around the world, not having roots. He's found deep roots. Of course, the trauma of divorce—something again that I have a problem with—and it's hard for me to understand how he could have done it. But, on the other hand, I would not have him lead the rest of his life unhappily burying his own needs, and he has made his choice. The only problem I have with the divorce is his separation from my grandchild. And we're doing our best with that.

Life itself has been rather fulfilling for me —busily writing, constantly writing, constantly teaching and lecturing. So that if one could look back on where you would like to be when you're at the twilight of your career, I don't think I could have planned it any better. . . . I planned well.

Does your wife have plans for retirement? No! She wants to go as long as she can. She is wonderful; it's wonderful. Of course she has it programmed well so that she doesn't have the pressures of a normal five-day job. She has it planned. But she finds it very rewarding. . . .

How is your relationship with your wife? Very good. *You said there had been some trouble.* We dealt with it. We've had a very close relationship for the last 20 years. Not quite 20 years. We've become closer. We know each other. When you're married over 40 years you get to know the worst and the best. And what you learn to do is understand the worst. You might fight. Our relationship is not without argument. I'm a strong-willed person; I believe I'm right. She is a strong-willed person. She believes that she is right, and often she believes that I don't give her credit for being right. So that will generate contests. But there is a lot of joy in our lives. A lot of fun. And the saving grace to our marriage is an enormously tuned sense of humor. *What do you do that is fun?* First of all the epitome of our elation, of our joy, is being with our son and his family. It wasn't so in the past because of the terrible relationship that he had. But his new marriage [changed that]; so that's one. Two, we have some wonderful friends—a small coterie of friends who are exciting people, intellectually stimulating and cultured people and we enjoy that. We go to the theatre, we go to the ballet or to the opera, but more so we have a very good feeling of where we are at this stage of our life. We are two different people. And I cannot ex-

pect her to be me. . . . What kept us together? The feeling of family, the feeling of responsibility, our dedication to our son, our dedication to our family, her family, my family; I'm talking about mother and father. . . .

Did her going to work make a difference? Oh yes! I think it did indeed; I think it made a big difference. *What about it?* Well, because I think she found something beyond the house; she found not only a career, but a sense of self. . . . Now she found fulfillment in her work. When she comes home at the end of the day, she's tired but she knows what has happened there, and there is much interplay there. . . . *Last time, 10 years ago when we talked, you and your wife were not having sexual relations. Has that changed?* Yes, and we're doing fine. Well I say fine; we're doing as well as most people do, without exaggerating. We have a loving relationship. We've made an effort, both of us, and there are many problems involved in that hiatus that we had, that short hiatus that we had. But life is much better, and I'd like to have 40 more years so I wouldn't make some of the mistakes I made. *But you are having sexual relations?* Yes! *On a fairly regular basis?* On a regular basis. . . .

Is your mother still alive? Yes, she is. She doesn't know where she is, but it's nice to have her. I see her regularly. *What is her situation?* She's in a home. She has Alzheimer's. She doesn't know where she is, but when I come she knows that I'm someone important in her life. Often she'll call me her grandson, more often it's the son, sometimes her husband, and sometimes her father. But she has, in that fog, a very positive feeling about life although, you know, with the Alzheimer's you have the paranoia that comes along with it and you have to understand it. She gets frightened at times. But I see her regularly; my sister sees her regularly; the family sees her regularly. She still is a human being. The real question is, ''Do you want to end up that way?''—not that you have a choice. What would you do if you had the choice? If you knew that you were going to have Alzheimer's to the degree where you didn't know where you were, you didn't know who people were, you forgot a minute afterwards that your son was visiting you, you were incontinent sometimes—do you want to end up that way? I don't want to end up that way! The concept of a living will is a very important one for me. I haven't come to grips with it yet, but I know I will. I don't want the pipes in me. I don't want to live other than as a thinking human being, as a feeling human being. I don't want to live in fear and in a cloud, in a fog. So I come to grips with that when I visit my mother. But on the other hand it's nice that she's there, to hold her hand. She's alive! It's nice for me; but I'm not sure where she is.

Were there some tough times in her illness? Very! I had to make a decision which I could not make until a couple of years ago. I put her in a home. *Where was she then living?* I had an apartment for her right near me. When I first got her the apartment, this was a self-sufficient woman—very positive person; was out constantly. And then we saw the signs. It was very, very rough. She would not accept help—we wanted to get help when we saw the signs of Alzheimer's and I had it diagnosed. And the paranoia: "You're trying to put me away!" I could not come to grips with that. But she didn't eat; she didn't clean herself. And I had to be there regularly. I'd come home from work, go over and make sure she ate. During the day she would not eat; but she said she ate; she could not remember what happened. And I had to come through a very difficult time. And I only lost my cool one time, when she accused me of trying to put her away. I was not going to put her away; in fact I couldn't deal with it and I walked out on her. And then I called her back and I said, "How are you feeling?" and I knew nothing could be done the way we were doing it. Then she got ill and we had to put her in the hospital and that was the time to do it. She got

ill for another reason, you know a physical reason—although Alzheimer's is physical. And I made the move right from the hospital to a home. And it was very difficult. . . .

At the moment your health is fine? Very good. I don't exercise. But it's very good.

You indicated that things have changed a great deal here at your position. Ten years ago there was . . . Yes. I had a confrontation, a difference of perspective on how to manage the company. And I have a feeling about the selling of the self—and the selling of the soul. I could not do that. I could have sat back and gone along with what I thought was wrong; but I fought. It was very daring to somebody who tells you that they are concerned about security and stability. I wasn't concerned enough to sell out. I use the term "sell out"—in other words, to go along. And it was a terrible time, working for people who are different in their perception of how to treat people. And I fought. And it changed; the leadership changed. I didn't win. The leadership changed and I went on. So there were many productive years in that period even though it was a trying time. . . . It was a terrible period; I thought of leaving here; I thought of changing my career; I didn't do it. I had many offers. I stayed with what I was doing, but I developed my other outlets at the same time, so that worked out fine. I now am in a position where I'm a senior thinker, senior advisor, often referred to as a dean, even though this is not an academic environment—the dean of my discipline, if you will. And that's nice. And I keep receiving wonderful honors. So my career has blossomed as a result of the confrontation with the former administration. I was able to thrive and survive not by hanging on by my fingernails, but thrive by fighting back. *Sometimes it pays to fight.* Indeed! And it's interesting—if you were to look back at all the things I've told you, you wouldn't think I was equipped to do that, because one, I'm concerned about stability; two, I am concerned about financial matters and you really risk a lot when you fight back in an organization. So I'm proud of that, very proud of that. It worked out.

Somehow I sense a parallel between what went on here in your occupation and what went on at home in your marriage — stability, sticking to it, working it out, finding ways to make it suit you. You're absolutely right, even though I said to you just before that you would have supposed that maybe I would have held on by my finger nails rather than fight back. I fought back in my marriage. And my wife did too; my wife did too. Yes, there is a direct parallel; it's the same thing. . . . But you're right, I didn't think of it in those terms, but it's not surprising.

Do you have good friends? I have very, very good friends. *Which you confide in?* Uh, confide in? Yes. I have many, many friends who I have a loving relationship with. Many people that respect me. A smaller group of close social friends. A very large group of friends throughout the country and the world who I consider friends; and in the smaller group of friends, social friends, there are one or two people that I confide in. I hesitate to use the word "confide." I am not, absent these interviews, one who is able to converse about the trials and tribulations in one's life. . . .

You mentioned also a sister? My sister. My relationship with my sister got better too. I had a lousy relationship with my sister. But we rallied together when my mother went into the home. . . . We are close because of what I see her now doing that she didn't do before, and that's being close to my mother. Although my mother always loved her. But there's no question that we both share the burden and the joy of our mother living to such an old age. So I see her. We visit my mother at least three times a month. And we go together and it's nice. And we like each other now. We didn't — maybe my

sister liked me, but I didn't really admire my sister. . . . I admire her now. Maybe it's not because she changed. Maybe it's because I see it differently. And she's my only family, my only sibling. And we have such a small family. It's only my mother, my sister, myself, and a couple of cousins . . . that's all there are.

I guess, being able to admire someone is important? When you came to admire her that relationship changed? That's right. The same with my wife. . . . But admiring people becomes a little different with me. And now we are talking about those people who challenge me intellectually — so that my closest friends are intellectuals. Yeah. Turns out that way.

Your wife can do that some? Yes, indeed. Indeed.

And your son? My son is a *bona fide* intellectual. He is a thinker. He has a creative mind. . . . He's developed into a whole human being; he's put it all together. And therefore it's always a challenge and a rewarding experience to be with my son. We discuss things other than the normal things of a father, of a son, and the marriage, what have you. We discuss things that go to the larger arena of life. And he really challenges me. If I were on a deserted island and I could have one person to be with me, it would be my son — even though my wife would be more comforting. To be able to continue the joy of the dialogue — which brings me back to my concern and dealing with death — that if I can't have that dialogue, if my mind fails, I don't want to be there.

What sort of a person is his wife? One hundred and eighty degrees from his first wife. She is a caring, loving, family-oriented, mature individual who sees life as a joy. . . . My wife is so happy. She has a relationship with her daughter-in-law now.

Do they have children? Not yet. Not yet.

Are they about the same age? Yes. The biological clock is ticking. They probably will.

It will be an interesting facet of their relationship—and a concern with what will that do to my granddaughter who is separated from them now. Very interesting times ahead.

How is it you'd like things to be in 10 years? I'd like to be healthy. I'd like my wife to be healthy. I am not concerned, my son will be healthy. I'd like to be able to move around more, to travel and still be able to occasionally make a contribution to thinking in my field. And I absolutely believe that's possible. Even though I will be close to 75 ten years from now. If my mind is sharp I will be able to do that. I would like to be able to be financially secure—should have put that right after healthy. (Laughs) Healthy first. Seeing my mother I worry about what could happen and seeing friends die of heart attacks, of cancer, the concern for health is foremost. And I'd like my son to continue to be happy and to be secure. I will always be as sensitive about his family, I don't think I'll change. And maybe I'll be visiting my mother, 10 years from now, when she's in her hundreds. . . .

One last question. I wonder if being interviewed like this has made any difference in your life? I've been frightened to go back to the last two interviews. I am not happy with—the same problem I had with psychiatry—I am not happy talking about my life to someone, a stranger. I am not a humble man. So its not a matter of humility. In fact people often think of me as cocky. But not innermost thoughts, feelings. Having shared with you what I shared with you has troubled me—my marriage, my sex life, my son, some of the things that I think should be kept personal. So that I used to move your books around. You see that I have a large library, and I keep it here [at the office]. I once took the book home. I don't know why and then I brought it back to my office. And I move it around. I then had an—interesting that you asked me this question—urge to share the two interviews with my son. But I decided not to—no way—I've shared a lot of personal things with my son. And I can do that. But I think it would be too confusing to him. I may in the final analysis, give him a view of this when I pass on. It may be interesting to him, but it's not important. He sees the living me, he doesn't have to see the written confession. But I did pick the book up yesterday, both of them, because I wanted to know what I had said and it was very interesting to go through it. It was interesting to look at myself from this vantage point, back when I was 48, and when I was 54. So that, uh, it doesn't change my life to read it and I am not surprised at what I said because it was a reflection of my life, but it's on a page there and I'm not sure—it's like reading somebody writing a biography of me. I don't want to read my obit and I don't want to read my biography.

CHAPTER 6

Work, Retirement, and Leisure

> Freud was once asked what he thought a normal person should be able to do well. The questioner probably expected a complicated, "deep" answer. But Freud simply said, *"Lieben und arbeiten"* ("to love and to work"). (Erikson, 1968, p. 136)

C ertainly these two aspects of human life are central during most of the years of adulthood. They encompass Erikson's stages of Intimacy versus Isolation and Generativity versus Stagnation. This lengthy period of generativity—which includes not only productivity and creativity in work but also the production and caring for offspring—extends from the resolution of the identity phase to the beginning of the final stage in Erikson's framework—Integrity versus Despair.

In the last chapter we discussed the first part of Freud's response, "to love"; here we turn our attention to the occupation, the job, or the career that occupies approximately 40 hours a week (but often up to twice that many hours) for 30 to 45 or more years of the life cycle. Perhaps such a large amount of time is a sufficient reason to take a careful took at the interaction between the occupation and the person during the middle years. But we are also interested in the interaction between the occupation and the family and in the role that the occupation plays in the final resolution of the identity issues. We want to explore the importance of paid employment in the lives of women, many of whom are mothers. We are also interested in the occupational cycle, in the process of occupational choice, and in the process of socialization by which the individual is prepared for an occupation and comes to accept the roles and status that the occupation entails.

Next, we note that since more people are living past age 65 today than ever before and since this trend will undoubtedly continue, more people are able to work until the traditional age of retirement and often beyond. In addition, the mandatory age for retirement has been lifted from most occupations. Moreover, more people are retiring and are living in retirement for a greater number of years or are entering a new career late in life. One effect of greater longevity has been to increase the prevalence of retirement as a developmental milestone; we examine this milestone in detail in a later section of this chapter.

Then we examine the relation of nonwork time to leisure. Many interacting factors, including technological advances such as automation and computers, have increased the amount of productivity for each hour a person works. The result of this change has been an evolving trend to increase the amount of *nonwork time* during an individual's life span. Longer preemployment training keeps large numbers of young people out of the labor market; longer vacations, shorter work weeks, and shorter work days reduce the number of hours a person works during the year; and earlier retirement shortens the total number of years of work. This trend is likely to continue, resulting in an increase in the amount of time potentially devoted to leisure (at least until the "baby boom" generation retires from the work force). We discuss leisure in the final section of this chapter. But first let us look at work, the occupational cycle, and retirement.

Work and the Life Cycle

The proportion of women in the labor force has been increasing, especially in recent years, while the proportion of men has been decreasing because of earlier retirement and a variety of other factors (Figure 6.1). Black women have historically had higher employment rates than White women; today, White women are approaching the same high levels. The rates for Hispanic men and women closely parallel the rates for White men and women. As is also true for men, Black and Hispanic women are much more likely to be unemployed and looking for work than White women (Taeuber & Valdisera, 1986; U.S. Bureau of Labor Statistics, 1977).

For women today, the trend is to enter the work force earlier and to work considerably longer than was true at the turn of the century. The opposite pattern is true for men; they tend to enter the work force later and to retire earlier today than in 1900 (Neugarten & Moore, 1968). However, because more people are living longer with better health today, the actual number of years that an average man spends working has *lengthened* about eight years since the turn of the century (U.S. Bureau of Labor Statistics, 1977, Table 60).

Identity and Generativity

Particularly for men, but for most women as well, the occupation involves a great investment of time, emotional energy, and commitment. Often the man is highly engaged in his occupation during the middle years of the family cycle, while the woman is expected to be highly involved in the home and family—even if she is working too. These intense involvements mark the final phase of the identity issue

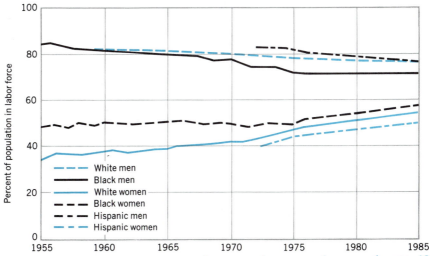

FIGURE 6.1 Labor force participation rates of women and men, annual averages, by race, 1955 to 1985, and Spanish origin, 1973 to 1985. (*Source*: U.S. Bureau of Labor Statistics, 1977, Chart 5; Taeuber & Valdisera, 1986, Figs. 3 and 4.)

for both men and women in Erikson's scheme of the eight ages of life. Success and satisfaction in the occupation and family reaffirm the individual's sense of identity and also provide social recognition for that identity. Clearly, the job is an important aspect of one's identity, ranking in importance along with one's name, gender, and citizenship. Although this close tie between one's identity and one's occupation may be more true for those in the professions ("I am a lawyer . . . doctor . . . teacher . . ."), we know that certain occupational characteristics (such as "blue collar" or "white collar") are reflected in attitudes, values, and political views. In addition, for most people the occupation reflects such factors as social class and amount of education.

Entry into the adult occupational and parenthood roles also marks the beginning of Erikson's stage of Generativity versus Stagnation. Thus, as these issues begin to become important, the central focus in the individual's developmental progression during the early years of the working life shifts to the combination of the *Generativity versus Stagnation* issue with the previous issue of *Intimacy versus Isolation*. During the later years, the focus shifts to *Generativity versus Stagnation* combined with *Integrity versus Despair*. This shift may occur perhaps during the midlife transition. This perspective suggests that the struggle regarding satisfaction versus frustration and success versus failure in one's job or in rearing one's children and managing a home not only brings the resolution of the identity issues, but also affects intimate relationships and may lead to a sense of leaving one's mark in the world in some way. This period might be termed, somewhat awkwardly, a "generativity crisis," as a parallel to the earlier "identity crisis."

Occupation and Family

The interaction between the family and the occupation may be seen as a system of mutually interacting factors that can add to or compensate for dissatisfactions in either sphere. That is, a frustrating job, in depersonalizing surroundings, with no opportunity for a sense of pride or accomplishment often promotes the importance of the family (and of leisure time) as a source of satisfaction and feeling of competence. The strain that may result as the frustrations are transferred from the workplace to the family may counteract the person's needs, however, by adding to family tension and thus enlarging the degree of frustration felt not only by the worker, but by the entire family. In addition, the requirement that the family provide satisfactions of such a degree as to compensate for the lack of satisfaction in the occupation is likely to overburden the family and may snowball into a family crisis reflecting, in this example, job frustration.

In the other direction, an unsatisfying family interaction and marital disharmony may shift the burden to the job as the primary source of satisfactions and rewards. Thus, the occupation may be used as an effective escape from the frustrations of family life, leading the person to acquire a second job, work longer hours, spend evenings entertaining clients, or be out of town as a substitute source of satisfactions. Sometimes, also, the family and the job are competing in their demands for the individual's time and loyalty. For example, the young executive or professional may be called upon to sacrifice a part of his or her family life to obtain advancement or to establish a career that may, of course, produce family tension.

There are many interacting influences between work and the family; some are almost obvious once pointed out, but others are more subtle and require careful analysis. Hoffman (1986) reviewed the research on the effects of work on the family and noted 10 general processes by which work affects the family:

1. Material resources that result from the income generated by work affect the family in important ways. For example, parenting style may reflect whether housing is adequate, the availability of time-saving appliances, the importance of broken items, and general vulnerability to economic stress. Punishing children for unintentional breakage, for example, may reflect economic reality, not personality.

2. The worker's self-concept and status in the family, as well as the family's status in the community, are affected by employment status. A steady job may carry more weight in some families than a high salary does in others. Conversely, loss of a job does not necessarily have negative effects; for example, adolescents in middle-class families before the depression of the 1930s who were affected by financial stress showed *positive* effects compared with adolescents whose families were not affected — presumably because of greater responsibility and family cooperation (Elder, 1974, 1982).

3. Work-related behavior may parallel behavior at home. Teachers who lecture their children or a minister who preaches at home are stereotypic examples. It is not clear if this reflects the influence of the job, or whether the individual personality affects both occupational choice and behavior with the family. Points 4 and 5 expand on this idea.

4. Work experiences influence child-rearing patterns. A series of studies by Kohn and his colleagues (e.g., Kohn & Schooler, 1982) has suggested that social class differences in the ways parents punish their children and the values they teach reflect the expectations the parents experience at work (e.g., self-direction and independence versus obedience and conformity).

5. The worker's personality is affected by work experiences; changes affect family behavior and child-rearing styles. Worker participation in making decisions and solving problems, for example, increases communication skills, interpersonal skills, and listening ability (Crouter, 1984); this probably affects family interaction patterns. Likewise, other studies have found that a mother's self-confidence is increased by paid employment.

6. Patterns of authority at work are replicated in parent–child interaction. The supervisor's rules may seem arbitrary and absolute to a low-status worker who, in turn, applies the same type of authority at home. Since a variety of variables (e.g., education and income) are also related, it is likely that the effect of work is only one contributing factor to family interaction patterns, however.

7. The effect of the work environment on the worker's mood can carry over into the family. This has been difficult to test because mood is subjective and the

same person reports similar moods at work and at home. A dissertation by Repetti (1985) found that average moods of workers in similar jobs and respondents' ratings of the work environment were related to the respondents' levels of depression, anxiety, and self-esteem. This may affect mood at home, of course.

8. The family and work may complement each other as sources of satisfaction for various personal needs. Much energy and enthusiasm may be devoted to parenting, for example, because the needs for warm interaction, joy, high performance standards, play, and a sense of accomplishment may not be satisfied by the job. In these areas, moods from work may not carry over, or may be dissipated.

9. There is no simple relationship between family involvement and time spent at work. The demands of work take time away from the family if they are excessive. Fathers' involvement in the family may be reduced by overinvolvement in a profession, long periods away from home, and by night-shift work. Too little work—unemployment or not working—may also produce stress. Part-time work for women has been found to have more positive effects on children and the marital relationship than either full-time work or nonemployment.

10. Stress is sometimes produced by work, or by family demands (e.g., several children, a handicapped child, an aged infirm parent). It can have negative effects on the children, on the marital relationship, and on parent–child interactions. Boys appear to be more vulnerable to stress than girls and interactions

Parenting satisfies needs for warm interaction, joy, play, and a sense of accomplishment that may not be satisfied by the job.

between parent and son, compared with parent and daughter, are more likely to be adversely affected when the parents are under stress (Hetherington, 1979). This may reflect boys' tendency to be more noncompliant and active than girls, which may be difficult for parents during periods of stress; it may also reflect the belief that boys are hardier than girls and therefore need less protection from the parental stress (Hoffman, 1972, 1984).

Each of these points requires further study, especially to identify when one particular process is involved (e.g., work-related moods) or when other influences are operating (e.g., personality). We return to a discussion of stress in our discussion of health psychology in Chapter 7.

Women in the Work Force

Women have always worked in a variety of tasks that have differed only in terms of cultural norms and economic necessities. Nye (1974) pointed out that women made substantial economic contributions in the work force during the Industrial Revolution and in Colonial America. It has been the exception in history for women to be confined to domestic responsibilities; in many cases, this was a privilege granted only to the wealthy who, in turn, employed female servants and bought goods manufactured by female workers. Even in recent American life, wives of farmers shared all the work with their husbands and children, combining work in the fields with work in the home. Until recently, however, women have frequently not been paid for their work and few have directly competed with men for the same jobs at the same pay. Instead, middle-class women were given the opportunity to spend the time made available by smaller families and time-saving housekeeping devices in a variety of voluntary activities — much as was the case for upper-class women with servants a few decades earlier. However, today the labor force is swelling with substantially greater numbers of women seeking paid employment, while services that were built on feminine voluntarism are turning to public financing to hire paid workers and are seeking to attract student and retired volunteers. At the same time, previously all-male occupations are slowly allowing women to enter and are beginning to face the complex set of issues that this involves.

In 1985, 51.1 million women over the age of 16 were in the civilian labor force, compared with 37 million in 1975. Two out of three women work over 35 hours a week; 48 percent work year-round full-time. Over 70 percent of all women between age 20 and 44 were either working or looking for work. Even 62 percent of women with children under age 6 were in the labor force in 1985, although many worked part-time. Between 1950 and 1976, the number of married women in the labor force increased nearly threefold to 21.6 million; by 1985 it was 27.7 million, or 54 percent of the total number of women in the labor force (Taeuber & Valdisera, 1986).

A number of interrelated changes have combined to produce the growing proportion of working women in this country. One important change has been the availability of birth control and family-planning information. This has given women control over when they become pregnant—and therefore how long they work before the first child is born—as well as the number of children they have. To a large extent, this has given women control over their life-style and, ultimately, their own life course has come to reflect women's greater control over childbirth. Perhaps the long and difficult struggles Margaret Sanger and others had to fight to develop and publicize birth control early in the twentieth century were fundamentally related to issues of economic power and a woman's right to control her own destiny.

Other changes have also led to the increase in working women today. The economic opportunities of the "baby boom" generation have not been as great as for their parents (in the postwar affluence of the 1950s), so two incomes may be needed today to live as well as families did on one income in the 1950s. Moreover, the postwar baby boom has increased the number of young women, and many are postponing marriage and childbirth longer than in the past, perhaps because of increased economic and marital competition within this cohort (Easterlin, 1980). In addition, a growing proportion of women are attending college and are closing the gap in educational level between men and women. Greater life expectancy of the population has increased the need for workers in the general areas of health care and human services; many of these job opportunities have been taken by women. The decline in industrial occupations and the growth in service occupations had also created more equal employment opportunities for women.

As a result of these trends, and the entrance of the baby boom generation into the labor market, a large number of jobs have been created during the past decade that are being filled by women.

> Between 1980 and 1985, 6.9 million new jobs were created in the female-dominated sectors of sales and services, while 500,000 jobs were lost in the male-dominated sectors of manufacturing, mining, construction, and transportation. Over this same period, the female labor force grew by 5.6 million and the male labor force by 3 million. (Barrett, 1987, p. 113)

It is uncertain how many of these new jobs will remain if there is an economic decline in the future, however.

Women in Various Occupations

Between 1970 and 1980 there has been some increase in the proportion of women in male-dominated occupations (in which men made up 60 percent or more of the total employment in 1970). Table 6.1 shows those occupations in which women had the largest net employment gains during this period. The occupations with the largest percentage increases were: male-dominated managerial and professional specialties; male-dominated technical, sales, and administrative support; male-dominated service occupations; farm workers; bakers; telephone installers and repairers; bus drivers; and stock handlers and baggers. Some of these occupations are relatively low paying (e.g., farm workers, janitors, and cleaners); others are predominately part-time (e.g., school bus drivers). In other fields, women gained in proportion to men (e.g., lawyers), but the actual number of women entering those occupations

TABLE 6.1 Occupations with Major Employment Gains for Women: 1970–1980 (Numbers in thousands)

Occupation	Employment Gain[a]	Percent Female	
		1980	1970
All occupations	13,807.3	42.6	38.0
Managerial and professional specialty	4,191.9	40.6	33.9
Male dominated:			
Salaried managers and admin., n.e.c.	900.3	26.9	15.6
Accountants and auditors	227.2	38.1	24.6
Other financial officers	133.2	44.9	25.4
Personnel, training, and labor rel. spec.	114.9	47.0	33.4
Female dominated:			
Registered nurse	491.0	95.9	97.3
Elementary school teacher	482.9	75.4	83.9
Technical, sales, and administrative support	6,283.9	64.4	59.0
Male dominated:			
Sales supervisors	219.6	28.2	13.7
Real estate sales	202.3	45.2	31.2
Computer operators	192.0	59.1	33.9
Other business service sales	126.4	37.4	8.4
Sales (mining, mfg., wholesale)	114.9	14.9	7.0
Stock and inventory clerks	90.3	34.7	24.3
Female dominated:			
Secretaries	1,145.0	98.8	97.8
General office clerks	800.1	82.1	75.3
Cashiers	756.1	83.5	84.2
Service occupations	1,936.8	58.9	59.7
Male dominated:			
Janitors and cleaners	293.0	23.4	13.1
Bartenders	95.5	44.3	21.2
Female dominated:			
Child-care workers	405.3	93.2	92.5
Nursery aides	382.4	87.8	87.0
Farming, forestry, and fishery	174.3	14.9	9.1
Male dominated:			
Farm workers	56.5	21.7	14.9
Farmers	48.6	9.8	4.7
Precision production, craft, and repair	231.9	7.8	7.3
Male dominated:			
Supervisors, production occupations	128.8	15.0	9.9
Bakers	23.5	40.7	25.4
Telephone installers and repairers	22.9	11.5	2.8
Operators, fabricators, and laborers	988.4	27.4	25.9
Male dominated:			
Machine oper. (misc. and not specified)	244.5	33.4	30.2
Bus drivers	103.8	45.8	28.3
Stock handlers and baggers	79.3	21.0	12.5

[a]Male-dominated occupations are defined as those in which men accounted for 60 percent or more of total employment in the occupations in 1970; female-dominated occupations are defined as those in which women accounted for 60 percent or more of total employment in the occupations in 1970. Occupations selected experienced the *largest* net employment gains (by rank order) between 1970 and 1980 and together accounted for 50 percent or more of the change in the male-dominated and female-dominated occupations.

Source: Taeuber & Valdisera (1986), Table 14.

was relatively small, and so are not shown in this table. There has also been a slight increase in the proportion of men in some female-dominated occupations in which large numbers of women gained employment (registered nurse and elementary school teacher).

Thus, although women have made significant gains in some occupations, one may be impressed with either these advances toward more participation in the male-dominated labor market or the continuing concentration of women in traditionally female-dominated jobs. For example, 70 percent of all full-time employed women in 1985 were in those occupations where over three-quarters of the employees were women (Barrett, 1987).

Earnings Gap between Women and Men

In general, women earn less than men; this is termed an **earnings gap**. For example, when only full-time workers who worked year-round are compared, the ratio of female to male earnings was 65 percent in 1987 (Figure 6.2). The gap tends to narrow somewhat during periods of economic recession, which have a particularly significant effect on lowering the income of the male-dominated high-wage segment of the economy (Barrett, 1987); for example, in 1982 the gap was 62 percent. There is some evidence that this earnings gap is closing faster among younger workers, age 18–24: from 76 percent in 1980 to 88 percent in 1984. The gap between Black and White women's earnings has narrowed since 1955, but the gap persists, as it does between the earnings of Black and White men. The gap for Hispanic women is slightly greater than for Black women (Taeuber & Valdisera,

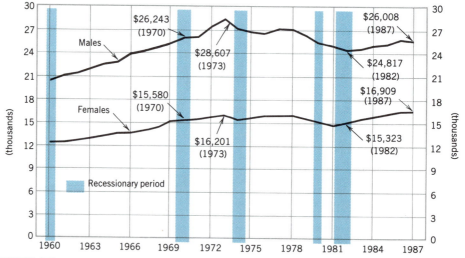

FIGURE 6.2 Median earnings: 1960–1987 (in 1987 dollars; year-round, full-time workers). (*Source*: U.S. Bureau of the Census. Money income and poverty status in the United States: 1987. *Current population reports*, Series P-60, No. 161. Washington, DC: U.S. Government Printing Office, 1988, Fig. 5, p. 6.

1986). There are a variety of influences on these data about median income. For example, Barrett (1987) noted that the wage gap increases with age, as promotions and seniority play more important roles in determining income.

There are two main reasons for this earnings gap between men and women. First, there is a preponderance of women in low-paying jobs that have been traditionally held by women and that offer restricted opportunity for advancement. Second, the dramatic increase in working women has meant that there are a large proportion of women who have entered their job recently and have not yet had time to advance to higher income levels (U.S. Department of Labor, 1976). In addition, women who leave the work force during child-rearing may also reduce their earning potential, and men are much more likely to work overtime than women.

Sexton (1977) examined this earnings gap in detail and found considerable evidence of how discrimination operates against women. For example, women start their career at almost the same level of income as men but, by the middle years, women earn only about half as much as middle-aged men earn. This suggests that women tend to be assigned to dead-end jobs and to be barred from career ladders that offer promotions to higher-status jobs with higher earnings. Sexton found that some companies assumed that women did not want to be promoted; others raised the salary of good female secretaries instead of promoting them, whereas male clerical employees would be promoted. Also women were often unaware of opportunities for promotions because these were not widely advertised and often were based on favoritism that could easily discriminate against women. In addition, women were usually not given training on the job for higher-status positions because it was assumed they would not be long-term employees. Subtle forms of discrimination such as these have formed the basis for legislation regarding sex discrimination and legal suits that have reduced some of these types of discrimination in some organizations.

More difficult to modify, however, is the **dual labor market** — one for women and one for men (Sexton, 1977). For example, women have been overrepresented in certain important occupations such as elementary school teachers, secretaries, nurses, and clerical workers, where the pay and working conditions may not have been attractive to men. These occupations have allowed women to move from place to place and find employment when their husband's job required a transfer; they also may have allowed women to leave for a period of child care and then return to work. These occupations also have been relatively low paying, but were filled because women could not enter higher-paying jobs in the primary labor market. Today, however, many women are not confined to a secondary labor market. Thus, it is likely that occupations where women have been overrepresented in the past will need to increase the salary greatly if they are to attract competent women (and men) who now have other job opportunities open to them.

Dual-Career Couples

Over 54 percent of all women living with their husbands were in the labor force in 1985. They make a substantial financial contribution to the family income, although the lower earnings of women as compared with men are clear, especially in White families (Table 6.2). Child-care arrangements, other practical issues such as sharing of household responsibilities, and providing support for each other's job-related stresses can complicate the lives of couples where both partners work (Gilbert, 1985).

Sekaran (1986) described **dual-career families** as those where both partners pursue careers that demand commitment to the work role, continual updating of job-related knowledge, and expectations of promotion. In contrast, *dual-earner* families are those where one or both partners have jobs that do not require a high degree of commitment to building a career.

There has been considerable research on dual-career families since the term was coined by Rapoport and Rapoport (1969). Reviewing the studies on dual-career families, Sekaran (1986) noted five general issues that are faced by these couples: (1) *Role Overload* produced by the multiple roles each spouse/parent/jobholder must maintain; (2) *Identity Dilemma* that results from the conflict between roles one was trained to hold during socialization earlier in life and the roles that one attains in the career and family; (3) *Role-Cycling* that is required for those who want both a family and a career, such as how many children and how to time their birth to fit with career development; (4) *Social Network Dilemma* that reflects the limited time available to develop ties with others and with the community; (5) *Normative Pressures* that result from life as a nontraditional family, especially if there are no children, or if other normative expectations are not met.

Advancing in one's career often requires geographic mobility, since a promotion or a more desirable occupation frequently involves moving to another part of the country. As long as one member of the couple (and this includes both homosexual and heterosexual couples) is willing to accept whatever employment is available, the couple can move together to maximize the career of the other partner. This pattern is characteristic of the dual-earner family and has been one reason women have tended to hold low-status jobs; they exist wherever the couple happens to

TABLE 6.2 1986 Median Family Income by Type of Family, for White, Black, and Hispanic Families

Type of Family	Median Family Income		
	White	Black	Hispanic
All families[a]	$30,809	$17,604	$19,995
Married couple	33,426	26,583	23,912
Wife in paid labor force	38,972	31,949	30,206
Wife not in paid labor force	26,421	16,766	17,507
Other families			
Male householder (no wife present)	26,247	18,731	20,894
Female householder (no husband present)	15,716	9,300	9,432

[a]Families as of March 1987.

Source: U.S. Bureau of the Census. *Current population reports*, Series P-60, No. 157. Money income and poverty status of families and persons in the United States, 1986. Washington, D.C.: U.S. Government Printing Office, 1987.

move, so women who hold these traditionally female occupations are seldom hampered by their need to move (if their husbands move) or by their immobility if the husband remains in one location (Van Dusen & Sheldon, 1976).

In contrast, the task of maximizing the career of two persons in high-status occupations is often difficult; this is the task faced by dual-career couples. Some couples may agree to remain in the same community, even if one or both limits his or her advancement by that decision. Other couples may strive to maximize first one career and then the other. And some couples find it necessary to establish separate households in different cities, spending only weekends and vacations together for brief or more extended periods. Perhaps the difficulty of managing two separate high-status careers has been one reason women's work has traditionally been limited to managing the home, providing practical and emotional support to her husband, and working in a secondary labor market when financially necessary.

Work, Family, and the Child

The proportion of mothers who are working has risen dramatically in recent years. By 1978, half of all mothers with children under 18 were in the labor force; in comparison, only 18 percent of similar women were working in 1946; by 1984, the proportion had risen to 60 percent (Hoffman, 1986, Table 2). Single mothers are more likely to be working than mothers with a husband present as long as the child is over age 3 (Table 6.3). The most rapid gains, however, have been among mothers with preschool-age children (Figure 6.3). Many working mothers are employed part-time, of course.

TABLE 6.3 *Percentage of Mothers in the Labor Force by Marital Status and Age of Child, 1984*

Marital Status of Mother and Age of Child	Percentage Employed
Mothers with children 6–17 only	
Married, husband present	65.4[a]
Widowed, divorced, separated	76.5[b]
Mothers with children under 6	
Married, husband present	51.8[c]
Widowed, divorced, separated	53.2
Mothers with children under 3	
Married, husband present	48.3[d]
Widowed, divorced, separated	45.0

[a]Of these, 65.8% were full-time, 29.2% were part-time, and 5.0% were "unemployed but looking."
[b]Of these, 73.4% were full-time, 14.7% were part-time, and 11.9% were "unemployed but looking."
[c]Of these, 58.9% were full-time, 32.2% were part-time, and 8.9% were "unemployed but looking."
[d]Of these, 57.8% were full-time, 32.8% were part-time, and 9.4% were "unemployed but looking."
Source: U.S. Department of Labor, Bureau of Labor Statistics. Data supplied by E. Waldman, Senior Economist. Reported in Hoffman (1986), p. 195. © American Psychological Association. Reprinted with permission.

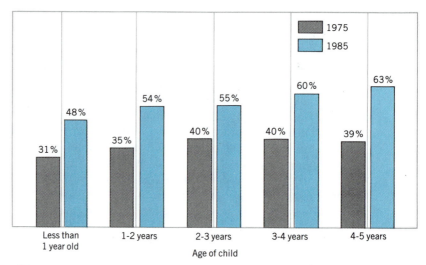

FIGURE 6.3 Women in labor force with young children (women 16 years old and over). (*Source*: Taeuber & Valdisera, 1986, Fig. 10.)

Care for children while the parents work has gained increased attention as the number of working mothers has grown. Considering only children under age 5, in 1982, relatives provided much of the care. In two-parent families where the mother worked, 52 percent of the children were cared for by a family member; the figure was 63 percent among only those mothers who worked part time (Cherlin, 1987). Nonparental relatives provided much of this care—11 percent in the child's own home, and 18 percent in another home; of these, 17 percent were grandparents. Group care centers were used by 20 percent of the unmarried mothers and by 13 percent of married mothers. In addition, 23 percent of the employed mothers were able to provide parental care for the child—14 percent by the father, and 9 percent by the mother while she was working (U.S. Bureau of the Census, 1983). Presser and Cain (1983) reported that "shift work" allowed some parents to provide child care: at least one spouse worked some period other than a regular day schedule in about one-third of two-parent families with a child under age 5 where both parents worked.

What are the effects of maternal employment on the child? We would expect that cultural background, social class, whether the mother is living with a spouse or the sole support of the family, level of education, number and age of the children, patterns of relationships within the family, and the psychological needs of the husband and wife would be among the factors that influence the impact of maternal employment on the children and the family. Lois Wladis Hoffman has been one of the leading researchers on the effects of the employment of mothers on the family for over 25 years. In a lecture in 1986 she summarized the research on the effects of parental employment on the family, giving particular attention to the effects of the employment of mothers.

Much of the care for children with working parents is provided by relatives. However, group care centers provide care for a substantial minority of all children with working parents. Some companies have begun to offer child care centers for their employees.

With respect to the husband–wife relationship, the data do not indicate any clear association between employment status and the affective bond, but there is some empirical support for an increase in egalitarianism, rather than husband dominance, in the families with employed mothers and clear support for a modest increase in the father's participation in household tasks and child care. It was suggested that the greater role of employed mothers in family decisions may be part of the explanation for the finding that the daughters of employed women are more likely to see women as competent and effective and to name their mothers as their adult models, whereas the less traditional division of labor in the family may be a link to the less stereotyped sex role attitudes of working mothers' children.

Research on the effects of employment on morale indicates that employment can provide either a psychological boost or a stress. Most studies do indicate a higher level of satisfaction among employed mothers, but stress can result when the demands of the dual role are excessive. Several researchers have tried to show that when there is congruence between the actual role and the woman's desired role, there are positive effects on the child, but the direction of causality is ambiguous in this research.

In considering mother-child interaction, . . . although employed mothers have less time with their children, the quality is not diminished and may be enhanced. . . .

One observation that can be made from these findings is that several family patterns that are associated with maternal employment seem to be beneficial for daughters: the more egalitarian power between parents, which may lead daughters to hold the female status in higher esteem, the less traditional division of labor, which may lead daughters to hold a less restricted view of their own role; the fact that mothers provide models more consistent with the roles the daughters themselves are likely to occupy; the greater encouragement of independence; and the possibility that daughters receive more parental attention even as infants. . . . The greater independence training may not be an advantage for boys, and some studies suggest that it is in the nonworking-mother family that young sons receive more attention. It is possible that the greater involvement of fathers in child care is an advantage for boys and that the household responsibilities and rule-governed households would benefit both sexes, but the situation for sons is more mixed than for daughters. (Hoffman, 1986, pp. 208–209)

These findings need to be put in perspective by considering at least four general comments in Hoffman's review:

1. Research on maternal employment focuses only on whether the mother worked or not; it rarely has focused on actual work experience or on particular kinds of work.

2. Employed mothers are more likely to be from lower income groups, but are better educated than average within their income group. They are more likely to have been divorced, to have fewer and older children, and are more likely to be African American than nonworking mothers.

3. Although most mothers work, almost 40 percent do not. A small family with a nonemployed mother is quite different from the "traditional" American family (with several children, few time-saving appliances, nondisposable diapers, few prepared foods, etc.). Thus, the child with an employed mother may receive as much attention as a child in a large family, even today, if the nonemployed mother has many household chores and has to divide her attention among several children.

4. Most studies do *not* find differences between children of working and nonworking mothers. Thus, maternal employment in itself is not a very "robust" variable. It is necessary to take into account a variety of other aspects and conditions before assuming that the mother's work is relevant.

The Occupational Cycle

When we view occupations from a developmental perspective, we are sensitized to their progression over time and to potential turning points or crisis points in the **occupational cycle**. This cycle is more easily seen in careers that follow a relatively orderly sequence—the advancement up a "career ladder," for example. However, many people do not experience a simple orderly progression in their occupation, in either one particular field or one particular company. Often, there are shifts from one career ladder to another, or from one kind of work to another. The plant may close, or the job may be replaced by automation and the worker may have to find other work, or be retrained for a different type of job. Thus, there are many individual paths between the two clearly marked points on the occupational cycle —entry and retirement. Because of the importance of retirement as a major shift in

the life cycle, we discuss it in detail in a later section of this chapter. Her
on the point of entry into the occupation, as well as some of the factors
occupational choice. Also, we look at variations in patterns of occupation
ment and the concept of the career clock.

Occupational Choice

The process of entering an occupation is not a simple matter of choosing
a process by which a person becomes matched with an occupation.
individual and the occupation are fitted together by the individual's sele
occupation to meet his or her needs and also by the socialization proce
by the new occupational roles and expectations. This usually involves ;
training or preparation (anticipatory socialization), and the role deman
itself also produce some degree of resocialization.

In addition, part of the earlier socialization process in childhood
cence serves to prepare the individual for eventual occupational requir
roles. Although this "personnel office" model is an oversimplification o
ization process, it calls attention to the ways in which schools and oth
tion agents influence occupational choice. For example, Cicourel :
(1968) pointed out how high schools define "academic careers" and '
careers" for their students and type the students according to "college p
or "vocational" goals. This social typing defines many of the academic, c
social experiences available and expected for each type of student. In
racial or sexual discrimination in employment begins with this kind of i
well as in more subtle ways during childhood socialization that prescr
able roles, activities, and dreams for boys, or girls, or certain "kinds c

Thus, the process of **occupational choice** in reality begins many
an actual job is selected; and the factors that are involved in this "cho
usually include the (impossible) task of deciding among the thousands
occupations. Instead, background factors (reflecting the effects of ear
tion), role models, experience, interests, personality, and the person's o
into occupations are some of the important factors that influence the se
occupation. We will discuss each factor here and later discuss the resoc
the individual upon entry into the occupation to complete the recipr
the matching process.

Background Factors

Socioeconomic status, ethnic origin, intelligence, gender, and race ten
in complex and often illegal ways to limit the range of occupations
individual. Many times a person may find a way to open the door to an
and be less bound by these background factors than others, but educ:
ground, contacts with a particular occupation through one's ethnic
groups and family members, and discrimination operate for or agains
ual's movement into an occupation. In general, these factors operate s
way they do in the choice of a marital partner: by setting general boun

which one searches for an occupation (or a mate). In addition, since many occupations require specialized training or specific education, they are unavailable to persons lacking those requirements. Thus, the occupational decision is usually between accepting a job at one's present level of preparation or getting more preparation that will allow entrance into a new range of possible occupations. The boundaries thus created are often unfair to particular groups of people (notably African Americans, Hispanics, and the poor), especially when individuals are unable to acquire the necessary skills at a later point because their prerequisites were denied in childhood and in adolescence by the socialization process and these background characteristics. However, there are at least two ways in which these boundaries may be overcome in childhood and adolescence: by selecting a role model in an occupation outside the usual range, or by having an experience different from the usual range for individuals of similar backgrounds that is related in some way to one's eventual occupation. Clearly, these solutions do not resolve the social problem involved in institutionalized racism in its subtle and overt forms, and that problem must be faced and dealt with; but our analysis here is intended to be general enough to also include persons who strive to move into an occupation out of the usual realm for their family and peers but who are not held back by racism.

Role Models

Frequently one selects an occupation on the basis of a **role model** — a respected person with whom one identifies and seeks to emulate. Often this role model is a relative; in more traditional societies one frequently followed in the footsteps of one's father or mother. Some still do. However, the selection of and identification with a role model who does not share one's background is one powerful way to move into an occupation outside the common experience of one's peers. An example of this process is given by Brown (1965) in *Manchild in the Promised Land* in which one staff member in a school for boys had a lasting effect on him and his subsequent involvement in getting an education. Thus, a laborer's son or daughter may aspire to become a teacher or a doctor because of early role models and later find another role model who leads the person on to a career in biochemistry, for example.

Experience

Similarly, an individual may choose a job on the basis of a particular experience. A woman may become a police officer because she saw her older brother killed in a gang war or a firefighter may choose that occupation because his grandmother's house was destroyed by fire. Again, one may move out of the range of jobs common to one's peers because of a unique response to a particular experience. An example would be the decision to work with older people because of an opportunity to be a volunteer in a senior citizen's center when taking a course on adulthood and aging.

The influence of experience and role models on occupational choice was clearly shown in a study of psychiatrists, psychoanalysts, psychologists, and psychiatric social workers (Henry, Sims & Spray, 1971).

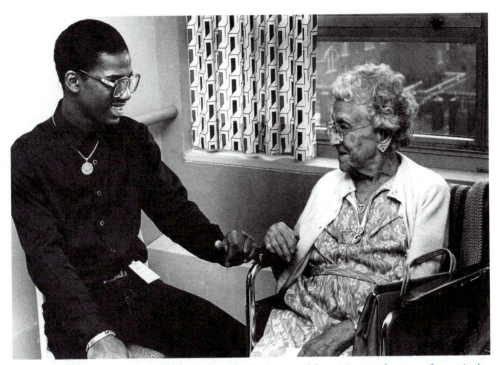

One may select a career that is outside the range of jobs typical for one's peers because of a particular experience — such as working in a senior citizen's center or nursing home during a high school or college fieldwork program.

Comparatively speaking, both psychiatrists and psychoanalysts, but especially analysts, were directed toward the general field of medicine primarily through "familial dynamics" — either by way of identification with a relative (most frequently a parent) who was a doctor, or through the setting of the goal of becoming a doctor by a parent (who was not in medicine). In short, the influences on psychiatrists and psychoanalysts operated early, consisted of persons rather than experiences, and were expressed through close relationships.

In contradistinction, clinical psychologists and psychiatric social workers were directed to their general fields at a later time and essentially equally by persons and experiences. For psychologists the most important person was the teacher, the most important experiences were training and reading, and the most important mode of influence was intellectual stimulation. For social workers the key figure was the nonrelated professional social worker, the crucial experience was the job, and the chief modes of influence were exposure to the field and the opportunity to recognize their ability and pleasure with the work. (Henry, Sims & Spray, 1971, pp. 111–112)

It is interesting to note that, for these psychotherapists, a second specialized occupational choice was also made, usually at a later point. That is, after deciding on medicine, psychology, or social work, they later decided to specialize in psychoanalysis or psychiatry, clinical psychology, and psychiatric social work, respectively. The influences for this specialized decision were generally drawn from within the profession. The influence of the parent was largely replaced by the influence of peers, although teachers, supervisors, and experiences were also important influences.

Interests

Obviously the individual's interests, preferences, and values play a large part in the choice of an occupation, as least insofar as there is an actual choice to make. In the case of psychotherapists, individuals in any of the professional disciplines would tend to be drawn to psychotherapy by similar interests (e.g., understanding and helping people); but, conversely, these interests could be satisfied in several different occupations and professions. In general, a person's interests, values, and preferences partly reflect the effect of role models and individual experiences; they also reflect the unique range of past accomplishments, talents, and abilities, as well as the sense of "who I am" and "what I want to do with my life." Bolles (1972, 1988), in his best-selling manual for persons seeking jobs or thinking of changing jobs, points out the importance of taking an inventory of yourself in terms of your goals and skills. He suggests a number of practical ways to do this, including reflecting on memories of your past, your feelings about the present, and your visions of the future.

1. Your interests, wishes and happiness determine what you actually do well more than your intelligence, aptitudes, or skills do. . . . Maybe the word "feelings" or "wishes" sounds just too erratic, in your ears. OK, then borrowing a word from biology, let's speak instead of "tropisms"; things which living creatures instinctively go toward, or away from. Man is no exception, and in addition each one of us has his own personal, unique tropisms. You must know: what do you feel drawn toward, what do you instinctively go away from? Your own personal tropisms are determinative for your first, second (third, or fourth) career.

2. If you do work you really enjoy, and at the highest level that you can legitimately claim, you are bound to do an outstanding job, and be of genuine help to others. . . .

3. No tests or other instruments have been devised yet, that measure what you want so effectively as just *asking you* or having you *ask yourself.* (Bolles, 1972, p. 85)

Personality

In addition, occupational choice often reflects a "fit" in some sense between the person and the job. A number of studies have sought to identify the personality characteristics of adults in various types of occupations in order to specify how personality factors correspond with the pattern of attributes and roles involved in different occupations. (Curiously, male psychologists tend to be the oldest child in the family and to have a younger sister; Conger, 1977, p. 441.) For example, Holland (1973) proposed six matching personality types and occupational environments. They are succinctly stated by Hall (1976):

1. *Realistic*—Involves aggressive behavior, physical activities requiring skill, strength, and coordination. (Examples: forestry, farming, agriculture.)

2. *Investigative*—Involves cognitive (thinking, organizing, understanding) rather

than affective (feeling, acting, or interpersonal and emotional) activities. (Examples: biology, mathematics, oceanography.)

3. *Social*—Involves interpersonal rather than intellectual or physical activities. (Examples: clinical psychology, foreign service, social work.)

4. *Conventional*—Involves structural, rule-regulated activities and subordination of personal needs to an organization or person of power and status. (Examples: accounting, finance.)

5. *Enterprising*—Involves verbal activities to influence others, to attain power and status. (Examples: management, law, public relations.)

6. *Artistic*—Involves self-expression, artistic creation, expression of emotions, and individualistic activities. (Examples: art, music, education). (Hall, 1976, p. 13)

Of course, people do not fit neatly into any category of types, and both individuals and occupations may be thought to combine these types in a variety of ways. Thus, a clinical psychologist who conducts research might combine types 2 and 3 (investigative and social); one who also teaches might combine types 2, 3, and 6 (artistic, investigative, and social); whereas one who works in a mental hospital might combine types 3 and 4 (conventional and social). In that sense, it is important to note that any occupation involves considerable variation within its general characteristics and often allows individuals to integrate their own personal style with the occupational role.

Holland (1985) organized these codes into a hexagon pattern, forming a two-dimensional grid that led to the development of a Self-Directed Search. This is a self-administered assessment booklet that helps the person identify the combination of three codes that best represents the individual's characteristics. The person then matches the code with a list of occupations. There are several safeguards built in to minimize the risk of errors or harmful outcomes (Holland & Rayman, 1985).

One interesting example of the correspondence between an occupation and certain personality characteristics is seen in a study by Henry (1965) of professional actors and actresses. He expected that this group would show many signs of "identity confusion" since their occupation consists of the portrayal of roles and, he reasoned, they may be attempting to compensate for a basic confusion about their own identity by taking on the roles of others. It was found that, indeed, this group of professional actors was lower on a measure of identity than comparison groups of nonactors; that the lower the identity score (i.e., the more identity confusion), the more likely the person was to be successful as an actor; and that identity scores rose during the several weeks of play rehearsal preceding an opening performance. These findings suggest that, at least for some actors, the occupation may serve as a source of satisfaction of (or compensation for) certain personality characteristics. It is also interesting that most of these persons chose acting as their career because the very first time they acted a part in a play, they felt that they wanted to be actors; it is as if the choice was so good for them that they could almost hear it "click" the very first time (similar to George's occupational choice of dancing in the first Interlude).

For persons who do not find this clear a response to an occupational field, vocational tests that compare one's response to a variety of questions with the typical responses of persons in various fields may be useful. However, the process of self-examination suggested by Bolles (1988) may be very helpful also because many successful persons are not necessarily typical personalities in that occupation. Some relevant dimensions include: Do you like working with persons, or with ideas, or with things — or a mixture of two or three of these? Do you prefer working alone or with others? How much, and what kind of satisfactions do you need? How much frustration can you accept before it is balanced by satisfaction, and how long can you wait for the satisfaction? These dimensions, and other "personal tropisms" (Bolles, 1972), provide important cues to the characteristics you will want to pay attention to when you begin researching occupations.

Research about Occupations

High schools and colleges teach students how to research all kinds of topics for class papers and projects. Although they usually leave it up to the student to discover that these same research methods are useful for finding information about personally relevant topics such as occupations, there are undergraduate courses in career selection (Ware & Millard, 1987).

Bolles (1988) provided a number of suggestions about ways to begin one's research into careers; it typically involves reading and interviewing a variety of sources and cross-checking the information to be sure it is accurate. One of the most helpful ways to research an occupation is to talk with people in the occupation to find out what it is like and how they acquired the training and the job. If one has the opportunity, firsthand experience in the prospective occupation is also very useful, for example, through fieldwork programs in high school or college, or as a volunteer. This can provide valuable information about how you respond to the job and will give you a chance to talk to people who are working in that field. It can also provide valuable experience that may be required to gain paid employment in that field.

Entry into the Occupation

In some cases one learns most of the skills required for the occupation on the job. But often one learns and practices many of the roles involved in the occupation during a period of *anticipatory socialization* before entering the job for the first time. Then, at the point of entry, the *real* demands of the job, the *real* expectations, and the *real* rewards are found. Probably, these will differ somewhat from what were expected; and there may be some conflict between the idealism of the earlier expectations and the actuality of the job. Consider, for example, a psychiatric social work student meeting her first patient in a mental hospital as a social work intern. She may not have been in a hospital ward before; she needs to define the situation and to define her role in it; usually role models and *resocialization* by other staff members help her with these tasks during the first few weeks of the entry period. But during the first few months, she may begin to realize that her skills, the state of psychological knowledge, and the resources of the hospital are less than ideal, and that the needs of the patients are often greater than the resources available. She begins to feel that she may not be as helpful as she hoped she would be; perhaps she will not be able to solve the problems she sees around her because there is not enough time, enough staff, or enough money to provide effective treatment within the walls of the hospital, let alone to do preventive or after-discharge work in the community. Thus, although her idealism may persist, she must readjust her expectations to the real demands of the actual situation. She may become frustrated and angry, she may become "radicalized" and begin working to change the situation, or she may decide to become the most effective social worker she can be and do her job with as much innovation and enthusiasm as possible. She might also look for a higher-paying job in a different type of work, or consider beginning a private practice of psychotherapy.

In a similar way, a police officer, an accountant, and a factory worker are resocialized by the demands of their new jobs and go through a period of "adjustment" and potential emotional upset during the first weeks or months in their first full-time job. "Boot camp" for army inductees would be a more extreme example of this resocialization process because, although the same process is involved, the situation is full-time, more intense, and less consistent with the inductee's previous roles and identity (Janowitz, 1965).

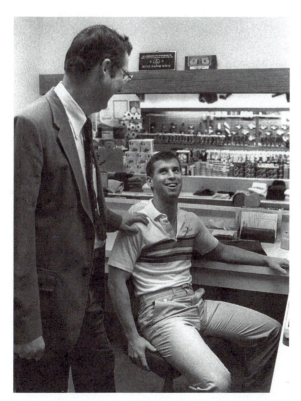

Entry into a job involves changes in oneself through the process of resocialization. If one's occupational role is a cornerstone of one's sense of identity, one's sense of competence and others' evaluation of one's performance are very important.

From a symbolic interaction perspective, the individual is developing a new *me* during this period of resocialization into the occupation. This involves taking the attitude of the others (employer, co-workers, and customers) toward oneself and learning the role behavior that is expected. At the same time, one sees oneself and reacts to oneself in this role. This process, which G. H. Mead called *self-consciousness,* allows one to analyze the correspondence between *I*'s inner feelings about the *me* in the occupation and the way one sees oneself behaving. For example, the social work intern discussed earlier might feel some inconsistency between her behavior and her expectations about herself. Her *I* might experience this inconsistency, and she would attempt to find a *me* that fits both her expectations and the demands of the situation. Thus, on one hand, if one feels that one's occupational *me* is relatively unimportant (e.g., one is just working to make money) then the inconsistency will be relatively trivial. On the other hand, if one's occupational *me* is a cornerstone of one's sense of identity—as a "doctor," a "psychologist," or an "artist"—then when *I* perceives the *me* as unsatisfying, or if *I* perceives others' attitudes toward the *me* as unfavorable, the crisis may be much more serious.

Even if there is no particular inconsistency that is upsetting, the shift in the self involves *I*'s integrating this new *me* into the array of other *me*s and attending to the expectations of a new group of significant other people. Thus, during this initial period of entry and socialization into the occupation, the individual may find it necessary to readjust aspects of the *self* because of the actual demands of the job and his or her ability to deal effectively with them.

The point of occupational entry, therefore, is a crucial point not only because it marks the transition into adult status and a shift in roles but also because it may involve a major shift in one's *self* and the emotional crisis that such a shift entails.

One Life—One Career?

Sometimes it is assumed that well-adjusted, normal people find their occupation, make it a part of their identity, and remain in that same occupation as long as they live, or until retirement. This has been called the **one life–one career imperative** (Sarason, 1977). This notion may make the choosing of an occupation a very serious, almost fateful, matter. However, a longitudinal study of a representative sample of all civilian, noninstitutionalized men between the ages of 45 and 59 in the United States in 1966 found that 3 out of 4 had changed occupations since they began their first job after leaving school; over the five-year study (from 1966 to 1971) 1 out of 4 of these middle-aged men nearing retirement changed occupations (Kohen, 1975). Not surprisingly, professionals and technicians were least likely to change occupations, whereas clerical and sales workers were most likely to change. Those who moved from one firm to another were more likely to change occupations than those who remained working for the same company; and those who were dissatisfied with their job in 1966 were more likely to change occupations. For only 3 out of 10 who changed firms, and 1 out of 10 who remained with the same company, did this change in occupations result in downward mobility; upward mobility was also more likely for those with greater education. Surprisingly, men who were forced to seek another job were no less likely to move up in occupational

status than men who left their job voluntarily; and neither local l
conditions nor race affected the likelihood that a middle-aged man wo
the occupational ladder. However, Black men moved less far than the
did, and it was estimated that "if middle-aged black men had had acces:
advancement opportunities as whites, the blacks would have moved ne
far up the occupational hierarchy as they actually did" during this perio
to 1971 (Kohen, 1975, p. 149). Contrary to what might be thought, nc
age discrimination was found for this group in terms of promotion, c
hiring practices.

> Finally, the results indicate that there are indeed economic and psycholog
> occupational change, even among middle-aged men. The psychologic:
> terms of increased job satisfaction) are evident and strong only among
> mained with the same firm over the five-year period. But the economic ret
> of relative improvement in hourly earnings) prevail both among those
> employers and among those who did not. Moreover, the data provide s\
> thesis that some mobile middle-aged workers trade off gains in some job
> (e.g., earnings) for losses in others (e.g., satisfaction). (Kohen, 1975, p

These data indicate that most working men change occupations a
that midlife occupational change is not uncommon, and that few men r
occupation all of their working lives — at least among the cohort of wo:
retirement in 1971. Similar results were found from census data tl
women as well as men. One-third of all men and about one-quarter c
changed occupations between 1965 and 1970; conversely, about hal
and 4 out of 10 women were in the same occupation; the remainder
unemployed or died by 1970 (Sommers & Eck, 1977). Although th
differences between occupations, even in the most stable occupations
craftworkers, managers), less than two-thirds were employed in the s
tion in 1970 as they were in 1965. During the 1980s the shift in jot
manufacturing industries toward greater service-oriented and high-te
cupations has undoubtedly increased this trend toward career change
seems to be little evidence to support the belief in a one life – one caree

Variations in the Occupational Cycle

As may by now be obvious, when we discuss the occupational cycle, w
different ideas of the occupation itself. For example, when we think o:
consistent socialization through a long training period, or a job whose
advancement may interfere with family life, we think of a career in wh
distinct steps in the pattern of advancement. The kind of occupation
when we think of a frustrating, depersonalized job, however, tends to
routine job on an assembly line.

Thus, it seems that there are vast differences between certain occu
indeed, among various patterns of occupations. First, consider the **car**
there are well-defined steps of advancement, a hierarchical progressio:
one follows if one is successful. This pattern is one of vertical movem\
status ladder; it is a pattern of orderly progression, often within the sa:

over a period of years. Or, it may involve a horizontal progression of functionally related jobs with increased status (e.g., apprentice, skilled worker, plant manager). As in the study of occupational mobility discussed earlier, a person's socioeconomic status can be inferred directly from the occupational classification (Duncan, 1961). Second, consider a **disorderly work history** in which there is no pattern to the sequence of jobs an individual holds; there is neither a vertical nor horizontal progression that provides increased status. Wilensky (1961) defined these criteria as one way of exploring the obvious differences in types of work histories. He found that, at most, one-third of the "middle mass" (persons who are economically secure but not upper-middle class) have work histories that may be characterized as orderly careers. Thus, the majority of those working are not involved in long-term career aspirations and in progressing up a status ladder but, instead, are likely to move up primarily on the basis of seniority with little increased responsibility or status on the job. In addition, Wilensky found that these two patterns were reflected in greater community involvement and in overlapping patterns of social participation on and off the job for the orderly group compared to the disorderly group.

> Men who have predictable careers for at least a fifth of their worklives belong to more organizations, attend more meetings, and average more hours in organizational activity. Their attachments to the local community are also stronger—indicated by support of local schools and, to a lesser extent, by contributions to church and charity. . . .
>
> If we give a man some college, put him on a stable career ladder, and top it off with a nice family income, he will get into the community act. Give a man less than high school, a thoroughly unpredictable sequence of jobs, a family income of five to eight thousand and it is very likely that his ties to the community will be few and weak. (Wilensky, 1961, p. 338)

Finally, Wilensky suggested that the pattern of work history (orderly or disorderly) had more impact on a man's social life than any of the work positions that he may have picked up and dropped along the way. (We might note that this study, which obviously used data from the 1950s, may or may not apply to workers in the 1980s, but it is not irrelevant since many of the men described are among the retired today.)

These findings point to one important aspect of the variations among occupations. Of course, there are several other factors that are also significant such as motivation (money, sustenance, status, service, creativity, and so on) and sources of satisfaction (money, helping, status, skill, accomplishment, fame, and so on). Thus, potentially orderly careers such as physician, machinist, and engineer are characterized by a number of differing factors (such as motivations and satisfactions) that distinguish one from the other, despite the orderly progression common to each of them. Such differences between specific orderly careers may be as important as the similarities among them.

In addition, a third type of career progression may be suggested as an important variation of the orderly career. This type is a pattern in which the individual changes occupations in a relatively sudden and major way. Perhaps one does this out of frustration in an attempt to find a more satisfying career, or one does it from a position of success and accomplishment in an attempt to find new challenges. On one hand, this pattern differs from the disorderly pattern because there would be only one or two such shifts in an otherwise orderly career. On the other hand, the shift itself distinguishes this pattern from a strictly orderly career. Examples of this pattern include the business executive who switches to government service or the priest who enters a secular career. We expect that such individuals may have entered a career for which they were not suited, or which they outgrew; or perhaps they are less willing to stick with an unsatisfying job (Weiner & Vaitenas, 1977). They may also be better able to take risks, to face insecurity, and to deal with challenges than the individual who remains in an unsatisfying career (Krantz, 1977). Also, in some cases their accomplishment in one career may set the stage for entry into a different career—such as athletes who enter business and persons who enter politics or public service after achieving success in another field.

The Career Clock

In Chapter 3 we discussed the crisis or turning point that may occur in the occupational cycle during the middle years. This experience contains elements similar to the issues at the entry point, in that it involves readjusting one's goals and idealistic hopes to what, at this stage, is perceived as one's realistic future possibilities in light of how much time is left in the occupation. An example might be a university professor, hoping to be famous in his field and to contribute great books, who decided at the age of 50 that he had better begin on his first book if he is ever to write any! This crisis differs from the earlier transition into the occupation, however, because it involves what may be called the **career clock.** This "clock" is similar to the *social clock* (Neugarten, 1968) discussed in Chapter 2. It is the individual's subjective sense of being "on time" or "behind time" in career development. During the middle years (beginning around age 40–45 when about half of the typical worklife is over) many people become aware of the number of years left before retirement and of the speed with which they are attaining their goals. If they are markedly "behind time," or if their goals are unrealistic, they begin to adjust their goals to be more consistent with what is likely to be feasible. They may also decide to change jobs "before it is too late." Relatively little attention has been given to women's occupational "clock"; we would expect the "clock" to differ for single, married, divorced, and widowed women, and for those who are mothers compared with those who are not. For some, however, the pattern may be similar to the one described by Neugarten (1967b) for men:

> Men perceive a close relationship between life-line and career-line. Middle age is the time to take stock. Any disparity noted between career-expectations and career achievements—that is, whether one is "on time" or "late" in reaching career goals—adds to the heightened awareness of age. One 47-year-old lawyer said,
>
> "I moved at age forty-five from a large corporation to a law firm. I got out at the last possible moment, because after forty-five it is too difficult to find the job you want. If you haven't made it by then, you had better make it fast, or you are stuck." (p. 96)

In addition to the growing introspection involved in this period of taking stock and reassessment of career goals, Neugarten found a sense of mastery, competence, and control in her sample of middle-aged male business executives. Often successful men at this point in their career report a highly developed decision-making ability, built from experience in similar situations over a period of years; a prevailing theme is a sense of "maximum capacity and ability to handle a highly complex environment and a highly differentiated self. Very few express a wish to be young again" (Neugarten, 1967b, p. 97).

Once again, we see changes in the self very much involved in these events of the middle years of the occupational cycle. The effect of experience is very much in evidence, as we discussed in Chapter 2. There is *I*'s ability to take the attitude of the generalized other involved in the career clock—noting when it is the "right time" to change jobs or obtain a promotion if one is to reach one's goals. But also, the process of selecting another job, or gaining the training and resocialization involved in a promotion such as from sales to management, involves changes in the *me* and the active processes of *I* in selecting and integrating these changes in the self. In general, every step up a career ladder, or every job change that involves any resocialization, as well as every promotion that also involves moving to a new community, involves changes in the self. And *I* and *me* aspects of the self are always involved in these changes.

Of course, the career clock may also be involved in timing the milestones of career development (such as promotions and major advances); but it is less clear whether the career clock is a meaningful concept for understanding disorderly patterns of work history or whether its usefulness is limited to orderly careers. We might speculate that the awareness of age and of having little time left to work would increase for individuals with disorderly patterns during this middle-age period as well. The possibility of acquiring another job if one is laid off becomes more and more difficult as one approaches retirement age, since employers are hesitant to hire a person who may need to be retrained and who may receive a company pension but can only work for 10 or 15 years. Thus, the potential for an emotional crisis during this middle period of the occupation may be at least as great for the disorderly pattern as it is for the orderly career, especially if the change is "off time"—such as early forced retirement or being laid off and unable to find work at age 55 or 60. Also, it is likely that a dramatic midcareer shift—such as giving up a job in management in an urban area and moving to a small city to become a construction worker or innkeeper—would be a significant transition, even if it was a chosen one; it often involves marital disruption that probably increases the emotional crisis (Krantz, 1977).

In the next section, we focus on the conclusion of the work cycle: the milestone of retirement.

Retirement: A Major Milestone

Retirement is a major turning point in adult development since it is the social milestone marking the shift from the middle years to the later years of life. It may be seen as a transition point, similar to the transition point at high school or college graduation. Retirement usually marks the end of full-time work and the beginning of a period of relative leisure.

Retirement as an Event

Retirement is often marked as an event that signals a *transition* point from one social position to another. It may be celebrated publicly with a banquet and a token or appreciation. The event may be noted in the trade or union or employer publications. But, more often than not, retirement tends to be a social event without a precise social meaning. Instead, its meaning must be understood within the social life space of the individual (Maddox, 1966).

Because of Social Security legislation in 1935, retirement age has usually been placed at 65 in the United States. This age was apparently first selected by Otto Von Bismarck, who was the chancellor of the German Empire and was instrumental in creating an Old Age and Survivors Pension Act in 1889 (House Committee on Aging, 1977). However, in the United States, persons age 62 may become eligible for Social Security benefits (at reduced levels), so the majority of retirees in the 1980s retired before age 65 (Figure 6.4). In fact, some had already stopped working before they became eligible for benefits. For example, in 1985, just 72 percent of 60-year-old men were in the labor force; as were only 31 percent of men in the "traditional" retirement year, age 65 (Rones, 1985).

Economic incentives for retirement have been an important factor in early retirement. In the past, Social Security benefits increased only 1–3 percent for every year a person worked after age 65; up to 50 percent of earnings from paid employment was lost by a reduction in Social Security benefits; taxes were paid on earnings, but most Social Security benefits were tax free; and one may not have been eligible for a private pension if one continued to work (Burkhauser & Tolley, 1978). A number of these financial incentives for early retirement were reduced by

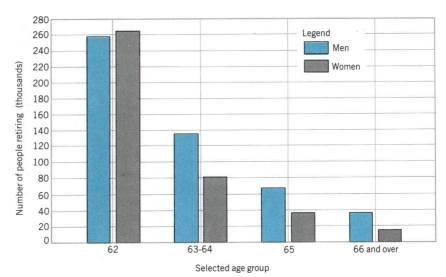

FIGURE 6.4 Workers retiring by selected age groups and sex (1982 survey). (*Source*: Sherman, 1985, Table B. Reprinted with permission of Basic Books, Inc. from M.C. Bernstein and J.B. Bernstein, *Social security: The system that works*, Fig. 8.1, p. 179. Copyright © 1988.)

legislation in 1986 and will gradually affect future retirees; we discuss Social Security in detail later in this chapter.

The Age Discrimination in Employment Act also affects retirement age. It was passed by the U.S. Congress in 1967 to protect workers over the age of 40 from discrimination. To partially offset the pressure to retire, the minimum legal age for mandatory retirement, as a form of age discrimination regulated by this act, was raised to 70 in 1979, and in 1986 it was removed altogether for most workers. Firefighters, law enforcement officers, tenured faculty in universities and colleges, executives who would retire with benefits over $44,000 per year, and employees in small companies are not covered by the legislation; the first three exemptions are subject to review and will expire in 1993 if no action is taken. Specific occupations where a claim of age-related fitness is made (e.g., airline pilots) may still have mandatory retirement; these policies must be justified and are subject to review by the Equal Employment Opportunities Commission (Sterns & Alexander, 1987). The intent of this legislation was to allow as many persons as possible the choice to continue working as long as they wished to work. Few are expected to take this option, but for those who do, it is often important for their sense of well-being and may provide important economic resources for them and important services to the employer.

Because of increased life span, the older population is growing rapidly (Figure

Mandatory retirement has been eliminated for most employees by federal legislation. Congressman Claude Pepper (D—FL) continued to work until his death at the age of 88. A tireless opponent of mandatory retirement, he also strove for the improved quality of life for older persons.

6.5). As a result, most individuals in the United States now reach retirement age and move into a period of retirement that is lasting much longer today than in the past. Since the birth rate declined following the period of high birth rate known as the baby boom, and that group will begin to reach age 65 at the turn of the century, the continued funding of the Social Security program has required sharp increases in workers' payments into the system.

The social ambivalence about retirement as a social event was clear in the attitudes expressed in a nationwide survey. Many retirees reported they missed something about working, usually the income and their friends at work (Table 6.4).

Since an understanding of retirement involves not only the influence of the event itself but also characteristics of the individual and his or her situation, it is important to examine the economic, biological, sociocultural, and psychological factors in retirement.

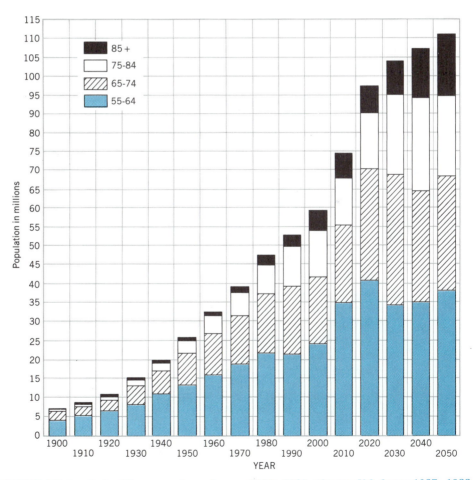

FIGURE 6.5 Population 55 years and over by age: 1900–2050. (*Source*: U.S. Senate 1987–1988, Chart 1–3, p. 11.)

TABLE 6.4 *The One Thing Missed the Most about the Job by Occupation*

	Prof./Mgr./ Prop.	*Clerical/ Sales*	*Skilled/ Foreman*	*Unskilled*
The money	20%	23%	42%	40%
The people	30%	27%	13%	24%
Feeling useful	11%	12%	6%	8%
Work itself	15%	11%	15%	10%

Source: Sheppard (1988), Table 9.9. Reprinted with permission of Springer Publishing Company, Inc. from *Retirement reconsidered*, R. Morris and S.A. Bass, Eds., © 1988.

Economic Issues

Having economic resources is undoubtedly an important factor in the complicated decision to retire from work, especially when retirement is voluntary. However, relatively few retirees give eligibility for Social Security as the primary reason for leaving their last job and even fewer give eligibility for a private pension as the reason for retirement (Sherman, 1985). Nonetheless, as noted earlier, eligibility for Social Security appears to be one factor in the selection of the age to retire. Conversely, it is likely that persons who need greater income may choose to continue working, since one may earn more than the Social Security benefits would provide (and after age 70, one may receive Social Security in addition to one's salary). In this section we briefly describe Social Security and private pensions.

Social Security

Supported by payments from employers and employees, the federal Social Security programs provide retirement benefits to insured workers and their spouses (Old-Age and Survivors Insurance), disability protection (Disability Insurance), and medical insurance (Medicare). Nearly all workers are covered by Social Security and participants build eligibility for benefits wherever they work. Disability protection is provided for disabled insured workers and many of their dependents. Medicare covers nearly all persons aged 65 and over (regardless of whether they are retired) as well as some younger persons eligible for disability benefits; we discuss Medicare in detail in Chapter 9.

> Social Security is a social insurance system. Employees pay contributions, matched by equal amounts from employers. These amounts earn eligibility, much as insurance premiums do. But, as *social* insurance, the recipients and amounts of benefits are determined in part by family relationships and common needs, factors that private insurance usually ignores.
> Social Security provides a partial income substitute as a return for past work and contributions rather than "demonstrated need." Demonstrated need means, in effect, turning one's purse inside out and spreading out personal papers (bank accounts,

insurance) for some official to measure against a yard stick by which a legislature defines "need." That is how the "needs-tested" (or "welfare") programs proceed — by ascertaining the income and assets of the elderly, the disabled, and families with dependent children. (Bernstein & Bernstein, 1988, p. 13)

In contrast to needs-tested programs, Social Security retirement benefits are based on a formula that considers the *age* at which the benefits begin (after age 62) and the individual's *average indexed monthly earnings.* The formula works so that people who always earned an average wage and retire at age 65 receive about 42 percent of their average working income; persons with lower than average wages get a higher proportion, whereas those with higher than average incomes get a lower proportion (Bernstein & Bernstein, 1988, p. 19).

The spouse of the insured worker also becomes eligible for benefits, which are based on a fraction of the worker's benefits (25 to 50 percent, depending on the age of the spouse when benefits begin after age 62). Married persons receive the higher of either their own basic benefit or the fraction of the spouse's benefit to which they are entitled. Widowed survivors are eligible for the spouse's benefit at age 60, or if they have minor or disabled children; and children under age 17 also qualify for a benefit equal to 50 percent of the deceased parent's benefit.

Benefits rise automatically with an increase in the Consumer Price Index each July, as a means of offsetting the effects of inflation. In 1988, a 4 percent cost-of-living adjustment (COLA) raised the maximum monthly benefit in 1989 for a person retiring at age 65 to $899. Among the 38.4 million Social Security recipients in 1989, the average retiree aged 65 was expected to receive $537 a month — $6444 a year. It was projected that the average monthly benefit for an elderly couple would be $921; $943 for the typical disabled worker, spouse, and children; and $1112 for the average widowed mother with two children. The maximum Social Security tax paid by workers was increased to $3604.80, which is matched by the employer; self-employed persons pay at a higher rate (*New York Times,* 1988).

Persons receiving Social Security benefits may also earn income. For example, in 1989 a retiree could earn an income equal to an additional $8880. Over that amount, $1 was deducted from benefits for every $2 earned (in 1990 $1 is deducted for every $3 earned). After age 70, no reduction in benefits applies. For each year after age 65 that benefits are delayed, one receives a 3 percent additional credit (this gradually increases in 1990, reaching 8 percent in 2009). In contrast, if one begins receiving benefits at age 62 instead of age 65, the amount is reduced by 20 percent. The age defined as the "normal retirement age" at which full benefits are received (now age 65) is scheduled to increase to age 67 in two steps during the next century. Increasing incentives for persons to continue working will benefit persons in good health, but hurt minority populations with a lower life expectancy.

Social Security benefits are not taxed unless the individual's income from all sources exceeds a specified amount; if it does, then up to half the benefit from these high-income recipients is taxed and the money is returned to Social Security; most states exempt Social Security income from taxation (Bernstein & Bernstein, 1988, pp. 27–28).

Social Security provides a significant source of income for older persons — 38 percent in 1986 — and protects a large number of older persons from poverty

An older person may work part-time for economic reasons or to remain actively engaged and feel productive and busy. Those older workers who choose to continue working may be more productive than younger workers.

(Figure 6.6). The COLA increases have been especially important in reducing the level of poverty among the elderly since they began in 1975 (U.S. Senate, 1987–1988).

Obviously, the growing number of older persons, the longer life expectancy of older adults, and the COLA increases are raising the cost of the Social Security benefits. Moreover, the baby boom generation that will become eligible for Social Security in the next century is a cause of particular concern. In 1983 Congress enacted a number of changes to ensure the sound fiscal basis of this program. Under current predictions the Old-Age, Survivors, Disability Insurance (OASDI) programs "are in 'close actuarial balance' until the sixth decade of the next century (as far ahead as anyone looks)" (Bernstein & Bernstein, 1988, p. 88). Although no one can predict the future, and unforeseen economic or political events could affect Social Security, the program enjoys broad public support that should protect its survival.

Private Pensions

Until the Pension Reform Act was passed by Congress in 1974, many workers did not receive the pension they thought they were entitled to because of various loopholes, conditions, or inadequate funding of the pension plan. The 1974 law established

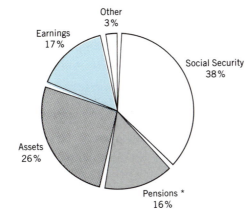

Other
3%

Earnings
17%

Social Security
38%

Assets
26%

Pensions *
16%

*Includes railroad retirement.

FIGURE 6.6 Income sources of persons or families aged 65 and older: 1986. (*Source:* U.S. Senate, 1987–88, Chart 2–14, p. 60.)

several controls over private pensions and also allowed individuals to set up individual retirement accounts (IRAs) with special tax benefits; self-employed persons can set up similar plans called Keogh accounts. The pension reform legislation established insurance for persons whose retirement plans are terminated with inadequate funds, provided mechanisms to regulate pension plans, required a disclosure statement to participants, and required reports to the Social Security Administration, which in turn notifies employees of their pension rights when they apply for Social Security benefits. In addition, the legislation provided minimal standards for vesting (Schulz, 1976). **Vesting** refers to the individual gaining rights to part or all of the pension benefits so that, if workers leave the job for any reason, their pension rights are protected. More recent legislation has reduced the length of service required for vesting and mandated other changes that became effective in 1989, but a number of significant problems remain.

> Private plans cover, at best, half the private work force. Small companies, with high installation and administrative costs, short corporate life, and high employee turnover, afford only sparse coverage, and that frequently disappears along with the demise of the enterprise. Service and other low-pay jobs provide little plan coverage and the many people with such jobs, principally women and minorities in part-time and part-year work, generally do not participate. No attention has yet been paid to the needs of agricultural workers.
>
> Plan participation rules have improved, but disparate treatment in favor of the highly paid remains permissible. Vesting, now mandatory after five years of employment, and after ten for those in multi-employer plans, salvages benefits formerly lost. But the dollar amounts that result frequently are small. . . . Vested benefits of separated employees do not participate in plan improvements; as a result chronic inflation constantly degrades their value even before payment starts. Similarly, inflation outpaces post-retirement benefit improvements which, in any event, are not required by law and are not the subject of mandatory bargaining. The absence of assured inflation-proofing continues as a major drawback of private plans. (Bernstein & Bernstein, 1988, pp. 145–146)

As shown in Figure 6.6, only 16 percent of the income of persons over age 65 was from pensions in 1986—about the same as the amount of earned income. However, forty percent received some income from public and/or private pensions, including 27 percent who received income from a private pension (U.S. Senate, 1987–1988).

Health

Physical health clearly affects the retirement process. The most obvious example of this is when poor health is the cause of retirement. Until recently, retirement was far less common than it is today because many persons died before reaching retirement age. Even among those men who began receiving Social Security benefits in the latter half of 1969, for instance, 43 percent had health-related work limitations; for those who began receiving benefits at age 62, 61 percent had health-related limitations (Rubin, 1976). Health problems were also significant for women who retired —one-third reported that health was the reason for leaving their last job (Reno, 1976). Comparable data in 1982 indicated the dramatic improvement in health during the last few years: 30.3 percent of the men and 27 percent of the women who retired gave health as the reason for leaving their last job; of those retiring at age 62, only 15 and 9 percent, respectively, gave health as the reason (Sherman, 1985, Table B).

Obviously, an extreme example of retirement hindered by health would be persons so incapacitated by poor health that they could neither find a part-time job nor enjoy travel and recreation during retirement. More often, retirement for health reasons indicates an inability to continue the old kind of work full-time, but may allow a reasonably full participation in other activities at least during the early years of retirement. Health also may improve during retirement after the demands of working have ended.

The interaction of health with other psychosocial factors was shown in a study of 1486 retired persons by the author and his colleagues (Kimmel, Price & Walker, 1978). Health was the major factor predicting retirement satisfaction; preretirement attitude about retiring was the second most predictive characteristic of satisfaction in retirement. Whether the person retired voluntarily or not was also important; voluntary retirees were likely to have higher income, higher occupational and health status, more positive feelings about retirement, and greater family support for retiring than nonvoluntary retirees. Voluntary retirees also had more positive attitudes about retirement and higher retirement satisfaction than those who did not retire voluntarily.

Clearly, physical limitations may be a major factor in a person's ability to find satisfaction in retirement. As we discuss in Chapter 7, various types of chronic disease are the major cause of changes associated with aging. If there is no disease, there are relatively few changes with age that impair a person's ability to function effectively, although "slowing down" (discussed in Chapter 4) and decrements in vision and hearing, and even lowered trust in one's body, may occur without apparent disease.

It is important to note, as discussed in Chapter 4, that there is no important decline in the types of everyday problem solving that are involved in many lines of work. Older workers may develop effective compensations for slower reaction time and any physical declines that might affect their performance. They may also seek the kinds of work that are best suited to their skills and expertise. If they retire from full-time work, an older person may seek part-time employment for economic reasons, or to remain actively engaged and to feel productive and busy. Since those older persons who continue working are likely to be a select sample, there is no reason to assume that they will be less productive than younger workers and they may, in fact, be more productive (Sterns & Alexander, 1987).

Finally, it should be pointed out that retirement does not, in itself, have a negative effect on an individual's health. Despite the widespread belief that retiring is harmful to one's health, nearly all studies have found that retirement leads neither to increased risk of death nor to deterioration in health (Ekerdt, 1987).

Sociocultural Factors

The meaning of retirement for the individual is also affected, to a large degree, by social variables and by the cultural meaning of retirement. For example, there has been a notable change in social attitudes about retirement in the last few years. As growing numbers of persons are retiring and retired life-styles have emerged as popular themes in the media, the stigma of not-working has been lifted to a large extent and replaced by a focus on retired persons as an untapped market of consumers. Likewise, research attention has begun to focus on the varieties of the retirement experience and on the positive aspects of retired life.

Palmore and his colleagues (Palmore, Burchett, Fillenbaum, George & Wallman, 1985) distinguished two differing types of retirement: *subjective retirement* based on the respondents' assessment of their own retirement status and *objective retirement* based on whether they worked less than full-time and received a retirement pension. They also noted a continuum based on the amount of time worked in the past year: full-time (not retired); less than full-time (partially retired); and no work (fully retired). Gibson (1987) identified another type, the *unretired-retired,* who are those persons over age 55 who are not working, but do not call themselves retired; this pattern is especially important for understanding African American retirees. There are also older persons (usually women) who are not working for pay, but are caring for aged parents or their spouse and may have "retired" from work to do so (Gibeau, 1988).

Sheppard (1988) called attention to the incentives for older persons to continue working based on a 1981 nationwide survey of retirees and those who continued working: higher income and lower risks of "dreariness, unhappiness, and low expectations of interesting and pleasant things in the future." He noted several types of occupations that are open to older persons and various community-based programs to find jobs for older men and women. Rothstein (1988) pointed out the emergence of agencies that place skilled older workers in part-time or short-term full-time jobs, the development of flexible work schedules to retain valued older workers, and the active recruitment of older workers by corporations such as McDonald's restaurants. In general, the image of the "retired" person has become as diverse as that of any other age group in our society. The end of mandatory retirement for most occupations and the continued trend toward "retirement" before age 65 assure that this diversity will continue.

Palmore et al. (1985) described the characteristics of retirees in the 1970s from several national longitudinal studies. Although these retirees may differ from persons currently retiring, they are among the population of older retirees today and therefore deserve attention. Few of the men were forced to retire; the majority retired early because either they felt their retirement income was adequate or their health limited their ability to work (p. 37). Although earlier cross-sectional studies reported a 50 percent decline in income, the decline shown in these longitudinal data was 25–28 percent when the actual preretirement income was considered. Early retirement had greater effects on income than retiring at age 65, perhaps because a greater proportion of early retirees did so as a result of health reasons. Health also decreased more among the early retirees, probably for the same reason; it is unlikely that retirement caused a decline in health since voluntary retirees had no declines in health compared to nonretirees. In general, "most of the supposed negative consequences of retirement are small or insignificant, but . . . early retirement has more effect than later retirement" (p. 49). Likewise, activity patterns did not change very much, except for the obvious decrease in time spent on the job and a compensating increase in time spent alone: "initial levels of activity were usually the strongest predictor of postretirement activity" (p. 48).

Few of the retirees in these nationwide samples showed poor adjustment. Moreover, the same variables affected the level of adjustment of retired and nonretired persons (e.g., income, health, friends, activities).

Between 27 and 37 percent of the men and 22 and 26 percent of the women worked after retirement, depending on their age. The need for additional income appeared to be the major reason they worked. There were large variations in the amount of work after retirement (p. 102). Those who did work seemed to enjoy the benefits of both working and of increased leisure time.

Gender Differences

Men and women appear to differ somewhat regarding retirement, although the nature of these differences is not clear. Palmore et al. (1985) suggest that the critical variables that would reveal these differences have not been examined and that a better theoretical analysis of gender differences is needed (p. 121). Atchley (1982) found modest gender differences, but noted that both men and women adjust well. Streib and Schneider (1971) found that women tended to be less willing to retire than men, and that single or married women tended to retire earlier than widowed or divorced women. Apparently, since the women generally had more education and a higher proportion were in professional occupations than the men in this study, they were less eager to retire. Single or married women would plan for retirement better than divorced or widowed women, so they were more likely to retire earlier than divorced or widowed women. O'Rand and Henretta (1982) found that women's work histories (later entry, lower-status occupations, and lower income compared with men) were likely to translate into lower retirement income for women. For example, more women are receiving retirement benefits based on their own work history today, but because of women's lower income, these benefits tend to be less than men receive. However, the development of "unisex" pension plans that provide equal payments for women over a longer expected life span as compared to men may improve the retirement income of single working women (Gohmann & McClure, 1987).

Retirement among African Americans

African American men and women have only begun to receive attention in studies of retirement. Two important themes stand out. First, for many African Americans, there is less discontinuity at retirement. Because of disadvantaged work patterns from young adulthood, there is an inherent ambiguity about retirement; for many (especially before age 65) they may describe their status as "disabled" instead of "retired" (Gibson, 1987). Second, raising the age at which one becomes eligible for Social Security would have a significant negative impact on African Americans because of shorter life expectancy in general. For many, this source of income provides greater financial stability than was available when they worked in the unstable labor market that was open to them (Jackson & Gibson, 1985, p. 216). African American women, for example, often worked in occupations that did not provide retirement benefits, and tended to be displaced by White women as they neared retirement age (Gibson, 1983). As a result of these conditions, many African Americans in a study by Gibson (1987) did not regard themselves as "retired" and earned income from sporadic work; this was true for both men and women. This is the reason they are typically excluded from studies of retirement.

In general, African Americans are a diverse population, often experiencing no dramatic change at the time of retirement, and frequently reporting a relatively high level of life satisfaction (Jackson & Gibson, 1985).

> They retire relatively early for reasons of poor health, find it necessary to supplement postretirement incomes with work, and rely heavily on governmental sources for income. Despite economic adversity, they were found to maintain moderately high levels of subjective well-being. (p. 213)

Retirement and the Family

The interaction of retirement and family relationships is also important. For example, if the spouse is living, retirement will thrust the couple into a more intense, full-time relationship than they have probably experienced for many years. Although Deutscher (1964) and others have reported that these postparental years are very happy years for couples in general, it may also be a difficult period for some. In either case, C. S. Lewis in *The Screwtape Letters* is probably accurate in noting that "when two humans have lived together for many years, it usually happens that each has tones of voice and expressions of face which are almost unendurably irritating to the other" (Lewis, 1943). An additional family issue for the retiring man is that he is leaving his world of work and is entering and spending much of his time in what has been his wife's realm — at least in the traditional family pattern. Is she going to be willing to share her domestic roles and duties with him, and will he accept them as meaningful for himself? Alternatively, if the wife continues working after the husband retires (or retains a range of community activities), the shifts in family roles for both spouses may provide an added source of potential upset to this developmental turning point. However, Hagestad (1988) reported that the passage of time may soften earlier conflicts in family relations, and that grandparent roles may provide important sources of satisfaction. Moreover, as Riley and Riley (1986) noted, the increased life span and other recent social and demographic changes have led to four potential opportunities: more complex social networks, greater duration of relationships, longer opportunities to gain experience, and new chances to fulfill and change role assignments. Each of these may enhance the family life of retired persons.

Preretirement Planning

One of the most important implications of studies on retirement is the importance of **preretirement planning**—or anticipatory socialization for the new set of roles that one will occupy when work roles are no longer present. Since this process takes some time, it should begin a decade or two before retirement. There is, in fact, evidence that workers begin to prepare psychologically for retirement about a decade before they retire: Cohn (1979) reported that data from a national cross-sectional survey indicated that the *relative* importance of intrinsic job satisfaction in determining one's global life satisfaction declines beginning about age 55; since actual amount of work satisfaction did not change, apparently other sources of satisfaction become relatively more important as retirement age nears. Nonetheless, relatively few preretirees make definite plans, although most "sometimes" think about it (McPherson & Guppy, 1979).

In our study of retirement, cited earlier, we suggested that preretirement counseling focus particular emphasis on health monitoring and maintenance and on attitudes about retirement, since these were clearly related to later retirement satisfaction (Kimmel et al., 1978). This planning should also involve many aspects, such as planning for a reliable source of income after retirement, anticipating the kinds of roles and activities that would be desirable and are available in the family and community, developing a few interests that may deepen into satisfying leisure pursuits (and possibly provide a new circle of friends to help replace those one is leaving at the job), and generally raising one's level of consciousness about retirement. Preretirement counseling programs also need to consider alternative work options, special issues that affect ethnic minorities, and resource networks (Dennis, 1984).

Psychological Factors

Retirement is a major social shift for an individual, but it does not usually involve a major psychosocial crisis. It clearly involves a process of anticipation and resocialization but, in general, the meaning of retirement reflects a complex array of social and cultural factors that reflect one's unique life situation and also one's perception of the social meaning of retirement.

In the Erikson framework, retirement may trigger the transition between Generativity versus Stagnation and Integrity versus Despair. Thus, the evaluation of one's contribution in the occupation and in the family gains importance as a crucial issue at the point of retirement. The sense of satisfaction, the sense of having produced something meaningful, and the sense of accomplishment in the occupation (as well as in the family) are therefore likely to become importance sources of a sense of integrity during this stage of life. Conversely, a sense of stagnation and of frustration will increase the difficulty of this stage. But, of course, the possibility for generativity does not end at retirement, nor is the issue of Integrity versus Despair suddenly important only after retirement. Instead, these two stages of the life cycle overlap; only the relative emphasis on generativity or integrity distinguishes one stage from the other. It may take many years after retirement before some of the other events occur that increase the importance of the issues involved in Integrity versus Despair. These events include the growing awareness of death as something personally relevant; some friends may have died, one's spouse may be ill or deceased, and one's own health may be failing. There may be extended periods of mourning over the loss of a friend or spouse, reawakening old memories that lead to a reevaluation of one's life. This introspective process may be called the life review (Butler, 1963b) and will be discussed in detail in Chapter 10.

With retirement there may be a shift away from a social world in which one played an important part to a smaller, less complex life involving a change in residence, a need to establish new social relationships, and different social tasks. However, there are considerable individual differences in the advantages and disadvantages of this change. For example, respondents in a nationwide study expressed very different views about retirement:

> A 66-year-old retired craftsman in Duluth, Minnesota, explained: "Retirement lets you enjoy life, go fishing, continue the hobbies you don't have time for when you work. . . ."
>
> An 80-year-old retired skilled craftsman in Kirkwood, Missouri, felt this way: "I really feel a person should work longer if they can. It gives them something to do. They feel like they have something to live for."
>
> A 78-year-old Mexican-American woman in Goodyear, Arizona, explained why she is opposed to early retirement: "Well, for one thing, I have seen in my family when people retire too early they tend to become useless and unwanted, unproductive. An emotional metamorphosis occurs, where people feel life has now passed them by and they are declining." (National Council on the Aging, 1975, pp. 219–220)

An individual's personality appears to be an important factor in the smoothness of the shift at retirement. Reichard, Livson, and Peterson (1962) reported, in a classic study of retired men, that three personality types were associated with good adjustment to retirement:

1. *Mature:* They moved easily into retirement and were relatively free of conflict, appeared to accept themselves realistically, and found considerable satisfaction in their activities and personal relationships. They took old age for granted, felt their lives had been rewarding, and made the best of it.

2. *Rocking-Chair Men:* They were generally passive, happy to be free of responsi-

bility and to satisfy their need to be passive in old age. Retirement brought them satisfactions that made up for any disadvantages.

3. *Armored:* These men maintained a complex system of defenses against passivity and helplessness; they appeared to avoid their fear of physical decline and aging by keeping active. In that sense, their defenses served to protect them from the fear of growing old.

There were also two types in their group of retired men who adjusted poorly:

4. *Angry Men:* They were bitter because they felt they had failed to achieve their goals, blamed others for their disappointments, and could not accept the fact they were growing old.

5. *Self-Haters:* These men felt their lives were disappointing and that they had failed; but they turned their anger inward and blamed themselves. They were likely to be depressed, especially since growing older increased their sense of worthlessness and inadequacy.

> With the exception of the mature group, many of whom had had difficulties in personal adjustment when they were younger, these personality types appeared to have been relatively stable throughout life. Poor adjustment to aging among the angry men and the self-haters seemed to stem from lifelong personality problems. Similarly, the histories of the armored and rocking-chair groups suggest that their personalities had changed very little throughout their lives. (Reichard et al., 1962, p. 171)

These data suggest that an individual's style of personality is relatively enduring and that it affects one's ability to adjust to a developmental turning point such as retirement. The data also suggest that retirement may have different meanings for persons with differing personalities and that a satisfying retirement for some (e.g., the ''rocking chair'' group) may be quite unpleasant for others (the ''armored,'' who felt they had to keep active). We will discuss personality and the relationship between personality and aging in Chapter 8, but this study sensitizes us to the variety of ways in which individuals differ and to the importance these personality differences may have.

In general, it should be noted that retired persons differ from one another at least as much as younger persons differ from one another. Thus, the personal needs, goals, satisfactions, and coping abilities differ among retired persons just as they do among all persons. This suggests that a satisfying life-style for one retired person — or for oneself — is not necessarily satisfying for another. Thus, the individual's preferences, interests, and personality need to be considered, respected, and allowed to maximize the variety of roles and styles of retired persons. Ideally, retired persons — as all individuals — should be able to strive for their most fully human potentials in an environment that supports and encourages their independence and growth.

For many retired persons, their increased nonwork time is often an opportunity for leisure. In the next section, we look at leisure and consider the relationship between leisure and work, or nonwork time. In addition, as the amount of time spent in activities that are unconnected with work during adulthood grows, the importance of an understanding of leisure becomes more and more significant for our society as a whole.

Retirement may have different meanings for persons of differing personalities; thus, a satisfying retirement for one type of person may be unpleasant for another.

Changing Leisure Values

Two differing definitions of leisure have evolved in our society as we have become more of a technological society that has, on one hand, provided more time away from work and, on the other hand, caused us to pay more attention to the quality of our lives. One definition of leisure has emphasized the distinction between **work** and **leisure** (Kelly, 1972). In this view, pure **leisure** is a *freely chosen* activity that is *not related to one's work.* It reflects the long struggle of the past century to free workers from long hours of toil at the mercy of their bosses and to provide them with greater **free time** to use as they choose. This view of leisure conflicts with the work-oriented values of our society in which free time has traditionally been seen as nonproductive, and potentially dangerous, idleness. Indeed, free time may be a problem for some persons—such as for some retired or unemployed persons. As a result, this view tends to focus on how one "spends" this leisure time and the implicit assumption is that it should be spent in productive, but not work-related, ways. This perspective also does not allow the possibility that one might be able to merge leisure with work to enhance the quality of work time as well as leisure time.

An alternative perspective on leisure, proposed by Neulinger (1980), does not define leisure in terms of its relation to work or nonwork time. Instead of focusing on free time, Neulinger focused on the *quality of life* that our technological society has made possible. **Leisure,** in this view, is a *state of mind* defined by two interrelated dimensions. The first dimension is *perceived freedom,* which is on a continuum from freedom to constraint in the activity the person is engaged in at the time. The second is the *motivation* the person experiences that leads to engaging in that activity. The motivational dimension is also a continuum from intrinsic (activities engaged in for the satisfaction of the activity itself) to extrinsic (activities engaged in for the external rewards they provide, such as money, prestige, success, etc.). For simplicity, the model can be presented graphically in six cells reflecting each of the four possible extreme types and two types of mixed intrinsic and extrinsic motivation (Figure 6.7). Thus, *pure leisure* is the extreme type reflecting perceived freedom of choice and intrinsic motivation.

Neulinger also used two different words for the occupation: the *job* is an activity one performs because one has to do it, and it provides no intrinsic reward in itself but only some extrinsic payoff. *Work* is an activity one performs because one has to do it, but it also provides a high degree of intrinsic motivation because the activity itself is personally satisfying to the individual. The other cells in the model are combinations of these three extreme types of activities and probably reflect the actual experience of most people most of the time; the extreme experiences of pure leisure, pure work, or pure job are probably fairly brief for most of us.

One of the most interesting aspects of Neulinger's model of leisure is that it not only allows but encourages the merger of one's leisure and occupation.

> Since leisure is no longer defined in contrast to work, it is no longer the opposite of a positive value; there is no longer a struggle between leisure and work, but rather a coexistence. (Neulinger, 1976b, p. 17)

Moreover, leisure in this model is not something one does or does not do, but instead it is a state of mind — an experience that one can achieve in many different situations given the right conditions (perceived freedom and intrinsic motivation). In Neulinger's view, some of us, or perhaps all of us, may need to learn how to achieve this state, either through leisure counseling or through education.

> Education for leisure . . . means to promote the conditions, within the person and within the environment, that will bring about a certain state of mind. It is a state where one fulfills oneself and feels fulfilled; it is a state where one ''works'' with something

Perceived freedom					
Freedom			Constraint		
Motivation			Motivation		
Intrinsic	Intrinsic and extrinsic	Extrinsic	Intrinsic	Intrinsic and extrinsic	Extrinsic
(1)	(2)	(3)	(4)	(5)	(6)
Pure leisure	Leisure work	Leisure job	Pure work	Work- job	Pure job
State of mind					

FIGURE 6.7 A psychological paradigm of leisure. (*Source*: Neulinger, 1976b, Table 2. Adapted and reprinted with permission.)

Leisure does not refer only to free time. It reflects the individual's free choice that provides intrinsic satisfaction. Some persons are able to integrate work with leisure.

one really likes to do; where things are done with enthusiasm, with joy, without haste or hurry, without undue pressure. . . . Leisure, conceived of in this way, takes on a high value, practical, moral, esthetic, and even religious. It is an ideal which we can never fully achieve, but which we can strive for. (Neulinger, 1976a, p. 4)

The challenge of this view of leisure is to discover those activities that are intrinsically satisfying to the individual, that can be realistically chosen, and that enhance the quality of life for the individual and perhaps, in an ideal sense, the quality of life for others as well. It does not suggest irresponsible self-indulgence, but instead implies greater self-knowledge about the ways in which one may fill one's productive life with leisure. This is very different from "killing" one's free time.

The emphasis in the Neulinger model is on the individual's state of mind, or experience of the activity. In that sense, Neulinger viewed it as a psychological model of leisure in contrast to the sociological model proposed by Kelly that emphasized classifying time periods rather than the individual's experience. Subsequently, Kelly (1982) provided a slightly different definition of leisure as "activity chosen primarily for its own sake" that combined two dimensions of relative freedom or choice and intrinsic meaning. In this view, leisure remains an *activity,* but the individual's state of mind is also taken into account. He found that adults tend to have certain activities that form a "core" of leisure. These activities usually are a central part of daily life and center around the home. Typically they include conversation and informal interaction with household companions, use of media (TV, radio, newspapers), reading, and walking. In addition, there are other activities that tend to "balance" opposite types of leisure: being quiet and activities, being alone and with others, engagement and relaxation. This balance may shift with the age of the person, reflecting the individual's self-definition, intentions, social aims, and opportunities (Kelly, 1983; Kelly, Steinkamp & Kelly, 1986).

In an application of his model of leisure, Kelly and his colleagues (1986) conducted telephone interviews with adults over age 40 in Peoria, Illinois, in 1983, using randomly selected numbers from the directory until he had reached 400 respondents who agreed to participate. He asked questions about 28 different categories of leisure. The responses were summarized according to eight general types and one global type, Overall Activity Level (Figure 6.8). It may be noted that the "core" types of leisure — family, social, and home-based activities — remained high with relatively less change even in the older age groups, compared with Overall Activity Level. Older women (probably widows) showed some decline in Family Leisure, and both groups showed some decline in Home-Based Activities, but the rate of participation was still fairly high. Cultural Activities, which included some that could be engaged in at home, also remained moderately high. Thus, they concluded that the "core" leisure activities tend to be maintained well into old age. Activity that involves social integration with others, or that does not require high levels of physical activity, is also maintained.

> The "balance" shifts somewhat toward social engagement and away from strenuous physical activity for the older segments of the sample . . . a shift away from organized and resource-based activity requiring considerable physical exertion and effort. (Kelly et al., 1986, p. 533)

The growing opportunity for leisure time — compared, for example, with the 1950s — has been made possible by shorter workweeks, longer vacations, earlier and longer retirement, time-saving appliances for household tasks, prepared foods to simplify meal preparation, and even periods of unemployment. However, it is not likely to allow many individuals to spend their time in ways that have always been possible for a few upper-class persons who live a "life of leisure," but it does raise the question of what all this nonworking time will mean to individuals in our society. And what will it mean for society? Does it mean additional time to watch television, more time for travel, or increased time for socializing with friends? Will it mean more time spent in education, participating in the arts, or in community service? It is likely that all these are true. In addition, many persons may be using this potential leisure time to get a second job to improve their style of living, or to pay educational expenses for their children. The essential question is whether the increase in nonwork time will become a source of growth and fulfillment that allows individuals to actualize their human potentials to the fullest. The challenge implicit in this question is whether we will be able to develop the conditions

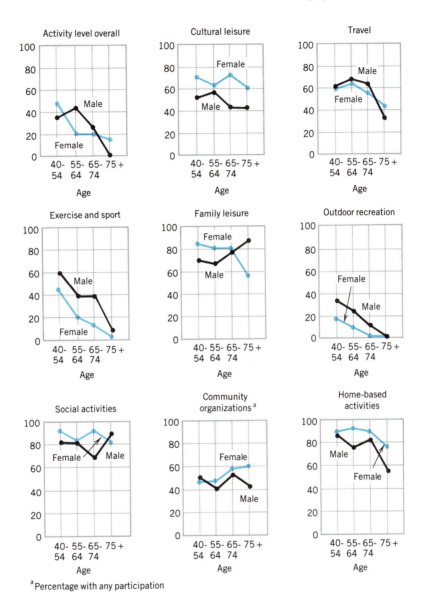

FIGURE 6.8 Percentages of respondents over age 40 reporting "high levels" of activity in various types of leisure. (*Source*: Kelly, Steinkamp & Kelly, 1986, Fig. 1. Reprinted with permission from *The Gerontologist*. Vol. 26, p. 533.)

necessary for leisure in our society, and whether these will be available to all persons or only to those who also have good jobs, good educations, and good health.

We now turn to an interview with Joan, age 67. Her pattern of work and leisure illustrates several of the themes in this chapter. In the next chapter we discuss biological processes of aging and health promotion, focusing on the emerging field of health psychology.

Chapter Summary

1. During the middle years of adulthood, involvement in one's family and career is a major source of identity that provides a sense of being intimately involved with others as well as being productive.

2. Family responsibilities and the occupational role may be seen as a system of mutually interacting sources of satisfaction and frustration. There are several ways in which work affects the family, including material resources, mood, and work-related behavior.

3. Two out of three women work over 35 hours a week in paid employment. There have been significant changes in the proportion of women in some occupations, but others remain limited primarily to women or to men. In general, women earn less than men.

4. Over half of all women living with their husbands were in the labor force in 1985. Dual-career families are those where both partners pursue careers that demand commitment to the work role. Dual-earner families are those where one or both partners have jobs that do not require a high degree of commitment to building a career.

5. Care for children while the parents work has gained increased importance as the number of working mothers has grown. The effects of working mothers on children seem beneficial for daughters and mixed for sons. Since most studies find no differences between children of working and nonworking mothers, other variables may be more important.

6. The process by which an individual chooses a career involves a process of socialization that begins during childhood. Many influences affect occupational choice, including one's background, role models, experience, interests, and personality.

7. Entering the job requires resocialization and may be a crucial point in the life cycle, not only because it marks the transition into adult status and a shift in roles, but also because it may involve a major change in one's *self*.

8. Most people change occupations at least once. Midlife occupational change is not uncommon and few people remain in one occupation all of their working lives.

9. We can recognize three patterns of the occupational cycle — the orderly career, the disorderly work history, and the sudden change in occupations.

10. The career clock, one's sense of being "on time" or "behind time" in career development, plays an important role in an individual's attainment of career goals.

11. Although mandatory retirement has been eliminated for most workers today, the majority of people retire before the age of 65. Because of earlier retirement and longer life span, the period of retirement is lasting much longer today than in the past.

12. Nearly all workers are covered by Social Security. After retirement, benefits

rise automatically to offset the effects of inflation. Social Security provides a significant source of income for older persons and protects a large number from poverty. Some retired persons also receive private pensions.

13. Health problems are a cause of retirement for some persons and may affect satisfaction in retirement. There is no evidence that retirement is harmful to health or leads to premature death. Many older persons are able to continue working long past the age of 65.

14. Retired persons are diverse in sociocultural characteristics. Some work; others do not work but also do not describe themselves as ''retired''; and the effects of past discrimination in salary and opportunities affect retirement. Preretirement planning should anticipate economic and family changes and consider postretirement goals and activities.

15. An individual's style of personality is relatively enduring and affects patterns of adjustment to retirement. The meaning of retirement and the characteristics of satisfying retirement differ among individuals, based on personality and other psychological variables.

16. Our technological society has provided more ''free time''away from work and also focused attention on the quality of life. Leisure may be defined as a freely chosen activity that is not related to one's work or as a state of mind, defined by two interrelated dimensions of perceived freedom and intrinsic motivation.

Key Words

career
career clock
disorderly work history
dual-career families
dual labor market
earnings gap
free time
leisure

occupational choice
occupational cycle
one life–one career imperative
preretirement planning
retirement
role model
vesting

Review Questions

Work and the Life Cycle

1. Which of Erikson's stages is/are related to the work experience? How?

2. Give examples of several ways in which work affects the family, based on your own family and drawing from the list of processes described by Hoffman.

3. What changes have combined to produce the growing proportion of working women in this country?

4. Summarize the influences that lead to the earnings gap between women and men. Do you think this gap will decrease in the future?

5. Who takes care of the children of working mothers?

6. Explain the conclusion that maternal employment in itself is not a very "robust" variable with regard to its effect on children. Why is this?

The Occupational Cycle

7. Describe five major influences that affect occupational choice. Give one example of each.

8. From a social interaction perspective, how does one's *self* change upon entering an occupational career?

9. Do most people have only one occupational career during their lifetime? Explain.

10. Contrast the concepts of a "career" and a "disorderly work history." What is one consequence of having an orderly or predictable career?

11. Define the career clock. Give some examples of how it functions.

Retirement: A Major Milestone

12. Why do many people choose to retire before age 65? Do you think this will change in the future, since employers can no longer force most workers to retire?

13. Why is the cost of Social Security increasing? What is the difference between Social Security and a private pension?

14. Why would raising the retirement age have a greater negative economic effect on Blacks than on Whites?

15. What are some of the important issues that preretirement planning should consider?

16. Describe the three personality types found by Reichard et al. that were associated with good adjustment to retirement. Describe the two personality types they found to be associated with poor adjustment to retirement.

Changing Leisure Values

17. Give two different definitions of leisure. How does "leisure" differ from "free time"?

18. Neulinger defined leisure as a state of mind. What does this mean? Define the terms in Figure 6.7 in your own words. Do you agree with this view of leisure?

INTERLUDE

Joan, AGE 67

Joan is a 67-year-old grandmother who lives in Harlem in New York City. She is one of 16 children; her mother was born during slavery in Georgia; she eventually moved to New York and brought Joan to the city as a young girl. Both Joan and her mother worked as "domestics" for a single family for 37 years, and Joan still works for them one day a week. Her mother died nearly 20 years ago at the grand age of 93, and Joan has five grandchildren; the oldest are in high school. Her proudest moment was the graduation of her two children from high school. She has some health problems now but works one day a week at a local Senior Center helping prepare the luncheon that is served daily.

Why did the milestones that she chose to discuss stand out in her memory? Does she choose different milestones from those a man might choose? What are some of the "timing events" in her life? In what sense are they "timing events"? What effect has her health had on her? Has she received adequate health care? How could it be improved? What are her feelings about death? How does living in Harlem affect her? In what ways has being African American affected her developmental milestones and course of life? In what ways has poverty affected her? Are there any practical ways in which a Senior Center or the community might increase her opportunities for fulfillment? Do her many assets and strengths make her an atypical "senior citizen"? She was interviewed in 1973. How have conditions changed since then, if at all?

As you look back over your life, what are some of the milestones that stand out? The education of my son and daughter; that's very

hard if you're Black. My son is 18 years in the Navy, and my daughter is 17 years with the telephone company, and I have five grandchildren. I'm 67 now. I was born January 1, 1906, in Georgia. I came to New York City as a young girl, attended school here, and then I started to work. And then I married and had my family. I never had any sickness until I reached my sixties. The doctor explained to me it comes with age — high blood pressure. He said high blood pressure gives me a blockage of the heart. When I feel so bad I go to the hospital and they give me treatments, you know; and he also discovered that I had sugar [diabetes] and I've been watching that. I have a diet that I don't really stick to, but I go in between — like if I eat bread one day, the next day I don't eat bread. He allows me three slices of bread a day, and no sodas, no beer, no alcoholic beverages, no jams and jellies. Plenty of fresh fruit, and so far I think that I'm in pretty good health excepting the high blood pressure. *Does that hinder you getting around at all?* No indeed. I can get out every day. He told me to walk 20 blocks a day, but walk slow. Don't walk against the wind. Stay in the bed two hours in the mornin' and one hour in the afternoon when I find myself getting dizzy. But other than that I get up, walk around the house, and do the shopping. Don't climb no subway stairs, no kind of stairs. And he says if I want to catch a bus, if I miss that one, just wait; no hurrying at all and no emotional upsets. And I find out it really pays off. I do an awful lot of reading, so that way it quiets my nerves.

What were some of the big events in your life? Well, the marriage of my two children; that was a very big event. And I had my son come home from Vietnam. He was in Vietnam for two years and when he came back I was very happy. And . . . I don't know. . . . *You have one son?* Yeah, and one daughter. They were born in the same year. I had two kids in one year; my son was born January 21, 1937, my daughter was born December 8, 1937. I had quite a time convincing the insurance company that I had two babies in the one year. That was quite an event in my life. With my first child I was in the hospital 21 days because I was in my thirties when he was born. The doctor explained to me that my pelvis didn't expand like a younger girl. But my daughter came in the ambulance. On December the eighth I went to the hospital and they said they didn't have a bed, so they put me in the ambulance and were taking me to _____ hospital and before we got there she was born; and I was ready to come home. They made me stay 10 days, but I was ready to come home. I came home and went right back to work and never had a sick day until I got in my sixties, you know the blood pressure and overweight.

What kind of work did you do? Domestic work; I cooked. You see, my mother came up before and she was a cook and then when I came up to public school, on the weekends I would go out to Long Island and cook there and then when the family moved back to New York City I continued to cook for them. Now I go in one day a week. But I just do ironing, or maybe they ask me to prepare a roast, a leg of lamb, you know, make something like that and leave it for them, 'cause all their kids are married now and it's just the two of them. So I run the wash through the machine and press his shirts, make a leg of lamb or something like that. I go one day a week, every Thursday. *You've worked with this same family for* . . . Over 37 years. My mother was in their family; so I go now. Sometime when they have somethin' special on the weekend I go and help them serve or cook. But they stopped entertainin' now because food is goin' up so high. They said no

more entertainin' now (laughs). So I just take it easy; and I go to the [Senior] Center and I cook Wednesdays and Fridays there [the Center serves lunch daily]. We finish about 2:00 or 2:30 and I come home, look at my stories [on TV], and that's it.

I don't go out at night no more, because . . . well, you know the reason why that is. *Why don't you go out at night?* I'm afraid of being mugged; and don't have anyone to go out with me, so I stay home and do my entertainin' in the house; the neighbors come visit one another and that's it. We don't go out in the night, that's all. Because you can't get a cab half the time; and there's no shows that I would like to go to downtown and pay taxi fare all the way back here. So nighttime I'm in the house; definitely! There's no way I'm goin' out. Sometimes I have friends that have cars; they come and get me and they take me back. Then if I go to my daughter, I get a cab in front of my house, get out in front of her door, and then she and her friend bring me back. That's the way we have to travel — but never just to catch a bus or walk out at night. It took me a long time to get it through my head not to go out at night (she laughs). *Why is that; did something happen once?* Not only once. I've been very fortunate in that, you know. I went out one Saturday night and they told me to take a taxi home. So I stood on the corner and hollered "Taxi, taxi"; so I said I'll walk over to Eighth Avenue and get the bus. And I saw these two fellas and I got to the corner of Eighth Avenue and 23rd Street and one fellow asked me if I had a cigarette or somethin' and I said I don't smoke and he grabbed me and said, "Yes, you do," but when he went to grab at me I screamed and there's a hotel right across the street. There was a lady looking out the window and she started to scream; so when they turned around to see where the noise was comin' from — there's a restaurant right down there — and I ran into that. So I asked the cashier would he come out so I could get a cab. So he got a cab and I came home and that was all right. Then, another time, I was comin' home and got off the Eighth Avenue bus and a fellow ran up to me; I had a pocketbook. I don't know why I pulled back 'cause there was nothin' in it at all. My keys was in my coat pocket and I just had tissues and a compact and comb—stuff like that. So, when he grabbed at the pocketbook, I hauled off and hit at him. He was so young! It was unbelievable to think that a young kid like that could do somethin' like that. So when I saw him I said this is nothin' but a little kid. He was pullin' and I gave him a shove and he fell backwards. Naturally, I ran, screaming as usual, you know. Well, he didn't follow me; and I got to the corner; a couple of people was on the corner and they were laughin'. They said, "I don't think he'll snatch a pocketbook any more" (she laughs). I looked back and he was still layin' down. Another time too; so my daughter said, "That's it!" That's why I tell you I don't go out at night no more. You don't push your luck too far. That's why I said when you're comin', push my buzzer; if I didn't know you was comin' I wouldn't answer that buzzer.

Oh, then in 1960—that's another happy event— I was picked as a delegate to go to San Francisco, California, with my Eastern Star. So, my son and daughter tricked me into taking a flight; instead of taking an ordinary flight, I took a jet. I was in San Francisco before my daughter could get from Kennedy Airport to the Bronx. *Sounds like a big trip.* A wonderful trip! Six weeks. I was a delegate. From San Francisco we went to Tijuana. You see, we flew there, but I wouldn't get back on, so they made arrangements to come back through the country, which was beautiful. Anywhere I go now, I travel on a Greyhound bus; no plane. I haven't had a trip since 1960, besides ordinary ones to [New] Jersey and Atlantic City, like that.

Were there any other big moments in your life? The biggest one was when my son came home from Vietnam. When he was 17

years old he enlisted in the Marines; he was in high school and decided he wanted to be a pilot; when he graduated in June, he changed over to the Navy and when he was 18 years old he was in Capetown, Africa. Really, he had never been away from home and he wasn't 18 years old then when he was sent overseas. Then I started readin' about Formosa, those different little straits and islands. . . . So then I didn't hear from him in a long time and a letter came. He had came down with pneumonia; but he got well and everything and he went right back. He came home after a year. "I'm goin' back overseas," he said; he loved it. Well, he came back the third time and he got married. Then he was stationed in Rhode Island and New Jersey and his first kid was born in Rhode Island; his second kid was born in Florida; the third kid was born in California. From then on he left from San Diego for Vietnam. After he came back from Vietnam— he served two years—he was up for promotion; so now he has his office here in New York City. So it worked out beautifully.

How does it feel to become a grandmother? Well, it's a thrill! The first grandchild, I'm tellin' you. My birthday is January the first and he was born on December the thirty-first. So I had this big party to serve, and I said my daughter was goin' to the hospital, and I said if everything is all right then I'll serve the party. So I had her under the doctor's care and he said she will definitely deliver the latter part of December. She started her pains the thirtieth of December and I rushed her to the hospital, so the next morning at 3:28, she delivered. And they called me from the hospital. I was a nervous mother, believe it or not. I called the people who wanted me and said, "Go ahead, have the party; I'm a grandmother now." Oh, that was a happy evenin'. That was a happy time. Yes-siree, that was a happy evenin'.

She was married one week, my son was married the next week. My first grandchild was born in December; my second grandchild was born that March. They married together, they started havin' their families together, so I started becomin' a grandmother in December and then in March. I went up to visit my daughter-in-law with my second grandchild; the third one was born in Florida and I went down there; and I said, "Look, the next grandchild you have, I'm not comin' out." *Why was it such a special event?* That was a very happy occasion. I thank God I had lived to be a grandmother and to see my kids married, grown, and have their own family. And believe me, you will never have a lonely moment. Never. I could never tell anyone I'm lonely, because they're here with their records and their rock 'n' roll, they keep me up to date on everything and I do an awful lot of readin' myself, you know. And then with their homework, believe it or not, I'm being reeducated. Because when I was goin' to school, we didn't have the things that they have. And now, I'm really reeducatin' myself on their homework, you know, which is very good. It keeps me very young and very happy, I can truthfully say. [Two of her grandchildren live with her during the week so they can live closer to their high school.]

How old were you when you came from Georgia? I was in my teens when I came. World War I ended in November, 1918, and I came here the very next year in September, 1919. And then I went to public school and after that I went to high school for two years, but I didn't graduate. I had to work with my mother, 'cause times was very hard then. Then I was supposed to go to school at night, and I went for a while, but it was gettin' me, you know, so my mother said, "No, I won't punish you like this." So we had to go to work to help support the family.

This is why I say a happy event is when my son graduated from high school and when my daughter graduated from high school; and then my son went to college on Uncle Sam [G.I. benefits]. My daughter went to _____ Col-

lege, which I helped her pay for that. So, the education of my two kids is a really happy event in my life, 'cause that's what counts today, education. The work that I had to do, they don't have to do. Oh yes, that was a very happy event. He graduated one year and she graduated the next year. I don't know about other people, but that's a very happy thing; and they done it in three years.

What about some of the sadder points; have there been any crisis points in your life? The crisis points, well, when my mother had a stroke. She was in her nineties when she died. I had brought her to live with me then. She had her own apartment, but by workin' all day it was too hard for me to go to her apartment, cook, wash and iron, clean up, and ask the neighbor to look in on her, 'cause she didn't want to go in the hospital. So I brought her here to live with me, and she had her first stroke here. She was ninety in January, and in October she had her first stroke. Naturally, I had an ambulance come and take her to the hospital, and the doctor said that she was not able to be by herself any more, and I put her in a nursing home. She was out there, and she was able to get around a bit, not too much, in a wheelchair, and they worked on her. She was a wonderful musician; and she was born in slavery time too. So she was able to play for the Christmas carols and entertainment. The third year, she was 93, and in September she had her third stroke. It was on a Tuesday at 1:30, and on Wednesday at 2:30 she passed. That was sad because being close to your parents, you know, and my father went away when I was quite young. So, she was a mother and a father to us.

And then I had a brother, who was in the service also; he was in Italy with World War II; and he had a murmur of the heart, and he came back and his hair had turned snow white. He always said, "I guess it was those bullets that frightened me." He had had pneumonia twice, and while he was up my mother passed, and he came down with lobar pneumonia the third time, and he went in the hospital on a Friday, and he passed the next Wednesday. It was so quick, you know, it was a shock to us, 'cause we thought he'd pull through that, but he didn't. So that was another sad time. So now it's only three girls left.

My mother had 16 children. *Sixteen children!* But see, my mother was born in slavery. She was married when she was 13, she said; you see, my grandmother was a "house slave," and my mother married what you called a "yard slave." You see, they had different kinds of slaves then. And she married at the age of 13; she had 14 children by him. After he died my grandmother brought her and some of her kids —'cause some of them had died when they were quite young—to _____ Georgia. And she met my father, and she had two kids by my father, which is me and my brother. She raised us, and my sisters got married; one went to Chicago; one came to Baltimore; and then my mother used to go back and forth to Florida to work, go to Virginia to work. You know, she was a cook, so she worked seasonal, you know. So she finally decided she'd get us out of the South. *You went with her when she went to these different places?* No, you see, my older sister was takin' care of us. We had to go to school; and then somethin' happened—we had a lynchin' down there; it was frightening with the Klan and all. So my mother got me up here, then the next year she got my brother up here. Then my sisters got married and my brother got married up here. We had plots here in the cemetery and she said, "When I pass don't ever bring me back there; we got plots up here and bury me up here." So she never went back. But I went back. My brother wouldn't go back, but I went back (laughs), I certainly did. Yeah, my mother was 93 when she passed; and she had all her facilities 'til she was 90. She used to forget, but you know she never used a walkin' cane. *How old were you when she*

passed? Oh, let's see now. She's been dead now about 19 years.

You said you did get back to Georgia once? Yeah, I went back in 1949 but I didn't know it. I wanted my kids to see my home and their father's home, so I carried them to Savannah and I went to _____, Georgia, but I didn't know my home. It was changed around. But my son, when we got on the buses, it said "White to the front and Colored to the rear." My son was takin' a picture so he could bring it back to show and he said, "Momma, I'll never come back here any more" (she laughs). So I said, "Well Johnny honey, things will change in years to come." We went into a souvenir store 'cause I wanted to get some cards to send home. The girl refused to wait on me, a little white girl, you know. I went over to the manager and I said, "Mister, I would like to get some souvenir cards to send back to New York and the young lady won't give them to me." He goes over to her and says, "Look, if you don't want to work, you can go to the office and get your pay. This lady wants to buy some cards and you refused to wait on her." So the man waited on us.

Is your husband still alive? Yes. We separated over 20 years ago. *Twenty years ago?* When people try to stay together in New York, you know, I was considered to be very old-fashioned, bein' from the South. So we agreed to disagree. That's why I say when my son and daughter came out of high school I was very happy 'cause I worked very hard. I worked night and day; I used to cater parties at night and cook in the day. So when I saw them come up that aisle and get their diploma, believe me, my chest was out this big.

This question of welfare was. . . . I didn't go for that at all. *You didn't want any welfare?* No, no. Nobody in my family ever had any. Why should I have it? There's work here; there's work enough! If my heart wasn't bad now, I could probably do two or three hours work every day. But now Friday we serve 175 people every day for lunch. *At the Senior Center?* At the Center. Boy was I tired Friday afternoon. No, I could never work every day no more! 'Cause my breath is very short. I have my pills for my heart, you know, and I had an electrocardiogram not so long ago, and the doctor told me not to do strenuous . . . you know. He wanted to put me in the hospital and I said, "Oh, no. I'll take your advice." I come back here at 2:00 every afternoon and watch my stories on TV.

How long were you and your husband together? We were married in 1941. We married for the convenience of keeping him from going into the Army (she laughs); that's what I told him. We went together for three years and never got married; and when World War II broke out he said, "Oh, yes, we're goin' to get married," to my mother. They put him in 4E [classification for the draft] (laughs). *Was that a big day in your life when you got married, or not?* Yeah, we just went to City Hall. Got married and came back to my mother's house; we had presents and my mother baked a couple cakes and different friends came in. Now if you get married in a church you got to pay; I don't go in for things like that.

I don't like a whole lot of fancy things. This is why people say, "You're still staying in that dump [referring to the apartment]?" I say, "Look, the way they raise the rent, any apartment you move in now you're gonna pay over a hundred dollars." I've been here since February, 1933, so now why should I move? The landlord can't raise the rent, you know [some apartments in New York had their rent controlled by law so that increases were limited while the same tenant kept the apartment]. And I'm a Senior Citizen so I got [rent] exemption, 'cause my Social Security's only $103. So now I have to take my rent out of there and my telephone and gas and electric. *$103 a month?*

Yeah. My daughter takes care of the kids [who stay with her during the week] and the food and all like that, but as I say, I'm not well enough to work every day, and when I go in on a Thursday, they give me $12, so that helps out. And I don't need a whole lot of clothes 'cause I don't go nowhere. My daughter says, "Now, Momma!" I say I don't need it. I don't need a pocketbook 'cause they're gonna snatch it from me, right? What do I need all those clothes to put in the closet? They're gonna come in here and rob me and take your things, you know. She's always sayin', "Momma, you need . . ." and I say, "You shut up! I know what I want." *So you have managed to stay off welfare so far?* Yeah, thank God. *You'd really hate to go on welfare if you had to?* At my age I wouldn't. None of my family ever been on it. And we're makin' out. My son is in the service; my daughter is workin'. I say I don't need clothes, and Social Security can pay my rent, and my telephone is for my comfort, for my health too. My daughter says, "Momma, come give me your gas and electric bill." When my son comes home he says, "Momma, give me your telephone bill." He says, "You got money to last you?" I say yeah, you know. So I budget myself. I got a Medicaid card; so I go to Harlem Hospital. For my eyeglasses I go to the eyeglass place; so now why should I go on welfare. I'm not goin' in and lay my life on the line for a few dollars.

Were there a lot of crisis points in your marriage? Was that a pretty difficult time? Yes it was. It was a problem trying to get him to come home with the salary; sittin' down and trying to budget ourselves, you know. I was workin' and meetin' the bills. Also, my mother used to help me too. And when his sister first got married, she and her husband were roomin' in the back room there. They was young and didn't have enough money, so they couldn't pay no rent. So we had to carry the rent, and feed them, you know. After five years, that's long enough. That was a terrible family problem, you know. *There were a lot of arguments about that?* Don't ever shack up with your in-laws! Take it from me. I'm tellin' you. That's what I went through; that's my problems! *That really destroyed your marriage?* That, and then after that, well you know, New York got a lot of glamour girls and he used to go to the bar. That was all right, but I couldn't go into the bar; but then they got a little too bold. I didn't want the kids to see that. Right now his son and daughter respects him, but they tell him, "Daddy, you know what you did to Momma." They don't like that, you know.

You said that you worked with this one family for 37 years; have there been any crisis points in your job there? No, a wonderful family! I am one of their family, and my mother was one of the family, and my children and grandchildren are part of the family. When the older girl got married I served at the party and my grandson helped me; my granddaughter helped me; my daughter helped. We were just one of his family. *It sounds like you're going to continue working there as long as you want.* I only work there one day a week now. I'm my own boss. I have my keys. When they first bought a house in Fire Island I used to go every weekend. So I've had a happy life. Poor, but happy. As I say, I don't go for welfare. I'm not against anybody gettin' it, especially some elderly people that we know. They really deserve it because some people they used to work for didn't pay Social Security for them and that's really unfair. I know I talked to one lady and she said that she worked 47 years for one family, and all the time they told her they were payin' Social Security, and they didn't pay. Now that's unfair to her. My people paid it. So when I got sick when I was 62 years old they said why don't you wait until you're 65 and you'll get more. I said there was no guarantee that I'm gonna live 'til I'm 65.

I was sick, really sick then. And two years

ago I was takin' cancer tests. The doctor didn't tell me, but every test he would give me I would look it up, or ask my friends who are doctors or nurses and they told me what it was. I went and the last test I had was all the X rays. I was X-rayed a whole day; all different angles. And I came home; it was in July, I'll never forget it. I had a chill 'cause the hospital was air-conditioned and the metal tables that you lay on, you know. So I put on my clothes and got a cab and came home. Now I was in a terrible state for two weeks, waitin' for the hospital to send for me or get a letter. So I went back for a check-up, and they said my X ray hadn't come back, and the nurse told me not to worry. She said the X rays must have come back negative, otherwise they would have sent for you in a hurry. Well, that didn't satisfy me. In September I went back again, I said to the doctor, "Where's my X rays?" So he said, "Don't worry. How did you feel?" I said, "All right — Doctor, do I have cancer?" He said, "Get that out of your mind! Now go on home and enjoy yourself and if we need you we'll send for you." They never sent for me, so I go to the clinic for my weight and blood pressure now. *It must have been a pretty frightening time, though, waiting and not knowing.* . . . Yeah, this is the frightening part. In the meantime I had lost two friends that had cancer of the rectum.

Would you say that you've changed very much in the last few years? My reflexes — I could walk in the kitchen and forget what I go in there for, somethin' like that. I spoke to the doctor and he said, "Well, you realize . . . ." I said, "Don't you say that I'm gettin' old!" He said, "Do you want to stay like you were when you were 16?" So he said to stop worryin' about my reflexes. You know, I have to make a list to go to the supermarket. I have that list in my hand with the shoppin' cart, and I forget I have the list. But this comes with age.

Do you sometimes look back over your

life and kind of review and think about the things that have happened? Well, I look back over the good times that I had, you know. I look back on my family life. You see, we was a big happy family. Every Thanksgiving my mother had us over to her house and she served everything from soup to nuts. And then Christmas we all would be together. And after my son went in the service and my daughter got married, well, I was here alone, and then my mother passed. So then after my daughter had children, it kind of gave me a second hold on life, you know. 'Cause I sat here by myself after the children got married; I couldn't expect them to stay here, you know. And then my mother was gone and my brother was gone. I used to get up 5:30 in the mornin' for work, but on the weekend I'd get lonesome, and I didn't want to go up to my daughter's house all the time. But after they had kids I always have a crowd here. You see, my Thanksgiving's gonna be here now. I carried on after my mother; and my sister have Christmas dinner; and then my daughter have me for New Year's. So, it's happy moments in my life. I can truthfully say I'm happy. *As you look back over your life, are you satisfied?* I'm very satisfied! I don't have no regrets. The one regret, I couldn't get the education that I wanted; but it was hard on my mother, so I had to come and start workin' with her. But I saw that my kids and my grandchildren are gettin' it. But I tell you one thing, a lot of peoples that know me they say, "Well, I don't know where you cut yourself short of education, 'cause you got a lot of mother wit." They say I think fast, you know. And if you keep your head above water in New York City, you're doin' pretty good, believe me.

Do you feel like you've left your mark here someplace? Yes, I have no regrets at all. I have a happy life. I have grandchildren. I have a son and daughter. So, you know, I'm happy.

Do you sometimes think about death? No. I had a pain in my chest last week.

I was in the bed. I got up and said, "Oh, Lord, I'm not ready" (she laughs). It was pressin' down, you know. I said, "Oh, Lord, I'm not ready." So I called my sister. She burst out laughin'. She said, "What are you doing?" I said, "I'm sittin' up!" When I got up I took a small glass of 7-Up for the gas. The doctor told me don't let it worry me as long as I abide by his rules. *So you don't think about it very much at all?* No. That's why I stay in the house (laughs). No I don't think about it. *You're not ready for it yet?* No, these are my golden years. I can truthfully say, I am happy, 'cause I can lay down in the bed, I have money to pay my rent, gas, and electric — things like that — when before it was a struggle. But it's not a struggle at all. It's just contentment. That's why I can sit in this house seven days a week and have no worries, no worries at all. When I was young I had them. I don't think about death.

How does the future look to you? It looks rosy for me, if the President don't cut off our Social Security. 'Cause if he cut off mine, I would be right on his door-step in Washington, D.C., 'cause I work very hard. A dollar's taken out of this and out of that. Now if you go back to work, your Social Security check is goin' to stop. I think that's very unfair! It's not like money that they have to give you. That's money that the people had to pay in! Now why take that from us? I think it's ridiculous, things like this. So these are my happy years. I'm 67, and I don't have to work hard. When I was younger I had to work very hard. Now if I wake up in the mornin' and it's rainin' or snowin' I don't have to go to the Center or to work. I can stay in the house all day, 'cause as I said, the rent will be paid and that means a lot. I can make it.

According to staff members at the Senior Center, Joan died of heart failure three years after this interview. She had remained active in the Center until she was taken to the hospital after having a heart attack. She appeared to have been making a good recovery in the hospital and had a pacemaker installed to regulate the heart beat; she was in the hospital about a week before she died. She did live to see her grandson graduate from high school — she had raised him and her granddaughter since they were infants. The granddaughter also graduated from high school, and both now have good jobs. The grandson remained living in Joan's apartment until he married; he now has a child.

CHAPTER 7

Kathe Kollowitz, *Self Portrait*, 1934. Art Resource, Inc. N.Y.

Biological Aspects of Aging

hat does it mean to "grow old"? Why do humans and many domestic animals age and eventually die although other forms of life such as trees or single-celled organisms are able to live indefinitely? What causes human aging? What changes occur in this period of biological aging and decline—that is, in the period termed **senescence?**

Such questions are indeed puzzling, since we have not yet found satisfying answers to them. A great deal of research on aging today is focusing on attempts to find the basic causes of aging. Other research is studying the process of age-related change in various organ systems of the human body and much research is exploring aging in various animals such as the mouse and rat. Aging is also being studied in species as varied as plants, insects, and roundworms (Finch & Schneider, 1985). However, the actual cause of biological aging is not yet clear. We discuss several theories of aging in the first section of this chapter, as well as some of the social implications of increased longevity that may eventually result from this intensive research into the nature of human aging.

In addition to considering the biological processes of aging, this chapter also marks a shift in our focus to the later years of the life span, since biological factors play an important role in the characteristics and changes that occur during late adulthood. For example, with increased age, susceptibility to various chronic diseases increases dramatically. We examine the connection between aging and disease and review the most important diseases that are associated with aging.

As noted in Chapter 4, even in the absence of disease, however, there is a general slowing down in many aspects of functioning; this slowing may affect a variety of responses that can have effects on health, such as the risk of falls or accidents because one may not respond quickly enough to the loss of balance or the danger. Other changes—in vision, hearing, and the cardiovascular system—tend to be more common among older people; but are these changes caused by aging? In general, we make a crucial distinction between the changes that result from *disease* and those that result from *aging* in the absence of disease. Disease can affect vision, hearing, or cardiovascular functioning at any age. Age alone, as discussed in Chapter 4, has relatively little effect, except for the slowing down in central nervous system (CNS) functioning, as long as there is no disease present. Thus, to understand the effects of aging per se, the effects of disease must be separated from those changes that occur with age in the absence of disease. Otherwise, the effects of aging are confounded with the effects of disease.

We conclude the chapter with a discussion of health psychology and behavioral medicine. It is becoming more and more clear that many of the physical changes associated with aging are caused by behavior (such as smoking or lack of exercise), diet (e.g., cholesterol or lack of fiber), and certain forms of stress. Psychological interventions may also help reduce the effects of certain chronic conditions (such as pain or disability). We describe this emerging field and some of the careers that are now developing in this interface of medicine and psychology.

Theories of Aging and Mortality

There are many different types of aging noted by biologists: bacteria are able to continue living indefinitely, limited only by the supply of food and physical space; annual plants complete their life cycle in one year of well-defined, genetically programmed stages; trees continue to grow until they can no longer transmit the sap to the upper branches or until the lower branches no longer receive adequate sunlight; and animals in the wild generally do not grow old but are killed by predators or starve when their physical strength declines. Also, the various mammals have characteristic life spans, many exceeding their reproductive life only slightly, if at all, in the wild; however, African elephants and perhaps Indian elephants live long enough after becoming infertile to rear their young (Sacher, personal communication; cf. Laws, 1971).

However, the human life span, while clearly characteristic of the species, lasts long beyond the end of reproductive capabilities (menopause) and involves a period of senescence atypical among animals in their natural habitat. In general, aging leads to a growing inability of the organism to adapt to the environment and thus to survive. We discuss several aspects of this aging process, beginning with hereditary and external factors, and then we consider physiological theories of aging. Although none of these theories seems adequate to explain the process of aging at present, each makes a valuable contribution to our understanding of this elusive process.

Hereditary Factors

Clearly there is a hereditary component involved in the length of life that is characteristic of a particular species. However, the human life span exceeds the length that would be expected for a mammal of our size, and we are the longest-lived species of mammal. Comfort (1964) reported that Indian elephants are known to reach 60 years, and the horse, hippopotamus, and probably the ass are the only other mammals known to reach or exceed 50 years of age. Baboons, chimpanzees, and other primates (as well as large cats, bears, and the African elephant) may reach or exceed 30 years. The life span of whales and dolphins is probably between 30 and 50 years. In general, the length of life among various species of mammals is related to the size of the animal, with humans as the marked exception. This is not the case for birds (some owls, cockatoos, eagles, parrots, condors, and pelicans have been found to live more than 50 years) or among reptiles (tortoises have been reported to live from 70 to over 152 years). Sacher (1959) proposed that the ratio of brain weight to body weight is best related to the longevity of mammals, including humans. That is, the much larger size of the human brain (largely because of the cerebrum) may be an important biological asset associated with longevity (as body size is associated with longevity for other mammals).

From these observations it appears that the life span of a species is relatively set by genetic or hereditary characteristics that, according to the theory of evolution, have evolved over countless years. Sacher's observations suggest that human thinking capacities may be related to our long life span. However, it is not clear what

Aged persons would be likely to remember where food and water had been found during a severe drought many years earlier; thus, aging may have played a role in human evolution if it promoted the survival of the species.

evolutionary function is served by the long postreproductive life characteristic of the human species. Today the average woman lives about 25 years after menopause and about 45 years after the birth of her last child. What function could this postreproductive period have played in the survival of the human species? It would seem that the characteristics of this postreproductive period could not have been under evolutionary control since these old people are not passing their genes on to future generations. However, it has been árgued, notably by Weissman (1891), that the aging process may have evolved as a means to promote the survival of children and grandchildren through social instead of biological mechanisms. That is, the aged would remember, for example, where food and water were found during the drought many years earlier (M. Mead, 1970, 1972).

Others have argued that senescence results only from the "running out" of the genetic program and is not specifically developed through evolution. Instead, the greater mental ability of humans may simply have allowed them to live longer so that aging is a kind of "exhaustion of program." In that sense, our later years may be analogous to a rocket that was programmed to place a satellite in orbit and simply continues on for a time after accomplishing this programmed task until pulled back into the atmosphere by the earth's gravity (Comfort, 1964).

Another evolutionary model of aging was proposed by Birren (1960) in the **counterpart theory** of aging. This suggests that human senescence is the result of characteristics that had a primary adaptive importance earlier in life, prior to the end of reproductive ability, so that they would directly enhance the species survival. For example, nonreplacement of cells in the human nervous system may enhance the ability for memory and learning and thus be highly adaptive in terms of species survival; but it may also result in slowing of CNS functioning in old age, and may prevent indefinite functioning and life. Williams (1957) similarly recognized that genes that had positive effects early in life might become harmful later in life; the natural selection of the beneficial properties prior to having offspring would outweigh the harmful effects after child bearing was finished.

Thus, it is unclear whether the long life of the human species (and consequent period of senescence) evolved directly because of the importance of aging for survival of the species — perhaps because the elderly provided leadership, historical memory, and wisdom — or whether it resulted simply from the success of humans as an evolved species in mastering the environment and in surviving because of advanced cognitive abilities.

A different type of evidence of a hereditary component in longevity is found in a study of identical twins (Kallmann & Jarvik, 1959). Monozygotic (identical) twins tend to have more similar lengths of life than dizygotic (fraternal) twins; this indicates that even within the species, genetic factors play a role in an individual's length of life. This study also found striking physical similarities between identical twins well into old age, indicating the persistence of genetic influence even to changes in appearance during aging (Figures 7.1 and 7.2). In addition, many studies have found that offspring whose parents and grandparents were long-lived are also likely to live longer. However, although such data indicate a genetic component in longevity, it may not be a directly transmitted genetic trait; for example, increased vigor and resistance to disease may be the genetically transmitted potentials that also lead to a longer life. Among mammals, hybrids (rather than inbred animals), individuals with younger mothers (father's age does not seem to be relevant), and females generally live longer (Comfort, 1964).

In reviewing the studies on longevity, Kirkwood (1985) noted that it is unlikely that there is any simple hereditary cause of aging. There may be several thousand genes that are involved in the biology of aging, although a few key genes may control the *rate* of aging. Genes involved in maintenance and repair of body cells are possibly among those key genes since one theory is that aging results from the accumulation of somatic damage, especially within the cells.

Progeria, a genetic disease that produces some symptoms that resemble aging, has been thought to provide a key to understanding the physical process of aging. It does not, however, because it lacks some of the features of normal aging (Russell, 1987). Other inherited conditions, such as *Werner syndrome,* likewise produce symptoms that resemble some aspects of aging, but differ in other important characteristics (Tice & Setlow, 1985).

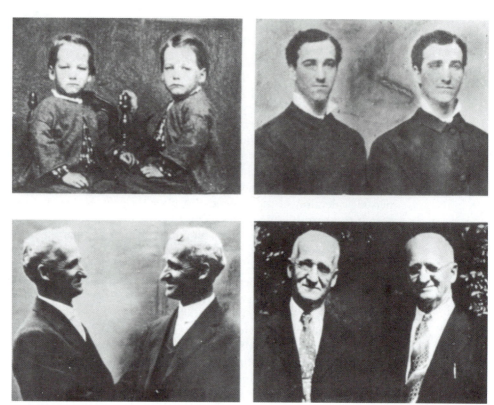

FIGURE 7.1 Identical twins at the ages of 5, 20, 55, and 86 years. (*Source*: Kallmann & Jarvik, 1959, Figure 8. Copyright © 1959. Reprinted with permission.)

External Factors

Hereditary factors are usually best seen as *potentials* that may only be realized to their greatest extent in a supportive environment. Obviously, an accident, disease, or lightning may terminate one's life regardless of the longevity of one's parents. For example, Jones (1959) estimated that external factors such as rural living or marriage increase the average length of life by 5 years whereas being overweight decreases the average life by 4 to 15 years (Table 7.1). The relative influence of hereditary factors, smoking, diet, and chronic disease may also be noted. As we discuss later in this chapter, individuals have begun to pay greater attention to those factors that can be modified—especially smoking, exercise, and diet. These behavior changes have led to a reduction in heart disease and contributed to an increased life expectancy for older adults in recent years.

Ionizing radiation has received some attention as a possible cause of aging since everyone is exposed to a small amount of cosmic radiation daily. Although much higher levels of radiation are required to damage the nucleus of cells, Curtis (1966) reported that the amount of damage to cells (measured by the amount of chromosomal damage) is related to the amount of life shortening produced. Numerous

FIGURE 7.2 Identical twins before and after long separations (between the ages of 18 and 65). (*Source*: Kallmann & Jarvik, 1959, Figure 9. Copyright © 1959. Reprinted with permission.)

studies have reported a connection between radiation and decreased life span caused by an acceleration of all forms of disease in animals (Lindop & Rotblat, 1961). However, in reviewing the research, Spiegel (1972) and Shock (1977) concluded that radiation does not appear to be related to ordinary aging processes. It is now thought that the life shortening produced by radiation differs from normal aging processes. That is, radiation intense enough to produce chromosomal damage tends to produce neoplasia (abnormal growth) that is generally the cause of the shortened life. Moreover, normal aging usually does not involve an accumulation of genetic mutations in cells (Tice & Setlow, 1985, p. 201).

Exposure to sunlight, which affects the aging of the skin and possibly the development of cataracts, is an example of an external influence that contributes to the physical changes that accompany aging, and one that can be controlled by the individual with sunscreen lotion, avoiding sunbathing, and the use of sunglasses. Gravity, the force that pulls our body toward the earth, is another example of an external influence; it affects the weight of the body, the effort required to pump blood when standing, and the shape of soft tissue in the body. It is likely that the

TABLE 7.1 *Effect of External and Physiological Factors on Length of Life*

Reversible		Permanent	
Comparison	*Years*	*Comparison*	*Years*
Country versus city dwelling	+ 5	Female versus male sex	+ 3
Married status versus single,		Familial constitutions	
widowed, divorced	+ 5	2 grandparents lived to 80	
Overweight		years	+ 2
25 percent overweight group	− 3.6	4 grandparents lived to 80	
35 percent overweight group	− 4.3	years	+ 4
45 percent overweight group	− 6.6	Mother lived to age 90 years	+ 3
55 percent overweight group	−11.4	Father lived to age 90 years	+ 4.4
67 percent overweight group	−15.1	Both mother and father lived	
Or: an average effect of 1		to age 90 years	+ 7.4
percent overweight	− 0.17	Mother lived to age 80 years	+ 1.5
Smoking		Father lived to age 80 years	+ 2.2
1 package cigarettes per day	− 7	Both mother and father lived	
2 packages cigarettes per day	−12	to age 80 years	+ 3.7
Atherosclerosis		Mother died at 60 years	− 0.7
Fat metabolism		Father died at 60 years	− 1.1
In 25th percentile of		Both mother and father died	
population having		at age 60 years	− 1.8
"ideal" lipoprotein		Recession of childhood and in-	
concentrations	+10	fectious disease over past	
Having average		century in Western	
lipoprotein concentrations	0	countries	+15
In 25th percentile of		Life Insurance *Impairment*	
population having		*Study*	
elevated lipoproteins	− 7	Rheumatic heart disease,	
In 5th percentile of popu-		evidenced by:	
lation having highest		Heart murmur	−11
elevation of lipoproteins	−15	Heart murmur + tonsilitis	−18
Diabetes		Heart murmur + strepto-	
Uncontrolled, before insulin,		coccal infection	−13
1900	−35	Rapid pulse	− 3.5
Controlled with insulin		Phlebitis	− 3.5
1920 Joslin Clinic record	−20	Varicose veins	− 0.2
1940 Joslin Clinic record	−15	Epilepsy	−20.0
1950 Joslin Clinic record	−10	Skull fracture	− 2.9
		Tuberculosis	− 1.8
		Nephrectomy	− 2.0
		Trace of albumin in urine	− 5.0
		Moderate albumin in urine	−13.5

Source: Jones, Hardin B. A special consideration of the aging process. Disease and life expectancy. In J. H. Lawrence and C. A. Tobias (Eds.), *Advances in biological and medical physics* (Vol. 4). New York: Academic Press, 1956. Reprinted with permission.

external characteristics of aging bodies would be different, and the reduction of muscular strength would be less important, in an environment with lower gravity. Perhaps one day there may be retirement communities on the moon to take advantage of this idea.

Usual versus Successful Aging

Individuals age in unique patterns as a result of hereditary and external influences. It is important to stress the diversity in aging, because the stereotype is that all older people decline in similar ways. In fact, a distinction can be made between **usual patterns of aging** that describe the average or typical older person and **successful patterns of aging** that describe individuals who show little decline or no change at all with aging in many aspects of physiological function. Feelings of being in control of important aspects in life, having social support to cope with the stress and hassles of living, healthful diet, and appropriate exercise are some of the factors that promote successful aging (Rowe & Kahn, 1987).

In this chapter we discuss the effects of chronic disease and note that it is useful to distinguish between patterns of aging that reflect pathological disease processes and those that characterize normal aging in the absence of disease. However, this tends to oversimplify the heterogeneity within the normal aging population—that is, it tends to lump everyone without apparent chronic disease into a single group called the "normal" aged. This normal group actually consists of a range of levels in functioning from those who run in marathons, conduct symphony orchestras, or manage multinational corporations to those who only occasionally walk for a few minutes, are relatively isolated from others, or spend the days waiting for something to happen.

Thus, many of the characteristics that typify aging for the *average* person may be absent or minimized for those who are aging successfully. In contrast, these characteristics can be exaggerated for other older persons for whom aging is a period of decline in a wide variety of functions. The implication of this idea is that *usual aging* should not be considered to be "normal"—in fact, it may be the result of low levels of functioning caused by a variety of extrinsic factors, including stereotypes about the way older people should feel or behave. These social stereotypes about older people may be manifestations of *ageism*. For example, if a doctor says, "You should expect this problem at your age," the older person is being encouraged to follow the pattern of usual aging. Instead, the individual may seek the goal of successful aging and not accept the normality of the condition. An exercise program, medical treatment, or appropriate ways of compensating for the condition may promote improved functioning and lead to successful instead of usual aging. Thus, we should take a balanced view: neither should we blame older people for the usual declines they may experience, nor should we accept usual aging as normal aging.

This perspective on the diversity of normal aging is important to keep in mind throughout this chapter as we discuss physiological theories of aging, disease, and typical changes with aging. We focus on some of the ways in which psychology is working to understand and promote successful aging in the final section of the chapter.

Physiological Theories of Aging

For humans as a species, the **force of mortality,** that is, the risk of death, is clearly related to age. Gompertz (1825) is credited with giving a mathematical representation to the relation between probability of death and age—a relationship that differs by constant parameters for different species (resulting from a different length of life) but that is relatively accurate for many species. From his mathematical relationship one observes an exponential increase in the risk of mortality with advancing age; it is on this principle that life insurance tables have been devised.

Physiological aging may be defined as "a decline in physiological competence that inevitably increases the incidence and intensifies the effects of accidents, disease, and other forms of environmental stress" (Timiras, 1972, p. 465). Thus, with the passage of time, there is a greater probability of dying (the Gompertz equation); an individual's death by "natural causes" means that enough important life-maintaining processes degenerate so that death results.

It is not clear whether there is a specific cause of aging, whether several potential causes operate together, or if aging is simply an accumulation of physiological deficits. The various physiological theories of aging we present next may each provide cues to the eventual understanding of this process. One likely possibility is that there is no single cause of aging, but instead different causes for the various organ systems (Shock, 1977).

Wear and Tear

Perhaps the most commonsense theory of aging is that the body simply wears out, similar to a machine. This view of aging was first proposed by Pearl (1924). In modern form there are at least three different theories implicit in this view; the first two have largely been discounted today, despite their superficial attractiveness.

The first theory is that aging is the result of the gradual deterioration of the various organs necessary for life. This idea has given rise to an interest in the replacement of vital organs such as the heart and kidney. Certainly, transplants and surgical repair of diseased organs may prolong life for specific individuals. However, it is not likely that "spare-parts replacement" will lengthen the human life span in general to an appreciable degree. Aging involves the interrelation of the various systems in the body and, for people in general, this interrelationship is more significant than the failure of any particular organ that could be replaced.

Likewise, there is no conclusive evidence to support the second theory that hard work or increased stress alone is responsible for shortening an individual's life span (Curtis, 1966). In contrast, there is growing evidence that appropriate exercise, moderate stress involved in maintaining relationships, and assertive striving to keep a sense of control over one's life can reduce some of the effects associated with aging (Buskirk, 1985; Rodin, 1986a, 1986b).

The third version of this view does remain a major theory of aging, however.

Current research in molecular biology and genetics has shifted the focus of "wear and tear" to the accumulation of damage to the DNA that is responsible for the replication of cells in many organs of the body (Harrison, 1985). That is, most organs are made up of cells that repair damage and reproduce themselves so that the organ can continue to function adequately. A decline in the efficiency of this repair process, or biochemical reactions that interfere with DNA molecules, may be responsible for the changes associated with aging. In this sense only "wear and tear" remains a viable theory of aging.

The role of DNA repair systems in aging is unclear, however. The capacity of cells to function effectively and to reproduce accurately depends on the integrity of DNA. Considerable research is focusing on this topic, but the results are contradictory. It is difficult to determine measures of the precise types of damage to DNA that might be related to aging (Tice, 1987).

Biochemical processes may affect cell function, and these are also receiving considerable research attention. *Free radicals* are highly reactive chemicals that are produced randomly in normal metabolism. This theory of "wear and tear" was suggested in 1954 by Harman (1987). It proposed that these biochemicals produce cellular damage that impairs the organism's ability to function. A modified form of this theory hypothesized that free radicals play a role in the diseases that are among the leading causes of death. These diseases include emphysema, atherosclerosis, cancer, arthritis, cirrhosis, and diabetes (Pryor, 1987). Free radicals may also play a role in DNA damage (Saul, Gee & Ames, 1987). These modern versions of "wear and tear" theories remain active areas of research.

Cellular Aging

A common misconception of aging is that cells of the body begin dying at a faster rate than they are produced some time in young adulthood, and that this decline continues until there are no longer enough cells to function and death results. The situation is hardly this simple. In fact, many cells in an old person are the same age as similar cells in a young person! Although some cells seldom or never reproduce (notably cells in the brain, nervous system, and muscles), most cells continue to reproduce themselves and theoretically allow the organism to live indefinitely.

When cells from an old animal are transplanted to a young animal, it appears that "a large number of tissue types are capable of functioning normally well beyond donor life spans" (Harrison, 1985, p. 349). This suggests that aging of cells results from some interaction between the cell and the environment, not from some characteristic intrinsic within the cell (Figure 7.3). In particular, it is striking that these cells may be capable of living several times longer than the animal from which they were transplanted.

In contrast to the transplantation experiments, Hayflick (1965, 1966, 1970) found that cells grown in laboratory culture dishes ("aging under glass") undergo a finite number of doublings (about 50), which suggests that a finite growth potential of cells might be a mechanism of aging. In addition, the doubling capacity of cells in cultures decreases with the age of the organism from which they were taken (about 45 at birth to age 10; about 30 by 80 to 90 years of age). The relationship of these

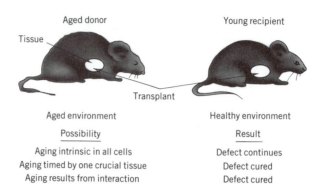

Aged donor   Young recipient

Tissue

Transplant

Aged environment   Healthy environment

Possibility   Result

Aging intrinsic in all cells   Defect continues
Aging timed by one crucial tissue   Defect cured
Aging results from interaction   Defect cured

FIGURE 7.3 Transplanting old tissue into young recipients and measuring its function may be used to test whether the change with age is intrinsic within the old tissue. (*Source*: Harrison, David E. 1982 (February). Must we grow old? *Biology Digest*, 8(6), 11–25, Fig. 8, p. 19. Reprinted with permission of Plexus Publishing Inc.)

experiments to the transplantation studies, or to human aging, is not clear, however. For example, some old adults have cells that double as often as those of young adults, and most old donor cells double at least 20 times in these experiments (Harrison, 1985, p. 326).

It may be more important to focus on those cells that do not reproduce than on those that do in order to understand aspects of aging especially relevant to humans. Specifically, those highly differentiated cells such as in the CNS may have evolved to provide continuity and regularity of performance and experience important for survival of younger individuals before they produced offspring. But, in old age, these same characteristics may be vulnerable to inefficient repair mechanisms and damage to DNA that may bring about eventual cellular inefficiency or death. This may be an example of Birren's (1960) counterpart theory of aging in that evolutionary adaptations that grant positive survival value to young organisms bring about negative results in old animals. One of the important results of these changes may be an increase in the *chemical noise* within the cell that impairs its function as an information system (Comfort, 1968). This may be a cause of the slowing down in CNS functioning speed discussed in Chapter 4.

A related observation is that virtually all organs have an extraordinary reserve capacity to continue functioning despite possible cellular damage. Thus, we can turn the question around from "Why do humans age?" to a question that makes the same point from another perspective: "Why do humans live so long after their prime reproductive years have passed?" It may be that a large degree of redundancy in DNA functioning, established by natural selection, is present in cells so that random errors are not critical, and that cells are able to function much longer than necessary for allowing the human to produce offspring. In that sense, aging is a kind of "coasting" on the redundancy present in human cells and organs. We develop for about 30 years, then "coast" for a maximum of 75 years (Hayflick, 1987). A similar view has been expressed by a Director of the National Institute on Aging:

> My current view, subject to challenge, is that, once we or other animals reach true maturity, we are more or less "coasting," with probably no built-in, evolutionarily

required, self-destructive processes. Such declines as we encounter and suffer from as we proceed through life are due rather to the impacts of environmental assaults, poor choices of life style (e.g., smoking, poor nutrition, decreased exercise), and disease processes, which we can more and more identify and at least potentially prevent or treat. (Williams, 1987, p. x)

Homeostatic Imbalance

Comfort (1964) proposed that the efficiency of crucial homeostatic mechanisms that maintain vital physiological balances in the body (such as the pH and sugar levels of the blood) is central to the process of aging. Thus, in his view, "aging is characteristically an increase in homeostatic faults" (p. 178). Although there is little change in these mechanisms of self-regulating equilibrium between young and older persons under *resting conditions,* Shock (1960) demonstrated that the rate of readjustment to normal equilibrium after stress is slower in old subjects than in young. For example, the capacity of the kidneys for maintaining homeostasis, the ability to maintain body temperature during exposure to heat or cold, and the efficiency of blood sugar regulation decrease with age (cf. Timiras, 1972, pp. 558–561). Because of such changes, medication levels for the elderly are frequently different from the level tolerated by young adults. Also, older persons are more likely to die from cold (hypothermia) than younger people because their body may not detect or respond to the lowering of body temperature as efficiently and they do not recognize that they are cold and may not begin shivering to increase body heat. Likewise, the elderly are more affected by hot weather (Weg, 1983).

This lessened efficiency of the physiological response to stress is perhaps the most general theory of aging and provides the clearest link between physiological, social, and psychological aspects of aging. As noted earlier, stress does not cause aging. However, the self-regulating mechanisms decrease in efficiency with age (Shock, 1977). As a result, the body is less able to respond efficiently to stress — either physical, emotional, or a combination of both — and to return to prestress levels within a reasonable period of time (Weg, 1983). If the stress is too great, it may lead to breakdown and disease, or even to death (Figure 7.4).

In 1977 Nathan Shock concluded that those theories of aging that focus on regulating and control mechanisms were very promising since they emphasize aging process in the total organism. Although the causes and effects of these age-related physiological changes are not yet fully understood, the neuroendocrinology of aging has become an established field of research (Finch & Landfield, 1985). Changes in the autonomic nervous system and in the endocrine system continue to be seen as key aspects of the aging process. It is not clear whether they are major causes of aging, or are primarily symptoms of more basic aging processes. In either case, understanding these changes can aid in the care and treatment of vulnerable elderly persons.

Dietary Restriction

One of the most interesting lines of research in biological aging is based on the observation that food restriction appears both to increase life expectancy and to prolong life span in rodents under laboratory conditions (Masoro, 1988). This

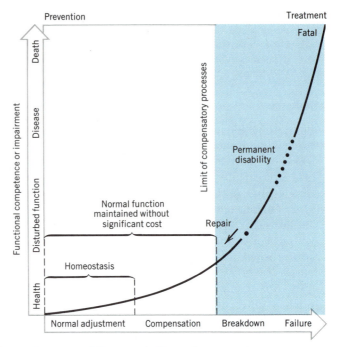

FIGURE 7.4 Progressive stages of homeostasis from adjustment (health) to failure (death). In the healthy adult, homeostatic processes ensure adequate adjustment in response to stress, and even for a period beyond this stage compensatory processes are capable of maintaining overall function without serious disability. When stress is exerted beyond compensatory capacities of the organism, disability ensues in rapidly increasing increments to severe illness, permanent disability, and death. When this model is viewed in terms of homeostatic responses to stress imposed on the aged and to aging itself, a period when the body can be regarded as at the point of "limit of compensatory processes," it is evident that even minor stresses are not tolerable, and the individual moves rapidly into stages of breakdown and failure. (*Source*: Timiras, 1972, Fig. 28–1. Reprinted with permission of Macmillan Publishing Co., Inc. Copyright © 1972 by Paola S. Timiras.)

technique requires a diet that avoids malnutrition but that restricts calories to 20 to 60 percent less than the animal would eat if allowed to eat at will. It appears that caloric intake is the key, because when protein was restricted, for example, but not calories, there was little effect on longevity (except that kidney disease was reduced). A variety of different diets have shown the effects of caloric restriction, so it seems clear that food components are not responsible for the effect (e.g., fat, minerals, protein, or contaminants). Moreover, it appears that even if food restriction is not begun until adulthood, it still has as great an effect as if it begins early in life (Maeda et al., 1985).

It is reasonable to think that food restriction affects the aging process through its effect on the neuroendocrine systems (Masoro, 1988). Previously it was thought that aging may have been slowed because metabolic rate was reduced by food restriction (Sacher, 1977). Likewise, it has been suggested that free radicals were reduced by the supposed slower metabolic rate associated with food restriction

(Harman, 1981). Masoro (1988) discounted these theories in the light of research suggesting that it is the amount of nutrition per mouse (or rat), not nutrition per unit metabolic mass, that is critical; thus metabolic rate is irrelevant to the slowing of aging. However, research is continuing on the concept that damage from free radical biochemical reactions may be reduced by this type of laboratory food restriction.

Four conclusions from this research were noted by Masoro (1988):

1. Life expectancy is increased under conditions of food restriction. This suggests that the rate of premature death (e.g., from disease) is reduced. The *apparent life span* is also increased, suggesting that the process of aging is slowed. Since no species of animals may yet reach their ultimate potential life span, we can conclude only that the usual maximum life span of the animals is increased.

2. A large range of ordinary age changes in these animals is retarded; but not all age-related changes are slowed. This suggests that food restriction affects some primary aging processes. Its breadth of effect does not shed any light on the nature of such primary aging processes, however.

3. Most age-related diseases in these animals are either postponed or their progression is slowed by food restriction. It is not clear whether the increased life span results from this delay of disease or from slowing some primary aging process, although research is consistent with the latter idea that aging is decelerated.

4. Future research on aging in rodents might profit from using food restriction to prevent or delay diseases and thereby provide an animal that is likely to be a model of relatively disease-free aging.

Weindruch and Walford (1989) have proposed that similar processes may apply to human aging and argue that research is required to study whether dietary restriction can lengthen human life.

Implications

A great deal of complex research is currently investigating the nature of aging and the physiological changes that may provide a key to the underlying processes of aging. It appears that there is no simple path to understanding this phenomenon. Many ideas have been suggested, but so far none has provided a definitive key. Caloric restriction with adequate nutritional levels, if it works in humans as it does in rodents, may provide a means to extend the life span and postpone diseases associated with aging; but we do not understand why this affects aging processes, if it does.

A variety of techniques have been used—without success—in an attempt to prolong life. Humans seem often to fear aging, death, and the loss of youthfulness. Potions, sexual rituals, herbal and folk medicine, and some animal parts have been used in attempts to prolong life—often without regard to the survival of the species of animal whose horn or organ was thought to be the secret of longevity. The "fountain of youth" has long provided fascination, leading even to the discovery of Florida by Ponce de León. Modern versions of the "elixir of youth" include Gerovital, cells from lamb embryos, ginseng root, and a variety of other rejuvenation techniques (Weg, 1983).

If any key is found to slowing the aging process, there are profound social and ethical issues that will be raised. The most obvious is *overpopulation*. Already, the reduction in disease is allowing more and more people to live into old age; if the life span were extended, this situation would be compounded. Although the problems of the growing number of older persons, as well as the worldwide growth of the human population, will have to be faced in any event, other serious problems would be raised. For example, would this "pill" (or whatever) be available to all, or would it be so expensive as to be used only by the rich? Will we have to choose between having children or living indefinitely? If so, who will decide who lives and who has how many children? And, most important of all, will this involve not only adding years to life but also adding life to years? It would be important that these added years of life be relatively free of disease, and also years that can be used to find economic, social, and psychological satisfactions if these added years are to be truly beneficial.

One of the most important themes of human aging—and one that has been relatively deemphasized in this discussion of biological aspects of aging—is that there are significant differences between individuals.

> The older population is heterogeneous. There is no "the aged." Older people are less alike than ever before, fulfilling a unique heredity within a particular lifestyle. Individuals age at different rates from one another; within the same individual, each organ system ages both differently and in coordination with other systems under the integrative control of the neuroendocrine system. Therefore, although it is useful to calculate and compare the average decline of a function(s), it is equally important to keep in mind that any one person may not fit that specific picture.
>
> Differences within the group aged 65–90 are frequently greater than the differences that exist between the middle-aged group, 40–64 years old, and the older group. For example, they differ in regard to mobility, energy level, work activity, health, and whether housebound or in the community. (Weg, 1983, p. 248)

In the next section, we focus on one important aspect of this dimension of individual differences, namely, disease.

Disease: A Most Important Consideration

The distinction between aging and disease has long been recognized in Western thought. Aristotle (384–322 B.C.) noted that "aging is not disease, because it is not contrary to nature" (Guillerme, 1963). Cicero (106–43 B.C.), in response to the observation that some old persons are invalids, noted: "But a disability of this degree is not peculiar to old age; it is rather the usual concomitant of ill health" (trans. 1967, p. 21).

Nonetheless, it is very difficult to separate the physiological, social, and psychological effects of aging from the effects of disease since aging and disease are highly correlated. That is, as individuals age they often experience chronic diseases (such as arthritis, heart disease, or diabetes). They also typically experience social losses (job, friends, spouse), and there may be a decrease in hearing and vision. These effects compound each other. For example, accidents are more prevalent and bones break more easily and take longer to heal for an aged person than for younger adults.

However, it is important to distinguish between the changes that result from aging per se, from disease, and from other social, psychological, and physiological factors. Otherwise, if these different variables are not disentangled, we are easily misled into equating aging with disease, as if sick old people are the only kind of old people there are. If we make that error, then we not only overlook the old people who are healthy, but we also do not know whether the characteristics of sick old people result from their advanced age, from their illness, or from the interaction of both. One example of this is that although religious feelings and beliefs do not decline with age, church attendance does decrease with advanced age (Moberg, 1965). This change could be interpreted in a variety of ways; but it might simply reflect the fact that chronic illness may make attendance at religious activities difficult for more and more people with advancing age.

In this section we describe a classic study that attempted to separate the effects of aging from the effects of disease. Then we describe the prevalence and effects of disease among the aged. In general, disease is a very potent factor in aging. In the absence of disease, the effects of aging are relatively minor; but when even a mild amount of chronic disease is present, a wide range of negative changes results. **Disease** will be defined as a disorder of bodily functions that may occur with a broad age range. **Aging,** in contrast, involves changes that are caused solely by the passage of time. Although there is a statistical relationship between aging and disease, this relationship varies in different environmental conditions. That is, the relationship between aging and disease is different today than it was in 1900; and it is different in the less developed and in the industrialized countries today.

Aging versus Disease among Healthy Elderly Subjects

Even though aging and disease typically occur together, the theories of biological aging presented earlier in this chapter suggest changes in cellular or homeostatic functioning that are a consequence of age alone and do not necessarily involve disease. Thus, to uncover the physiological changes that occur with age alone, it is necessary to separate out those changes that are primarily caused by disease. Put another way, what changes occur with aging in the absence of disease? The data we will present make two important points: (1) many of the changes usually attributed to aging are better seen as the result of disease; and (2) even in the absence of disease there are important changes in physiological functioning with age, although there is far less impairment than is commonly observed among the aged in the general population.

This classic study was carried out by Birren, Butler, Greenhouse, Sokoloff, and Yarrow (1963); the subjects were restudied 11 years later by Granick and Patterson (1971). Birren and his associates gave lengthy and extended examinations on a wide range of medical, physiological, psychological, and social variables to a sample of very healthy men between the ages of 65 and 91. The first important (and serendi-

Optimally healthy older persons are as vigorous and capable of exercise as average younger persons.

pitous) finding was that this healthy sample actually consisted of two different groups: *Group 1,* those in optimal health in every regard, and *Group 2,* those without clinical symptoms of disease but with mild (subclinical) diseases that were discovered only through intensive medical examination. It was clear from their data that the difference between Group 1 ($N = 27$) and Group 2 ($N = 20$) proved to be one of the most important differences in the study. On nearly all the subsequent tests, the optimal health group differed from the subclinical disease group in a positive direction. These findings make it abundantly clear that the presence of even a mild degree of chronic disease has major consequences for the aged on a wide variety of functions.

We discussed these data briefly in Chapter 4 with regard to the slightly slower speed of information processing that accompanies aging in the absence of disease. Some of the additional important findings were the following:

1. A considerable number of variables showed no difference between the optimally healthy aged men and standards for young men. For example, measures of cerebral blood flow and oxygen consumption during exercise did not differ, and

the elderly subjects (mean age 71 years) were as vigorous and capable of exercise as young men (mean age 21 years). However, the important measure of cerebral blood flow differed between the young and the Group 2 subjects, suggesting that even their subclinical degree of disease may affect the efficiency of brain functioning.

2. Even among the most healthy old people, the electroencephalogram (EEG) — a measure of electrical activity of the brain — was found to change with age, although all the EEG patterns were within the normal range for younger persons. In general, the average frequency spectrum of these old subjects was approximately one cycle slower than the comparable young-adult rate. The EEG of the Group 2 subjects differed from Group 1 in the same direction as the general-age trend. Thus, there was some evidence of slowing down of the electrical activity of the brain with age, and disease seemed to increase this trend.

3. The less-healthy group performed consistently less well on several personality tests than the optimally healthy group. That is, even this slight degree of illness affected the degree to which they terminated responses appropriately, adhered to the task goal, and showed an ordered sequence of thought. However, the optimally healthy respondents did not differ noticeably from young adequately functioning persons.

4. The amount of loss suffered by the respondents in their personal environment was also related to psychological and psychiatric functioning. That is, men who had suffered marked losses, especially the loss of significant persons, tended to perform less adequately on the psychometric and personality tests and to be more likely to have been rated as depressed.

5. Slowing down (on psychometric tests) was related to less adequate daily functioning (i.e., the planful aspects of daily behavior and the nature of social interaction). Perhaps individuals who showed greater slowing down were, in a sense, physiologically "older."

Implications

One of the major implications of this study is the integrated pattern of interrelations among various systems (medical, cerebral, psychological, social-psychological, and psychiatric) in the aging person. That is, although no single factor of aging was found, the pattern was one of interacting factors reinforcing or canceling the effects of other factors in a complex interdependency. However, three aspects of the aging process (in the absence of disease) were particularly striking: (1) the slowing down, or decrease in speed on psychological tests and on reaction time measures (described in Chapter 4); (2) the effect of personality style and the degree of social loss on psychosocial and cognitive performance, depression, self-perceptions, and adaptive responses to aging; and (3) the widespread effects of a mild degree of disease, especially the development of a kind of condition that may precede Alzheimer's disease (which causes severe cognitive impairment; see Chapter 8).

Overall, the major finding was that, for the aged, the presence of even asymptomatic disease increased the statistical dependency of the psychological capacities on the physiological status of the organism. That is, moderate disease led to a greater correlation between psychological capacities and physiological status, compared with relatively low correlation in the absence of disease. Perhaps, as the homeostatic imbalance theory of aging suggests, with advancing age the organism's ability to function becomes more marginal so that it is less able to adapt to stress; thus, even a small amount of disease may upset the balance, and many functions suffer.

Eleven-Year Follow-up Study

These same subjects were retested after 11 years by a different team of investigators (Granick & Patterson, 1971). Two major findings stand out from this study of actual age changes.

First, about half of the original sample had died. Most (70 percent) of the Group 2 subjects did not survive, but most (63 percent) of the very healthy Group 1 subjects did survive. Clearly, the mild degree of disease that differentiated these two groups was important in terms of eventual mortality. Most of the differences initially found between the two groups were also related to survival: higher intelligence, faster reaction time, better personality adaptation, and lower social loss. In general, two measures taken together correctly predicted 80 percent of both the survivors and the nonsurvivors. These were: greater organization of daily behavior (organized, planned living and gratifying pursuits in the living pattern) and not smoking cigarettes. Although it is difficult to be certain whether both of these variables are related to physical health, they seem to indicate the harmful effects of cigarettes as well as the importance of psychosocial factors. Could this indicate a marked psychosomatic factor in mortality?

Second, among the surviving subjects there was a "remarkably limited amount of change" (p. 132) with age; average age at that point was 81. However, the increased correlation between psychological and physiological functioning was even more marked than previously. In general, there was a gradual decline in "reserve capacities" of energy and of general physical status (such as a greater vulnerability to psychosocial stresses). Also, the decline in the speed of functioning was, again, found to be related to age.

Thus, on one hand, changes with aging alone seem to be relatively minor in the absence of disease, but, on the other hand, these changes may have wide-reaching effects insofar as they involve increased vulnerability to stress and to disease.

In the next section we discuss a variety of ordinary age-related changes in the body that are not necessarily caused by aging or disease alone, but by an interaction of many factors including accidents, aging, disease, environmental stimuli, nutrition, and physical injuries.

Physical and Physiological Changes with Aging

To be sure, some of the most obvious changes with aging are in such physical characteristics as graying or loss of hair, wrinkling of the skin, decrease in height, and loss of teeth; in such sensory modalities as decreased vision and hearing; and in the slowing of CNS functioning. Some of these changes have major effects on the concept of the self; others, especially decreased perceptual acuity and CNS slowing, have more widespread effects on psychosocial adjustment. There is much individual variation in the extent of these changes and they probably reflect the effects of both disease and aging combined. Also, nutrition, heredity, health care, exposure to sunlight, and variations in exercise are each important factors related to the extent of these physical changes in any particular individual. Yet, in general, these changes are age-related in the sense that they affect a greater proportion of individuals in each successive age group.

Since these changes are typically associated with aging, they tend to be seen as negative changes in our society. Thus, we need to be sensitive to *ageism* when we focus on these physical changes. That is, smooth, unwrinkled, clear skin *could* be negatively valued in a culture that valued old age since these characteristics may indicate inexperience, unfamiliarity with life's pain and pleasures, and irresponsibility. Conversely, an old face may be seen as reflecting a personal history that is written in the wrinkles and folds that are so uniquely individual to that face. In this section we review the major changes in the body that are often associated with growing older.

Smooth, unwrinkled skin can be viewed as a sign of inexperience, naiveté, and innocence. An old face may be seen as reflecting a personal history written in the unique pattern of wrinkles and folds. The preference for youth over age in our society is a reflection of ageism.

Physical Characteristics

The skeleton is fully formed by the early twenties and there is no change in individual bones after that time (Bromley, 1966), yet there may be a slight loss of height in old age because of changes in the discs between the spinal vertebrae caused by changes in collagen with age. **Collagen** is a fibrous protein that is one of the components in connective tissue and is found throughout the body. Connective tissues function in many important ways, such as mechanical support of the body and in repair of injury. Collagen undergoes continuous change with age and has received much research attention (Kligman, Grove & Balin, 1985). The loss of height also may be exaggerated by stooping as a result of muscular weakness. Still another factor exaggerating the loss of height is the recent population trend toward increased stature as a result of improved nutrition and other influences during childhood. This *cohort effect* caused people to grow taller in the last several decades, compared with earlier in this century; so older people are shorter than younger people today. Of course, the skeleton of older persons also reflects previous damage, disease, and nutritional deficiencies. Two diseases that affect the skeleton are osteoporosis and rheumatoid arthritis, which are discussed in later sections.

One of the most apparent changes in old age is the increased paleness, change in texture, loss of elasticity, dryness, and appearance of spots of pigmentation in the skin; many of these changes are attributed to change in collagen with age. The effect of exposure to sunshine appears to be responsible for many of these changes in the skin, and it is thought that the effective use of sunscreens would prevent most of them (Kligman, Aiken & Kligman, 1982). Moreover, wrinkling of skin is exaggerated by reduced elasticity of the skin and loss of muscular tissue, so skin that once covered muscles snugly may hang in folds in old age. Dry skin can be a serious problem — with itching that may become a preoccupation affecting sleep and causing scratching that can induce bacterial infections. The other effects of aging skin are primarily emotional and can influence the individual's self conception and social relationships (Kligman et al., 1985). The so-called "age spots" are produced by a group of substances, *lipofuscins,* that build up in some nerve cells with age and give rise to pigments in these cells (Curtis, 1966).

Loss of teeth is a frequent marker of entry into old age and, undoubtedly, the surgery required and the adjustment to dentures may be a time of significant age-related reassessment of the self-concept. Although the use of fluoride and advances in dentistry have prevented much tooth decay and premature loss of teeth in recent years, especially among young people, these advances do not necessarily reduce the loss of teeth from the other major adult dental problem, *periodontal disease* of the gum and supporting tissue. Greater education is being devoted to informing young and middle-aged adults about the prevention and treatment of this major cause of tooth loss. When it begins, and it generally does to some degree in all adults, surgical treatment may be required. Certainly, natural teeth are far more effective than dentures for chewing, but sound teeth in old age require lifetime care, proper diet, and periodic treatment. Perhaps the failure of teeth is basically a result of their evolutionary selection under different dietary conditions when the average life span was much shorter. They may have evolved to last through the childbearing years, but now we need them to last twice as long!

Graying and thinning of the hair is another obvious change associated with aging. In addition, the pattern of body and facial hair may change from its young adult pattern, with some loss and some increase for reasons not fully understood (Kligman et al., 1985). Bromley (1966) suggested that the gradual decline in secretion of the adrenal glands after the late twenties may be related to the loss of hair, although blood circulation in the scalp may also be involved. Gray hair results from the absence of pigment in the hair, presumably because the melanocytes that provide the pigment granules for the hair eventually run out of these granules, or do not produce new ones. Genetic factors have long been recognized to determine hair pigmentation and loss of hair in men.

Changes in the voice, which is often less powerful and more restricted in range in old age, seem to result from gradual bodily changes that may limit the capacity and control of expelled air, from upper respiratory congestion, or from atrophy of the muscles of the larynx (Timiras, 1972).

The digestive system is little affected by ordinary aging (Bromley, 1966), although an age-related decline in sensitivity to smell or taste may decrease the appetite. In particular, there is no evidence of an increase in constipation with age, despite the impression (and stereotypes supported by TV commercials) that old people may complain more about it. These complaints may reflect cohort factors of rigid toilet habits stressed during their childhood rather than actual constipation, since there are marked individual differences in bowel function. Also, Bromley (1966) reported an increase in red blood cells and hemoglobin in later life, suggesting little general need for ''iron'' tonics for the aging.

Sleep

Changes have been found in sleep patterns with age, and the topic is complex. Spontaneous interruption of sleep, relatively infrequent through adolescence, increases with age and the amount of time spent awake in bed increases after the fourth decade; the aged often compensate by spending more time in bed. Although the proportion of REM (rapid eye movement) sleep remains constant until extreme old age, the NREM (non-REM stage 2 and slow-wave stages 3 and 4) decrease in the elderly (Dement et al., 1985). The importance of these changes is not understood, but it is clear that many older persons are troubled by sleeping problems and seek medical help. In general, the problem tends to be circular: after waking early and being unable to fall asleep again, the person might nap during the day and might also go to bed early the next night, increasing the chances of waking early once again. Instead, current research in sleep disorder clinics suggests the following:

1. The person should stay awake until feeling sleepy.
2. If waking and unable to return to sleep, the person should engage in some sedentary activity until feeling sleepy and not be concerned about ''loss'' of sleep.

3. The same time of awakening each day is more important for setting the sleep–wake cycle than going to bed at the same time each night, so the person should avoid "sleeping late" some days.

4. Short naps during the day (under 50 minutes) have little effect on ability to fall asleep, and add to the amount of daily sleep.

5. Older people may require less sleep than younger people, and if they nap during the day, less sleep time is needed at night.

6. The use of sleeping medications may increase the severity of the sleep disorder, as may caffeine or alcohol. (Davies, Lacks, Storandt & Bertelson, 1986; Woodruff, 1985; Aber & Webb, 1986)

Sense Organs

Older persons are more likely than younger persons to show decrements in at least four of the five senses as well as in the sense of balance. Although it is not clear how much of this decrement results from aging alone, the change is at least partly the result of higher thresholds of stimulation that are required for perception, suggesting that the sense receptors become less efficient with age. Thus, in general, the aged require higher levels of stimulation in vision, audition, taste, and smell for the sense receptors to perform as well as a young person's senses. These decrements, especially in vision and hearing, are important to note since they not only influence the individual's ability to function in the physical environment but also can create a kind of sensory deprivation and social isolation that might have important psychological and social effects. As a result, many older persons seem to move more cautiously than younger persons. Although this may result from decreased vision and hearing, the sense of balance may also be impaired by ear infections or decreased blood flow to the inner ear. Thus, falls and accidental injuries are more likely for older persons (Strehler, 1977). Also, the slowing of information processing by the central nervous system reduces the speed with which visual input is scanned and perceived, so that older persons may respond to sensory information less rapidly and efficiently than younger persons, further increasing the risk of accidents and falls (Ochs, Newberry, Lenhardt & Harkins, 1985).

Vision

Several aspects of vision decline with age (Fozard, Wolf, Bell, McFarland & Podolsky, 1977). Visual *acuity,* the ability to see clearly at a distance, typically reaches its maximum in the late teens, remains fairly constant until 45–50, then declines gradually. The threshold for *adaptation to darkness* rises with age, indicating a decline in the ability to see clearly when illumination is low (as in night driving), and, in general, the ability of light to penetrate the lens, cornea, and vitreous humor of the eye declines with age. Also, *accommodation* of the lens of the eye to focus on near objects decreases from age 5 to age 60 at a constant rate (Hofstetter, 1944). This is commonly noted in the growing necessity for bifocal glasses or reading glasses in middle age — as some individuals describe it, "My arms seemed to grow shorter so that I couldn't hold the newspaper far enough away to read it!''

Although the incidence of visual dysfunction increases with age, most older people are not affected by severe visual impairment. Usually, the changes are gradual and can be compensated for by glasses or by surgery. Development of a **cataract** is a frequent cause of surgery on the eye. The condition is not a normal aspect of aging, and may be exacerbated by extensive exposure to sunlight (so the proper use of sunglasses is important). The cause is not known, but a cataract results from the lens of the eye becoming opaque. During surgery the lens is removed and a special lens is inserted in its place. Glaucoma and senile macular degeneration (SMD) also increase with age. There is no treatment for SMD, or for blindness associated with diabetes, which also becomes more prevalent with aging. However, routine screening for glaucoma is recommended so that its treatment can begin before significant damage occurs (Kline & Schieber, 1985).

Hearing

As with vision, the sense of hearing is complex. Sound, which consists of waves of air pressure (as sight consists of visible light waves), must be translated into neural impulses that are understood by the brain; this takes place in the organ of Corti in the inner ear. The loss of hair cells and reduced flexibility of membranes in this

Ronald Reagan wore a hearing aid while he was President; at 77, he was the oldest of all U.S. presidents.

organ are thought to be the primary cause of hearing loss with aging (Olsho, Harkins & Lenhardt, 1985). In general, the highest frequencies show the greatest decline (Weiss, 1959). Long-term exposure to noise is probably a factor in addition to probably lowered sensitivity of the auditory receptors. Certain high-frequency sounds in speech, bird songs, and electronic telephone "beeps" may not be heard at all. The understanding of speech may be especially difficult for an older person when there is much background noise (as in a restaurant). Simply talking louder seldom helps, and may embarrass both the speaker and the listener. Hearing aids can be useful, but are often regarded as less acceptable than eyeglasses as they seem to imply a stigma of being deaf, which may be associated with being "deaf and dumb." It is likely that extensive exposure of the young to loud sounds (e.g., from earphones or discotheques) may produce even greater hearing impairment in old age than is the case with the current cohort of elders.

Taste and Smell

Similar to the threshold increase found for vision and hearing, higher levels of stimulation of taste and smell receptors are thought to be required for older persons than is the case for younger persons (Strehler, 1977). In line with this idea, Spitzer (1988) reported an increase with age in taste thresholds for sour, salt, and bitter. Likewise, the number of taste buds was found to decrease with age, based on studies of the tongues of cadavers (Miller, 1988). There was also a greater threshold for smell found among older persons in a study comparing subjects between the ages of 70 and 90 with those between 18 and 24 years old (Stevens & Cain, 1987). These differences in smell and taste thresholds may affect the dietary habits and nutritional well-being of elderly persons, especially those living alone who base their meals on taste and convenience. Since eating is largely a social activity, if one eats alone, taste and smell of the food may outweigh nutritional considerations. And, as we note in Chapter 8, malnutrition can be a cause of mental impairment, often misdiagnosed as "senility" in the elderly.

Pain

The clinical impression is that sensitivity to pain might decrease with age, partly because some older persons experience more frequent pain from chronic diseases (such as arthritis) than do younger persons and because the threshold for other kinds of stimulation increases with age. However, empirical studies have not validated this impression. For example, Harkins, Price, and Martelli (1986) found that middle-aged persons showed a lower sensitivity to pain than either young or elderly persons in a study that used heat on the forearm as the stimulus. In general, they found that similarities among the age groups were more striking than the differences, and there was no indication that the older group had lower pain sensitivity.

Implications

Once again we must note individual differences in the extent and importance of these changes. A variety of factors, including disease and environmental influences, interact to produce these changes. Age alone is not a reliable predictor of the extent of change in vision, hearing, taste, or smell. We need to be sensitive to the possibility of these changes, however, and respond in an appropriate way. Many vision and hearing problems can be corrected and eye or ear diseases benefit from early detection and treatment. Changes in taste and smell may reduce the attractiveness of food and lead to malnutrition, or excessive use of salt and other seasonings. Simple awareness of these changes combined with conscious attention to nutritional requirements for older persons can effectively prevent either inadequate nutrition or overeating of sweet foods (which are less affected by changes in taste and smell sensitivity). Greater attention to visual and esthetic aspects of food presentation as well as social interaction may help to compensate for these changes in taste and smell perception.

Osteoporosis

Beginning perhaps as early as age 25, age-related bone loss, known as *osteoporosis,* results from a variety of interacting physiological factors; heredity also plays a role (Weg, 1983). If not available in the diet, the calcium necessary for maintaining homeostatic functioning of the body is taken from the bone mass in the skeleton, where it is stored. As a result the bones become lighter, thinner, more porous, and thus more likely to break. Hip fractures are one of the possible outcomes of this change; this can result in a serious health impairment as a result of surgery, the loss of mobility, and fear of additional fractures. Loss of height is often an early sign and the fracture of spinal vertebrae and a curving of the spine (sometimes called ''dowager's hump'') may occur. Increased amounts of calcium in the diet (milk and dairy products, dark-green leafy vegetables such as spinach, salmon, sardines, oysters, and tofu), vitamin D, and exercise are generally recommended to prevent and treat osteoporosis (Jarvik & Small, 1988).

Osteoporosis is more serious in women than in men. The decline in estrogen after menopause plays a major role in the loss of bone with aging in women. In addition, men typically have more bone mass than women and are therefore less vulnerable to this condition than women (Exton-Smith, 1985). For some women, estrogen-replacement therapy may be appropriate after menopause (we discussed this in Chapter 5).

In one study of a sample of recently postmenopausal women, bone loss appeared to be reduced by treatment that combined calcium supplement with low-dosage estrogen therapy (Ettinger, Genant & Cann, 1987). Over the three-year period of this study, after comparing various treatments it was found that neither calcium supplement nor estrogen treatment alone prevented bone loss entirely. Surprisingly, in this study, calcium supplementation alone appeared to have no effect; but the implications of this finding are not clear—for example, calcium supplement might be effective for older women, but not for women shortly after menopause.

Prevalence of Disease among the Aged

Older persons in general are less often afflicted with *acute* diseases, more often afflicted with *chronic* diseases, and are more likely to suffer disability restrictions because of their health than younger persons.

An **acute disease** is a temporary illness such as one caused by an infection by a virus (e.g., cold, flu, pneumonia). These diseases are much more frequent in childhood than at any other age. Their prevalence decreases with age for both men and women (Figure 7.5). Likewise, days of restricted activity because of acute conditions also decrease with age. The control of these illnesses by vaccines, antibiotics, and improved health conditions has been the major advance in medical science in this century. Most of the change has come since the 1940s, so older people today had to survive some of those diseases with little medical assistance. Since they are "survivors" in that sense, they may be somewhat hardier than younger generations. In addition, the control of infectious diseases has markedly increased the average life span at birth, but has had relatively little effect on the average life span for those who survive to age 65. Acute disease may be the cause of death for frail old persons, but does not shorten the average life span very much.

A **chronic disease,** in contrast, is a long-term illness that cannot be fully cured; only the symptoms can be treated. These conditions are much more common in adulthood and old age than among young people. Arthritis, hypertension (high blood pressure), and heart conditions are the most prevalent chronic diseases affecting persons over age 65, and they increase in prevalence with age (Figure 7.6). It is apparent that these chronic diseases may lead to restricted activity; and heart conditions, as well as high blood pressure, are associated with the leading causes of death. It should be noted that these diseases may also affect younger persons so they are correlated with, but not caused by, aging. **Arthritis,** for exam-

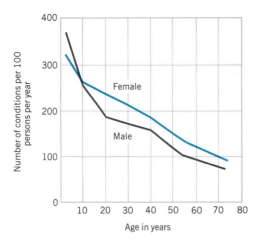

FIGURE 7.5 Incidence of acute conditions per 100 persons per year by sex and age, July 1974 to June 1975. (*Source*: National Center for Health Statistics. *Vital and health statistics*, Series 10, No. 114, Fig. 2. Washington, D.C.: U.S. Government Printing Office, 1977.)

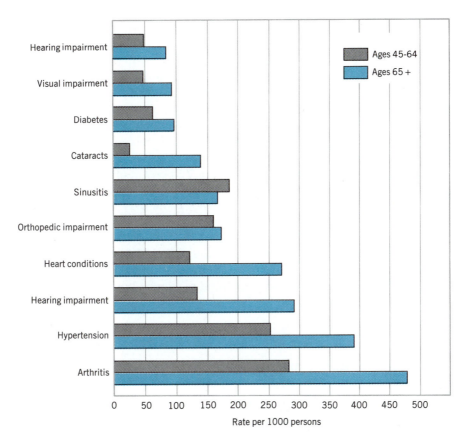

FIGURE 7.6 Morbidity from top ten chronic conditions: 1986. (*Source*: U.S. Senate, 1987–1988, Chart 4–2.)

ple, is the inflammation of a joint (e.g., wrist, elbow, hip) that may be caused by any of a number of diseases and may begin at any age, sometimes after a joint is injured. One of the most common forms is *rheumatoid arthritis,* which is caused by the inflammation of membrane of the joint, and usually begins in middle age; it should be treated as soon as it is diagnosed to reduce damage to the joint. **Osteoarthritis** is more properly called *degenerative joint disease* because the joint is usually not inflamed. It is related to wear and stress of the joint, heredity, and being overweight, which adds to the stress on the weight-bearing joints. Stiffness of the joint often is reduced by activity and may recur after rest. Treatment of arthritis may involve physical therapy, daily exercise, joint-replacement surgery, and medication to reduce inflammation and to control pain (Jarvik & Small, 1988).

Chronic impairments also increase in prevalence with age. These include hearing impairment, visual impairment, and reduced ability to get around because of orthopedic impairment (Figure 7.6). Chronic diseases such as arthritis, hypertension, or heart disease may also reduce mobility. Various kinds of injuries, especially accidental falls, are an important cause of chronic impairment. Again, these impairments are usually caused by disease or by environmental factors (e.g., diabetes or glaucoma; accidents or excessive noise); they are not directly caused by aging itself.

Only a minority of aged persons suffer restrictions in their ability to get around in the community, however. One measure of activity limitation is the number of days an individual is confined to bed (Table 7.2). Over 62 percent of persons over age 65 reported they had not been confined to bed at all; and only about 9 percent were confined to bed for more than a month. Activity limitation is greater for older persons: for those over age 85, about 14 percent of community-residing elderly were confined to bed for a month or longer. Likewise, data from the National Health Interview Survey in 1984 found that 77 percent of persons over age 65 reported no difficulty with personal care activities and 73 percent reported no home management activities that were difficult; for those over age 85, the percentages were 51 and 45 percent, respectively (Dawson, Hendershot & Fulton, 1987).

In general, longitudinal studies of aging (Dovenmuehle, Busse & Newman, 1961; Dovenmuehle, 1970) have found that, although physical disabilities are more common among the aged than among the young or middle-aged adult, there is great individual variation. Socioeconomic factors both affect and result from these impairments.

Major Causes of Death

The proportion of deaths from the three leading causes varies by age (Figure 7.7). Accidents are the major cause of death for adolescents and young adults (AIDS has also become a leading cause of death in this age group in some urban areas during the 1980s). In contrast, over 50 percent of deaths after age 75 are attributed to heart and cerebrovascular disease. Cancerous neoplasms account for a greater proportion of deaths during middle age than at other ages. Since a greater number of people die in old age than at younger ages, the cause of death for the overwhelming majority of people is heart and cerebrovascular disease.

TABLE 7.2 *Percentage of the 65-Plus Population in the Community Confined to Bed: 1984*

	Age			
Bed Days in Year	*65 to 74*	*74 to 84*	*85 plus*	*65 plus*
0	63.5	61.3	55.8	62.2
1 to 6 days	14.5	12.9	12.1	13.8
7 to 13 days	6.7	7.4	8.7	7.1
14 to 27 days	6.5	7.0	6.3	6.6
28 to 365 days	7.8	9.9	13.9	8.9
Always	1.0	1.6	3.4	1.4

Source: U.S. Senate (1987–1988), Table 4.4.

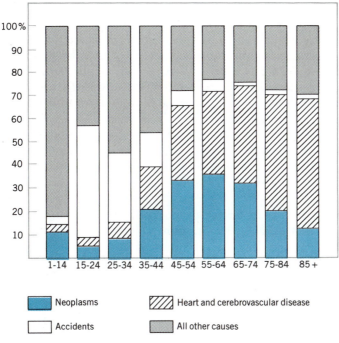

FIGURE 7.7 Mortality from malignant neoplasms (cancer), heart and cerebrovascular disease, and accidents in the United States, 1987, expressed as a percentage of total mortality by age group. (*Source*: National Center for Health Statistics. Monthly vital statistics report, Vol. 36, No. 13. Annual survey of births, marriages, divorces, and deaths, United States, 1987, Table 8, pp. 18–19. Hyattsville, MD: Public Health Service, 1988.)

In 1987, the 10 leading causes of death and death rates per 100,000 population in the United States, according to the National Center for Health Statistics (1988), were:

1. Diseases of the heart: 313.4
2. Malignant neoplasms (cancer): 196.1
3. Cerebrovascular diseases: 61.3
4. Accidents: 39.0
5. Chronic obstructive pulmonary diseases: 32.2
6. Pneumonia and influenza: 28.8
7. Diabetes mellitus: 15.6
8. Suicide: 12.7
9. Chronic liver disease and cirrhosis: 10.7
10. Atherosclerosis: 9.5

The death rate for **heart disease** declined by 18 percent between 1979 and 1986; nonetheless, it accounted for about one-quarter of all deaths in 1986 (Associated Press, 1989). Strehler (1977) pointed out that with age there is a decrease in pumping efficiency of the heart, a change in the elasticity of arteries, and the deposit of fatty substances such as cholesterol in the arteries, leading to the deposit of calcium salts that reduce the efficiency of the circulatory system. An example of this condition, known as *atherosclerosis,* is shown in Figure 7.8. *Arteriosclerosis* results from decreased elasticity of the blood vessels. *Hypertension,* or high blood pressure, may result from either of these conditions, or from other factors; it is more common among African Americans for reasons not fully understood.

Diet is thought to be related to atherosclerosis since animal fats, egg yolks, and certain vegetable oils are particularly high in cholesterol; however, one type of cholesterol (HDL) may reduce the risk of heart disease. Reduction of sodium (salt) in the diet, weight reduction, exercise, and medication are used to treat hypertension. However, the complex interaction between age, heredity, cholesterol level, body weight, diet, and exercise are not fully understood (Jarvik & Small, 1988, p. 61). We discuss behavior and cardiovascular disease in the final section of this chapter.

Conclusion

There has been a dramatic change in the health of older persons in recent years. As noted in Chapter 1, life expectancy at age 65 has increased markedly since the 1970s; much of this change is a result of the reduced death rate from heart disease.

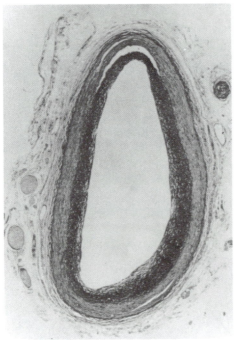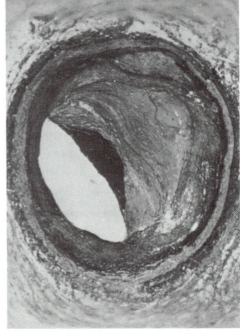

FIGURE 7.8 Cross sections of coronary arteries. Left, a near normal artery; right, an artery partially blocked by atherosclerotic plaques. (*Source*: National Heart, Lung, and Blood Institute.)

In addition, advanced surgical procedures, improved techniques for detection and diagnosis of disease that allow earlier treatment, and higher rates of successful treatment for some diseases (including some forms of cancer) have added years of healthy life to many older persons. For example, mortality from strokes decreased 52 percent from 1968 to 1984 (Baum & Manton, 1987).

Nonetheless, one of the concomitants of growing older is the greater susceptibility to chronic disease. Although many persons retain generally good health into the seventies and eighties today, many also manifest the symptoms of one or more chronic impairments and may be disabled to some degree as a result. Even when there is little apparent disability, decreased hearing, impaired vision, or the pain and reduced mobility resulting from diseases such as arthritis can isolate the old person from social interaction. Research now is focusing on the positive ways in which older persons cope with whatever degree of disability, if any, may be present. It is also calling attention to the "old-old"—those over age 85—who are most susceptible to health impairments.

Since behavior change in dietary habits, exercise, smoking, and stress management has been associated with improved health in recent years, we focus on the emerging field of health psychology and behavioral medicine in the next section.

Psychology and Health

In recent years, the complexity of factors involved in health and illness has become recognized and greater attention has been given to the importance of psychological factors. Today it is understood that all diseases and physical disabilities have psychological effects, and that a variety of psychosocial influences play a role in the individual's health and ability to cope with disease or disability.

An emerging field of *health psychology* is focusing on the contributions of psychology to promote and maintain health, to prevent and treat illness, and to identify etiological and diagnostic correlates of health, illness, and related dysfunctions; it also is focusing on improving the health care system and influencing the formation of health policy (Matarazzo, 1980).

Health psychology is related to *behavioral medicine* and is considerably broader than the classic idea of *psychosomatic* illness in which a disease was thought to be caused by psychological factors. Among the topics studied in health psychology are the following: healthful behavior patterns, compliance with prescribed treatments, educational programs about prevention of disease, personality characteristics associated with certain conditions such as "Type-A behavior" and heart disease, the role of stress reactions in disease, the effect of different styles of coping with symptoms, and the willingness to seek treatment early in the illness.

One of the chronic diseases that most clearly indicates the role of health psychology is **acquired immune deficiency syndrome (AIDS).** Most researchers agree that AIDS is caused by a virus that is transmitted by the exchange of bodily fluid during sexual contact or by the sharing of intravenous (IV) needles and syringes that are contaminated by blood infected with the virus. It can be passed on to unborn children, or through blood infected by the virus. No medical cure is now known, so the only effective means of curtailing the disease is through education

Education and assistance in changing behavior to more healthful practices have played a major role in reducing the effect of some diseases, such as AIDS and heart disease.

that produces healthful behavior change that prevents the spread of the virus. Thus, psychological techniques of effective education that promote appropriate change in sexual practices and reduce unsafe IV drug use are the most effective method of controlling this disease and saving lives. Until an effective treatment or vaccine is discovered, health psychology is at the forefront in the fight against this disease. Psychologists have played important roles in establishing health policies and in providing health care for persons with HIV infection (cf. Batchelor, 1984; Morin, 1988). Since some older people are infected with the virus and others who are presently infected will grow older, it is likely that this disease may become a significant health concern with regard to aging.

Another chronic disease in which health psychology has played a major role in prevention is heart disease, which, as noted earlier, is the leading cause of death in the United States.

> Beginning in 1968, a striking and unexpected drop was noticed in mortality resulting from the diseases of the heart. The best current evidence indicates that this drop is continuing, and is likely to do so well into the next century. . . . [M]ost of the reduction in mortality (and, it is likely, in morbidity as well) should be credited to changes in our behavior and our health habits, rather than to curative medical interventions. (Avorn, 1986, p. 284)

This reduction in heart disease is the result of reduced smoking, changes in diet, increased exercise, greater education regarding blood pressure, and (to be sure) improved medication — and compliance with medication recommendations — as well as better medical treatment of heart disease.

Other diseases of the circulatory system and lung cancer are similarly related to behavioral interventions. Likewise, early detection of cancer as a result of improved education and motivation may reduce mortality. Dietary factors and exercise are important in the prevention of osteoporosis, in combination with estrogen replacement therapy in some cases. Other dietary changes, such as increased fiber, are suggested as important for reducing the risk of other diseases, such as colon cancer. Thus, it is becoming more and more obvious that psychology, broadly applied, is highly relevant to physical health and must be involved in the promotion of health among persons as they grow older (Siegler, 1989).

In this section we focus on some of the major themes in health psychology that are relevant to aging. At the outset, however, it is important to stress that one must be careful to avoid "blaming the victim" by attributing disease to the individual's behavior (Siegler & Costa, 1985). As noted earlier, disease is caused by a variety of factors and, at most, one may only increase or decrease the risk of a disease by engaging in those behaviors that are implicated in the disease.

Cardiovascular Disease

Smoking, especially cigarette smoking, is clearly associated with the risk of heart attacks (Figure 7.9). Other risk factors include elevated blood pressure, high cholesterol levels, obesity, advancing age, and being male (Siegler, Nowlin & Blumenthal, 1980). In addition, a behavioral pattern has long been thought to be

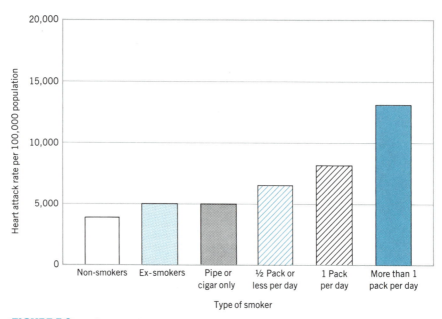

FIGURE 7.9 Smoking and heart attack risk. With other known risk factors controlled, the relative risk of suffering a heart attack increases in direct proportion to the number of cigarettes smoked per day. (*Source*: Matarazzo, 1984, Fig. 2, p. 19. © American Psychological Association. Reprinted with permission.)

associated with coronary disease. In the 1960s Friedman and Rosenman described a constellation of behaviors that they termed the "Type A" pattern that was found to be associated with coronary heart disease (CHD). In a longitudinal study of over 3500 employed men, 80 out of 113 men (71 percent) diagnosed with CHD were assessed by interviewers who did not know the respondents' heart condition as showing the Type A pattern (Rosenman et al., 1964). Of those who were free of CHD at the beginning of the study, Type A participants developed CHD at a rate 2.37 times the rate of non-Type A participants, called "Type B" (Rosenman et al., 1975). When other risk factors, such as smoking, age, blood pressure, and serum cholesterol, were controlled, the relative risk was still about twice as great (1.97) for the Type A participants (Brand, 1978). Other studies reported an association between the Type A pattern and extent of coronary atherosclerosis, based on autopsy analysis (Friedman, Rosenman, Straus, Wurm & Kositchek, 1968), and with severity of coronary artery disease (Blumenthal, Williams, Kong, Schanberg, & Thompson, 1978).

In the original study, Type A behavior was determined from a structured interview. In general, the **Type A behavior pattern** was described as one of excessive competition, desire for recognition, heightened aggressiveness, and a habitual tendency to speed up the pace of living (Rosenman et al., 1964). The **Type B behavior pattern** was described as the opposite. The classification reflected in part the speed and volume of the respondent's speech (Scherwitz, Berton & Leventhal, 1977; Schucker & Jacobs, 1977). A variety of other measures of this behavior pattern were also developed. One version, a multiple-choice, self-administered questionnaire, is the Jenkins Activity Survey, which is intended to determine the extent of the following characteristics:

> excesses of competitiveness, striving for achievement, aggressiveness (sometimes stringently repressed), time urgency, acceleration of common activities, restlessness, hostility, hyperalertness, explosiveness of speech amplitude, tenseness of facial musculature and feelings of struggle against the limitations of time and the insensitivity of the environment. (Jenkins, Rosenman & Zyzanski, 1974, p. 1271)

Bloom (1988) noted that this widely used measure does not correlate as highly with CHD as the original structured interview. Moreover, not all individuals with Type A patterns have heart attacks, and many with Type B patterns do.

Matthews (1982) pointed out that the Type A/B patterns should not be considered as personality characteristics, but are a set of behaviors that individuals display in an appropriate challenging environment. On the basis of this perspective, Rodin (1986b) suggested that:

> A coronary-prone behavior pattern may thus be described as a characteristic style of responding to environmental events that threaten an individual's sense of control. Type A's are engaged in a struggle for control, whereas Type B's are relatively free of such concerns and hence free of characteristic pattern "A" traits. (p. 146)

Health and a Sense of Control

Another major theme in health psychology research is the perception of *control*. For over a decade Judith Rodin (1986a, 1986b) has studied the interrelation of feelings of being in control in one's daily life and various aspects of health. Her research demonstrated the connections between psychological perceptions of one's relation to the environment, physiological functions, and physical health. She stressed that there are important individual differences in the preference for this sense of control. Some persons may strive for control in ways that can characterize the Type A pattern and thereby increase their risk of illness. Others may feel stressed when they are feeling a high degree of control and thus can increase their risk of disease. Nonetheless, for many persons, the maintenance of their individually appropriate sense of control appears to be health promoting. Her general perspective with regard to health, control, and aging is that:

1. Considerable data show the negative effect of loss of control, regardless of age, on the development of disease and the course of recovery from illness or surgical procedures.

2. There is evidence for increasing physical vulnerability in old age.

3. Biological decline associated with old age is capable of being reduced by changing the environment in ways that enhance an individual's perceived control over one's personal environment.

4. Therefore it is likely that biological decline with aging has been overestimated because environmental and personal events associated with old age so commonly produce a loss of control. (Rodin, 1986b, p. 140)

Rodin (1986b) noted that a wide variety of uncontrollable events may be related to psychological distress and ill health, if those events are also undesirable. However, positive events do not have negative effects on health, in general (Suls, 1982). For example, excessive work load or job responsibility may affect health, but only if they are near the limits of the person's capacity to remain in control of their work (House, 1975; Jenkins, 1971, 1976). Likewise, events that are uncontrollable are more likely to be perceived as stressful, and are associated with more physical complaints and physician visits (Wack, 1982). Research with animals in the laboratory also indicated that when a stressful stimulus cannot be avoided, the development of cancerous tumors appears to be enhanced, and in other studies, the immune system is affected. Rodin's studies on immunosuppression with 300 subjects between the ages of 62 and 91 also suggested a link between sense of control and the ability of the immune system to respond effectively in older adults (Rodin, 1986b, p. 158).

Being ill and undergoing medical procedures may also reduce a person's sense of control. Several studies have focused on ways to enhance an individual's control in such circumstances.

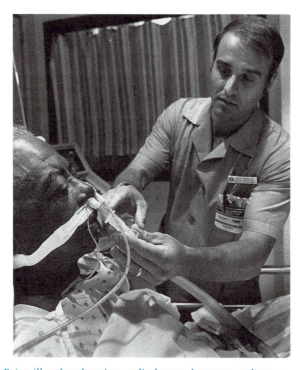

Being ill and undergoing medical procedures may reduce a person's sense of control; providing information in advance, enhancing feelings of competence, and giving greater responsibility for decisions appears to enhance recovery and promote health.

Looking at recovery from illness, several studies have suggested that those who are depressed and feel helpless take longer to recover from illness or are more likely to die from serious illnesses. Feeling out of control is thought to affect physiological processes in a deleterious way, to interfere with the mobilization of energy, or to result in unwillingness to cooperate with treatments that may be painful or may require physical effort. The opposite of depression, taking an active, involved role has been linked with faster recovery in a variety of situations. (Rodin, 1986b, pp. 147–148)

Two types of interventions are frequently used to enhance the patient's sense of control. One technique is to provide information about the details of the procedure to the patient in advance. This appears to reduce the degree of pain, the need for medication after surgery, and the time required for recovery (Johnson, 1975). It is thought that this technique helps shift attention from one's emotional reactions as a passive recipient of treatment to an active collaborator with the health care staff. A second technique is a *cognitive reappraisal* procedure in which individuals are encouraged to feel confident about their ability to handle whatever is encountered. This technique also was found to lead to less distress and less use of medication (Langer, Janis & Wolfer, 1975).

In a classic study by Langer and Rodin of the effects of a sense of control with nursing home residents, the group given greater responsibility for daily decisions became more active, felt less unhappy, and—after 18 months—improved significantly in health, and even showed a marginal difference in death rate in comparison with another group that was encouraged to let the staff care for them and satisfy their needs (Langer & Rodin, 1976; Rodin & Langer, 1977). In a later study, coping skills were taught to nursing home residents in an effort to enhance their sense of personal control. The result was lower feelings of stress, increased problem-solving ability, and reduction in corticosteroid levels among the experimental group; 18 months later, the group showed improved health compared with a control group (Rodin, 1983).

Continuing this line of research, Rodin and her colleagues used a family interaction task to enhance the sense of control over the decision to enter a nursing home in a randomly selected group of persons scheduled to enter nursing homes after being hospitalized. (As a result of this task some decided not to enter the home, in fact.) One year later, the degree of perceived control over the decision to enter the nursing home was found to be more important than severity of illness upon entry to the study in predicting who had returned home from the nursing homes (Bers, Bohm & Rodin, unpublished data cited in Rodin, 1986b, pp. 152–153).

On the basis of these and related studies, Rodin (1986b) concluded:

Interventions aimed at enhancing a sense of control and developing coping strategies appear to mitigate environmental challenges to the older person's adaptive resources, thus reducing harmful physiological reactions and lessening the chances of disease development. Given these findings, we and others continue trying to specify the mediating physiological processes. (Rodin, 1986b, p. 160)

Stress and Health

It is almost common sense to assume that stress is related to mental and physical health. For example, Bloom (1988), citing previous studies, noted:

One finding that has contributed to the development of behavioral medicine is the increasingly strong evidence that psychosocial factors that can be described as stressful can have adverse effects on physical health (Kaprio et al., 1987; Miller, 1983). Stress has been identified as a crucial factor in both physical and emotional disorders, and such stressful life events as job loss, bereavement, and marital disruption have been shown to increase the risk not only of psychological disorders such as depression, but also of minor infections and of many other more serious conditions (Elliott & Eisdorfer, 1982). (p. 75)

Stressful life events have been found to produce significant changes in physiological variables among healthy participants in a longitudinal study of aging (Willis, Thomas, Garry & Goodwin, 1987). Fifteen respondents answered a request to contact the study within a month of a major life crisis (such as death of a relative, diagnosis of a relative's serious illness, or hospitalization for surgery). Since participants in this larger study had annual physical examinations and various physiological measures were taken yearly, comparisons with their previous medical records could be made to determine the effects of the stress that resulted from the major life crisis. The fifteen respondents differed from the other study participants only in the higher proportion of women in the sample reporting the life crisis. In comparison with the previous annual examination (precrisis) and six months postcrisis levels, at the time of the crisis there was a significant loss in weight, reduced caloric intake, and decreased level of circulating lymphocytes that reflect immune system functioning; there was also an increase in psychological distress and in the level of cortisol that indicates stimulation of the hypothalamus, pituitary, and adrenal glands (Figure 7.10). It is thought that the risk of illness and death may be increased by reduced food intake, weight loss, lower efficiency of the immune system, and heightened activation of the hypothalamus–pituitary–adrenal system (Dorian et al., 1982). Thus the stress-related changes in these measures, and their subsequent return to precrisis levels after a six-month period of adaptation, suggest that major life crises can affect physiological processes related to health.

Yet, as noted earlier in this chapter, stress is not necessarily harmful—at least as a theory of biological aging—and the extent to which individuals feel "in control" may be more relevant than the amount of stress they are experiencing. Also, some persons may be accustomed to higher levels of stress than others, or have more efficient methods of coping with high levels of stress. So the study of stress and health is a complex topic.

A typical approach has been to take the "stress temperature" of the individual by examining the life events across a broad range of stress experiences (Chiriboga, 1980). Such an examination needs to take into account the period of life span in which the individual is located, however. Many of the typical measures of stress have demonstrated the link between stress and health, but miss much of the critical stresses of later life. One measure of stress that attempted to include stress-producing events throughout the adult life span is the Life Events Questionnaire (Horowitz & Wilner, 1980). This measure also asks about the recency of the event, giving higher scores to more recent stressful life events (Table 7.3).

Moreover, it is useful to distinguish between the respondent's perception of the stress as a **positive stress** or a **negative stress** associated with life events. To

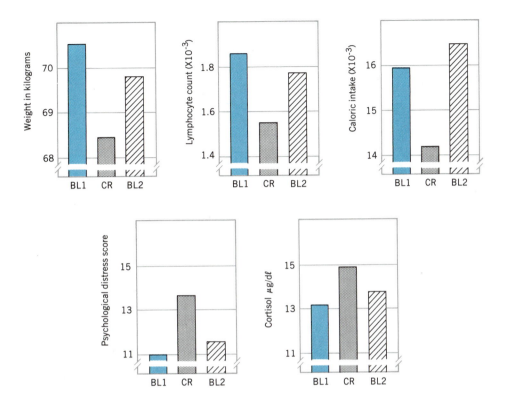

FIGURE 7.10 Histogram showing means of the five response measures for the three sampling periods: precrisis (BL1), crisis (CR), postcrisis (BL2). (*Source*: Adapted from Willis, Thomas, Garry & Goodwin, 1987, Fig. 1. Reprinted with permission from the *Journal of Gerontology*, Vol. 42, p. 629.)

illustrate, in a longitudinal study of adults during four periods of transitions (high school age preparing to leave home, newlywed, middle-aged with child preparing to leave home, retirement age), Chiriboga and Cutler (1980) found that middle-aged and retirement groups reported greater *negative* stress than the high school or newlywed groups; this reflected especially increased stress regarding the family. But the middle-aged group also had the greatest increase in *positive* stress; this was associated with their marital relationship. Thus, the "empty nest" period showed the greatest increase of both positive and negative stress, suggesting that it is a period of challenge and crisis. In contrast, respondents in the retirement period reported not only more negative stress but also less positive stress. Analyzing the styles of stress in the study of adults during four periods of transitions, Chiriboga and Cutler (1980) described a fourfold typology:

1. *Avoiders*, for whom both positive and negative stresses have declined.
2. *Lucky*, for whom positive stress increased while negative stress declined.
3. *Overwhelmed*, for whom negative stress increased while positive stress declined.
4. *Stress-prone*, for whom both negative and positive stress increased.

TABLE 7.3 Life Events Questionnaire—Short Form (Center for the Study of Neuroses, U. of California, San Francisco)

Short Form: Equivalent Weights (Combined Sex and Age Groups)

The checklist below consists of events which are sometimes important experiences. Read down the list until you find events that have happened to you personally. Check box under the column which indicates how long ago the event happened. Check each event as many times as it happened. For deaths (the first three items) there are several boxes in each time period; mark the additional boxes if more than one occurred. For events which continued for a long period of time, such as pregnancy, check the beginning date and the ending date and then check the boxes in between. If you can't remember the exact dates, just be as accurate as you can.[a]

	Weights				
	Within 0–1 mo.	Within 1–6 mo.	Within 6–12 mo.	Within 1–2 yr.	Over 2 yr.
Death of a child or spouse (husband, wife, or mate)?	90	81	67	50	32
Death of a child or spouse (husband, wife, or mate)? (2nd)	90	81	67	50	32
The death of a parent, brother or sister?	79	70	51	34	22
The death of a parent, brother or sister? (2nd)	79	70	51	34	22
The death of a parent, brother or sister? (3rd)	79	70	51	34	22
The loss of a close friend or important relationship by death?	70	53	36	22	12
The loss of a close friend or important relationship by death? (2nd)	70	53	36	22	12
Legal troubles resulting in being held in jail?	82	65	51	37	27
Financial difficulties?	60	43	26	13	7
Being fired or laid off?	68	46	27	16	8
A miscarriage or abortion (patient or spouse)?	71	53	31	18	11
Divorce, or a breakup with a lover?	76	63	45	29	16
Separation from spouse because of marital problems?	75	61	41	24	14
Court appearance for a serious violation?	70	41	23	13	5
An unwanted pregnancy (patient, wife, or girlfriend)?	72	57	42	25	15

TABLE 7.3 (*Continued*)

	Weights				
	Within 0–1 mo.	*Within 1–6 mo.*	*Within 6–12 mo.*	*Within 1–2 yr.*	*Over 2 yr.*
Hospitalization of a family member for serious illness?	69	46	26	14	8
Unemployment more than one month (if regularly employed)?	57	42	20	10	6
Illness/injury kept in bed for week or more, hospital or emergency room?	65	48	25	12	5
An extra-marital affair?	62	50	37	25	17
The loss of a personally valuable object?	47	26	13	8	5
Involvement in a lawsuit (other than divorce)?	61	41	23	13	7
Failing an important examination?	62	37	19	9	5
Breaking an engagement?	65	47	27	14	7
Arguments with spouse (husband, wife, or mate)?	59	40	26	17	11
Taking on a large loan?	42	29	20	14	10
Being drafted into the military?	62	51	39	30	17
Troubles with boss or other workers?	50	23	9	4	3
Separation from a close friend?	49	36	24	16	10
Taking an important examination?	45	12	5	2	2
Separation from spouse because of job demands?	65	51	38	26	15
A big change in work or in school?	49	30	16	9	5
A move to another town, city, state or country?	46	32	20	10	5
Getting married or returning to spouse after separation?	60	45	34	23	18
Minor violations of the law?	31	15	7	3	2
Moved home within the same town or city?	25	13	7	3	2
The birth or adoption of a child?	52	39	26	18	15

(*Continued*)

TABLE 7.3 (*Continued*)

	Weights				
	Within 0–1 mo.	*Within 1–6 mo.*	*Within 6–12 mo.*	*Within 1–2 yr.*	*Over 2 yr.*
Being confused for over 3 days?	62	34	15	10	
Being angry for over 3 days?	52	25	10	5	
Being nervous for over 3 days?	48	23	10	5	Internal Events
Being sad for over 3 days?	46	24	12	6	
Spouse unfaithful?	68	55	40	27	19
Attacked, raped or involved in violent acts?	72	57	42	25	18

[a] These are the instructions to subjects who just indicate occurrence and frequency of events. The numbers are the weightings later applied to these subjects' check marks. Scores for internal events and external events are added separately. Investigators interested only in external events could simply delete internal events.
Source: Horowitz & Wilner (1980), p. 371. © American Psychological Association. Reprinted with permission.

These styles suggest differing ways in which people manage, and even seek out, stress.

In addition to measuring the amount of stress, it is also useful to consider the *coping abilities* of the individual. For example, one distinguishing characteristic among these four types was that the stress-prone tended to have problems in social relations, especially true for the younger men and women in the sample. Other personality characteristics also differed among these types:

> For example, among the older women, 100% of the stress-prone, as opposed to 57% of the avoiders, were high on a dimension labeled Flamboyance. Ninety percent of the avoiders were high on a dimension labeled Peace and Quiet, as opposed to 18% of the overwhelmed. Ninety percent of the lucky, and 80% of the stress-prone were high on a Play dimension, as opposed to only 42% of the overwhelmed. Seventy percent of the stress-prone were high on Intellectual Challenge, as compared to 33% of the overwhelmed. (Chiriboga & Cutler, 1980, p. 354)

Still another dimension of stress is **hassles** — those seemingly trivial events that are associated with children, health, finances, friends, neighbors, parents, social activities, spouse, relatives, and time pressure. Chiriboga and Cutler (1980) noted that women reported more family hassles than men at each of the four life stages; and newlyweds were more hassled about family matters than any other group. The older respondents reported more health hassles and also greater preoccupation with family stress (including hassles with children) than the other groups. Thus, when these data are combined with those presented earlier, this study suggested that older persons experience more stress than younger persons.

However, the change associated with stress was not always negative; improved adaptations were also indicated on several measures in this study (Chiriboga & Cutler, 1980). In a later analysis of these respondents, Chiriboga (1987) reported that those persons who experience relatively greater levels of stress show more evidence of change, either positive or negative — including change in health status — than those who report lower levels of stress. In general, the extent of change is greater on measures of morale or well-being; it is lower on measures of mental or physical health; and it is lowest on measures of one's self-concept.

Adaptive styles of coping with stress may evolve throughout the life cycle, and different styles may be appropriate for various types of stress. Individual differences in stress management are also relevant. For example, providing information about stressful medical procedures may increase discomfort for some by giving more detail than the individuals want, especially if they are unable to manage their fears and anxieties (Melamed, 1984). Similarly, *denial* was found to be a more effective coping style than the problem-focused style in a study of women with breast cancer (Cohen, 1980). Likewise, at least in institutional settings, passive strategies appear to be more prevalent among elderly persons than active coping styles (Cutler & Chiriboga, 1976); also they seem to lead to a greater sense of well-being (Felton & Kahana, 1974). However, several studies have suggested that institutionalized elderly persons and cancer patients may live longer if they show aggressive, complaining, and fighting emotional reactions as a coping style (Lazarus, 1984; Tobin, 1987).

Thus, the links between stress, coping style, and life circumstance are complex. One's sense of personal control, individual coping patterns, social support, life stage, and the nature of the illness are among the key variables now being studied.

Personality, Health, and Self-Reported Symptoms

Research on health is problematic because objective measures (such as laboratory tests) and subjective reports of symptoms do not always agree. Some people complain about health problems, but medical specialists can find nothing wrong, or vice versa. Many studies of older people rely on self-reported health status, as if this was a reliable indicator of physical health. In some studies the statistical correlation between self-rated and physician-rated health is not very high (Costa & McCrae, 1985). Moreover, objective measures of health are not always the most relevant measures. For example, behavior may reflect one's perception of wellness more than it reflects the physician's perspective of one's health.

This issue is especially troublesome when an individual reports many physical symptoms but shows no overt signs of illness. Such individuals may be suffering from **hypochondriasis,** which is characterized by an unfounded belief that they are in ill health (Barsky & Klerman, 1983). The origins of this belief are not clear, but Costa and McCrae (1985) suggested that it is strongly related to a personality trait they termed *neuroticism*. On the basis of data from the Baltimore Longitudinal Study of Aging (BLAS) in which the participants are a generally healthy, community-

The correlation of objective and subjective measures of health is not always high. Some persons complain of health problems, but specialists can find nothing wrong. Others function better than their objective health status would predict.

living sample, Costa and McCrae (1980a) found that men with higher scores on a measure of neuroticism also reported more complaints on a measure of medical symptoms (Figure 7.11). They argued that since personality is generally stable in adulthood (see Chapter 8), it is unlikely that poor health leads to personality change, and therefore personality characteristics probably lead to the degree of symptom reporting, instead of vice versa.

This topic is especially relevant for the elderly, who typically have more physical symptoms and therefore are at risk for being seen as hypochondriacs. Costa and McCrae (1985) phrased the issue concisely:

> If older individuals, or some identifiable subset of them, are in fact hypochondriacs, steps should be taken to redirect them from medical to psychiatric treatment. If, however, the elderly are *not* prone to hypochondriasis, then health care practitioners should be made aware of this and should reconsider their preconceptions. The presumption that older people exaggerate complaints may lead to halfhearted examination and treatment and may needlessly endanger the health of this segment of the population. (p. 24)

From the BLAS data, Costa and McCrae (1985) concluded that there are enduring individual differences in symptom reporting: those who reported few symptoms earlier in the study also reported relatively few later in the study; those who reported many symptoms continued to report many. Individual differences, then, related in part to neuroticism, were more important than age differences in predict-

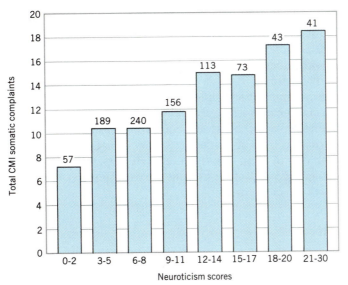

FIGURE 7.11 Mean somatic complaints on the Cornell Medical Index (CMI) for men grouped by neuroticism scores. *N*s given above bars. (*Source*: Costa & McCrae, 1985, Fig. 1, p. 21. © American Psychological Association. Reprinted with permission.)

ing the number of physical complaints. Moreover, hypochondriasis did not appear to be any more prevalent in old age than at younger ages in this study.

Behavioral Medicine

The field of behavioral medicine integrates the psychological study of behavior and biomedical science with the goal of promoting health and improving diagnosis, prevention, and treatment of illness and rehabilitation following disease or injury. It is possible here only to give a few examples of applications in this rapidly expanding field that are especially relevant to older persons.

Relaxation Therapy

Relaxation has long been recommended as a method for coping with stress and for promoting healing (Bloom, 1988). The use of natural mineral baths, spas, and hot tubs to promote relaxation is widely practiced. *Meditation* is also widely used to promote relaxation. **Biofeedback** is a procedure by which individuals learn to modify physiological functioning through auditory or visual feedback; this can be used to reduce muscle tension or other physical symptoms. *Progressive muscle relaxation* is a technique that involves successive tensing and relaxation of several muscle groups; once learned it can be linked with a cue to recall the experience. These techniques have been used with a variety of different symptoms, including insomnia, headaches, hypertension, anxiety, and pain. The systematic study of these techniques with older adults is relatively neglected, however.

One study by Arena, Hightower, and Chong (1988) illustrated the usefulness of the technique of progressive muscle relaxation with a small group of men and women between the ages of 62 and 80 who had experienced tension headaches for at least 10 years. Seven of the 10 subjects reported an improvement of 50 percent or greater on a diary record of headache activity over a period of three months following treatment; two of these reported complete cessation of headaches. This preliminary study suggested that older persons are as responsive as younger people to this type of behavioral medicine.

Compliance with Treatment

Any treatment procedure depends on the ability and willingness of the individual to cooperate with the treatment. A variety of factors affect the extent of **compliance.** Bloom (1988) estimated that one-third to one-half of patients do not follow a medical treatment program completely. He noted that patients often remember little of what physicians tell them, often as little as half of what was said; and adherence to treatment is related to the ways patients feel about how they are treated by health care professionals. Compliance is increased by patient education programs, tailoring the treatment to reduce the likelihood of the individual forgetting or losing track of dosage (such as a system of pill reminders), and the use of specific reinforcements such as praise to reward compliance.

None of these issues is unique with the elderly, but many may be especially relevant for them. A mild hearing difficulty may interfere with understanding the treatment; low income may make the treatment too costly; several different medications may get confusing or may produce unpleasant interactions. Thus, the physician can prescribe medication, but if it is not purchased, or not taken correctly, or taken in combination with certain foods, alcohol, or other medications, the result will not be effective; also it might produce adverse effects. Inadequate communication between the person and the physician may be at least partly responsible, and the physician may not be aware that the person is not following the treatment plan.

In one study, 141 persons between the ages of 65 and 74 who were living at home, retired, with above-marginal family income, and not bedridden were interviewed once a month for six months about their use of medications (Folkman, Bernstein & Lazarus, 1987). It was found that 48 percent of this relatively affluent and well-educated sample misused drugs at least once during the course of the study. The misuse involved lack of compliance, interactions between drugs (including over-the-counter medications and alcohol), and the use of multiple drugs of the same type. The results led to the following two recommendations:

> The first is that health care professionals and elderly persons themselves be made aware that seemingly innocent practices such as having an evening cocktail or taking over-the-counter medications in combination with particular prescribed drugs can lead to un-

wanted psychological and somatic symptoms. Particular care in this regard should be taken when psychoactive drugs are involved.

The second recommendation is that health care professionals and elderly persons be made aware that symptoms of psychological distress, including those associated with anxiety and depression, may not always be the side effects of a single drug or psychogenic in origin. Instead, these symptoms may be the result of drug misuse due to inappropriate usage, interactions, or the use of multiple drug agents from the same pharmacologic class. Rather than treating these symptoms with yet more drugs, health care professionals might consider that the problems may be due to misuse. (Folkman, Bernstein & Lazarus, 1987, p. 373)

Pharmacists can play an important role in educating customers about drug interactions and ways to avoid medication misuse, and in fact some pharmacies use computers to call attention to drug interactions among prescribed medications. But for older persons who take medication for a variety of symptoms, the potential for drug misuse is very real and at least one physician or pharmacist should be aware of all the drugs the individual is taking.

Finally, it should be noted that older persons are clearly capable of complying with treatment under suitable conditions. A study of antihypertensive medication to reduce rates of stroke among 551 persons over the age of 60 achieved compliance rates of over 80 percent over a one-year period (Black, Brand, Greenlick, Hughes & Smith, 1987). Compliance was measured by self-report, pill count, and urine tests. Although other studies have also reported high levels of compliance in older samples (and higher than for younger samples), a variety of strategies were used in this study to enhance compliance. These included a package of materials that explained the study and gave instructions; each of the participants was interviewed to assess their knowledge of the medication schedule, to reinforce compliance, and to identify any barriers to compliance; and frequent visits, with personal contact at each visit. A compliance self-report questionnaire also probably enhanced the level of compliance with the treatment. These techniques are examples of behavioral medicine that can be applied outside a research setting to enhance compliance with medical advice. Other practical suggestions include encouraging the patient to write out questions before the appointment, so that anxiety or shyness about relating to a professional does not inhibit effective communication.

Conclusion

Education and motivation for behavior change are critical aspects of effective medical treatment for persons of all ages. Since older persons are more likely than younger persons to require medical treatment, and may be receiving treatment for several conditions (possibly by several different health-care professionals), education and effective communication are especially important for older patients. For this reason, an integration of psychological principles of behavioral medicine with customary medical care is useful in general, but especially in geriatric medicine. The role of topics summarized in this section—such as Type A/B behavior, positive and negative stress, and personality characteristics—can be important in the prevention and treatment of many diseases, especially chronic diseases that cannot be cured by medical treatment but that rely on compliance and management of symptoms.

The next interlude illustrates many of these points since it is an interview with an older person who has experienced considerable stress during his life; the effect of stress on his health seems apparent. In addition, he is currently coping with the stress of bereavement and is continuing to work despite some chronic illness.

Chapter Summary

1. Each species of animal has a characteristic life span. Humans are the longest-lived mammal. Few species live much beyond their reproductive years (menopause in humans). Perhaps greater thinking capacity and memory provided an advantage during human evolution.

2. Heredity and aspects of the external environment influence the life span of individuals. Children of long-lived parents have a longer potential life span. Smoking, excess weight, urban living, and chronic disease reduce an individual's chances of longevity.

3. Diversity in patterns of aging is often overlooked. It is important to distinguish between usual characteristics of aging and successful patterns of aging within the normal population. Factors that contribute to successful aging include autonomy, social support, healthful diet, and exercise.

4. Aging is not simply the result of the body wearing out, or the loss of cells with age. Although there is no agreement about the cause of aging, considerable research has focused on physiological processes that may be involved. It is likely that different factors are responsible for aging in different organ systems.

5. Biochemical processes (such as free radicals) may affect cell function or play a role in diseases associated with aging. Decreased efficiency of processes that regulate the balance of the body's internal environment (homeostasis) is thought to reduce the body's ability to recover from physiological stress with advancing age. Changes in cellular processes with aging may interfere with the replication and functioning of cells. Dietary restriction appears to prolong life in rodents for reasons not fully understood.

6. Disease is a disorder of bodily function that may occur at any age. Although aging usually includes a greater risk of chronic disease, many of the changes often attributed to aging are better seen as the result of disease. Even in a healthy group of older persons, a subclinical level of disease brings important changes in physiological functioning.

7. Nutrition, heredity, health care, exposure to sunlight, and variations in exercise affect the extent of physical changes associated with aging such as graying or loss of hair, wrinkling of the skin, decrease in height, and loss of teeth. These changes may be seen as negative because of ageism in our society.

8. Changes in sleep patterns occur with age. The importance of specific changes is not understood, but many older persons are troubled by spontaneous interruption of sleep. Changes in behavior are more effective than medication in correcting sleep problems.

9. In general, higher levels of stimulation in vision, hearing, taste, and smell are required for older sense organs to perform as well as for younger persons. There is considerable individual variation in these changes. Most older people compensate effectively with glasses, hearing aids, creativity, and accurate information.

10. Bone loss known as osteoporosis increases with age, especially for women after menopause. Exercise and increased amounts of calcium in the diet are generally recommended, perhaps in combination with low-dosage estrogen-replacement therapy for postmenopausal women.

11. Chronic disease, such as arthritis, is more prevalent with aging. Death rates from heart disease are much greater than the rate for any other cause. Cancer is also a major cause of death, but it accounts for a greater proportion of deaths in middle age than in old age.

12. An emerging field of health psychology and behavioral medicine focuses on promoting and maintaining health, preventing and treating illness, and improving the health care system through changes in health policy. Education and behavior change are basic tools of health psychology.

13. Smoking, elevated blood pressure, high cholesterol levels, and obesity are associated with the risk of heart disease. Changes in behavior linked with these risk factors have played a major role in reducing the death rate from heart disease in recent years. Behavior related to the Type A personality also appears to be linked with heart disease.

14. Maintenance of an appropriate sense of control appears to be health promoting. Since aging and disease can reduce feelings of control, older persons may be especially vulnerable. Research has focused on ways to enhance an individual's sense of personal control.

15. Stress is not necessarily harmful, since most persons cope with it effectively. The ratio of positive to negative stresses, nature of daily hassles, coping style, social support, and life stage appear to affect how one manages stress.

16. Personality characteristics reflect individual differences in complaining about health problems. In general, older persons are no more likely than younger persons to report symptoms that are unfounded. However, persons who scored high on a measure of neuroticism were more likely to report medical symptoms than those who scored low.

17. Relaxation therapy using meditation, biofeedback, or progressive muscle relaxation is thought to be helpful in treating insomnia, headaches, hypertension, anxiety, and pain. Behavioral medicine has developed techniques to increase compliance with medical treatment through better understanding, communication, and motivation.

Key Words

acquired immune deficiency syndrome (AIDS)	force of mortality
	hassles
acute disease	heart disease
aging	hypochondriasis
arthritis	negative stress
biofeedback	osteoarthritis
cataract	physiological aging
chronic disease	positive stress
chronic impairments	senescence
collagen	successful patterns of aging
compliance	Type A behavior pattern
counterpart theory	Type B behavior pattern
disease	usual patterns of aging

Review Questions

Theories of Aging and Mortality

1. What is the counterpart theory of aging? How does it relate to evolution of the human species?

2. Give an example of how aging and longevity may be affected by (a) hereditary factors and (b) external factors.

3. Identify four theories of physiological aging and discuss two of them.

4. What would be some social consequences of a lengthened life span?

Disease: A Most Important Consideration

5. In the study by Birren et al. of healthy elderly men: (a) What was the difference in health between Group 1 and Group 2? (b) How did the two groups compare to each other? (Refer back to Chapter 4, where the data on speed of response were discussed.) (c) What did the study conclude about the effects of aging in the absence of disease?

Physical and Physiological Changes with Aging

6. How are physical characteristics affected by the combination of aging and disease-related changes that are common among older people?

7. What are the effects of aging on sleep patterns? Summarize the recommendations for dealing with sleeping problems.

8. How are the sense organs affected by aging?

9. What is osteoporosis? What measures can be taken to minimize it?

10. How prevalent are each of the following among older persons: (a) acute

diseases? (refer to Figure 7.5); (b) chronic diseases? (refer to Figure 7.6); (c) chronic impairments?

11. Describe Figure 7.7 in your own words. What is the leading cause of death for older persons?

Psychology and Health

12. Give some examples of how health psychology has been effective in the AIDS epidemic and in reducing the incidence of heart disease.

13. What is the Type A behavior pattern?

14. Describe some of the possible causes of a reduction in the sense of control among older people. What effects can this have on health?

15. Take your "stress temperature" (use Table 7.3). What coping strategies have you used to deal with the stress and hassles of life?

16. If older people complain about health problems, is it because of their age, their personality, or physical illness? Are older people more likely to be hypochondriacs?

17. Cite some techniques that can improve communication with medical professionals and some ways that compliance with medical treatment can be enhanced.

Henry, AGE 75

Henry is a 75-year-old man who recently suffered the death of his wife of 52 years when he was interviewed in 1973. He has continued to work because he could not manage on Social Security alone and because he will soon be eligible for a small pension from his union; he would have received a pension earlier, but he was unable to work for a time and lost the pension payments that he had built up; now he must work two more months in order to fulfill 15 continuous years work and receive his pension. He works as a waiter in a small restaurant, but when he was interviewed his feet were "burning" with arthritis after finishing his day's work, so our interview was ended prematurely. He is also suffering an increasing loss of hearing, which may reflect a general decline in health. He does not see how he will be able to continue working. And, with the death of his wife, he has suffered a severe emotional upset.

What will the future hold for him? What resources might he have to offset the loss of his wife and confidant? In what ways does he seem typical of old people in this country today? In what ways is he atypical? Why did he choose to talk about the milestones he picked — is there a sex difference in the milestones that men and women seem to choose to discuss? Is his difficulty in getting a pension a frequent problem for old people today? If he is no longer able to work, what do you think he will do? What could a social worker or a friend do to help?

What are some of the milestones that stand out in your life as you look back? What do you mean by "milestones"? *Some of the important events?* Was very important when I was married and had a nice son,

a school teacher, a very nice man. And I was very happy 'til 1972 when my wife passed away; I lived with her 52 years. *She just passed away?* Yeah, in November the 21st. *That must have been a very sad time for you.* That was very sad, a very sad time for me. And now life is not so much interested where it used to be. *How is your life different now?* Well, for a senior citizen, it's a very great difference when you lose your wife and you lose your companion; it is not so easy. When you're young you don't mind so much, but when you get old, it's pretty tough. *In what way is it so tough for you?* Tough in every way. In general, in life and everything. You've got no companionship; in everything. When I go home now I'm all by myself. Just coming into the house . . . making a little dinner for myself, and straighten out the house; see everything should be in order; and watch television, read a book. Don't sleep so good no more. *You were married 53 years ago now?* It's going on 53. I was married in 1920, October the 24th, 1920. *Was that a big event in your life?* Oh yeah. I had a beautiful wife, good looking, smart woman in every way; and I enjoyed life even though I wasn't a rich man. I was a poor man, but I enjoyed my life.

Were you born in this country? No, no. I was born in Russia. *How old were you when you came to this country?* I was about 18 years. *Was that a big event for you?* It was very surprising for me. I was studying, I don't know how they call it in English, not a rabbi, [the man] who kills the cattle — kosher, and all that. That's what I was supposed to be, but they drag me to the army because my brother and me was twins. One remain home, the other go because my father needed him for work, and I went to the army. I was in the army six months and I came to this country. Oh, it wasn't so easy. *Tell me about it.* When I came to the Russian Army, I was there six months, and then after six months when you take the second oath, they let you go in the city. Before I went to the city I wrote a letter home to my sister that I hate to be in the army. It's very tough to be in the Russian Army. So she said, "All right, I'll try to get together a few dollars and get an agent and we'll take you out of there." But it's very dangerous, because God forbid if you get caught —no court-martial, nothing; they shoot you right there on the spot. But finally I take the chance. I took that chance and came to the city. She wrote me where, and the agent was waiting for me, and he took me over and took off my uniform and everything, and he sent me away to a different city. Even if they should catch me without the clothes they would shoot me right away. Yes, martial law. *And then you came to America?* Yes, then I came here. It took me a long time. I came here with the boat. I was sailing about 26 days and nights and I lost . . . I weighed 160 pounds when I left; when I came here I weighed 120 pounds. I lost on the boat, because I couldn't eat and I couldn't drink nothing. I was vomiting. I couldn't take the sea. Seasick.

And what did you do when you came here? So when I came here I got a little job, you know, in the grocery store, because I couldn't speak. I got sick after that. I got a tumor and I lost my speech. That's why I became the counterman in the waiter business; my buddy who was singing in the Hebrew College, I learned with him, he was the sexton in the temple. I couldn't make it [as a cantor] on account of my voice. Finally I had an operation. At that time years ago they did not know so much about cancer, and Dr. B. operated on me and took out that growth; and it took me three years to get back my voice and my speech, and

then I was off my track. It was too late already to go again.

Then I worked as a grocer for three-and-a-half dollars a week, but 12 hours a day or more, six-and-a-half days a week; no, no, too many hours. It was very tough, very tough. And then I bought myself a suit for two dollars. An old one, secondhand; you could put two like me in there [it was so big]. I went to the man and I paid him a quarter a week; eight quarters; in eight weeks I paid him off for the suit and then I bought myself a pair of secondhand shoes. You shouldn't wear no secondhand shoes. I didn't have the money. What can I do? I slept by a shoemaker on the floor for a dollar a week. *Could you speak English?* No. I went to night school to learn a little; but I was so tired. As soon as I came into school I fell asleep right away. So the teacher say it's no good for you; you come to school, you sleep, you don't learn. So I says to her I try to learn by myself, and I did. I used to get books and learn by myself little by little; it takes me a long time, but I learned. Well, of course, I speak a little bit an accent, you know.

Then my brother came along from Russia too, so after a few years we work together. He was a carpenter, and I went with him to help him bring the lumber. So we saved a little money and then we opened up a candy store. And I was in the candy store and he was working as a carpenter. So I was making a little money. I was making that time about nine, ten dollars in the candy store and it was a tough life. Used to get up five o'clock in the morning and work 'til two o'clock in the morning. Oh, it was very tough.

When did you get married? I got married about eight years later. I met the girl in the candy store. She was a nice girl; she came to buy a piece of candy so I got acquainted with her and she brought another friend. So the friend my brother took . . . he should rest in peace, he's dead already . . . and I took this one here. So that's how it is. *Was it a big moment when your children were born?* I have only son. Of course I was very surprised. It was a boy. And my wife said, "Well, once you sell the candy store you buy another candy store, you fix up the candy store, you can't have too many children because you're moving around; one is enough." So we had one child.

Were there any other big moments in your life? Yes, I remember some. Three . . . (he counts on his fingers) . . . three years and eight months [ago] I went to Russia to see my brother, the youngest one. I had a very nice time. I was in Moscow, in Kiev, and Leningrad. And I met my brother and I enjoyed myself very nicely because I haven't seen him close to 60 years. And he remained alive. All the other family, my sisters and brothers, Hitler killed them. There was about 220 people from the family; everybody was killed. But this trip I enjoyed very very much. That was a great surprise in my life.

Do you have any grandchildren? Yes, one grandson. He goes to college. Oh, a beautiful boy; he was on the hockey team; a powerful kid, very nice boy. And I got my daughter-in-law; she is a manager in a department store; very nice person.

How about crisis points; were there any very difficult points for you? Difficult? Oh, yeah; was plenty of problems. When my son was drafted I felt very very bad. He was drafted and he was sent away on the other side and I didn't hear from him about six months. And I felt very bad and I got from loneliness — I figured that maybe I lose my son — I got like a paralytic stroke on my right side. Oh, was terrible! It took me about a year to get better. One day I was downstairs with a cane and I see under the door there's a telegram laying for me. I was so upset I couldn't take out the telegram, so I had the next door neighbor come over. So she took out the telegram, she says okay, your son is in the hospital. Thank God, you know,

my son was in the hospital, he isn't killed. But he was very sick; he was there with malaria, very bad sickness.

What happened with your paralysis? I went to a chiropractor. And he takes my leg and brings it over here to my head in the back and I fainted. He went over and got a pitcher of cold water and washed me down and I came to and he said, "Don't worry, you wouldn't die." And he take the same leg and bring it here. Finally he gave me about 25 adjustments. Every day I supposed to come there and I couldn't ride a taxi because I couldn't take the shaking; that was terrible. *Did he cure you?* He did! *You weren't able to work then, were you?* No, I couldn't bend! I couldn't walk! No, I didn't work. Was no financial money; my brother-in-law helped me a little, but that time was no union, nothing to help you. So [one day] when I came home my wife wasn't home so she prepared me something to eat and I walked into the house; instead of eating the sleep went on me. I couldn't keep my eyes open. So I crept into the bed with my clothes and I laid down and I fell asleep and I slept maybe five, six hours. And then when I get up, I get off the bed like a new man. I got off the bed and I started walking. I could walk! *And that was it?* So, I called the doctor and he said, "Go to work! And come to me once a week and then I'll massage you." And then I went to work.

What kind of job did you go to then? I worked in a restaurant. I worked there quite a number of years. Then the restaurant went under, and I went to work for a man on Broadway, and I'm working for him 28 years already. And to him it's just like I came today. He don't give a damn! No pension, no nothing.

No pension? No pension, because I'm in the union not even 15 years. I worked without a union. And I can't work; I got to retire. I can't work. Impossible for my legs. Don't forget, I'm 75 years old. I can't work, and I've got no pension. *Why don't you have a pension at 75?*

I'm trying to finish up yet; another couple week maybe, to pay into the union, to the pension. It's got to be paid in $160 and I haven't got the money to pay. *How long do you have to work before you get a pension?* You got to work at least 15 years in the union. *How much longer do you have to go?* The union says another couple months. And I can't do it. Here I'm sitting now. My feet are really burning like fire. *So you're just living on Social Security now?* Yeah, I get $165.20 a month. *Is that enough?* No. I need what I make here. I make here a couple dollars. But if I wouldn't work, then it would be tough for me. And from the union I could get, if I do get a pension, I get $52.75 a month. *That's not much.* Sure not. Especial the way, oh years ago — about 30 years ago — it would be fine, because the rent is very high. My rent is $150 a month. *So that's almost all your Social Security right there for rent.* Yeah, and then you got electric, telephone! And lodge money, insurance. Big expense! *What do you think is going to happen?* I have to go on welfare. They wouldn't take me. They wouldn't give me welfare. *Have you ap-*plied for welfare? Yeah, they wouldn't give me. *How would you feel about going on welfare if you have to?* I don't want to; I don't want to; I hate that. Maybe Medicare would be better for me — the medicines and doctor bills, because it's a lot of medications. It costs a lot of money. I'm trying this (he stands up) — maybe this way it should be better circulation; oh, it [his feet] feels burning. Okay Professor, we're going to go!

I talked with Henry about six months after this interview and learned that he had received his pension after working only a couple of additional weeks; his employer paid the necessary amount to the union pension fund and did not require Henry to work the remaining time. He seemed to be feeling well, and his health had improved after he no longer had to work everyday. However, I was unable to contact him in 1979; although the union had no record that he had died, he did not respond to my letter requesting an interview and his telephone had been disconnected.

CHAPTER 8

Personality and Psychopathology

A t a commonsense level we probably all assume that the human adult is a complex creature who possesses a unique and relatively stable *personality*. For example, some adults seem to be particularly daring, bold, and extroverted; others seem to be quiet, conservative, and introverted; and still others impress us with their sensitivity, their warmth and generosity, their dependability (and so on). Each of us, it would seem, has an individual style, a uniqueness, a characteristic set of attributes that distinguish us from others and also help to make us recognizably similar in different situations and at different times over the years. Such assumptions are clearly useful since most people are rather consistent in their behavior patterns from day to day (and those who are not tend to be labeled "mentally ill"). Moreover, the existence of relatively stable personalities is obviously a necessary assumption for human interaction to proceed smoothly. Consider the chaos that would result if we all woke up each morning with a new personality: one's cheerful, cooperative spouse today might be a demanding tyrant tomorrow; the capable, efficient boss of yesterday might be an indecisive, guilt-ridden neurotic today and a dictator tomorrow; the calm, reliable newscaster last night might become a biased bigot the next morning; and one's trusted friends, the national leaders, and the corner druggist might all become totally unpredictable. In such a situation, human interaction as we know it would become, at least, unpredictable and immensely difficult; at worst, it would be totally impossible. If we could not rely on some kind of predictability of the personality characteristics of oneself and of others, we would be as unable to interact with each other in meaningful ways as would be the case (pointed out in Chapter 2) if we all stopped playing social roles; in either case, each interaction would have to begin anew without the great advantage of prior experience and a set of expectations. It would be an impossibly confusing world indeed!

There are several different definitions of **personality,** but most of them emphasize three major characteristics. First, personality reflects an individual's *uniqueness* as a person. Whatever attributes are seen as making up an individual's personality, they set him or her apart from other individuals or groups of individuals and they describe that person or that "type" of person as someone different from other persons or other types of persons. Second, personality theories focus on those attributes of a person that are fairly *stable* over a long period of time and across many different situations. It seems that our Western culture is based on the assumption that an individual's personality is reasonably stable under ordinary circumstances. That is, unless there are mitigating circumstances, or one is mentally ill, one should behave in a manner consistent with one's past personality. Third, personality is seen as the *link between the person and the social and physical environment;* in that sense, it reflects the individual's pattern or style of adaptation to the environment. This does not necessarily imply that the person is passively adapting to an all-powerful environment; instead, the individual may best be seen as actively interpreting, creating, and modifying the environment while at the same time the environment affects the individual.

Although each of the several differing approaches to personality tends to emphasize these three characteristics, most focus greater attention on only one or two of them. For example, anthropologists emphasize the link between the person and the social and physical environment—as in studies of differences between individuals in farming societies compared with hunting and gathering societies, or the effects of urbanization on personality patterns. Freudian psychoanalysts stress the continuity of personality, examining links between early childhood experiences and adult behavior. Personality psychologists are frequently interested in identifying characteristics that make people different from one another, thus emphasizing personality traits such as the factors involved in occupational choice (discussed in Chapter 6). Behavioral psychologists and sociologists tend to emphasize the role of the environment, sometimes almost to the exclusion of a focus on the uniqueness of the person or the continuity of personality in different situations. And developmental psychologists tend to study the stability and change of personality over time, often paying little attention to the uniqueness of specific individuals and sometimes ignoring the effects of the social and physical environment in which the person is developing. As may be apparent from the general perspective of this book, the view we will emphasize here includes all three of these characteristics of personality. The Interludes in between the chapters emphasize the uniqueness of individuals; the interdisciplinary approach focuses on the link between the person and the environment; and the developmental framework calls attention to the issue of continuity and change in personality.

Throughout this chapter we pick up themes mentioned earlier in the book—the simultaneous processes of stability and change during adulthood, the notion of transitions, the dialectical model of development, the effects of changes in the family and the occupation, and the effects of physiological and biological changes. In that sense, this chapter pulls together many ideas we have discussed separately, and it also sets the stage for a discussion of the experience of growing old in our society that will be the topic of the next chapter. We begin with a discussion of personality differences between men and women. Then we turn to an examination of the nature of personality in adulthood and describe patterns of stability and change with aging. We conclude the chapter with a discussion of atypical changes in personality that sometimes require treatment by mental health professionals.

Gender Differences in Personality

Differences between men and women may be seen as the result of an interaction among physiological factors (e.g., hormones before and after birth), psychological influences (e.g., relations with parents and other role models), and social experiences (e.g., socialization). Each factor is influenced by the others, and the result is different from each of the separate factors. Because of the interaction of these factors, men and women differ in a variety of ways that are known as gender differences. Many of these gender differences are the result of pervasive and subtle sex-related norms and expectations in our culture. Gender differences in behavior are even greater in other cultures (such as Hispanic or Moslem countries or in Japan), and are less extensive in some other cultures (such as Israel or Scandinavia). The term **gender** is used instead of *sex* with regard to these differences because they do not result from biological sex alone, but from the interaction of social, psychological, and physiological factors.

At the same time that we discuss gender differences, we need also note that men and women are probably at least as similar as they are different and there is considerable individual variation. Thus, men and women need not be assumed to be *opposite* to one another: active versus passive, rational versus emotional, independent versus dependent, and so on. Instead of this commonly assumed oppositeness, we stress both the similarities and the differences. For example, a well-adjusted man or woman may be high on both "masculine" and "feminine" qualities. Both sets of characteristics can be defined to consist of traits that are not opposite each other: a man can be both tender and strong, and a woman can be both assertive and sensitive, for example. Similarly, one woman may be less "feminine" than another, but need not be any more "masculine." As long as it is clear that "masculine" is not necessarily the opposite of "feminine," both sets of personality characteristics may involve positive, adaptive, and different qualities.

We feel that less confusion results if it is kept in mind that men and women are probably as similar as they are different; they share many of the basic human characteristics of individuals in our society, and they share many of the same social values and attitudes. For this reason we prefer not to term them "opposite sexes." Women are one sex (gender) and men are the *other* gender, and vice versa.

Gender Roles and Stereotypes

An individual's culture defines what it means to be a man and a woman. Gender roles are not the same in every society, however. Margaret Mead (1949/1967), in her classic study *Male and Female,* described the variety of gender roles in different cultures:

> In every known society, mankind has elaborated the biological division of labour into forms often very remotely related to the original biological differences that provided the original clues. Upon the contrast in bodily form and function, men have built analogies between sun and moon, night and day, goodness and evil, strength and tenderness, steadfastness and fickleness, endurance and vulnerability. Sometimes one quality has been assigned to one sex, sometimes to the other. Now it is boys who are thought of as infinitely vulnerable and in need of special cherishing care, now it is girls. In some societies it is girls for whom parents must collect a dowry or make husband-catching magic, in others the parental worry is over the difficulty of marrying off the boys. Some peoples think of women as too weak to work out of doors, others regard women as the appropriate bearers of heavy burdens, "because their heads are stronger than men's." The periodicities of female reproductive functions have appealed to some peoples as making women the natural sources of magical or religious power, to others as directly antithetical to those powers; some religions, including our European traditional religions, have assigned women an inferior role in the religious hierarchy, others have built their whole symbolic relationship with the supernatural world upon male imitations of the natural functions of women. In some cultures women are regarded as sieves through whom the best-guarded secrets will sift; in others it is the men who are the gossips. Whether we deal with small matters or with large, with the frivolities of ornament and cosmetics or the sanctities of man's place in the universe, we find this great variety of

An individual's culture defines what it means to be a man or woman.

ways, often flatly contradictory one to the other, in which the roles of the two sexes have been patterned. (pp. 7–8)

Differences between the gender roles of women and men in the United States have been conceptualized as stereotypes that portray masculinity and femininity as opposite to each other on a number of characteristics. For example, Rosenkrantz and his colleagues (Rosenkrantz, Vogel, Bee, Broverman & Broverman, 1968) found that 41 items were agreed on by at least 75 percent of a college sample as either "masculine" or "feminine" (Table 8.1).

Such stereotypes tend to be internalized by the person as guides for one's behavior and feelings. Since the "feminine" traits tend to be less highly valued than "masculine" traits, women who adopt these traits may tend to have lower self-esteem than men (Broverman, Vogel, Broverman, Clarkson & Rosenkrantz, 1972, p. 75). In addition, many women tend to place greater importance on external or interpersonal sources of esteem and, consequently, less emphasis is placed on competitive achievement. This difference need not have negative effects on women's self-esteem, except that in our society objective accomplishment tends to be valued more than interpersonal skill. Thus, "masculine" characteristics and "masculine" sources of esteem tend to be more highly valued than "feminine" characteristics and sources of esteem.

TABLE 8.1 Stereotypic Sex-Role Items (Responses from 74 College Men and 80 College Women)

Competency Cluster: Masculine pole is more desirable

Feminine	Masculine
Not at all aggressive	Very aggressive
Not at all independent	Very independent
Very emotional	Not at all emotional
Does not hide emotions at all	Almost always hides emotions
Very subjective	Very objective
Very easily influenced	Not at all easily influenced
Very submissive	Very dominant
Dislikes math and science very much	Likes math and science very much
Very excitable in a minor crisis	Not at all excitable in a minor crisis
Very passive	Very active
Not at all competitive	Very competitive
Very illogical	Very logical
Very home oriented	Very worldly
Not at all skilled in business	Very skilled in business
Very sneaky	Very direct
Does not know the way of the world	Knows the way of the world
Feelings easily hurt	Feelings not easily hurt
Not at all adventurous	Very adventurous
Has difficulty making decisions	Can make decisions easily
Cries very easily	Never cries
Almost never acts as a leader	Almost always acts as a leader
Not at all self-confident	Very self-confident
Very uncomfortable about being aggressive	Not at all uncomfortable about being aggressive
Not at all ambitious	Very ambitious
Unable to separate feelings from ideas	Easily able to separate feelings from ideas
Very dependent	Not at all dependent
Very conceited about appearance	Never conceited about appearance
Thinks women are always superior to men	Thinks men are always superior to women
Does not talk freely about sex with men	Talks freely about sex with men

Warmth-Expressiveness Cluster: Feminine pole is more desirable

Feminine	Masculine
Doesn't use harsh language at all	Uses very harsh language
Very talkative	Not at all talkative
Very tactful	Very blunt
Very gentle	Very rough
Very aware of feelings of others	Not at all aware of feelings of others
Very religious	Not at all religious
Very interested in own appearance	Not at all interested in own appearance
Very neat in habits	Very sloppy in habits
Very quiet	Very loud
Very strong need for security	Very little need for security
Enjoys art and literature	Does not enjoy art and literature at all
Easily expresses tender feelings	Does not express tender feelings at all easily

Source: Broverman et al. (1972), p. 63. Copyright © 1972. Reprinted with permission

Women . . . tend to esteem themselves only insofar as they are esteemed by those they love and respect. Unlike the man, who is considered successful when he has achieved within his occupation, the woman who achieves is generally not considered successful unless she also has a husband and children. (Bardwick, 1971, p. 158)

Simone de Beauvoir (1953) analyzed the role of women as an *object,* by which she meant more than a "sex object" (although it is only recently that men have been seen as sex objects in magazine pictures and on television). She argued that men function as a *subject*—active, manipulating, controlling, and generally taking an active stance toward the world of objects that includes women. Women, however, are like objects—they are looked at, manipulated, and are generally passive.

These stereotypes about men and women in Western cultures a few decades ago provided the basis for a significant reconceptualization of gender roles during the 1970s. Enhanced by the Civil Rights movement of the 1960s and widely available methods of birth control that women could use on their own, women and men began to explore new ways of thinking about gender differences. It also became clear that women were not the only sex that was limited by its gender role.

Pleck and Sawyer (1974) noted that the male stereotype means that "getting ahead" is an important theme for boys and men. Whether it is through grades in school, prowess in sports, or success at work, men's performance is tested in competition with other men. Winning once is not enough, for men often feel they have to keep winning, continue evaluating themselves in relation to other men and, as a result, never really win once and for all. This may leave many men dissatisfied with their lives. Another major theme is "staying cool, no matter what." That is, men do not cry; they show excitement only in particular settings such as sports events, and they tend to repress their emotions even to the extent of not showing tenderness or fear, and muting or controlling their joy and anger. As a result, men may not fully experience their emotions, may ignore signs of physical or emotional distress, and tend to place greater stress on their body through the denial of feelings.

Other elements of the male role stereotype were suggested by David and Brannon (1976, p. 12):

1. No Sissy Stuff: The stigma of all stereotyped feminine characteristics and qualities, including openness and vulnerability.

2. The Big Wheel: Success, status, and the need to be looked up to.

3. The Sturdy Oak: A manly air of toughness, confidence, and self-reliance.

4. Give 'Em Hell!: The aura of aggression, violence, and daring.

These characteristics suggest that the male role is achieved by continual effort. In that sense, "masculinity" may be threatened at any point by "sissy stuff" or by not being sufficiently independent, self-reliant, and powerful. This implies an element of chronic insecurity and vulnerability that may affect a wide range of behaviors and interpersonal relationships. For example, feelings of competition, fears of homosexuality, distrust of openness and vulnerability, and a lack of close friendship with other men may be the result of this male role stereotype (Lewis, 1978). It may also lead men to engage in behaviors that are hazardous. Waldron (1976) estimated that in the 1970s the male role contributed about 75 percent to the shorter life expectancy of men and women, as compared with women; cigarette smoking alone con-

The male stereotype can lead men to think that masculinity requires avoiding any "sissy stuff."

tributed between one-third and one-half of the difference. The difference in the ratio of men and women who smoke cigarettes is less today, and lung cancer has surpassed breast cancer in prevalence among women. However, women still outlive men, on the average, by several years.

Personality Similarities: Androgyny

Stereotypes about men and women assume that masculinity and femininity are opposite one another; that is, the more masculine one is, the less feminine one is. But are men and women really opposite each other in personality characteristics? Several theoretical analyses of human development have argued that both men and women have different degrees of similar characteristics, not different sets of characteristics, and that maturity involves establishing a blend of both masculine and feminine attributes (Bakan, 1966; Jung, 1933). This approach began to receive a great deal of attention in the 1970s and remains a compelling perspective for understanding gender during adulthood and old age.

If we assume that masculinity and femininity are not opposite characteristics (a bipolar model), but that they are parallel sets of characteristics (a duality model), then an individual may be higher on one than on the other, or equally high or low on both. In this approach, a masculine person would be high on characteristics associated with masculinity and low on characteristics associated with femininity; a feminine person would be high on femininity and low on masculinity; and an *androgynous* person would be high on both masculinity and femininity, or at least

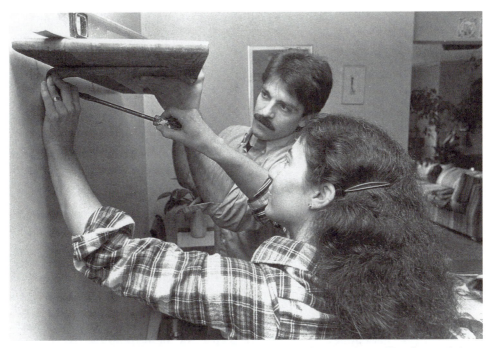

Androgyny may be defined as a blending of both masculine and feminine personality characteristics.

equal in the degree of masculinity and femininity. Thus, **androgyny** may be defined as a mixture or blending of both masculine and feminine personality characteristics. It implies that an individual may be both assertive and compassionate, for example, depending on the situation, or that a person may be able to act assertively while at the same time being sensitive to the impact of the action on the relationships with the other people involved. This approach implies that many important human characteristics are not, and should not be, confined to either one gender or the other. Also, it implies that a man may be no less masculine, but possibly more fully human, if he is androgynous; or that a woman may be no less feminine, but perhaps more completely human, if she is androgynous. Obvious examples include fathers caring for and reacting sensitively to their children and spouse, or mothers who are able to achieve success in a "masculine" career.

Two slightly different methods have been used to measure androgyny. In both, an inventory of gender-role characteristics, such as the list of stereotypes presented earlier (Table 8.1), is given to a group of men and women. The most widely used are the Bem Sex Role Inventory (Bem, 1974, 1977) and the Personal Attributes Questionnaire (Spence & Helmreich, 1978; Spence, Helmreich & Stapp, 1975). Scores on a scale of masculinity and on a separate scale of femininity are then analyzed. One method of classifying the respondents is to compare the difference between an individual's scores on the two scales (Bem, 1974). This results in five groups:

1. Feminine: much higher on femininity than on masculinity.

2. Masculine: much higher on masculinity than on femininity.

3. Near-feminine: slightly more feminine than masculine.

4. Near-masculine: slightly more masculine than feminine.

5. Androgynous: equal on masculinity and femininity.

In a study of 723 college students, Bem (1975) found that about one-third of the males and one-quarter of the females were androgynous. Thirty-six percent of the males were distinctly masculine with almost no feminine characteristics, and 34 percent of the women were distinctly feminine with almost no masculine characteristics. Very few of the respondents described themselves primarily by characteristics of the other gender (Table 8.2).

The second method of analyzing the scores divides the sample into those who are above and below the average score on the separate masculinity and femininity scales (Spence et al., 1975). This produces four groups: masculine (high on masculinity and low on femininity), feminine (low on masculinity, high on femininity), androgynous (high on both), and undifferentiated (low on both). In a study of 715 college students, Spence and Helmreich (1978) found that the proportions in the androgynous, feminine, and masculine categories were quite similar to those in Bem's findings. That is, 27 percent of the women and 32 percent of the men were androgynous; one-third of the women were feminine; one-third of the men were masculine; and about one-quarter of the respondents were in the undifferentiated category (low on both masculinity and femininity).

Androgynous persons have been found to have greater maturity in moral judgment (Block, 1973), greater self-esteem (Spence, et al., 1975), higher levels of both independence and nurturance when appropriate (Bem, 1975), and are able to perform cross-gender behavior with little reluctance or discomfort (Bem & Lenney, 1976).

Both Bem (1977) and Spence et al. (1975) found self-esteem to be related to these gender-role characteristics. Androgynous and masculine respondents were

TABLE 8.2 *Percentage of College Student Respondents in Each of the Five Sex-Role Categories*

Sex Role	Females (N = 444)	Males (N = 279)
Feminine	34	6
Near-feminine	20	5
Androgynous	27	34
Near-masculine	12	19
Masculine	8	36

Source: Bem (1975), Table 1. Copyright © 1975 by the American Psychological Association. Adapted and reprinted with permission.

higher in self-esteem than feminine or undifferentiated respondents among both men and women (Table 8.3); Spence and Helmreich (1978) found a similar relationship.

Thus, gender role may be more important than biological sex in understanding gender differences in self-esteem. However, this perspective allows the analysis to be carried a significant step further—it also allows an analysis of the interaction between sex and gender role. That is, using the respondents' actual scores on masculinity and femininity, Bem (1977) found different patterns for men and women on self-esteem. In men, self-esteem was related to masculinity, but unrelated to femininity. In women, self-esteem was associated with both masculinity and femininity. This suggests that self-esteem is associated with masculine characteristics for both men and women. However, men were high on self-esteem if they were high on masculinity, regardless of whether they were high or low on femininity, whereas women were highest on self-esteem if they were high on both masculinity and femininity and lowest if they were low on both. We must be cautious in generalizing this finding for two reasons, however. First, Spence and Helmreich (1978) reported data that contradicted Bem's findings. They found that for both sexes, masculinity (M) and femininity (F) scores were positively related to self-esteem. Thus, persons high on both M and F (androgynous) had higher self-esteem; persons low on both M and F had lower self-esteem. Both men and women who were high on either M *or* F tended to have higher self-esteem than those persons who were low on both. Second, recalling the Livson (1976) study discussed in Chapter 3, the "traditional" women appeared to experience less turmoil during middle age than the "independent" women; it is this latter group who might be termed androgynous, but their self-esteem and psychological health were relatively low during their forties—not until age 50 did their self-esteem match the higher level of the traditionally feminine women.

Considerable research followed from these ideas. Several studies have focused on changes during adulthood. One study (Hyde & Phillis, 1979) used the Bem Sex Role Inventory with a sample of 289 men and women between the ages of 13 and 85

TABLE 8.3 *Self-Esteem Scores as a Function of Sex-Role Classification*

	Bem Study		Spence et al. Study	
Sex Role	*Females (N = 71)*	*Males (N = 93)*	*Females (N = 270)*	*Males (N = 234)*
Androgynous	126.0	117.1	98.7	93.7
Masculine	115.6	119.8	92.2	87.0
Feminine	107.6	100.6	75.4	74.6
Undifferentiated	99.5	103.5	69.7	66.8

Note: In these two studies, self-esteem was measured by using different versions of the Texas Social Behavior Inventory.
Source: Bem (1977), Table 2; Spence et al. (1975), Table 4. Copyright © 1977, 1975 by the American Psychological Association. Adapted and reprinted with permission.

years. They found older men to be more androgynous than younger men, whereas women showed the opposite trend (Table 8.4). Another study (Sinnott, 1982) found that 53 percent of the 364 respondents (senior center members; age range 60–90 years) were androgynous; men had more nearly equal scores on the masculine and feminine scales than did women, however. When compared with data from other studies with different age groups, the older women had the highest scores on femininity of any group (Figure 8.1). Since we do not know the femininity scores of these older women earlier in their lives, they may have been even more feminine earlier in life and, like the men, have become more androgynous (the data in these studies are cross-sectional so that historical or cohort changes and age-related changes are impossible to separate). We discuss changes in gender role with aging from a different perspective later in this chapter.

In Sinnott's (1982) study, the androgynous group of men and women had more desirable scores on items reflecting mental health and successful aging; masculinity (M) scores were more highly associated with these items than femininity (F) scores were — as has been found in younger samples noted earlier. However, both sexes who had high F scores and low M scores tended to be more stressed and disadvantaged, whereas those with high M scores and low F scores had signs of greater life advantages (e.g., income, education, health). Perhaps, therefore, older women had higher F scores in part because they were more stressed and had lower life advantages; these factors may also partially explain the link between higher M scores and better mental health.

In another analysis of these data, Sinnott (1984b) noted that there were only three areas of disagreement between men and women about their *most important* characteristics. "Thus, the two sexes described themselves in very similar ways that included both "M" and "F" attributes" (p. 849).

Cunningham and Antill (1984) found that involvement with work and educational study was more important than family "stage" in terms of gender role. Some of their findings, using a sample of 582 Australian adults, were:

TABLE 8.4 *Percentages of Males and of Females Who Are Androgynous, Masculine, Feminine, or Undifferentiated according to the Categorical Scoring Procedure*

		Females					Males			
Age	n	Andro-gynous	Mascu-line	Femi-nine	Undiffer-entiated	n	Andro-gynous	Mascu-line	Femi-nine	Undiffer-entiated
13–20	56	26	16	46	13	47	9	49	6	36
21–40	42	31	10	50	10	25	4	52	4	40
41–60	37	11	22	46	22	32	31	59	0	9
61 and over	30	7	13	73	7	20	40	35	0	25
Total	165	20	15	52	13	124	18	51	3	28

Source: Hyde & Phillis (1979), Table 1. © American Psychological Association. Reprinted with permission.

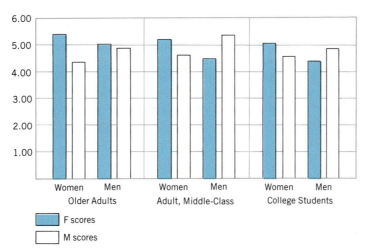

FIGURE 8.1 Comparison of BSRI scores across age and sex. (*Source*: Adapted from Sinnott, 1982, Table 1. Reprinted with permission.)

When the woman was employed, she had lower femininity scores, and her partner slightly lower masculinity scores, than when she was not. The presence of children in the home had no effect on women's or men's self-descriptions. . . .

[T]hose women who are supported financially by a man—wives who are not employed—scored lowest on masculinity of all women. Employed mothers had substantially higher masculinity scores . . . than nonemployed mothers. . . .

Motherhood did not make women more feminine or less masculine; fatherhood did not make men more masculine or less feminine. (p. 1140)

We should note that the data in these studies do not allow us to determine whether masculine or feminine personality characteristics reflect these differences in income, education, employment, and parenthood—or whether persons high on M characteristics are drawn more to education and high-income employment than are persons high on F characteristics. That is, these correlational data do not permit conclusions about cause and effect relationships between variables.

Moreover, Sinnott (1988) noted that we must not jump to conclusions that responses on a scale will predict behavior. Although the responses to these gender-role questionnaires do appear to be meaningful, and androgyny may be the most adaptive response in many circumstances, we cannot define precisely what role these M and F scores play in actual behavior, especially in different social situations, and at different ages. Later in this chapter we discuss stability and change in personality and will return to gender differences and androgyny.

In conclusion, studies on androgyny promise to be an interesting area of research in the future. Since there is considerable evidence that men and women are similar in many ways, there is little reason to assume that their personalities are made up of opposite characteristics. Instead, the differences may be more a matter of circumstance, cohort, and place in the life span than of a simple dichotomy between masculine and feminine. Many people appear to merge masculine and feminine characteristics into an apparently adaptive personality style. Thus, continued research into androgyny throughout the life span may be particularly useful now that men and women are individually exploring the meaning of masculinity and femininity and the mixture of the two for their own self-realization through the life cycle.

In the next two sections of this chapter we shift our focus from gender to age differences and consider the processes that produce continuity and change in adult personality over time.

Continuity and Change in Personality over Time

Throughout earlier chapters we have suggested numerous ways in which an individual's personality would be likely to change as one moves through transitions in adulthood, for example, the resocialization of parenthood, occupational socialization, the midlife transition, and the response to physical disability or chronic disease. Yet, the concept of personality emphasizes continuity and implies that individuals are not changed in important ways by such events. This raises several interesting questions: Does personality remain fairly stable over 10 or 20 or more years? What aspects of personality are highly stable? What are the processes that bring about this stability? Conversely, how much change is there in personality over time and in what aspects of it?

In Chapter 2, we discussed the process of stability and change in detail. We concluded that continuity and change are simultaneous processes, so that individuals change in some ways while they also remain stable in many ways. We noted that *change* may be brought about by change in the external environment, by changes in social roles or by socialization and resocialization, or by changes within the self. *Continuity* results from the memory of past experiences and habitual patterns that work efficiently in social situations, the selection of fairly consistent social environments, the tendency to perceive situations as consistent even when they are not, and the tendency to pay more attention to situations that confirm what we expect while ignoring those that conflict with our expectations. In Chapter 1, we introduced the dialectical perspective that suggested that these processes of stability and change may be seen as a continuous dialectical interaction. That is, development consists of an ongoing struggle between stability and change. In this view, continuity is only a period when the various aspects of one's life are synchronized; discontinuity, or change, is much more frequent since all dimensions of one's life are seldom in total harmony. Most of this discontinuity is fairly mild; but during periods of transition the discontinuity is more dramatic, and significant changes sometimes result (as discussed in Chapter 3).

Taken together, these perspectives suggest that personality has two distinct facets—change and stability (or continuity). To a large extent, which aspect of personality one observes is determined by the "lenses" one uses. If one looks for continuity (as with Freudian lenses), it will be observed. If one seeks change (as

Personality has two distinct aspects: change and stability. Whether one sees change or stability depends upon which aspect one looks for.

with behaviorist lenses), it also can be found. In reality, both processes occur simultaneously, and the development of an individual's personality probably results from this dialectical struggle between change and continuity over time. Perhaps that dialectical process cannot be observed directly, so we are forced to choose between viewing it through continuity lenses or change lenses, or alternating from one to the other. Thus, there may always be an element of uncertainty inherent in the unique ways humans link themselves to their social and physical environment. Similar to the uncertainty principle in physics, there may be an uncertainty principle in the study of personality.

An example of this *uncertainty principle* is seen in a study by Woodruff and Birren (1972), who found no statistically significant age changes in the scores of 85 respondents on a measure of self-adjustment over a 25-year age span; that is, there was no significant difference in the way in which the respondents described themselves in 1944 (at age 19.5) and their self-descriptions in 1969 (at average age 44.5). However, they also found that their respondents' *retrospective* descriptions of themselves in 1969 (as they thought they had answered in 1944) were markedly different — lower in personal and social adjustment — from the *actual* score in 1944 (Figure 8.2). Apparently these respondents perceived that they had changed (and in positive ways) since young adulthood, although this change was not present in their actual responses. Perhaps the test that was used and the statistical analyses employed reflected the *continuity* lenses, whereas the respondents were using *change* lenses when they looked back over the 25 years. Clearly the people felt they had changed, but the test did not show it; the people had been quite stable in their self-perceptions, but they did not feel this was the case. We might conclude that people are more stable in their self-perceptions then they believe themselves to be; or that objective tests of self-perceptions reveal more continuity than is actually experienced. Perhaps we cannot be certain because both conclusions are accurate, depending on which lenses we use to analyze the data.

In practical terms, this uncertainty principle implies that, even though our society is based on the assumption that individuals are fairly stable throughout their lives, we can never completely predict an individual's behavior in the future. Much of the continuity we see in ourselves and in others probably results from our socially encouraged and perhaps biologically based predisposition to use continuity lenses when we interact with others and with the social and physical world in which we live. Human evolution and social life as we know it would be impossible if we used

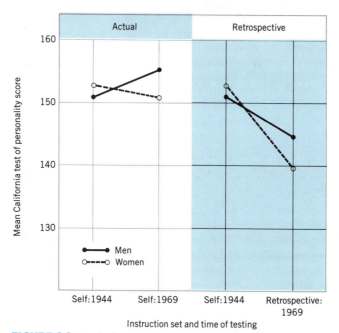

FIGURE 8.2 Level of personal and social adjustment as measured by the California test of personality scores in 1944 and 1969 for the 1924 cohort in the actual and retrospective condition. (*Source*: Adapted from Woodruff & Birren, 1972, p. 255. Reprinted with permission from *Developmental Psychology*, copyright © 1972 by the American Psychological Association.)

change lenses continually, because we would never recognize similarities and patterns in the world. At the same time, there is more change and complexity in the world than we ordinarily pay attention to. Certainly, much of the excitement in human relationships results from the unpredictability, freshness, and new facets we experience with the other person; but a relationship would not be possible without trust in the continuity and stability of the person and the relationship over time.

Let us explore the processes that are involved in personality continuity and change. First we discuss the trait perspective, which tends to emphasize continuity; second we discuss the behavioral perspective, which tends to emphasize change. However, both contribute important concepts to our view of adult personality as a system of interacting components.

Personality Trait Perspective

In the psychological view of personality, a number of relatively enduring characteristics, traits, or temperaments are seen as providing individual uniqueness and continuity over long periods of time. They link the individual with the world in two ways. First, they are thought to develop as a result of experience, usually during early childhood, often as a result of parental influence and child-rearing techniques. Second, they produce characteristic ways in which individuals respond to their environment throughout life.

Research by Paul Costa, Robert McCrae, and their colleagues has called attention to the stability of personality traits over many years. Much of their research has focused on three domains of personality: neuroticism, extraversion, and openness.

> The neuroticism scale is composed of subscales measuring anxiety, hostility, depression, self-consciousness, impulsiveness, and vulnerability; the extraversion scale includes measures of warmth, gregariousness, assertiveness, activity, excitement-seeking, and positive emotions; and openness is assessed in the areas of fantasy, aesthetics, feelings, actions, ideas, and values. (McCrae & Costa, 1986, p. 392).

McCrae and Costa (1986) used these personality types in two studies of a total of over 400 adults (age 21–91) on styles of coping with losses, threats, or challenges. Different personality types were found to use different coping styles. These differences help to suggest the meanings of these three personality scales.

> In both studies, neuroticism is associated with increased use of hostile reaction, escapist fantasy, self-blame, sedation, withdrawal, wishful thinking, passivity, and indecisiveness. Extraversion is correlated with rational action, positive thinking, substitution, and restraint. Open individuals are more likely to use humor in dealing with stress; closed individuals are more likely to use faith. (McCrae & Costa, 1986, p. 392)

Earlier studies by Costa and his colleagues also help clarify the nature of these personality types. *Neuroticism* was associated with heavy smoking, drinking problems, complaints about health, difficulties in sexual adjustment, financial troubles, separation and divorce, unhappiness, and dissatisfaction with life. *Extraversion* was linked with occupational choice, such as advertising or law for extraverts and architect or physicist for introverts; extraverts tended to be happier than introverts.

Openness was related to occupations such as psychologist, psychiatrist, or minister; the "open" men were also more likely to quit a job or begin a new line of work; their lives tended to be more "eventful" than those of the "closed" men (Costa & McCrae, 1980b, pp. 72–73).

Several studies have demonstrated that there is considerable stability in these personality traits during adulthood. One of the most dramatic studies was based on a nationwide sample of 10,149 adults ranging in age from 32 to 88 years; 37.5 percent were men and 13.5 percent were African American. The average score on measures of these personality traits by 10-year age groups for this sample is shown in Figure 8.3. Although there are significant differences because of the very large sample size (e.g., younger persons are higher on all three compared with older people), the actual differences are quite small. The graphs provide striking evidence for *stability* of personality: there were essentially no age differences over the 50-year age span in the distribution of these three personality traits among this sample of the United States population — in spite of any cohort effects that would be expected to affect such a cross-sectional study. Likewise, the data by one-year age

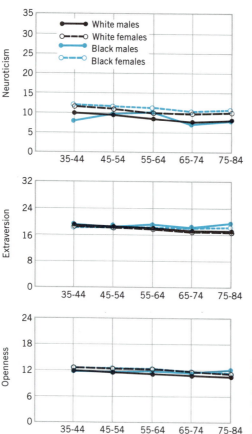

FIGURE 8.3 Mean levels of neuroticism, extraversion, and openness to experience for 10-year age groups of White men, Black men, White women, and Black women, aged from 35 to 84 years. (*Source*: Costa et al., 1986, Fig. 1. © American Psychological Association. Reprinted with permission.)

groups for the period of life when many theories predict a "midlife crisis" showed very little evidence of any age-related personality differences.

However, we should be cautious in drawing conclusions from these data about stability and change in personality among individuals. Studies of large groups of respondents that average scores on personality variables tend to find stability because individual variation is lost in the average scores. In contrast, studies of small groups of persons who differ on critical variables, such as stress, tend to find change (cf. Fiske & Chiriboga, 1985). Thus, additional data regarding individual patterns of change and stability over time are required before we can conclude that personality is stable throughout adulthood.

Another set of data reported by Costa and McCrae (1988) that was based on longitudinal studies of these personality characteristics provides more compelling evidence of personality stability for the same individuals over time. They obtained scores on their questionnaire from 365 men aged 25–91 and 270 women aged 21–96 in 1980 as a part of the Baltimore Longitudinal Study of Aging. Of the total 635 respondents, 447 provided data in 1983 (including two additional scales) and 398 provided data on all five scales in 1986. The results indicated a high degree of stability in personality for these respondents. Costa and McCrae also obtained ratings by the respondents' spouse for 167 individuals in this study. Six-year retest correlations of these scores were also very high. They concluded this study by making a very strong statement about the stability of personality:

> It appears from the data of many longitudinal studies that aging itself has little effect on personality. This is true despite the fact that the normal course of aging includes disease, bereavement, divorce, unemployment, and many other significant events for substantial portions of the population. (Costa & McCrae, 1988, p. 862)

Similarly, based on their analysis of the national cross-sectional data set described earlier, they argued that the stability of personality traits, not personality change, should be the focus of research:

> Gerontologists have devoted considerable time and energy to theory and research on personality change in adulthood, hoping to find either discrete stages of adult development, or maturational trends that would result in a characteristic personality profile for older individuals. Inspection of Figure [8.3], which portrays cross-sectional data from a large national sample covering a span of 50 years suggests that—at least for the dimensions of neuroticism, extraversion, and openness to experience—personality is predominately stable, and future research might better be focused on the mechanisms and implications of personality stability. (Costa et al., 1986, p. 148)

Similar, but more moderate, correlations have been found in various other measures of personality stability over time. For example, Filipp and Klauer (1986) found considerable stability in self-described traits related to the self-concept among 131 men in five birth cohorts (from 1905, 1912, 1925, 1935, and 1945) over a three-year longitudinal study (from 1980 to 1983) in West Germany. Correlation coefficients were between .61 and .74. Similar levels of correlation coefficients were reported in another study of self-concept by Mortimer, Finch, and Kumka (1982).

Moreover, similar moderately high correlations have been found between personality characteristics of *identical twins* (Table 8.5); this suggests that a genetic factor may be contributing to personality characteristics (Thompson, 1968). That is, the correlations between identical twins (Mz or monozygotic) are generally somewhat higher than for fraternal twins (Dz, or dizygotic). Gottschaldt (1960), in a study of the stability of a number of personality characteristics from adolescence to adulthood among twin pairs, found that age seemed to increase the importance of the genetic factor in these characteristics. Thus, heredity may play a role in at least some personality traits (Tyler, 1978). These genetic factors may be partly responsible for the stability of an individual's personality over time.

Behavioral Perspective

The approach to personality that emphasizes the potential for change much more than stability is social or psychological **behaviorism.** In both frameworks the internal characteristics of the person, such as personality traits, are seen as largely irrelevant, since the important influences on behavior are located in the environment. For example, in the sociological model, personality consists of an individual's unique collection of *social roles.* These roles are maintained by social sanctions and social expectations and are transmitted to the individual through the process of socialization (discussed in Chapter 2). Thus, in **social behaviorism,** an individual's roles and other social behaviors are maintained by the social and interpersonal consequences of one's behavior — if the behavior fits the expectations of others, it is reinforced; if it is not appropriate to the situation, then the behavior is eventually shaped to the expected or appropriate behavior. Clearly, change is easily explained, and consistency results from the stability of social expectations. Notably, in this perspective personality seems to vanish into a collection of roles (Heine, 1971). For example, one need not know a police officer's personality to know that she will, if necessary, risk her life to save you; or that a clinical psychologist will spend a great deal of time and effort attempting to help a patient whom he would ignore if he

TABLE 8.5 Similarities in Personality Traits between Monozygotic and Dizygotic Twin Pairs

	Mz	Dz	
		Like Sex	*Unlike Sex*
Neuroticism	.63	.32	.18
Self-sufficiency	.44	−.14	.12
Introversion	.50	.40	.18
Dominance	.71	.34	.18
Self-confidence	.58	.20	.07
Sociability	.57	.41	.39

Source: Carter, H. D. Twin similarities in emotional traits. *Character and Personality*, 1935, *4*, 61–78. Copyright © 1935. Reprinted with permission of the Duke University Press.

were to have first encountered that person on a bus acting only slightly strangely. If seems that role theory is quite powerful in explaining behavior — particularly if other variables such as age, gender, occupation, ethnicity, and education are also considered.

Similarly, psychological behaviorism views behavior as maintained by the consequences of that behavior, so that (as in social behaviorism) behaviors that are reinforced in some way will be maintained. To change behavior, one need know little about the individual except the question of what rewards are reinforcing; then the appropriate consequences (e.g., rewards) may be linked to the desired behavior. Thus, personality, insofar as it exists in this view, is seen as a collection of behaviors; in the social model, it would be a collection of social behaviors. This approach is especially powerful in producing desired behavior change, such as for residents in nursing homes who are overly dependent, abusive, or show other inappropriate behaviors (Block, Boczkowski, Hansen & Vanderbeck, 1987).

Personality as Process

Is it possible to integrate these differing views of personality? To do so we need to consider the interaction of genetic, physiological, cognitive, social, and environmental factors. We also need to focus on the simultaneous process of change and continuity as individuals progress through their life span. This approach requires an interactionist or dialectical perspective that views personality as a continuing process of transactions between the person and the environment over time.

Tyler (1978) described the process model of personality, tracing its philosophical origins to the work of Alfred North Whitehead (1929/1969) and Susanne Langer (1967, 1972). This perspective, similar to that of G.H. Mead (1934/1964), sees humans as active beings that select their actions, instead of as machinelike beings that are programmed and can behave only in predetermined ways. Thus, individuals select and organize their environment; there is an element of unpredictability or chance in behavior; and future behavior is a spontaneous creation.

> Individuals create themselves. To understand a person completely, we would need to trace the road he or she has taken on one occasion after another. It is development we must study, but the development of the shaper rather than the shaped. Obviously such complete understanding of an individual, especially of oneself, is impossible, but it is not unrealistic to hope that an expanded theory and technology for studying individuality will enable us to assess more accurately what has been created in an individual so far through the endless process of becoming what one is, to appreciate more deeply the value of human diversity, and to utilize the unique contributions of individuals to enrich the pattern of our common social fabric. (Tyler, 1978, pp. 233–234)

Her view incorporated the contributions of hereditary factors — seen as a process instead of a compound of ingredients, cognitive processes that act as ''mental screens'' that individuals use to process input from the environment, and cognitive strategies that individuals employ to deal with different situations in their life. Combined with the effects of social interactions and individual experience, these factors suggest that personality is an ongoing process and that behavior of an individual cannot be assumed to be completely predictable, even in principle. This idea does not require the dialectical perspective, which we discuss next, but it is compatible with it.

Dialectical Model of Personality

The dialectical view proposed by Klaus Riegel (1976), described in Chapter 1, suggests a perspective that combines models of personality presented in this chapter. In this approach, the individual is a "changing being in a changing world" (Riegel, 1976, p. 696). Thus, personality is seen as a continuing *dialectical* struggle between various influences: inner-biological, individual-psychological, cultural-sociological, and outer-physical. This process occurs over time, so that this approach is inherently developmental. For example, an individual's hereditary dispositions and physiological processes are the *inner-biological* dimension; personality traits are the *individual-psychological* dimension. One's social interactions and social environment represent the *cultural-sociological* dimension; and the physical environment is the *outer-physical* dimension. Personality would then be the dialectical evolution of these dimensions as a complex interaction of the individual *self* with the social and physical environment over time.

Susan Krauss Whitbourne (1985) developed a life span model of adaptation that conceptualizes development as a dialectical process. In this model, **adaptation** is defined as the preservation of psychological well-being and physical health of the individual. *Stress* disrupts the usual life patterns and therefore requires an adaptation. A variety of life events can produce stress, depending on the individual's *cognitive appraisal* of the event; that is, the way in which individuals interpret the experience affects their reaction to it. Physical stress, social transitions, and external challenges represent other examples of life events that appear to be consistent with the model Whitbourne proposed.

Individual *resources* at the time of the event, including social and personal characteristics, may facilitate or hinder adaptation. Linda George (1980) proposed four general types of personal resources that foster problem solving: finances, health, social support, and education. The significance of these resources for the individual's coping with life events reflects a variety of factors. For example, Elwell and Maltbie-Crannell (1981), in data from a national sample of adults over age 50, reported that social participation was a critical social resource in dealing with life events for women, but financial security was more important for men.

Coping with life events is necessary for adaptation. In the model proposed by Whitbourne, coping is based on the individual's appraisal of the event, positive or negative, and on the expected effects of the event and of the coping strategy. She assumed that individuals seek to solve problems of living effectively and to experience a sense of accomplishment. Thus, coping may involve attempts to change the environment, as well as to adjust oneself. A challenge may heighten one's sense of well-being; so a placid sense of equilibrium is not necessarily the goal of coping or adaptation.

These variables can be conceptualized in a dialectical model similar to the one described in Chapter 1. That is, life events, resources, and adaptation can be schematically represented in terms of the individual-psychological, inner-biological, cultural-sociological, and outer-physical dimensions (Box 8.1). The individ-

BOX 8.1	*Dialectical Model of Coping with Life Events*		
Dialectical Dimension	*Life Event*	*Resource*	*Adaptation*
Individual-psychological	Cognitive and affective meaning	Education	Happiness
Individual-biological	Physical stress	Health	Recovery
Cultural-sociological	Transition	Social support	Involvement
Outer-physical	Challenge	Finances	Rebuilding

ual's coping thus represents the dialectical process of maintaining adequate balance and challenge among those dimensions to fit the sense of identity as the individual subjectively defines it.

On the basis of this model of adaptation, Whitbourne has used techniques of "life drawing" to help persons review their lives, clarify expectations about the future, and adapt to life events. She also has employed a clinical interview to assess identity style as a way of understanding the process of adaptation to aging (Whitbourne, 1987).

This dialectical view of personality is a relatively new perspective, yet it has elements in common with the views expressed by Henry Murray (1938) in his book titled *Explorations in Personality*. Robert White (1987), in his *Memoir,* described the thrust of this book:

> It teaches us to be serious about taking people as wholes, as they are and as they think they are. Another of its messages is the dynamic one: people have needs, they are engaged in strivings, they are trying to produce end-states and reach goals. Furthermore, *Explorations* speaks for the importance of development over time; personality is not a fixed thing but a configuration undergoing perpetual change. Lastly, this seminal book was a powerful argument for proaction, as contrasted with reaction. Its vision of human nature included the planning, organizing, building, imagining, dreaming, creating activity without which we cannot understand either individuals or the civilization they have constructed. (White, 1987, p. 18)

Likewise, Bernice Neugarten (1968), one of the pioneers in the study of adult personality, called attention to the complex nature of personality in one of her provocative questions:

> What terms shall we use to describe the strategies with which . . . [a business executive, age 50, who makes a thousand decisions in the course of a day] manages his time, buffers himself from certain stimuli, makes elaborate plans and schedules, sheds some of his "load" by delegating some tasks to other people over whom he has certain forms of control, accepts other tasks as being singularly appropriate to his own competencies and responsibilities, and, in the same 24-hour period, succeeds in satisfying his emotional and sexual and aesthetic needs? (Neugarten, 1968, p. 140)

Continuity Theory of Aging

As noted earlier in this chapter, stability and change are both present throughout the life span; whether we see change or stability depends on which we look for — which "glasses" we use. We have described perspectives that reflect relative stability (personality traits) and relative change (behavioral perspectives). We also have noted that personality can be seen as a process of self-creation that is never fixed and fully predictable. And we just reviewed the dialectical perspective that views personality as only one dimension within the ceaseless flux of human life. To conclude this discussion of personality processes in adulthood, we describe the perspective called the **continuity theory;** it focuses on the efforts of adults to maintain and preserve the basic structures of their lives as they grow older.

Robert Atchley (1989) described *continuity* as a dynamic process within a basic structure of life that involves both internal aspects (such as one's sense of identity) and external aspects (such as one's enduring relationships). In his view, normal aging (in the absence of disabling mental or physical disease) is characterized by continuity: applying familiar strategies to daily life, using past experience as a helpful guide, and maintaining relative stability in the external environment (activities, friends, neighborhood, etc.).

A sense of *internal continuity* is important during middle age and aging for four reasons: (1) it provides a sense of competence, mastery, predictability, and control that promotes effective day-to-day functioning; (2) it facilitates a sense of integrity, the feeling that one's life has been a meaningful adventure, according to Erikson's theory (see Chapter 1); (3) it helps provide a sense of self-esteem; and (4) it facilitates the interaction with others because one is relatively predictable and comfortable to be around.

External continuity is important in terms of one's ongoing roles in the family and community as well as in the circle of family and friends who provide and depend on the individual's social support. Continuity in the external environment also facilitates affirmation of one's self-esteem by long-term relationships, and allows one to compensate effectively for decline with aging by performing in domains of one's expertise (as discussed in Chapter 4). Moreover, continuity of goals helps one cope with difficult changes such as retirement or widowhood.

> Thus, continuity is a preferred strategy for dealing with aging for a wide variety of reasons. Both internal and external continuity help individuals focus on and maintain their strengths and minimize the effects of deficits as normal aging occurs. (Atchley, 1989, p. 186)

This concept of continuity does not imply a "boring sameness," but instead is a "comforting routine and familiar sense of direction" (p. 188). It may reflect a desire to maintain a stable environment because physical surroundings, habitual patterns of activity, and community resources are known and dependable. It may reflect the maturation of relationships, especially with friends and one's spouse, that provide opportunity for belonging, mutual aid, and intimacy.

Disruption of continuity can have serious implications. It can produce discontinuity in one's sense of identity if one can no longer function as before; yet this may be a matter of degree and of self-definition. Some persons may be able to redefine their identity after a serious illness or disability in a way that reflects considerable continuity with their previous identity. Likewise, moving from one's neighborhood, losing close friends, and other disruptions of continuity can be especially upsetting or may be redefined to minimize discontinuity. In some cases, persons seek to maintain continuity even when it is no longer appropriate, at least from an outsider's point of view:

> Nurses may be turned into "mom" or "sister," perhaps by trying to evoke a familiar response from strange caregivers. Elders, especially frail ones, often try to get others to respond to them in terms of what they were — and still are trying to be — not in terms of the altered or broken or disabled person seen by staff or visitors.
>
> As Atchley points out, internal discontinuity can destroy mental health. (Huyck, 1989, p. 149)

The continuity perspective must be balanced by the perspective of the adventurous aged (Kahana & Kahana, 1982). Some older persons seek change and move great distances to find environmental discontinuity. For example, elderly persons emigrating from the United States to Israel and those migrating to Florida showed evidence of both continuity and discontinuity:

> Those relocating to Israel view themselves, for the most part, as "going home" to live their remaining days in the land of their people and to actualize their prayers and religious wishes. (p. 215)
>
> The Florida-bound older person often welcomes the end of the need to work and of involvement with children and grandchildren, although many of the movers welcome visits from family during the holidays. Going to Florida may have been a life's dream or a relatively recent desire, but, in any event, many view it as a gift they give themselves after the hardships of younger years. . . .
>
> There are some noteworthy similarities among those who relocate to Israel and Florida. Risk-taking is a common feature of both these groups. They do not mind having to learn new features of behavior, adaptation, and life-styles. Both groups feel capable of emotionally investing themselves in their new environments and are willing to part with many of their lifelong neighbors and friends as well as family. (Kahana & Kahana, 1982, p. 216)

Conclusion

David Chiriboga (1987), in a discussion of personality in later life, made a plea for an end to the controversy between "stability" and "change" and urged researchers to search for the factors that produce each: "for assuredly there is ample evidence for both in the developmental literature" (p. 148). In an analysis of data from a study of adults going through periods of expected developmental transition, Chiriboga (1984) noted that personality components were relatively stable over the entire 11-year follow-up. Despite this, analysis of individual life stress revealed a great deal about patterns of change. For example, persons with low stress tended to change less than persons with high stress. Moreover, in his study of persons going through a divorce there was evidence of a "chaining of life events" in which one event triggered the next. As a result, a change as such a divorce tends to produce additional change so that divorcing persons experienced both positive and negative changes in many areas of life as one change brought on another. In his view, all theories of transitions assume a kind of dialectic between the individual and the environment so that situational conditions can provide a strong influence not only for stability but also for change through the unfolding of personality characteristics.

Likewise, we view personality as a complex process that involves both continuity and change. It reflects the unique individual and his or her unique social environment. Thus, as defined earlier in this chapter, *personality* reflects individual uniqueness, tends to be relatively stable, and involves the dynamic interaction between the individual and the social environment. Whether we focus on change or on stability depends on the lenses we use when we look at the individual in interaction with the environment. The dialectical and process views of personality are probably unacceptable for those who adhere to strict behaviorist (change) or trait (stability) models, but they seem consistent with the dynamic continuity perspective proposed by Atchley.

Perhaps *individual differences* in personality characteristics provide the key. Some persons may prefer stability or continuity but adjust to change when necessary. Others may seek change and cope with the invigoration they receive from new environments by relatively continuous patterns of adaptation and functioning.

Patterns of Personality Stability and Change in Adulthood

Since there is both stability and change during adulthood, the goal in this section is to find some patterns of stability and some general patterns of change in adulthood and aging. We first describe some classic studies that set the stage for current research. Next we summarize conclusions from studies dealing with changes in self-conceptions with aging and the effects of stress. Then we describe the important role of a close friend in coping with changes such as retirement or widowhood.

Kansas City Studies of Adult Personality

One of the major studies of personality change and continuity in adulthood was conducted by a group from the Committee on Human Development at the University of Chicago in the mid-1950s. We discuss this study in detail because it attempted to investigate developmental change in personality structure. That is, instead of studying changes in specific personality characteristics, the researchers sought to investigate age-related changes in the total personality system. Although a major shortcoming of the study is the absence of data on physiological and health factors, in many ways this study is a classic because it was one of the first large-scale studies of "normal" community residents, and it contains both cross-sectional and longitudinal data on personality change in adults. Some of the major publications based on these data are Cumming and Henry (1961), Havighurst, Neugarten, and Tobin (1963/1968), and Neugarten and Associates (1964). They obtained a sample of nearly 700 respondents between the ages of 40 and 90 who were in relatively good health and who were living in homes or apartments (not institutions) in Kansas City. Respondents were selected on the basis of age, sex, and economic status and were interviewed repeatedly over a period of up to seven years. The studies found three age-related personality changes: a shift in gender-role perceptions, a personality shift toward "increased interiority," and a shift in the coping styles of personality. In addition, they found a number of personality aspects that did not change with age.

Thus, there are data on both change and on stability in personality; many of these findings have been supported in smaller studies of adult personality. We begin our discussion of these data with the findings of stability; we will then deal with the specific age-related changes that were also found.

Stability of Adaptive Personality Characteristics

Since *age* was a major variable in the Kansas City studies, one of the central findings was that some personality characteristics did not change with age of the respondent whereas other personality aspects did change. Those characteristics that did *not* change seemed to share a common theme — they dealt with "adaptive, goal directed, and purposive qualities of personality" that Neugarten (1964) described as **socioadaptational characteristics** of personality. That is, general adaptation (based on interview data), adaptive characteristics of the personality (such as integrity or adjustment or cognitive competence based on responses to projective tests), and general personality structure (based on personality tests) differed between individuals regardless of their chronological age. For example, they administered a personality test that, when the results were analyzed, yielded four general personality types: "integrated," "armored-defended," "passive-dependent," and "unintegrated." However, there were no consistent age differences among the respondents in each of these types. Similar data were obtained in another study on a different sample conducted by Reichard, Livson, and Peterson (1962) in which they found no clear differences among their five personality types (these were discussed in Chapter 6: "mature," "rocking-chair men," "armored," "angry men," and "self-haters"); instead, these personality patterns seemed to be consistent patterns of adaptation in the histories of the men in their sample. Other data on "adjustment" to aging found no age-related differences in a sample of healthy old men (Butler, 1963a). Indeed, in that study (discussed in Chapter 7) *disease* was identified as a far more important variable than chronological age.

Likewise, another study, based on the Kansas City samples, found no relationship between age and the person's degree of **life satisfaction,** which is a measure of adaptive adjustment to aging (Havighurst et al., 1963/1968). However, personality type was related to life satisfaction (Table 8.6). That is, respondents who were high on the "integrated" style of personality had high life satisfaction regardless of whether they were active in a variety of social roles. At the other extreme, "unintegrated" types were low or medium in life satisfaction whether they were active or not. "Armored-defended" types who were high or medium in activity were high on life satisfaction. "Passive-dependent" types tended to be medium on life satisfaction regardless of their degree of activity. Thus, personality characteristics seemed to be pivotal dimensions for whether successful aging is one of maintained activity or gradual disengagement from activity and social involvement (Neugarten, Havighurst & Tobin, 1965).

Thus, the data seem to indicate that there is little predictable change in these socioadaptational characteristics with advancing age. We interpret this finding as indicating that the adaptive interaction between the person and the social environment remains fairly stable. That is, an old person seems to adapt and interact with

TABLE 8.6 Personality Type in Relation to Activity and Life Satisfaction (N = 59)

Personality Type	Role Activity	Life Satisfaction		
		High	Medium	Low
Integrated	High	9	2	
	Medium	5		
	Low	3		
Armored-defended	High	5		
	Medium	6	1	
	Low	2	1	1
Passive-dependent	High		1	
	Medium	1	4	
	Low	2	3	2
Unintegrated	High		2	1
	Medium	1		
	Low		2	5
	Total	34	16	9

Source: Neugarten, Havighurst, & Tobin (1965/1968), Table 1. Reprinted with permission.

the environment with as much satisfaction as a middle-aged person, at least for generally healthy adults living in the community. There are a variety of ways in which a relatively stable personality can adjust and adapt to changes in roles and status while remaining generally stable. Neugarten summarized this conclusion in the following way:

> In a sense, the self becomes institutionalized with the passage of time. Not only do certain personality processes become stabilized and provide continuity, but the individual builds around him a network of social relationships which he comes to depend on for emotional support and responsiveness and which maintain him in many subtle ways. . . .
>
> Behavior in a normal old person is more consistent and more predictable than in a younger one— . . . as individuals age, they become increasingly like themselves— and, on the other hand, . . . the personality structure stands more clearly revealed in an old than in a younger person. (Neugarten, 1964, p. 198)

Change in Personality with Age

Three sets of data in the Kansas City studies indicate related changes in personality processes with age. In general, this change is one of **increased interiority** of the personality (Neugarten, 1968). This change seems to begin in middle age in a tendency toward increased self-reflection and introspection (in the decade of the fifties for most persons). It becomes more marked in later life, perhaps leading to the reminiscence characteristic of many aged persons (Butler, 1963b; this reminiscence and the "life-review process" will be discussed in detail in Chapter 10). Two of these studies (each of which we will discuss) suggest this increased interiority; one study found a decrease in "ego energy" with age, and the second found a shift in "ego style" with age. A third study found a shift in gender-role perceptions and a growing responsiveness to inner impulses with age. Each of these studies was based on data from projective tests (in which pictures were presented to the respondents who were then asked to tell a story about the picture and to describe the characters) and each dealt with "intrapsychic" processes of personality in contrast with the "socioadaptational" aspects of personality discussed in the previous section.

Rosen and Neugarten (1964) analyzed the responses of Kansas City respondents to five of the pictures in the Thematic Apperception Test (TAT) on four measures of *ego energy:* introduction of nonpictured characters into the story told about the card, introduction of conflict into the story, extent of vigorous activity ascribed to the characters, and the intensity of emotion (affect) described for the characters. It was assumed that each of these four variables tapped the amount of psychic energy that the respondent devoted to the task of making up a story about the picture presented; hence, low ratings suggest that the respondent invested little energy in the task. Their data show a consistent decline with age on all four measures; differences between age groups were statistically reliable. Although these findings were obtained from a cross-sectional sample, since many of the respondents were interviewed subsequently it was also possible to obtain longitudinal data on these dimensions. Lubin (1964) administered the same TAT cards to 93 of the subjects five years later and found a significant decline on a combined measure of ego energy over the five-year test retest interval. Thus, these findings add considerable support to the notion that ego energy, which is available for tasks in the outer world, does decline with advancing age and that older persons tend to respond to inner stimuli moreso than younger persons (Rosen & Neugarten, 1964).

A change with age that is closely related to the decrease in ego energy is a shift in *ego style* from active mastery to passive mastery and magical mastery styles. Gutmann (1964), again using TAT responses, rated the stories on these three ego mastery styles separately for men and women. The three mastery types were seen as points on a continuum of ego strength in which "active mastery represents the most vigorous, effective style of ego functioning and magical mastery represents stress-laden, maladaptive ego functioning" (Gutmann, 1964, p. 119). The data show a shift with age toward passive and magical mastery styles for both men and women (Figure 8.4). In subsequent studies of these same dimensions of ego style, Gutmann found similar patterns for aging men in various different cultures, including subsistence corn farmers in a remote Mexican province (Gutmann, 1967) and Native Americans (Krohn & Gutmann, 1971). This suggests a developmental shift in personality processes with age that is not related to the culture in which the individual grows old.

In another report on many different cultures, Gutmann (1977) found added support for this change in men, but determined that the shift could occur in the opposite direction for women; thus, the cross-cultural evidence appears to contra-

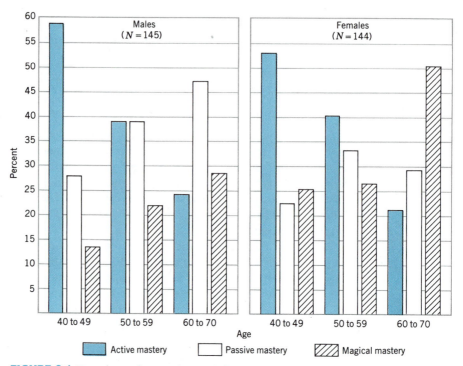

FIGURE 8.4 Percentage of respondents exhibiting active, passive, and magical mastery styles by age and sex. By the chi-square test, the distribution of active, passive, and magical mastery totals by age groups is significantly different from chance at the .02 level. (*Source*: Adapted from Gutmann, 1964, Tables 6.1 and 6.2. Reprinted with permission of the Aldine Publishing Company.)

dict the shift in ego style found for women in Kansas City. However, Gutmann (1987) reexamined these data for the Kansas City women and noted that those high in "magical mastery" were also highest in life satisfaction; their "feisty, combative stance" seemed more consonant with *active mastery* and different from passive mastery, in contrast with the pattern for men. This difference between women and men was also consistent among various cultures in his analysis. Therefore, he concluded:

> Whereas adult males start from a grounding in Active Mastery and move toward Passive Mastery, women are at first grounded in Passive Mastery, characterized by dependence on and even deference to the husband, but surge in later life toward Active Mastery, including autonomy from and even domination over the husband. Across cultures, and with age, they seem to become more authoritative, more effective, and less willing to trade submission for security. (Gutmann, 1987, p. 133).

Similar findings were obtained for a group of women between the ages of 43 and 51 (Cooper & Gutmann, 1987). Those who were no longer engaged in active parenting (post-empty nest) were found to be higher in the measure of active mastery compared with the women who had children living at home (pre-empty nest). These data are consistent with the idea that the end of the parenting responsibility allows a shift in personality so that women are "more free to express some of the masculine qualities of assertion, aggression, and executive capacity which they had had to repress in the service of parenthood" (p. 352). Gutmann (1987) asserted that this release from a "parental imperative" was the basic factor in the shift of gender role with aging in a variety of cultures.

In a third study with the Kansas City sample that focused on *gender-role perceptions,* Neugarten and Gutmann (1958) asked respondents to describe each of four figures shown on a TAT card prepared especially for this study (Figure 8.5). The descriptions given by older respondents (age 55–70) differed significantly from descriptions given by younger respondents (age 40–54) when describing the old man and the old woman in the picture. The most striking differences were that the perception of the old man shifted in the direction of increasing submissiveness when seen by older respondents (both men and women) as compared with younger respondents; and the old woman's role shifted from a subordinate to an authoritative position when seen by older respondents as compared to younger ones. Essentially the same findings were obtained in a later study by Singer (1963) for a different sample of 47 old men. Of course, these projective data (in which respondents are describing figures in a picture instead of their own behavior) must be interpreted with caution in terms of actual changes in gender-role behavior among older persons. Nonetheless, Neugarten and Gutmann (1958) felt these data implied significant personality changes:

> For example, women, as they age, [seem to become more tolerant] of their own aggressive, egocentric impulses; while men, as they age, [seem to become more tolerant] of their own nurturant and affiliative impulses. To take another example, with increasing age in both men and women, ego qualities in the personality seem to become more constricted—more detached from the mastery of affairs and less in control of impulse life. (p. 89)

The implication of these changes is that men and women become more similar in terms of gender role as they grow older, possibly related to the decreased importance of parental roles after their children are grown, leading to "the normal unisex of later life" (Gutmann, 1977, p. 311).

These findings, based on a variety of research approaches, are especially striking because they support Jung's clinical observations three decades before the Kansas City studies:

> Man's values, and even his body, do tend to change into their opposites.
>
> We might compare masculinity and femininity and their psychic components to a definite store of substances of which, in the first half of life, unequal use is made. A man consumes his large supply of masculine substance and has left over only the smaller amount of feminine substance, which must now be put to use. Conversely, the woman allows her hitherto unused supply of masculinity to become active. (Jung, 1933, p. 16)

However, as noted earlier in the discussion of gender roles and androgyny, not all studies find that older women are more androgynous than younger women (Sinnott, 1982); thus, the shift toward androgyny with age may be more pronounced for men and may reflect cohort differences, especially for women.

FIGURE 8.5 TAT picture designed for the Kansas City Study of Adult Life. (*Source*: Neugarten & Gutmann, 1958, Figure 1. Copyright by the Committee on Human Development, University of Chicago. Reprinted with permission.)

As men and women grow older, there is an increased tendency to incorporate characteristics of the other gender into one's self-conception.

In summary, on the basis of these studies we can speculate that the development of the personality system appears to progress from a period of maximal expansion (learning new roles, developing new roles, and attending to feedback from others about the "rules of the game") in young adulthood through a period of relative balance between internal processes and external demands in middle age to an increasing focus on internal processes in old age. This view is consistent with the basic findings in studies of midlife transitions discussed in Chapter 3. However, although general developmental changes such as increased interiority and loss of some social roles may be typical for older individuals, their personality and their active *I* continue to reveal individuality and to influence their interaction with the physical and social environment. That is, old persons, though they may show some similar developmental changes, remain (and perhaps become even more) like themselves. Thus they are no more like "older people" than young persons are like other members of their age group.

Aging and Self-Conceptions

Bengtson, Reedy, and Gordon (1985) reviewed nearly 100 studies of personality in adulthood and aging. They viewed personality in a manner consistent with our symbolic interactionist framework (discussed in Chapter 2) in which individual self-conceptions and personality characteristics are seen as *me* aspects of the self. That is, whether the persons describe themselves or answer items on a questionnaire that are mathematically combined into a personality trait, the data refer to thoughts, feelings, and behaviors that reflect characteristics of the person's self. *I* aspects of the self are not able to be studied in these ways. They also noted the many methodological issues involved in these studies; for example, cross-sectional data probably reflect cohort differences, average levels probably conceal individual change, and moderate correlations imply both stability and variation in the trait. On the basis of their review, they suggested a number of conclusions; three of these present information on personality dimensions we have not discussed:

> Cohort membership, gender, social/cultural trends, and life-stage experiences have more significant impact on self-conceptions than maturation does. (Bengtson et al., 1985, p. 573)
>
> The majority of studies showed either no age differences in self-esteem or higher self-esteem in older cohorts. This fact suggests either that today's older cohorts started out with a more favorable self-evaluation than did younger generations, or, more possibly, that self-esteem typically is maintained or increased as individuals age. (p. 578)
>
> Mean-level change in longitudinal research has been found in many variables: autonomy, self-competence, self-confidence, excitability, and humanitarian concern, all of which tend to increase from young adulthood at least into middle age; energy, which can decrease as early as the 40s; and social responsibility, which in older men's self-conceptions tends to decrease. (p. 586)

Stress and Personality in Adulthood

Marjorie Fiske, David Chiriboga, and their colleagues conducted a series of studies on stress and personality in adulthood. In one study, about 200 women and men were interviewed in 1969–1970 and four times after that until 11 years later in 1980 (Chiriboga, 1982b). At the beginning of the study they were selected because they were about to face one of five transitions: leaving their parents' home, first-time parenthood, departure of last child from home, and retirement from work. In a second study, 125 men and 185 women who were separated from their spouse and in the process of divorcing were interviewed; their age range was 20–79, with the average age in the mid thirties. A follow-up interview was conducted with 283 of the respondents about 3½ years later. The Life Events Questionnaire (described in Chapter 7) was used to assess positive and negative stress and a variety of other questionnaires were used to measure morale, psychological symptoms, self-criticism, overall life evaluation, and health status.

In the 11 years of the transitions study, on the one hand, "there was as much evidence for stability as there was for change in emotional experiences" (Chiriboga, 1982b, p. 16); on the other hand: "It was frequently the case that what appeared to be evidence for stability over the eleven years of contact actually represented the averaging of highly divergent trends across groups" (p. 25). When these groups were separated, considerable variation seemed evident. For example, stress had a different effect on the reported happiness of younger compared with older men over the first three years for which data had been analyzed (Figure 8.6). That is, older

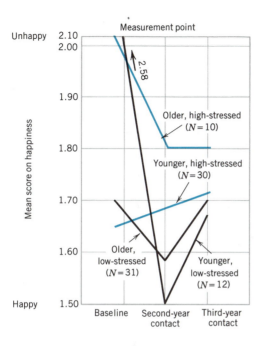

Measurement point

Unhappy

Mean score on happiness

2.58

Older, high-stressed
(*N* = 10)

Younger, high-stressed
(*N* = 30)

Older,
low-stressed
(*N* = 31)

Younger,
low-stressed
(*N* = 12)

Happy

Baseline   Second-year   Third-year
contact   contact

FIGURE 8.6 The interaction of life-stage and stress across time, showing mean scores for happiness (men only): transitions sample. (*Source*: Fiske & Chiriboga, 1985, Fig. 9.2. Reprinted with permission of Academic Press.)

men (middle-aged parents and preretirees at the beginning of the study) appeared more vulnerable to stress than younger men (high school seniors and new parents at the beginning of the study). The older men with high stress were the most unhappy at the second- and third-year contact, whereas older men with low stress were relatively happy. Younger men with low stress began the study as the most unhappy group, but at the third year contact were happier than those with high stress. In contrast, women who reported lower stress were happier than those who reported higher stress at each point (Fiske & Chiriboga, 1985, p. 199).

Comparing respondents from the divorce study with those in the transitions study who had not divorced, Fiske and Chiriboga (1985) noted that the divorcing sample showed greater evidence of psychosocial disruption. This supports the idea, suggested in Chapter 3, that nonnormative events are more disruptive than normative transitions. Other stressful events also affected the divorcing respondents and, not surprisingly, men and women with lower stress between the beginning of the study and the follow-up interview were happier than those with high stress. Age was also related to change in happiness:

> Men in their 40s improved most—from being quite unhappy at baseline to being the happiest group 3 years later. The two younger groups of men, those in their 20s and 30s, improved least, and while those of 50 or older did become somewhat happier at follow-up, they were still the least happy. . . . (Fiske & Chiriboga, 1985, p. 200)

> Similarly, women of all ages were generally happier by follow-up, but women in their 40s and over were happier than those in their 20s and 30s. Here we do find a difference from the men, since the oldest men in the divorce study ended up being the least happy group. Like the men, however, those women who experienced the greatest

stress between baseline and follow-up were less happy at both contacts. Once again we have evidence that stress is not only causally related to levels of happiness, but is itself predicted by characteristics of the people and situation. (p. 204)

Three other findings from these studies were also of interest. First, men seldom noted *stresses experienced by others* as a source of stress, but these were important sources of stress for women. Second, some *nonevents* (e.g., not having a grandchild) were perceived as stressful. Third, older persons tended to perceive stress in broader perspective than younger persons; they were less likely to become preoccupied with minor stress, perhaps because they had experienced more stress and more severe experiences during their lifetimes.

In Chapter 7, we discussed the link between stress, coping ability, and health. For example, in one longitudinal study major life crises appeared to affect physiological processes related to risk of illness (Willis, Thomas, Garry & Goodwin, 1987). However, the high risk level of the group experiencing crisis appeared to be reduced by the availability of social support, especially a confidant (Thomas, Goodwin & Goodwin, 1985). We discuss social support and the confidant relationship as a buffer against the major stresses of life in the next section.

Importance of a Confidant and Social Support

Lowenthal and Haven (1968) found that the presence of an intimate relationship — being able to confide in someone and to talk about yourself or about your problems — is highly important for older people (as it probably is for all of us). They found, in a study of 280 persons aged 60 and older who were living in the community, that the presence of such a **confidant** serves as a *buffer* against losses such as loss of role or a decline in social interaction. That is, those respondents who had a stable intimate relationship were less likely to be depressed (and more likely to be satisfied) than respondents without a confidant, even if their level of social interaction or their level of role status had decreased. This intimate relationship even seemed able to buffer these respondents against such significant losses as retirement and widowhood (Table 8.7). In fact, a slightly higher percentage of respondents who were widowed but had a confidant stated they were ''satisfied'' than those who were married but had no confidant. Similarly, a retired respondent with a confidant was as likely to be satisfied as a respondent who was still working but had no confidant. In addition, psychiatrists' ratings (for a subsample of 112) of the mental health of the respondents also showed the importance of a *stable* intimate relationship. That is, although the presence of a confidant was only slightly related to psychiatric status, 80 percent of the respondents who maintained the *same* confidant during the past year were rated ''unimpaired'' (compared with 20 percent rated ''impaired''). Thus, the maintenance of a stable, intimate relationship seems to serve an important function in protecting the individual's morale and mental stability against the various social losses that are associated with aging and with social disengagement (cf. Lemon, Bengtson & Peterson, 1972.)

However, as shown in Table 8.7, a confidant does not seem to buffer the individual against the psychological effects of physical illness. It appears that physi-

The presence of a confidant serves as a psychological protection against social and emotional losses, including retirement and widowhood. A long-term relationship with a confidant is especially helpful; the person may be a spouse, a child, or a friend.

ological decline, and particularly the onset of disease, is a process of such significance that even the buffer provided by a confidant is unable to prevent the loss of morale. The overpowering impact of disease was a central theme in Chapter 7; and even with an illness a confidant would be an important asset and possibly a caregiver for the aging person.

Women were somewhat more likely to have a confidant than men (69 and 57 percent, respectively). Married persons were more likely to have one than widows, who were more likely to have a confidant than single persons. The confidant was about equally likely to be a spouse, a child, or a friend. Lowenthal and Haven suggested that this gender difference may contribute to the greater longevity of women, as well as to their lower rate of suicide and their lower rate of mental illness following widowhood, as compared with men.

Although the practical implications of these findings are apparent—that aged persons who have intimate relationships benefit from maintaining close ties and the loss of a confidant has a more negative effect on morale than any other social

TABLE 8.7 *Effect of Widowhood, Retirement, and Physical Illness on Morale in the Presence and Absence of a Confidant (Age 60+)*

	Morale	
	Satisfied *(percent)*	Depressed *(percent)*
Widowed within 7 years:		
Has confidant	55	45
No confidant	(27)[a]	(73)
Married:		
Has confidant	65	35
No confidant	(47)	(53)
Retired within 7 years:		
Has confidant	50	50
No confidant	(36)	(64)
Not retired:		
Has confidant	70	30
No confidant	50	50
Serious physical illness within 2 years:		
Has confidant	(16)	(84)
No confidant	(13)	(87)
No serious illness:		
Has confidant	64	36
No confidant	42	58

[a]Percentages are placed in parentheses when the numbers on which they are based are under 20 ($N = 14-19$).
Source: Lowenthal & Haven (1968), Table 5. Reprinted with permission.

losses — there are three related points. First, some persons have maintained adequate levels of functioning with relative isolation over a long period of time; they seem no more prone to mental illness than nonisolates (Lowenthal, 1964). These isolates may also have high morale, but the majority of those who had lost a confidant are depressed. Second, loss of a confidant may result from a general dislocation (such as moving into a retirement community or a nursing home) that represents a double loss — a loss of social interactions and roles as well as loss of the confidant. Thus, when a confidant is needed most, he or she may be unavailable. Third, gaining a confidant may help some, but the importance of a stable relationship seems most significant.

Research on social support has proven to be complex and the findings are not as easy to interpret as this early study of the importance of a confidant. For example, social support is usually helpful, but it may also be a burden, especially if it involves conflictual interactions, providing care, or inequitable relationships. In general, patterns of social support appear to differ based on gender, age, ethnicity, and social class (Vaux, 1985). There is some evidence that social support enhances feelings of control if the support is not too extensive; beyond average levels, however, support appears to reduce feelings of control (Krause, 1987). Social support may also promote self-esteem (Pearlin, Menaghan, Lieberman, & Mullan, 1981).

Considerable research has explored the importance of social support for the elderly (Kahn, Wethington & Ingersoll-Dayton, 1987) and, in general, the data affirm that social support is an important determinant of well-being. Also, there is evidence that social support does provide a kind of buffer, especially for those persons who were recently widowed or are physically dependent.

Aging and Psychopathology

Up to this point, we have been focusing primarily on normal or typical processes of development during adulthood. **Psychopathology** is the study of abnormal personality functioning; it seeks to understand the nature and causes of psychological disorders or dysfunctions in emotional responses, thinking patterns, and ordinary daily functioning. It overlaps with the study of *social deviance* in sociology and with the study of *psychiatry* in medicine. Thus, it is an interdisciplinary field and may be studied from a developmental perspective. However, because it is such a large field, we can only present a brief overview of some of the topics that are most relevant for understanding aging and mental illness. We begin first with the most visible group of elderly persons with psychological disorders — those in institutions such as nursing homes. Second, we outline the variety of factors that can lead to psychological difficulties in old age. Third, we describe the most important types of psychological disturbance among older adults. Finally, we discuss psychotherapy and other forms of mental health treatment for older adults.

Institutionalized Elderly Persons

First impressions of nursing homes and mental hospital wards suggest that the aged comprise a relatively large proportion of persons with psychological problems. There are two factors involved: some persons have been hospitalized for many years and literally grow old in institutions or are maintained in the community through outpatient services or in nursing homes. In addition, a sizable proportion of admissions to nursing homes involve Alzheimer's disease or other psychological problems. Moreover, since the mid 1960s, mental health policy has been to "deinstitutionalize" patients from mental hospitals; for many older persons, this has meant reinstitutionalizing them in adult homes, single-room occupancy hotels, or nursing homes (Kermis, 1986). Many of these older people do not receive mental health services because they are in institutions that do not routinely provide psychological or psychiatric care.

> Nursing homes are the single largest place of care for the chronically mentally ill elderly. It is estimated that 56 to 80 percent of the 1.4 million residents of nursing homes in the United States have diagnosable mental conditions. In addition, nursing homes house a sizable population of individuals now having, or at risk of having, behavioral problems. Eight to ten percent of the nursing home residents are former residents of state mental hospitals or longterm-care specialty hospitals. Among the most

common diagnoses and forms of behavior in the nursing home are Alzheimer's disease, confusion, depression, wandering, disorientation, agitation, withdrawal, lethargy, frustration, stress reaction, dependency, apathy, guilt, irritability, rise and fall of self-esteem, persistent talk of a wish to die, paranoid delusions.

Against this backdrop of need, we know that in most nursing homes recognition and treatment of psychiatric conditions is unavailable or inadequate. . . .

The recognition of mental disorder in nursing homes is restricted by regulations that limit the number of residents with a primary psychiatric diagnosis. If more than half the residents of a nursing home have a psychiatric diagnosis, for example, the home is classified as an "Institution for Mental Disease," and the range of services it can provide will be refined. (Lebowitz, 1988, p. 54)

Mental health services are also restricted in nursing homes through lower levels of Medicare reimbursement, lack of training in geriatric mental health, lack of collaboration with Community Mental Health Centers, and other general reasons discussed at the end of this chapter. Even many nursing homes operated by the Veterans Administration, which recommends including psychologists on the staff, have only minimal training in geropsychology (Kupke, 1986).

Psychological Disorders and Biological Changes

Chronic disease and impairments, physiological changes, malnutrition, and even medication can play an important part in psychological disorders, especially among the aged. A number of factors are involved. Decreased hearing, sight, or physical mobility affect the kind of interactions one can have with others and also affect the inner experience of sensory stimulation. In addition, the general "slowing down" of reaction time, associated with aging and compounded by disease, makes it difficult to respond as fast as younger people. Sometimes these changes make one less sure of oneself, more isolated from stimulation, and more likely to get confused at fast-paced tasks in daily life (such as counting out change in a supermarket). Taken together, and combined with feelings of decreased social status, such changes can lead to feelings of "persecution" that, in extreme form, could resemble psychopathology. One example of this perhaps common experience in old age is from a fictional story:

They were all squabbles of one kind or another. The milkman had begun counting out the wrong change for me. The postman had held back my mail. The paper boy had delivered my newspaper or not, as the inclination struck him. And the clerks at the grocery store had amused themselves by playing petty tricks on me, breaking a few of my eggs as they packed the carton in a bag, or speaking so softly I could not hear them. The milkman wanted money, the postman and the newspaper boy convenience, the clerks amusement. To keep me from insisting on justice and courtesy, they relied on the precariousness of an old person's reputation, on the skepticism with which the word of the old is regarded, on my fear and feebleness. But I caught each of them up, and I did insist. (Webber, 1963)

It is, of course, impossible to determine how much of this "persecution" was actual (and related to the lower status of the aged) or was exaggerated because of some hearing loss, social isolation, and slower cognitive processes. However, more marked physical impairment can lead to a high degree of social isolation and also to mental illness. Lowenthal (1964) reported that a sample of aged respondents in a mental hospital were "considerably sicker physically" than a community sample of respondents of the same age (three-fourths reported "physical illness" as a major life-change since age 50). She also found that although lifelong extreme isolation did *not* seem to produce mental illness in old age, late-developing isolation and physical illness seemed to be related to mental illness. This suggested that physical illness may precede and cause both relative isolation and psychological disturbance in old age. Butler (1963a) reported significant interrelationships among "contemporaneous environmental deficits" (largely losses of significant persons), response time to psychomotor tasks, and depression as rated by psychiatrists. It seems that there is an important interaction among physiological, psychological, and social variables in the development of mental illness in the aged.

In the absence of Alzheimer's disease and other dementias, however, aged persons seem to be subject to the same range of psychopathology as young and middle-aged adults. Certainly physical illness and social trauma in the adult years could be relevant precipitating events for psychopathology in late life. Also, marital difficulties, identity problems, or bereavement can be important issues for young, middle-aged, and old adults. It is important, we feel, not only to try to understand what persons are "up against" regardless of their age, but also to be sensitive to particular crisis points from a developmental perspective as well. It may be true that different forms of therapy are useful for different types of issues and at different ages, but the general forms of psychopathology seem to be generally unrelated to age. However, there are three exceptions: depression, suicide, and dementia.

Depression

A widely used diagnostic manual described major **depressive syndrome** as including at least *five* of the following symptoms nearly every day during a period of two weeks (American Psychiatric Association, 1987, p. 222). Either (1) depressed mood or (2) loss of interest or pleasure must be one of the symptoms:

1. Depressed mood.
2. Loss of interest or pleasure in most activities.
3. Significant weight loss or decrease in appetite when not dieting, or weight gain or increase in appetite.
4. Insomnia, or sleeping much more than usual.
5. Agitation or restlessness, or being slowed down in movement or speech.
6. Fatigue or loss of energy.
7. Feelings of worthlessness or excessive or inappropriate guilt.
8. Reduced ability to concentrate, or increased indecisiveness.
9. Frequent thoughts of death, suicidal thoughts, or suicide attempt or plan.

Bereavement, even if it includes symptoms of a major depressive syndrome, is not ordinarily considered a mental disorder, unless it includes specific serious symptoms such as suicidal thoughts, or is of unusual duration (see Chapter 9).

La Rue, Dessonville, and Jarvik (1985) reviewed aging and mental disorders and noted that depression is one the most prevalent and most treatable of the mental disorders affecting the elderly. They reported that often the symptoms of depression in the elderly respond well to treatment with antidepressive medication. Psychotherapy is also often effective in treating depression. However, depression may not be diagnosed accurately because some of these symptoms may be assumed to be a ''natural'' consequence of aging; thus it may be underdiagnosed, or misdiagnosed as dementia. Clinical depression may result from physical illness, or lead to a cycle of emotional and physical illness if untreated. La Rue et al. (1985) stressed that clinical depression should be distinguished from mild depressions and sadness. In general, severe depression does not result from bereavement since the symptoms of bereaved persons are usually fewer and less severe than those of persons hospitalized for depression. Likewise, isolation, retirement, and relocation to new housing does not ordinarily produce depression. A variety of factors, such as the presence of social support, especially a confidant, are important in buffering the individual from this type of social loss. They concluded: "Only a small minority of older people are clinically depressed, and adaptation, rather than decompensation, appears to be the modal reaction to any single loss such as bereavement or retirement" (p. 676).

Suicide

Although depression and suicide are not necessarily related, many suicides in old age result from severe depression, sometimes in association with other psychotic symptoms such as delusions. In some cases, suicide may seem to be a solution to an

Depression is one of the most prevalent and most treatable of the mental disorders affecting the elderly.

intolerable social situation or physical illness; that is, suicide is sometimes attempted when the depression seems intolerable and the person feels there is no chance for improvement, or because there is a decreased ability to function or to recover from terminal illness.

Suicide attempts are much more common than actual suicides among younger persons, but suicide attempts among older persons almost always reflect an intent to die (Pfeiffer, 1977). Suicide death rates increase steadily with age for White males (Figure 8.7). Although there is a marked difference between the rates for men and women among White persons, this difference is much less marked for Black persons, and the increase with age is seen only for White men. Butler and Lewis (1977) speculated that "the explanation lies in the severe loss of status (ageism) that affects white men, who as a group had held the greatest power and influence in society. Black men and most women have long been accustomed to a lesser status (through racism and sexism) and ironically do not have to suffer such a drastic fall in old age" (p. 68).

Marshall (1978) analyzed suicide rates for persons between 65 and 74 years old and found that there had been a dramatic decline in the rate for White males between 1948 and 1972 in the United States, although it was still much higher than for White women (data for Black persons were not sufficient to be included in his analysis). He then compared the rising income status of the aged with the declining suicide rate and concluded that the change in the White male suicide rate was highly related to their income. Thus, improved economic well-being of older men ap-

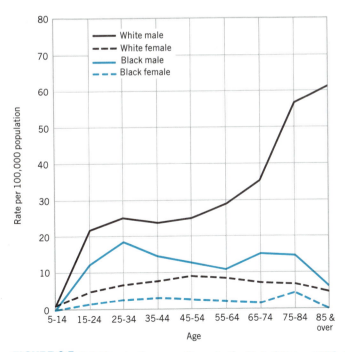

FIGURE 8.7 Suicide rates by age and race in the United States, 1985. (*Source*: Adapted from National Center for Health Statistics. *Health, United States, 1987*, DHHS Pub. No. PHS 88–1232, Table 31, pp. 74–75. Washington, D.C.: U.S. Government Printing Office, 1988.)

peared to have substantially reduced their suicide rate. However, since social and political attitudes about aging, as well as general physical health, may have also improved during this period, we cannot conclude that greater income alone explains the decline in suicide — or that the loss of status with age in general is the cause of the high suicide rate for White men. For example, Miller (1978), in a study of White male suicides after age 60 in Arizona between 1970 and 1975, noted that the men who committed suicide were likely to have been widowed, to have lost a confidant or never have had one, and to have recently seen a physician; over half had given some clue of their suicidal intention. This suggested that the loss of a confidant, perhaps combined with physical complaints, an inability to discuss their problem with their physician, or lack of assistance from the physician were related to the suicide. Difficulty in coping with retirement also seemed to be a major problem for many of these men.

With regard to both depression and suicide, psychological factors (coping styles, personality integration, and past experiences), social factors (losses of roles, status, and significant others), and physical factors (disease, physiological changes that affect emotional reactions, and loss of hearing or sight or mobility) combine and interact to produce the reactions that may be so painful for the person that they may lead to a loss of desire to continue living.

It should be noted that although the *rate* of suicide is highest for older White males, it is matched by young Native Americans. Also the *number* of suicides is higher for young persons (age 20 – 24) — who also comprise a larger proportion of the population. Moreover, the increase in suicides in this younger age group has been very large, whereas the suicide rate of older persons has been declining (Kastenbaum, 1985). In a study of changes in suicide rates between 1962 and 1981, the two populations with the greatest increase in risk of suicide were the oldest-old (age 85+) and nonwhite men. The increase for nonwhite men of all ages, 37.3 percent, was over twice the increase for White men during this period (Manton, Blazer & Woodbury, 1987).

Alzheimer's Disease, Dementia, and "Senility"

Senility is not a medical diagnosis, but it is often used as a "wastebasket" category for any old person with symptoms of severe memory loss, confusion, and disorientation. In recent years the term Alzheimer's disease has tended to be used in the same way; sometimes it is even mispronounced as "old-timer's disease" — implying that it is a condition caused by old age. Gatz and Pearson (1988) noted that Alzheimer's may represent a new form of age bias: it is the focus of considerable media attention, its prevalence is greatly overestimated, and it is overdiagnosed by clinicians. Although we cannot discuss this complex disease in detail, the goal of this section is to dispel many of the myths about senility and to point out some the most important aspects of dementia and aging.

Perhaps 1.5 million persons in the United States suffer from severe dementia, including Alzheimer's disease and other forms of major cognitive impairment, including about 25 percent of the population over age 85; the number of persons afflicted with dementia is expected to increase as the population over age 85 increases (Roybal, 1988). **Dementia** is defined by the American Psychiatric Association (1987) by the following symptoms:

1. Impairment of short-term memory (inability to learn new information) and long-term memory (inability to remember past personal information such as birthplace or occupation).
2. Impairment of abstract thinking, judgment, certain "higher" mental abilities, or personality change.
3. The disturbance interferes with work, usual social activities or relationships with others.
4. Not associated with the condition known as delirium (i.e., the person is conscious and alert).
5. Evidence of physical (organic) cause or not caused by some nonorganic disorder such as depression, malnutrition, or medication.

There are several forms of dementia, such as *multi-infarct dementia*, caused by several small strokes (cerebrovascular disease), *dementia of the Alzheimer type* (DAT), and a variety of other less common types such as Pick's disease and Jakob-Creutzfeldt disease. The only certain method to diagnose DAT is by autopsy of the brain after death. Thus, the diagnosis of type of dementia can be made only on the basis of clinical examination including a careful history of the condition. Medical tests can be useful in ruling out a variety of possible causes of the condition (La Rue et al., 1985). Psychological tests are also useful in identifying those persons who have mild DAT and in predicting those with mild DAT who would develop moderate or severe DAT within 12 months (Berg et al., 1984; Storandt, Botwinick, Danziger, Berg & Hughes, 1984).

It is particularly important to differentiate dementia from other conditions that may produce similar symptoms (Box 8.2). In particular, it is important to distinguish conditions associated with **delirium** and those associated with **reversible dementia,** since these can often be treated.

> Delirium is marked by disturbed mental functioning which frequently includes dramatic symptoms such as hallucinations, delusions, disorientation, increased or decreased alertness, attention deficits, and disturbed sleep patterns. There are rapid fluctuations in symptoms and their severity. In contrast, reversible dementia has been described as involving symptoms of memory loss which are virtually indistinguishable from irreversible dementia. . . .
>
> [The most frequent causes of delirium and reversible dementia in older persons] include toxic effects of medications or interactions between drugs, brain tumor, infections, electrolyte imbalances, malnutrition, and metabolic and endocrine disorders. . . . Symptoms may also occur following surgeries, fractures, head injuries, strokes, or environmental changes, including being moved to a nursing home or after the death of a spouse. . . . When the cause of the symptoms can be treated, the outcome is generally good, and complete recovery is not uncommon. If left untreated however, many of these conditions will lead to permanent brain damage and/or to death. (Zarit, Orr & Zarit, 1985, pp. 19–20)

Robert Butler (1975) was among the first geriatric psychiatrists to call attention to these conditions:

BOX 8.2 *Causes of Memory Loss*
Definitions of Dementia, Delirium, Depression and Normal Aging

Term	*Definition*	*Other Names*
Dementia	A syndrome involving memory and other impairments in cognition and behavior. Dementia may be irreversible when caused by a degenerative brain disease, or may be potentially reversible if caused by treatable conditions such as metabolic or toxic disorders.	Dementing illness, organic brain syndrome (O.B.S.), chronic brain syndrome (C.B.S.), senility, senile dementia
Alzheimer's disease	The most frequent cause of irreversible dementia.	Senile dementia of the Alzheimer type (SDAT), primary degenerative dementia
Multi-infarct dementia	A type of dementia caused by multiple small strokes (also called transient ischemic attacks or t.i.a.'s).	Vascular dementia
Delirium	A syndrome involving fluctuating mental function and disturbances of consciousness, attention, and cognition. Delirium can be caused by many conditions, including drugs, infections, fractures, metabolic disorders, malnutrition, and environmental stress.	Acute brain syndrome (A.B.S.), acute confusional state, toxic psychosis

---

The failure to diagnose and treat *reversible brain syndromes* is so unnecessary and yet so widespread that I would caution families of older persons to question doctors involved in care about this. . . .

Unfortunately many doctors dismiss the symptoms, assuming that the person is demonstrating typical confusion from chronic brain syndromes caused by hardening of the arteries or senile brain disease, and fail to treat the patient. (pp. 175–176)

Even in institutions such as nursing homes, "acting senile" can result from depression, overmedication, lack of emotional stimulation, or be a withdrawal from an unpleasant environment. Butler and Lewis (1977) noted that physician-induced reversible and irreversible dementia can be caused by certain drugs such as cortisone and extended use of tranquilizers; and even small amounts of medications may have marked negative reactions in older people.

Considerable research is currently focusing on the nature and causes of **Alzheimer's disease** (dementia of the Alzheimer type, or DAT). The condition was

---

BOX 8.2 *(Continued)*

Term	Definition	Other Names
Nonprogressive brain injury	Brain damage caused by head trauma, or other injury. Cognitive impairments depend on site and severity of the injury. Impairment does not get worse over time.	
Depression	Persistent feelings of sadness or dysphoric mood; often accompanied by lack of energy, loss of appetite, insomnia, withdrawal from usual activities. In the elderly, depression sometimes presents without overt complaints of sadness.	Depressive dementia, pseudodementia, dementia syndrome of depression, affective disorder, unipolar depression
Normal aging	The normal changes in behavior that occur with aging and in the absence of a dementing illness. These changes have a benign impact on cognitive functioning.	Senescence

Source: Reprinted with permission of New York University Press from *The hidden victims of Alzheimer's disease: Families under stress* by Steven H. Zarit, Nancy K. Orr, and Judy M. Zarit, Table 2.1. Copyright © 1985 by New York University.

---

first noted by Dr. Alois Alzheimer in 1907 and was once thought to affect only persons younger than age 65. Now it is known to involve a similar type of brain pathology as in the majority of older dementia patients. The characteristic markers of the disease involve *senile plaques, neurofibrillary tangles,* and *granulovacuolar structures;* there is also an overall loss of neurons (Figure 8.8). The normal brain cell (1) contains a nucleus and there is an axon that is a long projection radiating out from the cell resembling a tree.

In Alzheimer's disease, abnormal tangled protein fibers, the neurofibrillary tangles, appear in the cell body (2). Usually, when there are tangles, there are also senile plaques nearby (2). Plaques are masses of degenerated cell matter which occur in the spaces between cells and interfere with the messages that are sent from cell to cell.

If you think of a normal cell (1) as a tree, then the tangles are like a disease from within and the plaques are like a pest outside. What happens to the cell is very much like what happens to a tree being defoliated (3), (4). It swells and becomes gnarled; then it shrivels (5) to a stump (6). . . .

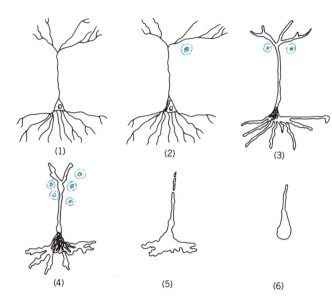

FIGURE 8.8 Progressive degeneration of a brain neuron in Alzheimer's disease. (*Source*: Reprinted with permission of New York University Press from *The hidden victims of Alzheimer's disease: Families under stress* by Steven H. Zarit, Nancy K. Orr, and Judy M. Zarit, Fig. 2.1. Copyright © 1985 by New York University.)

The other characteristic change in Alzheimer's disease, the granulovacuolar structures, are sacs filled with fluid and granular material that accumulate in the cell bodies of pyramidal cells in the hippocampus but rarely in other parts of the brain. Thus, impairment resulting from Alzheimer's disease appears selective for certain areas of the brain and types of cells. (Zarit et al., 1985, p. 12).

It was once thought that "senility" resulted from hardening of the arteries that in turn resulted in a lack of oxygen to the brain. Now that the nature of DAT is better understood, attention is focusing on the disruption of neurotransmitter systems, especially the role of *acetylcholine,* which is thought to be associated with learning and memory (La Rue et al., 1985). However, as of 1989 no treatment had been found to reverse the effects of DAT despite a major focus of research on the disease.

There are several ideas about the cause of Alzheimer's disease, but so far none has been clearly established. It is clear that there is an inherited factor in some cases where there is evidence of a family history of the disease. Recently the location of the genetic material associated with the hereditary transmission of this disease has been identified, but the implications of this finding are not clear at present (Jarvik, 1988).

Another theory about the cause of Alzheimer's disease is that there is some infectious agent involved, such as a "slow" virus or similar particle that requires a long incubation period from initial infection to ultimate development of the disease; if the person lives long enough and is infected, it would then develop late in life. Still another theory involves some toxin such as aluminum (from cooking utensils, cans, and products that contain aluminum salts) that somehow manages to pass through the blood–brain barrier and accumulate in neurons as neurofibrillary tangles; this may be the result instead of the cause of the disease, however. Reduced blood flow might also play a role, as might the decline in acetylcholine. As in

Malnutrition, depression, moving from one's familiar environment, or lack of emotional stimulation can lead to symptoms that resemble senility in an older person, but this condition can be reversed if it is diagnosed and treated appropriately.

cancer, there may be multiple factors involved, including but not limited to hereditary predispositions and these other plausible, but unproven, explanations (Wurtman, 1985). Likewise, DAT may consist of several different diseases that we are currently unable to differentiate (La Rue et al., 1985). Moreover, one study indicated that changes in mental performance may precede the diagnosis of dementia by as much as 20 years (Jarvik & La Rue, 1979). All these ideas have been inconclusive as of 1989.

Treatment of persons with dementia focuses primarily on controlling the symptoms and helping the caregivers to cope with the problems associated with the symptoms. It is especially important to diagnose and treat the reversible dementias, and also to diagnose and treat *depression,* which may appear to be dementia, or may coexist with the dementia.

Limited but important community supports are available to aid caregivers and the Alzheimer's and Related Disease Association organizes peer support groups in many communities (the national office is at 700 East Lake Street, Chicago, IL 60601). Caring for a person with Alzheimer's is often a considerable burden on the caregiver (Anthony-Bergstone, Zarit & Gatz, 1988; Zarit et al., 1985). Useful types of assistance include education about the disease, help in solving practical problems, and social support. Professional counseling for the caregivers, often including structured family meetings, and support groups also have been found to be beneficial (Zarit & Zarit, 1982).

The eventual course of the disease may require institutional care. Unfortunately, Medicare and most private insurance does not provide for "custodial" care since skilled nursing care is not necessary. We have already noted that nursing homes seldom provide mental health services. In the next chapter we discuss home health care and list community resources that may be available.

Mental Health Services and Older Adults

Margaret Gatz (1989) noted that one of the most interesting aspects of providing mental health services to older adults is that so many factors are involved and diagnosis of the relevant issues is so complex. In addition, often both the aging client and the extended family are in need of services.

> Another aspect that makes working with older adults interesting and rewarding is that often these are individuals or families who have been very ordinary or normal their entire lives and now are faced with an extraordinary, abnormal situation. In short, although clinical psychologists cannot cure dementia, these are people who can be helped. (Gatz, 1989, pp. 84–85)

There is considerable evidence that older adults do not receive as much mental health care as would be desirable (Flemming, Rickards, Santos & West, 1986; Santos, & VandenBos, 1982; Roybal, 1988). Ethnic minority elders are even less well served (Fellin & Powell, 1988). The reasons for this inadequate level of services are complex, but they do not necessarily include a bias against older persons (Gatz & Pearson, 1988). For example, the present cohort of elders may be reluctant to seek aid for emotional problems; funding to community mental health centers does not stimulate effective outreach to older adults; training programs in some mental health professions (such as psychology) do not emphasize geriatric specialization; and there are presently few financial incentives for many private practitioners to seek out older patients (Medicare offers only limited reimbursement for psychotherapy, primarily to psychiatrists).

Nonetheless, studies have found that chronological age is not a very important factor in determining outcome of mental health treatment; older persons may, in fact, improve as much or more than younger persons (Knight, 1983, 1988). Traditional and innovative forms of psychological treatment and therapy have been shown to be effective with elderly persons (Gottsegen & Park, 1982). A variety of group therapy approaches also have been found to be effective with older adults as outpatients in the community and in institutions (MacLennan, Saul & Weiner, 1988; Tross & Blum, 1988). Training practitioners to work with older persons and their families will be one of the most critical needs for the mental health professions in the 1990s.

We discuss the variety of roles in which students may be trained to provide a range of services to older adults at the conclusion of the next chapter. But first we pause for another interlude—an interview with an older person who has been a caregiver for a spouse with Alzheimer's disease for 10 years.

Chapter Summary

1. Definitions of personality involve three characteristics: the uniqueness of a person, attributes that are fairly stable over long periods of time and across different situations, and the adaptation of the individual to the social and physical environment.

2. Differences between men and women reflect the interaction of physiological, psychological, and social influences. Sex-related norms and expectations differ between cultures. Nonetheless, men and women share many characteristics and individual women and men vary in the extent to which they adopt socially prescribed gender roles.

3. Stereotypes usually define men and women as opposite to each other (e.g., independent versus dependent). Women's role stereotype is that of a passive object that is looked at and manipulated. Men's role stereotype emphasizes getting ahead, staying cool, and avoiding any "sissy stuff." Gender-role stereotypes have been linked with lower self-esteem for women and shorter life expectancy for men.

4. The study of androgyny focuses on the relation between biological sex and gender role. Androgynous men and women combine "masculine" and "feminine" characteristics in their self-description. Older men tend to be more androgynous than younger men. Androgyny in older men and women appears related to better mental health and successful aging.

5. Personality has two distinct facets — continuity and change. Both processes occur simultaneously, which is described as the "uncertainty principle." Thus, depending on the lenses used to view personality, one tends to emphasize either change or continuity. Moreover, we can never fully predict an individual's behavior in the future.

6. The study of personality traits or characteristics emphasizes individual uniqueness and the continuity of personality over time. Some personality traits (neuroticism, extraversion, and openness) have been found to be very stable over time for individuals and show little evidence of cohort or developmental change during adulthood.

7. Behavioral perspectives emphasize the potential for personality change as a result of environmental factors and social reinforcements that influence behavior. The process model emphasizes an individual's creation of personality through a unique life course. The dialectical view focuses on adaptation to stress and various coping strategies.

8. The continuity theory of aging stresses dynamic adaptation within a basically stable structure of life. It implies that maintaining a sense of internal and external continuity is a preferred strategy for aging. However, some older people seek adventure and may relocate to find change. Individual personality may account for this difference.

9. The Kansas City studies found that characteristics that deal with adaptive, goal-directed, and purposeful aspects of life remain generally stable with aging. Ego

energy that is available for tasks in the outer world declines. Ego style shifts from active to passive mastery. Individuals show increased introspection and "interiority."

10. Research on stress and aging suggested that nonnormative events (divorce) and nonevents (not having a grandchild) are stressful. Stresses experienced by others are more important sources of stress for women than for men. Older persons perceive stress in broader perspective and focus less on minor stress than younger persons.

11. The presence of an intimate relationship — a confidant — is important for the morale of many older people. It serves as a buffer against loss of roles, decline in social interaction, and widowhood. However, a confidant does not protect an individual against the psychological effects of physical illness.

12. Psychopathology is the study of abnormal personality functioning. Physical disease, social isolation, and losses of significant persons increase the risk of psychological disorder in old age. Many residents of nursing homes have mental conditions and behavioral problems. Most do not receive adequate treatment for mental illness.

13. Depression is one of the most prevalent and most treatable of the mental disorders affecting the elderly. It is often assumed to be a "natural" consequence of aging, however, and not diagnosed at all or misdiagnosed as dementia — without appropriate treatment. It is not ordinary sadness and usually does not result from bereavement.

14. Although younger people account for a higher number of suicides, suicide rates increase dramatically with age for White males. Loss of social status, reduced income, loss of a confidant, and increased health problems are among the factors that may lead to suicide. The suicide rate is growing fastest among those over 85 and nonwhite men.

15. "Senility" is not a medical diagnosis, but is often used as an excuse for not treating the physical, psychological, or social problems of old people. In recent years the term Alzheimer's disease has been used in the same way, implying that it is a condition caused by old age. This may represent age bias and interfere with treatment.

16. There are several forms of dementia. It is important to differentiate dementia from other conditions that may produce similar symptoms, such as delirium and reversible dementia, since these two conditions can often be treated. Malnutrition, dehydration, and many other causes can lead to chronic brain impairment if not treated.

17. Considerable research is focusing on the nature and causes of Alzheimer's disease. Treatment focuses primarily on controlling the symptoms and helping caregivers cope with problems associated with the symptoms. Community resources and self-help groups can provide support for caregivers.

18. Providing mental health services to older persons and their families is interesting and rewarding in part because many have been normal and ordinary persons all their lives and now are faced with extraordinary situations. Older per-

sons generally improve as much or more than younger persons from mental health treatment.

Key Words

adaptation
Alzheimer's disease (DAT)
androgyny
behaviorism
confidant
continuity theory
delirium
dementia
depressive syndrome

gender
increased interiority
life satisfaction
personality
psychopathology
reversible dementia
social behaviorism
socioadaptational characteristics

Review Questions

1. Define personality in three different ways.

Gender Differences in Personality

2. What do Margaret Mead's descriptions of gender differences in various cultures suggest about the interaction of physiology and the social environment in the process of becoming a man or a woman?

3. Define androgyny and explain what is meant by the statement that this is a duality model rather than a bipolar model of gender differences.

4. List some of the characteristics that have been found to be higher among persons who are androgynous; note the age and gender of the sample described.

Continuity and Change in Personality over Time

5. How can there be continuity and change in an individual's personality at the same time?

6. What is the evidence to support Costa and McCrae's conclusion that "aging itself has little effect on personality"?

7. Describe the difference between the personality trait perspective and the behavioral perspective.

8. Explain Tyler's statement: "Individuals create themselves" as an example of the process view of personality.

9. Summarize the major themes of the dialectical model of personality. Describe Box 8.1 in your own words.

10. What are the advantages of aging according to the continuity theory? Do you know persons who fit this model? Would you like to be an example of the adventurous aged? Why or why not?

Patterns of Personality Stability and Change in Adulthood

11. According to the Kansas City studies, what is the common theme in those personality characteristics that do not change with age? Define this characteristic. Is it compatible with the continuity theory?

12. Describe the changes in personality identified in the Kansas City studies.

13. How are the gender roles of older men and women described by middle-aged and older respondents? Compare Gutmann's statement about the "normal unisex of later life" with the concept of androgyny.

14. Cite some examples from the research on self-conceptions and the research on stress that suggest differences between younger and older people.

15. Define a confidant. What is the effect of having a confidant in later life if one (a) experiences a social loss or (b) has a major illness?

Aging and Psychopathology

16. What are the symptoms of depression? How can it be treated?

17. In your opinion, what accounts for the dramatic differences in suicide rates shown in Figure 8.7?

18. Why should the label "senile" be avoided? What are some causes of reversible dementia? Why is it important to diagnose promptly?

19. Cite some reasons why older persons do not receive adequate mental health services.

INTERLUDE

David, AGE 65

David is a leader and organizer of a local support group for persons who care for someone with Alzheimer's disease. His wife developed the disease 10 years ago, and David's own struggle led him to recognize the concerns faced by caregivers and the importance of peer support. The support and the organizing efforts played an important role in his own ability to cope with this tragedy. He was interviewed in 1989 at his office in the high school where he has been principal for many years.

This interview raises several questions relevant to the previous chapter. How has this long-term stressful transition affected his personality? What personality characteristics have helped him to cope with the situation? Have his work and volunteer activities helped him maintain his own mental health? Is the course of his wife's illness typical for the disease? If he could not afford to hire someone to care for his wife, what would happen?

As you look back over your life, what are some of the milestones that stand out? My high school; my college; my service in the U.S. Navy during World War II; my marriage; the birth of my children; my career; my wife's illness; and the birth of my grandchildren. That about sums it up. *How old are you?* Sixty-five.

You mention your high school; what about that was a milestone in your life? Well, high school was the time of my life when I made the closest friends who remain with me; that's where I met my wife. That's when I first became aware of what I thought my potentials were; and matured. *And then World War II?* Well, that was a trial by fire, literally.

First of all, there was a sort of an ideological decision; I mean I enlisted and I insisted on seeing action even though my mother, like a typical Jewish mother, was trying to find ways to keep me in the States. And then I was thrown together with people of all different kinds and had experiences that are literally unforgettable. Anybody who goes through a war is bound to remember that's the highlight, or lowlight, of his life. *Were you injured?* No, except in a fistfight, that's all.

Then you mentioned the birth of your children as a milestone. How many children do you have? Three. *Can you tell me anything about that period?* Yes. My children were exceptional, are exceptional. My wife and I, I guess, had good genes. Two went to Harvard, one went to Northwestern; they did very well and we're very proud of them. What else is there in a parent's life but to feel pride in children?

You mentioned also your career as being a milestone? What particular things? When I got out of the Navy, I went back to finish college and I was for a while undecided whether I wanted to go into teaching or pursue what I had done in the Navy. I was a radio operator mechanic. But I decided to go into teaching and found it was something very much to my liking and was very successful at it and was promoted several times until I have my present position, which I find is the best of all. It is the kind of work that I love doing and in many ways, it's the most important part of my present therapy in dealing with my wife's illness. *Do you have plans to retire?* Yes, but not within the next couple of years (laughs). I don't have any real plans. I know that someday I will retire, but right now I'm enjoying it too much and finding it easier and easier each year, which is after 18 years as a principal. So I imagine I will keep going for at least two, maybe longer. *Is there any mandatory age limit?* No, I can stay on as long as I'm sane and can walk and breathe (laughs).

You mentioned another milestone was your wife's illness. Yeah, well, I think my wife's illness was the most traumatic experience of my life. It was diagnosed almost 10 years ago, so for the past 10 years I've been finding ways to cope with that illness and the effect it's had on me and my family and on other people with whom I've come into contact who are facing similar problems. *The illness is what?* Alzheimer's disease.

We can return to that a little later; you mentioned also the milestone of the birth of grandchildren. Yeah, well, just as my children were the highlight of my life, I'm finding that it's almost a second life watching the grandchildren grow. I have five. The oldest is only three years of age. So they're little ones. I guess I derive as much pleasure from them as I do from anything else. I have two who live near me. And two who live in New York with my son and daughter-in-law. And one little girl living in Holland, in Amsterdam, with my daughter who moved there about six years ago and got married a little over a year and a half ago. They sort of renew the spirits and give you a never-ending source [of joy]—I mean, any grandparent will tell you this—you never get tired of playing with them, seeing them, and things like that.

What about crisis points? Were there any crisis points that stand out? Obviously, most of these crisis points are in connection with my wife. You know, as the disease progresses you have to constantly find new strategies to cope with the new problems that are arising. But

other than that, I wouldn't say that my life has been filled with crisis other than the normal things that happen to anybody—[like] the death of parents. *Was that particularly difficult for you?* I don't think it was any more difficult than for anyone else. I mean, fortunately when my father died, my wife was still ok. So she was a support in that situation. When my mother died my wife was already in the middle stage of Alzheimer's disease, so that was a little more difficult. But, I don't see it as any major trauma.

Have there been any particular crisis points with your wife's illness? I guess the worst part of the ordeal was the first several years when she was still able to speak somewhat, but almost every day I could see a decline in her ability to write, to read, to speak, to think, to dress, to walk. And then I guess the worst point of it was about six years ago when she had emergency surgery for a perforated ulcer which could have resulted in her death if I hadn't gotten her to the emergency room at the time that I did. She had been complaining about pain, but she couldn't localize it. You know, when you'd ask her, "Where is it?" She'd say, "All over." I took her to two doctors; they didn't find anything. Stupidly, they never thought to take an X-ray. It was only when a housekeeper that I had called me at school to tell me that my wife seemed to be in great pain and couldn't get out of bed that I rushed home and rushed her to the emergency room. That was the worst phase of her illness because she came out of the hospital, as Alzheimer's patients always do, much worse than she went in—mentally that is. The disease seems to take a sharp downturn after any kind of hospitalization.

The difficulty is getting satisfactory care for her at home while I'm away at work, or at play—whatever that may be. There's also the sometimes intense feeling of loneliness and loss of companionship and loss of sexual experience, call it what you will, that goes with losing a spouse, you know, not to death, but to what amounts to a death. So that's part of the pain that you suffer. *It was because of Alzheimer's disease that she couldn't tell you about the pain?* That's right. She couldn't express it; she couldn't tell where it was. We attributed the thing either to imagination or — we had also been a part of a double-blind experiment in drug treatment at _____ Hospital at the time; we thought it might be the effects of the medication that she was taking there, so we discontinued that. Later on I learned she was only on the placebo anyway; but that's what we thought it might be. And then discovered that it was something really serious. *Is she living at home now?* Yeah. She's been home right along.

Have there been any crisis points in your occupation? Not really. I can't think of anything that I'd call a crisis point. *Has the way people react to you changed over the years?* Sure. *In what ways?* They treat me like a grown man (laughs). Well, I don't know, I guess it's since I've been principal for so long and been associated with the school for so long, I have special status here, as well as in the city as a whole. I mean, all the high school principals in the city know me; I'm by now the second senior principal. And I guess I've been fairly successful in my work, so I've earned respect from the community, the teachers, the children, and so on, colleagues. It hasn't always been easy. When I first took over the job I had all kinds of minor irritations with unions, with this problem, that problem, but I've overcome all of that. I feel very comfortable; very secure and very content with what I'm doing. I think people react to that. Also, you know, when you get older you get gray hair and wrinkles and people see you're still able to walk and are physically healthy, that earns you some respect, too. So, I would say that as I've grown older, I guess I've grown better.

How is life different now than it was a few years ago for you? You mean, before my wife got sick? *Ok.* Well, it was very different. First of all, I think probably every waking moment of the day for the past 10 years somewhere in my mind there's been the thought of my wife and the disease: how is she doing, and what are we doing to deal with this disease, or find a treatment, or find a prevention, a cure, something like that. I've become very active in the Alzheimer's Association as a result of it. I just finished a two-year term as president of the Philadelphia chapter. I've been conducting support groups for the past seven years, I guess, eight. I organized them in my part of the city. So a lot of my spare time has been devoted to the Alzheimer's Association. So that's consumed a good part of my energy and thought.

I think also as a result of my wife's illness, I've sort of thrown myself more wholeheartedly into my work, my job, my children. I think in some ways, it's probably made me a stronger person. It's sort of made me realize, as it does anybody who has to do what I'm doing, that we have all kinds of resources that we're not even aware of — strength and powers — that we can call upon that we've never had to use in other circumstances. It's given me also kind of a philosophical outlook on life. I tell my friends at every opportunity, "Don't postpone. If you want to do something, do it now. The future has all kinds of surprises for you."

I guess it's made me very compassionate for other people who have this problem or something like it. The fact that I hadn't kept it a secret: on many occasions I've been prominent on television programs, lectures, whatever, so that I think most of the kids in school and all the faculty know what my home situation is like. I think that probably has given them a feeling of appreciation, respect, awe — call it what you will — that somebody who has this sort of problem is still able to function. You know, as I said before, it is a disease that can make you very lonely and very bitter sometimes. I've gone through periods of depression and self-pity. But I've come through them. *How did you cope with those?* Well, sometimes, I'd have a little drink of bourbon (laughs); I try to be physically active, so I've been playing tennis every Sunday for umpteen years. I try to get out of the house as much as possible. Fortunately I've been able to employ full-time home health aides so that I can get out, or even go away for a two-week vacation once a year. And, just recently, I've even begun dating; there you are. *You've had to pay for the home health aides yourself?* Right. About $20,000 a year, at least.

Is sex as important to you now as it used to be? Maybe more (laughs). *You mentioned that you'd just begun dating.* Yeah, dating; not sex, just dating. *How do you mean, "maybe more"?* Well, maybe more because of the absence of it, you know. You sort of wonder, well, are my days over, or is there another life for me, that's all.

Would you say that you have a pretty firm sense of who you are? ·Um-hum, yup. *How long have you felt that way?* The last five minutes (laughs). Oh, I don't know, I suppose, I guess I would say the past six years, ever since I decided that instead of bemoaning my fate and brooding over it, I was going to go out and help other people deal with their problems. That's when I started the support groups. I guess since then. *That made a real difference to you?* Yes, I think so. *Before your wife became ill, did you have a sense of who you were then?* Yes, I think I did. I mean I always had the feeling that I could rise to the top, put it that way. I always had the feeling that I was, you know, in some ways gifted as a teacher, and that I was probably brighter than most of the people with whom I associated; other people had the same feeling, I'm sure. So, you know, I guess I had a lot of self-confidence most of my life. I was always also sort of outspoken and

articulate. So, yes, I had a sense of who I was; but I guess more so now than ever before.

Have you had a close intimate relationship with someone? With my wife, yes, very close, very warm. Many people have told us that we are the best-matched couple they've ever seen; and I think we were in many ways. Even my children feel that way; who's a better judge? *What is your relationship with her now?* With my wife? There is no relationship. I just see that she gets care. She's totally unable to do anything. Her mental faculties are all gone. So I'm just like a supervisor of her physical care. Well, it's not quite accurate. I mean I still have the same tender feelings toward her that I always did. I'm constantly kissing her, stroking her, you know, talking to her even though it's a one-way relationship. That's what I mean; it's not two-ways, it's one-way.

In general in your life, do you have a sense of being particularly productive, of having left your mark? Yup. I think so. On my school, on my children, friends, associates, on the Alzheimer's Association. *Do you sometimes look back over your life and kind of review it?* Sure. *How does it look to you?* Well, I think I've done the best I could under the circumstances. It looks ok. I don't think there's anything I would do any differently, except maybe I would have done more traveling, seen more things, spent more time with my wife if I had known that she was going to get ill at such a young age. *She's about the same age you are?* About a year and a half younger.

Has life been a meaningful adventure for you so far? Um-hum. Unfortunately, yes. *How do you mean?* Well, unfortunately because what's made it so meaningful is this tragedy that's befallen us, and my life since. *Can you say a little bit more?* Well, I think that that event is probably the key event to understanding me and my whole life and my whole personality. And it's sad that it had to be something like that—you know, that in a sense my wife had to pay the price of my own fulfillment, I don't know what other word to call it. *It's really made a big difference in your life?* Definitely. *Given it a lot more meaning in a sense?* A lot more depth. A lot more meaning.

Do you sometimes think about death? My own, or somebody else's? *Either, both.* Very often. I think mainly, probably in connection with my wife, you know, what is it going to do to me? How am I going to cope with it? There are also times that one feels that it might be best, you know, a blessed release in some ways. And then in connection with my own possible death, I have a lot of concerns—as everybody else does who is a caregiver—what will happen to my wife if I should predecease her. So, yeah. I don't think I have morbid concern with death, you know, brood over it a lot; sometimes.

There was a time maybe eight or ten months ago when I thought my wife was losing the ability to swallow; that's part of the final stage—she's in the last stage now. Then, you know, I began thinking, well, what's my next move? Am I going to feed her through a nasal-gastric tube, or am I going to feed her with an abdominal tube, or am I not going to do that. I attended a variety of meetings, discussing questions like this. You know, life-support systems, the ethics of not feeding, and so on. Then I came to the conclusion that I was not going to put a tube in her, if she lost the ability to swallow. Fortunately, she regained it; she's able to swallow now. When and if she loses that ability, I'll simply give her liquid intravenously; I would not give her a nasal-gastric tube because that causes suffering, and I'll not give her an abdominal tube for the same reason; and I'll take my chances. If it results in death, it results in death. It's hard. It may sound callous. But sooner or later you reach a point where you have to look at things objectively and realistically.

With regard to your own death, have you made any preparations, a will? I'm having my will revised. As a matter of fact, I just went to an attorney the day before yesterday to revise my will, to make provisions for the estate in the event that I should die before my wife—power of attorney, the deed for the house, you know. I should have done it years ago, but I kept putting it off, saying I don't need it. I finally broke down and did it. You know, I realize that at my age, who knows, anything can happen. So, yeah I think about it a little bit; not too much, though.

Was there any particular thing that led you to do it a few days ago? There was nothing in particular, really. I had met an attorney about two years ago, I guess. We were both in a documentary film about Alzheimer's disease and he was well-disposed toward me and offered his services free of charge. I said, "No, not free of charge." But anyway, I kept him in mind and every time we go to support group meetings this question arises, you know, about legal matters, and being eligible for Medicaid and so on. So I finally called him a couple of months back and made an appointment, as it happened for the day before yesterday. So anyway, things on the legal front seem to be in pretty good shape as far as I'm concerned. I think I'll be able to die comfortably without any undue anxiety. My kids will be provided for, my wife will be provided for if she's still alive.

How does the future look to you? Oh, I don't know. The future looks ok, I guess. I think mainly the fact that I'm in good physical health gives me a sense of optimism about the future. And the fact that my children are all doing so well also. And I have, luckily for me, no economic worries, no financial problems; I'm well provided for, an excellent pension. I have investments. So I'm not worried about putting bread on my table or a roof over my head. I don't know; whatever will happen will happen. If my wife should pass away, well, I don't know, I probably will remarry. The fact that I've begun to date has given me a new sense of optimism. And it's also helping the lady I'm dating because her husband has the same problem my wife has. So we have a lot in common. Just last night we went to the movies together, so that's nice. You can't—I keep telling people this, I don't always do it myself—you can't lock yourself up away from the world, you can't pretend that you're sick too when you're not sick. You can't sacrifice two lives for one. You know, I tell people these things; I don't always do it. Yeah, the future looks ok, everything looks all right.

What would you like to be doing in five years? In five years? Oh, I don't know; I'd like to be traveling; I'd like to be playing tennis; I'd like to be more actively involved in the Alzheimer's Association—raising money, helping families; maybe being remarried—that's a possibility. So there is a future.

CHAPTER 9

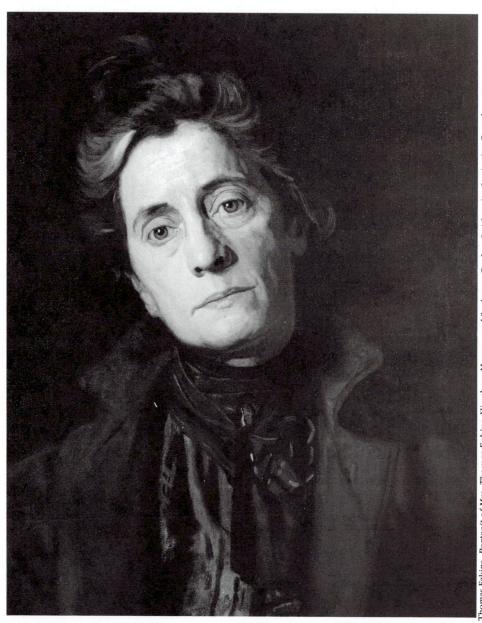

Growing Old in a Changing World

*I*t is striking: more and more people are growing old today, but they appear to be taking a longer time to do it. Improved health care, better nutrition, and the large reduction in mortality earlier in life are allowing greater numbers of people to live into old age. These changes have also slowed the disease processes often associated with aging so that a decade or more of active life has been added to the life span of many people in our society, effectively pushing the beginning of old age from the sixties up to the seventies or eighties. At the same time, attitudes about aging are changing so that older people are being seen more positively now than they were earlier in this century. To be sure, some negative stereotypes continue to exist about old people, but these are being challenged in part because older people are more numerous today, and in part because they are more active, are leading a wider variety of life-styles, and are in better health than persons of the same age were a few decades ago. As we look toward the next century, the aging population is likely to be different than it is today, or than it was in the past. By the year 2030, perhaps as many as one in three persons in the United States will be over age 55 and one in five over age 65 (U.S. Senate, 1987–1988). Moreover, the older population of the future will have had more formal education, more knowledge about health-promoting behavior, better health care, and better nutrition during childhood and adult years than is the case for older people in general today.

This chapter will examine aging within the perspective of cultural and social influences. Our changing world affects the experience of aging, and the growth of the older population is bringing about some of the important social changes around the world. We begin this chapter with a discussion of aging in cultures that differ from our own. Then we examine the link between aging and society in our own culture. Next we focus on some of the most important issues faced by older people today—including income, health care, and the more general issue of the quality of life, which necessarily involves housing, transportation, and fear of crime. The final section describes some of the educational and occupational opportunities for work with older persons.

Cross-Cultural Perspectives on Aging

It is frequently assumed that aging is a more positive experience in other cultures —especially in nonindustrial societies such as those that are based on agriculture, rearing animals, or hunting and gathering for food. Similarly, it is often assumed that industrialization has led to a breakdown of traditional social supports so that older persons are especially vulnerable in modern, highly developed societies, whereas older people were protected within a close-knit community in simpler times and simpler societies. However, the situation is actually far more complex than these assumptions suggest and, on balance, the elderly in today's modern societies are probably about as well cared for as old people have ever been. Of course, there are some cultures where it is better to grow old than others, and persons of higher socioeconomic status generally are treated better than persons of lower socioeconomic status in all societies. We discussed some of the differences among modern industrialized cultures in Chapter 5; for example, the care of old persons is primarily the responsibility of the family in Japan, but organized community resources play a more important role in Scandinavian countries. In this section, we focus on aging in a variety of different cultures, the effects of industrialization on the status of older people, and studies on groups of supposedly long-living people.

Aging in Different Cultures

Two central conclusions may be drawn from cross-cultural studies on aging. First, the meaning, status, and experience of aging differ greatly among cultures. It has been reported that some cultures honor their elderly; others honor only those older persons who are wealthy or powerful; still others leave the aged to die when they cannot care for themselves; and in a few societies the elderly live very much like younger people (Beauvoir, 1972; Simmons, 1945). Second, the nature of aging is

The status of older people is determined by different standards in various cultures. In many cultures, women age with less difficulty because family ties may last longer than a man's wealth or power.

intertwined with other cultural patterns of each society, so that the status and treatment of older persons depend on the nature and structure of the society. For example, in some cultures prestige is based on the number of wives a man has; this results in a delay in age of marriage for young men (because all available women are already married), and an accumulation of wives among older men. In some of these societies, older persons arrange marriages for the younger men, and the oldest man in the household may also count the wives of his sons as if they were his wives. All of this would seem to provide older men with greater power and prestige. However, wives may be lost to other men, return to their kin after menopause, or die and not be replaced. Thus, the aging man in these cultures may lose his prestige sometime after middle age, or he may remain head of a household consisting of many wives while his son takes over much of the actual power and responsibility of the household (Goody, 1976).

As this example implies, the status of aged men may differ from and be based on characteristics different from those that determine the status of aged women; this also depends on the nature of the cultural patterns within the particular society. Keith (1985) argued that women generally age with less difficulty than men do. On one hand, women are faced with less discontinuity in duties and expected behaviors as they get older, as compared to men.

> Hunting or heavy agricultural work may be difficult for old men to perform and their efficiency noticeably less than that of younger men. Old women may more easily continue food preparation and child care and, in addition, by performing these domestic jobs, free younger, stronger women for gathering or gardening. The hours and years invested in child care pay off for women in another way as well. The affectionate bonds created between women and their children and between women and their grandchildren are often a guarantee of both material and emotional comfort in later years. Men's power in earlier years may ensure them support to the letter of the law, but not foster the emotional ties that encourage care beyond the call of duty and are a satisfaction in themselves. (Keith, 1985, p. 235)

On the other hand, when there is normative age-related change in role behaviors, it tends to favor women, who also may be more experienced at adjusting to changed expectations, according to Keith (1985). For example, in many cultures, men lose the status they built up earlier in life, whereas women as they age shift from a timid bride to a powerful household head (p. 236).

Even a **gerontocracy,** which is government *by* the old and which is always male, is not necessarily government *for* the elderly, according to Fry (1985); the interests of family, class, friends, and corporate associates may take precedence over age-mates in political matters. Thus, a male gerontocracy does not necessarily benefit the old, nor the old men who are not involved in the government.

Historical records contain examples of several cultures that have extremely harsh or extremely reverent attitudes toward aging people. Beauvoir (1972) described some of the cultures in which it has been reported that old people were killed or allowed to die when they were no longer productive. These events usually were said to involve a ceremony of some kind, were usually seen as a way to enhance the old person's life after death, or sometimes were viewed as a sacrifice for the well-being of the community.

Anthropologists point out that these examples are very difficult to interpret accurately for several reasons. First, cultural *beliefs* and actual *practices* may not be the same. Thus, killing or abandonment might be acceptable under certain conditions, but actually occurred only rarely in these cultures. Second, the behavior may be explained not by a hostile attitude toward the elderly but by explanations as diverse as emotional disturbance associated with harsh environments, cultural beliefs about the meaning of death, and the valued role of self-sacrifice in the culture. Third, nearly all societies (including our own) contain examples of *both* positive and negative treatment of the elderly. Generally, it was the decrepit, not the well-functioning elderly that received nonsupportive or death-hastening treatment; the loss of family support was the most frequent cause of this treatment. Intact elderly who have not lost their strength or attractiveness were typically not vulnerable to this type of harsh treatment (Fry, 1985; Glascock & Feinman, 1981).

At the other extreme, a number of cultures have been reported to treat their elderly with great respect. The reasons for this are as varied as the reasons for the harsh treatment in other cultures. In some cases, the old people play an important part in ceremonies and rituals; in other cultures it is part of the religious tradition to honor the elders; and in still others they gain respect because of their memory of ancient myths or cultural history.

> Old people often acquire a high, privileged status because of their memories. This is the case among the Miao, who live in the high forest and bush country in China and Thailand. At one time the Miao began to evolve a high degree of civilization, but their development was checked, no doubt by wars. The family is patriarchal, and the son does not leave his father's roof until he is thirty. Theoretically the head of the house has the right of life and death over all of its members, but in fact the relationship between father and son is very good, each taking the other's advice. The Miao run to large families, and the grandparents look after the grandchildren. Women, children and old people are very well treated. If, having outlived his descendants, an old person is quite by himself, he will seek the protection of the head of an important family; he is always accepted, even though he is a burden. The Miao think that the souls of the dead live in the house and guard it, and that they are reincarnated in the new-born. It is the old who hand on the traditions, and the respect in which they are held is chiefly based on the ability to do so; their memory of the ancient myths can provide them with a very high standing. They are the community's guides and counsellors. (Beauvoir, 1972, p. 71)

Beauvoir noted several other societies where high status was granted to the elderly —the Navajo in North America, the Jivaro in South America, the Lile and Tiv in Africa, and the Mende in Sierra Leone. Of course, the traditional Japanese and Chinese cultures provide high status to the elderly, and this has been maintained, at least in Japan, to a great extent despite the dramatic industrialization of that country in this century (Palmore & Maeda, 1985). Even so, not all aged persons in these cultures actually receive high status. For example, the presence of children and the extent of family resources affect the extent of care aged persons receive in China and Taiwan (Ikels, 1980).

Between the extremes of high and low esteem of the elderly, there is wide diversity in their status and treatment. A good example of the sometimes subtle cultural factors that affect aging is Harlan's (1964) report on the status of the aged

in three different villages in India. In one village, the oldest male had great authority, but only until about age 65; he lost his status if his wife died because she played
the key role in his control over the household. However, when that role was taken
over by the wife of the eldest son, the son then gained the authority once held by
his father. Thus, age alone did not provide status, for it depended also on marital
status and the nature of intergenerational relations. In community matters, prestige
was based largely on economic status and education; age was not particularly
relevant.

In a second village, the oldest man had great authority in only two-thirds of the
families; here the status of the old woman was highly dependent on her husband
being alive — as long as he lived, no one dared to mistreat her. After her husband
died, a woman would retain her prestige as long as she was able to aid the family
(perhaps through a hidden cache of jewelry or gold that would be given to family
members after her death), performed useful services for the family, and behaved
well to appease other family members.

In the third village, respect was given to older people only on formal occasions,
but in day-to-day life they were not shown particular respect; the son often ran the
house even though the father was regarded as the head of the family. Thus, Harlan
concluded that the status of older people depends on a wide variety of factors, even
within nonindustrialized societies. He noted that special attention should be given
to the level of prestige granted old persons based on their socioeconomic status, that
actual family and community power or authority may differ from the reported norms
of the culture, and that many factors other than the degree of urbanization or
industrialization may contribute to the difference in status of the elderly between
urban industrialized countries and rural nonindustrial societies.

Effects of Industrialization

A number of studies have suggested that the status of older persons is lower in
"modern" industrialized societies than it is in "traditional" agricultural societies
(Cowgill & Holmes, 1972). The assumption is that aging is less prestigious in
modern societies for a number of reasons: the knowledge older people have is out of
date when social change is rapid; their memory is no longer needed when cultural
traditions are written down; increased education and training makes their skills
easily replaceable; and the sheer growth of their numbers makes aging itself less
unique and revered (Hauser, 1976).

One refinement in this debate is to differentiate *modernization* of the society
from the individual's *contact with modernity*. For example, one study focused on
attitudes of young people toward the aged in six "developing" nations — three were
relatively industrialized and three were more traditional (Bengtson, Dowd, Smith &
Inkeles, 1975). The young people in each country were from three different occupational groups: (1) rural farmers who had little contact with modern industrialization; (2) factory workers who had direct contact with modern industrialization; and
(3) urban nonindustrial workers. It was found that attitudes about aging did not
differ between these three occupational groups. If anything, the data tended to show
that those individuals who had more contact with modern life had more positive

attitudes about aging and the aged than those who had less contact. However, on the general cultural level, those persons in the more industrialized countries were found to have less positive attitudes about aging than those young people in the less industrialized countries. Thus, industrialization appeared to affect general cultural attitudes about aging, resulting in lower prestige and status of the aged. But individual contact with modern industrialization within a culture did not appear to lead to less positive attitudes about aging on an individual basis.

This study concluded with the suggestion that industrialization only initially brings greater cultural disorganization and devaluation of the elderly; eventually the higher productivity and standard of living may improve the quality of life for everyone in the society. That is, old people benefit from improved nutrition, sanitation, health care, and transportation at least as much as young people do; they may lose some relative status in comparison with the young, but still wind up better off than their grandparents were. Other research has also found evidence of this cyclical pattern of initial decline and subsequent improvement in the status of the elderly (Fry, 1985).

In general, it is important to be cautious about romanticizing "the good old days" within any culture, including our own. Laslett (1985), reviewing the data on societal development and aging, concluded:

> Then, as now, a place of their own, with help in the house, with access to their children, within reach of support, was what the elderly and the aged most wanted for themselves in the preindustrial world. This was difficult to secure in traditional England for any but fairly substantial people. It must have been almost impossible in many other cultural areas of the world. (pp. 229–230)

In contrast, some industrialized countries such as the United States have made this goal potentially available to many elderly persons in the society.

Studies of Communities with Long-Living People

Are there communities with unusually large numbers of old people? If so, the conditions in those communities might suggest ways of promoting aging or models for enhancing the quality of life as more and more people live to become old in our society.

Cross-cultural research on aging has focused on some specific groups of people that were thought to have unusually long life spans. One frequently reported example was the Abkhasians in the Caucasus region of the Soviet Union. Similar groups of supposedly long-living people have also been studied in other areas of the world. Although these relatively isolated communities of people have attracted attention because they have unusually large numbers of people who claimed to be very old, this claim was usually not supported by written birth records, so the determination of their actual age has been questioned (Medvedev, 1974). Usually, researchers could rely only on the old persons' memory of recorded past events they claimed to have witnessed; but there was always the possibility that the person was reporting events that had been relayed by others and not directly experienced, so it was often not possible to be certain that the people were as old as they claimed to be. Moreover, these people may have exaggerated their age because old age was given high status in their community.

Recent research has generally concluded that these explanations of the findings are more compelling than any other explanation (Schneider & Reed, 1985, p. 46). For example, Palmore (1984) reported that Soviet gerontologists closely examined the previous studies and "the results of this reevaluation clearly show that the earlier reports of extreme longevity in Abkhazia were erroneous and that there is no more longevity in Abkhazia than in the U.S.A." (p. 95). Thus, these long-lived people were not as old as they were thought to have been and, therefore, they have not provided any evidence of an unusual longevity that is different from people in other communities.

This research provides an interesting example of the difficulties of conducting cross-cultural studies on aging, especially in cultures that have few written records and different concepts of age than we have. In addition, it suggests that there are no cross-cultural models for our aging society with its growing proportion of very old persons.

Conclusion

There is great diversity around the world in the patterns of aging. In some societies, aging appears to be a very good experience, especially if one has power, money, or some kind of magic, and the society values these things. In many societies, recent improvements in health care, education, standard of living, and living conditions have improved life for the elderly, even if there has been loss in relative status. In general, aging is a mix of positives and negatives in most cultures (Fry, 1985). There is considerable debate and no clear consensus about the factors that differentiate cultures to make them positive toward aging or negative toward it; but even these terms are too simplistic when the great diversity of cultures and the complexity within a culture are recognized. However, those very old persons who are very frail and are no longer protected by a powerful spouse or family are likely to be at risk for lowered status in many traditional cultures (Keith, 1985).

As noted in Chapter 1, the growth of a large aged population is a new pattern in human history. Thus, it may not be sensible to extrapolate from previous styles of the treatment of old persons when we consider modern societies. For example, Keith (1985) noted that anthropological studies in the United States have suggested that the increasing numbers and official recognition of older persons in recent years have led to a new ethic regarding aging: one's visible care of aged relatives is as important in terms of one's evaluation by others in the community as is one's care of children. In the next section, we return to our own culture and begin a detailed examination of aging in the United States.

Aging and the Social Context

Clearly, there is a complex relationship between aging and society. In general, the social status of older persons within a particular society reflects the political and economic structure of that society, as well as the cultural values, traditions, and beliefs of the society. Changes in economic and political conditions, or changes in cultural values, can affect the status and characteristics of the aged. Conversely, changes in the relative proportion of older persons within a society or changes in the characteristics of older persons — such as better health — can affect the economic and political structure of society. All these factors are closely intertwined in a complex system of interacting forces. An invention, such as the automobile or the computer, can radically alter social and cultural patterns that, in turn, may affect the relationship between generations within a society. For example, the automobile not only encouraged families to move apart, but also allowed them to remain in contact. Similarly, the computer has played a major role in low-cost, long-distance telephone service, jet travel, and medical advances; each in its own way has helped to maintain relationships between generations, even as each has helped to transform relationships. Thus, to understand aging, we need to examine the changing social context in which it occurs. We begin with a brief historical overview of aging in the United States since 1900. Next, we focus on the growth of the older population and its impact on society. Then, we examine the ways in which the social structure of our society affects the aging process of persons with different socioeconomic status, ethnic-group membership, and gender.

Historical Overview: 1900 to 1990

Earlier in this century, older persons were looked upon as worn out, useless, a drain on the nation's productivity, and a hindrance to advancing technology. Many were in poor health and relatively few survived to ages that we now consider to be old. There were no Social Security or welfare programs, so being retired meant being out of work and living on savings, depending on one's family, or taking charity. This was a period of rapid change, and older persons had to cope with the revolutionary impact of the automobile, electricity, and industrialization.

Gruman (1978) traced the historical patterns in attitudes about older people and concluded that the origins of present-day negative views of aging date back to the close of the Western frontier of the United States in the 1890s. At that time, the national emphasis was on becoming a strong, aggressive country and on conquering new territories; the young were seen as a vital resource, whereas the old were weak and inadequate. He noted that it was "standard practice for industry to shut out workers over the age of 40" and that immigration quotas restricted the entry of older persons to the United States. These were also the days of "sweatshops," child labor, and growing unionization of workers. Life in urban areas often meant living in a tenement with only cold running water on the ground floor and an "outhouse" in the backyard. Tuberculosis and pneumonia were very serious diseases and often fatal; millions of persons died in the flu epidemic in 1918. Old people were especially vulnerable to many of these social conditions.

After World War I, rapid social change affected a large range of traditional values as women received the right to vote, young people began a dramatic sexual revolution, and the migration from farms into the cities began in earnest. The Great Depression of the 1930s, combined with a serious drought in the midwestern farmlands, wiped out the savings of a lifetime for many and brought about disloca-

Earlier in this century, older people in the United States were relatively rare and were often looked at as worn out and old-fashioned. If they could not care for themselves, they had to depend on their family or on charity. Life was especially difficult for the elderly during the Great Depression of the 1930s.

tion and poverty. In comparison to other historical periods, this period probably produced the lowest status of older persons in this century. They still made up only 5 percent of the population—unchanged from the turn of the century—but often their poverty was extreme, savings were gone, and older workers were seen as holding on to jobs needed by younger men who were out of work. Retirement was established by the creation of Social Security in 1935 to move old workers "out to pasture." President Franklin Roosevelt attacked the "nine old men" on the Supreme Court as hindering the country's progress. Many older people lived with their children's families because they could not afford to live alone. Partly to remain active, and partly to repay this charity, they often helped out with chores and odd jobs around the house. However, others were less fortunate and wound up living in "poor farms" or in state mental institutions—nearly the only facilities available in those days. Thus, during the first four decades of this century, the aged were seen as a social problem: What should be done with those few old people who have outlived their usefulness, needed care, but did not have families to take them in?

From the 1940s to the 1970s, the number of older people grew rapidly, largely because of medical advances such as the discovery of penicillin (for treating bacterial infections) in 1928 and streptomycin for treating tuberculosis in 1943. As the "problem of the aged" became more acute, social resources began to be organized to meet their needs; this led to a dramatic growth in federal and community programs to relieve these problems. At the same time, during the 1960s and 1970s, there was a great increase in research on the characteristics of older people, on the nature of aging processes, and on the problems of the elderly. Clark Tibbitts, one of the early scholars in the emerging field of gerontology, reviewed these historical changes in 1979 and argued that there had been a gradual improvement in the status of older people since World War II.

> My thesis is that over the past 30 to 40 years American society has been transforming itself from one in which older people were held in increasingly low esteem and characterized by a multiplicity of derogative stereotypes to one in which the roles and styles of life of older adults will be viewed as positive and contributive to the quality of life for themselves, for their communities, and for the total society. (Tibbitts, 1979, p. 10)

Today, it seems we are evolving new perspectives with regard to aging. The distinctions we used to make about age are becoming less important (Neugarten, 1982). Likewise, the *problems* of older people are being seen as symptoms of the problems of people in general. For example, health care for older persons is now being seen as a symptom of the greater social problem of health care for all persons. Thus, Medicare, created to help persons over age 65 cope with medical expenses, may eventually be replaced by a system of comprehensive national health insurance for all persons. Similarly, affordable housing, accessible transportation, fear of crime, and economic uncertainty are no longer special problems of the elderly, but are now recognized as problems faced by a wide range of adults. In this sense, the perspective has shifted during the 1980s from emphasizing age-related issues to an analysis of issues confronting our whole society. Thus, the old may now be seen as harbingers of future social policy issues that are only beginning to emerge on the horizon for the general population.

In addition, today we are recognizing that the elderly are as diverse a group as young or middle-aged persons and therefore not all that different from other people. They may, on average, be more vulnerable to problems that seem less serious to young people — such as icy sidewalks, the rising cost of medications, or economic inflation, and they may be more handicapped by physical barriers, such as steps, inadequate lighting, or loud background noise, but the vast majority lead lives that attest to the irrelevance of chronological age as long as they are in generally good physical health. Although some negative attitudes about older people persist, during the past decade the growing proportion of healthy, well-functioning older persons has successfully called public attention to the inaccuracy of past stereotypes that all older people are sick, impaired, dependent, or troubled.

Growth of the Older Population

One of the primary reasons for the changes in social attitudes toward older persons in our society since the 1940s has been the rapid growth of the older population. In earlier chapters we noted the rising proportion of older persons, in our country resulting from increased life expectancy (see Figure 1.5), and the growing number of older persons (see Figure 6.5). Thus, it may come as a surprise that the proportion of persons over 65 in the United States (12.7 percent in 1990) is relatively low in comparison with other industrialized countries; Austria, Belgium, France, Great Britain, Norway, and Sweden have higher proportions—some as high as 14 percent. In Africa, Asia, and Latin America the proportion is much lower—as few as 3 percent in some countries. Generally, those countries with *high birthrates* have lower proportions of older persons, and those with *low birthrates* have greater proportions of older persons. Immigration can contribute to the *number* of older persons, and many of the older people in the United States today came to this country during the period of high immigration around the turn of the century; but they usually have children and grandchildren, so immigration does not increase the *proportion* of older persons very much. Similarly, decreased mortality does not necessarily increase the proportion of older persons, contrary to what one might expect, unless the decrease in mortality affects the older age groups much more than other age groups. Thus, the future age structure of the population is determined primarily by fertility or *birthrate*. As a result, those born during the baby boom (after World War II) will swell the ranks of older age groups during the years 2010 to 2030, when this cohort reaches age 65.

The dramatic increase in the older population is a worldwide phenomenon, with different impacts in different nations (Figure 9.1). Myers (1985) differentiated four types of patterns: *Type 1* countries (such as France and Sweden) began the growth in the proportion of the older population before the turn of the century and the percentage over age 65 in the population has already begun to level off in these countries. *Type 2* countries (such as the United States and Greece) began to show the change early in this century and the proportion over age 65 will continue to increase at least up to the year 2025. *Type 3* countries (Japan and Argentina) began the increase after the end of World War II; Japan is expected to have one of the highest proportions of aged persons in the world by the year 2025. *Type 4* countries (such as Sri Lanka and the Republic of Korea) are developing countries with a declining birthrate; they are only beginning to show the dramatic increase in the aged population that is expected in the next century. Overall, the growth of the older population will be especially dramatic in less developed countries.

> While older persons in the more developed countries will increase by 58 percent between 1970 and 2000, those in the less developed countries will almost triple. In consequence, whereas the less developed countries had only 45 percent of the world's aged in 1970, they would have 58 percent by the century's end. (Hauser, 1976, p. 74)

Thus, the *number* of older persons is increasing more rapidly in those nations with high birthrates whose population is also growing rapidly; these societies also tend to be less economically developed, so the growth of the aged population is more likely to be an economic burden. The *proportion* of older persons is increas-

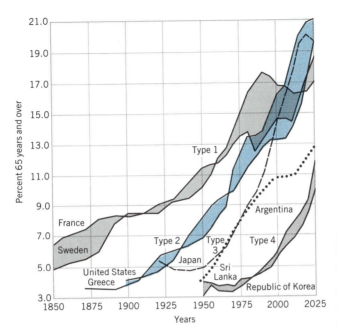

ing more rapidly in those nations with a declining birthrate—for example, in Europe and North America. In the United States, the oldest segments of the population are growing most rapidly. Between 1980 and 1986, the age group between 65 and 74 increased 11 percent; 75- to 84-year-olds increased by 17 percent; and those over age 85 grew by 25 percent (U.S. Senate, 1987–1988, p. 16).

In the United States, one of the most dramatic characteristics of the older population is the growing proportion of women over age 65. In 1987, there were only 68 men for every 100 women over age 65; this meant 5.6 million more women than men. The difference is far greater for older age groups, reaching 40 : 100 over age 85 (U.S. Bureau of the Census, 1988). As noted in Chapter 5, men have higher death rates than women at all ages, so the ratio of men to women declines steadily with age (Figure 5.2). At the same time, life expectancy has been increasing more rapidly for women than for men, so the greater growth of the older female population probably reflects various health-related gender differences (including greater cigarette smoking among men until recently). However, until 1930 there were about as many men as women over 65. The relative balance between men and women over 65 earlier in this century resulted from the heavy, predominately male immigration before World War I (U.S. Bureau of the Census, 1976a).

Another significant characteristic of the older population in the United States today is the growing level of formal education. In 1986, 49 percent of all persons over age 65 were high school graduates—up from 33 percent in 1975; this compares with about 75 percent of all persons over 25 in 1986—up from 60 percent in 1975 (Uhlenberg, 1977; U.S. Senate, 1987–1988, p. 142). Nearly half of all persons over age 65 in 1990 are likely to be high school graduates and 70 percent of those entering old age in the year 2000 will have graduated from high school, including over 25 percent who will have had some college education (Uhlenberg, 1977). In addition to these cohort factors, a sizable number of older people today were foreign-born and tend to have higher illiteracy rates and lower educational levels than native-born older persons; because of reduced immigration earlier in this century, the proportion of foreign-born older persons will decrease in the future and will begin to reflect the cultural background of more recent immigrants. These changes in educational background may affect many aspects of aging, including use of free time and ability to influence political institutions.

Finally, let us look at one measure of the effect of the growth of the older population on the rest of the population. The **dependency ratio** reflects the relative burden of older ''dependents'' on those persons who are economically ''productive.'' Of course, not all persons over 65 are dependent, nor are all persons between 18 and 64 economically productive, but if we compare the relative size of these groups, the dependency ratio has risen steadily and is expected to level off at about 19 persons over 65 for every 100 persons between 18 and 64 before the year 2000; however, it will increase sharply to 29 per 100 in 2030 when the postwar baby boom reaches age 65. This suggests that a considerable economic burden may fall on the shoulders of working men and women in the future as a result of the growth of the older population. However, there has also been a decrease in the proportion of the other ''dependent'' segment of the population, children under age 18 (Figure 9.2). When both groups of dependents are considered, the dependency ratio is found to have been at its highest point in the mid-1960s and is not expected to be as high during the next 60 years as it was in 1964 (Kingson, Hirshorn & Cornman, 1986). Thus, the burden of intergenerational dependency is shifting from care of children to care of the elderly, but the overall burden is not increasing. In fact, since the elderly often have resources of their own and actually provide some care to younger generations, there is evidence of greater equity between generations in the future than has been true in the past.

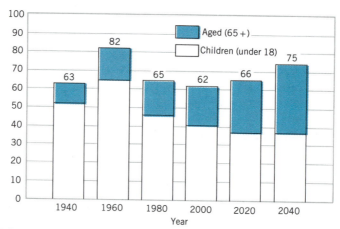

FIGURE 9.2 Overall dependency ratio: number of children and aged per 100 adults, 18–64: 1940–2040. (*Source*: Kingson, Hirshorn & Cornman, 1986, Chart 8–2, p. 140. Reprinted with permission from *Ties that bind: The interdependence of generations. A report from the Gerontological Society of America.*)

Aging and the Social Structure

The social meaning of aging reflects the individual's location within the social structure of society. In our society, an individual's socioeconomic status, ethnic-group membership, gender, and age may be seen as indices of that person's position in the social structure. In turn, the individual's location in the social structure influences his or her "life chances." **Life chances** reflect "the probability that an individual will be born healthy, or live to age 75, or get married, or have children, or have a comfortable income" (Bengtson, Kasschau & Ragan, 1977, p. 331). Growing older does not remove the importance of these social status characteristics; it may, in fact, add the additional dimensions of "retired" or "senior citizen" to the indices that determine the person's social status.

As a result of these social differences, older people are not a homogeneous population, contrary to stereotypes about them. That is, older people typically retain much of the diversity in social status that they experienced in middle age, but have added to this the considerable diversity that has resulted from their individual variability in health, family relationships, income, religion, ethnicity, gender, and even age. For example, very old persons over the age of 85 are, in general, different from "old" persons under age 75, especially in terms of frail health, widowed marital status, gender (female), living alone, and low income. Thus, we cannot describe the aged as a single homogeneous social group, but instead must examine the variations among older people in terms of those social characteristics that influence their status in society. In this section, we examine the ways in which three indices of social status — gender, socioeconomic status, and ethnic-group membership — affect aging in our society.

Gender Differences in Aging

As noted earlier, women generally live longer than men and are more likely to be widowed. Bengtson, Kasschau, and Ragan (1977) reviewed studies of gender differences in patterns of aging and noted that older women are more likely than men to be living on their own, less likely to be living with a spouse, and likely to have suffered a greater decrease in income. Perhaps as a result, older women were found to have more negative self-images and more negative views of aging and of other old people than is true for older men. However, older women seem to be more involved than older men in social activities, religious organizations, and community groups. Women also tend to have more friends and to be more involved in family relationships than is the case for men.

Two of the major events related to aging — retirement and widowhood — also differ considerably for men and women. Since a woman's status often reflects her husband's social position, her husband's retirement or her widowhood may affect the woman's social status more than the wife's retirement or death would affect the man's status. This often translates directly into income differences. In general, older women represent one of the lowest income levels in American society (Dressel, 1988; Minkler & Stone, 1985).

If the woman's retirement involves the end of full-time child-rearing rather than the end of an occupational career, it would occur several years before a man retires from his job and would involve different changes at a different time in her life than is the case for men. Widowhood might mean that the woman must take over the economic and financial responsibilities once managed by her husband. For example, half of all millionaires are women, and it is likely that many of these women are managing estates accumulated before their husband's death (Streib, 1985).

Moreover, when a woman is widowed late in life, she is likely to find a group of similar widowed women who can provide support and a network of friendships, but there are very few unmarried men in her age group. When a man is widowed, he is likely to find that most men his age are married and that he is greatly outnumbered by widowed women so that he has many opportunities to remarry if he wishes to do so.

Thus, many aspects of aging differ between men and women in our society. Although some of these differences seem to favor men and have been called the **double standard of aging** (Sontag, 1972), others appear to favor women. That is, older men are less likely to lose as much social status and income in old age and have more opportunity for heterosexual social and sexual partnerships, but women have more extensive friendship networks and are more likely to be involved in community activities—frequently with other widowed women. In addition, women are usually the caregivers to infirm parents, in-laws, and spouses. Despite this, some have observed that social policies for older persons have not taken these gender differences into account: "Invisible in culture and in law, older women have increased in number but their numbers have not informed social policy" (Rodeheaver, 1987, p. 745). In particular, the economic problems of older women who live alone have not received attention (Commonwealth Fund, 1987).

Socioeconomic Differences in Aging

Socioeconomic status (SES)—reflecting income, education, and occupation—has dramatic effects on patterns of aging in our society. It also has an important influence on an individual's "life chances" in terms of longevity, health, housing, and marriage. In general, the negative changes with aging typically occur later in life among persons of higher SES levels. Whether the measure is health status, life expectancy, days of disability per year, or limitation of activity, individuals with higher income have an advantage over persons with lower income—at least to age 75, when many of these differences are equalized (Bengtson, Kasschau & Ragan, 1977). Lifetime patterns of nutrition, health care, living conditions, and occupational hazards are some of the factors that cause these differences. Since many of these factors continue in old age, problems of inadequate nutrition, health care, and housing often characterize the aging experiences for persons of lower SES—as well as for persons whose level of income has dropped sharply in old age.

In general, less attention is given to the characteristics of middle-class elderly, who often own their own homes and have accumulated a modest amount of savings by retirement age. When their income drops after retirement, property taxes, medical expenses, and economic inflation that makes all products more expensive may be major concerns. This group is neither affluent enough to be free of financial worries nor poor enough to be eligible for public assistance. Moreover, older people often hope to leave an inheritance to their children; Chen (1973) reported that about 3 out of 4 older homeowners desired to do so, and many were sacrificing their own expenditures in the hope of leaving money to their heirs.

In many ways, higher levels of lifetime income increase an individual's range of choices and available options for aging. The very affluent can live wherever they please, afford the best health care, and lead a life-style that buffers them against many of the problems of aging. Less affluent middle-class people may choose to live in a retirement community, remain in a home that may be paid for by that time, or sell the home and move to a smaller house, apartment, or mobile home. In contrast, low-income older persons may be trapped in a home or apartment in a deteriorating part of a city or rural area and be unable to afford to move.

Bengtson, Kasschau, and Ragan (1977) noted that lower SES persons report more negative views of aging, are more likely to view themselves as "old" (rather than "middle-aged") if they are elderly, and see "old age" beginning earlier, compared with higher SES persons. Lower SES persons also report lower life satisfaction than higher SES persons, largely because of the differences in income (Edwards & Klemmack, 1973). Persons in lower SES levels have less frequent and less extensive contacts with friends, neighbors, and family who live separately, but are more likely to live with their children, compared with higher SES persons. Middle-class older persons are more likely to provide monetary help to their kin, whereas lower-class older persons are more likely to give various kinds of service assistance. In addition, older people are less likely to be involved in community activities if they have lower socioeconomic status; but there is no difference between higher and lower SES groups in participation in religious activities (Bengtson, Kasschau & Ragan, 1977).

Ethnic Differences and Aging

Greater attention has been given to the mosaic of ethnic backgrounds among older adults in the United States in recent years. Instead of thinking of our society as a "melting pot" in which ethnic differences blend into a new American identity, since the 1960s popular culture began emphasizing the cultural origin of many groups — for example, African Americans, Japanese Americans, or Mexican Americans. Such categories are defined by the individual and arise from boundaries drawn and maintained through patterns of within-group interaction and out-group opposition. These boundaries may become more or less important during various daily activities or during the course of the life cycle (Fry, 1985).

When ethnicity is combined with minority racial background in the United States it often is associated with social stigma and the risk of reduced opportunities in many areas of life. Racial and ethnic discrimination leads to lower-paying, low-prestige jobs and underemployment among minority groups. Those groups that have experienced greater discrimination because of their racial or cultural heritage are also likely to have shorter life expectancy at birth, poorer health, more physical impairment, and an earlier onset of diseases associated with aging as a result of lower income, less education, and lower-status occupations that have led to less adequate nutrition, housing, and health care.

For this reason, differences between ethnic and racial groups frequently reflect SES characteristics in our society. "For example, about 22 percent of all elderly Hispanics, 32 percent of all elderly blacks, 20 percent of elderly unmarried white women, and 57 percent of elderly black women living alone had below-poverty incomes in 1984" (Kingson et al., 1986, p. 43). Similarly, there are differences in level of education between some racial and ethnic groups. These differences are likely to remain for several years until gains in education among younger cohorts of ethnic minorities are reflected as they grow into old age.

In a major study of 1269 African American, Anglo American, and Mexican American persons between the ages of 45 and 74, Bengtson, Kasschau, and Ragan (1977) found that health problems, feelings of being old, and negative views of aging were more common among the minority groups. For example, Anglo Americans were much less likely to report poor health in all age groups, and the contrast was greater among the older respondents (Table 9.1). Older African Americans were more likely to have difficulty walking up three flights of stairs than Anglo Americans. About half of the African Americans and Mexican Americans reported that they retired because of poor health, compared with 27 percent among the Anglo Americans. The Mexican American respondents were likely to consider themselves "old" or "elderly" (rather than "middle-aged" or "young") at earlier ages than African American or Anglo American respondents (Figure 9.3). Both African Americans and Mexican Americans had the most negative evaluations of the quality of their own lives—greater sadness and worry, feelings that life is not worth living, and a belief that things get worse as one gets older; this was also related to feelings of being "old" among Mexican Americans, but not among African Americans or Anglo Americans. Other differences between these groups—in community participation, interaction with family, and friendship patterns—parallel the ethnic differences discussed in Chapter 5.

However, as we noted in Chapter 1, there is a **cross-over effect** such that the life expectancy for African American men and women at age 65 is about equal to life expectancy for Anglo Americans and, by age 75, African American, Pacific Asian, and

Table 9.1 *Percentage of African American, Mexican American, and Anglo American Respondents Who Consider Their Health to be Poor or Very Poor, by Ethnicity and Age*

	Ethnicity		
Age	*African American (N = 413)*	*Mexican· American (N = 449)*	*Anglo American (N = 407)*
45–54	13.8%	16.9%	1.7%
55–64	15.2	20.8	9.1
65–75	27.0	23.2	4.0

Source: Bengtson, Kasschau & Ragan (1977), Table 1. Copyright © 1977 by Litton Educational Publishing, Inc. Copyright © 1982 renewed by Van Nostrand Reinhold. All rights reserved. Adapted and reprinted with permission.

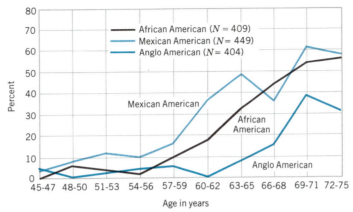

FIGURE 9.3 Percent of African American, Anglo American, and Mexican American respondents considering themselves "old" or "elderly." (*Source*: Bengtson, Kasschau & Ragan, 1977, Fig. 1. Copyright © 1977 by Litton Educational Publishing, Inc. Copyright © 1982 renewed by Van Nostrand Reinhold. All rights reserved. Reprinted with permission.)

Native American elderly actually have greater life expectancy than Anglo Americans (Cool, 1987, pp. 270–271). It may be that those who live long enough to reach old age are a select group of unusually fit individuals, especially among disadvantaged minorities. Gibson (1986) suggested several possible explanations for these survivors, including biological vigor, psychological strength, or resources in coping with stress, such as religious practices that also may link the individual to a community. Also, as noted in Chapter 8, Blacks have lower suicide rates than Whites (although rates among nonwhite men are increasing sharply).

It is important, therefore, to distinguish between the negative effects of minority status and ethnicity. *Ethnicity* is also potentially a positive characteristic of a group since "ethnic groups are composed of sets of individuals who interact and feel bonds of attachment to each other based on shared traits" (Cool, 1987, p. 265).

> Boundaries that exclude can also include. Those excluded from full participation in Wasp-Anglo institutions are included in a larger identity with a social organization and a web of social relations that work for its benefit. Although we should not romanticize poverty, we also should not underestimate the strengths concealed behind ethnic/minority borders. . . . For older people, ethnicity may actually be an advantage. . . . In addition to shielding them from majority attitudes, ethnicity provides the ethnic elderly with a source of esteem. (Fry, 1985, p. 233)

Moreover, it is important to note the wide diversity within ethnic groups, especially in terms of socioeconomic status, the relative proportion of elderly persons, and cultural background. For example, Hispanics (defined as Spanish-speaking persons in the United States) include groups from many different cultures. Blacks differ from one another in cultural background, SES, and from one geographic area to another. Likewise, differences in immigration patterns and birthrates affect the age distribution of each ethnic group in the United States.

The emerging field of *ethnogerontology* cautions against uncritical acceptance of any stereotype about ethnicity and aging (cf. Gelfand & Barresi, 1987; J. J. Jackson, 1980; J. S. Jackson, 1988; Markides & Mindel, 1987). For example, George (1988) reviewed the research on social support and aging comparing Blacks and Whites; she suggested the following conclusions:

1. Although there are few systematic comparisons of the friendships of older Blacks and Whites, the differences reported are small, with no difference in satisfaction. Women report more friends than men and this difference is much larger than race or age differences. SES essentially explains any racial differences found.

2. Older adults provide as well as receive social support and maintain relations with their children and other relatives. Differences between Blacks and Whites are modest in comparison with the similarities: women in both groups have more contact with the family and receive more support from it; kinship relations and gender determine who gives and receives support in both groups. Some studies have found Blacks have more family interaction and support than Whites, but others find that when SES differences are taken into account, the difference disappears.

3. A greater proportion of older Blacks live with relatives other than or in addition to their spouse, are more likely to live with their children, and to live in a household where one member is under the age of 18, compared with Whites. SES explains most, but not all of these differences.

4. Most studies find there are no significant differences in religious affiliation or frequency of church attendance between older Blacks and Whites. Although some studies find greater religious involvement among Blacks, substantial geographic regional differences and differences among specific religious denominations need to be considered before drawing any conclusions about racial differences in religious involvement.

5. Older Whites are more likely to be married than older Blacks; only among the never-married are the groups similar. Gender differences are much greater than racial differences, however. Thus, older Black women are least likely to be married, followed by older White women; older White men are most likely to be married, followed by older Black men. (pp. 110–118)

Other major areas of research related to differences between patterns of Black and White aging also have little reliable data available and need further study. For example, it is likely that there is tremendous variability among African Americans on the dimensions relevant for aging and human development (J. S. Jackson, 1988). Cultural differences in food selection and preparation may affect health, such as the risk of obesity and hypertension, which is higher in African Americans (Jerome, 1988). The prevalence of dementia such as Alzheimer's disease in older African Americans is not known (Baker, 1988). Moreover, little research has focused on patterns of health-seeking among rural elderly African Americans (Gibbs, 1988).

Finally, the complexity of interacting factors in research on ethnicity and aging may be demonstrated by a study of low-income African American, Mexican American, and Chinese American elderly:

Chinese and Mexican elderly are more likely than either Black or White elderly to share housing and receive help from an adult child. This phenomenon is believed to be the result of two major factors: cultural values and economic need. When acculturation level was examined, it indicated that the closer one's ties to traditional culture, the greater the parent–child supportive behavior. However, this relationship may also be confounded by economic need. Inability to speak English tends not only to maintain stronger cultural ties but also to inhibit use of other types of formal services. Limited English-speaking skills may also aggravate an elderly individual's low socioeconomic circumstances, requiring greater assistance from the elders' children, including provision of living arrangements. (Lubben & Becerra, 1987, p. 141)

Thus, ethnic differences, degree of acculturation, language ability, and economic status of the older person and the children may all be relevant to the likelihood of an intergenerational living arrangement. The authors of this study conclude with a suggestion that a measure of the degree to which the older person is "Americanized" should be included in studies of ethnicity and aging.

We conclude that the mosaic of ethnic diversity among the population of older persons in the United States is an important consideration, but one that is very difficult to understand without falling into stereotypes about cultural differences. It is useful to consider the considerable similarities across ethnic groups as well as to

There is a mosaic of ethnic diversity among the aged.

be sensitive to subtle differences within them. Minority status as well as SES differences are also major contributors to differences among older people, both within and between ethnic groups. Moreover, gender differences are, many times, at least as significant as any of the social-cultural differences we have discussed in this section.

Aging in an Aging Society

There has been no historical precedent for the aging of the population as we enter the twenty-first century. Concerns about the environment, education of the young, rebuilding the arteries of the cities, the federal budget deficit, and the shift from an industrial to a service labor force are among the issues at the forefront of our national agenda. But ranking among these top issues is the unprecedented growth of the older population. Never before have there been so many older people relative to the number of younger people; never before have people been so healthy and expected to live so long; never before has medical care been so good, and so expensive. Who will care for the aged? And how will we pay the bills?

This extraordinary situation requires complex analysis and effective public policies, or we may find that simple-minded solutions pit one age group against another, or stimulate conflict between the relatively younger minority populations who are concerned about children, education, economic opportunities and the relatively older White population who are retired and receiving Social Security, Medicare, and special "senior citizen" discounts. Fernando Torres-Gil (1988), former staff director of the U.S. House of Representatives Select Committee on Aging, identified four central challenges for the 1990s (Box 9.1). These issues are beginning to receive detailed examination because they have profound social, political, and ethical implications for the kind of world in which we will grow old (e.g., Foner, 1984; Kingson, et al., 1986; Neugarten, 1982; Pifer & Bronte, 1986). Four themes that are based in gerontological research may shed some light on these complex issues.

First, the elderly are a diverse population and will become more varied in the future. Age, socioeconomic status, gender, ethnicity, minority status, health, and marital status are the most obvious differences. Moreover, older persons are now more likely to have a surviving parent since the oldest age group (85+) is the fastest-growing segment of the elderly population and a growing number of people are surviving into their tenth or eleventh decade (it was estimated that 25,000 individuals were over the age of 100 in 1986, up from 15,000 in 1980; U.S. Senate, 1987–1988).

Second, most older persons are experiencing the same kinds of problems that persons of any age may encounter. By addressing these issues of health, housing, nutrition, crime, social support, income, accessibility to meaningful activities, and the quality of life, persons of all generations will benefit. These issues may be more apparent for persons of any age who are disabled or who experience discrimination, but they are generic issues that may be seen in sharp focus for the elderly because they are more at risk for these problems.

Third, attention needs to be given to the needs of specific segments of the elder

BOX 9.1   *Challenges for Aging Policy in the Twenty-First Century*

1. A restructuring of the current system of benefits and eligibility.   The current system of public benefits and services uses an extraordinary amount of public resources. Most of those benefits, particularly Social Security, have been earned by today's generations of elders. But in times of serious budget deficits and limited expansion of government, the large-scale entitlement programs become very visible to those who want to reduce government expenditures. Especially now that most older persons are reasonably healthy, well educated, and independent, serious consideration will be given to raising eligibility criteria and age. In addition, issues and targeting and means-testing benefits on criteria other than age will probably occur during the 1990s. Those criteria may center around need and functional ability rather than age. Serious examination of the organization and financing of services to the elderly will also occur.

2. Provision of health and longterm-care coverage. . . .   Not just because older persons desperately need longterm-care services, but because families with elders will realize that it is in their best interest to have those services available, and they may even be willing to pay for them, through public taxation. Also important is the increasing number of Americans without any healthcare coverage. If we adopt some form of comprehensive health care coverage for all Americans, regardless of age, it will help merge the political and social concerns of all generations.

3. Accepting a multiracial and multigenerational society.   A major demographic change in the cultural and social profile of the nation will be its ethnic diversity coupled with its aging. By 2010, a large proportion, perhaps a majority, of the U.S. population will be descendants of Hispanics, blacks, Asians and Pacific Islanders, and native Americans. . . .   They will compose a large component of the labor force, and on them will lie the burden of maintaining productivity and economic prosperity. But if they remain a poorly trained and poorly educated group, faced with serious obstacles to full participation in American social and political institutions, then the next century will see the fearful results of neglecting their well-being. . . .

4. Preparing the population for the aging society. . . .   If we no longer see 65 as old and view the 60s and even the 70s as active years, we can erase the stigmas attached to aging and be better prepared politically to make fundamental changes in the current system of public benefits and services for older persons.

(*Source:* Torres-Gil, 1988, pp. 7–8)

population, including the frail, those living in poverty, and those caring for infirm family members. Nursing home residents, old persons living alone, older women, older minorities, elderly in rural areas, and the very old are especially vulnerable.

Fourth, the issues of aging are intergenerational issues. We give and receive help to older and to younger generations throughout our lives. All generations benefit from social policy that promotes healthy children, good education, and employment opportunities and that buffers the family from burdens of care for the elderly. We all benefit when the generations work together for the good of all; and we risk losing this strength if we believe that one age group is less worthy of support than any other age group.

To understand these issues, let us focus on concrete issues of important concern to older people: income, health care, and quality of life.

Income

As with many other dimensions, there is great variation in income among older persons. For example, in 1984 about 1 in 5 older persons had an income under $5000 — approximately the poverty level as defined by the Census Bureau; 3 percent had incomes over 10 times as much, $50,000; and the median total income was $10,170 for the group of persons over age 65. Income is usually much higher for married couples than for nonmarried (e.g., widowed) persons (Social Security Administration, 1986). Income also reflects age, gender, ethnic or racial background, and living arrangement (Figure 9.4). One way to describe these differences is that the proportion of persons with incomes below the "poverty level" was nearly twice as great for persons over age 85 than for persons between ages 65 and 74. The "poverty rate" over age 65 was nearly three times as great for Black persons and over twice as great for Hispanic persons compared with White persons. In general, women, minorities, those living alone, and the oldest old — the three fastest-growing segments of the older population — have greater poverty rates than the average older person. These multiple factors combine so that, for example, 63.7 percent of African American women living alone over age 72 had incomes below the "poverty level" in 1986 (U.S. Senate, 1987–1988).

The proportion of older persons living below the "poverty level" has declined

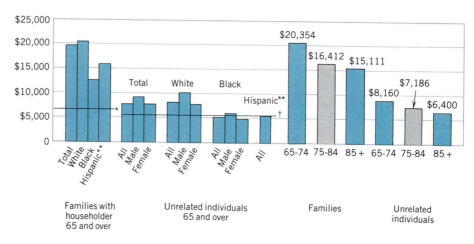

* Poverty level for elderly two-person families in 1986 was $6,630.

† Poverty level for elderly individuals in 1986 was $5,255.

** Hispanic persons may be of any race. Data were not available for Hispanic male and female unrelated individuals at press time.

FIGURE 9.4 Median annual income of families and unrelated individuals age 65 and older by race, Hispanic origin, sex, and age, compared to poverty levels: 1985–1986. (*Source*: U.S. Senate, 1987–1988, Charts 2–2 and 2–10.)

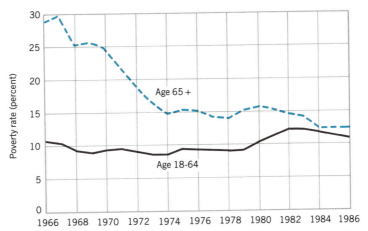

FIGURE 9.5 Poverty rates for elderly and nonelderly adults: 1966–1986. (*Source*: U.S. Senate, 1987–1988, Chart 2–12, p. 56.)

as a result of increased Social Security benefits and other factors in recent years (Figure 9.5). However, according to a study by the Commonwealth Fund (1987), the poverty rate for persons over age 75 living alone will probably increase from about 22 percent today to 25 percent by the year 2000 and then level off; this represents an increase in older poor people living alone from 1.7 million people in 1987 to 2 million in 2020. The greatest proportion of this at-risk population are widows. The Commonwealth Fund study focused on older widows and identified three main causes of poverty:

1. Many were poor before their spouse died. However, over half experienced poverty for the first time after their husband died.

2. Medical and funeral expenses used up financial resources. Also pension income was lost. (Recent changes in laws regarding pensions should reduce the chance that survivor benefits are lost in the future.)

3. Husbands were in poor health and retired early. They also tended to earn less when they did work and were able to set aside fewer assets for the surviving widow.

To reduce the incidence of poverty in old age, government assistance programs such as SSI (see the next section) need to reach those in need of economic benefits; however, at present some eligible recipients do not apply for the benefits and in other cases the eligibility standards for the program are too stringent for those who need assistance to qualify for benefits. Also in some states the benefits are not sufficient to raise income even to the "poverty" level. In addition, greater opportunities for employment on a part-time basis and increased private pension coverage would help reduce the incidence of poverty among the elderly in the future (Commonwealth Fund, 1987).

For older people in general, the largest source of income is Social Security (see Chapter 6 for a description of the program). For example, in 1986, 3 out of 10 depended on it for 80 percent or more of their income. Substantial income was also received from assets, pensions, and earnings from work. However, there was considerable variation among the elderly in these sources of income. For example, one-third reported no income from assets; persons between 65 and 69 earned much greater proportions of their income from working than did older persons; and only 1 in 4 received income from a private pension (U.S. Senate, 1987–1988, p. 61).

A number of benefits supplement the income of older people. Health insurance is provided through Medicare for nearly all persons over age 65 and some with very low income are also eligible for Medicaid (these programs are described later). About half of all older persons had incomes that did not require them to pay federal income taxes in 1986. Those who did owe tax, however, paid more on the average than younger taxpayers; and new taxes have recently been imposed on older persons with higher incomes. Some towns also provide special property tax exemptions, reduced transit fares, and other small benefits; private stores, pharmacies, and restaurants sometimes provide ''senior citizen'' discounts. In addition, a few older persons benefited from programs such as assistance with heating expenses (7%) or food stamps (6%), lived in public housing (4%), or received assistance with rent payments (2%) in 1986. When all these benefits are considered, the average income of older people is closer to that of younger persons (U.S. Senate, 1987–1988).

Many older people have accumulated sizable assets, but usually these are not available for day-to-day living expenses; they may be in savings accounts to cover unexpected expenses such as an illness or to leave as a legacy. About three-quarters of all older people own their own home or have equity in it; although this represents a considerable financial asset, there is seldom any way to use this equity for improving one's present standard of living unless one is willing to sell or mortgage the home (Schulz, 1976, p. 44).

Spending is generally lower for older persons than for younger persons; they have less income to spend, fewer people in the household, and different needs. In general, older persons spend 60 percent of their income on housing, utilities, food, and medical care; younger adults expend 40 percent of the income on these items. The only expense that is greater for persons over age 65 is out-of-pocket costs for health care, including payment for optional Medicare insurance coverage for physician visits and supplemental coverage, prescription drugs and supplies, and non-reimbursed costs for medical services. Even with Medicare the average person over age 75 pays about twice the amount of health care costs as an adult under age 65 (U.S. Bureau of Labor Statistics, 1986).

Overall, the income of older persons is dependent on forces beyond their control. In particular, high rates of inflation can erode the buying power of any fixed income. Social Security and Medicare programs are dependent on government policy. Other key threats to financial security include health crises of oneself or one's spouse, and death of a spouse (especially for women). In the next section we discuss a program that is designed to provide income security for older persons.

Supplemental Security Income (SSI)

Persons who are legally blind, over age 65, unable to work for 12 months or longer, or suffering from a deteriorating medical condition that will result in death may be eligible to receive **Supplemental Security Income (SSI).** This program is administered by the Social Security Administration, but its funds come from general tax revenues, not Social Security trust funds. These benefits, like Social Security, may increase annually through the cost-of-living adjustment. In 1989 the maximum monthly federal SSI payment increased to $368 for an individual and $553 for a couple (*New York Times*, 1988). Many states supplement the federal benefits; in New York state, the 1989 monthly supplement works out to $86 for an individual and $122.50 for a couple.

Unlike Social Security, this is a **means-test program** so that individuals who qualify must have low income and only a small amount of savings. Each state sets its own guidelines for eligibility; 1988 eligibility levels for SSI and Medicaid in New York are shown in Box 9.2. Social Security benefits and any other income (minus a small amount — $20 in 1988) are deducted from the SSI payment. Thus an individual living alone who received $320 in Social Security would have been eligible in New York for an additional $125.91 from SSI (to total $425.91 + $20) provided he or she did not exceed the cash resources, burial fund, or automobile limits and applied for the benefits. Persons eligible for SSI are also eligible for Medicaid and may receive food stamps (other persons may also be eligible for these benefits, depending on the state's regulations).

These benefits may not provide enough income to lift the older person above poverty — in 1987 the maximum federal benefit provided only 76% of the "poverty level" income for individuals and 90% for couples. Moreover, half of the eligible elderly poor do not apply for SSI benefits (Harris, 1986). Thus, to reduce poverty

---

BOX 9.2 *Eligibility Levels for SSI and Medicaid in New York: 1988*

Supplemental Security Income (SSI)

	Maximum Income
Individual living alone	$425.91 + $20
Couple living alone	$624.53 + $20
Individual living with others	$371.24 + $20
Couple living with others	$572.53 + $20
Individual living in another's household	$253.24 + $20
Couple living in another's household	$395.20 + $20
Maximum amount of cash resources, one person	$1900
Maximum amount of cash resources, couple	$2850
Maximum amount of burial fund (each person)	$1500
Maximum value of automobile	$4500

Medicaid

Number in household	*Maximum Income*	*Resources*
1	$434 + $20	$3100
2	$625 + $20	$4750
3	$634 + $20	$5300

Note: For aged, blind, or disabled persons the first $20 of income is not counted toward eligibility.
Source: Arlene Kochman, SAGE, Inc., New York, NY.

among the most vulnerable elderly—especially among the oldest, minorities, and widows living alone—two changes are required. First, the level of federal SSI benefits needs to be increased to the "poverty level." Second, effective methods need to be found to enroll a much greater proportion of eligible elderly in the SSI program (Commonwealth Fund, 1987).

Implications for the Future

Although significant improvements have been made in Social Security and in laws regulating private pensions, mandatory retirement has been eliminated for most workers, and persons over age 70 can earn income without affecting Social Security benefits (see Chapter 6), gaps remain that make the dream of a "golden age" in retirement a cruel hoax for many. At the same time, there are those who argue that other age groups, or other segments of the population, are not benefiting from federal programs to the same extent as the elderly. The staggering federal deficit and the cost of various government programs is leading to a close examination of national priorities. As noted earlier, the *dependency ratio* is growing if only the elderly are considered as dependents; but if children are also included as dependents, there is no increase projected in the burden on the working-age segment of the population for the next six decades (Figure 9.2). Nonetheless, the aged are a vulnerable minority who are economically dependent on Social Security and other federal programs. Since we are all growing older, it is in our national interest to

The elderly are a vulnerable minority group who are economically dependent on Social Security and Medicare. They are often a strong voice in political decisions concerning issues that affect them directly.

protect the income of the elderly. Although the economic and political considerations that are involved in that goal are complex, the goal of a secure retirement is no less important than the goal of healthy children, good education, full employment, strong national defense, and lifelong health care. All of these are intergenerational issues that reflect the strength of our diverse multiracial and multicultural nation as it faces the challenge of the unprecedented growth of the aging segment of the population.

Health Care

Until a relatively few years ago, older persons in the United States had only the protection of their savings, private insurance, and charity to buffer them against their increasing susceptibility to disease. In 1965 **Medicare** was established and it now provides benefits to any person over age 65 who is entitled to Social Security or railroad retirement benefits. Various provisions also exist for some persons under age 65, and surviving spouses or dependent spouses may also be covered. **Medicaid** provides health care to all recipients of public assistance (regardless of age) and to the "medically needy" as defined by each state—such as persons who have resources for daily living, but not for needed medical care, and all children under 21 whose parents cannot afford medical care.

In 1984, nearly half of all medical expenses of older people was paid by Medicare; 25 percent was paid by the older person, 13 percent by Medicaid, 7 percent by other insurance, and 6 percent by other government programs such as the Veterans Administration (U.S. Senate, 1987–1988). On the average, the older person paid $1059 in 1984 out-of-pocket expenses (excluding insurance premiums). The major expenses older people must pay for themselves include nursing homes, care not covered by Medicare or private insurance such as prescription drugs and prescribed health aids, physician fees, and hospital charges above the amount paid by Medicare or insurance (Figure 9.6).

One of the gaps in the current income protections places the middle class at risk for losing their accumulated savings and even their home if a health catastrophe strikes. For example, if one spouse develops Alzheimer's disease, requires extended nursing home care, or expensive prescription drugs, most of the cost for these

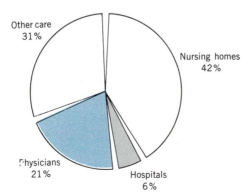

Other care
31%

Nursing homes
42%

Physicians
21%

Hospitals
6%

FIGURE 9.6 Where the out-of-pocket health care dollar for the elderly goes: 1984. (*Source*: U.S. Senate, 1987–1988, Chart 4–13, p. 130.)

services falls on the family. In the worst situation, the family resources are used up to the low level at which the person is eligible for Medicaid; as a result, the limited income that is allowed may not be adequate to meet mortgage, tax, and living expenses so the house may have to be sold. The "Catastrophic Health Care Bill" passed by Congress in 1988 was intended to relieve the burden of out-of-pocket expenses and to reduce the fear of poverty resulting from the cost of catastrophic illness; it is too soon to know how effective it will be. These concerns have also led to private insurance that is intended to cover nursing homes and expenses not covered by Medicare; however, many of these plans have been criticized for providing severely restricted coverage and inadequate benefits (Tolchin, 1988).

In this section we provide a brief overview of Medicare and Medicaid. Then we turn to the small minority of older persons who receive care in nursing homes; an equal number receive care in their own homes. Most older persons do not need special care, but may benefit from greater knowledge about nutrition, exercise, and medications. We can only summarize these topics here, but there are several books available that discuss a variety of issues about aging and health in practical terms (e.g., Jarvik & Small, 1988; Portnow & Houtmann, 1987; Silverstone & Hyman, 1982).

Medicare

The Medicare program is funded by the Health Insurance trust fund administered by Social Security. A percentage of the Federal Insurance Contributions Act (FICA) taxes paid by every employee and employer covered by Social Security provides funds for this program. The Medicare Catastrophic Coverage Act of 1988 modified the coverage. As of 1989, *Part A* theoretically provides unlimited hospitalization for approved care, limited extended care in a skilled nursing facility (with or without prior hospitalization), necessary home health care six days a week (seven days for a limited period) if prescribed by a doctor, unlimited hospice care (see Chapter 10), and a few other specialized services. Medicare *Part B* is optional insurance and helps to pay for doctors' bills, outpatient hospital services, medical supplies and services, home health services, outpatient physical therapy, some prescription drugs, and other health care services including up to 80 hours a year of home care to allow a respite to family caregivers if certain requirements are met *(The Medicare Handbook*, 1989).

About one quarter of the expenses for Medicare Part B are funded by a monthly premium paid by the recipient who elects to participate; the rest comes from general tax revenues (Bernstein & Bernstein, 1988, p. 82). In 1989 this monthly premium was set at $27.90. In addition, all participants in Medicare Part A must pay a nonvoluntary monthly premium of $4 to help finance the Catastrophic Health Care coverage. These amounts are deducted from Social Security benefits. Beginning in 1989, individuals who are eligible for Medicare Part A and also pay federal income taxes may be required to pay an additional supplemental premium of up to $800 for an individual (scheduled to rise in subsequent years), depending on the amount of income tax owed. Although the improved coverage in the 1988 change is important, this additional charge was an unexpected burden on middle-income retired persons and evoked considerable opposition.

Both parts of the Medicare program have significant deductible amounts and some programs have coinsurance that must be paid by the participant. For example, the plan that covers "most" prescription drugs beginning in 1991 requires a deductible of $600 and 50 percent coinsurance paid by the individual. Part B not only requires payment of "coinsurance" but limits the "approved charges" for services, so if the physician charges more than this amount, the individual must pay the difference (plus the coinsurance). Many older persons therefore purchase "Medi-Gap" insurance from private companies to offset the cost of deductible and other costs that Medicare does not pay. Beginning in 1990, Medicare Part B theoretically will limit an individual's out-of-pocket expenses to $1370 per year (to increase annually) based on the schedule of "approved charges"; if the physician does not accept this rate, of course, the individual must pay the difference, even over the $1370 cap (*The Medicare Handbook*, 1989).

A few months after the preceding discussion was written in 1989, Congress repealed the provisions of the Catastrophic Coverage Act of 1988. This unusual reversal resulted from the intense opposition of many older persons who felt they would not receive enough benefit from the changes to justify the increased cost to them. For example, many older persons were already receiving similar coverage from their previous employer's pension program or from private insurance. Clearly it is not possible to predict the exact coverage that will be provided by Medicare in the future.

Medicaid

A substantial proportion of public health care expenditures for older persons is paid through the Medicaid program. As may be seen in Figure 9.7, over two-thirds of Medicare spending goes to reimburse hospitals for care of older persons. In contrast,

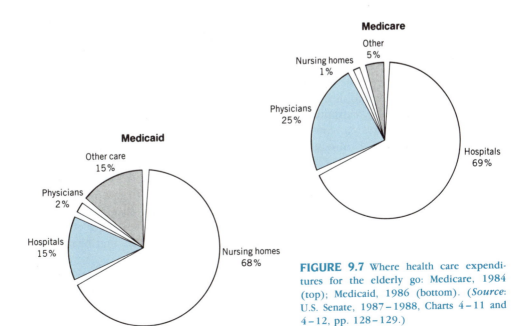

Medicare

Other 5%
Nursing homes 1%
Physicians 25%
Hospitals 69%

Medicaid

Other care 15%
Physicians 2%
Hospitals 15%
Nursing homes 68%

FIGURE 9.7 Where health care expenditures for the elderly go: Medicare, 1984 (top); Medicaid, 1986 (bottom). (*Source:* U.S. Senate, 1987–1988, Charts 4–11 and 4–12, pp. 128–129.)

over two-thirds of Medicaid spending for older persons goes to reimburse nursing homes. For example, many persons in nursing homes are supported by Medicaid, often because the cost of nursing home care has depleted their savings.

Medicaid is funded jointly by federal and state governments from general tax revenues and is available to persons of all ages who qualify for benefits on the basis of a *needs test*. Each state has its own financial requirements to qualify for Medicaid. For example, in New York state, individuals living alone with total income under $454 per month ($5448 a year) and less than $3100 in resources (including life insurance) were eligible for Medicaid in 1988 (see Box 9.2). It covers costs for physicians, dentists, other professionals, hospitals, nursing homes, outpatient or clinic services, home care, drugs, eyeglasses, and so on. Of course, not all health professionals accept Medicaid reimbursement. Payment is direct to the medical person or service, and there is usually no out-of-pocket expense. The important exception, however, is that if a person receives more than the maximum income allowed (such as in Social Security benefits), the difference must be spent on medical expenses before Medicaid covers the balance. In an extreme case, this may not leave enough income for the family and the surviving spouse may become impoverished as a result. Some nursing homes do not accept Medicaid, but in most a substantial proportion of residents are receiving care that is paid for by the program.

Nursing Homes

It is estimated that the chance of living in a nursing home at some point in one's life is about 30 percent for persons under age 45; it rises gradually to about 40 percent for persons age 75–80 and 46 percent for age 85–90; it then declines because of the higher risk of death after age 90 (Liang & Tu, 1986). In general, about 5 percent of persons over age 65 were living in a nursing home at the time of a 1985 survey, but the proportion differed greatly by age: 1 one percent of those age 65 to 74, but about 22 percent of those over age 85 (Hing, 1987). The population of residents in nursing homes is expected to increase in the future as more and more people grow old; this is especially true for the proportion of residents who are over age 85 (Figure 9.8).

A complex interplay of forces affects the nature of nursing homes in the United States. For example, the number of nursing home beds has been restricted in nearly all states to slow the rapid growth that followed the enactment of Medicare and Medicaid. Also, most states have an admission screening program to ensure that residents are "in need" of nursing home care and will be eligible for coverage under these programs or by private insurance. The result has been that the average level of functioning of nursing home residents has decreased dramatically since the 1970s (Mor & Spector, 1988). In addition, the "deinstitutionalization" of mental health care that began in the 1960s has shifted the burden of geriatric mental health care to nursing homes without providing resources for mental health services, as noted in Chapter 8.

In the past there were three types of nursing homes: *skilled nursing facility (SNF)*, *intermediate care facility (ICF)*, and *custodial care facility*. The distinction between the first two was eliminated by federal nursing home reform legisla-

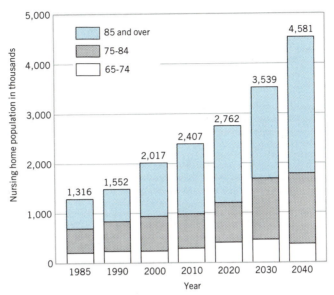

FIGURE 9.8 Projections of the nursing home population 65 years and older by age group: 1985 – 2040. (*Source*: U.S. Senate, 1987 – 1988, Chart 4 – 8, p. 120.)

tion in 1987 so that by October 1990 all nursing homes reimbursed by Medicaid must have a licensed nurse on duty at all times and a registered nurse on duty eight hours a day, seven days a week. Custodial care facilities are not reimbursed by Medicare or Medicaid, but SSI payments are increased in some states to pay for care in these facilities (Brown, 1989).

Since most of the cost of nursing home care is borne by Medicaid, there is considerable concern about "cost-containment"; this is often in conflict with ideals of humane care and regulations that set minimum standards of service. Likewise, since most of the cost of hospital care of older persons is borne by Medicare, there is similar pressure to reduce costs by discharging the patient "quicker and sicker" — often into a nursing home. At the same time, little attention may be given to staff training, motivation, and retention. The result is that nursing homes vary widely in quality, some offering little more than basic nursing and custodial care, whereas others provide a variety of services to restore and maintain the residents' ability to function.

One study in which psychological consultation was provided to a nursing home found that high turnover rates among the staff and poor staff morale resulted from "poor communication, distorted staff perceptions, and difficult work with little extrinsic reward" (Sbordone & Sterman, 1983, p. 248). Following a 12-week series of staff meetings and training of supervisors, turnover was substantially reduced and morale improved dramatically. Improving interpersonal communication among the staff and aiding the supervisors to establish positive reinforcement techniques were changes that seemed especially important.

In our study, we found that staff (particularly aides) were denied the opportunity to communicate feedback to supervisory personnel. The supervisory personnel, who controlled the formal communication network in the facility, excluded employee feedback, particularly at the nurse's aide level. This permitted the development of an informal communication network among nonsupervisory personnel, which alienated them from supervisory personnel. This network frequently produced passive-aggressive behavior by the nonsupervisory employees and was an indirect way to communicate their frustration and anger to supervisory personnel. This behavior reinforced the belief that the nonsupervisory employees were "lazy and stupid," and the supervisory personnel retaliated by giving nonsupervisory personnel the most difficult work assignments; openly calling them "dumb," "stupid," or "lazy" in front of their peers; refusing to acknowledge them as part of the staff; threatening them with dismissal; and generally demoralizing them. This communication style resulted in distorted perceptions of staff at each hierarchical level and fostered a negative reinforcement system of administrative control. (Sbordone & Sterman, 1983, p. 248)

In this brief discussion we can focus on only three key points. First, the choice of a nursing home is very important. A helpful guide, *How to Select a Nursing Home*, is available from the Consumer Information Center, Department 152-M, Pueblo, CO 81009. There is a long-term-care **ombudsman** available in the state or local office of aging and the telephone number should be posted in the home. This person investigates complaints and takes corrective action. The American Civil Liberties Union publishes a handbook that describes the legal rights of nursing home residents (Brown, 1989). Widely available practical books include guidelines and questions to ask when selecting a nursing home (e.g., Jarvik & Small, 1988; Portnow & Houtmann, 1987, Appendix G; Silverstone & Hyman, 1982).

Second, nursing homes may be viewed as *total institutions* (Goffman, 1961) that exert considerable control over the residents. As such, the adaptation of the resident is important to consider and the staff, other residents, and the family can enhance this process (Silverstone & Hyman, 1982). The predictors of good psychological adjustment are not obvious, however, since some of those who adapt best may also be more likely to die sooner (Janoff-Bulmann & Marshall, 1982). Also, nursing homes may be seen as *communities* whose subsystems interact with the broader social policy dimensions of the larger community (Smyer, 1988). For example, a study of a high-quality nursing home in the United States and one in Scotland revealed a lower quality of care in the U.S. home. This difference was attributed to three components: government insurance programs, training in geriatric care, and the availability of a well-coordinated structure of care (Kayser-Jones, 1982). Thus, to improve nursing home care we must focus both inside the nursing home itself and also on the national community of which it is a part.

Third, the role of the family needs attention. In comparison with persons over age 65 in the community, nursing home residents are more likely to be widowed, never married, and female; also over one-third do not have living children (Table 9.2). However, some are married and most do have children.

Pratt, Schmall, Wright, and Hare (1987) noted that families usually experience extensive burden providing day-to-day care for an older person before institutionalization is considered. Often, the caregiver's own health is at risk. Nonetheless,

TABLE 9.2 *Selected Characteristics of Nursing Home and Community Residents 65 Years and Older: 1985 and 1984*

	Living in Nursing Homes, 1985	Living in Community, 1984
Total 65+:		
Number (thousands)	1,316	26,343
Age:	(Percent)	(Percent)
65 to 74	16.1	61.7
75 to 84	38.7	30.7
85+	45.2	7.6
Sex:		
Male	25.4	40.8
Female	74.6	59.2
Race:		
White	93.1	90.4
Black	6.2	8.3
Other	0.7	1.3
Marital status[a]		
Widowed	64.2	34.1
Married	16.4	54.7
Never married	13.5	4.4
Divorced or separated	5.9	6.3
With living children	63.1	81.3
Requires assistance in:		
Bathing	91.2	6.0
Dressing	77.7	4.3
Using toilet room	63.3	2.2
Transferring[b]	62.7	2.8
Eating	40.4	1.1
Difficulty with bowel and/or bladder control	54.5	NA[c]
Disorientation or memory impairment	62.6	NA
Senile dementia or chronic organic brain syndrome	47.0	NA

[a]For nursing home residents, marital status at time of admission.
[b]Getting in or out of bed or chair.
[c]Although comparable data are not available 6 percent of the community-resident older population had difficulty with urinary control or had urinary catheters. NA-Not available.
Source: U.S. Senate (1987–1988), Table 4-11.

moving the person to a nursing home does not end the stress. Respondents in their study of family caregivers to Alzheimer's patients expressed this stress:

> It was easier to bury my first husband than to place my second husband in the nursing home [72-year-old wife].

Now that my husband is in the nursing home, I am lonely, but I just couldn't take it anymore. My back hurt constantly, I was cross with him, and cried a lot [75-year-old wife].

There are no words to express the trauma of finally having to accept the fact that you cannot care for him any longer [76-year-old wife].

When the time comes that you can't continue there is no choice but the nursing home. It does relieve the physical burden but the mental anguish continues. The caregiver may be burned out and not survive as long as the patient. This nearly happened in our case [69-year-old husband]. (Pratt et al., 1987, p. 206)

There may also be realistic concerns about the financial drain caused by the cost of nursing home care. The spouse may fear that the family house might be lost, or that resources will not be adequate for the future.

There are several ways of considering the family as "client" (instead of focusing only on the resident's adjustment) that can be helpful. The caregivers may be helped to regard placement in a nursing home as the solution to burdensome physical care, but not as an end to caring (Pratt et al., 1987, p. 209). Education and social support, perhaps as part of a group of caregivers, are often important. Specific personal problems of the caregiver may also need attention.

Tobin (1987) described the importance of considering institutionalization as a family process. Although we usually expect some feelings of guilt, the reaction

Although family members may have many mixed feelings about placing a relative in a nursing home, including relief, anger, and inadequacy, institutionalization is a family process that includes both negative and positive aspects.

actually may be more complex. It often involves many mixed feelings, including relief, but also a sense of heightened inadequacy combined with deep feelings of rage: "rage at oneself for being inadequate and rage toward the elderly person for inducing feelings of inadequacy" (p. 42). Nonetheless, family visits to nursing home residents are extremely important. Face-to-face contact can help the person know who they are and to remember their unique past history. Even if the confused elderly person does not seem aware of the visit, staff may note signs after the visit that it had an effect. Unless this information is given to the family, however, they may feel the visits are meaningless and serve only to increase their feelings of guilt, inadequacy, and rage (p. 49).

One strategy Tobin has used to help cope with these mixed feelings was to provide a "good" figure (a social-work intern) who could satisfy the family's desire for individualized care for the resident, and to provide a "bad" figure (the administration) who could tolerate the family's anger at their feelings of inadequacy, shame, and guilt. Another strategy may be to facilitate the perception of the move into the home as a *voluntary decision* and that the new environment is similar to one's ideally preferred environment; although these beliefs may be distortions of reality, they appear to enhance adaptation. In addition, Tobin noted a "unique psychology of the very old" in which aggressiveness, suspiciousness, and even nastiness may facilitate adaptation to relocation — if the staff is able to tolerate and even encourage these behaviors and to see their absence as a cause of alarm (Tobin, 1987; cf. Lieberman & Tobin, 1983; Tobin & Lieberman, 1976).

Home Health Care

A nationwide survey of long-term health care in 1982 found that families, spouses, other relatives and friends provide a great deal of care for older persons who live in the community. Adult children and spouses each provide over one-third of the care (Figure 9.9). Seventy percent of caregivers were women; 74 percent of caregivers live with the recipient; and 64 percent had provided care for at least a year. Older care recipients receive more care from "formal" (e.g., home health services) sources and from other family members and less from a spouse, compared with younger recipients (U.S. Senate, 1987–1988). A variety of services are available in most communities to assist the person with some disabilities to remain in the community as long as possible. These include:

Social work services

Visiting nurses for help with acute and chronic illness

Homemaker-home health aides to cook hot meals, coordinate shopping assistance, and provide companionship

Meals on Wheels that delivers a hot meal several days a week

Telephone reassurance services — a daily phone call at a prearranged time to see that everything is ok

Escort and transportation services to appointments, church, meetings, etc.

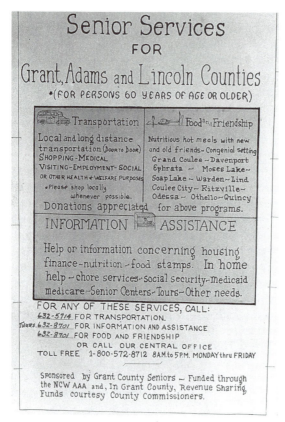

Senior Services
FOR
Grant, Adams and Lincoln Counties
*(FOR PERSONS 60 YEARS OF AGE OR OLDER)

Transportation
Local and long distance transportation (Door to Door) SHOPPING - MEDICAL VISITING - EMPLOYMENT - SOCIAL OR OTHER HEALTH + WELFARE PURPOSES
*Please shop locally whenever possible.

Food and Friendship
Nutritious hot meals with new and old friends - Congenial setting Grand Coulee ~ Davenport Ephrata ~ Moses Lake ~ Soap Lake ~ Warden ~ Lind Coulee City ~ Ritzville ~ Odessa ~ Othello ~ Quincy

Donations appreciated for above programs.

INFORMATION ASSISTANCE

Help or information concerning housing finance - nutrition - food stamps. In home help - chore services - social security - medicaid medicare - Senior Centers - Tours - Other needs.

FOR ANY OF THESE SERVICES, CALL:
632-5714 FOR TRANSPORTATION.
Thurs. 632-8701 FOR INFORMATION AND ASSISTANCE
632-8701 FOR FOOD AND FRIENDSHIP
OR CALL OUR CENTRAL OFFICE
TOLL FREE 1-800-572-8712 8A.M. to 5 P.M. MONDAY thru FRIDAY

Sponsored by Grant County Seniors ~ Funded through the NCW AAA and, In Grant County, Revenue Sharing Funds courtesy County Commissioners.

A variety of services are available to provide home health care to persons who require it. Some are provided by volunteer agencies or by government-supported programs, others must be purchased by the individual unless the person qualifies for Medicaid or the service is covered by Medicare.

Chore services for minor repairs and household tasks such as lawn mowing or putting up storm windows

Friendly visiting for companionship on a regular basis

Occupational and physical therapy services. (Silverstone & Hyman, 1982, pp. 187–193)

Some of these services are covered by Medicare or Medicaid for eligible persons; others are available from volunteer organizations in the community. Often the individual must pay at least part of the cost. In general, however, the services are not adequate to meet the need and the quality of service is difficult to monitor. Nonetheless, they provide a vital lifeline for fortunate elders who need care at home because they can receive a wide range of high-quality services.

In addition to these services at home, there are a variety of services available in the community. These include:

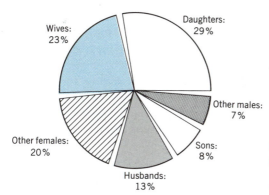

FIGURE 9.9 Distribution of informal caregivers by relationship to elderly care recipient: 1982. (*Source*: U.S. Senate, 1987–1988, Chart 4–9, p. 122.)

Congregate meals, for example, at Senior Centers at lunchtime

Senior Centers that provide a variety of social activities

Transportation services provided at reduced cost or by volunteers such as a high school driving class

Legal services at reduced rates or at no charge for those eligible

Day hospitals and day-care centers for persons who need some help, but not full-time care; these may provide a broad range of services, and provide extensive care for persons whose caregiver works during the day. (Silverstone & Hyman, 1982, pp. 193–196)

These services are financed by private contributions, by local, state, and federal money, and by various religious and service groups. Some communities have developed innovative programs of day care such as the model developed by the Brookdale Center on Aging in New York City (Quinn & Crabtree, 1987) and home health services such as the Nursing Home without Walls (Lombardi, 1988).

Psychological research on caregiving has been problematic (Smyer, 1988). In general, little attention has been given to the stage of disability that is involved, or to the type of illness involved. Caring for one recovering from a mild stroke may be a very different psychological experience than caring for one developing progressive Alzheimer's disease, for example. Caregivers who are part of an organized support group are often studied, but they probably differ from caregivers who are too busy to attend. Spouses, who themselves may be elderly, differ from adult children supporting families, who, in turn, differ from those adult children who may be retired and caring for parents in their eighties or nineties. Thus, caregivers are a very heterogeneous group and any attempt to generalize is probably inappropriate.

An excellent report on caregiving was prepared for the U.S. House of Representatives Select Committee on Aging by Stone (1987); some of the major themes are summarized in Chapter 5. One key point is that a vast amount of care is provided to the elderly by the family and other "informal" caregivers. Over all, only 1 in 5 aged persons with long-term care needs are living in nursing homes; only 1 in 4 noninstitutionalized elderly requiring care rely in part on "formal" care—3 in 4 rely only on "informal" caregivers (Liu, Manton & Liu, 1986). Nonetheless, only 35 states provide some very limited form of payment to family caregivers and federal assistance is also very limited, especially for low-income caregivers. Likewise, very few employers provide assistance for employees caring for elderly persons (Stone, 1987).

Another excellent review of aging and social care by Cantor and Little (1985) noted that the formal support system for home care in the United States is essentially a "non-system":

> In the United States, social services tend to be fragmented, with diverse funding sources and eligibility criteria, and there is rarely a single entry point to services. . . . In contrast, western European systems are better developed, have a stronger public welfare base, and tend to have clearly defined gateways to services, known to both older people and their families. (p. 772)

Nutrition

Nutrition involves more than food. It involves "motivation towards eating, customary and cultural attitudes and practices, general mental and physical health, isolation, availability of food, geography, transportation, economics, and education in the use of food" (Weg, 1978, p. 133). To take only one example, Rawson, Weinberg, Herold, and Holtz (1978) noted that the low intake of calcium found in their nationwide study of persons over age 60 may have resulted from low consumption of milk because the respondents often depended on family and neighbors for shopping; as a result, they did not purchase perishable items frequently enough to have fresh milk available. In addition, they seemed to be unaware of alternate sources of necessary nutrients.

A set of dietary guidelines for older persons is given in Box 9.3; it shows some of the alternate sources of various nutritional elements. Meals need not occur three times a day, so the total food intake may include snacks or be divided into five or six smaller meals; this may help to reduce boredom as well as to aid digestion (Bailey, 1978).

BOX 9.3   *Guidelines and Meal Patterns for the Middle and Later Years*

Daily Nutrition

Try, each day, for at least:

1 serving each meal of whole grain cereal, bread, or macaroni product.

2 glasses of skim milk, or its equivalent, such as milkshake, soups, pudding, custard made with skim milk; ice milk; low fat cheeses such as cottage, hoop, or farmer.

2 servings of meat or meat substitutes of high-quality protein: lean beef, veal, or lamb (preferably a maximum of 2 times/week), fish, poultry, peas, beans, legumes, nuts, seeds; eggs (not more than 3 times/week).

2 servings of fresh fruit including at least one that is especially rich in vitamin C—e.g., grapefruit, orange, cantaloupe, papaya, guava, strawberries.

2 servings of vegetables, one of which should be a leafy, dark green type—e.g., spinach, romaine lettuce.

BOX 9.3 *(Continued)*

6–8 glasses of liquids, including water. Weak tea or herb tea, decaffeinated coffee, skim milk, consomme, or other light, nonfatty soups, fruit juices, and watery fruits (watermelon) and vegetables all contribute to this total.

Note:
Nonfat dry milk is useful as a protein supplement in soups, other fluid drinks, casseroles, or mixed into water for reconstituted milk.
Eat a wide variety of foods. Use fresh foods whenever possible.
Minimize or eliminate the use of refined sugar and salt.

Methods of Preparation

Broiling is superior to frying. Frying increases the fat load of the meal, increasing empty calories, and makes food harder to digest.
Baking is superior to boiling for preserving whatever vitamins exist. Boiling tends to lose vitamins of food to the water, which is usually discarded.
Remove excess fat present close to skin of poultry, and on meats to insure the excellent source of essential amino acids without the potentially harmful fat food.

Note:
An average serving of bread is 1 slice.
An average serving of cereal is ½ to ¾ cup.
An average serving of fruits or vegetables is approximately ½ to ¾ cup.
An average serving of cooked meat is 3 oz.

Meal Pattern Suggestions

Breakfast
Fresh fruit
Egg or cereal[a] or both
Whole wheat toast or bread and margarine
Artifically sweetened jam or jelly
  occasionally
Skim milk, weak tea, decaffeinated coffee

Lunch
Salad[b]
Main dish—meat or poultry or cheese
Whole wheat bread or roll and margarine
Fresh fruit
Skim milk, weak tea, decaffeinated coffee

Dinner
Salad[b]
Main dish (meat, fish, poultry, or cheese)
Yellow or green vegetable
Baked potato
Whole wheat bread or roll with margarine
Dessert: fresh fruit and ice milk or plain
  cookies (no sugar icing or creamy filling))
Skim milk, weak tea, decaffeinated coffee

[a]Cereals, preferably whole grain and hot; if cold, nonsugared.
[b]Salads: one (1) salad/day is generally adequate to provide its quota of vitamins, minerals, and fiber. Important that a mixture of leafy vegetables be included: dark green spinach and a variety of lettuce.

   Snacks, e.g., carrots, celery, unsweetened grapefruit or apple juice, an orange or tomato, could make healthful additions to daily food intake, modified and selected according to individual caloric and specific nutrient needs.

   Some people feel better, and use food more satisfactorily, if total intake is divided into five or six small meals. This may be advantageous to digestion and to reducing overeating tendency or hunger pangs over a period of several hours.

Source: Weg (1985), Table 8.7. Reprinted with permission of John Wiley & Sons, Inc. from *Depression in the elderly*, Copyright © 1985.

Nutrition, exercise, and health are interrelated, and many older persons do not exercise enough to maintain their health. Thus, they may eat too much and are at risk for being overweight and for some chronic diseases. A combination of appropriate exercise and nutrition — and avoidance of high-risk behaviors such as cigarette smoking — is probably the best available prevention for premature aging and chronic disease.

It should also be noted that eating is a social activity (Weg, 1985). Probably no one enjoys eating alone, and cooking for one is dull. It is hard to buy fresh food for one person's balanced diet. For this reason, older persons may be at risk for malnutrition — even if they eat regularly, they may not receive adequate nutrition. Thus, the availability of low-cost meals at Senior Centers and through programs such as **Meals on Wheels** that deliver prepared food to homebound elderly persons can be vital. Malnutrition can be one of the causes of reversible brain syndrome (see Chapter 8).

Drug Use

Older people consume a disproportionate share of prescription medication, including both psychotropic drugs (e.g., antidepressants and tranquilizers) and drugs for chronic diseases such as hypertension or pain relief. Frequently persons who use prescription drugs also use medications purchased without restriction in stores, such as pain medication, cold remedies, or nose drops. Some also drink alcohol a few times a week. Although most use these drugs appropriately, there can be a danger when drugs are used in combination with each other or with alcohol (Guttmann, 1977).

> Alcohol, itself a drug, mixes unfavorably with many other drugs, including those sold by prescription and those bought over the counter. In addition, use of prescription drugs may intensify the older person's reaction to alcohol, leading to more rapid intoxication. Alcohol can dangerously slow down performance skills (driving, walking, etc.), impair judgment, and reduce alertness when taken with drugs. . . .
>
> Anyone who drinks even moderately should check with a physician or pharmacist about possible drug interactions. (Jarvik & Small, 1988, p. 209)

Even seemingly innocuous medications, such as nose drops, can lead to serious drug interactions. Jarvik and Small (1988) suggest the guidelines in Box 9.4 as common-sense precautions against drug interactions and misuse. It is useful to take notes when the physician explains the way medication is to be taken, and to inquire about some kind of "daily pill box" to keep the medication regimen on schedule. Compliance with prescribed medical treatment was discussed in Chapter 7.

Quality of Life

It is apparent that old age is often a negative social position in our country. One way of seeing this position is to consider the combination of negative social statuses that may characterize an older person. First, there is clearly the negative status of being old — bad enough in our youth-oriented society, characterized by what Butler

BOX 9.4   *How to Use Medicines Safety*

Take exactly the amount of drug prescribed by the doctor, and follow the dosage schedule as closely as possible. (Call your doctor or pharmacist if you have questions.)

Never take drugs prescribed for a friend or relative, even though your symptoms may be the same.

Always tell the doctor about past problems you have had with drugs. When the doctor prescribes a new drug, be sure to mention all other medicines you are taking currently. It is best to bring a list.

Keep a daily record of the drugs you are taking.

If childproof containers are hard to handle, ask the pharmacist for easy-to-open containers. Always be sure, however, that they are out of the reach of children.

Make sure directions printed on a drug container are understandable and that the name of the medicine is clearly printed on the label.

Discard old medicines; many drugs lose their effectiveness over time.

When starting a new drug, ask the doctor or pharmacist about side effects, about special rules for storage, and about foods or beverages, if any, to avoid, or if they should be taken before or after the medication.

Avoid discontinuing a medicine until the doctor says so. If you do have to stop or forget to take a dose, check with your doctor on how to start again.

Always call the doctor promptly if you notice unusual reactions.

Source: Jarvik & Small (1988), p. 153. Reprinted with permission.

(1969) termed *ageism*. Add to this the other negative statuses that may be present: not working, poor, ethnic or racial minority, and female (probably widowed). The result is a compounding of negative social positions that is frequently intensified by chronic illness and loneliness—especially among the "old-old" population. In large cities, there may be the advantages of activities, programs, and services that result from the concentration of older persons in urban areas, but there are also disadvantages such as the fear of crime, decaying neighborhoods, indifferent land-lords, and disruptive neighbors. In rural areas, although the physical situation is quite different, the problems are no less severe—transportation, lack of nearby medical care, and physical as well as possibly social isolation. In short, many aspects of aging in our country can reduce the quality of life for older people.

However, the problems faced by some older people are only part of the total experience of aging in the United States. At the other extreme are those older persons for whom aging appears to bring extraordinary benefits. Because these examples contrast so sharply with stereotypes about aging, they are often reported in the news media; this one is from the *New York Times*.

> A year and a half ago, Alberta Hunter, an obscure, retired nurse, set out to resume her previous career as a jazz and blues singer, a career she abandoned more than 20 years ago in order to study and practice nursing. Miss Hunter's remarkable comeback at 82 was officially launched in October of 1977 at Barney Josephson's Cookery when she began a limited engagement that has become an indefinite run. Moreover, Miss Hunter's new career is running at full throttle with television appearances ("60 Minutes," "The Mike

Douglas Show,'' ''Camera Three'' and the recent Kennedy Center gala), and a new Columbia soundtrack recording of the film ''Remember My Name.'' . . .

Her 83-year-old voice remains a strong, flexible instrument, and she projects an authoritative, hard-hitting approach to the blues that eclipses the work of many contemporary performers decades her junior. (Lissner, 1979, p. D-23)

To be sure, Miss Hunter was a remarkable woman; she performed until the year before she died at age 89. But there are similar, if much less dramatic, examples of older men and women in all racial and ethnic groups who find that aging is an exciting, challenging, and fulfilling time of life.

Thus, as we focus on the quality of life for older persons, we need to consider both the positive and negative extremes, as well as the majority in between who are aging, despite the obstacles, with a sense of satisfaction and meaning. In an anthropological study of a community of elderly Jews in California, Myerhoff (1979) pointed out that younger people often see aging only from the outside, so that it appears to be a tragic series of losses; but the anthropological perspective provides a view of aging from the older person's own frame of reference as a challenging *career* that has meaning in itself.

The women were describing some of the strategies they had cultivated for coping with their circumstances — growing old, living alone and with little money. Each in a different way, with a different specialization, had improvised techniques for growing old with originality and dedication. For these women, aging was a career, . . . a serious commitment to surviving, complete with standards of excellence, clear, public, long-term goals whose attainment yielded community recognition and inner satisfaction. (Myerhoff, 1979, pp. 250–251)

She also found that the older persons' own behavior often contrasted sharply with the stereotypes about aging, including those that they expressed themselves.

> Even those who stated flatly that old age was a curse, with no redeeming features, could be seen living engaged lives, passionate and original. Nearly every person in the Center community—men and women—had devised some career, some activity or purpose to which he/she was committed. They had provided themselves with new possibilities to replace those that had been lost, regularly set new standards for themselves in terms of which to measure growth and achievement, sought and found meaning in their lives, in the short run and the long. (Myerhoff, 1979, p. 251)

In addition to the factors that have been discussed in earlier chapters such as the family network, leisure, and health, four issues are especially important to the quality of life for older persons: housing, transportation, fear of crime, and elder abuse.

Housing

Just as there is no substitute for an adequate income if individuals are to be able to exercise free choice about the style of their lives, there is no substitute for a variety of alternate housing arrangements for older people to exercise their freedom of choice. The poor, minority, disabled, and rural aged are particularly in need of adequate and well-maintained housing and neighborhoods. But it also needs to be the kind of housing that meets their personal, health, and economic needs, as well as housing that is located where they want to live and where they can readily visit places of interest.

Golant (1984) interviewed a random sample of persons over age 60 in a middle-class suburb of Chicago to determine their satisfaction with housing and their environment. He found that most of the older people were satisfied with their neighborhood, community, and housing. They felt their home or apartment provided comfortable experiences, were satisfied with the community services, and experienced "good times" in the community. Nonetheless, a sizable minority reported negative or unpleasant experiences with their environment.

> For instance . . . 16 percent of the elderly felt their houses were too big; 4 percent often felt fatigued as a result of caring for their homes; 8 percent frequently felt annoyed about having no place to rest while doing their shopping; 33 percent persistently felt frightened about going out at night because of crime; 18 percent persistently worried about being attacked or robbed while walking and 19 percent worried that a thief might break into their home; 26 percent were frequently bothered by cold weather and snow and 18 percent persistently postponed their plans because of bad weather; 16 percent often were discouraged from going out at night because of poor street lighting; 12 percent did not go places in their community because they were not within walking distance; 9 percent frequently felt lonely; 13 percent were dissatisfied with how far they lived from their family and relatives; and 14 percent felt they could not count on someone to help them with chores around their house. (Golant, 1984, pp. 336–337)

Many urban elderly live in apartments, sometimes paying moderate rents or benefiting from rent subsidies, but receive less than adequate services; or they are forced to move because the single-room-occupancy (SRO) building is being torn down and rebuilt or turned into a condominium they cannot afford. Some public housing projects reserve apartments for the elderly, but often the location and fear of crime keep older persons from moving in. Even in well-designed housing there may be subtle physical barriers that make shopping trips, visits to neighbors, and travel to places of interest very difficult for those older persons with physical disabilities. Stairs, unguarded streets or intersections without crosswalks, and high curbs or broken sidewalks can be significant barriers. In the design of housing for the elderly, it is also important to consider the availability of stores and their pricing policies, the access to public transportation, and physical characteristics of the building that increase security (Blank, 1979).

Ethnic elderly often have neighborhood and housing preferences that are important. How available are the preferred foods? Can family ties be maintained? Are there other persons who speak their language? For these reasons, many old persons prefer to remain in their deteriorating family homes or apartments; others stay for sentimental reasons or because the neighborhood is familiar. It may also be cheaper to stay. But in urban areas, this too often means that the neighborhood is decaying around them, fear of crime makes them a prisoner in their home, and friends and family may have moved away. Many rural elderly live in a community where the young are migrating to the cities; the doctor and dentist may have died or left, as many as 1 out of 5 residents may also be old, and their housing often lacks basic necessities.

It is useful to think of the range of housing for older persons to lie along a continuum from independent living in one's home to total care in a nursing home (Streib, Folts & Hilker, 1984). A variety of options exist for supportive housing, but these provide a relatively small proportion of living arrangements for older people (Table 9.3). **Retirement communities** exist in a variety of forms and provide a variety of services, usually including security, home maintenance, social activities, and community facilities. They range from loosely organized trailer parks to high-rise buildings and hotels. Often they require the older person to be self-sufficient and able to get around independently. Some provide meals and recreational facilities.

Shared living homes are receiving more attention today and provide a creative solution to two problems: older persons who live in a home that is too large to manage alone, and older persons who cannot afford to live alone. These homes vary in cost, size, and organization but generally consist of unrelated persons who neither are able to live independently nor need institutional care. Each home tends to work out arrangements for providing privacy and for sharing space (West, 1985). Most have a small paid staff who manage meals and maintenance, and may provide other services; but personal care and medical care are not provided (Streib et al., 1984). A national organization, The Shared Housing Resource Center in Philadelphia, provides information and technical assistance to local groups that want to establish such housing.

Boarding homes and similar facilities are often operated by local residents for modest profit. Although they may provide some personal care, since most are not

TABLE 9.3 *Continuum of Living Arrangements: From Private Home to the Nursing Home*

Least Supportive[a]
  Houses
  Condominiums
  Apartments
More Supportive
  Mobile Home Parks (retirement)
  Retirement Villages
  Retirement Apartments (high-rise)
  Retirement Hotels
  Shared Living Homes
  Board and Care Homes
Most Supportive
  Life Care Facilities
  Nursing Homes

[a]Conventional housing comprises about 80% to 90% of elderly housing.
Source: Adapted from Streib, Folts & Hilker (1984), Fig. 2.1.

licensed, the quality of care is uneven and one should be cautious.

Life care facilities offer a comprehensive range of housing, from self-sufficient living in an apartment to acute or chronic nursing care in one location. They are not permitted in all states and may involve a considerable financial investment. One should check the legal contract with a lawyer and exercise prudent judgment before making a commitment. If appropriate, they can provide the most complete range of housing alternatives in one location, but are able to meet the needs of only a small proportion of the elderly population (Streib et al., 1984).

Transportation

There are three obvious facets to the problems of transportation for older persons. First, whether it is available near their residence and is economical so that it is truly available; second, whether it is safe, convenient, and designed to accommodate the special needs of disabled persons; and third, whether there is any place worth going on it. Certainly, the elderly, like all of us, depend on transportation to participate in spiritual, cultural, social, and recreational activities; and lack of transportation implicitly denies full participation in the community. For example, a study conducted in Philadelphia found that 30 percent of older persons who were participating in senior centers or other programs for the elderly reported that they needed more transportation than was available; 1 out of 5 of these older persons needed transportation to attend church on Sunday (Stirner, 1978).

As with other problems, income issues are paramount, since with limited income older people frequently live in areas that are not well served by mass transit, and they often do not have resources for taxi fares or for private automobiles. For some, even transit fares may be a large expense. Also, there are several physical and psychological barriers to most forms of mass transit: steps to climb, closing doors to dodge, jerking trains or buses, waiting in the rain or cold, the painfully high step into many buses, infrequent service, slow travel, long walks, and fear of crime. Adequate transportation is an especially severe problem in rural areas, and distance may be a major barrier to health care, social interaction, and community participation.

Programs are being developed in many communities to help meet the transportation needs of older people and persons who are disabled. Some of these include specially designed vans or "Medicabs" for persons in wheelchairs, "dial-a-ride" programs in which eligible persons can arrange a reduced-fare taxi ride by reservation, reduced transit fares for older persons, and high school driver education classes that provide rides to individuals who request them in advance.

Crime and Elder Abuse

Nationwide surveys have indicated that about half of all older persons fear crime, compared with 41 percent of those under age 65; 69 percent of older women and 34 percent of older men said they were afraid. Fear of crime was found to be higher among Blacks than among Whites; and urban elderly were more fearful than older persons in smaller cities and towns, suburbs, or rural areas (Clemente & Kleinman, 1976).

However, persons over age 65 were less likely to be victimized than other age groups, according to a national survey that asked representative samples of persons about their experiences with crime. Older persons were less likely to be subject to violent crimes, and were no more likely than other age groups to be robbed on the street. Nonetheless, they were more likely to experience "predatory incidents" such as robbery or mugging in or near their home and were more likely to be victims of unplanned attacks by young, inexperienced criminals who were unarmed, acting alone, and unknown to the victim, as compared to other age groups (Antunes, Cook, Cook & Skogan, 1977; Cook, Skogan, Cook & Antunes, 1978).

Although older persons were not found to suffer larger financial losses or greater physical harm than other age groups, their *relative* financial losses compared with monthly income were larger than for middle-aged persons but lower than for younger persons (age 33–39). They were also less likely to be attacked than other age groups, but if they were attacked, older persons were more likely to be injured, to suffer internal injuries, and to lose consciousness, but were less likely to suffer wounds and broken bones or teeth than other age groups. The cost of medical care as a result of crime was no higher for older persons, but it was a larger proportion of their income than that of other age groups. Thus, the degree that crime affects the elderly more than other age groups is largely a consequence of the lower income of older persons, so that losses resulting from crime have a greater relative impact on older persons than middle-aged persons (Cook et al., 1978). Nonetheless, the fear of crime remains high among the elderly; this is probably heightened by media coverage of dramatic crimes against them.

Another form of crime against the elderly has also come to public attention as more concern has focused on abuse of older persons by their caregivers.

Domestic abuse of the elderly by families, relatives, and other caretakers has recently been viewed as a serious social problem, perhaps because of the rapid increase in the numbers of "old-old," vulnerable individuals in our population. Accurate data on the extent and nature of elder abuse are scarce. Unclear definitions of elder abuse, professional and public unawareness, and the victim's reluctance to take action are all believed to contribute to underreporting. . . .

The typical abused elderly person is depicted as age 75 or over, female, and dependent on others for care and protection. (Salend, Kane, Satz & Pynoos, 1984, p. 61)

In a large-scale random sample study, 2020 community-dwelling elderly were interviewed; the prevalence rate of abuse was found to be 32 per 1000 persons. Spouses were the most frequent perpetrator and roughly equal numbers of men and women were victims, contrary to earlier impressions (Phillemer & Finkelhor, 1988).

Several states have laws regarding **elder abuse**, but there are many complex issues that are involved in their enforcement—as there are with child abuse and spouse abuse statutes. If abuse is suspected in a nursing home, the state Nursing Home Ombudsman should be notified. In other cases, the Information and Referral Service of the Area Agency on Aging should be able to provide assistance. In emergencies, call the police.

Conclusion

Older people in the United States today are such a diverse group of individuals that it is important to avoid both positive and negative stereotypes about the elderly— either stereotype may reflect *ageism*. Large differences exist in terms of income and health status, and these differences interact with the individual's social and psychological resources, bringing still greater heterogeneity. In turn, this interaction of strengths, resources, and problems is intertwined with the changing patterns of life today. Thus, the problems of urban elderly reflect, often in intensified ways, the problems of life in American cities—such as crime, housing, and transportation. The economic problems of some older persons also reflect nationwide issues of poverty, racism, and the unique vulnerability of very old women. Similarly, the need for health care among older persons reflects the need for comprehensive health insurance for all persons.

In our rapidly changing world, future generations of older persons are likely to be better educated, in better health, and even more diverse than older people today. They will be more numerous, more will be in the "old-old" age group, more will be "people of color" from ethnic and racial minority groups, and they will reflect the varied life-styles of younger people today grown old. They will, after all, be ourselves.

Ideally, there should be greater freedom of choice among a wider variety of constructive alternatives for older persons so that the diverse needs of this varied group of people can be met according to their own desires, abilities, and resources. How can we play a role in improving the quality of life for older persons—and for ourselves if we are fortunate enough to grow old? This will be the focus of the brief final section of this chapter.

Education and Occupations in Gerontology

There is scarcely a profession that is not directly or indirectly connected with the needs of aging persons. In the fields of psychology, sociology, social work, medicine, nursing, and psychiatry there are specialities in gerontology or geriatrics that train persons to provide direct service to the aged (Peterson, 1987). In biology and physiology there is a great need for research on the basic mechanisms of aging. In anthropology there is a need for research on the effects of cultural variations on the aging process—both in different cultures and in different subcultures within our society. In fields such as architecture and engineering there are great challenges for designing barrier-free environments, housing, and transportation for the elderly. Ethical issues in hospital and nursing home care of terminally ill persons and the greater importance of aging in public policy have increased the importance of philosophy and political science to the field of gerontology. In history, literature, drama, and the arts (to mention some less obvious examples) there are fascinating studies or applications waiting to be made concerning aging—one example may suffice: How have films portrayed aging and how is it portrayed presently? What symbols are used and how have they changed in recent years?

The past decade has seen the emergence of a number of training programs in adult development and aging, or human development, or gerontology, or geriatrics. They have been established in a number of universities across the nation and have emerged in a variety of settings—both in established academic disciplines such as sociology, psychology, and social work as well as in interdisciplinary programs that draw faculty and students from a range of specialities. It is obvious that these training and research programs are important for advancing our understanding of the aging process and for equipping professionals to work with the aged.

The past decade has also seen an increase in the membership of professional organizations concerned with the aged, such as the American Society on Aging and the Gerontological Society of America, as well as several regional gerontological societies. These organizations are made up of persons concerned with social policy, services, and research in the natural and social sciences concerning aging. They serve as important forums for the exchange of research and ideas about the field of gerontology and as major centers for information about this growing field. A variety of other national and international organizations focus on issues related to aging and many professional societies, such at the American Psychological Association, have sections devoted to gerontology.

There are also a number of occupations that serve the aged directly in various contexts such as hospital administration, medicine, nursing, and public administration. Accounting, clerical work, and computer science are other fields that are important in hospital or nursing home management, in city, state, and federal offices for the aging, and in organizations for the aged. Lawyers, accountants (especially for taxes), dentists, podiatrists, chiropractors, optometrists, and clergymen all serve the aged professionally and might even specialize in the aged or volunteer their services for the elderly. In addition, several occupations are involved with the aged in hospitals and nursing homes. These occupations include, in addition to the ones already mentioned, physical therapists, occupational therapists, recreational therapists, music or dance therapists, and speech therapists. Dietitians, pharmacists, beautitians, and the entire health services field are represented in some of the best hospitals and homes for the aged. In many of these fields there are excellent opportunities for employment and advancement as well as for personal satisfaction. ''Gerontology, the study of the process of aging and the needs and care of the elderly, has become one of the fastest-growing career opportunities for the next decade'' (Fowler, 1988).

There are a variety of ways in which students may be trained to work with the elderly (or with adults generally). There are also paraprofessional jobs and roles being developed for persons without a bachelor's degree. Some of these include work in the community to improve the quality of community life and to maximize the independence of older persons. Nearly every senior citizen center and home or hospital for the aged or chronically ill appreciates volunteers for a variety of roles. Actually, there is little better way to gain an understanding of an area such as adulthood and aging than by directly experiencing it; volunteer roles provide this opportunity as well as an important additional benefit—they allow a person to test out some of the jobs that are interesting and to talk with persons who are actually doing that kind of work.

Since one of the keys to aiding the minority aged is having trained minority persons (often bilingual) who can provide direct services to the aged and can serve as resource persons on ways to improve the condition of the aged they know best, it is clear that minority students need to be attracted into these fields. A heterogeneous group of aged persons demands a heterogeneous range of trained professionals and paraprofessionals.

Education of young persons in gerontology is complemented by education of middle-aged and older persons in a variety of fields of lifelong learning, including gerontology.

But education of young persons is only one aspect of the occupational needs in this area. Middle-aged and older persons can also benefit from greatly expanded educational opportunities — in reality, throughout one's life — not only to fulfill themselves, but also to acquire new skills to aid others. Certainly, the aged themselves represent a rich resource for services and programs for the elderly; and the range of skills needed to serve as representative members of groups on government boards setting priorities, establishing policies, and providing funding — or to provide direct services to the aged themselves — may require education in a variety of fields. Most colleges have opened their doors to older persons, and the impact of this concept might revolutionize thinking about the place and function of education in life and in our society.

As we look toward the future and imagine what kind of lives we want to have for ourselves in a diversified society that is faced with serious social problems and the fast pace of technological change, the opportunities and challenges are truly astounding. As years are added to life, will life be added to years? Perhaps the place to begin is with that older person who reminds us of what might happen to us if nothing changes to improve the quality of life as we grow old ourselves. Mrs. K. in the next Interlude illustrates some of the challenges that are involved in one's personal aging career.

Chapter Summary

1. Aging is likely to be different in the future than it was in the past. Perhaps as many as one in three persons in the United States will be over age 55 and one in five over age 65 by the year 2030. Older people in the future will have greater education, knowledge about healthful behaviors, and health care than today's elders.

2. The meaning, status, and experience of aging differ greatly among various cultures around the world. In general, the status and treatment of older persons depend on cultural beliefs and practices, the nature and structure of the society, and characteristics of the individual old person.

3. Industrialization of traditional agricultural societies, though possibly lowering the relative status of older people compared to younger people, often brings improved living conditions for all groups. Thus, after a period of initial decline in prestige, older people may wind up better off than their grandparents were.

4. Previous reports of groups of long-living people were found to have been erroneous. There is no historical precedent for the recent growth of a large aged population. In most cultures aging is a mix of positive and negative characteristics. New ethics regarding aging are likely to emerge as more and more people grow old.

5. Negative views of aging in the United States date back to the 1890s. Older people had especially low prestige during the Great Depression of the 1930s. In many respects, there has been a gradual improvement in the status of older people since the 1940s.

6. The growth of the older population began earlier in some countries and is only now beginning in others because of differences in birthrate, modern sanitation, and health care. In newly developing countries, the growth of the older population will be especially dramatic and may create significant social and economic problems.

7. The aged cannot be described as a single homogeneous social group. Older people typically retain much of the diversity in social status that they experienced in middle age; added to this is diversity that reflects individual variability in health, family relationships, income, religion, ethnicity, gender, and even age.

8. Minority status may have negative effects on individuals in society. Ethnicity is potentially a positive characteristic of a group. Degree of acculturation, language ability, and socioeconomic status interact with ethnic background and minority status to influence patterns of aging.

9. The problems of older people today are problems faced by all age groups, including health care, housing, transportation, fear of crime, and economic uncertainty. Problems of frail elderly, the very old, women living alone, and older minorities need particular attention. The issues of aging are intergenerational issues and affect everyone.

10. The largest source of income for older people is Social Security, which protects many elderly from poverty. Income also is received from investments or savings, working, and pensions. A number of benefits supplement the income of older people. Some are eligible for Supplementary Security Income (SSI), food stamps, and other programs.

11. Medicare provides health insurance to nearly all persons over age 65. It does not pay all costs, however, and monthly premiums must be paid, with an optional premium for coverage of physician fees and other services. A surcharge on income taxes of Medicare recipients has been proposed as an additional charge for many older persons with taxable income.

12. Compared with only one in twenty persons over 65, about 22 percent of persons over age 85 are living in nursing homes. Much of the cost is paid by Medicaid, the program for persons with low income and few financial resources. Families and spouses also provide a great deal of care for older persons in the community.

13. The quality of life for some old people is poor; but other older people find significant opportunities for fulfillment and lead highly satisfying lives. For many, aging is a kind of career that provides meaning through a commitment to survive with originality and the support of friends despite obstacles that may be present.

14. Choices among alternative types of affordable housing, access to transportation that goes where one wants to go, and freedom from fear of crime enhance an older person's quality of life. Housing and transportation problems are especially acute for the rural elderly; crime is a particular problem for urban elderly.

15. Greater attention to older persons has created a range of opportunities for education and occupations related to aging. Many specializations are relevant to working with older persons. Programs and courses in the field of gerontology offer a variety of resources for both older and younger students.

Key Words

boarding homes	Meals on Wheels
cross-over effect	means-test program
dependency ratio	Medicaid
double standard of aging	Medicare
elder abuse	ombudsman
gerontocracy	retirement communities
life care facilities	shared living homes
life chances	Supplemental Security Income (SSI)

Review Questions

Cross-Cultural Perspectives on Aging

1. What conclusions may be drawn from the studies of aging in different cultures? Give some examples of cultural variations in the treatment of older people.

2. What are the effects of modernization and contact with modernity in studies of attitudes about the aged during industrialization of developing nations? Do the aged benefit or suffer from modernization?

Aging and the Social Context

3. Where did the negative attitude toward the elderly in America originate? Why do you think this happened? Is it changing today?

4. What accounts for differences in the proportion of persons over 65 in different countries? What factors determine the future age structure of the population?

5. Why will the level of formal education be higher among the aged in the future? Name some aspects of aging that will be affected by this increase in educational level.

6. What is the "dependency ratio"? How does the growing proportion of older persons affect working people? Describe Figure 9.2 in your own words.

7. In what ways are the elderly not a homogeneous group? What are the factors that make them even more diverse as a group than young or middle-aged people?

8. Give some examples of the "double standard of aging." List some advantages and disadvantages with aging for each gender.

9. Give some examples of the ways ethnic background affects characteristics of aging. Describe Figure 9.3 in your own words.

Aging in an Aging Society

10. What are the major sources of income for older persons? Describe the difference between SSI and Social Security. How can poverty among the elderly be reduced?

11. Describe Medicare, Parts A and B. What is Medicaid and who is eligible to receive it?

12. What are some of the family issues raised by admitting a relative to a nursing home? Why are these reactions important to understand?

13. Who cares for older persons in the community? What services are available in your community and what additional kinds of help do caregivers need?

14. What contributes to inadequate nutrition for some older persons? Why is this a serious concern?

15. What problems may result from a pattern of multiple medication? How can this risk be reduced?

16. What factors contribute to a poorer quality of life for some older persons?

17. What does Myerhoff mean by "aging as a career"?

18. Describe some of the alternatives to institutionalized care for the elderly that exist or should be created.

19. What considerations should be taken into account when designing housing, transportation, and crime protection for the elderly?

Education and Occupations in Gerontology

20. Name a few of the ways students may be trained to work with older persons and some of the occupations where knowledge about older persons would be useful.

Mrs. K., AGE 89

Mrs. K. is an 89-year-old woman who lives in a nursing home; she has been in the home 11 years and is remarkably vigorous and independent. Her bed was covered with handcrafts she had made and she apparently works in her own private room. She is one of the longest residents in her home, living first in the small building next door (which she calls her "white house") until the new modern building was built a few years ago. The home seems close to an ideal nursing home; but like most of the patients in this private (proprietary) nursing home, she depends on Medicare and Medicaid to pay her expenses. Mrs. K. (no one called her by her first name) came to the United States 43 years ago and learned English on her own. She seems to have been quite independent and on her own for most of her life, although some of this independence may reflect the personality shift in the later years described in Chapter 8. She has outlived her husband by many years and has no children. After working until the age of 70 she had to "retire" and give up her apartment a few years later when her health failed.

This example raises important questions not only about her life but also about the problems of the aged in our society. If she were not living in a nursing home, where would she live? How could she pay the expensive rates for such excellent care without government help? Turning to her life, we wonder whether she married "late" for her time and, if so, why? Why did she and her husband (Karl) not have children? Was their marriage satisfying for her? Might her strong personality be related to her ability to cope with the several traumatic events in her later years (the death of her husband, her ill-

ness, giving up her apartment, and moving from the old nursing home to the new building) — and possibly with her longevity? Has she worked through her feelings about death? Does she have a sense of meaningfulness in her life?

As you look back over your life, what milestones stand out? What milestones; let me think. I think there are many things where I am really interested and was always interested since a child. I was a child more reserved. I don't know why. That time when I was young I didn't know what's what. But later when I knew more, then I knew I was — I can say — a special girl, special child. I always wanted to learn something. We lived that time in the country for several years because father was transferred from the city to the country; then after [that] we came to the city again. . . .

What things stand out in your memory of your life? What should I say? What kind of things stand out? . . . Having a job; of course this took most of my time; and then getting married is something different too; and then, the biggest moment was when we came to America. *That was really a big moment for you?* This was. This was an unexpected big moment, because my husband knew a gentleman from the German-American Consulate. And he asked my husband, "What do you do for a living? Would you like to go to America?" "No," my husband said, "this is not for us," because we made out good, you know. But then was the war [World War I]. We lost everything, so we couldn't make out anymore; and through that gentleman my husband came here in three weeks. Because my husband was in agriculture, diplomas he has, you know, he can work in big estates and everything. He comes himself from a big estate in Germany. He was always interested in horses; he raised horses and trained them. He was here in three weeks; I came here 10 months later, because I had to sell my household, you know. And this took me a little time. And then [I] came right away over too, and then I was working because I could not fulfill that job what I used [to] be, so I was sitting in the workroom and make dresses, and then after that . . . the worsest part was we couldn't speak English. That was the hindrance for me. Then, when I knew a little bit [of] English and I came higher up, and then I started as a fitter, you know . . . ladies' body dresses. I pinned them up . . . and all of them had girls sitting in the workroom and then I was all right. This I did until I was 70 years [old]. *You did that until you were 70 years old!* I'm older now. Naturally (she laughs). I'm 89. *Are you really! I never would have guessed.*

The last few years I grew older very much on account of my sickness, you know . . . swollen . . . (gestures to her legs) and it goes down and gets all flabby. Anyway . . . once we have to take something and I know this very well, so that's that. They leave me all alone; I can do just as I want. Of course, I don't do wrong things. I am very satisfied here and have a few nice, nice friends; and this makes me happy too. And I think I make them happy too, because they all look for me to talk with me. This makes me proud. Yesterday I received a card from a lady again. I met her in the hospital. She went to another residence; and through her I met her sister. Ever since then the sister comes and visits me and send me always money. She's good off. So I have two other wonderful friends I met here and this makes me happy. You know, they come always once in a while and [it] is happy. So, I can say I'm never lonesome. I'm always occupied and

happy so-called, you know. And that's the main thing, you know. And when I can have people I always try my best. This is not much, but. . . .

You've lived here for 15 years? No, 11; I'm here in this room 11 years. Only, I'm here 43 years in the United States. So, now I keep on as long as I can.

Do you have any children? No, I have no children. My husband is dead 26 years already. *I see.*

Then, I was still working, working, working, 'til I got sick and then I came here. I was very much crying when [I was] told in the hospital I come to the home. I had my apartment, but I couldn't go. So, they couldn't let me go home and I cried. And the social worker said to me, "You are a citizen. You must receive everything that other people get. It's coming to you." I said, "No, I cannot do it; I had so much saved I could live to 90 years old with my Social Security." And now came all different, took sick. Was laying down and they brought me to hospital. You see, unexpected comes, you know. *It was a very sad time for you when you had to leave your apartment.* Yah, I didn't see it any more. They brought me back here from the hospital and I never saw my apartment again. *You just went to the hospital and then came here.* Yah, it was two months. I was two months in hospital and then they sent me here [to the old building]. I call it my "white house." *Your "white house."* And then I make always about [it] little poems or little essays, you know. It's nothing much but I do the best. . . . And it comes here in the paper —we have a monthly paper here, we write everything. So I put it in there for Christmas and for holidays and so on . . . little poems. So I always occupy myself. I must have something which, you know, I must create this myself (she laughs).

Your husband, did he live on some kind of an agricultural farm? No, my husband was in the academy when he came . . . in the riding academy in _____ [town in Germany]. He taught ladies and children riding. And then after . . . there was not enough money. . . then I came over and my husband was there with his horses. We rode out with the lady here, there, and everywhere on the big estate and all that kind of things. Then he took off; it was not enough money. When I came over I made some myself, but it was very little because we couldn't speak English. And then my husband met a man; he was a painter . . . inside; he was German. He said, "Why don't you take [up] painting? You can make money." He learned my husband painting and my husband liked it very much and he made the nicest color, made everything nice and fine and even. We lived on _____ Street for 25 years until I took sick. We were always in New York.

Was getting married a big event for you? I married very late. I didn't want to get married at all because I had a wonderful position in Germany since 1910 and I could support myself. And I didn't want to take from a man money. I had plenty of opportunities to marry, but I said to my mother, "Nothing doing. I want to learn something. I want to make my own money. I don't want to take from a man. I just take what I want and do what I want, and that's good." So I did. I was 39 years old already. And I would have shoved him over also, but he was persistent. And I thank God for this, because through him I came to America; otherwise I would be destroyed in the Second World War. We came here in '29. See, when Hitler came, then we would have finished, you know. We didn't know him. But I have relatives over there and these [we] supported very much. I supported many many. I've never been [back] in Germany because, I say this cost a few thousand dollars and I'd rather give it to them because people need that more than. . . .

What kind of a profession were you in? I was in dressmaking. I was a directress in the best places in _____ [large German city] since 1910. And had girls sitting, eight girls apart more or less, in the workroom. I cut the dresses; I made the patterns; I fitted the dresses; and the girls would finish the dresses after that. It was a very good life. We had a few countesses; we had a few baronesses; we had one princess even, from Germany; this one I didn't fit because I was not a fitter. "Directress" we called it. I had a wonderful position for money. I didn't need to marry for money. Then when my husband was dead I was still working, always. Sure, I miss this, but as I say, I got sick and couldn't come [fit] in shoes; I get swollen. That was the hindrance.

So you had to stop working at 70? Yah, then I was sitting home. Seven years I was constantly in doctor's care; then he said, "I cannot help you anymore, Mrs. K. You must go into hospital; they have facilities which I am not allowed to use." So, then I was sitting seven years in my house not going . . . I didn't want to go in hospital. Then I fall together several times; then they picked me up and brought me to hospital and that was that. So this was the end and then I came here. Since then I was always happy here and worked, worked, worked.

Do you sometimes look back over your life and think about the things that happened? I think back and look back constantly, from a little child on . . . how it happened, why it happened. Yes, I do, but I do not regret. I'm alone, have nobody. Even if I would have children I wouldn't live with them. I would leave them alone. They should be happy. I wanted that too when I was young. I would leave them too. I would go in a home. *Do you wish that you did have children sometimes?* No, on account of the war [World War I], you know. We losed every penny; then, how can you get children? I had to work. And at least you want your children raised like you are raised, you know. And especial you would want a little decent, and this we couldn't do. Then was the big moment when we came here, you know. That was the biggest moment for me in the later years. I was glad to be here, and still am, you know.

Why was that such a big moment for you? You know, I never thought we could come to America! Imagine! We had a nice income and a flat [apartment], but through the war we lose everything; no work, no nothing. We had debts by my parents and this couldn't go on anymore. So, finally my husband met this man and through him he came here; and then, of course he sent the fare back to my mother. Then, months later I came, and I made my own money too. We saved a little. This was the biggest, the nicest moment. That's what I must say. I loved here when we came how cheap everything was. In Germany, it cost a pound of butter, two dollars — marks, we say; and here, we bought four pounds of butter from dollar. I say, "You bring it right back." He said, "You are a funny woman. Why don't you taste?" "It can't be good; you know how much cream you need for a pound of butter." He was an agricultural man, you know. Then he was stunned and thought it over. He said, "Taste it," and I tasted; it was the good butter. So, everything was so cheap here. Food! Oh, I love food. I always ate food, food, food. Every Saturday we bought food. Everything for the whole week. I like food still, all my life. *You still like food.* Oh, crazy about it! I cannot do without food.

How was your marriage? My marriage was fairly good. You know, there's always a little smoke in every kitchen; but this was overcome, you know. You must give in. My husband had his own mind and I had my own mind; but I always helped him. When something happened I always told him in advance what can happen and he didn't believe me. "Can't do nothing with that woman! Can't do nothing with that woman! Can't do nothing with that woman!" he always said. When sometimes trouble came, for instance, he wanted to participate with a partner. He wanted to make a little business.

We had a little money saved. Not much, but a little. I say, "Karl, you do not do that. We are strange in this country. We don't have the language exactly right and we don't know the rules and everything. We leave our hands off! You lose the money." Twice we lose and I say, "No; now I keep my money and you keep yours. You can do with it what you want, and I keep my money." And that's why sometimes we get trouble. We had a few troubles and I bawled him out in the right place in the right way. That's why he always said, "You're a smart woman!" But I said, "You don't listen when I tell you in advance, 'don't do it!'" That was really the idea, because I had the feeling in me, you know . . . I have the house of Cancer ruling me, you know. I made all the horoscopes. We learned to make all the horoscopes — a hell of a work. You need charts of the stars, where they are at this and that moment, and all the tables and all that. This I wouldn't want anymore, but that's why I said I feel. There are people who see, not directly, but they see. I feel; I feel in advance something is wrong, not coming right. And that's really true. I advised people and helped people. You think they did it? They didn't do it, see! You must always work, work and improve more and more and more; but they have not that ambition in them. That's what I believe . . . in the stars and how they stand in nature of the almighty universe. That is my special, how you say, work. If I could write very good as a writer I would make a nice book, but I'm not so intelligent so I can write. I make little things.

I get up in the morning [at] quarter to five. Bathe myself down every morning; nobody is up then. Then I'm finished; make my bed; pick everything up and then I sit here 'til seven and then get breakfast; and then we start working (she laughs). That's my life. *You work down in the craft shop?* No, I do not, because I'm on my own. *You work up here [in her private room]?* Yah, I'm all my own, because I could be the instructor of everything. I don't want to be under. They wanted me under them to show the others. But, I must say, I'm never—how should you say—high-headed. But this is what I worked out for myself, and this I keep. I didn't work under other people. I'm a creator in everything. What I do is all my own. *I get the feeling you've always been that way.* When I was a child already. But then I didn't know what's what. I had to learn first how to go, what is what. And then I figured out how, why, and so. Then I was able. So, no, I worked for things, but all on my own. I made recently for Mrs. D. a suit—crocheted suit with skirt and jacket, and she wears it once or two times, three times, four times. She's very pleased. I made very, very many things for Mrs. D., for her daughter, for her daughter-in-law; all sorts of dresses and outfits. Everything I make, everything. Other people cannot do that, you know. There are a few now [who can make] a little something, yes sure, but when they want really something now, then they ask me. And I gladly advise when I can help, sure.

Were you and your husband very close to one another? Oh yah. I loved my husband very much. And he loved me too. Because, what should I say, he was an educated man, came from a good family; he was also in the war and he had nice position there and he kept this. Yah, I loved my husband; we were happy, but as I said, sometimes was smoke in the kitchen (she laughs). *You had your arguments too?* Oh sure, sure. For instance, I tell you what was the biggest argument we had. When that damn, excuse me, Hitler was . . . and he heard from other German men on 86th Street . . . Saturdays he usually went there, or Sundays. And then he talked about everything, and he listened and listened. Now my husband was from a big estate, and he was the oldest son. He would have inherited it if he stayed. I said, "Karl, you leave the hands from it. We have no children; we are both alone. We have good work. We are satisfied and we want peace now." "No, no" he said. "I understand you stay in your house or you lose it, but imagine what you have to pay. You pay the trip over and you have to pay the man to look out for it. What is left for you—only work," I said. "Don't do it." No, he didn't want it [her advice]. And there was that Bund [club or association] from Hitler, and he would like to join that too, those meetings. [The German-American Volksbund, or Bund, was a pro-Nazi organization in the United States during the 1930s and 1940s.] I said, "You leave the hands from this," I said. "We are new in America. We do not participate in anything." "He promised you get back what you losed." I said, "Karl, don't you believe that!" "Yah, yah, yah, yah," he said. "I go over to Germany," he said. I said, "You go over from here to Germany? No!" And I talked with him over that often, very often. He insisted that he wanted to get his estate back. I told him everything as it comes and how it is away. I never believed in Hitler. I know. He said, "Yes, yes, yes." And I said, "No, Karl, let's make it here. You go over to Germany. I don't keep you. You know, I don't need you. I make my own money. I never needed no husband for making money. You go over. I don't keep you away. But once I tell you now in advance. I know you wouldn't like it. It won't come out as you think. You will be glad to come back here, but I don't give you a penny to come back. Stay there!" That was the biggest moment in all. Otherwise was nothing. *That was a big fight?* Oh yah, always fighting. And then finally when it came out what Hitler was and that Bund was, then he said, "I know you are a smart woman." I said, "Don't say that. You don't do when I tell you in advance." That was . . . oh . . . we had many fights. I would have let him go if he really wanted to go, but then find out a little bit before; so he stood here. Oh, yah, we had big fights. Now, how could we [have gone back to Germany?] . . . I was glad to be here, you know. Oh, I never liked that man [Hitler]. I didn't know him personally. . . . We were here already in '29 and he was there I think '33, you know, he started. No, I said, "Nothing doing." Otherwise, I said this was a very big moment—coming to America and having this event with him; he wanted to go.

Were sexual relations very important between the two of you? Oh, we were both [on] in years, you know, and—how should I say . . . I said to my husband before we were married, "One thing, think it over; when we marry don't go with other woman. If you cannot do this, we don't get married then." We never talked about this later . . . I don't think so. No, that's all right. That was not my main thing, you know. My main thing was working and learning. *Sexual relations weren't very important in your relationship then?* No, not so, not so. I could not say that. He was a very nice man with manners and so, and that's all.

Was his death quite a shock for you? Yes, very, yah, sure; because I was all alone here, and I just came from work and he was before me in the house, and we always had little dogs and they were always with him. They sat outside in the street and waited for me. So I came home and I wanted to go to the doctor because I get injection for my sickness. And I had the feeling that I don't like to go today. I'd rather go home. I went home, you know. Then I came, he was sitting in the sofa in the front, and sick. I said, "What's the matter, Karl?" He said, "Now I am finished." I said, "What's the matter?" "I have all here these things. It hurts me here, here, here. I have double pneumonia," he said. But I said, "It is not pneumonia." I said, "Come in the kitchen just the same," and I made him a wet pack and I knew this was not pneumonia; but I didn't know either what it was. So I did this and bedded him on the couch, and then he said, "Give me a little drink," and I gave him ginger ale. He drank that and I turned my back and wanted to set it on the table and then there was (she makes gasping, choking sounds) and I look back and I say, "Karl! You

are not dying!" And then . . . he was finished. He had the heart, how you say, blood clot on the heart. That was quite a . . . that was, of course, big moment. This was very . . . I was all alone then, but I was used to things. I could manage. I was courage person, you know. Of course, was a long time 'til you get over that, but I worked and a lady called me from the shop and said, "Mrs. K. you better come and work; you'll overcome the things better." I had everything regulated so far in advance back in my shop. Then after . . . little by little. You know how it is. Yes, this was hard moment. Since then I am all alone. Nothing was too much for me. Day and night I would work and everything. So now we sit here . . . and we see how long (she laughs). *We see how long we stay here.* Oh, here we stay; but when the death comes, you know.

Do you sometimes think about death? I often think and I pray always. There is nothing what I do without praying. Nothing. When I take something and do something, I always pray, pray, pray, pray. So, of course, I think often on the death; and . . . I always think about this; I always say, "If I die, I would wish to die nicely, quietly, without pain." That is my only wish, my last wish, nothing else. But this we don't know. *Right; but we can pray.* I hope, I hope. Yah, we hope the best. I do nothing without praying to God . . . nothing. People don't know. I say when the minister comes, you know. Those things I know, of course, I should do it and did it Sunday morning [go to services in the home], but usually not, because I know how I act, what I do, and that's enough. I think so at least. Maybe I'm wrong. I could be wrong, but that's all right.

Do you feel you left your mark here somewhere; that your life has been meaningful and productive? I think, if I understood right, I think . . . I was from child on already dedicated to help people. Now in my age I still do. I always helped, I always did, and nothing was too much for me. And still I'm this way; and I think I was a person who was so-called dedicated to do those things, otherwise you couldn't do. *So helping people has been very important for you; and you've done that?* Yes, I did plenty. Not with money so much, because I had to make my own living, but whatever I could help . . . helping them . . . doing things for them. I never took money from anybody, not a penny, not a penny. As long as I had what I needed. I'm not crazy for money. So I need a little—a certain amount to have this and this and that and many things that you do too, but not overdoing. It's not necessary. But give a poor old man something, a little bit; help poor people.

According to nursing home records, Mrs. K. died about a year after this interview in her room at 5:30 A.M. She had been suffering from diabetes and arteriosclerotic vascular disease, but her health had been generally deteriorating for some time before she died. Unfortunately, she did experience considerable pain before her death; it was described as "generalized body pain" that probably resulted from arthritis—she had complained of it for about a year. She chose not to go to a hospital to determine the cause of the pain, but wished to remain in her room at the nursing home. Her death was attributed to pulmonary edema—fluid in the lungs.

CHAPTER 10

Kathe Kollowitz, *The Hand of Death*, 1934. Private Collection. Art Resource, Inc. N.Y.

Dying and Bereavement

*I*n many ways, death is a subject that may be both frightening and deeply interesting at the same time. Perhaps the topic of death is an even more sensitive and avoided topic than sexuality is today. So it is probably realistic to begin our discussion somewhat slowly and to recognize from the outset that until recently death has been a topic not readily discussed in free and relaxed conversation in our society. At the deepest levels of our being, denial of death is probably necessary to function in a world where accidents, illnesses, wars, and killings are present. We may need to feel that these events will happen to others, not to us, or we would be unable to take risks, drive cars, or even leave the house. However, a pervasive denial of death that prevents any consideration of our own mortality and fears of death may affect our attitudes about living as well as our reactions toward older people (who tend to be seen as closer to death than younger people).

Perhaps most of us typically avoid thinking about death, the dying, and hence the aged or terminally ill person. Sometimes the avoidance of older persons, the tendency to push them out of sight — psychologically and socially — suggests that they are treated as if they were reminders of our common fate as mortal human beings. It is as if one might "catch" aging and death by touching or becoming too close to an older person. Thus, as we become more aware of our own mortality and our fears of death, we may become more comfortable in relations with older people and with terminally ill people of any age. In our own lives also, we may find that the uniqueness of each day may be more appreciated than if the finiteness of life is ignored and each day is seen as just one more of an endless flow of days.

We probably (and perhaps necessarily, at least in our "unconscious") feel that *we* shall surely never die — accidents, heart attacks, and fatal illnesses happen to others, but not to us. Yet death is obviously inevitable for every person, and we will probably experience the death of persons close to us during the course of our lives. Perhaps, then, this discussion of death will lead us to a more humane perspective toward the dying while only partially lifting the denial of our own mortality and death. The mystery and the fear of death are very real, but we can work toward understanding death and dealing with our own denial and fears of death. One result of the denial of death and avoidance of the topic is to avoid and sometimes to dehumanize those who are dying otherwise very human deaths.

He may cry for rest, peace, and dignity, but he will get infusions, transfusions, a heart machine, or tracheostomy if necessary. He may want one single person to stop for one single minute so that he can ask one single question — but he will get a dozen people around the clock, all busily preoccupied with his heart rate, pulse, electrocardiogram or pulmonary functions, his secretions or excretions but not with him as a human being. He may wish to fight it all but it is going to be a useless fight since all this is done in the fight for his life, and if they can save his life they can consider the person afterwards. Those who consider the person first may lose precious time to save his life! At least this seems to be the rationale or justification behind all this — or is it? Is the reason for this increasingly mechanical, depersonalized approach our own defensiveness? Is this approach our own way to cope with and repress the anxieties that a terminally or critically ill patient evokes in us? Is our concentration on equipment, on blood pressure our desperate attempt to deny the impending death which is so frightening and discomforting to us that we displace all our knowledge onto machines, since they are less close to us than the suffering face of another human being which would remind us once more of our lack of omnipotence, our own limits and failures, and last but not least perhaps our own mortality? (Kübler-Ross, 1969, p. 9)[7]

This view of the critically ill patient in modern hospitals and the provocative questions that it raises was written by Elisabeth Kübler-Ross in the introduction to her report on a seminar she conducted on death and dying with terminally ill patients, students from a theological seminary, and hospital staff. Her concern was to learn from the dying patients themselves about the process of dying and simultaneously to learn ways of helping persons with terminal illnesses resolve this very significant milestone of adult life in the most positive and humanistic way possible. We will discuss her work in considerable detail in the middle section of this chapter, for it has increased our awareness and understanding of the dying process and has shaken and opened to discussion a wide range of assumptions about dying in our culture; by implication it has also called attention to the assumptions and values about life in our society.

In reality, is the dying process any less important or meaningful an aspect of life than the birth process? Have we turned away from the actual process of birth in much the same way as we turn away from the process of dying? Do we favor birth in a hospital with anesthetics, with the husband separated from the wife, and with the actual birth behind closed doors? Perhaps there may be a parallel between the growing popularity of "natural childbirth" — still in a hospital, but with the parents jointly sharing this important event and hearing the first cries of the child — and the perspective Kübler-Ross might call "natural dying" — possibly in a hospital, but with the humanness of patients not obliterated by the machines and tubes and technology that seem almost to turn them into an extension of the machine. She does not, of course, advocate a denial of medical technology but, instead, affirms the dignity and humanity of dying persons who may need psychological, religious, and family support and the chance to resolve the issues involved in this final important event in their own meaningful ways. This perspective has led to the establishment of a variety of hospice programs where people can live to the fullest extent possible while being cared for during a terminal illness; we discuss these programs later in this chapter.

Indeed, if we come to humanize the dying process and to deal somewhat with our own fears of death (at least at a conscious level), perhaps we may also come to more fully humanize living. From the existential point of view, the reality of death is necessary for life to be meaningful; if death is denied, life is also denied. Yet we are inundated by statistics of death — on the highways, in disasters, and in the cities — and are exposed to countless TV deaths. If death has lost its sting, where is the value of living? In one particularly provocative passage, Kübler-Ross (1969) suggested: "Is war perhaps nothing else but a need to face death, to conquer and master it, to

---

[7] All quotations from Kübler-Ross (1969) are reprinted with permission of Macmillan Publishing Co., Inc., and Tavistock Publications, Ltd., from *On Death and Dying*, copyright © 1969 by Elisabeth Kübler-Ross.

come out of it alive — a peculiar form of denial of our own mortality?'' Moreover, perhaps an understanding of death in all its reality, rather than its denial, may bring with it ''a chance for peace'' and ''perhaps there could be less destructiveness around us'' (p. 13). Since her book was first published, there has been considerable interest and research on death, dying, and bereavement. However, her book appears to retain its popular appeal and is still widely available.

In this chapter we discuss three aspects of the stage of life that precedes death. We begin with the psychological issues and changes that appear to precede the actual dying process and that seem best understood as developmental changes timed by the approach of death. Next we present Kübler-Ross's insights and understanding of the dying process itself, which she sees as consisting of five characteristic reactions that both dying and bereaved persons may experience. In the last section we discuss the process of mourning and issues faced by the survivors and conclude with a brief discussion of the social view of death as a status passage for the dying person and also for the survivors. From time to time we quote from the classic short story by Leo Tolstoy (1828–1910), *The Death of Ivan Ilych,* an exceptional example of the parallel between the insight of the artist and the insight of the social scientist.

Developmental Changes Preceding Death

Up to this point in the book we have been discussing developmental changes, milestones, and sequential issues of adulthood with reference to the length of time the person has been alive — that is, *timed by the years since birth (age).* However, the data available so far suggest that the changes or developmental progression in the late years of life may not be timed entirely by chronological age, but rather they may be set in motion or *timed by the nearness of the individual to death.* For example, the Erikson stage of Integrity versus Despair, the last of his eight ages of life, would be the developmental issue faced by persons who are nearing death and in the later years of their lives, although they might be younger than 40 or older than 80. His theory states that the beginning of this final stage is triggered by the realization of one's approaching death and by the recognition that it is too late to change one's life in major ways for the time is too short to start over. Cues such as illness, advanced age itself, the death of one's cohorts, and perhaps inner cues of the approaching end of life would be likely to be involved in triggering this final turning point. In addition, some psychological processes have been found to change as death approaches, suggesting that nearness to death itself brings developmental change. Moreover, some of Neugarten's (1967b) data on middle-aged persons also point to a shift in time perspective during the middle years from ''time lived'' to ''time left to live'' as an important marker for timing and for regulating one's internal social clock.

> Both sexes, although men more than women, talked of the new difference in the way time is perceived. Life is restructured in terms of time-left-to-live rather than time-since-birth. Not only the reversal in directionality but the awareness that time is finite is a particularly conspicuous feature of middle age. . . .
>
> The recognition that there is ''only so much time left'' was a frequent theme in the

interviews. In referring to the death of a contemporary, one man said, "There is now the realization that death is very real. Those things don't quite penetrate when you're in your twenties and you think that life is all ahead of you. Now you know that death will come to you, too." (Neugarten, 1967b, p. 97)

Thus, in the later years a *future event* (death) may be a marker replacing, to some degree, the importance of the number of years since birth, which was a timing factor in earlier years.

Erikson's Eighth Stage: Integrity versus Despair

The last stage in Erikson's theory is described as the fruition of the previous seven stages. It involves "the acceptance of one's one and only life cycle and of the people who have become significant to it as something that had to be and that, by necessity, permitted of no substitutions" (Erikson, 1968, p. 139). In this framework, one would look back over one's life and deal with the question of the meaningfulness of one's life, the intersection of one's life with history, and the degree to which one's life was a worthwhile venture. One pole of the struggle is a sense of integrity; the other pole is a sense of despair: "Time is short, too short for the attempt to start another life and to try out alternate roads to integrity" (p. 140). Erikson viewed old age as providing the link between past heritage and future generations and thus giving perspective to the life cycle. The resolution of this stage involves *wisdom:* "ripened 'wits' . . . accumulated knowledge, mature judgment, and inclusive understanding" (p. 140). According to Erikson, the essence of wisdom is often provided by *tradition* and consideration of *ultimate concerns* that transcend the limitations of one's identity. As noted in Chapter 4, understanding one's role in the universe would be an example of *philosophical wisdom*; mature judgment reflects *practical wisdom* that focuses on personally relevant situations in daily life.

In Tolstoy's short story, *The Death of Ivan Ilych,* Ivan Ilych is slowly dying from the effects of an injury. In his career he was (as a fictional character) a judge in Russia in the late nineteenth century; thus there are political and religious themes written into the story, but Erikson's concept of a struggle between integrity and despair is clearly portrayed.

> Ivan Ilych saw that he was dying, and he was in continual despair.
>
> In the depth of his heart he knew he was dying, but not only was he not accustomed to the thought, he simply did not and could not grasp it. (Tolstoy, 1886, p. 131)
>
> It occurred to him that what had appeared perfectly impossible before, namely that he had not spent his life as he should have done, might after all be true. It occurred to him that his scarcely perceptible attempts to struggle against what was considered good by the most highly placed people, those scarcely noticeable impulses which he had immediately suppressed, might have been the real thing, and all the rest false. And his professional duties and the whole arrangement of his life and of his family, and all his social and official interests, might all have been false. He tried to defend all those things to himself and suddenly felt the weakness of what he was defending. There was nothing to defend.
>
> "But if that is so," he said to himself, "and I am leaving this life with the consciousness that I have lost all that was given to me and it is impossible to rectify it — what then?" (p. 152)

Existential Anxiety and Death

This view of the final struggle to resolve the meaning of life (in terms of Integrity versus Despair) seems similar to the **existential perspective** that people strive to find meaning in their great or mundane lives, and that the absence of a sense of meaning leads to despair. However, in the existential view, death is an ever possible choice that provides ultimate freedom—one is always walking along the edge of the abyss and is free to jump or to continue walking—and this ultimate freedom is at the core of the meaning of existence. Put another way, "one finds meaning in life when one is committed to something for which one is willing to accept death" (Barnes, 1959, p. 81). Similarly, "the confronting of death gives the most positive reality to life itself. It makes the individual existence real, absolute, and concrete" (May, 1958, p. 49). But death also represents the threat of nonbeing and thus brings existential anxiety as an essential characteristic of humans who, after all, are perhaps the only animals that can be aware of their own impending death. May (1958) defined this anxiety as "the subjective state of the individual's becoming aware that his existence can become destroyed, that he can lose himself and his world, that he can become 'nothing'" (p. 50).

As profound as these insights into the basic nature of the human condition may be, we wonder if they do not pertain to the contemplation of death by those for whom death is not actually imminent; that is, how could existential anxiety about death have the same impact on an aged, suffering, cancer patient as it would have on a healthy young person or a powerful middle-aged person who is not facing death? Do these views imply that patients in hospitals for the chronically ill (where nearly all the patients do not leave until they die) are actively contemplating the meaning of their lives and attempting to resolve their anxiety about becoming no-thing? Beauvoir (1972), a noted existentialist, in her treatise on old age, pointed out that death for the aged may not be feared because it is an acceptable alternative to a life that has become meaningless.

> Even if the old person is struck by no particular misfortune [physical suffering, outliving all those he loves], he has usually either lost his reasons for living or he has discovered their absence. The reason why death fills us with anxiety is that it is the inescapable reverse of our projects: when a man is no longer active in any way, when he has ceased all undertakings, all plans, then there remains nothing that death can destroy. It is usual to put forward wearing-out and fatigue as an explanation for the way some old people resign themselves to death; but if all a man needed was to vegetate he could put up with this life in slow motion. But for man living means self-transcendence. A consequence of biological decay is the impossibility of surpassing oneself and of becoming passionately concerned with anything; it kills all projects, and it is by this expedient that it renders death acceptable. (Beauvoir, 1972, p. 443)

Thus, it may be that anxiety about nonbeing, introspection about the meaning of one's life, and concern with the issue of Integrity versus Despair—in sum, resolution of the "death issue"—may not be highly significant *immediately* before death in old age (although it may occur when death seems imminent among younger persons). Instead, these issues may be more salient when death is not at the doorstep (so to speak), and our interest in life is high—for example, in late middle age when the imminence of death is not upon us, but its inevitability becomes apparent as parents, friends, and loved ones begin to die one by one. So although the Integrity versus Despair issue may be triggered by the realization of one's eventual death, we need not assume that the final days of a person's life (especially in old age) are spent in coming to a resolution of that crisis — it may occur a decade or two earlier. Let us examine some data on this question.

Studies on the Acceptance of Death

On the basis of their research, Lieberman and Coplan (1970) speculated that the acceptance of death is a more significant issue for middle-aged persons than it is for older people. Many of their aged respondents living in a nursing home or in the community had "worked out the meaning of death for themselves and most have developed a personal viewpoint toward their own death" (p. 83). These respondents were willing to talk openly about death, and most anxiety or disruption about death was related to change in their socioenvironmental conditions. That is, those respondents who (as it later turned out) were near to death and were living in the home or in stable environments in the community seemed to be dealing with the task of facing death without storminess or disruption; "it was as if they were dealing with a developmental task that they were coping with adequately" (p. 82). In contrast, persons who were waiting to enter the home or had only recently entered

Although older persons are often willing to talk about death, ordinary concerns are usually more important, and it is not a major psychological issue dominating the last decade or two of life.

felt much more anxiety and disruption, and many appeared to lack a personal philosophy about death. It was as if these changes in living arrangements had forced them to readjust once more and had perhaps disrupted their previous resolution of the death issue. Thus, although older persons are often willing to talk about death, it does not appear to be a major psychological issue dominating the last decade or two of life.

Bengtson, Cuellar, and Ragan (1977) studied fear of death among African American, Mexican American, and Anglo American persons selected to be representative of each group in terms of age (from 45 to 74) and socioeconomic status (low, medium, and high). Only about a quarter of the older respondents expressed fear of death, as compared with about half of the middle-aged respondents (young adults were not included in the study); gender, racial/ethnic group, and socioeconomic status had relatively little effect in comparison with age (Figure 10.1). There was no clear relationship between age and the frequency of thinking about death. Less than 1 in 5 respondents in any of these age–ethnic subgroups reported that they often thought about death; among Anglo Americans, less than 1 in 12. Clearly, these data support the notion that neither fear of death nor thoughts about death dominate the later years of life; instead, they seem to be more significant in middle age. However, there may be ethnic and racial differences reflecting cultural factors in attitudes and a denial of death. One example of these differences that may reflect denial of death is the respondents' expectation of the number of years they will live (Figure 10.2). Although life expectancy is lower for nonwhites, the African American respondents in this study had much greater expectations than did the Anglo American respondents; statistically, life expectancy at the time of the study for whites at age 50 was 26.4 years and at age 70 it was 12.2 years, and for nonwhites it was 23.8 and 12.0 years, respectively (Bengtson, Cuellar & Ragan, 1977). Thus, although Anglo Ameri-

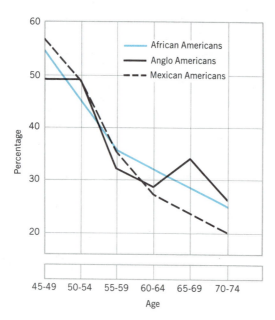

FIGURE 10.1 Percentage responding "very afraid" or "somewhat afraid" of death, by age and ethnicity. (*Source*: Bengtson, Cuellar & Ragan, 1977, Fig. 1. Reprinted with permission of the *Journal of Gerontology*.)

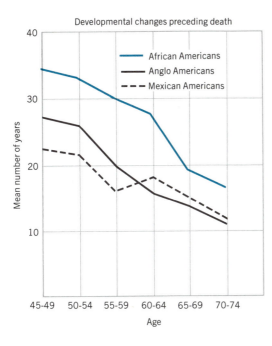

FIGURE 10.2 Mean number of years that respondents report they expect to live, by age and ethnicity. (*Source*: Bengtson, Cuellar & Ragan, 1977, Fig. 3. Reprinted with permission of the *Journal of Gerontology*.)

cans tended not to report that they thought about death very often, they predicted their future life expectancy fairly accurately. Mexican Americans tended to think about death more frequently than Anglo Americans, but also predicted their life expectancy fairly accurately. African Americans thought about death about as much as the Mexican American respondents, but were much more optimistic (and statistically unrealistic) in the prediction of the number of years they expected to live.

These findings suggest that research on the acceptance of death is very complex and that any simple conclusions are likely to be misleading. In the Bengtson study, one of the respondents, whom they called Mrs. Garcia, suggested that the meaning of death and the acceptance of death depend on one's life events and personal definition of dying.

> It's interesting you should ask me if I fear death. I don't want to die any more than you do, but I'm not afraid of death. Why? Because I'm a woman. I have lived with a man who drank too much and was always running around, and I've sent two sons to war. Every time the phone rang or there was a knock at the door I would die. I've died a thousand times. Why should I be afraid of death? But, I still don't *want* to die. (Bengtson, Cuellar & Ragan, 1977, p. 85)

In addition, these data are cross-sectional, so that the smaller proportion of respondents reporting fear of death may reflect less fear of death among people born around the turn of the century compared with those born in the 1920s. However, the interview data suggest that the difference does reflect developmental change. Although other studies have found that greater education is related to less frequent thoughts of death, especially among younger people, and to more positive attitudes about death (Riley, 1963), this tricultural study did not find education or other socioeconomic variables to be important (Bengtson, Cuellar & Ragan, 1977). Thus, the only clear conclusion we can draw is that older adults are less likely than the middle-aged adults to report that they are afraid of death; most other studies also support this finding (Kalish, 1976; Stevens, Cooper & Thomas, 1980).

Fear of death does not seem to be a major fear for most people. Kalish (1976) noted that only one out of four respondents in his multiethnic study reported a fear of death. Riley (1963), in a nationwide sample of 1500 adults, found that at all ages the attitude was more one of acceptance ("death is sometimes a blessing" or "death is not tragic for the person who dies, only for the survivors") than of fear ("death always comes too soon" or "to die is to suffer"). Over 60 percent of his respondents described death as "a long sleep." Generally, more religious people tend to have lower fear of death than less religious persons, although some studies have found that moderately religious persons, such as irregular churchgoers who possibly have uncertain religious beliefs, are more fearful of death than either devoutly religious or irreligious persons (Kalish, 1985).

There is also some evidence that preparation for death increases with age, especially for persons with higher education (Riley, 1963); these data from a nationwide survey suggest that persons with at least a high school education began making specific plans—such as making a will and funeral arrangements—during the decade of their forties or fifties; for persons with less than high school education, this planning did not begin until the decade of their sixties (Table 10.1). However, relatively few people prepare for death; Phalon (1978) reported that seven out of ten people die without leaving a will.

One interesting study of attitudes about death among college students found that those respondents most fearful of death were also afraid of aging (Salter &

TABLE 10.1 *Percentage with High Degree of Preparation for Death[a] by Age and Education (N = 1500)*

	Education			
Age	*Junior High School or Less*	*High School*	*College*	*"Effect" of Higher Education*
30 and under	0	1	3	+ 3
31 to 40	2	4	8	+ 6
41 to 50	8	14	22	+14
51 to 60	8	25	40	+32
61+	20	30	44	+24
"Effect" of older age	+20	+29	+41	

[a]Based on positive answers to questions about whether it is best in general to make any plans about death, and whether specific actions have been taken (discussing with those closest, making funeral or cemetery arrangements, making a will).
Note: The smallest base for any percentage is 45.
Source: Riley (1963), Exhibit 14.20. Reprinted with permission from *Aging and Society*, Vol. I, by Matilda White Riley, Anne Foner, and Associates, copyright © 1968 by Russell Sage Foundation.

Salter, 1976). However, anxiety about death was not associated with a rejection of the elderly, as might be expected — at least for the sample as a whole. Instead, it was related to agreement with the need for a "national awareness campaign" about the needs of the elderly, a willingness to visit older people, and to take them to religious services. This suggests that one effect of the fear of death may be to help older persons as a means of reducing one's own fears of aging and death. Although this optimistic conclusion is appealing, it may apply to only one group of the respondents; another smaller group may deal with their fear of death by rejecting the elderly, but this cannot be determined from the correlational analyses reported. A less optimistic conclusion was suggested by Eakes (1985), who found that anxiety about death was associated with negative attitudes toward the elderly among full-time nursing home staff members.

In summary, Erikson's concept of Integrity versus Despair is often seen as emerging only at the conclusion of life, but the available data indicate that the growing awareness of death and the reduction in the fear of death appear to begin during middle age. Although much more research is needed on the acceptance of death, it appears that this issue is gradually resolved over several decades and that fear of death during the last months or years of life may result from a crisis in the social environment that disrupts one's previous resolution of the issues involved in accepting death. Thus, though the resolution of questions about the existential meaning of life and the acceptance of death may be a typical task one undertakes as one begins to see the end of one's life on the horizon, apparently it does not dominate the last decade or two of life. The first emergence of the Integrity versus Despair issues may well be during middle age, perhaps as a part of the midlife transition (discussed in Chapter 3).

The Life Review Process

Another concept of the psychological tasks preceding death and triggered by one's closeness to death is the process of the life review, as suggested by Butler (1963b). The **life review** is defined as a "naturally occurring, universal mental process . . . prompted by the realization of approaching dissolution and death, and the inability to maintain one's sense of personal invulnerability." It potentially proceeds toward personality reorganization, including the achievement of such characteristics as wisdom and serenity in the aged; thus it is a potential force toward increased self-awareness. However, it may also lead to some pathological manifestations as well, such as depression, guilt, or obsessional ruminations about past events. The process consists of reminiscence, thinking about oneself, reconsideration of previous experiences and their meanings, and "mirror gazing" (this may serve as one of the best indications that the process is taking place). One example of mirror gazing (i.e., pausing to look into a mirror, perhaps for several moments and perhaps with some verbal comments intended for one's self) was reported by Butler (1963b): "I was passing by my mirror. I noticed how old I was. My appearance, well, it prompted me to think of death — and of my past — what I hadn't done, what I had done wrong." A similar episode is described in Tolstoy's Ivan Ilych:

Pausing to look in the mirror for several moments may indicate that the life review process is taking place. This type of reminiscence may be an adaptive response to change in oneself.

Ivan Ilych locked the door and began to examine himself in the glass, first full face, then in profile. He took up a portrait of himself taken with his wife, and compared it with what he saw in the glass. The change in him was immense. Then he bared his arms to the elbow, looked at them, drew the sleeves down again, sat down on an ottoman, and grew blacker than night. (Tolstoy, 1886, p. 127)

The symbolic interaction interpretation of this process would be that the person is actively working to integrate the new (physical) *me* into the relatively continuous sense of self and is, in a sense, attempting to gain mastery and integration of the changed physical *me* and the internal experiencings. The *I* is striving for a new integration based on this different *me*, memory of past *me*s, and current bodily experiencings. Possibly, the body *me* is changing as rapidly as it ever did (e.g., at adolescence), and these changes may require a reintegration of rather massive proportions. Thus, the past is reviewed as one attempts to sense the consistency between past *me*s, present *me*s, and future *me*s in the light of current reality and future potential. Perhaps the feedback from others (such as a "confidant," discussed in Chapter 8) would be important in this process. That is, just as one's sense of identity is the crucial issue during adolescence and young adulthood and feedback from others is significant, feedback may also be important for this later, potentially massive reorganization of the self in preparation for death.

However, Butler's concept of the life review emphasizes not only the potential reorganization of the self but also the adaptive aspects of reminiscence among the aged. Often this reminiscence might be seen as beyond the older person's control, or as an escape from the present, or as simply filling up empty time; but he sees the life review as an important and characteristic step for those, whether old or young, who expect death (and it may be a general response to other types of crises as well). Although Butler does not draw the parallel between this life review process and Erikson's stage of Integrity versus Despair, it seems clear that a central aspect of this stage involves looking back over one's life. This psychological reorganization, which might involve ignoring or selectively recalling old memories in the search for meaning, would be deeply involved in the eventual resolution of the Integrity versus Despair crisis. Tolstoy (1886) also illustrates the life review quite explicitly; it is one major source of Ivan Ilych's despair.

> He lay on his back and began to pass his life in review. . . . (p. 152)
> And in imagination he began to recall the best moments of his pleasant life. But strange to say none of those best moments of his pleasant life now seemed at all what they had then seemed — none of them except the first recollections of childhood. There, in childhood, there had been something really pleasant with which it would be possible to live if it could return. But the child who had experienced that happiness existed no longer, it was like a reminiscence of somebody else.
> As soon as the period began which had produced the present Ivan Ilych, all that had then seemed joys now melted before his sight and turned into something trivial and often nasty.
> And the further he departed from childhood and the nearer he came to the present the more worthless and doubtful were the joys. (p. 147)

Although the concept of the life review is associated with reminiscence among older persons and may be seen as a part of the Integrity versus Despair issues during the second half of life, reminiscence clearly occurs among people of all ages. For example, Cameron (1972) interviewed respondents by interrupting them and asking them what they were just thinking about, the topic of their thoughts, and whether they were thinking about the past, present, or future. He interviewed three different groups varying in age from 18 to 65+ at their home, at work, or on a beach. At all ages the most frequent orientation was present, followed by the future, and then the past. Thus, he found no evidence that old people think about the past more than the present or the future, or that they think about the past more than young people do. Similarly, Giambra (1977) interviewed about 1100 men and women between the ages of 17 and 92 about their daydreams and whether the daydreams were oriented toward the present, past, or future; he also found no correlation between age and the number of past-oriented daydreams. However, he found differences among age groups in the *proportions* of daydreams that dealt with the past as compared with the present or future. When he compared the ratio of daydreams concerned with the past to those concerned with the present, he found that both his youngest (ages 17–23) and his oldest (60+) respondents tended to be equally concerned with past and present, whereas those in between were much more likely to daydream about the present than the past (Figure 10.3). When he compared past with future, he found that his youngest respondents were much more likely to daydream about the future than about the past, whereas his older respondents—especially females—were more likely to daydream about the past than about the future (Figure 10.4). Thus, the relative proportion of daydreams about the past appears to increase with age, especially in comparison with daydreams about the future. However, as in Cameron's study, thoughts about the past do not dominate the daydreams of older persons; they appear to increase to the point of approximately equalling daydreams about the present (and younger people also daydream about the past as much as the present).

Studies have also explored the relationship between reminiscence and the resolution of the Integrity versus Despair issues. Havighurst and Glasser (1972) found that there was an association among positive feelings about reminiscence,

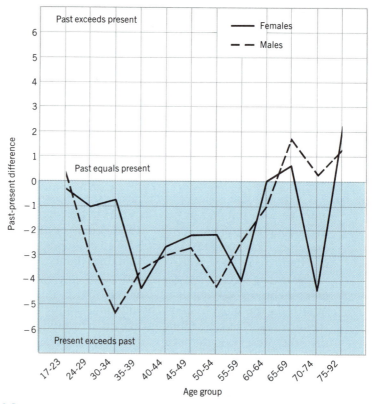

FIGURE 10.3 Differences between past and present orientation in daydreams for individual respondents, by age and sex. (*Source*: Giambra, 1977, Fig. 1. Reprinted with permission of *The Gerontologist*.)

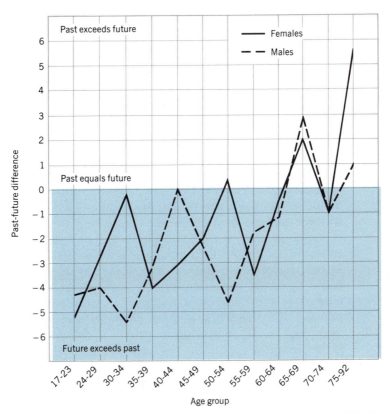

FIGURE 10.4 Differences between past and future orientation in daydreams for individual respondents, by age and sex. (Source: Giambra, 1977, Fig. 2. Reprinted with permission of *The Gerontologist.*)

frequent reminiscence, and "good personal-social adjustment" in various relatively elite samples of older persons; however, it was not clear whether frequent reminiscence caused good adjustment or vice versa. Another study focused explicitly on Erikson's concept of integrity in terms of reminiscence (Boylin, Gordon & Nehrke, 1976). Their respondents were elderly men living in a Veterans Administration hospital. They found that about two-thirds of their respondents reminisced occasionally but, unlike in the Havighurst and Glasser study, their respondents reported negative feelings about the content of their memories, especially about those memories from their fifties and sixties. However, frequency of reminiscing was significantly related to their measure of integrity (e.g., "life has been good," "would not change my life if I lived it over," "accept myself the way I am"). Thus, they speculated that these men were reviewing and evaluating their life in both its positive and negative aspects and were achieving, or at least working toward, a sense of integrity through reminiscence. Perhaps the physical reasons for their hospitalizations played a part in their negative feelings about their memories, but even this negative aspect of reminiscing was related to integrity.

Haight (1988), however, noted that ordinary reminiscence is a very different process from the kind of life review that guides an older person through personal memories. She conducted a well-designed study that found positive effects of a therapeutic life review process with a sample of elderly homebound persons. The participants were 51 recipients of a Meals-on-Wheels program. After being informed about the study and agreeing to take part, the participants were randomly placed in one of three groups: (1) Life Review (the experimental group); (2) Friendly Visiting (the control group); and (3) No Treatment. In the first two groups, a trained student visited one hour a week for six weeks. In the first group, a structured life review was conducted so that it was a lengthy integrative process lasting one hour a week for six weeks; sample questions are shown in Table 10.2. In the second group, friendly visiting consisted of informal conversations about current events, health problems, television shows, and the weather for one hour a week for six weeks. In all three groups a series of measures assessing life satisfaction, psychological well-being, depression, and activities of daily living were administered by a researcher (who did not know which group the individual was in) one week after the person agreed to participate and again in seven weeks. This series of questionnaires six weeks apart was the extent of the participation for the no-treatment group. She found that life satisfaction and psychological well-being were significantly improved by the life review process, in comparison with the control and the no-treatment groups. There was no evidence of severe depression in the sample, and participation in the life review process had no effect on levels of depression — suggesting that it is not a risky procedure with homebound elderly persons. Moreover, the interviewers reported that the participants were ready to terminate the contact when they had finished the life review procedure. Thus, this study indicated

TABLE 10.2 *Sample Questions from the Life Review and Experiencing Form* (LREF)

Childhood

What is the very first thing you can remember in your life? Go as far back as you can.

Did you have any brothers or sisters? Tell me what each was like.

Adolescence

When you think about yourself and your life as a teenager, what is the first thing you can remember about that time?

What were the pleasant things about your adolescence?

Adulthood

What was life like for you in your twenties and thirties?

Tell me about your work. Did you enjoy your work? Did you earn an adequate living? Did you work hard during those years? Were you appreciated?

Summary

On the whole what kind of life do you think you've had?

If you were going to live your life over again, what would you change? Leave unchanged?

What was the hardest thing you had to face in your life? Describe.

Source: Haight (1988), Table 1. Reprinted with permission from the *Journal of Gerontology: Psychological Sciences*, Vol. 43, p. 41.

that life review can be a therapeutic aid for older persons and that its use should be explored more fully.

Psychological Changes Predicting Nearness to Death

Although the study of psychosocial aspects of the dying process is fairly new, there is a growing body of data indicating that there are important changes associated with nearness to death—that is, changes that are brought on not by age alone, but by the closeness to death. These data are particularly interesting since they suggest that developmental changes occur in the last few years of life and are apparently timed by impending natural death. In addition, these data indicate that in many cases psychological changes may serve as better predictors of the nearness to death than medical or physical factors alone. The studies are conducted by giving a series of psychological tests, usually over a period of several months or years, and comparing those persons who later are found to die within a specified period of time with those who remain alive.

Lieberman (1965) conducted some early research in this area and reported developing an interest in possible psychological changes preceding death when one of the nurses in a nursing home where he was working displayed a "remarkable accuracy" in predicting the death of residents several months in advance and before there were any pronounced physical changes. She was unable to identify what led to her predictions except that a person approaching death "just seemed to act differently."

To explore this phenomenon, he administered several psychological tests to a group of 25 elderly volunteers. The data suggested a decline in energy, complexity, and organization in drawings made by persons who died less than three months after completing at least five drawings three or four weeks apart (Lieberman, 1965). Two subsequent studies using larger numbers of aged persons (Lieberman, 1966; Lieberman & Coplan, 1970) failed to replicate the earlier findings, but they did find related differences in a range of psychological realms between those who were a year or less away from death and those who were at least three years away from death. In both studies respondents were "matched" so that all comparisons could be made between similar respondents in the death-near and death-far groups. They found a decline in various measures of cognitive functioning, in emotional complexity, in introspection, and in several aspects of self-image among the death-near respondents, compared to their matched death-far "control" (Lieberman & Coplan, 1970). These results supported the hypothesis that distance from death, rather than chronological age, appeared to be the most useful time dimension for organizing changes in psychological functioning in the aged.

This hypothesis must be examined very closely, however, because many other studies have not considered the chronological age of the respondents (Lieberman and Coplan did consider age in matching the death-near and death-far groups). That is, if the changes occur normally with advancing age and the persons near death are also older, then this decline could be caused by either age, nearness to death, or both. For example, several studies have reported various terminal declines in intelligence between those who died within a few months, or a few years, compared with those who remained alive. In an 11-year longitudinal study of a random sample of people over age 70 in Gothenberg, Sweden, Berg (1987) found a clear connection between proximity to death and decline in measures of "verbal meaning" and "reasoning" (Figures 10.5 and 10.6). The data across several studies have been inconsistent, however—one study found that decline affected only those who died within one year (Reimanis & Green, 1971), another found that it affected only those who died after one year (Wilkie & Eisdorfer, 1974), and others found it was much more marked for those under age 70 (Riegel & Riegel, 1972; White & Cunningham, 1988). Palmore and Cleveland (1976) pointed out that aging changes must be distinguished from terminal changes; they found that intelligence shows "a large aging decline and a small but significant terminal decline" (p. 81)—similar to the data, but not the conclusion, reported by Riegel and Riegel (1972). Thus, sophisticated research and analyses will be required to clarify these death-related psychological changes.

In a preliminary, but carefully designed, study that included age of the respondent, Botwinick, West, and Storandt (1978) attempted to determine which psychological tests and questionnaires would allow prediction of those respondents near to death. Using a group of 732 persons who had applied for housing in a senior citizens' apartment complex, they found that 13 psychological measures and two medical health ratings differentiated those respondents who died within five years and those who were still living after five years. However, none of these measures alone predicted survivorship as well as all of them together. A combination of eight of the psychological test and questionnaire items together was able to correctly

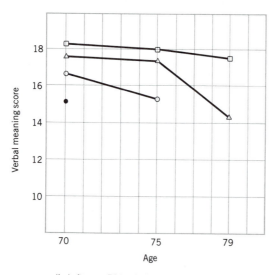

• died after age 70 but before age 75 ($N = 49$)
○ died after age 75 but before age 79 ($N = 56$)
△ died after age 79 but before age 81 ($N = 21$)
□ still alive at age 81 ($N = 154$)

FIGURE 10.5 The relation between survival and results of an intelligence test of verbal meaning ($N = 280$). (*Source*: Berg, 1987, Fig. 44–1. Reprinted with permission of Springer Publishing Company, Inc. from *Aging: The universal human experience*, G.L. Maddox & E.W. Busse, Eds., © 1987.)

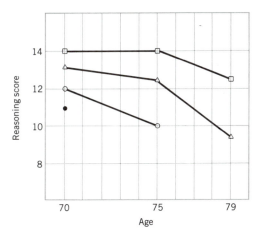

FIGURE 10.6 The relation between survival and results of an intelligence test of reasoning (*N* = 280). (*Source*: Berg, 1987, Fig. 44–2. Reprinted with permission of Springer Publishing Company, Inc. from *Aging: The universal human experience*, G.L. Maddox & E.W. Busse, Eds., © 1987.)

• died after age 70 but before age 75 (*N* = 49)
○ died after age 75 but before age 79 (*N* = 56)
△ died after age 79 but before age 81 (*N* = 21)
□ still alive at age 81 (*N* = 154)

classify 71 percent of the living respondents and 64 percent of those who had died, even though they varied in age. There was no evidence of a decline over time on any of these measures, so that the first administration of the tests and questionnaires was used as the basis for the classification of the living and the deceased respondents five years later. Administration of all eight procedures requires about 30 minutes; three involve speed of response, two involve learning and memory, one measures depression, one asks "what degree of control do you feel you have over things," and one asks about the respondent's self-rated health (from poor to excellent). They found that physicians' ratings were not as predictive of survival as the respondent's own self-rating; a clinically assessed health measure and age did predict survival, but not as accurately as the eight other procedures combined. They concluded that these measures can serve as a "medical alert" for older persons, calling the physician's attention to possible health problems that may have been overlooked; this may be particularly important since the physicians' ratings were not accurate predictors of survivorship. However, further validation of these findings is necessary, in part because it is not clear why these particular measures predict survival. For example, Siegler, McCarty, and Logue (1982) found that a different set of measures (verbal tests on the Wechsler Memory Scale and Wechsler Adult Intelligence Scale) predicted survival in another study. Nonetheless, the data clearly suggest a *psychosomatic* interaction in which bodily decline and progression toward death affect psychological processes. The earlier findings of Lieberman and Coplan (1970) also deserve further study since they make a similar point and may provide additional measures that could be combined with these measures to further increase the accuracy of prediction.

The Dying Process

Elisabeth Kübler-Ross, who described herself as "a country doctor," was a psychiatrist at the University of Chicago (which operates a teaching-research hospital) when she was approached by some graduate students in theology for help on a paper on terminally ill patients. Her approach was, "if you really wish to share and experience what it is like to have a very limited time to live, sit with your dying patients and listen" (Kübler-Ross, 1970). A seminar on death and dying developed from this idea, as dying patients were invited to talk with her or other participants, sometimes observed through a viewing window by various members of the "helping professions" (doctors, nurses, chaplains, rabbis, priests, social workers, and so on). If necessary, patients were interviewed in their beds with whatever medical attention was needed (transfusions, infusions, and so on).

Initially the project met with a great deal of resistance since it seemed to be generally assumed, as another pioneer in studying death was asked, "Isn't it cruel, sadistic, and traumatic to discuss death with seriously ill and terminally ill people?" (Feifel, 1963, p. 9). Kübler-Ross reported initially insurmountable difficulties and hostility:

Elisabeth Kübler-Ross.

Suddenly, this big teaching hospital did not have a single dying patient!

During the first year of this undertaking it required an average of ten hours per week to search for a patient—and to get permission from a physician. . . .

In general, the very young physicians or the very old ones were more amenable to our requests, the nurses and nurses' aides the most interested, and the patients themselves the most enthusiastic. With few exceptions, the patients were surprised, amazed, and grateful. Some were plain curious and others expressed their disbelief that "a young, healthy doctor would sit with a dying old woman and really care to know what it is like." In the majority of cases the initial outcome was similar to opening floodgates. It was hard to stop them once the conversation was initiated and the patients responded with great relief to sharing some of their last concerns, expressing their feelings without fear of repercussions. (Kübler-Ross, 1970, pp. 157–158)

Much of Kübler-Ross's work can be seen as an attempt to humanize the dying process, to counteract the tendency in North America of depersonalizing the dying person, and to reinstate the process of dying back into the full course of human life. Part of the difficulty, she argued, is that death is feared and denied in our unconscious: "In simple terms, in our unconscious mind we can only be killed; it is inconceivable to die of a natural cause or of old age. Therefore death in itself is associated with a bad act, a frightening happening, something that in itself calls for retribution and punishment" (Kübler-Ross, 1969, p. 2). But also, this anxiety about

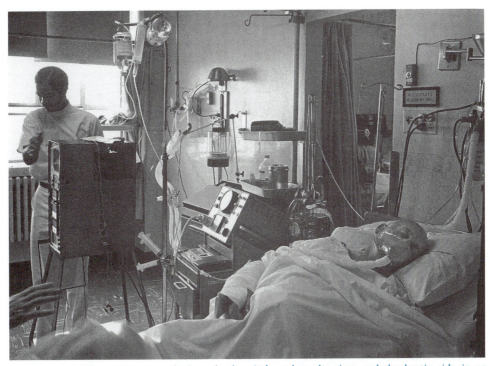

Often, gravely ill persons are rushed to the hospital, endure the siren and the hectic ride in an ambulance, and are subjected to busy hospital routines, tests, x-rays, and CAT scans, and may overhear discussions of their case, but have no real chance to participate in the discussion.

death is aided by our highly developed technology that attempts to find a "solution" for every "problem"—so that, too often while attempting to preserve life, we tend to turn the patient into a "thing" in which something has "gone wrong" and that needs to be "fixed." Often someone else makes the decision that individuals require hospitalization; they are then rushed to the hospital, endure the siren and hectic rush in an ambulance, and are subjected to busy hospital staff, tests, X rays, CAT scans, and so forth. They may overhear discussions of their "case" but have no real chance to participate in the discussion; they are the "case," the "object." And once in the hospital, they must learn the rules and regulations of that institution and, in short, become resocialized into the role of patients—especially in chronic or geriatric hospitals.

She reported (1969) one extreme and memorable case of a woman who seemingly had to resort to a "psychotic break" to prevent one last operation that might prolong her life although she was prepared to die and wanted only to die in peace. Questions of "mercy killing" and relations between physician and patient, between nurse and patient, and between family and patient all come to be provocative and unanswered issues. Medical schools have begun to do more to train physicians to deal with the incurably ill and dying patient, but too often the emphasis is—understandably—on preserving life and on maintaining health; in a sense, death is a medical failure. Perhaps nurses, clergy, aides, and orderlies should be given some opportunity to work through their own feelings about dying patients so that they might be more helpful. Perhaps psychologists, psychiatrists, and other hospital staff might be better able to facilitate the final communication between the patient and family. Kübler-Ross argued that, though hope of recovery needs to be maintained, patients often would be aided by being told that the illness is very serious (they usually know it anyway) in a manner that respects their dignity yet allows them to complete their life without being forced into deceptions and lies. Tolstoy has Ivan Ilych making this point quite eloquently.

> What tormented Ivan Ilych most was the deception, the lie, which for some reason they all accepted, that he was not dying but was simply ill, and that he only need keep quiet and undergo a treatment and then something very good would result. He however knew that do what they would nothing would come of it, only still more agonizing suffering and death. This deception tortured him—their not wishing to admit what they all knew and what he knew, but wanting to lie to him concerning his terrible condition, and wishing and forcing him to participate in that lie. Those lies—lies enacted over him on the eve of his death and destined to degrade this awful, solemn act to the level of their visitings, their curtains, their sturgeon for dinner—were a terrible agony for Ivan Ilych. . . . He saw that no one felt for him, because no one even wished to grasp his position. Only Gerasim recognized it and pitied him. And so Ivan Ilych felt at ease only with him. . . . Once when Ivan Ilych was sending him away he even said straight out: "We shall all of us die, so why should I grudge a little trouble?"—expressing the fact that he did not think his work burdensome, because he was doing it for a dying man and hoped someone would do the same for him when his time came. (Tolstoy, 1886, pp. 137–138)

Kübler-Ross reminds me considerably of Gerasim (Ivan's servant) in the story; but this aspect of her work is only a part of her contribution to our understanding of standing of death and dying. She also described five "stages" of the dying process that help us to understand the process of dying as she discovered it from her interviews with dying patients.

Reactions during the Dying Process

From her interviews with over 200 dying patients, Kübler-Ross (1969) distilled five characteristic reactions to terminal illness. Although she called these reactions "stages," it is not clear why they would necessarily occur in a regular sequence or why one person might not alternately express some or all of the reactions within a few hours. In a later book she clarified this point: "Most of my patients have exhibited two or three stages simultaneously and these do not always occur in the same order" (Kübler-Ross, 1974, pp. 25–26). Thus, these reactions may best be seen as characteristic responses in dealing with the reality of a terminal illness and as crucial issues that increase our understanding of the experience of the dying person. They should not be seen as developmental stages that dying persons should go through. This is important to note because some well-intentioned people may misinterpret this aspect of her work and try to push the person through the "stages"; another misinterpretation is to use these reactions to label and dismiss the response of the person (e.g., "patient in bed 12 is in anger stage"). Ideally, these five characteristic responses provide a few clues to help us begin to understand individuals as they cope with all that is involved in having a very serious, probably terminal, illness. These responses are *denial and isolation, anger, bargaining, depression, and acceptance;* through the entire period of the final illness, *hope* is a central theme. We will present each of these characteristic responses in summary form and use brief quotations from *The Death of Ivan Ilych* to illustrate the issues. Then we discuss some of the criticisms of her approach by other persons who have studied death and dying.

Denial and Isolation

The first response made by most of the patients she interviewed was: "No, not me, it cannot be true." Some felt a mistake had been made (the X ray or lab tests had been confused with someone else's—and we know of one case where this did occur); others would find another physician or go to many doctors or to faith healers in an attempt to obtain a more positive diagnosis (of course, seeking a second opinion would by a realistic response but a manifestation of denial nonetheless). **Denial** is seen as a healthy manner of coping with shocking, unpleasant news; it functions as a buffer in the short term, allowing the patient to develop less radical defenses to cope with long-term suffering and the reality of impending death. Only 3 of her 200 respondents maintained denial to the very end; most replaced it with "partial acceptance" after the central buffering function of denial had served its purpose. Clearly, when a patient is heavily invested in denial of the seriousness of the illness, attempting to discuss feelings about death would be threatening; hence, the patient's willingness to discuss dying may be the best indicator of readiness to begin dealing with the issue. Other patients may not be terminally ill, but may wish to deal with the possibility of death before it becomes an immediate reality. Also, the sensitive listener will note the times when the patient occasionally needs to deny the reality of impending death and to psychologically distance that reality from awareness; but after the initial shock gives way to partial acceptance, the periods of denial are usually transient. Examples of this type of denial are prevalent in the story of Ivan Ilych, for example:

> The progress of his disease was so gradual that he could deceive himself when comparing one day with another — the difference was so slight. But when he consulted the doctors it seemed to him that he was getting worse, and even very rapidly. Yet despite this he was continually consulting them.
>
> That month he went to see another celebrity, who told him almost the same as the first had done but put his questions rather differently. . . . A friend of a friend of his, a very good doctor, diagnosed his illness again quite differently from the others. . . . A homoeopathist diagnosed the disease in yet another way, and prescribed medicine which Ivan Ilych took secretly for a week. . . . One day a lady acquaintance mentioned a cure effected by a wonder-working icon. Ivan Ilych caught himself listening attentively and beginning to believe that it had occurred. (Tolstoy, 1886, p. 124)
>
> The syllogism he had learnt from Kiezewetter's Logic. "Caius is a man, men are mortal, therefore Caius is mortal," had always seemed to him correct as applied to Caius, but certainly not as applied to himself. (p. 131)

The other aspect of this stage, **isolation**, describes the response of hospital staff to the dying patient. Often they will close the door, avoid visiting except when necessary, or believe that the patient does not wish to discuss issues about death and dying.

Anger

When the realization that the illness is fatal registers, and the patient has some beginning acceptance of that fact — that is, when denial is less complete — the response is often **anger.** The central feeling is one of "Why me?" and may involve envy and resentment of those who are healthy. This anger is often very difficult to cope with for the family or the staff, yet from the patient's point of view it is quite understandable. It tends to be anger directed at anyone who happens to be available — doctors, nurses, staff, family, and visitors. Perhaps, as Kübler-Ross stated, all of us might well be angry if our lives were interrupted prematurely, we were confined to a hospital bed, and others rushed around doing things to and for us that indicated our helplessness and dependency. Part of the message of anger may be: "I am alive, don't forget that. You can hear my voice, I am not dead yet!" (Kübler-Ross, 1969, p. 52). Her suggestion to deal with this difficult situation is to provide respect and understanding to the patient instead of taking the anger as a personal message (which it frequently is not) or avoiding patients. Instead, they need to feel cared for and to feel that they will be visited not because they ring the bell or are angry but because they are valued and it is a pleasure to drop in for a short visit — especially when the result of such attention and visits is a reduction in their anger. Ivan Ilych shows considerable anger and rage when he begins to accept the reality of his dying and, as noted earlier, his servant Gerasim comforts him and relieves the anger and bitterness because he values Ivan as a human being.

"Death. Yes, death. And none of them know or wish to know it, and they have no pity for me. Now they are playing." (He heard through the door the distant sound of a song and its accompaniment.) "It's all the same to them, but they will die too! Fools! I first, and they later, but it will be the same for them. And now they are merry . . . the beasts!"

Anger choked him and he was agonizingly, unbearably miserable. "It is impossible that all men have been doomed to suffer this awful horror!" (Tolstoy, 1886, p. 130)

After that Ivan Ilych would sometimes call Gerasim and get him to hold his legs on his shoulders, and he liked talking to him. Gerasim did it all easily, willingly, simply and with a good nature that touched Ivan Ilych. Health, strength, and vitality in other people were offensive to him, but Gerasim's strength and vitality did not mortify but soothed him. (p. 137)

Bargaining

Kübler-Ross suggested that a particular response that she termed **bargaining** is helpful to the patient for brief periods of time. It is as if knowing that one cannot get what one wants by demanding (in anger), one turns to "asking nicely," hoping to strike a bargain — with God, or the staff, or with the illness itself. The notion is akin to "time off for good behavior" — but is successful for only short periods of time since the illness tends quickly to invalidate the "bargain." She gave a poignant example of a patient who wished to live long enough to attend the marriage of her oldest and favorite son. By efforts from several staff, she was taught self-hypnosis and could control the pain for several hours and, when the day came, she left the hospital to attend the wedding looking like "an elegant lady." "I will never forget the moment when she returned to the hospital. She looked tired and somewhat exhausted and — before I could say hello — said, 'Now don't forget I have another son!'" (Kübler-Ross, 1969, p. 83).

Examples of bargaining do not seem to be as obvious as the other stages, and possibly not all patients attempt to cope with dying in this way or, if they do, their bargains are relatively subtle. Yet such attempts, although rather short term, may be seen as positive attempts to cope with death and, insofar as they are appropriate, need not be discouraged. One possible instance of bargaining in Ivan Ilych indicates some of the forms it may take and also the subtlety of this stage.

He would say to himself: "I will take up my duties again — after all I used to live by them." And banishing all doubts he would go to the law courts, enter into conversation with his colleagues, and sit carelessly as was his wont, scanning the crowd with a thoughtful look and leaning both his emaciated arms on the arms of his oak chair. . . . But suddenly in the midst of those proceedings the pain in his side, regardless of the stage the proceedings had reached, would begin its own gnawing work. . . . He would shake himself, try to pull himself together, manage somehow to bring the sitting to a close, and return home with the sorrowful consciousness that his judicial labours could not as formerly hide from him what he wanted them to hide, and could not deliver him from *It*. (Tolstoy, 1886, pp. 132–133)

Depression

Another characteristic response is a great sense of loss that Kübler-Ross differentiated into two different reactions. **Reactive depression** results from past losses and may be accompanied by guilt or shame at the loss—such as a woman whose breast is removed because of cancer, or whose teeth have been removed, or whose body is disfigured by the illness. **Preparatory depression** involves the "preparatory grief" that is involved in giving up the things of the world and in preparing oneself for the final separation from the world. "The patient is in the process of losing everything and everybody he loves. If he is allowed to express his sorrow he will find a final acceptance much easier, and he will be grateful to those who can sit with him during this stage of depression without constantly telling him not to be sad" (Kübler-Ross, 1969, p. 87). This type of depression is often "a silent one" and frequently silent gestures and mutual expression of feelings and tenderness can be quite helpful. In contrast, the reactive depression may require some intervention, some "cheering up" and some support for the patient's self-esteem. Thus, it seems useful to distinguish between these types of depression. Kübler-Ross suggested that members of the helping professions and patients' family members should realize that this preparatory type of depression "is necessary and beneficial if the patient is to die in a stage of acceptance and peace" (p. 88).

Although most of Ivan Ilych's depression may be seen as despair (the negative pole of Erikson's Integrity versus Despair crisis) resulting from his meaningless life and his inability to find any semblance of integrity until the very end, there are also some examples of preparatory depression.

> No one pitied him as he wished to be pitied. At certain moments after prolonged suffering he wished most of all (though he would have been ashamed to confess it) for someone to pity him as a sick child is pitied. He longed to be petted and comforted. . . . Ivan Ilych wanted to weep, wanted to be petted and cried over. (Tolstoy, 1886, p. 138)

But Ivan remained in continual despair, and made little progress in working through this preparatory grief. Finally, near the end, "the screaming began that continued for three days, and was so terrible that one could not hear it through two closed doors without horror" (Tolstoy, 1886, p. 154).

Acceptance

A fifth experience in the Kübler-Ross scheme is a quiet culmination of the previous trials and preceding reactions that she termed **acceptance.** Here the patient, if he or she is able to work through the denial, anger, depression, and general fear/anxiety about death, comes to "contemplate his coming end with a certain degree of quiet expectation. He will be tired and, in most cases, quite weak" (Kübler-Ross, 1969, p. 112). This period is described as "almost void of feelings" and, as one of her respondents phrased it, of "the final rest before the long journey" (p. 113). This is the time, she suggested, when short visits, often in silence, sometimes holding the patient's hand, are the most helpful. She preferred to visit such patients at the end of the day when she too was tired and enjoyed a few minutes of peaceful silence. Visits with such patients may be meaningful for the visitor also, "as it will show him that dying is not such a frightening, horrible thing that so many want to avoid" (p. 114). It is also a time when the wishes and feelings of the patient may be more accepting of death than is true for the family. She cited one case we noted earlier in which the husband wished one last operation to save his wife, who had accepted death and wished to be left in peace; her only recourse was to develop a psychotic episode in the operating room that effectively prevented the operation. The next day she told Dr. Kübler-Ross in reference to her husband, "Talk to this man and make him understand" (p. 117).

Despite Ivan's three days of agonized screaming, there is some indication of his acceptance of death:

> This occurred at the end of the third day, two hours before his death. Just then his schoolboy son had crept softly in and gone up to the bedside. The dying man was still screaming desperately and waving his arms. His hand fell on the boy's head, and the boy caught it, pressed it to his lips, and began to cry. At that very moment Ivan Ilych fell through and caught sight of the light, and it was revealed to him that though his life had not been what it should have been, this could still be rectified. . . .
>
> And suddenly it grew clear to him that what had been oppressing him and would not leave him was all dropping away at once from two sides, from ten sides, and from all sides. He was sorry for them, he must act so as to not hurt them: release them and free himself from these sufferings. "How good and how simple!" he thought. "And the pain?" he asked himself. "What has become of it? Where are you, pain?" . . .
>
> He sought his former accustomed fear of death and did not find it. "Where is it? What death?" There was no fear because there was no death.
>
> In place of death there was light.
>
> "So that's what it is!" he suddenly exclaimed aloud. "What joy!" (Tolstoy, 1886, pp. 155–156)

Hope

Through all of the five reactions that, as indicated before, do not necessarily follow one another in sequence but instead may come and go, Kübler-Ross saw hope as an important, continuing factor. She suggested that it is the **hope** of eventual recovery (a new drug, a last-minute success in a research project, or some kind of cure — which, of course, *has* occurred; for example, in the discovery of insulin or penicillin) that maintains the patient through the weeks and months of suffering. She noted that patients showed greatest confidence in doctors who allowed some hope to remain, and also a majority of her respondents made a "comeback" in some way or another — often from talking about the seriousness of their illness and from regaining that glimpse of hope that they are not forgotten or rejected. Certainly this hope is not only for a recovery, but also the hope that one may die without pain and with the important issues worked through with family and loved ones. If the last bit of life can be valued and meaningfully comprehended by those left behind, and if there can be some real communication between the dying and the bereaved while there is still time left, she argued very persuasively that both the dying and the bereavement are made more humane and more meaningful.

> If this book serves no other purpose but to sensitize family members of terminally ill patients and hospital personnel to the implicit communications of dying patients, then it has fulfilled its task. If we, as members of the helping professions, can help the patient

and his family to get "in tune" to each other's needs and come to an acceptance of an unavoidable reality together, we can help to avoid much unnecessary agony and suffering on the part of the dying and even more so on the part of the family that is left behind. (Kübler-Ross, 1969, p. 142)

Critique of the Kübler-Ross Approach

As suggested earlier, the most frequent criticism of the Kübler-Ross (1969) approach to death and dying has been that the responses she described are not "stages" that occur in sequence; she later agreed that these reactions do not occur in any particular order. Perhaps they were first presented as a series of stages because there appears to be a kind of logical order to the reactions — denial would appear to be a typical first reaction; as denial subsides, anger is felt, and so on; likewise, acceptance seems to be a logical final stage. However, death, and the process of dying, is not logical. It is quite likely that the first reaction may be anger, or depression. Some persons may die shaking their fist at death, fighting to the end; this need not be wholly incompatible with acceptance, since acceptance of death does not mean wishing to die (Kalish, 1976). Therefore, the Kübler-Ross approach should not be seen as a kind of prescription for a successful death. Individuals die in individual ways and this should be respected to the greatest extent possible if we wish to humanize the dying process. This implies that individuals should not be fit into some predetermined mold, especially with regard to such a significant experience in their lives.

After describing the Kübler-Ross approach and noting that she does not provide any information about the proportion of respondents who experienced any or all of her "stages," Shneidman (1973), a therapist who worked with dying persons, pointed out that his experience revealed a much wider range of emotional reactions with no particular order to them at all.

> Rather than the five definite stages discussed above, my experience leads me to posit a hive of affect, in which there is a constant coming and going. The emotional stages seem to include a constant interplay between disbelief and hope and, against these as background, a waxing and waning of anguish, terror, acquiescence and surrender, rage and envy, disinterest and ennui, pretense, taunting and daring and even yearning for death —all these in the context of bewilderment and pain.
>
> One does not find a unidirectional movement through progressive stages so much as an alternation between acceptance and denial. Denial is a most interesting psychodynamic phenomenon. For a few consecutive days a dying person is capable of shocking a listener with the breathtaking candor of his profound acceptance of imminent death and the next day shock that listener with unrealistic talk of leaving the hospital and going on a trip. This interplay between acceptance and denial, between understanding what is happening and magically disbelieving its reality, may reflect a deeper dialogue of the total mind, involving different layers of conscious awareness of "knowing" and of needing not to know. (Shneidman, 1973, p. 7)

This critique suggests that the Kübler-Ross approach tends to be both too simple and too sanitized.

Kastenbaum (1975) pointed out that there are several important questions raised by the Kübler-Ross perspective that should be explored in future research. For example, what effect does the nature of the terminal disease have on the person's reactions? Are there differences between men and women in their reactions to dying? What is the effect of racial and ethnic background? How does personality or cognitive style affect coping with death? What are the effects of age or developmental level? How does the sociophysical milieu in which the person is hospitalized or living affect reactions to dying? For each of these questions, Kastenbaum suggested a number of factors and interesting bits of data that make these topics significant for further study. To take only one example, some preliminary findings in one of his studies indicated that women are disturbed more by the effect of their terminal illness on others, and men are concerned more with dependency, pain, and the effect of the illness on their occupational role. Thus, he was especially critical of the image of one single process of dying, with universal stages that are assumed to apply to all persons.

> It is always a specific person dying in a specific environment that has its own social and physical dynamics, and the person approaches death through one or more specific disease modalities, responding in terms of the idiosyncratic integration of personality, ethnic, sex-role, and developmental resources. Viewed in this light, each death is individual. The five stages, if they do exist, are found within the context of the situation but do not necessarily dominate it. (Kastenbaum, 1975, p. 44)

Previous research has clearly suggested that all individuals do not die in the same manner. For example, Hinton (1967) reported that about one-quarter of the persons dying in a general hospital showed a high degree of acceptance and composure, but circumstances surrounding the illness and hospitalization played an important role. He suggested that about half of the patients eventually come to acknowledge openly and to accept the end of their life (and it was more common among the elderly); a quarter expressed distress; and another quarter said little about it. Weisman and Kastenbaum (1968) reviewed the data on fear of death and offered a few tentative conclusions: "Only a few elderly subjects express fear of death . . . fear of death is more likely to be found among elderly people who are suffering from acute emotional or psychiatric disturbances . . . elderly people manifest a variety of orientations toward death, not a uniform pattern" (p. 35). They suggested two distinct patterns of dying among their chronic patients in a geriatric hospital: the ones who seemed to be aware of and to accept impending death and who slipped into withdrawal and inactivity until the final illness, and the ones who remained actively engaged in hospital activities until they were interrupted by death.

Moreover, it is obvious that many people die from accidents or experience sudden deaths that do not allow time for the Kübler-Ross "stages" to occur, except possibly in the most fleeting manner. In these situations, the reactions are more likely to be felt by the bereaved persons who are left to deal with the death; we will discuss these bereavement reactions later in this chapter.

In sum, these critiques of the perspective proposed by Kübler-Ross call attention to the need to expand her model to account for the variety of individual styles of dying and the complex reactions that this experience involves. One approach that might be helpful in this goal is the **psychological autopsy** described by Weisman and Kastenbaum (1968). They suggested that the persons involved in the care of a deceased person analyze the psychosocial aspects of the person's death with the aim of improving the psychosocial support that they might have provided. The psychological autopsy has five principal objectives: adequate medical care, encouragement of competent behavior, preservation of rewarding relationships, maintenance of a dignified self-image, and attainment of an acceptable and, if possible, appropriate death. They suggested that little attention has been paid to dying patients in the past, especially during the "preterminal" period, largely because little attention is given to the aged in general. Since the person in the hospital is likely to become "a patient" (a social role), attention needs to be given to the other roles the person maintains (parent, spouse, and so on) and to the social situation within the hospital so that the person's identity is not diminished to that of only "patient in bed number 14" or, worse, that the person becomes a "thing." They pointed out, "Many aged people suffer from devaluation, not disease" (p. 37). Of course, not all dying people are old, and some terminally ill people are stigmatized by their disease (such as AIDS or cancer), not by age (Katz et al., 1987).

Clearly, the work of Kübler-Ross and many others has focused attention on death and dying and has begun to bring greater awareness to the issues involved in this final stage of life. One of the most successful manifestations of this greater awareness is the growing acceptance of the hospice concept of care for persons who are terminally ill.

The Hospice Concept

In the Middle Ages throughout Europe, in large cities, at major river crossings and mountain passes, at monasteries, and along the route of pilgrimage to the Holy Land, one could find refuge at a *hospice.* Weary travelers, the sick, the poor, the orphaned, women in labor, and the dying were offered hospitality. They may have received some medical care, but primarily they were given protection, fellowship, and refreshment. The words hospice, hospitality, hospital, and hostel are from the original root *hospes*—" the mutual caring of people for one another" (Stoddard, 1978). In this century the term has been revived and is being used as a concept of caring for persons who are terminally ill. First in England, then in Canada and the United States, a number of hospices have been created as community-based systems of care for dying persons, especially those in pain who cannot be aided by modern medical technology and are expected to live at least several more days or weeks. In keeping with their ancient tradition, the modern hospice provides relief from the pain, a refreshing physical environment (or continuous support for the person at home), and the kind of fellowship and hospitality that a weary traveler longs to receive.

St. Christopher's Hospice in London and its founder, Dame Cicely Saunders, are perhaps the best known representatives of this concept. However, St. Christopher's is relatively new (construction began in 1971); its pioneering recreation of this concept of care grew out of St. Joseph's Hospice that had been welcoming dying patients in London since the early 1900s; it was there that Saunders, a physician, developed effective techniques for pain control (Stoddard, 1978). St. Joseph's had been founded by Mother Mary Aikenhead, who had opened a hospice in Dublin, Ireland, in the mid-1800s. The idea was brought to America in 1963 when Saunders was invited to speak at Yale University. Her talk inspired the formation of the first hospice in the United States in Connecticut. Saunders lectured extensively during the next decade and St. Christopher's became a center for educating leaders of the American hospice programs. The hospice concept of care was also influenced by Elisabeth Kübler-Ross and by Balfour Mount, director of a hospice in Montreal, Canada. In 1978 American hospice leaders created the National Hospice Organization (NHO), which holds the U.S. copyright to the name *hospice*. By the mid-1980s there were over 1500 hospice programs in the United States. Some were affiliated with hospitals, others were based in home health agencies, and some were freestanding community-based programs (Paradis & Cummings, 1986). In 1983 Medicare began providing limited coverage for hospice care, and in 1989 it began to provide theoretically complete coverage for eligible persons. Thus, it is clear that the hospice movement is rapidly emerging as a major resource for those terminally ill persons who desire and would benefit from this type of care. Most patients are suffering from cancer, but many programs are providing extensive services to persons with acquired immune deficiency syndrome (AIDS).

Mor (1987) described the general characteristics of the **hospice** model of care:

1. An interdisciplinary team, headed by a medical director and including specialists in nursing, social work, pastoral, and psychological services.

2. The availability of hospice services 24 hours a day, 7 days a week.

3. The ability to ensure continuity of care, whether the patient is at home, in a hospital, or in a temporary respite care facility.

4. The appropriate utilization of primary caregivers who are either family members, friends, or neighbors.

5. The appropriate utilization of community volunteers who have been carefully selected, trained, and supervised.

A successful hospice effort, then, will involve the development of an individualized care plan that is sensitive to the needs and wishes of the patient–family unit and that calls upon the skills of an interdisciplinary team of paid staff and volunteers. (pp. 19–20)

There are also two guiding principles: first, the patient and the family are the unit of care—not the patient alone; and second, the values, preferences, and outlook on life of the patient and family must be considered (p. 19). Moreover, according to the NHO, the basic components of care include "symptom management, palliative and supportive care, integrated inpatient and home care, educational programming for patients and families, bereavement services after the patient's death, and the use of volunteers" (Paradis & Cummings, 1986, p. 371). Inpatient units, which can be required for short periods of time, are designed to be homelike and cheerful and to include accommodations for relatives (Taylor, 1987).

Holden (1976) reported that pain control is the first priority at St. Christopher's Hospice. The person is made free of pain and of the memory of pain; this is usually achieved through a variety of pain-killing medications administered so that they effectively relieve the pain and are given frequently enough so that the patient need not fear that the pain will occur again. Once the pain has been removed, the dosage can often be reduced and patients generally manage their own medication. This effective pain control provides the patient with a sense of control over one of the most disturbing aspects of dying. In addition, the patient receives continual attention from the staff and volunteers in a pleasant environment where the person need never be alone or have to hide the seriousness of the illness from others. Stoddard (1978) noted that privacy is available for individuals or couples when they desire it.

Most of the patients return to their homes after the pain is under control and frequently they regain much of their ability to function on their own with whatever support is needed being arranged by the hospice. Thus, the care is physical, psychological, and social — with the reality of death clearly acknowledged and accepted as a familiar reality instead of something to be prevented or postponed at any cost. Assistance, if it is needed, is always available. The person's own physician ordinarily continues to provide medical care and, of course, the patient is free to enter a hospital for aggressive medical treatment if desired. However, the hospice concept emphasizes the person's physical and psychological comfort instead of futile attacks on the disease.

A National Hospice Study of 13,000 patients over a two-year period found that

Most hospice patients return to their homes with the necessary support arranged in cooperation with hospice volunteers, family, and friends.

nearly all had some form of cancer, most were married, over age 65, and tended not to have been in a nursing home. Older patients responded to hospice care as well as younger patients: they were as likely to die at home (indicating comparable support systems); were cared for by daughters, spouses, and siblings; there was no relationship between the caregiver's subsequent health problems and their age; and older and younger patients had comparable length of survival rates (Mor, 1987). Research has also focused on the positive effects of hospice nursing training (Lev, 1986), on the high degree of effectiveness in hospice training of volunteers (Wilkinson & Wilkinson, 1986–1987), and on the characteristics, motivations, and satisfactions of volunteers who are the key to most hospice programs (Patchner & Finn, 1987–1988).

The hospice concept began as a movement to reform medical care of people with terminal illness. Today it is a multimillion dollar "industry" and hospices are likely to emerge in health-maintenance organizations (HMOs) and in for-profit programs. Paradis and Cummings (1986) traced this rapid development and concluded, optimistically, that the end result is still positive.

> While hospice is part of the medical mainstream, there is no evidence that competition for the market created by dying people and their families automatically dehumanizes care of the dying. However, this is certainly an area warranting further investigation. Supporters of current trends within hospice maintain that although the movement has made peace with the medical mainstream because it must rely upon physicians, nurses and others for services, major concessions have been won from traditional providers. Hospice services have, in fact, been greatly expanded and are more widely available through Medicare and third party payers. Moreover, dying persons are treated differently by established providers, and many physicians now have a meaningful alternative to treat the terminally ill. (Paradis & Cummings, 1986, p. 381)

Critics of the program have focused especially on the view that since it is a "cost-effective" alternative to aggressive medical care for terminal patients, it may be abused by budget-conscious individuals and programs (Gibson, 1984). Nonetheless, it seems clear that the hospice movement has provided one important way in which the dying process may be brought back into the life of the community. As a result, fears and denial of death may be reduced, and dying made more fully human and humane.

Bereavement and Grief

Much of Kübler-Ross's work on dying and the hospice concept of care are aimed at helping the dying person to resolve the last issues and weeks of life with dignity and psychological integrity. However, these approaches clearly involve the family. A central theme is the importance of relatively open and honest communication between the hospital staff, the patient, and the family (at least to the extent that the patient is open and responsive to such honesty). Such communication aids the patient and also aids the family in saying good-bye to one another for the last time. Such a farewell involves many deep, complex, and sometimes conflicting emotions within each person, and the interaction of these deep feelings between the dying and the bereaved is even more complex. For example, as patients experience the reactions Kübler-Ross described, they may confuse, confound, and conflict with those of the family. They may express denial, anger, depression, and acceptance intermittently over a few days, while the family may be seeking acknowledgment that they are not being rejected and have behaved properly toward the person. Also the patient may experience such phases as preparatory depression and acceptance while the closest relatives may still be denying the imminence of death. Perhaps the bereaved also have reactions similar to those of the dying person, and it would be helpful if the family and patient could assist one another through these reactions. Yet often the anger (aimed in reality at the disease or at death) is misinterpreted as directed at the patient or at the family, or it may be choked back by feelings of guilt at being angry. Such guilt — at this anger, at the inability to prolong the life, at the inability to pay for some famous specialist, or at some real or imagined "wrong" that may have been done — can be a particularly heavy burden for the bereaved, and it would often be helpful for this feeling to be worked through while the patient can still participate. Thus, one therapeutic task might be to facilitate the discussion of such dysfunctional, conflicted, and uncompleted feelings between the family and the patient while there is still time. If that is possible, the burden may be less for the family. Somehow, helping the bereaved and the dying say farewell to one another —even though that farewell may involve some anger or resentment as well as sadness, grief, and loneliness — would seem to be a primary goal from a psychological point of view for the sake of both the dying and the bereaved. Also important would be the family's understanding of the dying process; for example, anger may be expressed by the patient and may be felt by the family, or the dying person may need to say good-bye to some persons earlier than others so that the fading energy may be focused on saying farewell to those very few that have been saved until last. But even these persons may erroneously feel rejected when the patient focuses nearly all energy inward in coping with oncoming death or has so little energy left that he or she cannot even squeeze the hand or acknowledge the kiss. The bereaved are often overly sensitive to clues about their value to the dying person and may leave the hospital feeling rejected, guilty, or depressed because their need for acceptance was not met; in reality, the dying person clearly has important internal issues to deal with and often little energy left.

A similarly important task during this period of final farewell is to begin the expression of grief before death actually occurs. That is, once some of the guilt, anger, and resentment have been resolved by the patient and by the family, they may then share together some of the preparatory grief, supporting one another in that process, and sharing this deep emotion with the one whose absence will be so keenly felt. We all know, for example, that pretense and facade that cover up honest feelings frequently block communication, require a great deal of effort, and make a close relationship more difficult. Perhaps then, during the last few days and weeks when a relationship with the dying person is possible, these facades (which the patient can probably see through anyway) may interfere with that relationship and might best give way to the genuine sadness and preparatory grief.

Psychological Reactions to Bereavement

We would expect that the reactions to bereavement would be related to a large number of variables. Was the deceased old, or "cut down before their time" (the social clock, again)? Was the dying sudden, of a few weeks duration, or a prolonged illness? What was the relationship of the bereaved and the deceased person? Is the bereaved a man or woman? Lesbian or gay? What age? How is his or her physical health? Was death discussed? Were plans made? What is the ethnic or racial or cultural heritage of the bereaved and relevant family members? Each of these deceptively simple questions conceals a wealth of possible factors that might affect the nature of bereavement. For example, the relationship between the bereaved and the deceased could be examined in terms of closeness, dependency, involvement, duration, storminess, openness, and so on. Or it could be explored in terms of relationship categories: parent whose child dies, child whose parent dies, gay partner or spouse of deceased, grandchild of deceased, and so forth. At once we expect that age would also be important, for example, in the death of a parent. Ethnic differences in the meaning of death and the social supports for bereavement would also be involved.

Few of these questions have been explored in a systematic way; instead, studies have tended to find a sample of bereaved persons and to determine the characteristics they have in common, or those that differ between bereaved and nonbereaved

The funeral service provides an institutionalized setting for expressing pent-up emotion and to confirm the reality of death. It also represents the ongoing stability of the family and the community.

persons. The **bereavement reactions** that have been found are sometimes of almost pathological intensity. Gorer (1965) reported that many of his respondents were unable to adjust to their loss and characterized the grieving of one-third of his respondents as "unlimited." Similarly, Lopata (1973) found that one-fifth of her widowed respondents felt that the grief lasts "always; never get over it." An early study by Lindemann (1944) of persons bereaved by an accidental fire at the Cocoanut Grove nightclub in Boston found that somatic distress, preoccupation with the image of the deceased, a sense of unreality, guilt, hostile reactions, loss of patterns of conduct, and irritability were characteristic of the bereaved. These relatively extreme symptoms may result in part from the accidental crisis that caused the deaths since other studies have found that these symptoms may be present but are not the most common ones. For example, a study by Clayton, Halikes, and Maurice (1971), based on interviews with 109 widowed persons during the first month of bereavement, found that the most common symptoms were crying, depressed feelings, and difficulty in sleeping; difficulty in concentrating or poor memory, lack of appetite or weight loss, and reliance on sleeping pills or tranquilizers were also noted in more than half of the randomly selected subjects in the study. However, more pathological reactions were relatively infrequent (Figure 10.7). About one-third of the respondents complained about the physician or hospital — often that the physician did not indicate the severity of the illness, especially if it was short and unexpected; and 21 percent reported guilt feelings. They reported that the bereaved indicated a benefit from reviewing the terminal illness during the study and suggested that reviewing the illness (perhaps with the physician) aids the bereaved by allowing them to express pent-up emotion and to confirm the reality of the death. Perhaps the funeral service provides a similar institutionalized setting for this process to occur. The respondents also reported that their children were the most helpful persons in their environment after the death, although the undertaker and the lawyer were also often viewed as helpful — perhaps because they aid the widowed person in the important task of making immediate decisions. Clayton et al. (1971) suggested that helping with immediate plans may be the most beneficial aid that can be given to the bereaved and that decisions about the future should be avoided, at least during the first month.

Bereavement and Health

Although many studies have found a relatively low incidence of suicidal thoughts among the bereaved in the first month, other studies have reported that the incidence of natural death among the recently widowed is higher than among married persons of the same age (Hinton, 1967; Rees & Lutkins, 1967). Schulz (1978) reported that several studies have confirmed these findings, both in the United States and in England. He concluded that the hopelessness, loss of will to live, and the "broken heart syndrome" probably are largely responsible for lowered resistance to disease or changes in behavior that may lead to death. Perhaps also the lack of attention to one's own physical health during a lengthy terminal illness of a relative or spouse aggravates one's own health problems. In contrast, McCrae and Costa (1988) examined data from a 10-year study of a national sample of married and

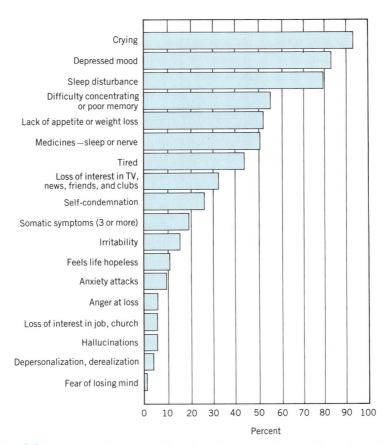

FIGURE 10.7 Percentage of randomly selected recently widowed persons reporting various symptoms of bereavement ($N = 109$). Somatic symptoms include headaches, blurred vision, dyspnea, abdominal pain, constipation, urinary frequency, dysmenorrhea, and other body pains. (*Source*: Adapted from Clayton et al., 1971, Table 1. Reprinted with permission.)

widowed persons aged 25 to 74. They found no difference in mortality rate between these groups when age and education were considered. The data suggested that most individuals respond to the stressful event of bereavement with psychological resilience. Similarly, Norris and Murrell (1987) found that bereavement had little lasting effect on physical health in a sample of 63 older adults (over age 55). It did produce considerable psychological distress, but most respondents handled it well. If there was an effect on health, it usually came before the death itself and reflected family stress.

Several studies have reported an increase in physical complaints and visits to physicians following bereavement. For example, Parkes (1987) reported that 3 out of 4 widows in his study had seen their physician within the first six months of bereavement — often for psychological difficulties associated with grief, but also for physical complaints — in all, there was a 63 percent increase in physician visits during the six months after bereavement, compared with the six months before. He felt that most of the complaints reflected tension or anxiety rather than organic illness, however. In addition, physical symptoms may have been ignored during the period before bereavement if the husband was sick. Similar conclusions were reached from the data about bereavement in the National Hospice Study (Mor, McHorney & Sherwood, 1986).

The ordeal of a prolonged illness may have a pronounced effect on the health of the surviving spouse. One study that examined the relative effects of short-term acute illness, short-term chronic illness (lasting less than six months), and long-term chronic illness (lasting more than six months) found that those persons with the long-term chronic illness prior to the bereavement reported more physician visits and greater incidents of illness without seeking medical help than either of the short-term groups; men were even more affected than women by an extended deathwatch (Gerber, Rusalem, Hannon, Battin & Arkin, 1975). The authors pointed out that these findings indicate that the presumed impact of sudden death may in fact be no more pronounced in terms of the health of the survivor than the impact of death caused by chronic illness. Thus, practitioners should pay close attention to both groups, especially widowed men and those who experienced long-term chronic illness. In addition, they concluded that the period of "preparatory grief" made possible by a long-term chronic illness did not appear to have a positive effect as the work of Kübler-Ross might predict; in fact, it had a negative effect. However, a deathwatch does not necessarily involve preparatory grief or any discussion of dying, bereavement, or plans for the future; since they did not measure the extent of mutual grieving in preparation for the death, this interpretation remains speculative. Nonetheless, a study of 95 widows over age 55 found that those who expected the death of their husband — and those that engaged in discussions about funeral arrangements, finances, feelings about being widowed, and future plans — adjusted to widowhood no better and, in some cases, worse than widows who did not expect the death or did not discuss plans (Hill, Thompson & Gallagher, 1988). Thus, in this study, widowhood that is on-time according to the social clock generally appears to be unaffected by whether the death is sudden or is anticipated for a month or more. Moreover, discussion and rehearsal for widowhood with the spouse prior to death did not appear to be beneficial, at least in terms of intensity of grief, physical health, and psychological health during the first year of bereavement. However, perhaps inadequate or inappropriate rehearsal strategies lead to poorer adjustment than no rehearsal at all.

The Process of Mourning

Bowlby (1960) distinguished five phases of grief and mourning: (1) thought and behavior directed toward the lost love object; (2) hostility toward the lost object or others; (3) appeals for help and support from others; (4) despair, withdrawal, regression, and disorganization; and (5) reorganization of behavior directed toward a new love object. He emphasized the importance of **mourning,** defined as the psychological process set in motion by the loss of the loved person, and **grief,** defined as subjective states that follow the loss and accompany the mourning. Both are required for the full resolution of the loss that leads to a reorganization of behavior. However, he maintained that a person may stall at any stage of the process. For younger adults, he noted that the reorganization directed toward a new love object may involve a period of promiscuity for both men and women. Although this may be true for younger persons, social pressures undoubtedly restrict promiscuity and the search for a new love object for the older person and may inhibit the process of reorganization following bereavement.

More recent research by Parkes (Glick, Weiss & Parkes, 1974; Parkes, 1987) suggested typical **phases of bereavement,** lasting about one year. Interestingly, some of these reactions are similar in humans and other animals. According to Schulz (1978), the *initial response* lasts a few weeks; it is characterized by shock and disbelief, followed by great sorrow with crying and weeping. Fears of "not making it" or having a breakdown are common. Some use alcohol or tranquilizers to control this anxiety; others try to keep busy. Sometimes social pressure to control one's emotions can inhibit grief behaviors with no negative effects, but it may also exaggerate the fears of not being able to overcome the grief. In general, however, allowing or encouraging the expression of grief is beneficial. The *intermediate phase* begins after several weeks and lasts during most of the first year of bereavement. It typically involves a repetitious reviewing of the death and events leading up to it and a search for the meaning of the death. There is also an uncanny kind of searching for the person who has died and often a comforting feeling that the person is still present.

> People who attempt to avoid painful reminders of the dead person by moving away usually come back, and the bereaved person who avoids reminders is aware of a sense of being pulled in two directions. One widow, for instance, moved into the back bedroom of her house to get away from her memories, but found that she missed her husband so much that she moved back into the front bedroom "to be near him." Two widows felt drawn towards the hospital where their husbands had passed their final illnesses, and one found herself walking into the hospital ward before she realized that he was not there. Another thought of her husband as being upstairs in the bed in which he had remained for many months before his death. She found herself listening out for him and sometimes thought she heard him calling for her. (Parkes, 1987, p. 72)

The *recovery phase* begins about one year after bereavement. Often there is a conscious decision to proceed with life, an increase in social involvement, and renewed feelings of strength and competence. Not infrequently, however, widowed persons may be treated as stigmatized persons. It is likely that this results in part from the fear others have that a similar fate may be in their future. It may also be that an "available" single person in a social world predominately filled with couples is inherently threatening. This also probably depends on the age of the widowed persons, whether they are male or female, and other ethnic and personal characteristics. Parkes (1987) also noted that a small proportion of bereaved persons develop atypical grief reactions and may benefit from professional help; a variety of self-help groups can give support to persons experiencing more typical grief reactions.

In sum, the psychological response to bereavement involves a period, often a year or two, of grief and mourning during which the person's ability to function is somewhat impaired, but it does not generally involve overt pathological symptoms (unless previous symptoms were present). Not all persons respond to bereavement in the same way, and the studies that have described typical phases of grieving undoubtedly over-simplify this process. Thus an individual's style of grief and mourning may be normal even if it differs from the phases of bereavement described earlier.

Reworking the events leading up to the death may often be helpful, especially with someone (such as the physician) who knew the deceased up to the end. Perhaps one of the most traumatic aspects of the loss would be the loss of a confidant, as discussed in Chapter 8; such a confidant generally seems to buffer the aged against losses and even against bereavement as well as the general difficulties of aging. When such a confidant is lost it is often a severe loss indeed, for there is no longer anyone to provide a buffer for the loss. Kübler-Ross (1969) suggested that the worst time for the bereaved may come when the funeral is over and the relatives have left, and one is all alone for the first time. It would seem that visits by family and friends during this long period of mourning might aid as much, if not more, than immediate aid and company after death. Yet the lonely hours of evening and night, the quiet home, and the empty bed are often reported to be the worst of all.

Social Aspects of Bereavement

In concluding this chapter, we briefly consider some of the social aspects of the dying process and of bereavement. Glaser and Strauss (1965) pointed out that death can be seen as a *status passage* that, like other institutionalized changes in status, involves a shift in social roles and presents some difficulties for the maintenance of the social system; for this reason, many aspects of the status passage are structured by society. For example, the complex legal process of inheritance and wills is institutionalized to ensure the continuance of a stable social structure and to provide for an acceptable distribution of the deceased's economic assets. Similarly, the **funeral** is a socially structured event to commemorate this status passage and to provide a means for public expression of grief. Mandelbaum (1959) listed three social functions of the funeral: disposal of the body, aiding the bereaved in reorienting themselves (i.e., beginning the resocialization process into their new roles), and publicly acknowledging the death of the person and the viability of the social group. In addition, he suggested several latent functions beside these manifest functions of the funeral: to reaffirm the stability of the social order, to demonstrate family cohesion, to affirm extended family ties, and to reaffirm the social character of of human experience. Kalish (1985) noted that funeral rites and related ceremonies are apparently in a state of transition; the sending of flowers is sometimes replaced by charitable donations, and cremation with the ashes sprinkled over land or water instead of burial has become more frequent. He felt these changes may represent the development of new sacred rituals and are not a secularization of death. Today, federal regulations require that the charges for funeral services be itemized; a sample listing a range of services is shown in Box 10.1.

Socially, recently bereaved persons are often treated as if they were sick themselves—they are given time off from work, visited by relatives, and others take

BOX 10.1 *Statement of Funeral Goods and Services Selected*

If you selected a funeral which required embalming, such as a funeral with viewing, you may have to pay for embalming. You do not have to pay for embalming you did not approve if you selected arrangements such as a direct cremation or immediate burial. If we charged for embalming, we will explain why below. Charges are only for these items that are used. If we are required by law to use any items, we will explain in writing below. If any law, cemetery, or crematory requirements have required the purchase of any of these items, the law or requirement is explained below.

Funeral Services for _____ Date of Death _____

A. CHARGE FOR SERVICES SELECTED:

Minimum services of staff	$_____
Additional staff services	$_____
Embalming	$_____
Other preparation of body	$_____
	$_____

Facilities and equipment:

Basic facilities	$_____
Use of facilities for viewing	$_____
Use of facilities for ceremony	$_____
Other use of facilities	$_____
	$_____

Automotive equipment:

Transfer of remains	$_____
Hearse	$_____
Other automotive equipment	$_____
Mileage @ $_____per mile	$_____
	$_____

Other services/facilities/
equipment
_____ $_____

TOTAL OF SERVICES SELECTED $_____

B. CHARGE FOR MERCHANDISE SELECTED:

Casket or other receptacle	$_____
Outer burial container	$_____
Acknowledgement cards	$_____
Register book(s)	$_____
Clothing	$_____
Cremation urn	$_____
Other merchandise_____	$_____

TOTAL MERCHANDISE SELECTED $_____

C. SPECIAL CHARGES:

Forwarding of remains to
_____ $_____
funeral home
Receiving of remains from
_____ $_____
funeral home

Immediate burial	$_____
Direct cremation	$_____

TOTAL OF SPECIAL CHARGES $_____

D. CASH ADVANCES:

Opening and closing grave	$_____
Cemetery charges	$_____
Crematory charges	$_____
Medical examiner fee	$_____
Transportation (describe)	$_____
Clergy honorarium	$_____
Musicians honorarium	$_____
Flowers	$_____
Paid death notices	$_____
Burial permit	$_____
Certified copies of death certificates	
_____ at $_____ each	$_____
Hairdresser	$_____
Telephone and telegraph	$_____
Others _____	$_____
_____	$_____
_____	$_____
_____	$_____
_____	$_____
_____	$_____

TOTAL CASH ADVANCES $_____

SUMMARY OF CHARGES

A. Services	$_____
B. Merchandise	$_____
C. Special Charges	$_____
D. Cash Advances	$_____

TOTAL OF ALL SELECTIONS $_____

Items ordered later of adjustments

_____	$_____
_____	$_____
_____	$_____

Balance due $_____

Reason for embalming_____
_____
_____
_____
_____

Source: Jordan Funeral Home, Ellsworth, ME.

over decision making. There are also social norms about proper behavior of the bereaved. Kalish and Reynolds (1976) interviewed 434 residents of Los Angeles about preferred mourning practices and found general agreement that one should wait at least one year before remarrying, and at least six months before dating; about one-third felt a few days off from work was preferred.

In general, the death of a friend or relative leads to some degree of resocialization, that is, it leads to some adjustment in one's *self*. There is a new relationship with the deceased now, one located primarily in the memory of past experiences. There is a new social identity if one becomes widowed; there are some *me*s that, in a sense, are stored away — for the other to whom they were significant is no longer present. There are new feelings of grief and shock and loss that are slowly integrated into the self by one's *I*. Some of these changes were discussed in Chapter 5, but these social and psychological shifts, changes, and reorientations are important to note again. Perhaps these "adjustments" (far too mechanistic a term for this process) begin with the death, perhaps during the period of preparatory grief with the dying person, perhaps with the funeral. They may be aided by the support of family and friends, and a confidant may be an important resource for those fortunate enough to maintain a close relationship. But these supports cannot satisfy the loneliness, and the bereaved have to do their grief work alone, often with the increased realization of their own impending death. Clearly there is a place for persons whom Strauss and Glaser (1970) term "Grief-Workers," who are sympathetic listeners or comforters helping the bereaved to work through their long mourning process. The Widowed Person's Service (Silverman, 1988) is one example of this type of program. In some cases short-term psychotherapy is also helpful. Also, books on widowhood and grief (e.g., Caine, 1975; Shuchter, 1986) can provide helpful advice and reassurance that one's bewildering array of reactions to bereavement is not that unique after all.

A variety of self-help groups, such as the Widowed Persons Service, are helpful for persons experiencing typical grief reactions.

Epilogue

When a relationship ends, it is important to spend a little time reviewing the meaning of the relationship with the other person, to affirm that it has been a worthwhile experience, and to say good-bye. This is true in psychotherapy relationships and in professional relationships in human services of all kinds. It may also be important in personal relationships, especially when they have been significant. Much of human development involves endings and beginnings. Perhaps, in a sense, the same is true with books. Some are like friends, and we pick them up again and again over the years. Others may have been worthwhile experiences that stay with us only in memory. Hopefully this has been one of those books.

We have covered much ground on our tour of adulthood and aging. We have explored some new perspectives, and perhaps some useful concepts have been discovered. Perhaps too, we have gained a deeper appreciation of older persons, and as a result have developed a greater awareness of our own life course. Our goal has been to raise the level of consciousness about the diversity, beauty, and potential of human development through all of the adult years—to add life to years at the same time that years are being added to life.

Knowing that one day we shall all surely die, let us smell the flowers, hear the birds, appreciate our relationships, and pay attention to those aspects of our lives that we cherish. This seems to be one important lesson that dying persons can teach us about living. So, may your lives be long, and your years full of life!

Chapter Summary

1. Some developmental processes during the second half of life appear to be affected by the individual's nearness to death, as well as by chronological age.

2. Erikson's eighth stage of development defines the issues of the last years of life as a struggle between a sense of integrity—experienced as an acceptance of one's life and a belief that it had meaning—and despair—the feeling that one's life was lived in vain and that it is too late to seek meaning because there is so little time left to live.

3. From an existential perspective, the possibility of death provides meaning to life. Existential anxiety about nonbeing, introspection about the meaning of one's life, and concerns with the issues involved in dying are important throughout life.

4. Fear of death does not seem to be a major concern for most people; in general, the attitude of adults is more one of acceptance than of fear. Older persons express less fear of death than middle-aged persons; but few persons in middle or old age report that they think about death frequently. Thoughts of death do not ordinarily dominate the later years of life.

5. The life review process, identified by Butler, consists of reminiscence, "mirror gazing," and a reinterpretation of one's past life. It is thought to be a naturally occurring mental process for individuals nearing death. Daydreams about

the past relative to the present increase with age, but thoughts and daydreams about the past do not dominate the lives of most older people. Reminiscence appears to be associated with feelings of integrity about one's past life, but for some older people it may involve negative feelings about the events or actions recalled. A structured life review can be therapeutic.

6. Nearness to death brings about psychological changes. A combination of psychological tests may be able to predict many of those older persons who would survive over five years compared with those who would die within five years. Various measures of cognitive functioning, emotional complexity, introspection, and self-image have been found to decline among persons who were a year or less away from death, compared to respondents who were at least three years away from death. Data on changes in intellectual functioning are inconsistent, however.

7. Kübler-Ross proposed five characteristic responses that are evident among terminally ill persons. Although the responses do not necessarily follow a particular sequence, they provide helpful clues to understanding the reactions of individuals who are facing death. These responses are: denial and isolation, anger, bargaining, depression, and acceptance; hope is also important throughout the dying process.

8. The Kübler-Ross model should not be seen as a prescription for successful dying. Emotional reactions to death are frequently very complex; the nature of the terminal disease and a variety of psychosocial factors may affect the reactions of the dying person.

9. A hospice is a system of care for dying persons, especially those who cannot be aided by aggressive medical treatment. The atmosphere of the hospice is one where dying is seen as a natural process and where both patient and family may find comfort and support during the dying process.

10. Bereavement brings a number of reactions that parallel the responses of dying persons. Crying, depressed mood, and sleep disturbance are common symptoms of bereavement. Increased health problems and a greater incidence of death after bereavement have been reported in several studies. A prolonged terminal illness may have as significant an impact on the bereaved spouse as a sudden death.

11. The process of mourning differs from one person to another; it often lasts about one year. The expression of grief and reviewing the events leading up to the death may be helpful. Frequently there is a searching for the deceased and a comforting feeling that the person is still present. The worst time is after the funeral, when one is left alone; sometimes there are fears of not being able to cope.

12. Many of the events surrounding death are structured by society, such as the funeral and the process of inheritance. These social aspects of death reaffirm the social character of human experience and demonstrate the cohesion and continuity of the family and society. Bereavement also brings a shifts in roles, resocialization, and some adjustment in the *self*.

Key Words

acceptance
anger
bargaining
bereavement reactions
denial
existential perspective
funeral
grief
hope

hospice
isolation
life review
mourning
phases of bereavement
preparatory depression
psychological autopsy
reactive depression

Review Questions

1. According to Kübler-Ross, why do we tend to dehumanize those who are dying?

Developmental Changes Preceding Death

2. Describe Erikson's eighth stage of development.

3. Summarize the findings of studies on the acceptance of death (refer to Figures 10.1 and 10.2).

4. What is the process of "life review" as proposed by Butler? What are some functions of this process?

5. What have studies on reminiscence shown about the prevalence of past versus present and future-oriented thought among young, middle-aged, and older individuals (refer to Figures 10.3 and 10.4)?

6. Describe the method used in studying psychological changes that are associated with nearness to death. Why must the age of the respondents in the study be considered in addition to nearness to death?

The Dying Process

7. Describe the five characteristic reactions of terminally ill persons that Kübler-Ross identified. Why is it important that these reactions not be seen as stages of dying?

8. How might the behavior of a person who is dying be misinterpreted by family members or the hospital staff?

9. What are some of the limitations and criticisms of the Kübler-Ross approach?

10. What is a hospice? How does it aid dying individuals and their families? What is your reaction to the hospice concept?

Bereavement and Grief

11. What are some common feelings and reactions of the bereaved person (refer to Figure 10.7)?

12. How are health and bereavement related? How does one affect the other?

13. Describe the process of mourning proposed by Bowlby. What are some of the characteristic reactions during the initial, intermediate, and recovery phases of bereavement?

14. Give some examples of how a "grief worker" might be helpful during this period.

References

Aber, Robert & Webb, Wilse B. 1986. Effects of a limited nap on night sleep in older subjects. *Psychology and Aging, 1,* 300–302.

Adams, Diane M. 1983. The psychosocial development of professional Black women's lives and the consequences of career for their personal happiness (Doctoral dissertation, Wright Institute, Berkeley, CA). *Dissertation Abstracts International, 44,* 3920B.

Adelman, Marcy (Ed.). 1986. *Long time passing: Lives of older lesbians.* Boston: Alyson.

Aizenberg, Rhonda & Treas, Judith. 1985. The family in late life: Psychosocial and demographic considerations. In J. E. Birren & K. W. Schaie (Eds.), *Handbook of the psychology of aging* (2nd ed., pp. 169-189). New York: Van Nostrand Reinhold.

Allen, Walter R. 1978. The search for applicable theories of Black family life. *Journal of Marriage and the Family, 40,* 117-129.

Almvig, Chris. 1982. *The invisible minority: Aging and lesbianism.* Utica, NY: Utica College of Syracuse University.

American Psychiatric Association. 1987. *Diagnostic and statistical manual of mental disorders* (3rd ed., revised). Washington, DC: Author.

American Psychological Association. 1982. *Ethical principles in the conduct of research with human participants.* Washington, DC: Author.

Anthony-Bergstone, Cheri R.; Zarit, Steven H.; & Gatz, Margaret. 1988. Symptoms of psychological distress among caregivers of dementia patients. *Psychology and Aging, 3,* 245–248.

Antunes, George E.; Cook, Fay Lomax; Cook, Thomas D.; & Skogan, Wesley G. 1977. Patterns of personal crime against the elderly: Findings from a national survey. *The Gerontologist, 17,* 321–327.

Arena, John G.; Hightower, Nancy E.; & Chong, Gary C. 1988. Relaxation therapy for tension headache in the elderly: A prospective study. *Psychology and Aging, 3,* 96–98.

Arlin, Patricia Kennedy. 1975. Cognitive development in adulthood: A fifth stage? *Developmental Psychology, 11,* 602–606.

Arlin, Patricia Kennedy. 1977. Piagetian operations in problem finding. *Developmental Psychology, 13,* 297–298.

Arlin, Patricia Kennedy. 1984. Adolescent and adult thought: A structural interpretation. In M. L. Commons, F. A. Richards & C. Armon (Eds). *Beyond formal operations: Late adolescent and adult cognitive development* (pp. 258–271). New York: Praeger.

Associated Press. 1989 (April 2). Death rate declines except for mortality related to smoking. *New York Times,* 23.

Atchley, Robert C. 1982. The process of retirement: The female experience. In M. Szinovacz (Ed.), *Women's retirement.* Beverly Hills, CA: Sage Publications.

Atchley, Robert C. 1989. A continuity theory of normal aging. *The Gerontologist, 29,* 183–190.

Avorn, Jerome L. 1986. Medicine: The life and death of Oliver Shay. In A. Pifer & L. Bronte (Eds.), *Our aging society: Paradox and promise* (pp. 283–297). New York: Norton.

Back, Kurt W. 1974 (October). *The three-generation household in pre-industrial society: Norm or expedient?* Paper presented at the meeting of the Gerontological Society of America, Portland, OR.

Bahrick, H. P.; Bahrick, P. O.; & Wittlinger, R. P. 1975. Fifty years of memory for names and faces: A cross-sectional approach. *Journal of Experimental Psychology: General, 104,* 54–75.

Bailey, Anne. 1978. The 7 day diet: A computer-analyzed diet for older Americans. In R. B. Weg, *Nutrition and the later years* (pp. 145–156). Los Angeles: University of Southern California Press.

Bakan, David. 1966. *The duality of human existence.* Chicago: Rand McNally.

Baker, F. M. 1988. Dementing illness and Black Americans. In J. S. Jackson (Ed.), *The Black American elderly: Research on physical and psychosocial health* (pp. 215–233). New York: Springer.

Baltes, Paul B. 1968. Longitudinal and cross-sectional sequences in the study of age and generation effects. *Human Development, 11,* 145–171.

Baltes, Paul B.; Cornelius, Steven W.; & Nesselroade, John R. 1980. Cohort effects in developmental psychology. In J. R. Nesselroade & P. B. Baltes (Eds.), *Longitudinal research in the study of behavior and development* (pp. 61–87). New York: Academic Press.

Baltes, Paul B. & Goulet, L. R. 1971. Exploration of developmental variables by manipulation and simulation of age differences in behavior. *Human Development, 14,* 149–170.

Baltes, Paul B.; Reese, Hayne W.; & Lipsitt, Lewis P. 1980. Life-span developmental psychology. *Annual Review of Psychology, 31,* 65–110.

Baltes, Paul B.; Reese, Hayne W; & Nesselroade, John R. 1977. *Life-span developmental psychology: Introduction to research methods.* Monterey, CA: Brooks/Cole.

Baltes, P. B. & Willis, S. L. 1979. The critical importance of appropriate methodology in the study of aging: The sample case of psychometric intelligence. In F. Hoffmeister & C. Müller (Eds.), *Brain functions in old age.* Heidelberg: Springer-Verlag.

Bankoff, Elizabeth A. 1983. Social support and adaptation to widowhood. *Journal of Marriage and the Family, 45,* 827–839.

Bardwick, Judith M. 1971. *Psychology of women.* New York: Harper & Row.

Barnes, Hazel E. 1959. *Humanistic existentialism: The literature of possibility.* Lincoln: University of Nebraska Press.

Barrett, Nancy. 1987. Women and the economy. In S. E. Rix (Ed.), *The American woman, 1987–88* (pp. 100–149). New York: Norton.

Barsky, A. J. & Klerman, G. L. 1983. Overview: Hypochondriasis, bodily complaints, and somatic styles. *American Journal of Psychiatry, 140,* 273–283.

Bart, Pauline B. 1971. Depression in middle-aged women. In V. Gornick & B. K. Moran (Eds.), *Women in sexist society* (pp. 99–117). New York: Basic Books.

Bartlett, James C. & Snelus, Paul. 1980. Lifespan memory for popular songs. *American Journal of Psychology, 93,* 551–560.

Basseches, Michael. 1980. Dialectical schemata: A framework for the empirical study of the development of dialectical thinking. *Human Development, 21,* 400–421.

Batchelor, Walter F. 1984. AIDS: A public health and psychological emergency. *American Psychologist, 39,* 1279–1284.

Baum, Herbert M. & Manton, Kenneth G. 1987. National trends in stroke-related mortality: A comparison of multiple cause mortality data with survey and other health data. *The Gerontologist, 27,* 293–308.

Beauvoir, Simone de. 1953 *The second sex.* (Translated by H. M. Parshley.) New York: Knopf.

Beauvoir, Simone de. 1972. *The coming of age.* (Translated by P. O'Brian.) New York: Putnam.

Bell, Alan P. & Weinberg, Martin S. 1978. *Homosexualities: A study of diversity among men and women.* New York: Simon & Schuster.

Bem, Sandra L. 1974. The measurement of psychological androgyny. *Journal of Consulting and Clinical Psychology, 42,* 155–162.

Bem, Sandra L. 1975. Sex role adaptability: One consequence of psychological androgyny. *Journal of Personality and Social Psychology, 31,* 634–643.

Bem, Sandra L. 1977. On the utility of alternative procedures for assessing psychological androgyny. *Journal of Consulting and Clinical Psychology, 45,* 196–205.

Bem, Sandra L. & Lenney, Ellen. 1976. Sex typing and the avoidance of cross-sex behavior. *Journal of Personality and Social Psychology, 33,* 48–54.

Benedek, Therese. 1952. *Psychosexual functions in women.* New York: Ronald Press.

Benedict, Ruth. 1946. *The chrysanthemum and the sword: Patterns of Japanese culture.* New York: New American Library.

Bengtson, Vern L. 1985. Diversity and symbolism in grandparental roles. In V. L. Bengtson & J. F. Robertson (Eds.), *Grandparenthood* (pp. 11–25). Beverly Hills, CA: Sage Publications.

Bengtson, Vern L.; Cuellar, José B.; & Ragan, Pauline K. 1977. Stratum contrasts and similarities in attitudes toward death. *Journal of Gerontology, 32,* 76–88.

Bengtson, Vern L.; Dowd, James J.; Smith, David H.; & Inkeles, Alex. 1975. Modernization, modernity, and perceptions of aging: A cross-cultural study. *Journal of Gerontology, 30,* 688–695.

Bengtson, Vern L.; Kasschau, Patricia L.; & Ragan, Pauline K. 1977. The impact of social structure on aging individuals. In J. E. Birren & K. W. Schaie (Eds.), *Handbook of the psychology of aging* (pp. 327–353). New York: Van Nostrand Reinhold.

Bengtson, Vern L. & Kuypers, Joseph A. 1971. Generational difference and the developmental stake. *Aging and Human Development, 2,* 249–260.

Bengtson, Vern L.; Reedy, Margaret N.; & Gordon, Chad. 1985. Aging and self-conceptions: Personality processes and social contexts. In J. E. Birren & K. W. Schaie (Eds.), *Handbook of the psychology of aging* (2nd ed., pp. 544–593). New York: Van Nostrand Reinhold.

Berg, Leonard; Danziger, Warren L.; Storandt, Martha; Coben, Lawrence A.; Gado, Mohktar; Hughes, Charles P.; Knesevich, John W.; & Botwinick, Jack. 1984. Predictive features in mild senile dementia of the Alzheimer type. *Neurology, 34,* 563–569.

Berg, Stig. 1987. Intelligence and terminal decline. In G. L. Maddox & E. W. Busse, *Aging: The universal human experience* (pp. 411–416). New York: Springer.

Berger, Raymond M. 1982. *Gay and gray: The older homosexual man.* Urbana: University of Illinois Press.

Bernstein, Merton C. & Bernstein, Joan Brodshaug. 1988. *Social security: The system that works.* New York: Basic Books.

Berzon, Betty. 1988. *Permanent partners: Building gay and lesbian relations that last.* New York: Dutton.

Biller, Henry B. 1982. Fatherhood: Implications for child and adult development. In B. B. Wolman (Ed.), *Handbook of developmental psychology* (pp. 702–725). Englewood Cliffs, NJ: Prentice-Hall.

Birren, James E. 1960. Behavioral theories of aging. In N. W. Shock (Ed.), *Aging: Some social and biological aspects* (pp. 305–332). Publication No. 65. Washington, DC: American Association for the Advancement of Science.

Birren, James E.; Butler, Robert N.; Greenhouse, Samuel W.; Sokoloff, Louis; & Yarrow, Marian

R. (Eds.) 1963. *Human aging: A biological and behavioral study.* Publication No. (HSM) 71-9051. Washington, DC: U.S. Government Printing Office.

Birren, James E. & Renner, V. Jayne. 1977. Research on the psychology of aging: Principles and experimentation. In J. E. Birren & K. W. Schaie (Eds.), *Handbook of the psychology of aging* (pp. 3–38). New York: Van Nostrand Reinhold.

Black, Dennis M.; Brand, Richard J.; Greenlick, Merwyn; Hughes, Glenn; & Smith, Jacqueline. 1987. Compliance to treatment for hypertension in elderly patients: The SHEP pilot study. *Journal of Gerontology, 42,* 552–557.

Blanchard-Fields, Fredda. 1986. Reasoning on social dilemmas varying in emotional saliency: An adult developmental perspective. *Psychology and Aging, 1,* 325–333.

Blank, Thomas O. 1979 (September). *Older people doing their shopping.* Paper presented at the meeting of the American Psychological Association, New York.

Block, Christopher; Boczkowski, Judith A.; Hansen, Nancy; & Vanderbeck, Michael. 1987. Nursing home consultation: Difficult residents and frustrated staff. *The Gerontologist, 27,* 443–446.

Block, Jeanne H. 1973. Conceptions of sex role: Some cross-cultural and longitudinal perspectives. *American Psychologist, 28,* 512–526.

Bloom, Bernard L. 1988. *Health psychology: A psychosocial perspective.* Englewood Cliffs, NJ: Prentice–Hall.

Blumenthal, James A.; Williams, Redford B., Jr.; Kong, Yihong; Schanberg, Saul M.; & Thompson, Larry W. 1978. Type A behavior pattern and coronary atherosclerosis. *Circulation, 58,* 634–639.

Blumstein, Philip & Schwartz, Pepper. 1983. *Amerian couples: Money, work, sex.* New York: Morrow.

Bolles, Richard Nelson. 1972. *What color is your parachute? A practical manual for job-hunters & career-changers.* Berkeley, CA: Ten Speed Press.

Bolles, Richard Nelson. 1988. *What color is your parachute? A practical manual for job-hunters & career-changers.* (Rev. ed.) Berkeley, CA: Ten Speed Press.

Botwinick, Jack. 1977. Intellectual abilities. In J. E. Birren & K. W. Schaie (Eds.), *Handbook of the psychology of aging* (pp. 580–605). New York: Van Nostrand Reinhold.

Botwinick, Jack; West, Robin; & Storandt, Martha. 1978. Predicting death from behavioral test performance. *Journal of Gerontology, 33,* 755–762.

Bowlby, John. 1960. Grief and mourning in infancy and early childhood. *Psychoanalytic Study of the Child, 15,* 9–52.

Boylin, William; Gordon, Susan K.; & Nehrke, Milton F. 1976. Reminiscing and ego integrity in institutionalized elderly males. *The Gerontologist, 16,* 118–124.

Brand, R. J. 1978. Coronary prone behavior as an independent risk factor for coronary heart disease. In T. M. Dembroski, S. M. Weiss, S. G. Haynes & M. Feinlab (Eds.), *Coronary prone behavior.* New York: Springer-Verlag.

Bransford, John D. & Stein, Barry S. 1984. *The ideal problem solver: A guide for improving thinking, learning, and creativity.* New York: Freeman.

Brim, Orville G., Jr. 1968. Adult socialization. In J. A. Clausen (Ed.), *Socialization and society* (pp. 182–226). Boston: Little, Brown.

Brim, Orville G., Jr. 1976. Theories of the male mid-life crisis. *Counseling Psychologist, 6,* 2–9.

Brim, Orville G., Jr. & Wheeler, Stanton (Eds.). 1966. *Socialization after childhood: Two essays.* New York: Wiley.

Brody, Elaine. 1977. *Long-term care of older people.* New York: Human Sciences Press.

Brody, Elaine M. 1985. Parent care as a normative family stress. *The Gerontologist, 25,* 19–29.

Brody, Elaine M. & Schoonover, Claire B. 1986. Patterns of parent-care when adult daughters work and when they do not. *The Gerontologist, 26,* 372–381.

Bromley, D. B. 1966. *The psychology of human ageing.* Baltimore: Penguin.

Broverman, Inge K.; Vogel, Susan Raymond; Broverman, Donald M.; Clarkson, Frank E.; & Rosenkrantz, Paul S. 1972. Sex role stereotypes: A current appraisal. *Journal of Social Issues, 28*(2), 59–78.

Brown, Claude. 1965. *Manchild in the promised land.* New York: Macmillan Co.

Brown, Robert N. 1989. *The rights of older persons: A basic guide to the legal rights of older persons under current law* (2nd ed.). Carbondale: Southern Illinois University Press.

Bühler, Charlotte. 1968. The developmental structure of goal setting in group and individual studies. In C. Bühler & F. Massarik (Eds.), *The course of human life* (pp. 27–54). New York: Springer.

Burgess, Jane K. 1988. Widowers. In C. S. Chilman, E. W. Nunnally & F. M. Cox (Eds.), *Variant family forms* (pp. 150–164). Newbury Park, CA: Sage Publications.

Burkhauser, Richard V. & Tolley, G. S. 1978. Older Americans and market work. *The Gerontologist, 18,* 449–453.

Burton, Linda M. 1985. Early and on-time grandmotherhood in multi-generation Black families. *Dissertation Abstracts International, 46,* 1409A–1410A. (Copies available exclusively from: Micrographics Dept., Doheny Library, University of Southern California, Los Angeles, CA 90089-0182.)

Burton, Linda M. & Bengtson, Vern L. 1985. Black grandmothers: Issues of timing and continuity of roles. In V. L. Bengtson & J. F. Robertson (Eds.), *Grandparenthood* (pp. 61–77). Beverly Hills, CA: Sage Publications.

Buskirk Elsworth R. 1985. Health maintenance and longevity: Exercise. In C. E. Finch & E. L. Schneider (Eds.), *Handbook of the biology of aging* (2nd ed., pp. 894–931). New York: Van Nostrand Reinhold.

Butler, Robert N. 1963a. The façade of chronological age: An interpretive summary. *American Journal of Psychiatry, 119,* 721–728.

Butler, Robert N. 1963b. The life review: An interpretation of reminiscence in the aged. *Psychiatry, 26,* 65–76.

Butler, Robert N. 1969. Age-ism: Another form of bigotry. *The Gerontologist, 9,* 243–246.

Butler, Robert N. 1975. *Why survive: Being old in America.* New York: Harper & Row.

Butler, Robert N. 1980. Ageism: A foreword. *Journal of Social Issues, 36*(2), 8–11.

Butler, Robert N. & Lewis, Myrna I. 1976. *Sex after sixty: A guide for men and women for their later years.* New York: Harper & Row.

Butler, Robert N. & Lewis, Myrna I. 1977. *Aging and mental health: Positive psychosocial approaches* (2nd ed.). St. Louis: Mosby.

Caine, Lynn. 1975. *Widow.* New York: Bantam.

Cameron, Paul. 1972. The generation gap: Time orientation. *The Gerontologist, 12,* 117–119.

Cantor, Marjorie & Little, Virginia. 1985. Aging and social care. In R. H. Binstock & E. Shanas (Eds.), *Handbook of aging and the social sciences* (2nd ed., pp. 745–781). New York: Van Nostrand Reinhold.

Caspi, Avshalom & Elder, Glen H., Jr. 1986. Life satisfaction in old age: Linking social psychology and history. *Psychology and Aging, 1,* 18–26.

Cavanaugh, John C.; Kramer, Deirdre A.; Sinnott, Jan D.; Camp, Cameron J.; & Markley, Robert P. 1985. On missing links and such: Interfaces between cognitive research and everyday problem-solving. *Human Development, 28,* 146–168.

Cerella, J. 1985. Information processing rates in the elderly. *Psychological Bulletin, 98,* 67–83.

Charness, Neil 1988. Expertise in chess, music, and physics: A cognitive perspective. In L. K. Obler & D. Fein (Eds.), *The exceptional brain: Neuropsychology of talent and special abilities* (pp. 399–426). New York: Guilford Press.

Chen, Y. P. 1973. A pilot survey study of the housing-annuity plan. Offset. Los Angeles: University of California, Graduate School of Management. (Cited in Streib, 1976.)

Cherlin, Andrew. 1987. Women and the family. In S. E. Rix (Ed.), *The American woman, 1987–88* (pp. 67–99). New York: Norton.

Cherlin, Andrew & Furstenberg, Frank F. 1985. Styles and strategies of grandparenting. In V. L. Bengtson & J. F. Robertson (Eds.), *Grandparenthood* (pp. 97–116). Beverly Hills, CA: Sage Publications.

Chilman, Catherine S. 1983. *Adolescent sexuality in a changing American society* (2nd ed.). New York: Wiley.

Chilman, Catherine S. 1988. Never-married, single, adolescent parents. In C. S. Chilman, E. W. Nunnally & F. M. Cox (Eds.), *Variant family forms* (pp. 17–38). Newbury Park, CA: Sage Publications.

Chiriboga, David A. 1980. Stress and coping: Introduction. In L. W. Poon (Ed.), *Aging in the 1980s: Psychological issues* (pp. 343–345). Washington, DC: American Psychological Association.

Chiriboga, David A. 1982a. Adaptation to marital separation in later and earlier life. *Journal of Gerontology, 37,* 109–114.

Chiriboga, David A. 1982b. Consistency in adult functioning: The influence of social stress. *Ageing and Society, 2*(Part 1), 7–29.

Chiriboga, David A. 1984. Social stressors as antecedents of change. *Journal of Gerontology, 39,* 468–477.

Chiriboga, David. 1987. Personality in later life. In P. Silverman (Ed.), *The elderly as modern pioneers* (pp. 133–157). Bloomington: Indiana University Press.

Chiriboga, David A. & Cutler, Loraine. 1977. Stress responses among divorcing men and women. *Journal of Divorce, 1,* 95–106.

Chiriboga, David A. & Cutler, Loraine. 1980. Stress and adaptation: Life span perspectives. In L. W. Poon (Ed.), *Aging in the 1980s: Psychological issues* (pp. 347–362). Washington, DC: American Psychological Association.

Cicero, Marcus Tullius. 1967. *On old age.* (Translated by F. O. Copley.) Ann Arbor: University of Michigan Press.

Cicourel, Aaron V. & Kitsuse, John I. 1968. The social organization of the high school and deviant adolescent careers. In E. Rubington & M. S. Weinberg (Eds.), *Deviance: The interactionist perspective* (pp. 124–135). New York: Macmillan Co.

Clark, Don. 1988. *As we are.* Boston: Alyson.

Clausen, John A. 1968. Introduction. In J. A. Clausen (Ed.), *Socialization and society* (pp. 1–17). Boston: Little, Brown.

Clayton, Paula J. 1971. Bereavement: Concepts of management. *Psychiatry/1971,* 59, 63. (Published by *Medical World News.*)

Clayton, Paula J.; Halikes, James A.; & Maurice, William L. 1971. The bereavement of the widowed. *Diseases of the Nervous System, 32,* 597–604.

Clayton, Vivian. 1982. Wisdom and intelligence: The nature and function of knowledge in the later years. *International Journal of Aging and Human Development, 15,* 315–321.

Clayton, Vivian P. & Birren, James E. 1980. The development of wisdom across the life span: A reexamination of an ancient topic. In P. B Baltes & O. G. Brim, Jr. (Eds.), *Life-span development and behavior* (Vol. 3, pp. 103–135). New York: Academic Press.

Clemente, Frank & Kleiman, Michael B. 1976. Fear of crime among the aged. *The Gerontologist, 16,* 207–210.

Cohen, Frances. 1980. Coping with surgery: Information, psychological preparation, and recovery. In L. W. Poon (Ed.), *Aging in the 1980s: Psychological issues* (pp. 375–382). Washington, DC: American Psychological Association.

Cohler, B. J. 1982. Personal narrative and the life course. In P. B. Baltes & O. G. Brim, Jr. (Eds.), *Life-span development and behavior* (Vol. 4, pp. 205–241). New York: Academic Press.

Cohn, Richard M. 1979. Age and the satisfactions from work. *Journal of Gerontology, 34,* 264–272.

Comfort, Alex. 1964. *Ageing: The biology of senescence.* New York: Holt, Rinehart & Winston.

Comfort, Alex. 1968. Feasibility in age research. *Nature, 217,* 320–322.

Comfort, Alex. 1974. Sexuality in old age. *Journal of the American Geriatrics Society, 22,* 440–442.

Comfort, Alex. 1976. *A good age.* New York: Crown.

Commonwealth Fund. 1987. *Old, alone and poor: A plan for reducing poverty among elderly people living alone.* Available from The Commonwealth Fund, 624 N. Broadway, Baltimore, MD 21205-1901.

Conger, John J. 1975. Proceedings of the American Psychological Association, Incorporated, for the year 1974: Minutes of the annual meeting of the Council of Representatives. *American Psychologist, 30,* 620–651.

Conger, John J. 1977. *Adolescence and youth* (2nd ed.). New York: Harper & Row.

Cook, Fay Lomax; Skogan, Wesley G.; Cook, Thomas D.; & Antunes, George E. 1978. Criminal victimization of the elderly: The physical and economic consequences. *The Gerontologist, 18,* 338–349.

Cool, Linda Evers. 1987. The effects of social class and ethnicity on the aging process. In P. Silverman (Ed.), *The elderly as modern pioneers* (pp. 263–282). Bloomington: Indiana University Press.

Cooley, Charles H. 1911. *Social organization.* New York: Scribner's.

Cooper, Kathryn L. & Gutmann, David L. 1987. Gender identity and ego mastery style in middle-aged, pre- and post-empty nest women. *The Gerontologist, 27,* 347–352.

Costa, Paul T., Jr. & McCrae, Robert R. 1980a. Somatic complaints in males as a function of age and neuroticism: A longitudinal analysis. *Journal of Behavioral Medicine, 3,* 245–257.

Costa, Paul T., Jr. & McCrae, Robert R. 1980b. Still stable after all these years: Personality as a key to some issues in adulthood and old age. In P. B. Baltes & O. G. Brim, Jr. (Eds.), *Life-span development and behavior* (Vol. 3, pp. 65–102). New York: Academic Press.

Costa, Paul T., Jr. & McCrae, Robert R. 1985. Hypochondriasis, neuroticism, and aging: When are somatic complaints unfounded? *American Psychologist, 40,* 19–28.

Costa, Paul T., Jr. & McCrae, Robert R. 1988. Personality in adulthood: A six-year longitudinal study of self-reports and spouse ratings on the NEO Personality Inventory. *Journal of Personality and Social Psychology, 54,* 853–863.

Costa, Paul T., Jr.; McCrae, Robert R.; Zonderman, Alan B.; Barbano, Helen E.; Lebowitz, Barry; & Larson, David M. 1986. Cross-sectional studies of personality in a national sample: 2. Stability in neuroticism, extraversion, and openness. *Psychology and Aging, 1,* 144–149.

Cowan, Alison L. 1989 (March 12). 'Parentood II': The nest won't stay empty. *New York Times,* 1, 30.

Cowan, Gloria; Warren, Lynda W.; & Young, Joyce L. 1985. Medical perceptions of menopausal symptoms. *Psychology of Women Quarterly, 9,* 3–14.

Cowgill, Donald O. & Holmes, Lowell D. (Eds.). 1972. *Aging and modernization.* New York: Appleton–Century–Crofts.

Craik, Fergus I. M.; Byrd, Mark; & Swanson, James M. 1987. Patterns of memory loss in three elderly samples. *Psychology and Aging, 2,* 79–86.

Crouter, Ann C. 1984. Participative work as an influence on human development. *Journal of Applied Developmental Psychology, 5,* 71–90.

Cumming, Elaine & Henry, William E. 1961. *Growing old: The process of disengagement.* New York: Basic Books.

Cunningham, John D. & Antill, John K. 1984. Changes in masculinity and femininity across the family life cycle: A reexamination. *Developmental Psychology, 20,* 1135–1141.

Curtis, Howard J. 1966. *Biological mechanisms of aging.* Springfield, IL: Charles C Thomas.

Cutler, L. & Chiriboga, D. 1976 (October). *Coping process in the organically impaired elderly.* Paper presented at the meeting of the Gerontological Society of America, New York. (Cited in Chiriboga, 1980.)

Datan, Nancy. 1986. Corpses, lepers, and menstruating women: Tradition, transition, and the sociology of knowledge. *Sex Roles, 14,* 693–703.

Datan, Nancy; Antonovsky, Aaron; & Maoz, Benjamin. 1981. *A time to reap: The middle age of women in five Israeli subcultures.* Baltimore: Johns Hopkins University Press.

David, Deborah S. & Brannon, Robert (Eds.). 1976. *The forty-nine percent majority: Male sex role.* Reading, MA: Addison–Wesley.

Davies, Ruth; Lacks, Patricia; Storandt, Martha; & Bertelson, Amy D. 1986. Countercontrol treatment of sleep-maintenance insomnia in relation to age. *Psychology and Aging, 1,* 233–238.

Dawson, Deborah; Hendershot, Gerry; & Fulton, John. 1987 (June 10). Aging in the eighties: Functional limitations of individuals age 65 years and over. *Advance Data* No. 133, National Center for Health Statistics. (Cited in U.S. Senate, 1987–1988, pp. 104–105.)

Dement, William; Richardson, Gary; Prinz, Patricia; Carskadon, Mary; Kripke, Daniel; & Czeisler, Charles. 1985. Changes of sleep and wakefulness with age. In C. E. Finch & E. L. Schneider (Eds.), *Handbook of the biology of aging* (2nd ed., pp. 692–717). New York: Van Nostrand Reinhold.

Dennis, Helen (Ed.). 1984. *Retirement preparation: What retirement specialists need to know.* Lexington, MA: Lexington Books.

Deutsch, Helene. 1945. *The psychology of women: A psychoanalytic interpretation. Vol. 2, Motherhood.* New York: Grune & Stratton.

Deutscher, Irwin. 1964. The quality of postparental life. *Journal of Marriage and the Family, 26,* 263–268.

Dittmann-Kohli, Freya & Baltes, Paul B. In press. Toward a neofunctionalist conception of adult intellectual development: Wisdom as a prototypical case of intellectual growth. In C. Alexander & E. Langer (Eds.), *Beyond formal operations: Alternative endpoints to human development.* New York: Oxford University Press.

Dorian, B.; Garfinkel, P.; Brown, G.; Shore, A.; Gladman, D.; & Keystone, E. 1982. Aberrations in lymphocyte subpopulations and function during psychological stress. *Clinical and Experimental Immunology, 50,* 132–138.

Dovenmuehle, Robert H. 1970. Aging versus illness. In E. Palmore (Ed.), *Normal aging* (pp. 39–47). Durham, NC: Duke University Press.

Dovenmuehle, Robert H.; Busse, Ewald W.; & Newman, Gustave. 1961. Physical problems of older people. *Journal of the American Geriatrics Society, 9,* 208–217.

Dressel, Paula L. 1988. Gender, race, and class: Beyond the feminization of poverty in later life. *The Gerontologist, 28,* 177–180.

Droege, Ruth. 1982. A psychosocial study of the formation of the middle adult life structure in women. *Dissertation Abstracts International, 43,* 1635B. (University Microfilms No. 82-23517.)

Duncan, Otis Dudley. 1961. A socioeconomic index for all occupations. In A. J. Reiss, Jr., et al. *Occupations and social status.* New York: Free Press of Glencoe.

Duvall, Evelyn M. 1971. *Family development* (4th ed.). Philadelphia: Lippincott.

Eakes, Georgene G. 1985. The relationship between death anxiety and attitudes toward the elderly among nursing staff. *Death Studies, 9,* 163–172.

Easterlin, Richard A. 1980. *Birth and fortune: The impact of numbers on personal welfare.* New York: Basic Books.

Edwards, John N. & Klemmack, David L. 1973. Correlates of life satisfaction: A re-examination. *Journal of Gerontology, 28,* 497–502.

Einstein, Albert. 1961. *Relativity: The special and general theory.* (Translated by R. W. Lawson.) New York: Crown.

Ekerdt, David J. 1987. Why the notion persists that retirement harms health. *The Gerontologist, 27,* 454–457.

Elder, Glen H., Jr. 1974. *Children of the Great Depression.* Chicago: University of Chicago Press.

Elder, Glen H., Jr. 1982. Historical experiences in the later years. In T. K. Hareven & K. J. Adams (Eds.), *Aging and life course transitions: An interdisciplinary perspective* (pp. 75–107). New York: Guilford Press.

Elliott, G. R. & Eisdorfer, C. (Eds.) 1982. *Stress and human health.* New York: Springer.

Elstein, A. S.; Shulman, L. S.; & Sprafka, S. A. 1978. *Medical problem solving: An analysis of clinical reasoning.* Cambridge, MA: Harvard University Press.

Elwell, F. & Maltbie-Crannell, Alice D. 1981. The impact of role loss upon coping resources and life satisfaction of the elderly. *Journal of Gerontology, 36,* 223–232.

Entwisle, Doris R. & Doering, Susan G. 1981. *The first birth: A family turning point.* Baltimore: Johns Hopkins University Press.

Erikson, Erik H. 1950. *Childhood and society.* New York: Norton.

Erikson, Erik H. 1968. *Identity: Youth and crisis.* New York: Norton.

Erikson, Erik H. 1976. Reflections on Dr. Borg's life cycle. *Daedalus, 105,* 1–28.

Ettinger, B.; Genant, H. K.; & Cann, C. E. 1987. Low-dosage estrogen combined with calcium prevents postmenopausal bone loss: Results of a 3 year study. In D. V. Cohn & T. J. Martin (Eds.), *Osteoporosis* (pp. 21–26). Amsterdam: Elsevier.

Exton-Smith, A. N. 1985. Mineral metabolism. In C. E. Finch & E. L. Schneider (Eds.), *Handbook of the biology of aging* (2nd ed., pp. 511–539). New York: Van Nostrand Reinhold.

Feifel, Herman. 1963. Death. In N. L. Farberow (Ed.), *Taboo topics* (pp. 8–21). New York: Atherton.

Fellin, Phillip A. & Powell, Thomas J. 1988. Mental health services and older adult minorities: An assessment. *The Gerontologist, 28,* 442–447.

Felton, Barbara & Kahana, Eva 1974. Adjustment and situationally-bound locus of control among institutionalized aged. *Journal of Gerontology, 29,* 295–301.

Field, Tiffany M. & Widmayer, Susan M. 1982. Motherhood. In B. B. Wolman (Ed.), *Handbook of developmental psychology* (pp. 681–701). Englewood Cliffs, NJ: Prentice–Hall.

Filipp, Sigrun-Heide & Klauer, Thomas. 1986. Conceptions of self over the life span: Reflections on the dialectics of change. In M. M. Baltes & P. B. Baltes (Eds.), *The psychology of control and aging* (pp. 167–205). Hillsdale, NJ: Erlbaum.

Finch, Caleb E. & Landfield, Philip W. 1985. Neuroendocrine and autonomic functions in aging mammals. In C. E. Finch & E. L. Schneider (Eds.), *Handbook of the biology of aging* (2nd ed., pp. 567–594). New York: Van Nostrand Reinhold.

Finch, Caleb E. & Schneider, Edward L. 1985. *Handbook of the biology of aging* (2nd ed.). New York: Van Nostrand Reinhold.

Fiske, Marjorie. 1978 (November). *Adult transitions: Theory and research from a longitudinal perspective.* Paper presented at the meeting of the Gerontological Society, Dallas.

Fiske, Marjorie & Chiriboga, David A. 1985. The interweaving of societal and personal change in adulthood. In J. M. A. Munnichs, P. Mussen, E. Olbrich & P. G. Coleman (Eds.), *Life-span and change in a gerontological perspective* (pp. 177–209). Orlando, FL: Academic Press.

Flemming, Arthur S.; Rickards, Larry D.; Santos, John F.; & West, P. R. 1986. Mental health services for the elderly: Report on a survey of community mental health centers. *Action committee to implement the mental health recommendations of the 1981 White House conference on aging* (Vol. 3). Washington, DC: American Psychological Association.

Folkman, Susan; Bernstein, Linda; & Lazarus, Richard S. 1987. Stress processes and the misuse of drugs in older adults. *Psychology and Aging, 2,* 366–374.

Foner, Nancy. 1984. *Ages in conflict: A cross-cultural perspective on inequality between old and young.* New York: Columbia University Press.

Fowler, Elizabeth M. 1988 (November 15). Gerontology: Big demand for workers. *New York Times,* D21.

Fozard, James L.; Wolf, Ernst; Bell, Benjamin; McFarland, Ross A.; & Podolsky, Stephen. 1977. Visual perception and communication. In J. E. Birren & K. W. Schaie (Eds.), *Handbook of the psychology of aging* (pp. 497–534). New York: Van Nostrand Reinhold.

Frenkel, Else. 1936. Studies in biographical psychology. *Character and Personality, 5,* 1–34.

Friedman, M.; Rosenman, R. H.; Straus, R.; Wurm, M.; & Kositchek, R. 1968. The relationship of behavior Pattern A to the state of the coronary vasculature: A study of fifty-one autopsy subjects. *American Journal of Medicine, 44,* 525–537.

Fromm, Erich. 1941. *Escape from freedom.* New York: Avon.

Fry, Christine L. 1985. Culture, behavior, and aging in the comparative perspective. In J. E. Birren & K. W. Schaie (Eds.), *Handbook of the psychology of aging* (2nd ed., pp. 216–244). New York: Van Nostrand Reinhold.

Furst, Kathryn A. 1983. Origins and evolution of women's dreams in early adulthood. *Dissertation Abstracts International, 44,* 2242B. (University Microfilms No. 83-26138.)

Furstenberg, Frank F., Jr. & Spanier, Graham B. 1984. *Recycling the family: Remarriage after divorce.* Beverly Hills, CA: Sage Publications.

Gatz, Margaret. 1989. Clinical psychology and aging. In M. Storandt & G. R. VandenBos (Eds.), *The adult years: Continuity and change* (pp. 83–114). Washington, DC: American Psychological Association.

Gatz, Margaret & Pearson, Cynthia G. 1988. Ageism revised and the provision of psychological services. *American Psychologist, 43,* 184–188.

Gelfand, Donald E. & Barresi, Charles M. (Eds.) 1987. *Ethnic dimensions of aging.* New York: Springer.

Gendlin, Eugene T. 1964. A theory of personality change. In P. Worchel & D.Bryne (Eds.), *Personality change* (pp. 100–148). New York: Wiley.

George, Linda K. 1980. *Role transitions in later life.* Monterey, CA: Brooks/Cole.

George, Linda K. 1988. Social participation in later life: Black-White differences. In J. S. Jackson (Ed.), *The Black American elderly: Research on physical and psychosocial health* (pp. 99–126). New York: Springer.

George, Linda K. & Weiler, Stephen J. 1981. Sexuality in middle and late life: The effects of age, cohort, and gender. *Archives of General Psychiatry, 38,* 919–923.

Gerber, Irwin; Rusalem, Roslyn; Hannon, Natalie; Battin, Delia; & Arkin, Arthur. 1975. Anticipatory grief and aged widows and widowers. *Journal of Gerontology, 30,* 225–229.

Germaine, Leonard M. & Freedman, Robert R. 1984. Behavioral treatment of menopausal hot flashes: Evaluation by objective methods. *Journal of Consulting and Clinical Psychology, 52,* 1072–1079.

Giambra, Leonard M. 1977. Daydreaming about the past: The time setting of spontaneous thought intrusions. *The Gerontologist, 17,* 35–38.

Gibbs, Tyson. 1988. Health-seeking behavior of elderly Blacks. In J. S. Jackson (Ed.), *The Black American elderly: Research on physical and psychosocial health* (pp. 282–291). New York: Springer.

Gibeau, Janice. 1988. Working caregivers: Family conflicts and adaptations of older workers. In R. Morris & S. A. Bass (Eds.), *Retirement reconsidered: Economic and social roles for older people* (pp. 185–201). New York: Springer.

Gibson, Donald E. 1984. Hospice: Morality and economics. *The Gerontologist, 24,* 4-8.

Gibson, Rose C. 1983. Work patterns of older Black female heads of household. *Journal of Minority Aging, 8,* 2-17.

Gibson, Rose C. 1986. Outlook for the Black family. In A. Pifer & L. Bronte (Eds.), *Our aging society: Paradox and promise* (pp. 181-197). New York: Norton.

Gibson, Rose C. 1987. Reconceptualizing retirement for Black Americans. *The Gerontologist, 27,* 691-698.

Gilbert, Jeanne G. & Levee, Raymond F. 1971. Patterns of declining memory. *Journal of Gerontology, 26,* 70-75.

Gilbert, L. A. 1985. *Men in dual-career families.* Hillsdale, NJ: Erlbaum.

Gilligan, Carol. 1982. *In a different voice: Psychological theory and women's development.* Cambridge, MA: Harvard University Press.

Ginsburg, Herbert & Opper, Sylvia. 1979. *Piaget's theory of intellectual development: An introduction* (2nd ed.). Englewood Cliffs, NJ: Prentice–Hall.

Glascock, A. P. & Feinman, S. 1981. Social asset or social burden: Treatment of the aged in non-industrial societies. In C. L. Fry (Ed.), *Dimensions: Aging, culture and health* (pp. 13–32). New York: Praeger.

Glaser, Barney G. & Strauss, Anselm L. 1965. Temporal aspects of dying as a non-scheduled status passage. *American Journal of Sociology, 71,* 48–59.

Glick, Ira O.; Weiss, Robert S.; & Parkes, C. Murray. 1974. *The first year of bereavement.* New York: Wiley.

Glick, Paul C. 1977. Updating the life cycle of the family. *Journal of Marriage and the Family, 39,* 5–13.

Glick, Paul C. 1980. Marriage experiences of family life specialists. *Family Relations, 29,* 111–118.

Glick, Paul C. 1988. Fifty years of family demography: A record of social change. *Journal of Marriage and the Family, 50,* 861–873.

Glick, Paul C. 1989a. Remarried families, stepfamilies, and stepchildren: A brief demographic profile. *Family Relations, 38,* 24–27.

Glick, Paul C. 1989b. The family life cycle and social change. *Family Relations, 38,* 123–129.

Glick, Paul C. & Lin, Sung-Ling. 1986. Recent changes in divorce and remarriage. *Journal of Mariage and the Family, 48,* 737–747.

Glick, Paul C. & Lin, Sung-Ling. 1987. Remarriage after divorce: Recent changes and demographic variations. *Sociological Perspectives, 30,* 162–179.

Goffman, E. 1961. *Asylums.* Chicago: Aldine.

Gohmann, Stephan F. & McClure, James E. 1987. Supreme Court rulings on pension plans: The effect on retirement age and wealth of single people. *The Gerontologist, 27,* 471–477.

Golant, Stephen M. 1984. *A place to grow old: The meaning of environment in old age.* New York: Columbia University Press.

Gompertz, B. 1825. On the nature of the function expressive of the law of human mortality on a new mode of determining life contingencies. *Philosophical Transaction of the Royal Society (London), Series A, 115,* 513–585.

Goodman, Madeleine J.; Grove, John S.; & Gilbert, Fred, Jr. 1978. Age at menopause in relation to reproductive history in Japanese, Caucasian, Chinese and Hawaiian women living in Hawaii. *Journal of Gerontology, 33,* 688–694.

Goody, Jack. 1976. Aging in nonindustrial societies. In R. H. Binstock & E. Shanas (Eds.), *Handbook of aging and the social sciences* (pp. 117–129). New York: Van Nostrand Reinhold.

Gorer, Geoffrey. 1965. *Death, grief and mourning in contemporary Britain.* London: Cresset.

Gottschaldt, K. 1960. Das Problem der Phanogenetick der Personlichkeit. In P. Lersh & H. Thomas (Eds.), *Personlichkeits Forschung und Personlichkeits Theorie, Handbuch der Psychologie* (Vol. 4). Göttingen: Hofgrefie. (Cited in Thompson, 1968.)

Gottsegen, Gloria B. & Park, Paul D. (Eds.). 1982. Psychotherapy in later life. *Psychotherapy: Theory, Research & Practice, 19* (Whole No. 4).

Gould, Roger L. 1972. The phases of adult life: A study in developmental psychology. *American Journal of Psychiatry, 129,* 521–531.

Gould, Roger L. 1978. *Transformations: Growth and change in adult life.* New York: Simon & Schuster.

Granick, Samuel & Patterson, Robert D. (Eds.) 1971. *Human aging II: An eleven-year followup biomedical and behavioral study.* Publication No. (HSM) 71-9037. Washington, DC: U.S. Government Printing Office.

Gray, Heather & Dressel, Paula. 1985. Alternative interpretations of aging among gay males. *The Gerontologist, 25,* 83–87.

Greeley, Andrew M. 1971. *Why can't they be like us.* New York: Dutton.

Gruman, Gerald J. 1978. Cultural origins of present-day "age-ism": The modernization of the life cycle. In S. F. Spicker, K. M. Woodward & D. D. Van Tassel (Eds.), *Aging and the elderly: Humanistic perspectives in gerontology* (pp. 359–387). Atlantic Highlands, NJ: Humanities Press.

Gubrium, Jaber F. 1976. Being single in old age. In J. F. Gubrium (Ed.), *Time, roles, and self in old age* (pp. 179–195). New York: Human Sciences Press.

Guillerme, J. 1963. *Longevity.* New York: Walker and Co.

Gutmann, David L. 1964. An exploration of ego configurations in middle and late life. In B. L. Neugarten & Associates (Eds.), *Personality in middle and late life* (pp. 114–148). New York: Atherton Press.

Gutmann, David L. 1967. Aging among the highland Maya: A comparative study. *Journal of Personality and Social Psychology, 7,* 28–35.

Gutmann, David 1977. The cross-cultural perspective: Notes toward a comparative psychology of aging. In J. E. Birren & K. W. Schaie (Eds.), *Handbook of the psychology of aging* (pp. 302–326). New York: Van Nostrand Reinhold.

Gutmann, David. 1987. *Reclaimed powers: Toward a new psychology of men and women in later life.* New York: Basic Books.

Guttmann, David. 1977. *A study of legal drug use by older Americans.* (NIDA Services Research Report). Washington, DC: U.S. Government Printing Office.

Haan, Norma. 1981. Common dimensions of personality development: Early adolescence to middle life. In D. H. Eichorn, J. A. Clausen, N. Haan, M. P. Honzik & P. H. Mussen (Eds.), *Present and past in middle life* (pp. 117–151). New York: Academic Press.

Hagestad, Gunhild O. 1981. Problems and promises in the social psychology of intergenerational relations. In R. W. Fogel et al. (Eds.), *Aging: Stability and change in the family* (pp. 11–46). New York: Academic Press.

Hagestad, Gunhild O. 1982a (Winter). Divorce: The family ripple effect. *Generations, 6,* 24–31.

Hagestad, Gunhild O. 1982b. Parent and child: Generations in the family. In T. M. Field et al. (Eds.), *Review of human development* (pp. 485–499). New York: Wiley.

Hagestad, Gunhild O. 1984. The continuous bond: A dynamic multigenerational perspective on parent–child relations between adults. In M. Perlmutter (Ed.), *Parent–child interaction and parent–child relations in child development* (pp. 129–158), The Minnesota Symposium on Child Psychology (Vol. 17). Hillsdale, NJ: Erlbaum.

Hagestad, Gunhild O. 1985. Continuity and connectedness. In V. L. Bengtson & J. F. Robertson (Eds.), *Grandparenthood* (pp. 31–48). Beverly Hills, CA: Sage Publications.

Hagestad, Gunhild O. 1987. Families in an aging society. *Zeitschrift für Sozialisationsforschung und Erziehungssoziologie (ZSE), 7,* 148–160.

Hagestad, Gunhild O. 1988. Able elderly in the family context: Changes, chances, and challenges. In R. Morris & S. A. Bass (Eds.), *Retirement reconsidered: Economic and social roles for older people* (pp. 171–184). New York: Springer.

Hagestad, Gunhild O. & Burton, Linda M. 1986. Grandparenthood, life context, and family development. *American Behavioral Scientist, 29,* 471–484.

Hagestad, Gunhild O. & Neugarten, Bernice L. 1985. Age and the life course. In R. H. Binstock & E. Shanas (Eds.), *Handbook of aging and the social sciences* (2nd ed., pp. 35–61). New York: Van Nostrand Reinhold.

Haight, Barbara K. 1988. The therapeutic role of a structured life review process in homebound elderly subjects. *Journal of Gerontology: Psychological Sciences, 43,* P40–P44.

Hall, Douglas T. 1976. *Careers in organization.* Pacific Palisades, CA: Goodyear.

Hamilton, Edith. 1940. *Mythology: Timeless tales of gods and heroes.* Boston: Little, Brown.

Harkins, Stephen W.; Price, Donald D.; & Martelli, Michael. 1986. Effects of age on pain perception: Thermonociception. *Journal of Gerontology, 41,* 58–63.

Harlan, William H. 1964. Social status of the aged in three Indian villages. *Vita Humana, 7,* 239–252.

Harman, D. 1981. The aging process. *Proceedings of the National Academy of Sciences USA, 78,* 7124–7128.

Harman, Denham. 1987. The free-radical theory of aging. In H. R. Warner, R. N. Butler, R. L. Sprott & E. L. Schneider (Eds.), *Modern biological theories of aging* (pp. 81–87). New York: Raven Press.

Harman, S. Mitchell & Talbert, George B. 1985. Reproductive aging. In C. E. Finch & E. L. Schneider (Eds.), *Handbook of the biology of aging* (2nd ed., pp. 457–510). New York: Van Nostrand Reinhold.

Harris, Louis. 1986. Problems facing elderly Americans living alone. (National survey cited in *Aging alone*, a report of the Commonwealth Fund commission on elderly people living alone, 1988.)

Harris, Mary B. & Turner, Pauline H. 1986. Gay and lesbian parents. *Journal of Homosexuality, 12*(2), 101–113.

Harris, Sidney J. 1965 (May 11). Strictly personal. *Chicago Daily News.* (Cited in Neugarten, 1967b/1968.)

Harrison, David E. 1985. Cell and tissue transplantation: A means of studying the aging process. In C. E. Finch & E. L. Schneider (Eds.), *Handbook of the biology of aging* (2nd ed., pp. 322–356). New York: Van Nostrand Reinhold.

Harry, Joseph. 1988. Some problems of gay/lesbian families. In C. S. Chilman, E. W. Nunnally & F. M. Cox (Eds.), *Variant family forms* (pp. 96–113). Newbury Park, CA: Sage Publications.

Hauser, Philip M. 1976. Aging and world-wide population change. In R. H. Binstock & E. Shanas (Eds.), *Handbook of aging and the social sciences* (pp. 59–86). New York: Van Nostrand Reinhold.

Havighurst, Robert J. & Glasser, Richard. 1972. An exploratory study of reminiscence. *Journal of Gerontology, 27,* 245–253.

Havighurst, Robert J.; Neugarten, Bernice L.; & Tobin, Sheldon S. 1963/1968. Disengagement and patterns of aging. In B. L. Neugarten (Ed.), *Middle age and aging* (pp. 161–172). Chicago: University of Chicago Press, 1968. (Paper presented at the meeting of the International Association of Gerontology, Copenhagen, August 1963.)

Hayflick, Leonard. 1965. The limited *in vitro* lifetime of human diploid cell strains. *Experimental Cell Research, 37,* 614–636.

Hayflick, Leonard. 1966. Senescence in cultured cells. In N. W. Shock (Ed.), *Perspectives in experimental gerontology.* Springfield, IL: Charles C Thomas.

Hayflick, Leonard. 1970. Aging under glass. *Experimental Gerontology, 5,* 291–303.

Hayflick, Leonard. 1987. Origins of longevity. In H. R. Warner, R. N. Butler, R. L. Sprott & E. L. Schneider (Eds.), *Modern biological theories of aging* (pp. 21–34). New York: Raven Press.

Heine, Patricke Johns. 1971. *Personality in social theory.* Chicago: Aldine

Henry, William E. 1965 (September). *Identity and diffusion in professional actors.* Paper presented at the meeting of the American Psychological Association.

Henry, William E.; Sims, John H.; & Spray, S. Lee. 1971. *The fifth profession: Becoming a psychotherapist.* San Francisco: Jossey-Bass.

Hertzog, Christopher & Schaie, K. Warner. 1986. Stability and change in adult intelligence: 1. Analysis of longitudinal covariance structures. *Psychology and Aging, 1,* 159–171.

Hetherington, E. M. 1979. A child's perspective. *American Psychologist, 34,* 851–858.

Higginbotham, Elizabeth. 1981. Is marriage a priority? Class differences in marital options of educated Black women. In P. J. Stein (Ed.), *Single life: Unmarried adults in social context* (pp. 259–267). New York: St. Martin's Press.

Hill, Connie Dessonville; Thompson, Larry W.; & Gallagher, Dolores. 1988. The role of anticipatory bereavement in older women's adjustment to widowhood. *The Gerontologist, 28,* 792–796.

Hing, Esther. 1987. Use of nursing homes by the elderly: Preliminary data from the 1985 National Nursing Home Survey. *Advance Data* No. 135, National Center for Health Statistics (May 14, 1987). (Cited in U.S. Senate, 1987–1988, p. 118.)

Hinton, John. 1967. *Dying.* Baltimore: Penguin.

Hobbs, Daniel F., Jr. 1965. Parenthood as crisis: A third study. *Journal of Marriage and the Family, 27,* 367–372.

Hobbs, Daniel F., Jr. & Cole, Sue P. 1976. Transition to parenthood: A decade replication. *Journal of Marriage and the Family, 38,* 723–731.

Hobbs, Daniel F., Jr. & Wimbish, Jane M. 1977. Transition to parenthood by Black couples. *Journal of Marriage and the Family, 39,* 677–689.

Hoffman, Lois Wladis. 1972. Early childhood experiences and women's achievement motives. *Journal of Social Issues, 28*(2), 129–156.

Hoffman, Lois Wladis. 1984. Marital employment and the young child. In M. Perlmutter

(Ed.), *Parent–child interaction and parent–child relations in child development* (pp. 101–128), The Minnesota Symposium on Child Psychology (Vol. 17). Hillsdale, NJ: Erlbaum.

Hoffman, Lois Wladis. 1986. Work, family, and the child. In M. S. Pallak & R. Perloff (Eds.), *Psychology and work: Productivity, change, and employment* (pp. 173–220). Washington, DC: American Psychological Association.

Hofstetter, H. W. 1944. A comparison of Duane's and Donders' tables of the amplitude of accommodation. *American Journal of Optometry and Archives of American Academy of Optometry, 21,* 345–363.

Holden, Constance. 1976. Hospices: For the dying, relief from pain and fear. *Science, 193,* 389–391.

Holland, John L. 1973. *Making vocational choices: A theory of careers.* Englewood Cliffs, NJ: Prentice–Hall.

Holland, J. L. 1985. *Professional manual for the self-directed search.* Odessa, FL: Psychological Assessment Resources.

Holland, John L. & Rayman, Jack R. 1985. The self-directed search. In W. B. Walsh & S. H. Osipow (Eds.), *Advances in vocational psychology. Volume I: The assessment of interests* (pp. 55–82). Hillsdale, NJ: Erlbaum.

Horn, J. L. 1970. Organization of data on life span development of human abilities. In L. R. Goulet & P. B. Baltes (Eds.), *Life-span developmental psychology: Research and theory* (pp. 423–466). New York: Academic Press.

Horn, John L. 1982. The aging of human abilities. In B. B. Wolman (Ed.), *Handbook of developmental psychology* (pp. 847–870). Englewood Cliffs, NJ: Prentice–Hall.

Horn, John L. & Cattell, Raymond B. 1967. Age differences in fluid and crystallized intelligence. *Acta Psychologica, 26,* 107–129.

Horn, John L. & Donaldson, Gary 1976. On the myth of intellectual decline in adulthood. *American Psychologist, 31,* 701–719.

Horowitz, Mardi J. & Wilner, Nancy. 1980. Life events, stress, and coping. In L. W. Poon (Ed.), *Aging in the 1980s* (pp. 363–374). Washington, DC: American Psychological Association.

House, James S. 1975. Occupational stress as a precursor to coronary disease. In W. D. Gentry & R. B. Williams, Jr. (Eds.), *Psychological aspects of myocardial infarction and coronary care* (pp. 24–36). St. Louis: Mosby.

House Committee on Aging. 1977. *Mandatory retirement: The social and human cost of enforced idleness.* (U.S. House of Representatives, Select Committee on Aging.) Washington, DC: U.S. Government Printing Office.

Huyck, Margaret H. 1977. Sex, gender and aging. *Humanitas, 13.*

Huyck, Margaret H. 1989. Give me continuity or give me death. *The Gerontologist, 29,* 148–149.

Hyde, Janet S. & Phillis, Diane E. 1979. Androgyny across the life span. *Developmental Psychology, 15,* 334–336.

Ikels, C. 1980. The coming of age in Chinese society: Traditional patterns and contemporary Hong Kong. In C. L. Fry (Ed.), *Aging in culture and society: Comparative perspectives and strategies* (pp. 80–100). New York: Praeger.

Inhelder, Bärbel & Piaget, Jean. 1958. *The growth of logical thinking from childhood to adolescence.* (Translated by A. Parsons & S. Milgram.) New York: Basic Books.

Jackson, Jacquelyne Johnson. 1980. *Minorities and aging.* Belmont, CA: Wadsworth.

Jackson, James S. (Ed.) 1988. *The Black American elderly: Research on physical and psychosocial health.* New York: Springer.

Jackson, James S. & Gibson, Rose C. 1985. Work and retirement among the Black elderly.

Current perspectives on aging and the life cycle (Vol. 1, pp. 193–222). Greenwich, CT: JAI Press.

James, William. 1892. *Psychology*. New York: Holt.

Janoff-Bulman, Ronnie & Marshall, Grant. 1982. Mortality, well-being, and control: A study of a population of institutionalized aged. *Personality and Social Psychology Bulletin, 8,* 691–698.

Janowitz, Morris. 1965. *Sociology and the military establishment* (rev. ed.). New York: Russell Sage Foundation.

Jaques, Elliott. 1965. Death and the mid-life crisis. *International Journal of Psychoanalysis, 46,* 502–514.

Jarvik, Lissy F. 1988. Aging of the brain: How can we prevent it? *The Gerontologist, 28,* 739–747.

Jarvik, L. F. & La Rue, A. 1979. *Prediction of the development of organic brain syndrome.* Invited address presented at the meeting "Life-Span Research on the Prediction of Psychopathology." (Cited in La Rue, Dessonville & Jarvik, 1985.)

Jarvik, Lissy & Small, Gary. 1988. *Parentcare: A commonsense guide for adult children.* New York: Crown.

Jenkins, C. David. 1971. Psychologic and social precursors of coronary disease. *New England Journal of Medicine, 284,* 244–255, 307–317.

Jenkins, C. David. 1976. Recent evidence supporting psychologic and social risk factors for coronary disease. *New England Journal of Medicine, 294,* 987–994, 1033–1038.

Jenkins, C. David; Rosenman, Ray H.; & Zyzanski, Stephen J. 1974. Prediction of clinical coronary heart disease by a test for the coronary-prone behavior pattern. *New England Journal of Medicine, 290,* 1271–1275.

Jerome, Norge W. 1988. Dietary intake and nutritional status of older U.S. Blacks: An overview. In J. S. Jackson (Ed.), *The Black American elderly: Research on physical and psychosocial health* (pp. 129–149). New York: Springer.

Johnson, Colleen L. & Barer, Barbara M. 1987. Marital instability and the changing kinship networks of grandparents. *The Gerontologist, 27,* 330–335.

Johnson, Colleen L. & Catalano, Donald J. 1983. A longitudinal study of family supports to impaired elderly. *The Gerontologist, 23,* 612–618.

Johnson, J. E. 1975. Stress reduction through sensation information. In I. G. Sarason & C. D. Spielberger (Eds.), *Stress and anxiety* (Vol. 2, pp. 361–378). Washington DC: Hemisphere.

Jones, Hardin B. 1959. The relation of human health to age, place and time. In J. E. Birren (Ed.), *Handbook of aging and the individual* (pp. 336–363). Chicago: University of Chicago Press.

Jung, Carl G. 1933/1971. The stages of life. (Translated by R. F. C. Hull.) In J. Campbell (Ed.), *The portable Jung* (pp. 3–22). New York: Viking.

Kahana, Boaz & Kahana, Eva. 1970. Grandparenthood from the perspective of the developing grandchild. *Developmental Psychology, 3,* 98–105.

Kahana, Eva & Kahana, Boaz. 1982. Environmental continuity, futurity, and adaptation of the aged. In G. Rowles & R. Ohta (Eds.), *Aging and milieu: Environmental perspectives on growing old* (pp. 205–228). New York: Academic Press.

Kahn, Robert L.; Wethington, Elaine; & Ingersoll-Dayton, Berit. 1987. Social support and social networks: Determinants, effects, and interactions. In R. P. Abeles (Ed.), *Life-span perspectives and social psychology* (pp. 139–165). Hillsdale, NJ: Erlbaum.

Kalish, Richard A. 1976. Death and dying in a social context. In R. H. Binstock & E. Shanas (Eds.), *Handbook of aging and the social sciences* (pp. 483–507). New York: Van Nostrand Reinhold.

Kalish, Richard A. 1985. The social context of death and dying. In R. H. Binstock & E. Shanas (Eds.), *Handbook of aging and the social sciences* (2nd ed., pp. 149–170). New York: Van Nostrand Reinhold.

Kalish, Richard A. & Reynolds, David K. 1976. *Death and ethnicity: A psychocultural study.* Los Angeles: University of Southern California Press.

Kallmann, Franz J. & Jarvik, Lissy F. 1959. Individual differences in constitution and genetic background. In J. E. Birren (Ed.), *Handbook of aging and the individual* (pp. 216–263). Chicago: University of Chicago Press.

Kaplan, Philip. 1974. Singles' bars and single men. Unpublished honors thesis, City College of The City University of New York.

Kaprio, Jaakko; Koskenvuo, Markku; & Rita, H. 1987. Mortality after bereavement: A prospective study of 95,647 widowed persons. *American Journal of Public Health, 77,* 283–287.

Karp, David A. 1988. A decade of reminders: Changing age consciousness between fifty and sixty years old. *The Gerontologist, 28,* 727–738.

Kastenbaum, Robert. 1975. Is death a life crisis? On the confrontation with death in theory and practice. In N. Datan & L. H. Ginsberg (Eds.), *Life-span developmental psychology: Normative life crises* (pp. 19–50). New York: Academic Press.

Kastenbaum, Robert. 1985. Dying and death: A life-span approach. In J. E. Birren & K. W. Schaie (Eds.), *Handbook of the psychology of aging* (2nd ed., pp. 619–643). New York: Van Nostrand Reinhold.

Katz, Irwin; Hass, Glen; Parisi, Nina; Astone, Janetta; McEvaddy, Denise; & Lucido, David J. 1987. Lay people's and health care personnel's perceptions of cancer, AIDS, cardiac, and diabetic patients. *Psychological Reports, 60,* 615–629.

Kausler, D. H. 1970. Retention-forgetting as a nomological network for developmental research. In L. R. Goulet & P. B. Baltes (Eds.), *Life-span developmental psychology.* (pp. 305–353). New York: Academic Press.

Kayser-Jones, J. S. 1982. Institutional structures: Catalysts of or barriers to quality care for the institutionalized aged in Scotland and the U.S. *Social Science and Medicine, 16* 935–944.

Keating, Daniel P. 1980. Thinking processes in adolescence. In J. Adelson (Ed.), *Handbook of adolescent psychology* (pp. 211–246). New York: Wiley.

Kehoe, Monika. 1988. Lesbians over 60 speak for themselves. *Journal of Homosexuality, 16* (Whole Numbers 3/4).

Keith, Jennie. 1985. Age in anthropological research. In R. H. Binstock & E. Shanas (Eds.), *Handbook of aging and the social sciences* (2nd ed., pp. 231–263). New York: Van Nostrand Reinhold.

Kelly, Jim. 1977. The aging male homosexual: Myth and reality. *The Gerontologist, 17,* 328–332.

Kelly, John R. 1972. Work and leisure: A simplified paradigm. *Journal of Leisure Research, 4,* 50–62.

Kelly, John R. 1982. *Leisure.* Englewood Cliffs, NJ: Prentice–Hall.

Kelly, John R. 1983. *Leisure identities and interactions.* London and Boston: Allen & Unwin.

Kelly, John R.; Steinkamp, Marjorie W.; & Kelly, Janice R. 1986. Later life leisure: How they play in Peoria. *The Gerontologist, 26,* 531–537.

Kermis, Marguerite D. 1986. The epidemiology of mental disorder in the elderly: A response to the Senate/AARP report. *The Gerontologist, 26,* 482–487.

Kimmel, Douglas C. 1978. Adult development and aging: A gay perspective. *Journal of Social Issues, 34*(3), 113–130.

Kimmel, Douglas C. 1979. Gay people grow old too: Life history interviews of aging gay men. *The International Journal of Aging and Human Development, 10,* 239–248.

Kimmel, Douglas C. 1988. Ageism, psychology, and public policy. *American Psychologist, 43,* 175–178.

Kimmel, Douglas C. & Moody, Harry R. In press. Ethical issues in gerontological research and services. In J. E. Birren & K. W. Schaie (Eds.), *Handbook of the psychology of aging* (3rd ed.). Orlando, FL: Academic Press.

Kimmel, Douglas C.; Price, Karl F.; & Walker, James W. 1978. Retirement choice and retirement satisfaction. *Journal of Gerontology, 33,* 575–585.

Kimmel, Douglas C. & Weiner, Irving B. 1985. *Adolescence: A developmental transition.* Hillsdale, NJ: Erlbaum.

King, Barbara. 1978 (June). Marriage at the top. *Town & Country, 132*(4978), 75–77.

King, P. M.; Kitchener, K. S.; Davison, M. L.; Parker, C. A.; & Wood, P. K. 1983. The justification of beliefs in young adults: A longitudinal study. *Human Development, 26,* 106–116.

Kingson, Eric R.; Hirshorn, Barbara A.; & Cornman, John M. 1986. *Ties that bind: The interdependence of generations. A report from the Gerontological Society of America.* Washington, DC: Seven Locks Press.

Kirkwood, Thomas B. L. 1985. Comparative and evolutionary aspects of longevity. In C. E. Finch & E. L. Schneider (Eds.), *Handbook of the biology of aging* (2nd ed., pp. 27–44). New York: Van Nostrand Reinhold.

Kitchener, Karen S. & King, Patricia M. 1981. Reflective judgment: Concepts of justification and their relationship to age and education. *Journal of Applied Developmental Psychology, 2,* 89–116.

Kliegl, Reinhold; Smith, Jacqui; & Baltes, Paul B. 1986. Testing-the-limits, expertise, and memory in adulthood and old age. In, F. Klix & H. Hagendorf (Eds.), *Human memory and cognitive capabilities: Mechanisms and performances.* Amsterdam: Elsevier.

Kligman, Albert M.; Grove, Gary L.; & Balin, Arthur K. 1985. Aging of human skin. In C. E. Finch & E. L. Schneider (Eds.), *Handbook of the biology of aging* (2nd ed., pp. 820–841). New York: Van Nostrand Reinhold.

Kligman, L. H.; Aiken, F. J.; & Kligman, A. M. 1982. Prevention of untraviolet damage to the dermis of hairless mice by sunscreens. *Journal of Investigative Dermatology, 78,* 181–189.

Kline, Donald W. & Schieber, Frank. 1985. Vision and aging. In J. E. Birren & K. W. Schaie (Eds.), *Handbook of the psychology of aging* (2nd ed., pp. 296–331). New York: Van Nostrand Reinhold.

Knight, B. G. 1983. Assessing a mobile outreach team. In M. A. Smyer & M. Gatz (Eds.), *Mental health and aging: Programs and evaluations* (pp. 23–40). Beverly Hills, CA: Sage Publications.

Knight, Bob. 1988. Factors influencing therapist-rated change in older adults. *Journal of Gerontology: Psychological Sciences, 43,* P111–P112.

Kohen, Andrew I. 1975 Occupational mobility among middle-aged men. In *The pre-retirement years, Volume 4: A longitudinal study of the labor market experience of men* (pp. 115–151). U.S. Department of Labor, Manpower R & D Monograph 15. Washington, DC: U.S. Government Printing Office (Catalog #L1.39/3:15/v4).

Kohn, Melvin L. & Schooler, Carmi. 1982. Job conditions and personality: A longitudinal assessment of their reciprocal effects. *American Journal of Sociology, 87,* 1257–1286.

Kramer, Deirdre A. 1983. Post-formal operations? A need for further conceptualization. *Human Development, 26,* 91–105.

Kramer, Deirdre A. & Woodruff, Diana S. 1986. Relativistic and dialectical thought in three adult age-groups. *Human Development, 29,* 280–290.

Krantz, David L. 1977. The Santa Fe experience. In search of a new life: Radical career change in a special place. In S. B. Sarason, *Work, aging, and social change: Professionals and the one life–one career imperative* (pp. 165–188). New York: Free Press.

Krause, Neal. 1987. Understanding the stress process: Linking social support with locus of control beliefs. *Journal of Gerontology, 42,* 589–593.

Krohn, Alan & Gutmann, David. 1971. Changes in mastery styles with age: A study of Navajo dreams. *Psychiatry, 34,* 289–300.

Kübler-Ross, Elisabeth. 1969. *On death and dying.* New York: Macmillan Co.

Kübler-Ross, Elisabeth. 1970. The dying patient's point of view. In O. G. Brim, Jr., H. E. Freeman, S. Levine & N. A. Scotch (Eds.), *The dying patient* (pp. 156–170). New York: Russell Sage Foundation.

Kübler-Ross, Elisabeth. 1974. *Questions and answers on death and dying.* New York: Macmillan Co.

Kuhlen, Raymond G. 1964. Developmental changes in motivation during the adult years. In J. E. Birren (Ed.), *Relations of development and aging* (pp. 209–246). Springfield, IL: Charles C Thomas.

Kuipers, B. & Kassirer, J. P. 1984. Causal reasoning in medicine: Analysis of a protocol. *Cognitive Science, 8,* 363–385.

Kupke, Thomas. 1986. Psychological services provided within Veterans Administration nursing homes. *Professional Psychology: Research and Practice, 17,* 185–190.

Labouvie-Vief, Gisela. 1985. Intelligence and cognition. In J. E. Birren & K. W. Schaie (Eds.), *Handbook of the psychology of aging* (2nd ed., pp. 500–530). New York: Van Nostrand Reinhold.

Langer, Ellen J.; Janis, Irving L.; & Wolfer, John A. 1975. Reduction of psychological stress in surgical patients. *Journal of Experimental Social Psychology, 11,* 155–165.

Langer, Ellen J. & Rodin, Judith. 1976. The effects of choice and enhanced personal responsibility for the aged: A field experiment in an institutional setting. *Journal of Personality and Social Psychology, 34,* 191–198.

Langer, Susanne K. 1967. *Mind: An essay on human feeling* (Vol. 1). Baltimore: Johns Hopkins University Press.

Langer, Susanne K. 1972. *Mind: An essay on human feeling* (Vol. 2). Baltimore: Johns Hopkins University Press.

La Rue, Asenath; Dessonville, Connie; & Jarvik, Lissy F. 1985. Aging and mental disorders. In J. E. Birren & K. W. Schaie (Eds.), *Handbook of the psychology of aging* (2nd ed., pp. 664–702). New York: Van Nostrand Reinhold.

Laslett, Peter. 1985. Societal development and aging. In R. H. Binstock & E. Shanas (Eds.), *Handbook of aging and the social sciences* (2nd ed., pp. 199–230). New York: Van Nostrand Reinhold.

Laws, R. M. 1971. Patterns of reproductive and somatic aging in large mammals. In G. A. Sacher (Ed.), *Aging in relationship to development and reproduction.* Argonne, IL: Argonne National Laboratory.

Lazarus, Richard S. 1984. The trivialization of distress. In B. L. Hammonds & C. J. Scheirer (Eds.), *Psychology and health* (pp. 125–144). Washington, DC: American Psychological Association.

Lebowitz, Barry D. 1988 (Spring). Mental health policy and aging. *Generations, 12,* 53–56.

Lebra, Takie S. 1976. *Japanese patterns of behavior.* Honolulu: University of Hawaii Press.

LeMasters, E. E. 1957. Parenthood as crisis. *Marriage and Family Living, 19,* 352–355.

Lemon, Bruce W.; Bengtson, Vern L.; & Peterson, James A. 1972. An exploration of the activity theory of aging: Activity types and life satisfaction among in-movers to a retirement community. *Journal of Gerontology, 27,* 511–523.

Lev, Elise L. 1986. Effects of course in hospice nursing: Attitudes and behaviors of baccalaureate school of nursing undergraduates and graduates. *Psychological Reports, 59,* 847–858.

Levinson, Daniel J. 1978. *The seasons of a man's life.* (With Charlotte N. Darrow, Edward B. Klein, Maria H. Levinson & Braxton McKee.) New York: Knopf.

Levinson, Daniel J. 1986. A conception of adult development. *American Psychologist, 41,* 3–13.

Levinson, Daniel J.; Darrow, Charlotte N.; Klein, Edward B.; Levinson, Maria H.; & McKee, Braxton. 1976. Periods in the adult development of men: Ages 18 to 45. *Counseling Psychologist, 6,* 21–25.

Lewis, C.S. 1943. *The screwtape letters.* New York: Macmillan Co.

Lewis, Robert A. 1978. Emotional intimacy among men. *Journal of Social Issues, 34*(1), 108–121.

Liang, Jersey & Tu, Edward Jow-Ching. 1986. Estimating lifetime risk of nursing home residency: A further note. *The Gerontologist, 26,* 560–563.

Libby, Roger W. 1978. Creative singlehood as a sexual life style: Beyond marriage as a rite of passage. In B. I. Murstein (Ed.), *Exploring intimate life styles* (pp. 164–195). New York: Springer.

Lieberman, Morton A. 1965. Psychological correlates of impending death: Some preliminary observations. *Journal of Gerontology, 20,* 181–190.

Lieberman, Morton A. 1966. Observations on death and dying. *The Gerontologist, 6,* 70–73.

Lieberman, Morton A. & Coplan, Annie Siranne. 1970. Distance from death as a variable in the study of aging. *Developmental Psychology, 2,* 71–84.

Lieberman, M. A. & Tobin, S. S. 1983. *The experience of old age: Stress, coping and survival.* New York: Basic Books.

Lindemann, Erich. 1944. Symptomatology and management of acute grief. *American Journal of Psychiatry, 101,* 141–148.

Lindop, Patricia J. & Rotblat, J. 1961. Long-term effects of a single whole-body exposure of mice to ionizing radiations. *Proceedings of the Royal Society (London), Series B, 154,* 332–349.

Lissner, John. 1979 (June 3). The robust artistry of Alberta Hunter. *New York Times,* D-23.

Litwak, Eugene. 1960. Geographic mobility and extended family cohesion. *American Sociological Review, 25,* 385–394.

Liu, K.; Manton, K.; & Liu, B. M. 1986. Home care expenses for the disabled. *Health Care Financing Review, 7,* 51–58. (Cited in Stone, 1987, p. 5.)

Livson, Florine B. 1976. Patterns of personality development in middle-aged women: A longitudinal study. *International Journal of Aging and Human Development, 7,* 107–115.

Livson, Florine B. 1981. Paths to psychological health in the middle years: Sex differences. In D. H. Eichorn, J. A. Clausen, N. Haan, M. P. Honzik & P. H. Mussen (Eds.), *Present and past in middle life* (pp. 195–221). New York: Academic Press.

Loevinger, Jane. 1979. Construct validity of the Sentence Completion Test of ego development. *Applied Psychological Measurement, 3,* 281–311.

Lombardi, Tarky, Jr. 1987 (Winter). Nursing home without walls. *Generations, 11,* 21–23.

Lopata, Helena Znaniecki. 1973. *Widowhood in an American city.* Cambridge, MA: Schenkman.

Lopata, Helena Znaniecki. 1981. Widowhood and husband sanctification. *Journal of Marriage and the Family, 43,* 439–450.

Lopata, Helena Znaniecki. 1988a. Support systems of American urban widowhood. *Journal of Social Issues, 44*(3), 113–128.

Lopata, Helena Znaniecki. 1988b. Widows and their families. In C. S. Chilman, E. W. Nunnally, & F. M. Cox (Eds.), *Variant family forms* (pp. 133–149). Newbury Park, CA: Sage Publications.

Lowenthal, Marjorie Fiske. 1964. Social isolation and mental illness in old age. *American Sociological Review, 29,* 54–70.

Lowenthal, Marjorie Fiske & Haven, Clayton. 1968. Interaction and adaptation: Intimacy as a critical variable. *American Sociological Review, 33,* 20–30.

Lowenthal, Marjorie Fiske; Thurnher, Majda; Chiriboga, David; & Associates. 1975. *Four stages of life: A comparative study of women and men facing transitions.* San Francisco: Jossey-Bass.

Lubben, James E. & Becerra, Rosina M. 1987. Social support among Black, Mexican, and Chinese elderly. In D. E. Gelfand & C. M. Barresi (Eds.), *Ethnic dimensions of aging* (pp. 130–144). New York: Springer.

Lubin, Marc I. 1964. Addendum to Chapter 4. In B. L. Neugarten & Associates (Eds.), *Personality in middle and late life* (pp. 102–104). New York: Atherton Press.

McAdoo, Harriette Pipes. 1978. Factors related to stability in upwardly mobile Black families. *Journal of Marriage and the Family, 40,* 761–776.

McCrae, Robert R. & Costa, Paul T., Jr. 1986. Personality, coping, and coping effectiveness in an adult sample. *Journal of Personality, 54,* 385–405.

McCrae, Robert R. & Costa, Paul T., Jr. 1988. Psychological resilience among widowed men and women: A 10-year follow-up of a national sample. *Journal of Social Issues, 44*(3), 129–142.

Macklin, Eleanor D. 1978. Review of research on nonmarital cohabitation in the United States. In B. I. Murstein (Ed.), *Exploring intimate life styles* (pp. 197–243). New York: Springer.

Macklin, Eleanor D. 1988. Heterosexual couples who cohabit nonmaritally: Some common problems and issues. In C. S. Chilman, E. W. Nunnally & F. M. Cox (Eds.), *Variant family forms* (pp. 56–72). Newbury Park, CA: Sage Publications.

MacLennan, Beryce W.; Saul, Shura; & Weiner, Marcella B. (Eds.). 1988. *Group psychotherapies for the elderly.* Madison, CT: International Universities Press.

McPherson, Barry & Guppy, Neil. 1979. Pre-retirement life-style and the degree of planning for retirement. *Journal of Gerontology, 34,* 254–263.

Maddox, George L. 1966. Retirement as a social event in the United States. In J. C. McKinney & F. T. de Vyver (Eds.), *Aging and social policy* (pp. 117–135). New York: Appleton–Century–Crofts.

Maeda, H.; Gleiser, C. A.; Masoro, E. J.; Murata, I.; McMahan, C. A.; & Yu, B. P. 1985. Nutritional influences on aging of Fischer 344 rats. II. Pathology. *Journal of Gerontology, 40,* 671–688.

Mandelbaum, David G. 1959. Social uses of funeral rites. In H. Feifel (Ed.), *The meaning of death* (pp. 189–217). New York: McGraw–Hill.

Manton, Kenneth G.; Blazer, Dan G.; & Woodbury, Max A. 1987. Suicide in middle age and later life: Sex and race specific life table and cohort analyses. *Journal of Gerontology, 42,* 219–227.

Marcus, Eric. 1988. *The male couple's guide to living together: What gay men should know about living together and coping in a straight world.* New York: Harper & Row.

Markides, Kyriakos S. & Mindel, Charles H. 1987. *Aging & ethnicity.* Newbury Park, CA: Sage Publications.

Marshall, James R. 1978. Changes in aged white male suicide: 1948–1972. *Journal of Gerontology, 33,* 763–768.

Marshall, Victor W. 1975. Organizational features of terminal status passage in residential facilities for the aged. *Urban Life, 4,* 349–368.

Masoro, Edward J. 1988. Food restriction in rodents: An evaluation of its role in the study of aging. *Journal of Gerontology: Biological Sciences, 43,* B59–B64.

Masters, William H. & Johnson, Virginia E. 1966. *Human sexual response.* Boston: Little, Brown.

Masters, William H. & Johnson, Virginia E. 1970. *Human sexual inadequacy.* Boston: Little, Brown.

Masters, William H. & Johnson, Virginia E. 1979. *Homosexuality in perspective.* Boston: Little, Brown.

Masters, William H.; Johnson, Virginia E.; & Kolodny, Robert C. 1988. *Human sexuality* (3rd ed.). Boston: Little, Brown.

Matarazzo, Joseph D. 1980. Behavioral health and behavioral medicine: Frontiers for a new health psychology. *American Psychologist, 35,* 807–817.

Matthews, Karen A. 1982. Psychological perspectives on the Type A behavior pattern. *Psychological Bulletin, 91,* 293–323.

May, Rollo. 1958. Contributions of existential psychotherapy. In R. May, E. Angel & H. F. Ellenberger (Eds.), *Existence: A new dimension in psychiatry and psychology* (pp. 37–91). New York: Basic Books.

Mead, George Herbert. 1934/1964. Mind, self, and society. In A. Strauss (Ed.), *George Herbert Mead: On social psychology* (pp. 115–282). Chicago: University of Chicago Press. (Originally published in C. W. Morris (Ed.), *Mind, Self, and Society.* Chicago: University of Chicago Press.

Mead, George Herbert. 1936/1964. Mind approached through behavior—Can its study be made scientific? In A. Strauss (Ed.), *George Herbert Mead: On social psychology* (pp. 65–82). Chicago: University of Chicago Press. (First published in M. H. Moore (Ed.), *Movements of thought in the nineteenth century* (pp. 386–404). Chicago: University of Chicago Press.)

Mead, Margaret. 1928. *Coming of age in Samoa.* New York: Dell (Laurel).

Mead, Margaret. 1949/1967. *Male and female.* New York: Morrow (Apollo ed.).

Mead, Margaret. 1970. *Culture and commitment: A study of the generation gap.* Garden City, NY: Doubleday.

Mead, Margaret. 1972 (December). *Long living in cross-cultural perspective.* Paper presented at the meeting of the Gerontological Society of America, San Juan.

The Medicare Handbook. 1989. Publication No. HCFA 10050. Baltimore: U.S. Department of Health and Human Services.

Medvedev, Zhores A. 1974. Caucasus and Altay longevity: A biological or social problem? *The Gerontologist, 14,* 381–387.

Melamed, Barbara G. 1984. Health intervention: Collaboration for health and science. In B. L. Hammonds & C. J. Scheirer (Eds.), *Psychology and health* (pp. 49–119). Washington, DC: American Psychological Association.

Meyrowitz, Joshua. 1985. *No sense of place: The impact of electronic media on social behavior.* New York: Oxford.

Miller, Inglis J., Jr. 1988. Human taste bud density across adult age groups. *Journal of Gerontology: Biological Sciences, 43,* B26–B30.

Miller, Marv. 1978. Geriatric suicide: The Arizona study. *The Gerontologist, 18,* 488–495.

Miller, Neal E. 1983. Behavioral medicine: Symbiosis between laboratory and clinic. *Annual Review of Psychology, 34,* 1–31.

Mindel, Charles H. & Habenstein, Robert W. 1976. *Ethnic families in America: Patterns and variations.* New York: Elsevier.

Minkler, Meredith & Stone, Robyn 1985. The feminization of poverty and older women. *The Gerontologist, 25,* 351–357.

Mitchell, Jim & Register, Jasper C. 1984. An exploration of family interaction with the elderly by race, socioeconomic status, and residence. *The Gerontologist, 24,* 48–54.

Moberg, David O. 1965. Religiosity in old age. *The Gerontologist, 5,* 78–87.

Money, John. 1988. *Gay, straight and in-between: The sexology of erotic orientation.* New York: Oxford University Press.

Mor, Vincent. 1987 (Spring). Hospice: The older person as patient and caregiver. *Generations, 11,* 19–21.

Mor, Vincent; McHorney, Colleen; & Sherwood, Sylvia. 1986. Secondary morbidity among the recently bereaved. *American Journal of Psychiatry, 143,* 158–163.

Mor, Vincent & Spector, William. 1988 (Spring). Longterm-care policy: Achieving continuity of care. *Generations, 12,* 47–52.

Morgan, Leslie A. 1976. A re-examination of widowhood and morale. *Journal of Gerontology, 31,* 687–695.

Morin, Stephen F. 1988. AIDS: The challenge to psychology. *American Psychologist, 43,* 838–842.

Mortimer, J. F.; Finch, M. D.; & Kumka, D. 1982. Persistence and change in development: The multidimensional self-concept. In P. B. Baltes & O. G. Brim, Jr. (Eds.), *Life-span development and behavior* (Vol. 4, pp. 264–313). New York: Academic Press.

Moss, Miriam & Moss, Sidney. 1989. Death of a parent. In R. A. Kalish (Ed.), *Midlife loss: Coping strategies.* Newbury Park, CA: Sage Publications.

Murdock, Steve H. & Schwartz, Donald F. 1978. Family structure and the use of agency services: An examination of patterns among elderly Native Americans. *The Gerontologist, 18,* 475–481.

Murray, Henry A. & Staff. 1938. *Explorations in personality.* New York: Oxford.

Myerhoff, Barbara. 1979. *Number our days.* New York: Dutton.

Myers, George C. 1985. Aging and worldwide population change. In R. H. Binstock & E. Shanas (Eds.), *Handbook of aging and the social sciences* (2nd ed., pp. 173–198). New York: Van Nostrand Reinhold.

National Center for Health Statistics. 1988. Annual survey of births, marriages, divorces, and deaths, United States, 1987. *Monthly Vital Statistics Report, 36*(13). Hyattsville, MD: U.S. Public Health Services.

National Council on the Aging. 1975. *The myth and reality of aging in America.* (Conducted by Louis Harris & Associates, Inc.) Washington, DC: National Council on the Aging, Inc.

Nesselroade, John R. & Labouvie, Erich W. 1985. Experimental design in research on aging. In J. E. Birren & K. W. Schaie (Eds.), *Handbook of the psychology of aging* (2nd ed., pp. 35–60). New York: Van Nostrand Reinhold.

Neugarten, Bernice L. 1964. Summary and implications. In B. L. Neugarten & Associates (Eds.), *Personality in middle and late life* (pp. 188–200). New York: Atherton Press.

Neugarten, Bernice L. 1967a (December). A new look at menopause. *Psychology Today, 1,* 42–45, 67–69, 71.

Neugarten, Bernice L. 1967b/1968. The awareness of middle age. In B. L. Neugarten (Ed.), *Middle age and aging* (pp. 93–98). Chicago: University of Chicago Press. (Originally published in R. Owen (Ed.), *Middle age.* London: British Broadcasting Corporation.)

Neugarten, Bernice L. 1968. Adult personality: Toward a psychology of the life cycle. In B. L. Neugarten (Ed.), *Middle age and aging* (pp. 137–147). Chicago: University of Chicago Press.

Neugarten, Bernice L. 1976/1970. Adaptation and the life cycle. *Counseling Psychologist, 6,* 16–20. (Revision of: Dynamics of transition of middle age to old age. *Journal of Geriatric Psychiatry, 4,* 71–87.)

Neugarten, Bernice L. 1982. Policy for the 1980s: Age or need entitlement? In B. L. Neugarten (Ed.), *Age or need? Public policies for older people* (pp. 19–54). Beverly Hills, CA: Sage Publications.

Neugarten, Bernice L. & Associates. 1964. *Personality in middle and late life.* New York: Atherton Press.

Neugarten, Bernice L. & Gutmann, David L. 1958. Age-sex roles and personality in middle age: A thematic apperception study. *Psychological Monographs, 72*(Whole No. 470).

Neugarten, Bernice L. & Hagestad, Gunhild O. 1976. Age and the life course. In R. H. Binstock & E. Shanas (Eds.), *Handbook of aging and the social sciences* (pp. 35–55). New York: Van Nostrand Reinhold.

Neugarten, Bernice L.; Havighurst, Robert J.; & Tobin, Sheldon S. 1965/1968. Personality and patterns of aging. In B. L. Neugarten (Ed.), *Middle age and aging* (pp. 173–177). Chicago: University of Chicago Press. (Originally published in *Gawein: Tijdschrift van de Psychologische Kring aan de Nijmessgse Universitiet, Jrg. 13,*249–256.)

Neugarten, Bernice L. & Moore, Joan W. 1968. The changing age-status system. In B. L. Neugarten (Ed.), *Middle age and aging* (pp. 5–21). Chicago: University of Chicago Press.

Neugarten, Bernice L.; Moore, Joan W.; & Lowe, John C. 1965. Age norms, age constraints, and adult socialization. *American Journal of Sociology, 70,* 710–717.

Neugarten, Bernice L. & Neugarten, Dail A. 1986 (Winter). Age in the aging society. *Daedalus, 115*(1), 31–49.

Neugarten, Bernice L. & Neugarten, Dail A. 1987 (May). The changing meanings of age. *Psychology Today, 21,* 29–33.

Neugarten, Bernice L. & Weinstein, Karol K. 1964. The changing American grandparent. *Journal of Marriage and the Family, 26,* 199–204.

Neugarten, Bernice L.; Wood, Vivian; Kraines, Ruth J.; & Loomis, Barbara. 1963. Women's attitudes toward the menopause. *Vita Humana, 6,* 140–151.

Neulinger, John. 1976a (March). An issue of attitude change. *Leisure Today,* 4–5.

Neulinger, John. 1976b. The need for and the implications of a psychological conception of leisure. *The Ontario Psychologist, 8*(2), 13–20.

Neulinger, John. 1980. *To leisure: An introduction.* Boston: Allyn & Bacon.

Neulinger, John. 1986. *What am I doing? The WAID.* Dolgeville, NY: The Leisure Institute (R.D. #1, Hopson Road, Box 416).

Newman, Gustave & Nichols, Claude R. 1960. Sexual activities and attitudes in older persons. *Journal of the American Medical Association, 173,* 33–35.

New York Times. 1988 (October 22). Social Security checks will rise 4%. p. 35.

Norris, Fran H. & Murrell, Stanley A. 1987. Older adult family stress and adaptation before and after bereavement. *Journal of Gerontology, 42,* 606–612.

Norton, Arthur J. & Glick, Paul C. 1981. Marital instability in America: Past, present, and future. In P. J. Stein (Ed.), *Single life: Unmarried adults in social context* (pp. 57–69). New York: St. Martin's Press.

Nydegger, Corinne N. 1973 (November). *Late and early fathers.* Paper presented at the meeting of the Gerontological Society of America, Miami Beach.

Nye, F. Ivan. 1974. Husband-wife relationship. In L. W. Hoffman, F. I. Nye & Associates (Eds.), *Working mothers: An evaluative review of consequences for wife, husband, and child* (pp. 186–206). San Francisco: Jossey-Bass.

Ochs, Alfred L.; Newberry, Janice; Lenhardt, Martin L.; & Harkins, Stephen W. 1985. Neural and vestibular aging associated with falls. In J. E. Birren & K. W. Schaie (Eds.), *Handbook of the psychology of aging* (2nd ed., pp. 378–399). New York: Van Nostrand Reinhold.

Offer, Daniel & Offer, Judith B. 1975. *From teenage to young manhood.* New York: Basic Books.

Offer, Daniel; Ostrov, Eric; & Howard, Kenneth I. 1981. *The adolescent: A psychological self-portrait.* New York: Basic Books.

Olsen, Kenneth M. 1969. Social class and age-group differences in the timing of family status changes: A study of age norms in American society (Doctoral dissertation, University of Chicago). (Cited in Hagestad & Neugarten, 1976.)

Olsho, Lynne Werner; Harkins, Stephen W.; & Lenhardt, Martin L. 1985. Aging and the auditory system. In J. E. Birren & K. W. Schaie (Eds.), *Handbook of the psychology of aging* (2nd ed., pp. 332–377). New York: Van Nostrand Reinhold.

O'Rand, A. & Henretta, J. 1982. Midlife work history and retirement income. In M. Szinovacz (Ed.), *Women's retirement.* Beverly Hills, CA: Sage Publications.

Owens, W. A. 1966. Age and mental abilities: A second adult follow-up. *Journal of Educational Psychology, 57,* 311–325.

Pachella, R. G. 1974. The interpretation of reaction time in information processing research. In B. H. Kantowitz (Ed.), *Human information processing: Tutorials in performance and cognition* (pp. 431–482). Hillsdale, NJ: Erlbaum.

Palmore, Erdman. 1972. Gerontophobia versus ageism. *The Gerontologist, 12,* 213.

Palmore, Erdman B. 1984. Longevity in Abkhazia: A reevaluation. *The Gerontologist, 24,* 95–96.

Palmore, Erdman B.; Burchett, Bruce M.; Fillenbaum, Gerda G.; George, Linda K.; & Wallman, Laurence M. 1985. *Retirement: Causes and consequences.* New York: Springer.

Palmore, Erdman & Cleveland, William. 1976. Aging, terminal decline, and terminal drop. *Journal of Gerontology, 31,* 76–81.

Palmore, Erdman, B. & Maeda, Daisaku. 1985. *The honorable elders revisited: A revised cross-cultural analysis of aging in Japan.* Durham, NC: Duke University Press.

Paradis, Lenora Finn & Cummings, Scott B. 1986. The evolution of hospice in America toward organizational homogeneity. *Journal of Health and Social Behavior, 27,* 370–386.

Park, Denise Cortis; Puglisi, J. Thomas; & Smith, Anderson D. 1986. Memory for pictures: Does an age-related decline exist? *Psychology and Aging, 1,* 11–17.

Parkes, Colin Murray. 1987. *Bereavement: Studies of grief in adult life* (2nd American ed.). Madison, CT: International Universities Press.

Passuth, P. M. & Maines, D. R. 1981. *Transformations in age norms and age constraints: Evidence bearing on the age-irrelevancy hypothesis.* Paper presented at the World Congress on Gerontology, Hamburg. (Cited in Hagestad & Neugarten, 1985.)

Patchner, Michael A. & Finn, Mark B. 1987–1988. Volunteers: The life-line of hospice. *Omega, 18,* 135–144.

Pearl, Raymond. 1924. *Studies in human biology.* Baltimore: Williams & Wilkins.

Pearlin, Leonard I. 1982. Discontinuities in the study of aging. In T. K. Hareven & K. J. Adams (Eds.), *Aging and life course transitions: An interdisciplinary perspective* (pp. 55–74). New York: Guilford Press.

Pearlin, Leonard I.; Menaghan, Elizabeth G.; Lieberman, Morton A.; & Mullan, Joseph T. 1981. The stress process. *Journal of Health and Social Behavior, 22,* 337–356.

Peterson, David A. 1987. *Career paths in the field of aging.* Lexington, MA: Lexington Books.

Pfeiffer, Eric. 1977. Psychopathology and social pathology. In J. E. Birren & K. W. Schaie (Eds.), *Handbook of the psychology of aging* (pp. 650–671). New York: Van Nostrand Reinhold.

Pfeiffer, Eric & Davis, Glenn C. 1974. Determinants of sexual behavior in middle and old age. In E. Palmore (Ed.), *Normal aging II: Reports from the Duke Longitudinal Studies, 1970–1973* (pp. 251–262). Durham, NC: Duke University Press.

Pfeiffer, Eric; Verwoerdt, Adriaan; & Davis, Glenn C. 1974. Sexual behavior in middle life. In E. Palmore (Ed.), *Normal aging II: Reports from the Duke Longitudinal Studies, 1970–1973* (pp. 243–251). Durham, NC: Duke University Press.

Phalon, Richard. 1978 (March 30). Family money. *New York Times,* C-9.

Phillemer, Karl & Finkelhor, David. 1988. The prevalence of elder abuse: A random sample survey. *The Gerontologist, 28,* 51–57.

Piaget, Jean. 1972. Intellectual evolution from adolescence to adulthood. *Human Development, 15,* 1–12.

Piaget, Jean & Inhelder, Bärbel. 1969. *The psychology of the child.* New York: Basic Books.

Pifer, Alan & Bronte, Lydia (Eds.). 1986. *Our aging society: Paradox and promise.* New York: Norton.

Plath, D. & Ikeda, K. 1975. After coming of age: Adult awareness of age norms. In T. R. Williams (Ed.). *Socialization and communication in primary groups.* The Hague: Mouton.

Pleck, Joseph H. & Sawyer, Jack (Eds.). 1974. *Men and masculinity.* Englewood Cliffs, NJ: Prentice–Hall.

Pocs, Ollie; Godow, Annette; Tolone, William L.; & Walsh, Robert H. 1977 (June). Is there sex after 40? *Psychology Today, 11,* 54–56, 87.

Polit, Denise F. & LaRocco, Susan A. 1980. Social and psychological correlates of menopausal symptoms. *Psychosomatic Medicine, 42,* 335–345.

Poon, Leonard W. 1985. Differences in human memory with aging: Nature, causes, and clinical implications. In J. E. Birren & K. W. Schaie (Eds.), *Handbook of the psychology of aging* (2nd ed., pp. 427–462). New York: Van Nostrand Reinhold.

Poon, Leonard W. & Fozard, James L. 1978. Speed of retrieval from long-term memory in relation to age, familiarity, and datedness of information. *Journal of Gerontology, 33,* 711–717.

Poon, Leonard W. & Fozard, James L. 1980. Age and word frequency effects in continuous recognition memory. *Journal of Gerontology, 35,* 77–86.

Poon, L. W. & Schaffer, G. 1982 (August). *Prospective memory in young and elderly adults.* Paper presented at the meeting of the American Psychological Association, Washington, DC. (Cited in Sinnott, 1986.)

Portnow, Jay & Houtmann, Martha. 1987. *Home care for the elderly: A complete guide.* New York: McGraw–Hill.

Pratt, Clara; Schmall, Vicki; Wright, Scott; & Hare, Jan. 1987. The forgotten client: Family caregivers to institutionalized dementia patients. In T. H. Brubaker (Ed.), *Aging, health, and family: Long-term care* (pp. 197–213). Newbury Park, CA: Sage Publications.

Presser, Harriet B. & Cain, Virginia S. 1983. Shift work among dual-earner couples with children. *Science, 219,* 876–879.

Pryor, William A. 1987. The free-radical theory of aging revisited: A critique and a suggested disease-specific theory. In H. R. Warner, R. N. Butler, R. L. Sprott & E. L. Schneider (Eds.), *Modern biological theories of aging* (pp. 89–112). New York: Raven Press.

Quinn, Terry & Crabtree, Jill (Eds.). 1987. *How to start a respite service for people with Alzheimer's and their families: A guide for community-based organizations.* New York: The Brookdale Foundation.

Raine, Mary J. 1989 (Winter). The reconstituted family: A Misnomer. *Mount Holyoke Alumnae Quarterly, 62,* 13–15.

Rapoport, Rhona & Rapoport, Robert N. 1969. The dual career family. *Human Relations, 22,* 3–30.

Rawson, Ian G.; Weinberg, Edward I.; Herold, Jo Ann; & Holtz, Judy. 1978. Nutrition of rural elderly in southwestern Pennsylvania. *The Gerontologist, 18,* 24–29.

Rebok, George W. 1987. *Life-span cognitive development*. New York: Holt, Reinhart & Winston.

Rees, W. D. & Lutkins, S. G. 1967. Mortality of bereavement. *British Medical Journal, 4,* 13–16.

Reichard, Suzanne; Livson, Florine; & Peterson, Paul G. 1962. *Aging and personality*. New York: Wiley.

Reimanis, Gunars & Green, Russel F. 1971. Imminence of death and intellectual decrement in the aging. *Developmental Psychology, 5,* 270–272.

Reno, Virginia. 1976. Retired women workers. In *Reaching retirement age: Findings from a survey of newly entitled workers 1968–70* (pp. 75–93). Washington, DC: U.S. Government Printing Office.

Repetti, Rena L. 1985. The social environment at work and psychological well being. *Dissertation Abstracts International, 46,* 4026B–4027B. (University Microfilms #86-01004.)

Riegel, K. F. 1973. Dialectic operations: The final period of cognitive development. *Human Development, 16,* 371–381.

Riegel, Klaus F. 1976. The dialectic of human development. *American Psychologist, 31,* 689–700.

Riegel, Klaus F. 1977. The dialectics of time. In N. Datan & H. W. Reese (Eds.), *Life-span developmental psychology: Dialectical perspectives on experimental research* (pp. 4–45). New York: Academic Press.

Riegel, Klaus F. & Riegel, Ruth M. 1972. Development, drop, and death. *Developmental Psychology, 6,* 306–319.

Riley, John W., Jr. 1963. Attitudes toward death. Unpublished. (Cited in M. W. Riley, A. Foner & Associates, *Aging and society. Vol. 1. An inventory of research findings.* New York: Russell Sage Foundation, 1968.)

Riley, Maltida White & Riley, John W., Jr. 1986. Longevity and social structure: The potential of the added years. In A. Pifer & L. Bronte (Eds.), *Our aging society: Paradox and promise* (pp. 53–77). New York: Norton.

Roberts, Priscilla & Newton, Peter M. 1987. Levinsonian studies of women's adult development. *Psychology and Aging, 2,* 154–163.

Rodeheaver, Dean. 1987. When old age became a social problem, women were left behind. *The Gerontologist, 27,* 741–746.

Rodeheaver, Dean & Datan, Nancy. 1988. The challenge of double jeopardy: Toward a mental health agenda for aging women. *American Psychologist, 43,* 648–654.

Rodin, J. 1983. Behavioral medicine: Beneficial effects of self-control training in aging. *International Review of Applied Psychology, 32,* 153–181.

Rodin, Judith. 1986a. Aging and health: Effects of the sense of control. *Science, 233,* 1271–1276.

Rodin, Judith. 1986b. Health, control, and aging. In M. M. Baltes & P. B. Baltes (Eds.), *The psychology of control and aging* (pp. 139–165). Hillsdale, NJ: Erlbaum.

Rodin, Judith & Langer, Ellen J. 1977. Long-term effects of a control-relevant intervention with the institutionalized aged. *Journal of Personality and Social Psychology, 35,* 897–902.

Rogers, C. Jean & Gallion, Teresa E. 1978. Characteristics of elderly Pueblo Indians in New Mexico. *The Gerontologist, 18,* 482–487.

Rogers, Carl R. 1972. *Becoming partners: Marriage and its alternatives*. New York: Dell (Delta).

Rollins, Boyd C. & Feldman, Harold. 1970. Marital satisfaction over the family life cycle. *Journal of Marriage and the Family, 32,* 20–28.

Rones, P. 1985. Using the CPS to track retirement trends among older men. *Monthly Labor Review, 108,* 46–49.

Rosen, Jacqueline L. & Neugarten, Bernice L. 1964. Ego functions in the middle and late years: A thematic apperception study. In B. L. Neugarten & Associates (Eds.), *Personality in middle and late life* (pp. 90–101). New York: Atherton Press.

Rosenkrantz, Paul S.; Vogel, Susan Raymond; Bee, Helen; Broverman, Inge K.; & Broverman, Donald M. 1968. Sex-role stereotypes and self-concepts in college students. *Journal of Consulting and Clinical Psychology, 32,* 287–295.

Rosenman, Ray H.; Brand, Richard J.; Jenkins, C. David; Friedman, Meyer; Straus, Reuben; & Wurm, Moses. 1975. Coronary heart disease in the Western Collaborative Group Study: Final follow-up experience of 8-½ years. *Journal of the American Medical Association, 233,* 872–877.

Rosenman, Ray H.; Friedman, Meyer; Straus, Reuben; Wurm, Moses; Kositchek, Robert; Hahn, Wilfrid; & Werthessen, Nicholas T. 1964. A predictive study of coronary heart disease. *Journal of the American Medical Association, 189,* 15–22.

Rothstein, Frances R. 1988. Older worker employment opportunities in the private sector. In R. Morris & S. A. Bass (Eds.), *Retirement reconsidered: Economic and social roles for older people* (pp. 148–158). New York: Springer.

Rowe, John W. & Kahn, Robert L. 1987. Human aging: Usual and successful. *Science, 237,* 143–149.

Roybal, Edward R. 1988. Mental health and aging: The need for an expanded federal response. *American Psychologist, 43,* 189–194.

Rubin, Leonard. 1976. Disabling health conditions among men. In *Reaching retirement age: Findings from a survey of newly entitled workers 1968–70* (pp. 65–74). Washington, DC: U.S. Government Printing Office.

Rubinstein, Robert L. 1986. *Singular paths: Old men living alone.* New York: Columbia University Press.

Russell, Richard L. 1987. Evidence for and against the theory of developmentally programmed aging. In H. R. Warner, R. N. Butler, R. L. Sprott & E. L. Schneider (Eds.), *Modern biological theories of aging* (pp. 35–61). New York: Raven Press.

Rybash, John M.; Hoyer, William J.; & Roodin, Paul A. 1986. *Adult cognition and aging: Developmental changes in processing, knowing and thinking.* New York: Pergamon.

Sacher, George A. 1959. Relation of lifespan to brain weight and body weight in mammals. In G. E. W. Wolstenholme & M. O'Connor (Eds.), *Ciba Foundation Symposium on the life span of animals.* London: Churchill.

Sacher, G. A. 1977. Life table modifications and life prolongation. In C. E. Finch & L. Hayflick, (Eds.), *Handbook of the biology of aging* (pp. 582–638). New York: Van Nostrand Reinhold.

Salend, Elyse; Kane, Rosalie A.; Satz, Maureeen; & Pynoos, Jon. 1984. Elder abuse reporting: Limitations of statutes. *The Gerontologist, 24,* 61–69.

Salter, Charles A. & Salter, Carlota deLerma. 1976. Attitudes toward aging and behaviors toward the elderly among young people as a function of death anxiety. *The Gerontologist, 16,* 232–236.

Salthouse, Timothy A. 1982. *Adult cognition: An experimental psychology of human aging.* New York: Springer-Verlag.

Salthouse, Timothy A. 1984. Effects of age and skill in typing. *Journal of Experimental Psychology: General, 113,* 345–371.

Salthouse, Timothy A. 1987. Age, experience, and compensation. In C. Schooler & K. W. Schaie (Eds.), *Cognitive functioning and social structure over the life course* (pp. 142–157). Norwood, NJ: Ablex.

Sanders, Catherine M. 1989. *Grief: The mourning after*. New York: Wiley.

Santos, John F. & VandenBos, Gary R. (Eds.). 1982. *Psychology and the older adult: Challenges for training in the 1980s*. Washington, DC: American Psychological Association.

Sarason, Seymour B. 1977. *Work, aging, and social change: Professionals and the one life-one career imperative*. New York: Free Press.

Saul, Robert L.; Gee, Pauline; & Ames, Bruce N. 1987. Free radicals, DNA damage, and aging. In H. R. Warner, R. N. Butler, R. L. Sprott & E. L. Schneider (Eds.), *Modern biological theories of aging* (pp. 113–129). New York: Raven Press.

Sbordone, Robert J. & Sterman, Lorraine T. 1983. The psychologist as a consultant in a nursing home: Effect on staff morale and turnover. *Professional Psychology: Research and Practice, 14*, 240–250.

Schaie, K. Warner. 1977. Quasi-experimental research designs in the psychology of aging. In J. E. Birren & K. W. Schaie (Eds.), *Handbook of the psychology of aging* (pp. 39–58). New York: Van Nostrand Reinhold.

Schaie, K. Warner. 1979. The primary mental abilities in adulthood: An exploration in the development of psychometric intelligence. In P. B. Baltes & O. G. Brim, Jr. (Eds.), *Life-span development and behavior* (Vol. 2, pp. 68–117). New York: Academic Press.

Schaie, K. Warner. 1983. The Seattle longitudinal study: A 21 year exploration of psychometric intelligence in adulthood. In K. W. Schaie (Ed.), *Longitudinal studies of adult psychological development* (pp. 64–135). New York: Guilford Press.

Schaie, K. Warner, 1987. Applications of psychometric intelligence to the prediction of everyday competence in the elderly. In C. Schooler & K. W. Schaie (Eds.), *Cognitive functioning and social structure over the life course* (pp. 50–58). Norwood, NJ: Ablex.

Schaie, K. Warner. 1988. Ageism in psychological research. *American Psychologist, 43*, 179–183.

Schaie, K. Warner & Hertzog, Christopher. 1985. Measurement in the psychology of adulthood and aging. In J. E. Birren & K. W. Schaie (Eds.), *Handbook of the psychology of aging* (2nd ed., pp. 61–92). New York: Van Nostrand Reinhold.

Schaie, K. Warner & Parham, Iris A. 1977. Cohort-sequential analyses of adult intellectual development. *Developmental Psychology, 13*, 649–653.

Schaie, K. W. & Strother, C. R. 1968. The effects of time and cohort differences on the interpretation of age changes in cognitive behavior. *Multivariate Behavioral Research, 3*, 259–294.

Schaie, K. Warner & Willis, Sherry L. 1986. Can decline in adult intellectual functioning be reversed? *Developmental Psychology, 22*, 223–232.

Scherwitz, Larry; Berton, Kent; & Leventhal, Howard. 1977. Type A assessment and interaction in the behavior pattern interview. *Psychosomatic Medicine, 39*, 229–240.

Schneider, Edward L. & Reed, John D. 1985. Modulations of aging processes. In C. E. Finch & E. L. Schneider (Eds.), *Handbook of the biology of aging* (2nd ed., pp. 45–76). New York: Van Nostrand Reinhold.

Schneider, Margaret S. 1986. The relationships of cohabiting lesbian and heterosexual couples: A comparison. *Psychology of Women Quarterly, 10*, 234–239.

Schucker, Beth & Jacobs, David R., Jr. 1977. Assessment of behavioral risk for coronary disease by voice characteristics. *Psychosomatic Medicine, 39*, 219–228.

Schulenburg, Joy. 1985. *Gay parenting: A complete guide for gay men and lesbians with children*. New York: Anchor Press/Doubleday.

Schulz, James H. 1976. *The economics of aging*. Belmont, CA: Wadsworth.

Schulz, Richard. 1978. *The psychology of death, dying, and bereavement*. Reading, MA: Addison–Wesley.

Sekaran, Uma. 1986. *Dual-career families.* San Francisco: Jossey-Bass.

Sexton, Patricia Cayo. 1977. *Women and work.* U.S. Department of Labor, R & D Monograph 47. Washington, DC: U.S. Government Printing Office.

Shanas, Ethel. 1979. Social myth as hypothesis: The case of the family relations of old people. *The Gerontologist, 19,* 3–9.

Shanas, Ethel & Sussman, Marvin B. 1981. The family in later life: Social structure and social policy. In R. W. Fogel et al. (Eds.), *Aging: Stability and change in the family* (pp. 211–231). New York: Academic Press.

Sheehy, Gail. 1976. *Passages: Predictable crises of adult life.* New York: Dutton.

Sheppard, Harold L. 1988. Work continuity versus retirement: Reasons for continuing work. In R. Morris & S. A. Bass (Eds.), *Retirement reconsidered: Economic and social roles for older people* (pp. 129–147). New York: Springer.

Sherfey, Mary Jane. 1972. *The nature and evolution of female sexuality.* New York: Random House.

Sherman, Sally R. 1985 (March). Reported reasons retired workers left their last job: Findings from the 1982 New Beneficiary Survey. *Social Security Bulletin, 48,* 27.

Shneidman, Edwin S. 1973. *Deaths of man.* New York: Quadrangle.

Shneidman, Edwin. 1989. The Indian summer of life: A preliminary study of septuagenarians. *American Psychologist, 44,* 684–694.

Shock, Nathan W. 1960. Some of the facts of aging. In N. W. Shock (Ed.), *Aging: Some social and biological aspects* (pp. 241–260). Publication No. 65. Washington, DC: American Association for the Advancement of Science.

Shock, Nathan W. 1977. Biological theories of aging. In J. E. Birren & K. W. Schaie (Eds.), *Handbook of the psychology of aging* (pp. 103–115). New York: Van Nostrand Reinhold.

Shuchter, Stephen R. 1986. *Dimensions of grief: Adjusting to the death of a spouse.* San Francisco: Jossey-Bass.

Siegler, Ilene C. 1989. Developmental health psychology. In M. Storandt & G. R. VandenBos (Eds.), *The adult years: Continuity and change* (pp. 119–142). Washington, DC: American Psychological Association.

Siegler, Ilene C. & Costa, Paul T., Jr. 1985. Health behavior relationships. In J. E. Birren & K. Warner Schaie (Eds.), *Handbook of the psychology of aging* (2nd ed., pp. 144–166). New York: Van Nostrand Reinhold.

Siegler, Ilene C.; McCarty, Sarah M.; & Logue, Patrick E. 1982. Wechsler Memory Scale scores, selective attrition, and distance from death. *Journal of Gerontology, 37,* 176–181.

Siegler, Ilene C.; Nowlin, John B.; & Blumenthal, James. A. 1980. Health and behavior: Methodological considerations for adult development and aging. In L. W. Poon (Ed.), *Aging in the 1980s* (pp. 599–612). Washington, DC: American Psychological Association.

Silverman, Phyllis R. 1988. Widow-to-widow: A mutual help program for the widowed. In R. H. Price, E. L. Cowen, R. P. Lorion & J. Ramos-McKay (Eds.), *14 Ounces of Prevention: A casebook for practitioners* (pp. 175–186). Washington, DC: American Psychological Association.

Silverstone, Barbara & Hyman, Helen Kandel. 1982. *You and your aging parent: The modern family's guide to emotional, physical, and financial problems.* New York: Pantheon.

Simmons, Leo W. 1945. *The role of the aged in primitive society.* New Haven, CT: Yale University Press.

Singer, Margaret T. 1963. Personality measurements in the aged. In J. E. Birren et al. (Eds.), *Human aging: A biological and behavioral study* (pp. 217–249). Publication No. (HSM) 71-9051. Washington, DC: U.S. Government Printing Office.

Sinnott, Jan D. 1981. The theory of relativity: A metatheory for development? *Human Development, 24,* 293–311.

Sinnott, Jan D. 1982. Correlates of sex roles of older adults. *Journal of Gerontology, 37,* 587–594.

Sinnott, Jan D. 1984a (August). *Everyday memory and the solution of everyday problems.* Paper presented at the meeting of the American Psychological Association, Toronto. (Cited in Sinnott, 1986.)

Sinnott, Jan D. 1984b. Older men, older women: Are their perceived sex roles similar? *Sex Roles, 10,* 847–856.

Sinnott, Jan D. 1984c. Postformal reasoning: The relativistic stage. In M. L. Commons, F. A. Richards & C. Armon (Eds.), *Beyond formal operations: Late adolescent and adult cognitive development* (pp. 357–380). New York: Praeger.

Sinnott, Jan D. 1986. Prospective/intentional and incidental everyday memory: Effects of age and passage of time. *Psychology and Aging, 1,* 110–116.

Sinnott, Jan D. 1988. Sex roles in adulthood and old age. In D. B. Carter (Ed.), *Current conceptions of sex roles and sex typing.* New York: Praeger.

Sinnott, Jan D. & Guttmann, David. 1978. Dialectics of decision making in older adults. *Human Development, 21,* 190–200.

Skard, A. G. 1965. Maternal deprivation: The research and implications. *Journal of Marriage and Family, 27,* 3.

Skinner, B. F. & Vaughan, M. E. 1983. *Enjoy old age: A program of self-management.* New York: Norton.

Smyer, Michael A. 1988 (August). *Nursing homes as a setting for psychological practice: Public policy perspectives.* Paper presented at the meeting of the American Psychological Association, Atlanta.

Social Security Administration. 1986. *Income and resources of the population 65 and over.* SSA Publication No. 13-11727. Washington, DC: U.S. Government Printing Office.

Sommers, Dixie & Eck, Alan. 1977 (January). Occupational mobility in the American labor force. *Monthly Labor Review,* 3–19.

Sontag, Susan. 1972 (September 23). The double standard of aging. *Saturday Review of the Society,* 29–38.

Spence, Janet T. & Helmreich, Robert L. 1978. *Masculinity and femininity: Their psychological dimensions, correlates, and antecedents.* Austin: University of Texas Press.

Spence, Janet T.; Helmreich, Robert; & Stapp, Joy. 1975. Ratings of self and peers on sex-role attributes and their relations to self-esteem and conceptions of masculinity and femininity. *Journal of Personality and Social Psychology, 32,* 29–39.

Spiegel, Paul Martin. 1972. Theories of aging. In P. S. Timiras (Ed.), *Developmental physiology and aging* (pp. 564–580). New York: Macmillan Co.

Spitzer, Mary E. 1988. Taste acuity in institutionalized and noninstitutionalized elderly men. *Journal of Gerontology: Psychological Sciences, 43,* P71–P74.

Stall, Ron D.; Coates, Thomas J.; & Hoff, Colleen. 1988. Behavioral risk reduction for HIV infection among gay and bisexual men: A review of results from the United States. *American Psychologist, 43,* 878–885.

Stanaway, Anne. 1987. The happiness and longevity club. *Japan Society Newsletter, 34*(7), 3–9.

Staples, Robert. 1976. The Black American family. In C. H. Mindel & R. W. Habenstein (Eds.), *Ethnic families in America* (2nd ed., pp. 217–244). New York: Elsevier.

Starr, Bernard D. 1985. Sexuality and aging. *Annual Review of Gerontology and Geriatrics, 5,* 97–126.

Starr, Joyce R. & Carns, Donald E. 1972 (February). Singles in the city. *Society, 9,* 43–48.

Sternberg, Robert J. & Berg, Cynthia A. 1987. What are theories of adult intellectual development theories of? In C. Schooler & K. W. Schaie (Eds.), *Cognitive functioning and social structure over the life course* (pp. 3–23). Norwood, NJ: Ablex.

Sterns, Harvey L. & Alexander, Ralph A. 1987. Industrial gerontology: The aging individual and work. *Annual Review of Gerontology and Geriatrics, 7,* 243–264.

Stevens, Joseph C. & Cain, William S. 1987. Old-age deficits in the sense of smell as gauged by thresholds, magnitude matching, and odor identification. *Psychology and Aging, 2,* 36–42.

Stevens, Scott J.; Cooper, Pamela E.; & Thomas, L. Eugene. 1980. Age norms for Templer's Death Anxiety Scale. *Psychological Reports, 46,* 205–206.

Stewart, Abigail J. & Healy, Joseph M., Jr. 1989. Linking individual development and social changes. *American Psychologist, 44,* 30–42.

Stewart, Wendy A. 1977. A psychosocial study of the formation of the early adult life structure in women. *Dissertation Abstracts International, 38,* 381B. (University Microfilms No. 77-14849.)

Stirner, Fritz W. 1978. The transportation needs of the elderly in a large urban environment. *The Gerontologist, 18,* 207–211.

Stoddard, Sandol. 1978. *The hospice movement: A better way of caring for the dying.* New York: Vintage Books.

Stone, Robyn. 1987. *Exploding the myths: Caregiving in America.* U.S. House of Representatives, Select Committee on Aging, Publication No. 99–611. Washington, DC: U.S. Government Printing Office.

Storandt, Martha; Botwinick, Jack; Danziger, Warren L.; Berg, Leonard; & Hughes, Charles P. 1984. Psychometric differentiation of mild senile dementia of the Alzheimer type. *Archives of Neurology, 41,* 497–499.

Strauss, Anselm (Ed.). 1964. *George Herbert Mead: On social psychology.* Chicago: University of Chicago Press.

Strauss, Anselm L. & Glaser, Barney G. 1970. Patterns of dying. In O. G. Brim, Jr., H. E. Freeman, S. Levine & N. A. Scotch (Eds.), *The dying patient* (pp. 129–155). New York: Russell Sage Foundation.

Strayer, David L.; Wickens, Christopher D. & Braune, Rolf. 1987. Adult age differences in the speed of capacity of information processing: 2. An electrophysiological approach. *Psychology and Aging, 2,* 99–110.

Strehler, Bernard L. 1977. *Time, cells, and aging* (2nd ed.). New York: Academic Press.

Streib, Gordon F. 1985. Social stratification and aging. In R. H. Binstock & E. Shanas (Eds.), *Handbook of aging and the social sciences* (2nd ed., pp. 339–368). New York: Van Nostrand Reinhold.

Streib, Gordon F.; Folts, W. Edward; & Hilker, Mary Anne. 1984. *Old homes — new families: Shared living for the elderly.* New York: Columbia University Press.

Streib, Gordon F. & Schneider, Clement J. 1971. *Retirement in American society: Impact and process.* Ithaca, NY: Cornell University Press.

Suls, J. 1982. Social support, interpersonal relations and health: Benefits and liabilities. In G. Sanders & J. Suls (Eds.), *The social psychology of health and illness* (pp. 57–71). Hillsdale, NJ: Erlbaum.

Sussman, Marvin B. 1985. The family life of old people. In R. H. Binstock & E. Shanas (Eds.), *Handbook of aging and the social sciences* (2nd ed., pp. 415–449). New York: Van Nostrand Reinhold.

Sussman, Marvin B. & Burchinal, Lee. 1962. Kin family network: Unheralded structure in current conceptualizations of family functioning. *Marriage and Family Living, 24,* 231–240.

Taeuber, Cynthia M. & Valdisera, Victor. 1986. *Women in the American economy.* Current

Population Reports, Series P-23, No. 146, U. S. Bureau of the Census. Washington, DC: U. S. Government Printing Office.

Talbert, George B. 1977. Aging of the reproductive system. In C. E. Finch & L. Hayflick (Eds.), *Handbook of the biology of aging* (pp. 318–356). New York: Van Nostrand Reinhold.

Taylor, Jean. 1987 (Spring). Hospice house: A homelike inpatient unit. *Generations, 11,* 22–26.

Thomas, Paula D.; Goodwin, Jean M.; & Goodwin, James S. 1985. Effect of social support on stress related changes in cholesterol level, uric acid level, and immune function in an elderly sample. *American Journal of Psychiatry, 142,* 735–737.

Thompson, William R. 1968. Genetics and personality. In E. Norbeck, D. Price-Williams & W. M. McCord (Eds.), *The study of personality: An interdisciplinary appraisal* (pp. 161–174). New York: Holt, Rinehart & Winston.

Thurstone, L. L. & Thurstone, T. G. 1949. *Examiners manual, SRA Primary Mental Abilities test (Form 11-17).* Chicago: Science Research Associates.

Tibbitts, Clark. 1979. Can we invalidate negative stereotypes of aging? *The Gerontologist, 19,* 10–20.

Tice, Raymond R. 1987. Summary and discussion of Part V. In H. R. Warner, R. N. Butler, R. L. Sprott & E. L. Schneider (Eds.), *Modern biological theories of aging* (pp. 211–215). New York: Raven Press.

Tice, Raymond R. & Setlow, Richard B. 1985. DNA repair and replication in aging organisms and cells. In C. E. Finch & E. L. Schneider (Eds.), *Handbook of the biology of aging* (2nd ed., pp. 173–224). New York: Van Nostrand Reinhold.

Timiras, P. S. 1972. *Developmental physiology and aging.* New York: Macmillan Co.

Tobin, Sheldon S. 1987. A structural approach to families. In T. H. Brubaker (Ed.), *Aging, health, and family: Long-term care* (pp. 42–55). Newbury Park, CA: Sage Publications.

Tobin, Sheldon S. & Lieberman, Morton A. 1976. *A last home for the aged: Critical implications of institutionalization.* San Francisco: Jossey-Bass.

Tolchin, Martin. 1988 (November 6). Pressure spurs move for better insurance on long-term care. *New York Times,* 1, 26.

Tolstoy, Leo. 1886/1960. The death of Ivan Ilych. In L. Tolstoy, *The death of Ivan Ilych and other stories* (pp. 95–156). New York: New American Library (Signet).

Torres-Gil, Fernando M. 1988 (Spring). Aging for the twenty-first century: Process, politics, and policy. *Generations, 12,* 5–9.

Troll, Lillian E. 1972. *Salience of family members in three generations.* Paper presented at the meeting of the American Psychological Association, Honolulu. (Cited in Troll & Bengtson, 1982.)

Troll, Lillian E. 1975. *Development in early and middle adulthood.* Monterey, CA: Brooks/Cole.

Troll, Lillian E. 1980. Grandparenting. In L. W. Poon (Ed.), *Aging in the 1980s: Psychological issues* (pp. 475–481). Washington, DC: American Psychological Association.

Troll, Lillian E. 1983. Grandparents: The family watchdogs. In T. Brubaker (Ed.), *Family relationships in later life* (pp. 63–74). Beverly Hills, CA: Sage Publications.

Troll, Lillian E. (Ed.) 1986. *Family issues in current gerontology.* New York: Springer.

Troll, Lillian E. & Bengtson, Vern L. 1982. Intergenerational relations throughout the life span. In B. B. Wolman (Ed.), *Handbook of developmental psychology* (pp. 890–911). Englewood Cliffs, NJ: Prentice–Hall.

Troll, Lillian E.; Miller, Sheila J.; & Atchley, Robert C. 1979. *Families in later life.* Belmont, CA: Wadsworth.

Troll, Lillian E. & Seltzer, Mildred M. 1985 (August). *Older women and poverty.* Paper presented at the annual meeting of the American Psychological Association, Los Angeles. (Cited in Troll, 1986.)

Troll, Lillian E. & Turner, Barbara F. 1976. The secular trends in sex roles and the family of later life. Paper presented at Ford Foundation conference, Merrill-Palmer Institute. (Cited in Troll, Miller & Atchley, 1979.)

Tross, Susan & Blum, June E. 1988. A review of group therapy with the older adult: Practice and research. In B. W. Maclennan, S. Saul, & M. B. Weiner (Eds.), *Group psychotherapies for the elderly* (pp. 3–29). Madison, CT: International Universities Press.

Turner, Barbara F. 1982. Sex-related differences in aging. In B. B. Wolman (Ed.), *Handbook of developmental psychology* (pp. 912–936). Englewood Cliffs, NJ: Prentice–Hall.

Tyler, Leona E. 1978. *Individuality: Human possibilities and personal choice in the psychological development of men and women.* San Francisco: Jossey-Bass.

Uhlenberg, Peter. 1977. Changing structure of the older population of the USA during the twentieth century. *The Gerontologist, 17,* 197–202.

Unger, Rhoda K. 1979. *Female and male: Psychological perspectives.* New York: Harper & Row.

U.S. Bureau of Labor Statistics. 1977. *U.S. working women: A databook.* Washington, DC: U.S. Government Printing Office.

U.S. Bureau of Labor Statistics. 1986. *Consumer expenditure survey: Interview survey, 1984.* Bulletin 2267. Washington, DC: U.S. Department of Labor.

U.S. Bureau of the Census. 1973. *Age at first marriage.* 1970 Census of the population, PC(2)-40. Washington, DC: U.S. Government Printing Office.

U.S. Bureau of the Census. 1976a. *Demographic aspects of aging and the older population in the United States.* Current Population Reports, Series P-23, No. 59. Washington, DC: U.S. Government Printing Office.

U.S. Bureau of the Census. 1976b. *Number, timing and duration of marriage and divorces in the United States: June 1975.* Current Population Reports, Series P-20, No. 297. Washington, DC: U.S. Government Printing Office.

U.S. Burean of the Census. 1977. *Marriage, divorce, widowhood and remarriage by family characteristics: June 1975.* Current Population Reports, Series P-20, No. 312. Washington, DC: U.S. Government Printing Office.

U.S. Bureau of the Census. 1983. *Child care arrangements of working mothers: June 1982.* Current Population Reports, Series P-23, No. 129. Washington, DC: U.S. Government Printing Office.

U.S. Bureau of the Census. 1988a. *Marital status and living arrangements: March 1987.* Current Population Reports, Series P-20, No. 423. Washington, DC: U.S. Government Printing Office.

U.S. Bureau of the Census. 1988b. *United States population estimates, by age, sex, and race, 1980 to 1987.* Current Population Reports, Series P-25, No. 1022. Washington, DC: U.S. Government Printing Office.

U.S. Department of Labor. 1976. *The earnings gap between women and men.* Washington, DC: U.S. Government Printing Office.

U.S. Senate. 1987–1988. *Aging America: Trends and projections* (1987–1988 ed.) Available from U.S. Senate Special Committee on Aging, Washington, DC 20510.

Vaillant, George E. 1977. *Adaptation to life.* Boston: Little, Brown.

van de Walle, Etienne. 1976. Household dynamics in a Belgian village, 1847–1866. *Family History, 1,* 80–94.

Van Dusen, Roxann A. & Sheldon, Eleanor Bernert. 1976. The changing status of American women: A life cycle perspective. *American Psychologist, 31,* 106–116.

Vaux, Alan. 1985. Variations in social support associated with gender, ethnicity, and age. *Journal of Social Issues, 41*(1), 89–110.

Wack, Jeffery T. 1982. Appraisals and patterning of affect and coping in encounters with everyday stressors. *Dissertation Abstracts International, 43,* 1601B. (University Microfilms No. 82-22332.)

Waldron, I. 1976. Why do women live longer than men? *Journal of Human Stress, 2,* 1–13.

Ware, Mark E. & Millard, Richard J. (Eds.). 1987. *Handbook on student development: Advising, career development, and field placement.* Hillsdale, NJ: Erlbaum.

Webber, Howard. 1963 (March 30). Games. *The New Yorker,* 42–46.

Wechsler, David. 1955. *Manual for the Adult Intelligence Scale.* New York: The Psychological Corporation.

Weg, Ruth B. 1978. *Nutrition and the later years.* Los Angeles: University of Southern California Press.

Weg, Ruth B. 1983. Changing physiology of aging: Normal and pathological. In D. S. Woodruff & J. E. Birren (Eds.), *Aging: Scientific perspectives and social issues* (2nd ed., pp. 242–284). Monterey, CA: Brooks/Cole.

Weg, Ruth B. 1985. Nutrients and nutrition. In G. M. Chaisson-Stewart (Ed.), *Depression in the elderly: An interdisciplinary approach* (pp. 214–240). New York: Wiley.

Weindruch, Richard & Walford, Roy L. 1989. *The retardation of aging and disease by dietary restriction.* Springfield, IL: Charles C Thomas.

Weiner, Yoash & Vaitenas, Rimantas. 1977. Personality correlates of voluntary midcareer change in enterprising occupations. *Journal of Applied Psychology, 62,* 706–712.

Weisman, Avery D. & Kastenbaum, Robert. 1968. *The psychological autopsy: A study of the terminal phase of life.* Community Mental Health Journal Monograph No. 4. New York: Behavioral Publications, Inc.

Weiss, Alfred D. 1959. Sensory functions. In J. E. Birren (Ed.), *Handbook of aging and the individual* (pp. 503–542). Chicago: University of Chicago Press.

Weissman, August. 1891. *Essays on heredity.* Oxford: Clarendon Press.

West, Sheree L. 1985. Sharing and privacy in shared housing for older people. *Dissertation Abstracts International, 46,* 1374A. (University Microfilms No. 85-15671.)

Whitbourne, Susan Krauss. 1985. The psychological construction of the life span. In J. E. Birren & K. W. Schaie (Eds.), *Handbook of the psychology of aging* (2nd ed., pp. 594–618). New York: Van Nostrand Reinhold.

Whitbourne, Susan Krauss. 1987. Personality development in adulthood and old age: Relationships among identity style, health, and well-being. *Annual Review of Gerontology and Geriatrics, 7,* 189–216.

White, Nancy & Cunningham, Walter R. 1988. Is terminal drop pervasive or specific? *Journal of Gerontology: Psychological Sciences, 43,* P141–P144.

White, Robert W. 1987. *A memoir: Seeking the shape of personality.* Marlborough, NH: Homestead Press.

Whitehead, Alfred North. 1929/1969. *Process and reality.* New York: Free Press.

Wilensky, Harold L. 1961. Orderly careers and social participation: The impact of work history on social integration in the middle mass. *American Sociological Review, 26,* 521–539.

Wilkie, Frances & Eisdorfer, Carl. 1974. Terminal changes in intelligence. In E. Palmore (Ed.), *Normal aging II: Reports from the Duke Longitudinal Studies, 1970–1973* (pp. 103–115). Durham, NC: Duke University Press.

Wilkinson, H. Jean & Wilkinson, John W. 1986–1987. Evaluation of a hospice volunteer training program. *Omega, 17,* 263–275.

Williams, G. C. 1957. Pleiotropy, natural selection and the evolution of senescence. *Evolution, 11,* 398–411.

Williams, Juanita H. 1977. *Psychology of women: Behavior in a biosocial context.* New York: Norton.

Williams, T. Franklin. 1987. Introduction. In H. R. Warner, R. N. Butler, R. L. Sprott & E. L. Schneider (Eds.), *Modern biological theories of aging* (pp. ix–x). New York: Raven Press.

Willie, Charles V. 1988. *A new look at Black families* (3rd ed.). Dix Hills, NY: General Hall.

Willis, Lee; Thomas, Paula; Garry, Philip J.; & Goodwin, James S. 1987. A prospective study of response to stressful life events in initially healthy elders. *Journal of Gerontology, 42,* 627–630.

Willis, Sherry L. & Baltes, Paul B. 1980. Intelligence in adulthood and aging: Contemporary issues. In L. W. Poon (Ed.), *Aging in the 1980s: Psychological issues* (pp. 260–272). Washington, DC: American Psychological Association.

Wilson, K. B. & DeShane, M. 1982. The legal rights of grandparents: A preliminary discussion. *The Gerontologist, 22,* 67–71.

Woehrer, Carol E. 1978. Cultural pluralism in American families: The influence of ethnicity on social aspects of aging. *Family Coordinator, 27,* 329–339.

Wood, Vivian & Robertson, Joan F. 1976. The significance of grandparenthood. In J. F. Gubrium (Ed.), *Time, roles, and self in old age* (pp. 278–304). New York: Human Sciences Press.

Woodruff, Diana S. 1985. Arousal, sleep, and aging. In J. E. Birren & K. W. Schaie (Eds.), *Handbook of the psychology of aging* (2nd ed., pp. 261–295). New York: Van Nostrand Reinhold.

Woodruff, Diana S. & Birren, James E. 1972. Age changes and cohort differences in personality. *Developmental Psychology, 6,* 252–259.

Wurtman, Richard J. 1985. Alzheimer's disease. *Scientific American, 252,* 62–74.

Zarit, Steven H.; Orr, Nancy K.; & Zarit, Judy M. 1985. *The hidden victims of Alzheimer's disease: Families under stress.* New York: New York University Press.

Zarit, Steven H. & Zarit, Judy M. 1982. Families under stress: Interventions for caregivers of senile dementia patients. *Psychotherapy: Theory, Research & Practice, 19,* 461–471.

Zeits, Carol R. & Prince, Robert M. 1982. Child effects on parents. In B. B. Wolman (Ed.), *Handbook of developmental psychology* (pp. 751–770). Englewood Cliffs, NJ: Prentice–Hall.

Glossary

Acceptance A quiet culmination of the dying process that is one of the typical reactions to a terminal illness, according to Kübler-Ross.

Acquired Immune Deficiency Syndrome (AIDS) A chronic disease that causes the body to become susceptible to several unusual and potentially fatal infections.

Acute Disease A temporary illness from which one recovers completely.

Adaptation An individual's attempt to preserve psychological well-being and physical health.

Ageism A form of social bias that can stigmatize individuals on the basis of chronological age.

Age norms Expectations about behavior that is appropriate for persons of particular chronological ages or at various points in the lifespan.

Age Simulation An experimental method that allows an investigator to manipulate variables affecting performance (e.g., typing speed) to identify factors that may be responsible for age differences.

Aging Changes that are caused solely by the passage of time.

Alzheimer's disease A common cause of *dementia* in which certain areas of the brain become impaired and there is an overall loss of neurons (also known as dementia of the Alzheimer type, DAT, or SDAT).

Androgyny Mixture or blending of both masculine and feminine characteristics in an individual's personality.

Anger One of the typical reactions to a terminal illness. Envy and resentment may be directed at anyone who is present and may be especially difficult for family members, who may also feel angry at the unfairness of the illness and the prospect of death.

Anticipatory Socialization The process of preparation for a change in role or status and learning the norms and expectations that will be associated with the new role or status.

Arthritis Inflammation of a joint (e.g., wrist, elbow, hip) which may be caused by a number of diseases (such as rheumatoid arthritis) and may begin at any age, sometimes after a joint is injured.

Bargaining One of the typical reactions to a terminal illness. The person thinks that a "bargain" can be struck to postpone or reverse the course of the illness.

Behaviorism The view that internal characteristics of the person are largely irrelevant since the important influences on behavior are the reinforcement contingencies in the environment.

Bereavement Reactions A person's characteristic reactions to the death of a spouse, beloved person, or similar loss.

Biofeedback A procedure by which individuals learn to reduce muscle tension or other physical symptoms through auditory or visual feedback.

Biological Age Whether one is relatively young or old based on the level of biological development and physical health.

Boarding Homes Facilities often operated by local residents for modest profit. The home may provide some personal care, but most are not licensed and the quality of care is variable.

Career An occupation that demands commitment to the work role, continual updating of job-related knowledge, and expectations of promotion.

Note. Words in *italics* denote separate entries in the Glossary.

Career Clock The individual's subjective sense of being "on time" or "behind time" in career development in terms of social norms and expectations.

Career Consolidation Achieving success, promotion, and recognition at work. The central theme during early adulthood in Vaillant's study of men.

Cataract An abnormal condition that results from the lens of the eye becoming opaque.

Chaining of Life Events One change precipitates another, and another in turn.

Child-rearing Phase Period of the family cycle when one or more children are living at home.

Chronic Disease A long-term illness that cannot be cured but whose symptoms can be treated.

Chronic Impairments Hearing impairment, visual impairment, and reduced ability to get around because of orthopedic impairment caused by chronic diseases, injuries, or falls.

Chronological Age The number of years since birth. It serves as an index of a large number of factors that interact to produce development.

Cognition The way we think about and know things. It includes paying attention to particular stimuli, memory, solving problems, and understanding the physical and social world.

Cohabitation Living with a person of the other gender in a sexually intimate relationship.

Cohort In developmental research, a group of people born at about the same time. As members of this cohort move through the life span together, they experience similar historical influences that differ from those experienced by members of other cohorts.

Collagen A fibrous protein that is one of the components in connective tissue and is found throughout the body. Connective tissues function in many important ways, such as mechanical support of the body and in repair of injury.

Compliance Voluntary cooperation with prescribed treatment procedures.

Confidant An intimate relationship in which one can confide in the person and talk about oneself or one's problems.

Contextualism The view that lifespan human development can best be understood within its multifaceted psychosocial context.

Continuity Theory The view that adults seek to maintain and preserve the basic structure of their life as they grow older.

Counterpart Theory Evolutionary view of human aging as a result of the late life effects (counterpart) of characteristics that had primary adaptive importance prior to the end of reproductive ability.

Cross-over Effect Reversal of a statistical difference after a particular age (e.g., Black versus White life expectancy).

Cross-sectional Study A research method in which information is gathered from individuals who represent a cross-section of ages at one point in time. Age differences found in this way are likely to reflect *cohort* effects.

Crystallized Intelligence Abilities that do not decline or may increase with age during adulthood, such as verbal comprehension, concept formation, and logical reasoning.

Delirium Disturbed mental functioning which frequently includes dramatic symptoms such as hallucination, delusions, disorientation, increased or decreased alertness, attention deficits, and disturbed sleep patterns. If the cause is treated, complete recovery is possible.

Dementia Severe cognitive impairment affecting memory, abstract thinking, judgment, or personality, caused by conditions such as Alzheimer's disease and cerebrovascular disease (multi-infarct dementia). If the cause is reversible, complete recovery is possible.

Denial A healthy psychological defense against shocking news that allows a terminally ill patient the opportunity to live for short periods of time as if the illness were not fatal.

Dependency Ratio Statistic showing the relative number of older or younger persons (presumed to be "dependent") compared to those persons between ages 18 and 64 (presumed to be economically productive).

Depressive Syndrome One of the most prevalent and most treatable of the mental disorders affecting the elderly. It is characterized by prolonged depressed mood or loss of interest or pleasure in life and a variety of related symptoms.

Development A progressive, sequential, unidirectional course of human life that follows essentially the same pattern generation after generation; it is also circular in that as each generation matures, it sows the seeds of succeeding generations.

Developmental Perspective A focus on factors that interact to cause growth and change throughout the lifespan; it stresses patterns of stability and change that describe characteristics of individuals in general at particular points in their life cycle.

Developmental Research Empirical research that focuses on change and stability over time, the order of sequential events, and the effect of factors linked to chronological age.

Dialectical Interaction The clash of ideas or opposite qualities within a person in which there is a tension between two or more opposing forces. The result of this interaction is a new synthesis that reflects not the sum of the forces, but a resolution of them in a way that is different from the original separate forces.

Dialectical Thinking Intellectual analysis that focuses on the conflict between interacting forces that are always changing.

Disease Disorder of bodily functions that may occur within a broad age range.

Disorderly Work History An employment pattern in which there is neither vertical nor horizontal progression that provides increased status in the sequence of jobs an individual holds.

Double Standard of Aging Some of the gender differences in aging seem to favor men, including social status, income, and opportunity for heterosexual social and sexual partnerships.

The Dream The inner sense one has of how one wants life to work out. This is a major theme in Levinson's description of the Early Adult Transition phase of adult development.

Dual-career Families Both partners pursue careers that demand commitment to the work role, continual updating of job-related knowledge, and expectations of promotion.

Dual Labor Market Women often were limited to occupations where the pay and working conditions were not attractive to men. These occupations also may have been relatively low-paying, but allowed women to find employment when their husband's job required a transfer.

Earnings Gap The difference between median income of women and men from paid employment for year-round, full-time work.

Eight Ages of Life. Erik Erikson's model of human development as a series of crucial turning points stretching from birth to death.

Elder Abuse Physical or psychological harm com-

mitted against an older person, for example by a caregiver, relative, or spouse.

Empirical Research Observation, inquiry about experience, and experiments that test hypotheses with data from direct observation or experience.

Encapsulation A model of cognition in which performance in specific areas of *expertise* does not reflect slowing in general processing rate with age because skill and knowledge enhance performance.

Erectile Dysfunction Inability to have an erection of the penis (sometimes called impotence).

Establishment Phase Period of the family cycle that begins with the partners living together as a couple and continues until the relationship is fairly well established or the first child is born.

Estrogen Replacement Therapy (ERT) Prescribed supplements of estrogens and progestins so that the post-menopausal woman's body has hormonal levels similar to those before menopause.

Event Related Potentials (ERP) A measure of electrical responses of the brain to specific stimuli.

Existential Perspective The philosophical view that people strive to find meaning in life, and that death is an ever-possible choice that provides a core of meaning to life.

Expertise Knowledge about a specific topic that has become intuitive, automatic, and highly skilled.

Extended Family Those individuals one is related to through blood or marriage, as well as "fictive kin" who are treated as family members even though they are not actual relatives.

Family Cycle Developmental stages in families marked by milestones such as marriage, birth of the first child, birth of the last child, last child leaving home, and widowhood.

Fluid Intelligence Abilities that decrease with age during adulthood, such as seeing relationships among stimulus patterns, drawing inferences from relationships, and comprehending implications.

Force of Mortality Mathematical representation of the relation between advancing age and the increased probability of death.

Formal Operations The most advanced stage in Piaget's theory of cognitive development characterized by mental abilities such as thinking about logical hypotheses, abstract objects, and future possibilities that are not concrete.

Free Time Traditionally viewed as nonproductive,

and potentially dangerous, idleness in our work-oriented society. It may be a problem for some retired or unemployed persons.

Funeral A socially structured event to commemorate the change in social status of the deceased (from life to death) and to provide a means for public expression of grief.

Gay Men Some men who are sexually attracted to men identify themselves as a part of the gay community and adopt this term as a positive label for their life-style.

Gender Man or woman; used instead of the term "sex" because female and male characteristics do not result from biological sex alone, but from the interaction of social, psychological, and physiological factors.

Generational Stake Each generation has an investment in the future that may differ from other generations. For example, parents want the next generation to carry on family traditions, whereas adolescents often feel a need to establish their own identity.

Generativity The seventh stage in Erikson's model, defined as having left one's mark by producing something that will outlive oneself in some way, usually through parenthood or in occupational achievements.

Gerontocracy Government by the old, but not necessarily government for the elderly.

Grief Subjective states that follow a significant loss and accompany the *mourning* process.

Hassles Seemingly trivial events that produce stress.

Heart Disease The leading cause of death in the United States; related to impaired blood flow to the heart muscle and a variety of other conditions.

Hope During a terminal illness, the wish, however unlikely, that a cure might be found for the disease threatening one's life, or at least for death without suffering and in the company of loved ones.

Hospice A model of care for terminally ill persons who would not benefit from surgery or similar aggressive medical treatment but who may need relief from pain, a refreshing physical environment, or support for caregivers at home.

Hot Flash Sensations of warmth and flushing in the skin accompanied by perspiration, experienced by many women from time to time after menopause (also known as hot flush).

Hypochondriasis Unfounded belief that one is ill.

I An aspect of the *self*, as described by G. H. Mead, that involves moment-by-moment experiencing, awareness, and consciousness of oneself. It provides a continuing source of creativity, surprise, and novelty to the self.

Identity An integrated view of one's talents, beliefs, and impact on other people; a sense of continuity and consistency of oneself over time; and reasonable certainty about the part one is playing in the scheme of life.

Idiosyncratic Transitions Changes in life patterns that are unique to a particular individual or for which there are no social expectations about when these unscheduled events should occur (e.g., winning a lottery or divorce).

Increased Interiority Personality changes with aging identified in the Kansas City studies that are characterized by increased self-reflection, introspection, and reminiscence.

Individual Variation Since general developmental trends apply to many people, but not equally to everyone, unique patterns can be examined to understand a particular person in a specific socio-cultural environment at a specific time in life.

Information Processing Perception, understanding, reaction, and response to a stimulus.

Integrity A sense of affirmation that one's life has been meaningful. As the final stage in Erikson's model, it is triggered by the nearness of death; the crucial task is to evaluate one's life and accomplishments.

Intelligence A characteristic of an individual that affects the ability to solve problems. It involves information encoding, cognitive processing, memory, and communicating the solution of the problem.

Interaction The effect of multiple forces in which the result is likely to be different from the sum of the parts.

Interaction Experience Knowledge gained from personal contact with a variety of people in different types of interpersonal relationships.

Interdisciplinary Perspective The use of different academic disciplines, such as anthropology, biology, sociology, or psychology, to examine a topic.

Intimacy A mutual relationship of affection and

trust that involves appreciation of each other's uniqueness and separateness. It does not require sexuality, but may involve friendship and mutual inspiration.

Kinkeepers Family members (usually women) who strive to maintain relationships within the multi-generational family.

Leisure (1) Freely chosen activity that is not related to one's work, according to Kelly. (2) A state of mind defined by two interrelated dimensions: perceived freedom of choice and the degree of intrinsic motivation for engaging in the activity, according to Neulinger.

Lesbians Some women who are sexually attracted to women identify themselves as a part of the lesbian and gay community and adopt these terms as positive labels for their life-style (some also use the term gay women).

Life Care Facilities Living arrangements that offer a comprehensive range of housing—from self-sufficient living in an apartment to acute or chronic nursing care—in one location.

Life Chances Statistical probabilities regarding health, longevity, marital status, family size, and income based on the individual's location within the social structure of society.

Life Review A process that may lead to increased self-awareness and involves reminiscence, thinking about oneself, reconsideration of previous experiences and their meanings, and pausing to look into a mirror.

Life Satisfaction An empirical measure of adaptive adjustment to aging based on responses to a questionnaire or interview.

Longitudinal Sequence A research technique in which a group of participants is studied for a few years, possibly over a period of time that might represent a developmental turning point.

Longitudinal Study A research strategy whereby a group of participants is selected appropriate for the question being studied, and data are collected from them periodically over several years.

Me An aspect of the *self*, as described by G. H. Mead, that consists of the objective characteristics of the person that can be observed, examined, touched, measured, or listened to during social interaction.

Meals on Wheels Local programs, sometimes affiliated with Senior Centers, that deliver prepared food to homebound elderly persons.

Means-test Program Economic or medical assistance available only to individuals who qualify because they have low income and a limited amount of savings. Each state government sets its own guidelines for eligibility.

Medicaid National program that provides health care to all recipients of public assistance (regardless of age) and to the "medically needy" as defined by each state government.

Medicare U.S. government program that provides specific health care benefits to any person over age 65 who is entitled to Social Security or railroad retirement benefits. Some persons under age 65, surviving spouses, or dependent spouses may also be covered.

Memory Learning, storage, and retrieval of mental information.

Menopause The ending of the menstrual cycle in women.

Mentor A person who is more experienced, typically older, who functions as a kind of sponsor or guide to lead the person into the field he or she is entering.

Metacognition Thinking about thinking (e.g., introspection) that is characteristic of advanced thinking abilities developed during adolescence.

Midlife Crisis A term coined by Jaques to describe psychological changes triggered in middle age by the growing awareness of personal mortality.

Milestone An event that stands out in one's memory, or in one's future plans, as a significant turning point, marker, or personal reference point in one's life history.

Modified Extended Family Interconnected *nuclear families* that provide close ties across generations and among siblings but maintain separate autonomous households.

Mourning The psychological process set in motion by the death of a loved person, or similar loss.

Multigenerational Households Extended family household in which three or more generations live together.

Negative Stress Life events which pose emotional or physical difficulties for the individual that are perceived as problematic or harmful.

New Parents Phase Period of the family cycle that begins with pregnancy and the birth of the first child.

Nonevent A normative event—such as the birth of a grandchild—that does not occur and may be a cause of stress.

Normative Transitions Changes that are expected according to the social norms for individuals at particular times of their lives, including events such as graduation from high school, marriage, grandparenthood, and retirement.

Norms A set of expectations about appropriate behavior that people use to regulate their behavior and to respond to others' behavior.

Nuclear Families Households consisting only of a mother, father, and their children.

Occupational Choice The process of selecting an occupation that usually involves personal background, role models, experience, interests, personality, and research into occupations.

Occupational Cycle Progression over time and potential turning points or milestones in the development of one's career.

Off-time Events Predictable occurrences during the course of an individual's lifetime that occur unusually early or unusually late, according to the *social clock*.

Off-time Transitions Changes or developmental events that occur either too early or too late according to social norms.

Ombudsman A person in the state or local Office of Aging who has authority to investigate complaints regarding long-term care and take corrective action.

One Life – One Career Imperative The assumption that people find their occupation, make it a part of their identity, and remain in that same occupation as long as they live, or until retirement.

On-time Events Social milestones that take place at the expected times according to the *social clock*.

Operation Mental actions that form a coherent and reversible system; for example, the union of two classes (mothers and fathers are parents), or addition or subtraction of two numbers.

Osteoarthritis Degenerative joint disease related to wear and stress of the joint, heredity, and being overweight; unlike arthritis, the joint is usually not inflamed.

Osteoporosis Loss of bone mass with aging, often related to the decline in estrogen after menopause and inadequate calcium in the diet.

Perceived Age The individual's perception of how old he or she feels.

Personality Characteristics that combine to make a person unique, are fairly stable over time, and reflect a person's style of adaptation to the environment.

Phases of Bereavement Typical reactions of grief and mourning that last a year or two following the loss of a loved person.

Physiological Aging Declining "physiological competence that inevitably increases the incidence and intensifies the effects of accidents, disease, and other forms of environmental stress" (Timiras, 1972, p. 465).

Pluralistic The view that developmental processes begin at different points in time and follow different courses depending on the aspect of development in question.

Positive Stress Life events which pose emotional or physical challenges to the individual that are perceived as beneficial or productive.

Postformal Operations Styles of thinking more advanced than the last stage in Piaget's theory of cognitive development.

Postparental Phase Period of the family cycle after the last child leaves home; it may also include grandparenthood and widowhood.

Preparatory Depression Grief that a dying person may experience that results from the prospect of giving up all the beloved things in the world.

Preretirement Planning Anticipatory socialization for retirement, including arranging for income and health care, anticipating roles and activities, and considering alternative work options.

Problem-finding Creative thought in discovering and formulating problems, raising questions about problems, and the process of thinking reflected in scientific curiosity.

Prospective Memory Remembering something in order to reach a goal or to accomplish an activity that requires planning.

Psychological Age Level of psychological development as measured by a series of developmental stages (e.g., Erikson's Eight Ages of Life).

Psychological Autopsy An analysis of the psychosocial aspects of the person's death with the aim of improving the support that caregivers might have provided.

Psychopathology The study of abnormal personality functioning that seeks to understand the nature and causes of psychological disorders.

Psychosocial Perspective The effect of social influences on individual development.

Reactive Depression Emotional response to actual losses caused by a serious illness. Support for the patient's self-esteem may be a helpful intervention.

Relativistic Thinking Information-processing skills such as those involved in analyzing complex interpersonal relationships that require an element of self-reference and subjectivity (e.g., emotions).

Resocialization Learning the norms and expectations that are associated with a new role or status.

Retirement The end of full-time paid employment.

Retirement Communities Living arrangements for older persons that range from loosely organized trailer parks to high-rise buildings and hotels. Some provide a range of services, usually including security, home maintenance, social activities, and community facilities.

Reversible Dementia Memory loss that is difficult to distinguish from irreversible *dementia*; however, if the cause is identified and treated, complete recovery is possible.

Role Behavior that is expected from a person occupying a social position (e.g., mother). Since many social positions have role behaviors associated with them, the social position is often called a role.

Role Model A respected person whom one identifies with and seeks to emulate.

Self A human characteristic that requires the capacity to interact with other persons in social settings through the use of communication and language, according to G. H. Mead. The self is a process that consists of two interacting aspects, *I* and *me*.

Self-consciousness The process by which an individual becomes aware of his or her *self* and reflects on it; it involves viewing oneself as if seen through the eyes of another person.

Self Experience Knowledge of oneself based on

introspection and personal reactions to a variety of individuals and situations.

Senescence Period of biological aging and decline.

Sequential Study A research method that combines *cross-sectional* and *longitudinal* strategies and requires a sophistical statistical procedure to analyze those factors that change with age, those that reflect the year the study was conducted, and those that reflect the year the person was born.

Shared Living Homes Living arrangements for a group of unrelated persons who neither are able to live independently nor need institutional care. Most homes have a small paid staff who manage meals and maintenance and may provide other services, but personal care and medical care are not provided.

Significant Symbols Words or gestures that have essentially the same meaning to everyone involved in the social interaction.

Situation Experience Knowledge gained from personal exposure to different cultural, geographic, and social circumstances.

Social Age An individual's status regarding socially defined milestones of development (e.g., working full-time, marriage, parenthood, grandparenthood).

Social Behaviorism The view that one's roles and other behaviors are maintained or modified by the social and interpersonal consequences of these behaviors.

Social Clock An internal sense of the best time to reach social milestones. It acts as a prod to speed up or as a brake to slow one's progress through the social events of the lifeline.

Socialization The process by which individuals learn to perform various social roles adequately and by which social norms, values, and expectations are transmitted from one generation to the next.

Socializee The person learning to perform various social roles adequately through the process of *socialization*.

Socializing Agent The person instructing others to perform various social roles adequately through the process of *socialization*.

Socioadaptational Characteristics Personality attributes that reflect goal directed and adaptive qualities and did not change with age in the Kansas City studies.

Special Woman/Man An important figure during the phase Levinson described as the Early Adult Transition. This person brings out affectionate, romantic, and sexual feelings and facilitates the individual's *dream* in a manner parallel to the *mentor*.

Speed-Accuracy Trade-off Sacrificing accurate responses for rapid responses or vice versa.

Speed of Response Length of time required to perceive, understand, and respond to a stimulus (also called reaction time).

Successful Patterns of Aging Characteristics of individuals who show little or no decline with aging in many aspects of physiological function.

Supplemental Security Income (SSI) National subsistence program supported by general tax revenues for needy persons who are legally blind, over age 65, unable to work for 12 months or longer, or suffering from a deteriorating medical condition that will result in death.

Symbolic Interaction The model developed by G. H. Mead to describe the development and maintenance of the *self* through symbols (such as language or gestures) used in social interaction.

Synthesized Intelligence Abilities that do not decline or may increase with age that emphasize problem-solving strategies and reflect the ability to deal with complex and important life tasks.

Taking the Attitude of the Other Understanding as fully as possible another person's experiencing (sometimes described as being in another person's shoes).

Timetable of Age-related Events Expected developmental schedule of one's own life and the lives of others.

Timing Events Experiences that cause one to modify one's view of oneself in an age-related way.

Transition A period of change, growth, and disequilibrium that serves as a kind of bridge between one relatively stable point in life and another relatively stable but different point.

Type A Behavior Pattern Excessive competition, desire for recognition, heightened aggressiveness, and habitual tendency to speed up the pace of living.

Type B Behavior Pattern The opposite set of characteristics to the *Type A behavior pattern*.

Usual Patterns of Aging Characteristics of average or typical older persons.

Vesting Employees gain rights to part or all of their pension benefits after a specific number of years so that if workers leave the job for any reason, their pension rights are protected.

Wisdom Ability to exercise good judgment about important but uncertain matters of life, ability to understand human nature, and knowledge that focuses on the meaning of life and the relation of human life to the universe.

Photo Credits

Beringer/The Image Works; (right) Chester Higgins Jr./Photo Researchers, Inc.   Page 361: Larry Ruben-stein/Bettmann Newsphotos.   Page 368: National Heart, Lung, & Blood Institute.   Page 370: Barbara Rios/Photo Researchers, Inc.   Page 374: Kathy Sloane/Photo Researchers, Inc.   Page 382: Bohdan Hrynewych/Stock, Boston.

CHAPTER 8

Page 399: Rick Smolan/Stock, Boston.   Page 402: Hazel Hankin/Stock, Boston.   Page 403: Michael Weisbrot/Stock, Boston.   Page 409: Lynn McLaren/Photo Researchers, Inc.   Page 427: Alexander Lowry/Photo Researchers, Inc.   Page 431: Positive Images.   Page 436: Harvey Stein.   Page 442: Rick Kopstein/Monkmeyer Press.

CHAPTER 9

Page 459: Stock, Boston.   Page 466: Photo Researchers, Inc.   Page 477: Elizabeth Crews.   Page 484: Positive Images.   Page 492: Bill Aron Photography/Photo Researchers, Inc.   Page 494: Eric Kroll/ Taurus Photos.   Page 500: Susan Kuklin/Photo Researchers, Inc.   Page 507: Elizabeth Crews.

CHAPTER 10

Page 527: John Maher/Stock, Boston.   Page 532: Eric Kroll/Taurus.   Page 540: UPI/Bettmann News-photos.   Page 541: George Gardner/Stock, Boston.   Page 552: Shirley Zeiberg/Taurus.   Page 555: Richard Baljer/Stock, Boston.   Page 562: Sybil Shelton/Peter Arnold, Inc.

Author Index

Subject Index